Ford Granada & Scorpio
Service and Repair Manual

Matthew Minter and Christopher Rogers

Models covered
Ford Granada & Scorpio; Hatchback, Saloon & Estate
1.8, 2.0, 2.4, 2.8 and 2.9 litre petrol engines

Does not cover 4x4, Diesel engine or 24V (Cosworth) models

ABCDE
F

2

(1245-9X6)

© Haynes Publishing 1995

A book in the Haynes Service and Repair Manual Series

ISBN 1 85960 170 7

British Library Cataloguing in Publication Data
A catalogue record for this book is available from the British Library.

Printed by J H Haynes & Co. Ltd, Sparkford, Nr Yeovil, Somerset BA22 7JJ

Haynes Publishing
Sparkford, Nr Yeovil, Somerset BA22 7JJ, England

Haynes North America, Inc
861 Lawrence Drive, Newbury Park, California 91320, USA

Editions Haynes S.A.
147/149, rue Saint Honoré, 75001 PARIS, France

Contents

Contents

Introduction

Introduction to the Ford Granada

The latest vehicles to carry the name Granada bear little visual resemblance to their predecessors, although some mechanical components have been carried over. Originally only one body style, a 5-door hatchback, was available but the range has now increased with the addition of Saloon models in January 1990 and Estate models in March 1992. Petrol engines offered are 1.8 and 2.0 litre 4-cylinder OHC and 2.4, 2.8 and 2.9 litre pushrod V6; all are well-tried units which benefit from the latest engine management systems. The 1.8 litre engine has a twin choke carburettor, the V6 engines have fuel-injection and the 2.0 litre is available in both carburettor and fuel-injection forms.

A 5-speed manual gearbox or a 4-speed automatic transmission is fitted. Drive is to the rear wheels via a conventional differential unit and open tubular driveshafts. A viscous-coupled limited slip differential is available as an optional extra. There is also a four-wheel drive version, but this is not covered in this manual.

Disc brakes are fitted all round, with Ford's new anti-lock braking system (ABS) standard on all models. ABS ensures that maximum braking effect is available under all road conditions, even in the hands of unskilled drivers. Suspension is fully independent.

Interior fittings and trim are of the high standard expected in vehicles of this class. Trim levels range from the relatively basic L, through GL and Ghia to the lavishly-equipped Scorpio. Refinements such as electrically-operated windows, control door locking and air conditioning are standard on the Scorpio.

Mechanically the vehicles are very easy to work on in most areas, and thought has obviously been given to the quick replacement of commonly required items such as the exhaust system. Routine maintenance requirements are minimal, a full service being necessary only every 12 000 miles or annually, with an oil change and a brief check at half this interval.

Ford Granada GLX

Ford Granada Estate LX

Acknowledgements

Thanks are due to Champion Spark Plug, who supplied the illustrations showing spark plug conditions. Certain other illustrations are the copyright of the Ford Motor Company and are used with their permission. Thanks are also due to Sykes-Pickavant Limited, who provided some of the workshop tools, and to all those people at Sparkford who helped in the production of this manual.

We take great pride in the accuracy of information given in this manual, but vehicle manufacturers make alterations and design changes during the production run of a particular vehicle of which they do not inform us. No liability can be accepted by the authors or publishers for loss, damage or injury caused by errors in, or omissions from, the information given.

General dimensions and weights

Dimensions

Overall length	4.669 m
Width:	
Including mirrors	1.963 m
Excluding mirrors	1.766 m
Overall height (maximum)	1.450 m
Wheelbase	2.761 m
Track:	
Front	1.477 m
Rear	1.492 m

Weights

Kerb weight (nominal):	
1.8 litre	1225 kg
2.0 litre carburettor	1255 kg
2.0 litre fuel-injection	1265 kg
V6, GL and Ghia	1340 kg
V6, Scorpio	1390 kg
Roof rack maximum load	75 kg
Maximum trailer weight*:	
1.8 litre	1475 kg
2.0 litre carburettor, manual	1525 kg
2.0 litre carburettor, automatic	1750 kg
2.0 litre fuel-injection	1750 kg
V6, manual and limited slip differential	1625 kg
V6, manual	1750 kg
V6, automatic	1825 kg
Trailer nose weight (all models max)	75 kg
Gross vehicle weight	Refer to VIN plate

*Subject to current legislation. Weights given allow re-starting on a gradient of 12% at sea level; vehicle laden with two occupants only

Safety First!

Working on your car can be dangerous. This page shows just some of the potential risks and hazards, with the aim of creating a safety-conscious attitude.

General hazards

Scalding

• Don't remove the radiator or expansion tank cap while the engine is hot.
• Engine oil, automatic transmission fluid or power steering fluid may also be dangerously hot if the engine has recently been running.

Burning

• Beware of burns from the exhaust system and from any part of the engine. Brake discs and drums can also be extremely hot immediately after use.

Crushing

• When working under or near a raised vehicle, always supplement the jack with axle stands, or use drive-on ramps. *Never venture under a car which is only supported by a jack.*
• Take care if loosening or tightening high-torque nuts when the vehicle is on stands. Initial loosening and final tightening should be done with the wheels on the ground.

Fire

• Fuel is highly flammable; fuel vapour is explosive.
• Don't let fuel spill onto a hot engine.
• Do not smoke or allow naked lights (including pilot lights) anywhere near a vehicle being worked on. Also beware of creating sparks (electrically or by use of tools).
• Fuel vapour is heavier than air, so don't work on the fuel system with the vehicle over an inspection pit.
• Another cause of fire is an electrical overload or short-circuit. Take care when repairing or modifying the vehicle wiring.
• Keep a fire extinguisher handy, of a type suitable for use on fuel and electrical fires.

Electric shock

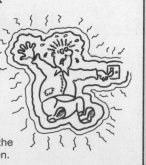

• Ignition HT voltage can be dangerous, especially to people with heart problems or a pacemaker. Don't work on or near the ignition system with the engine running or the ignition switched on.

• Mains voltage is also dangerous. Make sure that any mains-operated equipment is correctly earthed. Mains power points should be protected by a residual current device (RCD) circuit breaker.

Fume or gas intoxication

• Exhaust fumes are poisonous; they often contain carbon monoxide, which is rapidly fatal if inhaled. Never run the engine in a confined space such as a garage with the doors shut.
• Fuel vapour is also poisonous, as are the vapours from some cleaning solvents and paint thinners.

Poisonous or irritant substances

• Avoid skin contact with battery acid and with any fuel, fluid or lubricant, especially antifreeze, brake hydraulic fluid and Diesel fuel. Don't syphon them by mouth. If such a substance is swallowed or gets into the eyes, seek medical advice.
• Prolonged contact with used engine oil can cause skin cancer. Wear gloves or use a barrier cream if necessary. Change out of oil-soaked clothes and do not keep oily rags in your pocket.
• Air conditioning refrigerant forms a poisonous gas if exposed to a naked flame (including a cigarette). It can also cause skin burns on contact.

Asbestos

• Asbestos dust can cause cancer if inhaled or swallowed. Asbestos may be found in gaskets and in brake and clutch linings. When dealing with such components it is safest to assume that they contain asbestos.

Special hazards

Hydrofluoric acid

• This extremely corrosive acid is formed when certain types of synthetic rubber, found in some O-rings, oil seals, fuel hoses etc, are exposed to temperatures above 400°C. The rubber changes into a charred or sticky substance containing the acid. *Once formed, the acid remains dangerous for years. If it gets onto the skin, it may be necessary to amputate the limb concerned.*
• When dealing with a vehicle which has suffered a fire, or with components salvaged from such a vehicle, wear protective gloves and discard them after use.

The battery

• Batteries contain sulphuric acid, which attacks clothing, eyes and skin. Take care when topping-up or carrying the battery.
• The hydrogen gas given off by the battery is highly explosive. Never cause a spark or allow a naked light nearby. Be careful when connecting and disconnecting battery chargers or jump leads.

Air bags

• Air bags can cause injury if they go off accidentally. Take care when removing the steering wheel and/or facia. Special storage instructions may apply.

Diesel injection equipment

• Diesel injection pumps supply fuel at very high pressure. Take care when working on the fuel injectors and fuel pipes.

⚠️ *Warning: Never expose the hands, face or any other part of the body to injector spray; the fuel can penetrate the skin with potentially fatal results.*

Remember...

DO

• Do use eye protection when using power tools, and when working under the vehicle.

• Do wear gloves or use barrier cream to protect your hands when necessary.

• Do get someone to check periodically that all is well when working alone on the vehicle.

• Do keep loose clothing and long hair well out of the way of moving mechanical parts.

• Do remove rings, wristwatch etc, before working on the vehicle – especially the electrical system.

• Do ensure that any lifting or jacking equipment has a safe working load rating adequate for the job.

DON'T

• Don't attempt to lift a heavy component which may be beyond your capability – get assistance.

• Don't rush to finish a job, or take unverified short cuts.

• Don't use ill-fitting tools which may slip and cause injury.

• Don't leave tools or parts lying around where someone can trip over them. Mop up oil and fuel spills at once.

• Don't allow children or pets to play in or near a vehicle being worked on.

Jacking

Use the jack supplied with the vehicle only for wheel changing in an emergency - see *"Wheel changing"*. The jack locates in the jacking points positioned at the front and rear of the body sills on each side of the car. Ensure that the jack head is correctly engaged

before attempting to raise the vehicle **(see illustrations)**. Chock the wheel diagonally opposite the one being removed.

When raising the vehicle for repair or maintenance, preferably use a trolley or hydraulic jack with a wooden block as an insulator to prevent damage to the underbody. Place the jack under a structural member at the points indicated **(see illustration)**, never raise the vehicle by jacking up under the engine sump or transmission casing. If both front or both rear wheels are to be raised, jack up one side first and securely support it on an axle stand before raising the other side.

To avoid repetition, the procedures for raising the vehicle in order to carry out work under it is not included before each relevant operation described in this manual.

It is to be preferred and is certainly recommended that the vehicle is positioned over an inspection pit or raised on a lift. When such equipment is not available, use ramps or jack up the vehicle as previously described, but always supplement the lifting device with axle stands. **Never** work under, around, or near a raised vehicle, unless it is adequately supported in at least two places.

Vehicle jack head engaged in jacking point

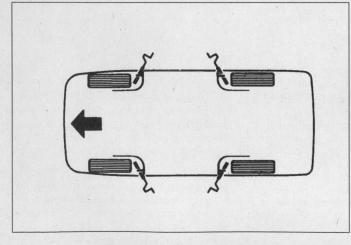

Swivel vehicle jack as shown for each position. Arrow points to front of vehicle

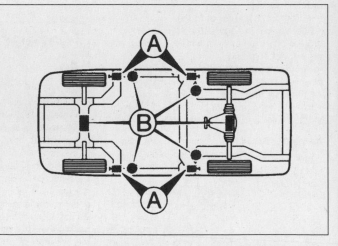

Underbody jacking points

A Vehicle jack   *B Trolley jack or axle stands*

Towing

Towing eyes are fitted to the front and rear of the vehicle for attachment of a tow rope **(see illustrations)**. Always turn the ignition key to the "ON" position when the vehicle is being towed, so that the steering lock is released, and the direction indicators and brake lights are working.

Before being towed, release the handbrake, and select neutral on manual gearbox models, or "N" on automatic transmission models. Note that greater-than-usual pedal pressure will be required to operate the brakes, since the vacuum servo unit is only operational with the engine running. Similarly, on models with power steering, greater-than-usual steering effort will be required.

Models with automatic transmission should be towed with the rear wheels off the ground, particularly if a transmission fault is suspected. If the vehicle is to be towed with its rear wheels on the ground, it must always be towed forwards at speeds not exceeding 30 mph (50 km/h) or for a distance no further than 30 miles (50 km).

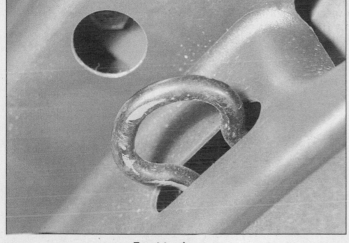

Front towing eye

Rear towing eye

Wheel changing

The spare wheel is located in the luggage compartment. The jack and wheelbrace are stored in the luggage compartment behind the right-hand side trim panel. For access to the spare wheel, proceed as follows:
a) Lift the luggage compartment floor covering to one side.
b) Release the wheel cover by turning its retainer anticlockwise one quarter of a turn.
c) Lift the spare wheel out of the floor well
To change a wheel, remove the spare wheel, jack and wheelbrace then proceed as follows.

Park on a firm flat surface if possible. Apply the handbrake and engage reverse gear or "P". Chock the wheel diagonally opposite the one being removed.

Remove the wheel trim, when applicable, for access to the wheel nuts. Prise the trim off if necessary using the plastic-tipped end of the wheelbrace. Use the other end of the wheelbrace to slacken each wheel nut by half a turn.

If the car is fairly new, the wheels and tyres will have been balanced on the vehicle during production. To maintain this relationship, mark the position of the wheel relative to the hub. (This is not necessary if the tyre is to be removed for repair or renewal, since the balance will inevitably be altered.)

Jack up the vehicle until the wheel is clear of the ground. Remove the wheel nuts and lift the wheel off the studs. Transfer the wheel centre cap on alloy wheels, then fit the new wheel onto the studs and secure it with the nuts. Tighten the nuts until they are snug, but do not tighten them fully yet.

Lower the vehicle and remove the jack. Carry out the final tightening of the wheel nuts in criss-cross sequence. See Chapter 1 Specifications for the recommended tightening torque.

Refit the wheel trim, when applicable, and stow the tools. If a new wheel has been brought into service, have it balanced on the vehicle if necessary.

Roadside Repairs

Identifying leaks

Puddles on the garage floor or drive, or obvious wetness under the bonnet or underneath the car, suggest a leak that needs investigating. It can sometimes be difficult to decide where the leak is coming from, especially if the engine bay is very dirty already. Leaking oil or fluid can also be blown rearwards by the passage of air under the car, giving a false impression of where the problem lies.

 Warning: Most automotive oils and fluids are poisonous. Wash them off skin, and change out of contaminated clothing, without delay.

HAYNES HiNT *The smell of a fluid leaking from the car may provide a clue to what's leaking. Some fluids are distictively coloured. It may help to clean the car carefully and to park it over some clean paper overnight as an aid to locating the source of the leak.*
Remember that some leaks may only occur while the engine is running.

Sump oil

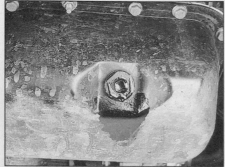

Engine oil may leak from the drain plug...

Oil from filter

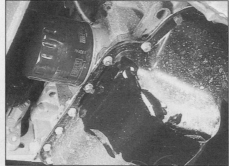

...or from the base of the oil filter.

Gearbox oil

Gearbox oil can leak from the seals at the inboard ends of the driveshafts.

Antifreeze

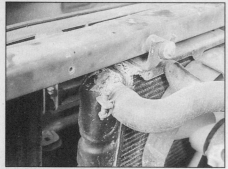

Leaking antifreeze often leaves a crystalline deposit like this.

Brake fluid

A leak occurring at a wheel is almost certainly brake fluid.

Power steering fluid

Power steering fluid may leak from the pipe connectors on the steering rack.

Buying spare parts

Spare parts are available from many sources, including maker's appointed garages, accessory shops, and motor factors. To be sure of obtaining the correct parts, it will sometimes be necessary to quote the vehicle identification number. If possible, it can also be useful to take the old parts along for positive identification. Items such as starter motors and alternators may be available under a service exchange scheme - any parts returned should always be clean.

Our advice regarding spare part sources is as follows.

Officially-appointed garages

This is the best source of parts which are peculiar to your car, and which are not otherwise generally available (eg badges, interior trim, certain body panels, etc). It is also the only place at which you should buy parts if the vehicle is still under warranty.

Accessory shops

These are very good places to buy materials and components needed for the maintenance of your car (oil, air and fuel filters, spark plugs, light bulbs, drivebelts, oils and greases, brake pads, touch-up paint, etc). Components of this nature sold by a reputable shop are of the same standard as those used by the car manufacturer.

Besides components, these shops also sell tools and general accessories, usually have convenient opening hours, charge lower prices, and can often be found not far from home. Some accessory shops have parts counters where the components needed for almost any repair job can be purchased or ordered.

Motor factors

Good factors will stock all the more important components which wear out comparatively quickly, and can sometimes supply individual components needed for the overhaul of a larger assembly (eg brake seals and hydraulic parts, bearing shells, pistons, valves, alternator brushes). They may also handle work such as cylinder block reboring, crankshaft regrinding and balancing, etc.

Tyre and exhaust specialists

These outlets may be independent, or members of a local or national chain. They frequently offer competitive prices when compared with a main dealer or local garage, but it will pay to obtain several quotes before making a decision. When researching prices, also ask what "extras" may be added - for instance, fitting a new valve and balancing the wheel may be charged on top of the price of a new tyre.

Other sources

Beware of parts or materials obtained from market stalls, car boot sales or similar outlets. Such items are not invariably sub-standard, but there is little chance of compensation if they do prove unsatisfactory. In the case of safety-critical components such as brake pads, there is the risk not only of financial loss but also of an accident causing injury or death.

Second-hand components or assemblies obtained from a car breaker can be a good buy in some circumstances, but this sort of purchase is best made by the experienced DIY mechanic.

Vehicle identification numbers

Modifications are a continuing and unpublicised process in vehicle manufacture, quite apart from major model changes. Spare parts lists are compiled upon a numerical basis, the individual vehicle identification numbers being essential to correct identification of the component concerned.

When ordering spare parts, always give as much information as possible. Quote the car model, year of manufacture, body and engine numbers, as appropriate.

The *Vehicle Identification Number (VIN)* plate is mounted on the right-hand side of the body front panel, and may be seen once the bonnet is open (see illustration). Besides the VIN it also carries information on vehicle equipment and permissible loads. The VIN is also stamped into the floor panel to the right of the driver's seat; an inspection cover is provided (see illustration).

The *engine number* is situated on the cylinder block. On SOHC engines it is on the right-hand side, near the alternator (see illustration); on DOHC engines it is stamped on the front of the block, below the upper timing chain cover (see illustration) and on V6 engines it is on the left-hand side, above the fuel pump blanking plate (see illustration).

The *transmission number* is situated on the top of the transmission casing.

Other identification numbers or codes are stamped on major items such as the final drive housing, distributor etc. These numbers are unlikely to be needed by the home mechanic.

Typical VIN plate

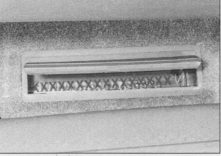

VIN is repeated next to driver's seat

Engine number (SOHC)

Engine number code sticker and engine number location (A) - (DOHC engine)

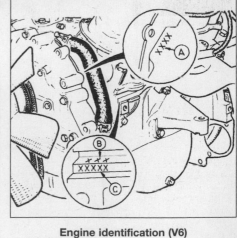

Engine identification (V6)
A Date code
B Engine code
C Engine Number

Roadside Repairs

Booster battery (jump) starting

When jump-starting a car using a booster battery, observe the following precautions:

A) Before connecting the booster battery, make sure that the ignition is switched off.

B) Ensure that all electrical equipment (lights, heater, wipers, etc) is switched off.

C) Make sure that the booster battery is the same voltage as the discharged one in the vehicle.

D) If the battery is being jump-started from the battery in another vehicle, the two vehcles MUST NOT TOUCH each other.

E) Make sure that the transmission is in neutral (or PARK, in the case of automatic transmission).

HAYNES HiNT *Jump starting will get you out of trouble, but you must correct whatever made the battery go flat in the first place. There are three possibilities:*

1 *The battery has been drained by repeated attempts to start, or by leaving the lights on.*

2 *The charging system is not working properly (alternator drivebelt slack or broken, alternator wiring fault or alternator itself faulty).*

3 *The battery itself is at fault (electrolyte low, or battery worn out).*

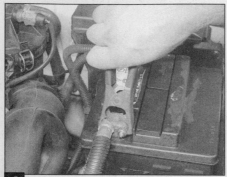

1 Connect one end of the red jump lead to the positive (+) terminal of the flat battery

2 Connect the other end of the red lead to the positive (+) terminal of the booster battery.

3 Connect one end of the black jump lead to the negative (-) terminal of the booster battery

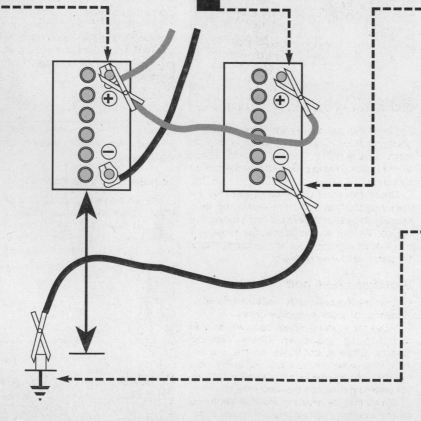

4 Connect the other end of the black jump lead to a bolt or bracket on the engine block, well away from the battery, on the vehicle to be started.

5 Make sure that the jump leads will not come into contact with the fan, drive-belts or other moving parts of the engine.

6 Start the engine using the booster battery, then with the engine running at idle speed, disconnect the jump leads in the reverse order of connection.

This is a guide to getting your vehicle through the MOT test. Obviously it will not be possible to examine the vehicle to the same standard as the professional MOT tester. However, working through the following checks will enable you to identify any problem areas before submitting the vehicle for the test.

Where a testable component is in borderline condition, the tester has discretion in deciding whether to pass or fail it. The basis of such discretion is whether the tester would be happy for a close relative or friend to use the vehicle with the component in that condition. If the vehicle presented is clean and evidently well cared for, the tester may be more inclined to pass a borderline component than if the vehicle is scruffy and apparently neglected.

It has only been possible to summarise the test requirements here, based on the regulations in force at the time of printing. Test standards are becoming increasingly stringent, although there are some exemptions for older vehicles. For full details obtain a copy of the Haynes publication Pass the MOT! (available from stockists of Haynes manuals).

An assistant will be needed to help carry out some of these checks.

The checks have been sub-divided into four categories, as follows:

1 Checks carried out **FROM THE DRIVER'S SEAT**

2 Checks carried out **WITH THE VEHICLE ON THE GROUND**

3 Checks carried out **WITH THE VEHICLE RAISED AND THE WHEELS FREE TO TURN**

4 Checks carried out on **YOUR VEHICLE'S EXHAUST EMISSION SYSTEM**

1 Checks carried out **FROM THE DRIVER'S SEAT**

Handbrake

☐ Test the operation of the handbrake. Excessive travel (too many clicks) indicates incorrect brake or cable adjustment.

☐ Check that the handbrake cannot be released by tapping the lever sideways. Check the security of the lever mountings.

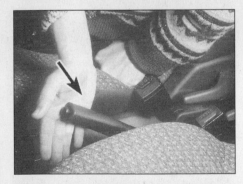

Footbrake

☐ Depress the brake pedal and check that it does not creep down to the floor, indicating a master cylinder fault. Release the pedal, wait a few seconds, then depress it again. If the pedal travels nearly to the floor before firm resistance is felt, brake adjustment or repair is necessary. If the pedal feels spongy, there is air in the hydraulic system which must be removed by bleeding.

☐ Check that the brake pedal is secure and in good condition. Check also for signs of fluid leaks on the pedal, floor or carpets, which would indicate failed seals in the brake master cylinder.

☐ Check the servo unit (when applicable) by operating the brake pedal several times, then keeping the pedal depressed and starting the engine. As the engine starts, the pedal will move down slightly. If not, the vacuum hose or the servo itself may be faulty.

Steering wheel and column

☐ Examine the steering wheel for fractures or looseness of the hub, spokes or rim.

☐ Move the steering wheel from side to side and then up and down. Check that the steering wheel is not loose on the column, indicating wear or a loose retaining nut. Continue moving the steering wheel as before, but also turn it slightly from left to right.

☐ Check that the steering wheel is not loose on the column, and that there is no abnormal

movement of the steering wheel, indicating wear in the column support bearings or couplings.

Windscreen and mirrors

☐ The windscreen must be free of cracks or other significant damage within the driver's field of view. (Small stone chips are acceptable.) Rear view mirrors must be secure, intact, and capable of being adjusted.

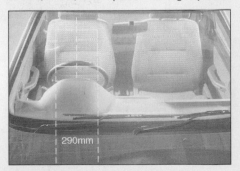

290mm

Seat belts and seats

Note: *The following checks are applicable to all seat belts, front and rear.*

☐ Examine the webbing of all the belts (including rear belts if fitted) for cuts, serious fraying or deterioration. Fasten and unfasten each belt to check the buckles. If applicable, check the retracting mechanism. Check the security of all seat belt mountings accessible from inside the vehicle.

☐ The front seats themselves must be securely attached and the backrests must lock in the upright position.

Doors

☐ Both front doors must be able to be opened and closed from outside and inside, and must latch securely when closed.

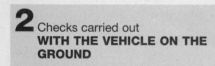

2 Checks carried out **WITH THE VEHICLE ON THE GROUND**

Vehicle identification

☐ Number plates must be in good condition, secure and legible, with letters and numbers correctly spaced – spacing at (A) should be twice that at (B).

☐ The VIN plate (A) and homologation plate (B) must be legible.

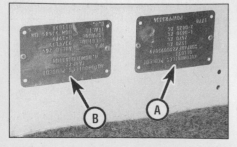

Electrical equipment

☐ Switch on the ignition and check the operation of the horn.

☐ Check the windscreen washers and wipers, examining the wiper blades; renew damaged or perished blades. Also check the operation of the stop-lights.

☐ Check the operation of the sidelights and number plate lights. The lenses and reflectors must be secure, clean and undamaged.

☐ Check the operation and alignment of the headlights. The headlight reflectors must not be tarnished and the lenses must be undamaged.

☐ Switch on the ignition and check the operation of the direction indicators (including the instrument panel tell-tale) and the hazard warning lights. Operation of the sidelights and stop-lights must not affect the indicators - if it does, the cause is usually a bad earth at the rear light cluster.

☐ Check the operation of the rear foglight(s), including the warning light on the instrument panel or in the switch.

Footbrake

☐ Examine the master cylinder, brake pipes and servo unit for leaks, loose mountings, corrosion or other damage.

☐ The fluid reservoir must be secure and the fluid level must be between the upper (A) and lower (B) markings.

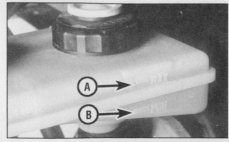

☐ Inspect both front brake flexible hoses for cracks or deterioration of the rubber. Turn the steering from lock to lock, and ensure that the hoses do not contact the wheel, tyre, or any part of the steering or suspension mechanism. With the brake pedal firmly depressed, check the hoses for bulges or leaks under pressure.

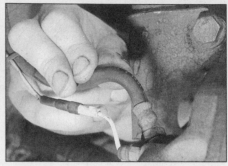

Steering and suspension

☐ Have your assistant turn the steering wheel from side to side slightly, up to the point where the steering gear just begins to transmit this movement to the roadwheels. Check for excessive free play between the steering wheel and the steering gear, indicating wear or insecurity of the steering column joints, the column-to-steering gear coupling, or the steering gear itself.

☐ Have your assistant turn the steering wheel more vigorously in each direction, so that the roadwheels just begin to turn. As this is done, examine all the steering joints, linkages, fittings and attachments. Renew any component that shows signs of wear or damage. On vehicles with power steering, check the security and condition of the steering pump, drivebelt and hoses.

☐ Check that the vehicle is standing level, and at approximately the correct ride height.

Shock absorbers

☐ Depress each corner of the vehicle in turn, then release it. The vehicle should rise and then settle in its normal position. If the vehicle continues to rise and fall, the shock absorber is defective. A shock absorber which has seized will also cause the vehicle to fail.

Exhaust system

☐ Start the engine. With your assistant holding a rag over the tailpipe, check the entire system for leaks. Repair or renew leaking sections.

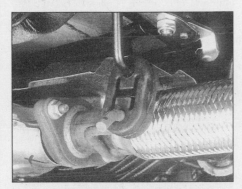

3 Checks carried out **WITH THE VEHICLE RAISED AND THE WHEELS FREE TO TURN**

Jack up the front and rear of the vehicle, and securely support it on axle stands. Position the stands clear of the suspension assemblies. Ensure that the wheels are clear of the ground and that the steering can be turned from lock to lock.

Steering mechanism

☐ Have your assistant turn the steering from lock to lock. Check that the steering turns smoothly, and that no part of the steering mechanism, including a wheel or tyre, fouls any brake hose or pipe or any part of the body structure.
☐ Examine the steering rack rubber gaiters for damage or insecurity of the retaining clips. If power steering is fitted, check for signs of damage or leakage of the fluid hoses, pipes or connections. Also check for excessive stiffness or binding of the steering, a missing split pin or locking device, or severe corrosion of the body structure within 30 cm of any steering component attachment point.

Front and rear suspension and wheel bearings

☐ Starting at the front right-hand side, grasp the roadwheel at the 3 o'clock and 9 o'clock positions and shake it vigorously. Check for free play or insecurity at the wheel bearings, suspension balljoints, or suspension mountings, pivots and attachments.
☐ Now grasp the wheel at the 12 o'clock and 6 o'clock positions and repeat the previous inspection. Spin the wheel, and check for roughness or tightness of the front wheel bearing.

☐ If excess free play is suspected at a component pivot point, this can be confirmed by using a large screwdriver or similar tool and levering between the mounting and the component attachment. This will confirm whether the wear is in the pivot bush, its retaining bolt, or in the mounting itself (the bolt holes can often become elongated).

☐ Carry out all the above checks at the other front wheel, and then at both rear wheels.

Springs and shock absorbers

☐ Examine the suspension struts (when applicable) for serious fluid leakage, corrosion, or damage to the casing. Also check the security of the mounting points.
☐ If coil springs are fitted, check that the spring ends locate in their seats, and that the spring is not corroded, cracked or broken.
☐ If leaf springs are fitted, check that all leaves are intact, that the axle is securely attached to each spring, and that there is no deterioration of the spring eye mountings, bushes, and shackles.

☐ The same general checks apply to vehicles fitted with other suspension types, such as torsion bars, hydraulic displacer units, etc. Ensure that all mountings and attachments are secure, that there are no signs of excessive wear, corrosion or damage, and (on hydraulic types) that there are no fluid leaks or damaged pipes.
☐ Inspect the shock absorbers for signs of serious fluid leakage. Check for wear of the mounting bushes or attachments, or damage to the body of the unit.

Driveshafts (fwd vehicles only)

☐ Rotate each front wheel in turn and inspect the constant velocity joint gaiters for splits or damage. Also check that each driveshaft is straight and undamaged.

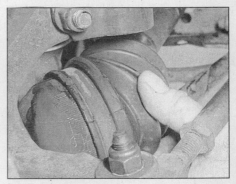

Braking system

☐ If possible without dismantling, check brake pad wear and disc condition. Ensure that the friction lining material has not worn excessively, (A) and that the discs are not fractured, pitted, scored or badly worn (B).

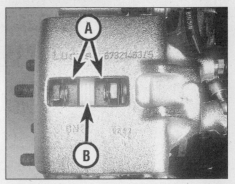

☐ Examine all the rigid brake pipes underneath the vehicle, and the flexible hose(s) at the rear. Look for corrosion, chafing or insecurity of the pipes, and for signs of bulging under pressure, chafing, splits or deterioration of the flexible hoses.
☐ Look for signs of fluid leaks at the brake calipers or on the brake backplates. Repair or renew leaking components.
☐ Slowly spin each wheel, while your assistant depresses and releases the footbrake. Ensure that each brake is operating and does not bind when the pedal is released.

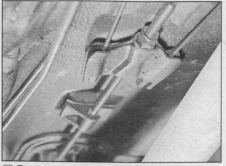

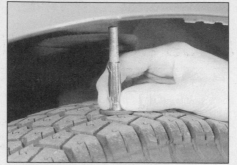

□ Examine the handbrake mechanism, checking for frayed or broken cables, excessive corrosion, or wear or insecurity of the linkage. Check that the mechanism works on each relevant wheel, and releases fully, without binding.

□ It is not possible to test brake efficiency without special equipment, but a road test can be carried out later to check that the vehicle pulls up in a straight line.

Fuel and exhaust systems

□ Inspect the fuel tank (including the filler cap), fuel pipes, hoses and unions. All components must be secure and free from leaks.

□ Examine the exhaust system over its entire length, checking for any damaged, broken or missing mountings, security of the retaining clamps and rust or corrosion.

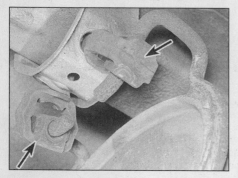

Wheels and tyres

□ Examine the sidewalls and tread area of each tyre in turn. Check for cuts, tears, lumps, bulges, separation of the tread, and exposure of the ply or cord due to wear or damage. Check that the tyre bead is correctly seated on the wheel rim, that the valve is sound and

properly seated, and that the wheel is not distorted or damaged.

□ Check that the tyres are of the correct size for the vehicle, that they are of the same size and type on each axle, and that the pressures are correct.

□ Check the tyre tread depth. The legal minimum at the time of writing is 1.6 mm over at least three-quarters of the tread width. Abnormal tread wear may indicate incorrect front wheel alignment.

Body corrosion

□ Check the condition of the entire vehicle structure for signs of corrosion in load-bearing areas. (These include chassis box sections, side sills, cross-members, pillars, and all suspension, steering, braking system and seat belt mountings and anchorages.) Any corrosion which has seriously reduced the thickness of a load-bearing area is likely to cause the vehicle to fail. In this case professional repairs are likely to be needed.

□ Damage or corrosion which causes sharp or otherwise dangerous edges to be exposed will also cause the vehicle to fail.

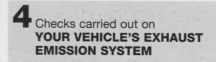

4 Checks carried out on **YOUR VEHICLE'S EXHAUST EMISSION SYSTEM**

Petrol models

□ Have the engine at normal operating temperature, and make sure that it is in good tune (ignition system in good order, air filter element clean, etc).

□ Before any measurements are carried out, raise the engine speed to around 2500 rpm, and hold it at this speed for 20 seconds. Allow the engine speed to return to idle, and watch

for smoke emissions from the exhaust tailpipe. If the idle speed is obviously much too high, or if dense blue or clearly-visible black smoke comes from the tailpipe for more than 5 seconds, the vehicle will fail. As a rule of thumb, blue smoke signifies oil being burnt (engine wear) while black smoke signifies unburnt fuel (dirty air cleaner element, or other carburettor or fuel system fault).

□ An exhaust gas analyser capable of measuring carbon monoxide (CO) and hydrocarbons (HC) is now needed. If such an instrument cannot be hired or borrowed, a local garage may agree to perform the check for a small fee.

CO emissions (mixture)

□ At the time or writing, the maximum CO level at idle is 3.5% for vehicles first used after August 1986 and 4.5% for older vehicles. From January 1996 a much tighter limit (around 0.5%) applies to catalyst-equipped vehicles first used from August 1992. If the CO level cannot be reduced far enough to pass the test (and the fuel and ignition systems are otherwise in good condition) then the carburettor is badly worn, or there is some problem in the fuel injection system or catalytic converter (as applicable).

HC emissions

□ With the CO emissions within limits, HC emissions must be no more than 1200 ppm (parts per million). If the vehicle fails this test at idle, it can be re-tested at around 2000 rpm; if the HC level is then 1200 ppm or less, this counts as a pass.

□ Excessive HC emissions can be caused by oil being burnt, but they are more likely to be due to unburnt fuel.

Diesel models

□ The only emission test applicable to Diesel engines is the measuring of exhaust smoke density. The test involves accelerating the engine several times to its maximum unloaded speed.

Note: *It is of the utmost importance that the engine timing belt is in good condition before the test is carried out.*

□ Excessive smoke can be caused by a dirty air cleaner element. Otherwise, professional advice may be needed to find the cause.

Chapter 1
Routine maintenance and servicing

Contents

Degrees of difficulty

Easy, suitable for novice with little experience	Fairly easy, suitable for beginner with some experience	Fairly difficult, suitable for competent DIY mechanic	Difficult, suitable for experienced DIY mechanic	Very difficult, suitable for expert DIY or professional

Ford Granada maintenance schedule

The maintenance intervals in this manual are provided with the assumption that you will be carrying out the work yourself. These are the minimum maintenance intervals recommended by the manufacturer for vehicles driven daily. If you wish to keep your vehicle in peak condition at all times, you may wish to perform some of these procedures more often. We encourage frequent maintenance, because it enhances the efficiency, performance and resale value of your vehicle.

If the vehicle is driven in dusty areas, used to tow a trailer, or driven frequently at slow speeds (idling in traffic) or on short journeys, more frequent maintenance intervals are recommended.

When the vehicle is new, it should be serviced by a factory-authorised dealer service department, in order to preserve the factory warranty.

Every 250 miles (400 km) or weekly

☐ Check the engine oil level (Section 3).
☐ Check the engine coolant level (Section 3).
☐ Check the brake fluid level (Section 3).
☐ Check the screen washer fluid level (Section 3).
☐ Visually examine the tyres for tread depth, and wear or damage (Section 4).
☐ Check and if necessary adjust the tyre pressures (Section 4).
☐ Check and if necessary top-up the battery electrolyte level - where applicable (Section 6).
☐ Check the operation of the horn, all lights, and the wipers and washers (Sections 5 and 7).

Every 6000 miles (10 000 km) or 6 months – whichever comes sooner

☐ Renew engine oil and filter (Section 8)
☐ Check brake pads for wear (front and rear) (Section 9)
☐ Check tightness of wheel nuts (Section 13)
☐ Check idle speed (1.8 litre only) (Section 15)
☐ Check idle mixture (not fuel-injection models) - at first 6000 miles only (Section 16)
☐ Clean oil filler cap (Section 14)
☐ Inspect engine bay and underside of vehicle for fluid leaks or other signs of damage (Section 10)
☐ Check function and condition of seat belts (Section 11)
☐ Check operation of brake fluid level warning indicator (Section 9)
☐ Check condition and security of exhaust system (Section 12)

Maintenance Schedule

Every 12 000 miles (20 000 km) or 12 months – whichever comes sooner

- ☐ Check operation of latches, check straps and locks; lubricate if necessary (Section 19)
- ☐ Check condition and tension of auxiliary drivebelt(s); adjust or renew as necessary (Section 21)
- ☐ Check tightness of battery terminals, clean and neutralise corrosion if necessary (Section 22)
- ☐ Check engine valve clearances (Section 23)
- ☐ Check tightness of inlet manifold bolts (V6 only) (Section 24)
- ☐ Renew spark plugs (Section 20)
- ☐ Clean air conditioning condenser fins (when applicable) (Section 25)
- ☐ Check air conditioning refrigerant charge (when applicable) (Section 26)
- ☐ Check manual gearbox oil level (Section 18)
- ☐ Check final drive oil level (Section 27)
- ☐ Lubricate automatic transmission selector/kickdown linkage (Section 28)
- ☐ Check security and condition of steering and suspension components, gaiters and boots (Section 29)
- ☐ Check condition and security of driveshaft joints (Section 30)
- ☐ Inspect underbody and panels for corrosion or other damage (Section 31)
- ☐ Inspect brake pipes and hoses (Section 32)
- ☐ Clean idle speed control linkage at throttle (when applicable) (Section 33)
- ☐ Road test and check operation of ABS (Section 34)
- ☐ Check automatic transmission fluid level (engine hot) (Section 17)
- ☐ Check engine for satisfactory hot starting (Section 37)
- ☐ Check that automatic choke is fully off with engine hot (not fuel-injection models) (Section 36)
- ☐ Check power steering fluid level (when applicable) (Section 35)

Every 24 000 miles (40 000 km) or 2 years - whichever comes sooner

- ☐ Renew air cleaner element (Section 38)
- ☐ Clean and inspect distributor cap, rotor arm, HT leads and coil tower (Section 39)
- ☐ Adjust automatic transmission brake bands (Section 40)
- ☐ Renew fuel filter (fuel-injection models only) (Section 41)
- ☐ Renew crankcase ventilation vent valve (carburettor models) (Section 42)

Every 36 000 miles (60 000 km) or 3 years - whichever comes sooner

- ☐ Renew brake hydraulic system seals and hoses if necessary (Section 43)
- ☐ Renew brake hydraulic fluid (Section 44)
- ☐ Renew camshaft drivebelt on SOHC models - recommended as a precautionary measure (Section 45)

Every 2 years - regardless of mileage

- ☐ Renew coolant (Section 46)

Lubricants and fluids

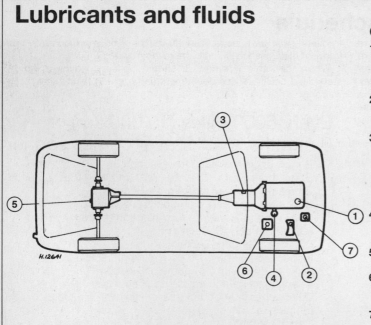

H.12641

Component or system	Lubricant type/specification
1 Engine	Multigrade engine oil, viscosity range SAE 10W/30 to 20W/50 to API SG/CD or better
2 Cooling system	Soft water/antifreeze to Ford spec. SSM 97B9103-A or SDM-M97B49-A
3 Manual transmission:	
N9	Semi-synthetic gear oil to Ford spec. ESD M2C175-A (80 EP)
MT75	Gear oil to Ford spec. ESD-M2C186-A
4 Automatic transmission	ATF to Ford spec. SQM-2C9010-A (TQ Dexron II)
5 Final drive	Gear oil SAE 90EP to API GL5
6 Brake hydraulic system	Hydraulic fluid to Ford spec. SAM- 6C9103-A
7 Power steering	ATF to Ford spec. SQM-2C9010-A (TQ Dexron II)

Capacities

Engine oil

SOHC:
  With filter . . . . .3.75 litres (6.6 pints)
DOHC:
  With filter . . . . .4.5 litres (7.9 pints)
  Without filter . . . . .4.0 litres (7.0 pints)
V6:
  With filte r . . . . .4.25 litres (7.5 pints)

Cooling system

OHC . . . . .8.0 litres (14.1 pints)
V6 . . . . .8.5 litres (15.0 pints)

Fuel tank

All models . . . . .70 litres (15.4 gallons)

Manual gearbox

All models . . . . .1.25 litres (2.2 pints)

Automatic transmission

All models (from dry) . . . . .8.5 litres (15.0 pints)

Final drive

7 inch crownwheel . . . . .0.9 litres (1.6 pints)
7.5 inch crownwheel . . . . .1.3 litres (2.3 pints)

Power steering

OHC . . . . .0.65 litres (1.1 pints)
V6 . . . . .0.75 litres (1.3 pints)

Under-bonnet view of a 2.0 litre SOHC Granada with fuel-injection

1 Battery
2 Engine oil dipstick
3 Inlet manifold
4 Throttle/kickdown cable bracket
5 Suspension turrets
6 Ignition coil
7 Air cleaner cover
8 Fuel pressure regulator
9 Vane airflow meter
10 Headlight covers
11 Tune-up label
12 Idle speed control valve
13 Oil filler cap
14 Spark plug leads
15 VIN plate
16 Radiator hoses
17 Horn
18 Windscreen washer pump
19 Windscreen washer reservoir
20 Alternator
21 Coolant expansion tank cap
22 Engine mounting
23 Heater hose
24 Automatic transmission fluid dipstick
25 Brake fluid reservoir cap
26 Brake hydraulic unit accumulator
27 Brake hydraulic unit valve block
28 Main fuse/relay box
29 Wiper motor (behind cover)
30 Heater blower cover

Under-bonnet view of a 2.0 litre DOHC Granada with fuel-injection

1 Windscreen wiper motor
2 Battery
3 Suspension strut top mounting
4 Brake fluid reservoir
5 Ignition distributor
6 Coolant expansion tank
7 Washer fluid reservoir
8 Automatic transmission fluid dipstick
9 Oil filler cap
10 Engine oil level dipstick
11 Air cleaner element housing
12 Idle speed control valve
13 Ignition module
14 Manifold Absolute Pressure (MAP) sensor
15 Throttle position sensor
16 Power steering fluid reservoir
17 Anti-theft alarm horn
18 Speed control system diaphragm
19 Speed control system vacuum pump
20 Vehicle identification (VIN) plate
21 Fuel pressure regulator
22 Air charge temperature sensor
23 Manifold absolute pressure (MAP) sensor vapour trap
24 Fuse/relay box

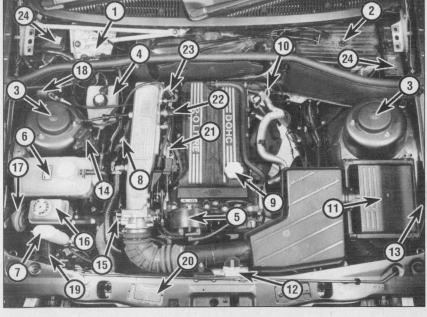

Maintenance Schedule

Under-bonnet view of a 2.8 litre V6 Granada

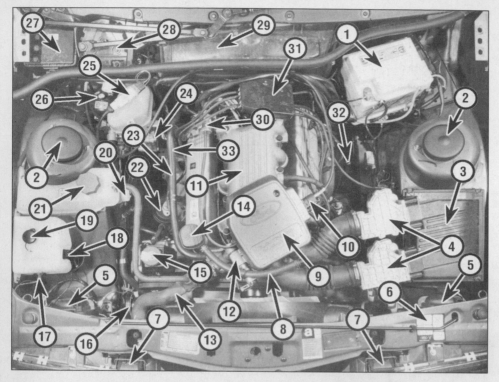

1 Battery
2 Suspension turrets
3 Air cleaner cover
4 Vane airflow meters
5 Headlight covers
6 Tune-up label
7 Auxiliary driving light covers
8 Crankcase ventilation hoses
9 Throttle linkage cover
10 Throttle cable and kickdown switch
11 Plenum chamber
12 Idle speed control valve
13 Radiator top hose
14 Oil filler cap
15 Power steering fluid reservoir
16 Horn
17 Washer fluid level switch
18 Windscreen washer pump
19 Windscreen washer reservoir
20 Coolant level switch
21 Coolant expansion tank cap
22 Engine mounting
23 Heater hose
24 Brake hydraulic unit valve block
25 Brake fluid reservoir cap
26 Brake hydraulic unit accumulator
27 Main fuse/relay box
28 Wiper motor (behind cover)
29 Heater blower cover
30 Fuel pressure regulator
31 Distributor screening lid
32 Engine oil dipstick
33 Automatic transmission fluid dipstick

Front underbody view of a 2.0 litre SOHC Granada with automatic transmission

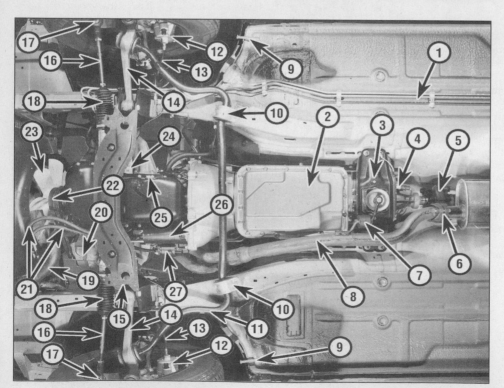

1 Brake and fuel pipes
2 Transmission sump
3 Transmission crossmember
4 Speedometer sender unit
5 Propeller shaft coupling
6 Exhaust flanged joint
7 Exhaust mounting
8 Exhaust pipe
9 Jacking points
10 Anti-roll bar clamps
11 Anti-roll bar
12 Brake calipers
13 Brake flexible hoses
14 Suspension lower arms
15 Front crossmember
16 Track rods
17 Track rod ends
18 Steering rack bellows
19 Radiator bottom hose
20 Alternator
21 Transmission fluid cooler hoses
22 Crankshaft pulley
23 Fan
24 Oil filter
25 Sump drain plug
26 Starter motor
27 Starter motor solenoid

Front underbody view of a 2.0 litre DOHC Granada with automatic transmission

1 Track rod end
2 Track rod
3 Steering gear gaiter
4 Water pump
5 Starter motor
6 Front suspension lower arm
7 Front suspension anti-roll bar
8 Exhaust downpipe
9 Exhaust gas oxygen (HEGO) sensor - models with catalytic converter
10 Front suspension crossmember
11 Sump drain plug
12 Power steering pump
13 Washer fluid reservoir
14 Radiator cooling fans
15 Catalytic converter (where fitted)
16 Catalytic converter heatshield (where fitted)
17 Transmission crossmember
18 Fuel feed and return pipes
19 Rear brake pipes
20 Steering gear feed and return hoses

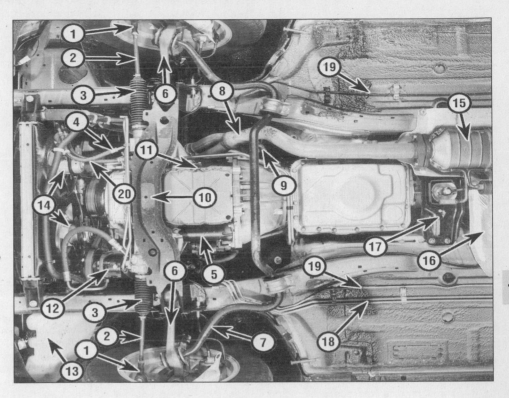

Rear underbody view of a 2.0 litre SOHC Granada with fuel-injection

1 Rear silencer
2 Fuel pump (fuel-injection)
3 Fuel filter (fuel-injection)
4 Fuel tank
5 Fuel tank straps
6 Anti-roll bar clamps
7 Final drive rear mounting
8 Anti-roll bar
9 Driveshafts
10 Driveshaft joints
11 Final drive unit
12 Handbrake cables
13 Suspension lower arms
14 Crossmember
15 Exhaust hanger
16 Guide plates
17 Propeller shaft
18 Propeller shaft universal joint
19 Brake and fuel pipes
20 Shock absorber lower mountings
21 Jacking points
22 Intermediate silencer
23 Exhaust pipe

Maintenance Procedures

1 Introduction

This Chapter is designed to help the home mechanic maintain his/her vehicle for safety, economy, long life and peak performance.

The Chapter contains a master maintenance schedule, followed by Sections dealing specifically with each task in the schedule. Visual checks, adjustments, component renewal and other helpful items are included. Refer to the accompanying illustrations of the engine compartment and the underside of the vehicle for the locations of the various components.

Servicing your vehicle in accordance with the mileage/time maintenance schedule and the following Sections will provide a planned maintenance programme, which should result in a long and reliable service life. This is a comprehensive plan, so maintaining some items but not others at the specified service intervals, will not produce the same results.

As you service your vehicle, you will discover that many of the procedures can - and should - be grouped together, because of the particular procedure being performed, or because of the close proximity of two otherwise-unrelated components to one another. For example, if the vehicle is raised for any reason, the exhaust can be inspected at the same time as the suspension and steering components.

The first step in this maintenance programme is to prepare yourself before the actual work begins. Read through all the Sections relevant to the work to be carried out, then make a list and gather together all the parts and tools required. If a problem is encountered, seek advice from a parts specialist, or a dealer service department.

2 Intensive maintenance

If, from the time the vehicle is new, the routine maintenance schedule is followed closely, and frequent checks are made of fluid levels and high-wear items, as suggested throughout this manual, the engine will be kept in relatively good running condition, and the need for additional work will be minimised.

It is possible that there will be times when the engine is running poorly due to the lack of regular maintenance. This is even more likely if a used vehicle, which has not received regular and frequent maintenance checks, is purchased. In such cases, additional work may need to be carried out, outside of the regular maintenance intervals.

If engine wear is suspected, a compression test will provide valuable information regarding the overall performance of the main internal components. Such a test can be used as a basis to decide on the extent of the work to be carried out. If, for example, a compression test indicates serious internal engine wear, conventional maintenance as described in this Chapter will not greatly improve the performance of the engine, and may prove a waste of time and money, unless extensive overhaul work is carried out first.

The following series of operations are those most often required to improve the performance of a generally poor-running engine:

Primary operations
a) Clean, inspect and test the battery (Section 6)
b) Check all the engine-related fluids (Section 3).
c) Check the condition and tension of the auxiliary drivebelt (Section 21).
d) Renew the spark plugs (Section 20).
e) Inspect the distributor cap, rotor arm and HT leads - as applicable (Chapter 5).
f) Check the condition of the air cleaner filter element, and renew if necessary (Section 38).
g) Renew the fuel filter (Section 41).
h) Check the condition of all hoses, and check for fluid leaks (Section 10).
i) Check the idle speed and mixture settings - as applicable (Chapter 4).

If the above operations do not prove fully effective, carry out the following secondary operations:

Secondary operations
a) Check the charging system (Chapter 5).
b) Check the ignition system (Chapter 5).
c) Check the fuel system (Chapter 4).
d) Renew the distributor cap and rotor arm - as applicable (Chapter 5).
f) Renew the ignition HT leads - as applicable (Chapter 5).

Weekly checks

3 Fluid level checks

Engine oil

1 Check the oil level as follows.
2 With the vehicle parked on level ground, and with the engine having been stopped for a few minutes, open and prop the bonnet. Withdraw the dipstick, wipe it on a clean rag and re-insert it fully. Withdraw it again and read the oil level relative to the marks on the end of the stick (see illustration).
3 The oil level should be in between the MAX and MIN marks on the dipstick. If it is at or below the MIN mark, top-up (via the oil filler cap) without delay. The quantity of oil required to raise the lever from MIN to MAX on the dipstick is approximately 1 litre. Do not overfill (see illustration).
4 The rate of oil consumption depends on leaks and on the quantity of oil burnt. External leakage should be obvious. Oil which is burnt may enter the combustion chambers through the valve guides or past the piston rings; excessive blow-by past the rings can also force oil out via the crankcase ventilation system. Driving conditions also affect oil consumption.
5 Always use the correct grade and type of oil as shown in "Lubricants and fluids".

Coolant

⚠️ **Warning: DO NOT remove the expansion tank pressure cap when the engine is hot, as there is a great risk of scalding.**

6 Check the coolant level as follows.
7 Open and prop the bonnet. Observe the level of coolant through the translucent walls of the expansion tank (on the right-hand side of the engine bay). The level should be up to the MAX mark when the engine is cold, and may be somewhat above the mark when hot.
8 If topping-up is necessary, wait for the system to cool down if it is hot. Place a thick rag over the expansion tank cap and slacken it

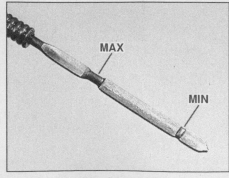

3.2 Dipstick markings

3.3 Topping up the engine oil

3.9 Topping up the cooling system

3.14 Removing the brake fluid reservoir cap

3.15 Topping up the brake fluid reservoir

to release any pressure. When pressure has been released, carry on unscrewing the cap and remove it.

9 Top-up to the MAX mark with the specified coolant **(see illustration)**. In an emergency plain water is better than nothing, but remember that it is diluting the proper coolant. Do not add cold water to an overheated engine whilst it is still hot.

10 Refit the expansion tank cap securely when the level is correct. With a sealed type cooling system like this, the addition of coolant should only be necessary at very infrequent intervals. If frequent topping-up is required, it is likely there is a leak in the system. Check the radiator, all hoses and joint faces for any sign of staining or actual wetness, and rectify as necessary. If no leaks can be found, it is advisable to have the pressure cap and the entire system pressure-tested by a dealer or suitably-equipped garage, as this will often show up a small leak not previously apparent.

Brake fluid

 Warning: Brake hydraulic fluid can harm your eyes and damage painted surfaces, so use extreme caution when handling and pouring it. Do not use fluid that has been standing open for some time, as it absorbs moisture from the air. Excess moisture can cause a dangerous loss of braking effectiveness.

Be sure to use only the specified brake hydraulic fluid, since mixing different types of fluid can cause damage to the system. See *"Lubricants, fluids and capacities"* at the beginning of this Chapter. When adding fluid, it is a good idea to inspect the reservoir for contamination. The system should be drained and refilled if deposits, dirt particles or contamination are seen in the fluid.

11 Check the brake fluid level as follows.

12 With the vehicle parked on level ground and the ignition switched off, pump the brake pedal at least 20 times or until the pedal feels hard.

13 Open the bonnet. Switch on the ignition: the hydraulic unit pump will be heard running. Wait until the pump stops, then switch off the ignition.

14 The fluid level in the reservoir should now be between the MAX and MIN marks. If topping-up is necessary, unplug the electrical connectors from the cap, then unscrew and remove it **(see illustration)**. Catch the hydraulic fluid which will drip off the level sensor with a piece of rag.

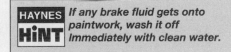 **HAYNES HINT** *If any brake fluid gets onto paintwork, wash it off immediately with clean water.*

15 Top-up with fresh brake fluid of the specified type **(see illustration)**. Do not overfill. Refit and reconnect the reservoir cap immediately.

16 The fluid level in the reservoir will drop slightly as the brake pads wear down during normal operation. If the reservoir requires repeated replenishment to maintain the proper level, this is an indication of a hydraulic leak somewhere in the system, which should be investigated immediately.

Washer fluid

17 When topping-up the windscreen or rear screen washer fluid reservoir, a screenwash additive should be added in the quantities recommended on the bottle.

4 Tyre checks

1 On later models tyres may have tread wear safety bands, which will appear when the tread depth reaches approximately 1.6 mm. Otherwise, tread wear can be monitored with a simple, inexpensive device known as a tread depth indicator gauge **(see illustration)**.

2 Wheels and tyres should give no real problems in use, provided that a close eye is kept on them with regard to excessive wear or damage. To this end, the following points should be noted.

3 Ensure that the tyre pressures are checked regularly and maintained correctly **(see illustration)**. Checking should be carried out with the tyres cold, not immediately after the vehicle has been in use. If the pressures are checked with the tyres hot, an apparently-high reading will be obtained, owing to heat expansion. **Under no circumstances** should an attempt be made to reduce the pressures to the quoted cold reading in this instance, or effective under-inflation will result.

4 Note any abnormal tread wear **(see illustration)**. Tread pattern irregularities such as feathering, flat spots, and more wear on one side than the other, are indications of front wheel alignment and/or balance problems. If any of these conditions are noted, they should be rectified as soon as possible.

5 Under-inflation will cause overheating of the tyre, owing to excessive flexing of the casing, and the tread will not sit correctly on the road surface. This will cause excessive wear, not to mention the danger of sudden tyre failure due to heat build-up.

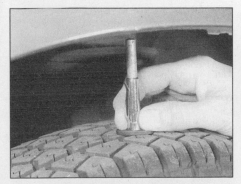
4.1 Checking the tyre tread depth

4.3 Checking tyre pressure

Tyre Tread Wear Patterns

Shoulder Wear

Underinflation (wear on both sides)
Check and adjust pressures

Incorrect wheel camber (wear on one side)
Repair or renew suspension parts

Hard cornering
Reduce speed!

Centre Wear

Overinflation
Check and adjust pressures

If you sometimes have to inflate your car's tyres to the higher pressures specified for maximum load or sustained high speed, don't forget to reduce the pressures to normal afterwards.

Toe Wear

Incorrect toe setting
Adjust front wheel alignment

Note: The feathered edge of the tread which characterises toe wear is best checked by feel.

Uneven Wear

Incorrect camber or castor
Repair or renew suspension parts

Malfunctioning suspension
Repair or renew suspension parts

Unbalanced wheel
Balance tyres

Out-of-round brake disc/drum
Machine or renew

6 Over-inflation will cause rapid wear of the centre part of the tyre tread, coupled with reduced adhesion, harsher ride, and the danger of shock damage occurring in the tyre casing.

7 Regularly check the tyres for damage in the form of cuts or bulges, especially in the sidewalls. Remove any nails or stones embedded in the tread before they penetrate the tyre to cause deflation. If removal of a nail does reveal that the tyre has been punctured, refit the nail so that its point of penetration is marked. Then immediately change the wheel, and have the tyre repaired by a tyre dealer. Do not drive on a tyre in such a condition. If in any doubt as to the possible consequences of any damage found, consult your local tyre dealer for advice.

8 Periodically remove the wheels, and clean any dirt or mud from the inside and outside surfaces. Examine the wheel rims for signs of rusting, corrosion or other damage. Light alloy wheels are easily damaged by "kerbing" whilst parking, and similarly steel wheels may become dented or buckled. Renewal of the wheel is very often the only course of remedial action possible.

9 The balance of each wheel and tyre assembly should be maintained to avoid excessive wear, not only to the tyres but also to the steering and suspension components. Wheel imbalance is normally signified by vibration through the vehicle's bodyshell, although in many cases it is particularly noticeable through the steering wheel. Conversely, it should be noted that wear or damage in suspension or steering components may cause excessive tyre wear. Out-of-round or out-of-true tyres, damaged wheels, and wheel bearing wear also fall into this category. Balancing will not usually cure vibration caused by such wear.

10 Wheel balancing may be carried out with the wheel either on or off the vehicle. If balanced on the vehicle, ensure that the wheel-to-hub relationship is marked in some way prior to subsequent wheel removal, so that it may be refitted in its original position.

11 General tyre wear is influenced to a large degree by driving style - harsh braking and acceleration, or fast cornering, will all produce more rapid tyre wear. Interchanging of tyres may result in more even wear. However, if this is completely effective, the added expense is incurred of replacing all four tyres at once, which may prove financially-restrictive for many owners.

12 Front tyres may wear unevenly as a result of wheel misalignment. The front wheels should always be correctly aligned according to the settings specified by the vehicle manufacturer.

13 Legal restrictions apply to many aspects of tyre fitting and usage, and in the UK this information is contained in the Motor Vehicle Construction and Use Regulations. It is suggested that a copy of these regulations is obtained from your local police, if in doubt as to current legal requirements with regard to tyre type and condition, minimum tread depth, etc.

5 Electrical system check

Check the operation of all the electrical equipment, ie. lights, direction indicators, horn, washers, etc. Refer to the appropriate Sections of Chapter 13 for details if any of the circuits are found to be inoperative.

Visually check all accessible wiring connectors, harnesses and retaining clips for security, and for signs of chafing or damage. Rectify any faults found.

6 Battery electrolyte level check

Caution: *Before carrying out any work on the vehicle battery, read through the precautions given in "Safety first!" at the beginning of this manual.*

1 The battery fitted as original equipment is "maintenance-free", and requires no maintenance apart from having the case kept clean, and the terminals clean and tight.

2 If a "traditional" type battery is fitted as a replacement, remove the old cell covers and check that the plate separators in each cell are covered by approximately 6 mm (0.25 in) of electrolyte. If the battery case is translucent, the cell covers need not be removed to check the level. Top-up if necessary with distilled or de-ionized water; do not overfill, and mop up any spillage at once **(see illustration)**.

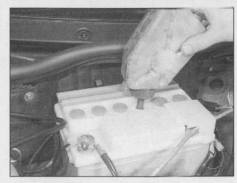

6.2 Topping up the battery

7 Wiper blade check

1 Clean the wiper blades and the windscreen, using a solution of concentrated washer fluid or methylated spirit. Similarly clean the headlight lens and wiper blades.
2 Check the condition of the wiper blades; if they are cracked or show any signs of deterioration, or if the glass swept area is smeared, renew them. At the same time, check the headlight wiper blades (where fitted) for condition, and renew if necessary.

> **HAYNES HiNT** *For maximum clarity of vision, windscreen wiper blades should be renewed annually, as a matter of course.*

3 To remove a blade, hinge the arm and blade away from the screen. Press the tab on the spring clip in the middle of the blade and unhook the blade from the arm.

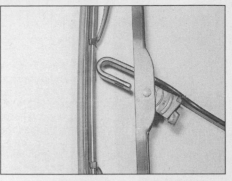

7.4 Fitting a windscreen wiper blade

4 Refit the blade by sliding it onto the hook on the arm **(see illustration)**.
5 Check that the windscreen washer jets operate correctly, and direct the washer fluid towards the upper area of the wiper blade stroke. If necessary, use a pin to reposition the washer jets.

3 Persistent need for topping-up the battery electrolyte suggests either that the alternator output is excessive. or that the battery is approaching the end of its life.
4 Further information on the battery, charging and jump-starting can be found in Chapter 5, and in the preliminary Sections of this manual.

Every 6000 miles or 6 months

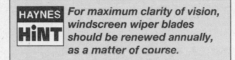

8 Engine oil and filter renewal

> **HAYNES HiNT** *Frequent oil and filter changes are the most important preventative maintenance procedures which can be undertaken by the DIY owner. As engine oil ages, it becomes diluted and contaminated, which leads to premature engine wear.*

1 Before starting this procedure, gather together all the necessary tools and materials. Also make sure that you have plenty of clean rags and newspapers handy, to mop up any spills. Ideally, the engine oil should be warm, as it will drain better, and more built-up sludge will be removed with it. Take care, however, not to touch the exhaust or any other hot parts of the engine when working under the vehicle. To avoid any possibility of scalding, and to

8.6 Fitting an oil filter

protect yourself from possible skin irritants and other harmful contaminants in used engine oils, it is advisable to wear gloves when carrying out this work.
2 Access to the underside of the vehicle will be greatly improved if it can be raised on a lift, driven onto ramps, or jacked up and supported on axle stands (see *"Jacking"*). Whichever method is chosen, make sure that the vehicle remains level, or if it is at an angle, that the drain plug is at the lowest point.
3 Slacken the drain plug about half a turn. Position the draining container under the drain plug, then remove the plug completely. If possible, try to keep the plug pressed into the sump while unscrewing it by hand the last couple of turns. As the plug releases from the threads, move it away sharply so the stream of oil issuing from the sump runs into the container, not up your sleeve. Recover the sealing washer from the drain plug.
4 Allow some time for the old oil to drain, noting that it may be necessary to reposition the container as the oil flow slows to a trickle.
5 After all the oil has drained, wipe off the drain plug with a clean rag. Check the sealing washer for condition, and renew it if necessary. Clean the area around the drain plug opening, and refit the plug. Tighten the plug to the specified torque.
6 Move the container into position under the oil filter. On SOHC engines, the filter is located on the left-hand side of the cylinder block in front of the engine bearer. On DOHC and V6 engines, the filter is located on the right-hand side of the cylinder block **(see illustration)**.
7 Using an oil filter removal tool if necessary, slacken the filter, then unscrew it by hand the rest of the way. Empty the oil from the old filter into the container, and discard the filter.

8 Use a clean rag to remove all oil, dirt and sludge from the filter sealing area on the engine. Check the old filter to make sure that the rubber sealing ring hasn't stuck to the engine. If it has, carefully remove it.
9 Apply a light coating of clean engine oil to the sealing ring on the new filter, then screw it into position on the engine. Tighten the filter firmly by hand only - **do not** use any tools. Wipe clean the filter and sump drain plug.
10 Remove the old oil and all tools from under the car, then lower the car to the ground (if applicable).
11 Remove the oil filler cap and withdraw the dipstick from the top of the filler tube. Fill the engine, using the correct grade and type of oil (see *"Lubricants and fluids"*). An oil can spout or funnel may help to reduce spillage. Pour in half the specified quantity of oil first, then wait a few minutes for the oil to fall to the sump. Continue adding oil a small quantity at a time until the level is up to the lower mark on the dipstick. Finally, bring the level up to the upper mark on the dipstick. Insert the dipstick, and refit the filler cap.
12 Start the engine and run it for a few minutes; check for leaks around the oil filter seal and the sump drain plug. Note that there may be a delay of a few seconds before the oil pressure warning light goes out when the engine is first started, as the oil circulates through the engine oil galleries and the new oil filter, before the pressure builds up.
13 Switch off the engine, and wait a few minutes for the oil to settle in the sump once more. With the new oil circulated and the filter completely full, recheck the level on the dipstick, and add more oil as necessary.
14 Dispose of the used engine oil safely, with reference to *"General repair procedures"* in the reference Sections of this manual.

1

9 Front and rear brake pad check

1 Firmly apply the handbrake, then jack up the front and rear of the car and support it securely on axle stands (see *"Jacking"*).
2 For a quick check, the front brake disc pads can be inspected without removing the front wheels, using a mirror and a torch through the aperture in the rear face of the caliper. If any one pad is worn down to the minimum specified, all four pads (on both front wheels) must be renewed.
3 It is necessary to remove the rear wheels in order to inspect the rear pads. The pads can be viewed through the top of the caliper after removing the spring clip. If any one pad is worn down to the minimum specified, all four pads (on both rear wheels) must be renewed.
4 For a comprehensive check, the brake pads should be removed and cleaned. The operation of the caliper can then also be checked, and the condition of the brake discs can be fully examined on both sides. Refer to Chapter 10 for further information.
5 At the same interval, check the function of the brake fluid level warning light. Chock the wheels, release the handbrake and switch on the ignition. Unscrew and raise the brake fluid reservoir cap whilst an assistant observes the warning light: it should come on as the level sensor is withdrawn from the fluid. Refit the cap.
6 On completion, refit the wheels and lower the car to the ground.

10 Fluid leak check

1 Visually inspect the engine joint faces, gaskets and seals for any signs of water or oil leaks. Pay particular attention to the areas around the rocker cover, cylinder head, oil filter and sump joint faces. Bear in mind that over a period of time some very slight seepage from these areas is to be expected but what you are really looking for is any indication of a serious leak. Should a leak be found, renew the offending gasket or oil seal by referring to the appropriate Chapter(s) in this manual.
2 Similarly, check the transmission for oil leaks, and investigate and rectify and problems found.
3 Check the security and condition of all the engine related pipes and hoses. Ensure that all cable-ties or securing clips are in place and in good condition. Clips which are broken or missing can lead to chafing of the hoses, pipes or wiring which could cause more serious problems in the future.
4 Carefully check the condition of all coolant, fuel and brake hoses. Renew any hose which is cracked, swollen or deteriorated. Cracks will show up better if the hose is squeezed. Pay close attention to the hose clips that secure the hoses to the system components. Hose

clips can pinch and puncture hoses, resulting in leaks. If wire type hose clips are used, it may be a good idea to replace them with screw-type clips.
5 With the vehicle raised, inspect the fuel tank and filler neck for punctures, cracks and other damage. The connection between the filler neck and tank is especially critical. Sometimes a rubber filler neck or connecting hose will leak due to loose retaining clamps or deteriorated rubber.
6 Similarly, inspect all brake hoses and metal pipes. If any damage or deterioration is discovered, do not drive the vehicle until the necessary repair work has been carried out. Renew any damaged sections of hose or pipe.
7 Carefully check all rubber hoses and metal fuel lines leading away from the petrol tank. Check for loose connections, deteriorated hoses, crimped lines and other damage. Pay particular attention to the vent pipes and hoses which often loop up around the filler neck and can become blocked or crimped. Follow the lines to the front of the vehicle carefully inspecting them all the way. Renew damaged sections as necessary.
8 From within the engine compartment, check the security of all fuel hose attachments and pipe unions, and inspect the fuel hoses and vacuum hoses for kinks, chafing and deterioration.
9 Where applicable, check the condition of the oil cooler hoses and pipes.
10 Check the condition of all exposed wiring harnesses.
11 Also check the engine and transmission components for signs of fluid leaks.

11 Seat belt check

Periodically check the belts for fraying or other damage. If evident, renew the belt.

If the belts become dirty, wipe them with a damp cloth using a little detergent only.

Check the tightness of the anchor bolts and if they are ever disconnected, make quite sure that the original sequence of fitting of washers, bushes and anchor plates is retained.

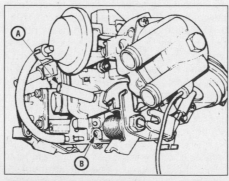

15.3 Idle adjustment screws - Pierburg 2V carburettor

A Idle speed   *B Idle mixture*

12 Exhaust system check

With the vehicle raised on a hoist or supported on axle stands (see *"Jacking"*), check the exhaust system for signs of leaks, corrosion or damage and check the rubber mountings for condition and security. Where damage or corrosion are evident, renew the system complete or in sections, as applicable, using the information given in Chapter 4.

13 Roadwheel security check

With the wheels on the ground, slacken each wheel nut by a quarter turn, then retighten it immediately to the specified torque.

14 Oil filler cap check

Remove and clean the oil filler cap of any sludge build-up using paraffin.

Inspect the vent hose for blockage or damage. A blocked hose can cause a build-up of crankcase pressure, which in turn can cause oil leaks.

15 Idle speed check - 1.8 litre SOHC

An accurate tachometer (rev. counter) will be needed to adjust the idle speed. The engine must be at operating temperature, the air cleaner element must be clean and the vacuum hoses fitted, and the engine valve clearances must be correct. The ignition system must also be in good condition.

Connect the tachometer to the engine as instructed by the manufacturers. Start the engine and allow it to idle. Read the speed from the tachometer and compare it with the value in the Specifications of Chapter 4 (Pierburg 2V carburettor).

If adjustment is necessary, turn the idle speed adjustment screw. Turn the screw clockwise to increase the speed, and anti-clockwise to decrease the speed **(see illustration)**.

16 Idle mixture check - carburettor models only

1.8 litre engine

1 An exhaust gas analyser (CO meter) or other proprietary device will be needed to adjust the idle mixture.
2 The engine must be at operating temperature, the air cleaner element must be clean and the vacuum hoses fitted, and the

16.12 Idle mixture adjustment screw (arrowed) - Weber 2V carburettor

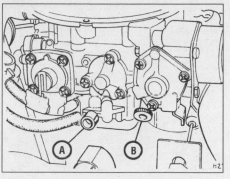

16.13 Idle adjustment screws- Weber 2V TLD carburettor

A Idle mixture   B Idle speed

engine valve clearances must be correct. The ignition system must also be in good condition.

3 Mixture adjustment is not usual on a routine basis. If the CO level is incorrect, proceed as follows.

4 Connect the exhaust gas analyser as instructed by the manufacturers.

5 Raise the engine speed to 3000 rpm approximately and hold it at this speed for 30 seconds, then allow it to idle. Repeat this procedure every 60 seconds until adjustment is complete.

6 Read the CO level when it has stabilised after the 3000 rpm burst. The desired level is given in the Specifications of Chapter 4 (Pierburg 2V carburettor).

7 If the idle mixture needs adjustment, turn the mixture adjusting screw. The screw may be covered by a tamperproof plug.

8 Recheck the idle speed after adjusting the mixture.

9 Stop the engine and disconnect the test gear.

10 Fit a new tamperproof plug to the mixture adjusting screw if required.

2.0 litre SOHC engine

11 If mixture adjustment is required, proceed as described for the 1.8 litre engine above.

12 **See illustration** for the location of the mixture adjusting screw on the Weber 2V carburettor fitted to this engine

DOHC engine

13 Proceed as described for the 1.8 litre engine, noting the following points **(see illustration).**

14 Refer to the Specification for the Weber 2V (TLD) carburettor in Chapter 4.

15 The air cleaner must be removed for access to the mixture adjustment screw.

16 Prise the tamperproof seal from the mixture screw.

17 Loosely refit the air cleaner, ensuring that the vacuum pipe and the camshaft cover breather hose are securely connected and free from restrictions (there is no need to secure the air cleaner in position).

18 On completion, fit a new tamperproof seal to the mixture screw (the service replacement plug is coloured blue) and refit the air cleaner assembly.

Every 12 000 miles or 12 months

17 Automatic transmission fluid level check

1 Fluid level should be checked with the transmission at operating temperature (after a run) and with the vehicle parked on level ground.

2 Open and prop the bonnet. With the engine idling and the handbrake and footbrake applied, move the gear selector through all positions three times, finishing up in position P.

3 Wait one minute. With the engine still idling, withdraw the transmission dipstick **(see illustration).** Wipe the dipstick with a clean lint-free rag, re-insert it fully and withdraw it again. Read the fluid level at the end of the dipstick: it should be between the two notches.

4 If topping-up is necessary, do so via the dipstick tube, using clean transmission fluid of the specified type **(see illustration).** Do not overfill.

5 Stop the engine, refit the dipstick and close the bonnet.

6 Note that if the fluid level was below the minimum mark when checked or is in constant need of topping-up, check around the transmission for any signs of excessive fluid leaks.If present, leaks must be rectified without delay.

7 If the colour of the fluid is dark brown or black this denotes the sign of a worn brake band or transmission clutches, in which case have your Ford dealer check the transmission at the earliest opportunity.

18 Manual gearbox oil level check

1 Place the vehicle over a pit, or raise and support it at front and rear. The vehicle must be level for an accurate check.

2 If the transmission is hot after a run, allow it to cool for a few minutes. This is necessary because the oil can foam when hot and give a false level reading.

3 Wipe clean around the filler/level plug, which is located on the left-hand side of the gearbox. Unscrew the plug with a square drive key and remove it

4 Using a piece of bent wire as a dipstick, check that the oil level is up to the bottom of the filler/level plug hole, or no more than 5 mm (0.2 in) below it.

5 Top-up if necessary using clean oil of the specified type. Do not overfill; allow excess oil to drip out of the plug hole if necessary. Refit and tighten the filler/level plug.

6 Frequent need for topping-up can only be due to leaks, which should be rectified. The rear extension oil seal can be renewed *in situ* after removing the propeller shaft (N type only).

7 No periodic oil changing is specified, and no drain plug is fitted.

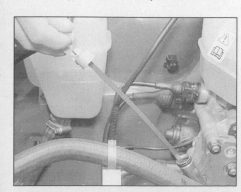

17.3 The automatic transmission dipstick

17.4 Topping up the transmission fluid

19 Hinge and lock check and lubrication

1 Work around the vehicle, and lubricate the hinges and locks with a light machine oil.
2 Lightly lubricate the bonnet release mechanism and exposed sections of inner cable with a smear of grease.
3 Check the security and operation of all hinges, latches and locks, adjusting them where required. Where applicable, check the operation of the central locking system.
4 Check the condition and operation of the tailgate struts, renewing them if either is leaking or is no longer able to support the tailgate securely when raised.

20 Spark plug renewal

SOHC and V6 engines

1 The correct functioning of the spark plugs is vital for the correct running and efficiency of the engine. It is essential that the plugs fitted are appropriate for the engine.
2 Make sure that the ignition is switched off before inspecting the HT leads to see if they carry their cylinder numbers - if not, number each lead using sticky tape or paint.
3 Pull the HT lead connectors off the plugs. Pull on the connectors, not on the leads.
4 Blow away any dirt from around the spark plug recesses in the cylinder head(s).
5 Unscrew and remove the plugs, using a proprietary plug spanner or a spark plug socket, extension and ratchet.
6 The condition of the plugs will tell much about the overall condition of the engine. If the insulator nose of the spark plug is clean and white, with no deposits, this is indicative of a weak mixture or too hot a plug (a hot plug transfers heat away from the electrode slowly, a cold plug transfers heat away quickly).
7 If the tip and insulator nose are covered with hard black-looking deposits, then this is indicative that the mixture is too rich. Should the plug be black and oily, then it is likely that the engine is fairly worn, as well as the mixture being too rich.
8 If the insulator nose is covered with light tan to greyish-brown deposits, then the mixture is correct, and it is likely that the engine is in good condition.
9 Apply a smear of anti-seize compound to the threads of the new plugs. Make sure that the insulators are clean and that the screwed HT lead adapters are tight. Pay particular attention to the plug seating surfaces on OHC engines, since these plugs have no sealing washers ("taper seat" type) and any dirt will cause a bad seal.
10 Screw each plug into its hole by hand. If a plug is reluctant to go in, do not force it with a spanner, but unscrew it and try again. If the plug is cross-threaded, it is the cylinder head which will be damaged.

HAYNES HiNT

It is very often difficult to insert spark plugs into their holes without cross-threading them. To avoid this possibility, fit a short length of 5/16-inch internal diameter rubber hose over the end of the spark plug. The flexible hose acts as a universal joint to help align the plug with the plug hole. Should the plug begin to cross-thread, the hose will slip on the spark plug, preventing thread damage to the aluminium cylinder head. Remove the rubber hose, and tighten the plug to the specified torque using the spark plug socket and a torque wrench. Fit the remaining spark plugs in the same manner.

11 Final tightening of the spark plugs should ideally be carried out using a torque wrench. The tightening torques are given in the Specifications. If a torque wrench is not available, tighten the plugs beyond the point where they contact the head as follows:

OHC (taper seat plugs) - One-sixteenth of a turn maximum

V6 (plugs with washers) - One-quarter of a turn maximum

12 If the taper seat type of plug is overtightened, the sealing faces will bite together and removal will be very difficult.
13 Refit the HT leads to the plugs, paying attention to the cylinder numbers. Push each connector firmly onto its plug.
14 Run the engine to verify that the HT leads have been refitted correctly.

DOHC engines

15 Proceed as described above whilst noting the following points.
a) *Remove the air cleaner as described in Chapter 4.*
b) *The minimal length of number 3 HT lead makes removal from the spark plug difficult. It is advisable to remove this lead from the distributor prior to removing it from the spark plug.*
c) *The spark plugs are deeply recessed in the cylinder head and it will be necessary to use a spark plug socket with a long extension bar. If possible, use a spark plug socket with a rubber grip inside as this will hold onto the spark plug once loosened and will enable the spark plugs to be withdrawn and refitted more easily.*

21 Auxiliary drivebelt check

SOHC and all V6 engines

1 All of these engines have one or two drivebelts which drive the water pump and alternator from the crankshaft pulley. When power steering is fitted, the same belts drive the steering pump. The air conditioning compressor, when fitted, is driven independently.
2 Periodically inspect the drivebelt(s) for fraying, cracks, glazing or other damage. Turn the engine so that the full length of the belt(s) can be viewed. Renew belts which are in poor condition. When twin drivebelts are fitted, both must be renewed together, even if only one is damaged.
3 Check the tension of the drivebelt(s) by pressing firmly with the fingers in the middle of the longest belt run (engine stopped). Tension is correct when the belt can be deflected by 10 mm (0.4 in) under firm finger pressure (see illustration).
4 Renewal and adjustment procedures for models with power steering are given in Chapter 11. For other models proceed as follows.
5 Disconnect the battery negative lead.
6 On models with air conditioning, remove the compressor drivebelt.
7 Slacken the alternator pivot and adjusting bolts. Swing the alternator towards the engine and slip the belt(s) off the pulleys.
8 Fit the new belt(s) over the pulleys. Move the alternator away from the engine until the belt tension is correct, then tighten the alternator adjusting strap and pivot bolts. If it is necessary to lever against the alternator to achieve the correct tension, only do so using a wooden or plastic lever **(see illustration)**.
9 Refit and tension the air conditioning compressor drivebelt, when applicable.
10 Reconnect the battery. If a new drivebelt has been fitted, run the engine for a few minutes, then stop it and recheck the tension.
11 Check the tension of new belts again after a few hundred miles.

21.3 Checking drivebelt tension

21.8 Tightening the alternator strap bolt

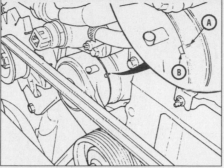

21.14a Water pump/alternator drivebelt tensioner indicator position - DOHC engine

A Indicator mark   B Block

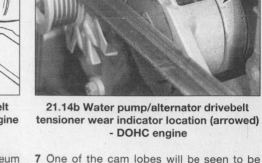

21.14b Water pump/alternator drivebelt tensioner wear indicator location (arrowed) - DOHC engine

DOHC engines

12 On this engine, the coolant/alternator drivebelt also drives the power steering pump and (where applicable) the air conditioning compressor. The drivebelt tension is set by an automatic tensioner assembly.

13 The condition of the drivebelt should be checked as described above.

14 An idea of the amount of wear which has taken place on the belt can be gained from the position of indicator mark (A) on the mounting bracket in relation to the block (B) on the tensioner arm **(see illustration)**. When the belt is new the mark should be aligned with the top of the tensioner block. As the belt wears, the tensioner arm moves and the block on the arm will move slowly up in relation to the mark on the bracket. When the mark aligns with the bottom of the tensioner arm block the belt can be regarded as worn and should be replaced **(see illustration)**.

15 To renew the belt, turn the automatic tensioner arm clockwise, using a 17 mm socket and a wrench on the boss in the centre of the pulley, and slide the belt from the pulleys, then slowly release the tensioner.

16 To fit a new belt, rotate the tensioner clockwise as during removal, then slide the belt over the pulleys. With the belt correctly located, slowly release the tensioner; the tensioner will automatically set the correct drivebelt tension.

22 Battery terminal check

Caution: *Before carrying out any work on the vehicle battery, read through the precautions given in "Safety first!" at the beginning of this manual.*

1 The battery fitted as original equipment is "maintenance-free", and requires no maintenance apart from having the case kept clean, and the terminals clean and tight.

2 To clean the battery terminals disconnect them, after having first removed the cover (later models) - negative earth first. Use a wire brush or abrasive paper to clean the terminals. Bad corrosion should be treated with a solution of bicarbonate of soda, applied with an old toothbrush. Do not let this solution get inside the battery.

3 Coat the battery terminals with petroleum jelly or a proprietary anti-corrosive compound before reconnecting them. Reconnect and tighten the positive (live) lead first, followed by the negative (earth) lead. Do not overtighten.

4 Keep the top of the battery clean and dry. Periodically inspect the battery tray for corrosion, and make good as necessary.

5 Further information on the battery, charging and jump-starting can be found in Chapter 5, and in the preliminary Sections of this manual.

23 Engine valve clearance check

SOHC engines

1 Valve clearances are checked with the engine cold.

2 On carburettor models, remove the air cleaner.

3 On fuel-injection models, remove the bracing strap which connects the inlet manifold to the right-hand side of the engine.

4 On all models, identify the HT leads and disconnect them from the spark plugs. Unclip the leads from the rocker cover.

5 Although not essential, it will make the engine easier to turn if the spark plugs are removed.

6 Remove the ten bolts which secure the rocker cover, noting the location of the different shapes of reinforcing plates. Remove the cover and gasket.

7 One of the cam lobes will be seen to be pointing upwards. Measure the clearance between the base of this cam and the cam follower, finding the thickness of feeler blade which gives a firm sliding fit **(see illustration)**.

8 The desired valve clearances are given in the Specifications. Note that the clearances for inlet and exhaust valves are different. Numbering from the front (sprocket) end of the camshaft, the exhaust valves are 1, 3, 5 and 7, and the inlet valves 2, 4, 6 and 8.

9 If adjustment is necessary, slacken the ball-pin locknut and screw the ball-pin up or down until the clearance is correct. Hold the ball-pin stationary and tighten the locknut **(see illustration)**. Recheck the clearance after tightening the locknut in case the ball-pin has moved.

10 Turn the engine to bring another cam lobe to the vertical position and repeat the above procedure. Carry on until all eight valves have been checked.

11 Access to some of the ball-pins is made difficult by the carburettor or fuel-injection inlet manifold. To avoid having to remove the offending components, double cranked spanners or cutaway socket spanners can be used **(see illustration)**.

12 When adjustment is complete, refit the rocker cover using a new gasket. Make sure that the dovetail sections of the gasket fit together correctly.

13 Fit the rocker cover bolts and reinforcing plates. Tighten the bolts as described in Chapter 2A Section 44, paragraph 11.

23.7 Measuring a valve clearance - SOHC engine

23.9 Adjusting a valve clearance - SOHC engine

1

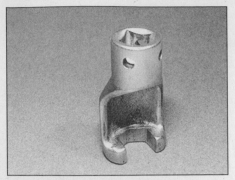
23.11 Cutaway socket spanner

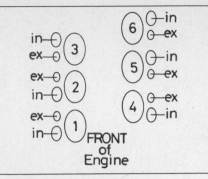
23.19 Inlet and exhaust valve location - 2.8 litre V6 engine

14 Refit the other disturbed components.
15 Run the engine and check that there are no oil leaks from the rocker cover.

2.8 litre engine

16 If the engine is in the vehicle, carry out the preliminary steps:
a) *Disconnect the battery negative lead*
b) *Remove the throttle mechanism cover, air cleaner cover, airflow meters and inlet trunking*
c) *Remove the HT leads from the spark plugs and unclip them from the rocker cover*
d) *Unbolt and remove the rocker covers*

17 Although not essential, it will be easier to turn the engine if the spark plugs are removed.
18 Valve clearances must be adjusted with the engine cold (less than 40°C/104°F).
19 Turn the engine, using a spanner on the crankshaft pulley bolt, until the crankshaft pulley timing mark is aligned with the TDC (zero) pointer on the timing cover and the valves of No 5 cylinder are overlapping, ie the exhaust valve is closing and the inlet valve is opening. (No 5 cylinder is the middle one on the left-hand bank - left being the vehicle's left, not necessarily to operator's.) **(see illustration).**
20 When the valves of No 5 cylinder are in this position, check the valve clearances of No1 cylinder by inserting a feeler blade of the specified thickness between the rocker arm and the valve stem. Adjust the clearance, if necessary, by turning the rocker arm adjusting

screw until the specified clearance is obtained **(see illustration)**. Inlet and exhaust valve are different.
21 If the engine is now rotated one-third of a turn clockwise at the crankshaft, the valves of No 3 cylinder will be overlapping and the valves of No4 cylinder can be checked and adjusted.
22 Proceed to adjust the clearances according to the firing order as follows. The cylinders are numbered **(see illustration)** and the valves are listed in their correct order, working from the front of the engine:

Valves overlapping	Valves to adjust
No 5 cylinder	*No 1 cylinder (in, ex)*
No 3 cylinder	*No 4 cylinder (in, ex)*
No 6 cylinder	*No 2 cylinder (in, ex)*
No 1 cylinder	*No 5 cylinder (ex, in)*
No 4 cylinder	*No 3 cylinder (ex, in)*
No 2 cylinder	*No 6 cylinder (ex, in)*

23 Refit the rocker covers, using new gaskets if necessary. Tighten the rocker cover bolts to the specified torque.
24 If the engine is in the vehicle, refit the other displaced components.

2.4 & 2.9 litre engines

25 The operation for these engines is essentially as described for the 2.8 litre engine, noting that the valve arrangement is changed **(see illustrations)**.

24 Engine inlet manifold security check - V6 only

Using a spanner of the appropriate size, check each manifold securing nut in turn whilst referring to the appropriate Sections in Chapter 2C for tightening sequences and torque loading figures.

25 Air conditioner condenser check

Remove the radiator grille and clean any leaves, insects etc. from the condenser coil and fins. Be very careful not to damage the condenser fins: use a soft brush, or a compressed air jet, along (not across) the fins **(see illustration)**.

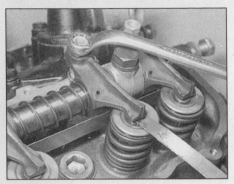
23.20 Adjusting a valve clearance - V6 engine

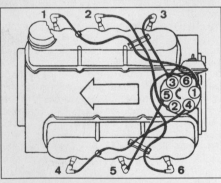
23.22 Cylinder numbering and HT lead connections - V6 engine
White arrow points to front of engine

23.25a Valve arrangement for RH cylinder head - 2.4 & 2.9 litre engines
Upper arrow points to front of engine

23.25b Valve arrangement for LH cylinder head - 2.4 & 2.9 litre engines
Upper arrow points to front of engine

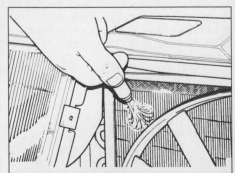
25.1 Cleaning the air conditioner condenser fins

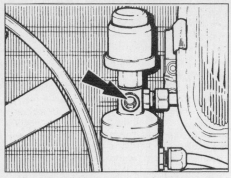

26.3 Refrigerant sight glass (arrowed)

27.3 Final drive oil filler/level plug (arrowed)

30 Driveshaft check

Position the vehicle over a pit, or raise it at front and rear on ramps or axle stands.

Examine the driveshaft joint rubber gaiters. Flex the gaiters by hand and inspect the folds and clips. Damaged or leaking gaiters must be renewed without delay to avoid damage occurring to the joint itself

Check the tightness of the final drive mounting bolts and the driveshaft flange screws.

26 Air conditioner refrigerant charge check

1 Remove the radiator grille being careful not to damage the condenser fins.
2 Check the refrigerant charge as follows. The engine should be cold and the ambient temperature should be between 18° and 25°C (64° and 77°F).
3 Start the engine and allow it to idle. Observe the refrigerant sight glass (see illustration) and have an assistant switch on the air conditioning to fan speed III. A few bubbles should be seen in the sight glass as the system starts up, but all bubbles should disappear within 10 seconds. Persistent bubbles, or no bubbles at all, mean that the refrigerant charge is low. Switch off the system immediately if the charge is low and do not use it again until it has been recharged.
4 Inspect the refrigerant pipes, hoses and unions for security and good condition. Refit the radiator grille.
5 The air conditioning system will lose a proportion of its charge through normal seepage typically up to 100 g (4 oz) per year - so it is as well to regard periodic recharging as a maintenance operation.

27 Final drive oil level check

1 Check the final drive oil level as follows.
2 Position the vehicle over a pit, or raise it at front and rear on ramps or axle stands (see "Jacking"). The vehicle must be level.
3 Wipe clean around the final drive filler/level plug (see illustration). Unscrew the plug with a hexagon key. Using a piece of bent wire as a dipstick, check that the oil is no more than 10 mm (0.4 in) below the plug hole.
4 If topping-up is necessary, use clean gear oil of the specified type. Do not overfill. Frequent need for topping-up can only be due to leaks, which should be rectified.
5 When the level is correct, refit the filler/level plug and tighten it.
6 There is no requirement for periodic oil changing, and no drain plug is provided.

28 Automatic transmission selector linkage lubrication

Lubricate the transmission selector and kickdown linkages with engine oil or aerosol lubricant.

29 Steering and suspension security check

1 Examine all steering and suspension components for wear and damage. Pay particular attention to dust covers and gaiters, which if renewed promptly when damaged can save further damage to the component protected.
2 At the same intervals, check the front suspension lower arm balljoints for wear by levering up the arms (see illustration). Balljoint free movement must not exceed 0.5 mm (0.02 in). The track rod end balljoints can be checked in a similar manner, or by observing them whilst an assistant rocks the steering wheel back and forth. If the lower arm balljoint is worn, the complete lower arm must be renewed.
3 Check the shock absorbers by bouncing the vehicle up and down at each corner in turn. When released, it should come to rest within one complete oscillation. Continued movement, or squeaking and groaning noises from the shock absorber suggests that renewal is required.

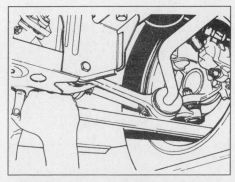

29.2 Checking a front suspension lower arm balljoint

31 Underbody inspection

1 Except on vehicles with a wax-based underbody protective coating, have the whole of the underframe of the vehicle steam-cleaned, engine compartment included, so that a thorough inspection can be carried out to see what minor repairs and renovations are necessary.
2 Steam-cleaning is available at many garages, and is necessary for the removal of the accumulation of oily grime, which sometimes is allowed to become thick in certain areas. If steam-cleaning facilities are not available, there are some excellent grease solvents available which can be brush-applied; the dirt can then be simply hosed off.
3 After cleaning, position the vehicle over a pit, or raise it at front and rear on ramps or axle stands.
4 Using a strong light, work around the underside of the vehicle, inspecting it for corrosion or damage. If either is found, refer to Chapter 12 for details of repair.

32 Brake pipe and hose check

Periodically inspect the rigid brake pipes for rust and other damage, and the flexible hoses for cracks, splits or "ballooning". Have an assistant depress the brake pedal (ignition on) and inspect the hose and pipe unions for leaks. Renew any defective item without delay.

33 Idle speed linkage clean

On 2.0 litre engines, good electrical contact between the carburettor stepper motor plunger and the adjusting screw is essential to maintain a regular idle speed.

Clean the plunger and adjusting screw contact faces with abrasive paper followed by switch cleaning fluid. Switch cleaning fluid is available from electronic component shops.

1

Every 24 000 miles or 2 years

34 Road test

Instruments and electrical equipment

1 Check the operation of all instruments and electrical equipment.
2 Make sure that all instruments read correctly, and switch on all electrical equipment in turn to check that it functions properly.

Steering and suspension

3 Check for any abnormalities in the steering, suspension, handling or road "feel".
4 Drive the vehicle, and check that there are no unusual vibrations or noises.
5 Check that the steering feels positive, with no excessive "sloppiness", or roughness, and check for any suspension noises when cornering, or when driving over bumps.

Drivetrain

6 Check the performance of the engine, clutch, transmission and driveshafts.
7 Listen for any unusual noises from the engine, clutch and transmission.
8 Make sure that the engine runs smoothly when idling, and that there is no hesitation when accelerating.
9 Where applicable, check that the clutch action is smooth and progressive, that the drive is taken up smoothly, and that the pedal travel is not excessive. Also listen for any noises when the clutch pedal is depressed.
10 Check that all gears can be engaged smoothly, without noise, and that the gear lever action is not abnormally vague or "notchy".

35.2 Removing the power steering fluid dipstick

Check the operation and performance of the braking system

11 Make sure that the vehicle does not pull to one side when braking, and that the wheels do not lock prematurely when braking hard.
12 Check that there is no vibration through the steering when braking.
13 Check that the handbrake operates correctly, without excessive movement of the lever, and that it holds the vehicle stationary on a slope.
14 Test the operation of the brake servo unit as follows. With the engine off, depress the footbrake four or five times to exhaust the vacuum. Start the engine, holding the brake pedal depressed. As the engine starts, there should be a noticeable "give" in the brake pedal as vacuum builds up. Allow the engine to run for at least two minutes, and then switch it off. If the brake pedal is depressed now, it should be possible to detect a hiss from the servo as the pedal is depressed. After about four or five applications, no further hissing should be heard, and the pedal should feel considerably firmer.

35 Power steering fluid level check

1 The power steering fluid dipstick is incorporated in the reservoir filler cap. The reservoir is mounted on the pump. Observe scrupulous cleanliness when checking the level or topping-up.
2 The system should be at operating temperature and the engine switched off. Wipe clean around the reservoir filler cap. Unscrew the cap, withdraw the dipstick and wipe it with a clean lint-free rag. Reinsert the dipstick, screw the cap home, then unscrew it again and read the level on the dipstick. It should be up to the MAX or upper HOT mark (depending on the dipstick markings) (see illustration).
3 Top-up if necessary with clean fluid of the specified type. Check for leaks if topping-up is frequently required.
4 If the level is checked cold, use the MIN or FULL COLD mark on the dipstick for reference. Recheck the level at operating temperature.

36 Automatic choke check

On carburettor models, remove the air cleaner cover and check that the automatic choke is opening fully when the engine is hot.

37 Hot starting check

Run the engine until it reaches normal operating temperature. Stop the engine and immediately restart it. If the engine fails to start cleanly and immediately then refer to either Chapters 4 or 5 and check fuel feed adjustments.

Every 24 000 miles or 2 years

38 Air cleaner filter element renewal

Carburettor models

SOHC engines

1 Remove the screws from the air cleaner cover (see illustration).
2 Release the spring clips (when fitted), then lift off the cover (see illustration).
3 Lift out the air cleaner element (see illustration). Wipe clean inside the air cleaner housing, but be careful not to sweep dirt into the carburettor throat.
4 Where it is necessary to remove the air cleaner body for cleaning or repair, first disconnect the cold air inlet trunking from the spout (see illustration).

5 Disconnect the vacuum pipe from the inlet manifold, and the hot air trunking from the spout or exhaust manifold shroud (see illustration).

6 Remove the remaining screw which secures the air cleaner to the valve cover, then lift off the air cleaner.
7 Refit by reversing the removal operations.

38.1 Removing an air cleaner cover screw (carburettor model)

38.2 Releasing an air cleaner cover clip (carburettor model)

38.3 Removing the air cleaner element (carburettor model)

38.4 Disconnecting the air cleaner cold air inlet trunking (carburettor model)

38.5 Air cleaner hot air trunking and manifold shroud (carburettor model)

DOHC engine

8 Proceed as described above whilst noting that the camshaft cover breather hose must be disconnected before the air cleaner can be removed.

Fuel-injection models

SOHC and V6 engines

9 Release the four spring clips which secure the air cleaner cover (see illustration).
10 Lift off the cover and move it aside. It is attached to the vane airflow meter(s): be careful not to strain the air trunking or meter wiring. To remove the cover completely, disconnect the meter(s) or unbolt the cover (see illustration).
11 Remove the air cleaner element, noting

which way up it is fitted (see illustration). Wipe clean inside the air cleaner body.
12 Where it is necessary to remove the air cleaner body for cleaning or repair, remove the three securing nuts which are accessible from inside the left-hand wheel arch. Disengage the body from the air pick-up hose and remove it.
13 Refit by reversing the removal operations.

DOHC engine

14 To renew the element, disconnect the battery negative lead.
15 Disconnect the wiring plug from the idle speed control valve at the front of the plenum chamber.
16 Loosen the clamp, and detach the air inlet hose from the air inlet tubing.
17 Unscrew the securing nut, and release the

air inlet tube from the bracket on the engine compartment front panel (see illustration).
18 Release the air cleaner lid securing clips, then lift away the air inlet tube, plenum chamber and air cleaner lid as an assembly, disconnecting the breather hose from the air inlet tube.
19 Lift out the air cleaner element, then wipe the inside of the air cleaner lid and casing clean (see illustration).
20 Fit the new element with the sealing lip uppermost.
21 Further refitting is a reversal of removal.
22 To remove and refit the air cleaner housing, refer to paragraph 12.
23 Refitting is the reverse of the removal procedure.

39 Ignition system component check

1 Before disturbing any part of the ignition system, disconnect the battery negative lead.
2 Identify and clearly mark all HT leads before disconnecting them from the spark plugs.

All engines except DOHC

3 On V6 models, remove the screening can lid (see illustration).
4 Remove the coil-to-distributor HT lead (sometimes called the king lead) by disconnecting it from the coil tower and the distributor cap.
5 Disconnect the other HT leads from the

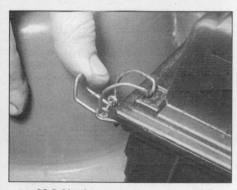

38.9 Air cleaner cover spring clip (fuel-injection SOHC and V6)

38.10 Airflow meter to cover bolts (arrowed) (fuel-injection SOHC and V6)

38.11 Removing the air cleaner element (fuel-injection SOHC and V6)

38.17 Air intake tube retaining nut (fuel-Injection DOHC)

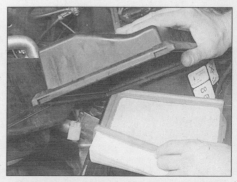

38.19 Removing the air cleaner element (fuel-injection DOHC)

39.3 Removing a distributor can screening lid - V6 engine

39.6 Removing a distributor screening can - V6 engine

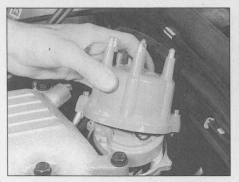

39.7 Removing a distributor cap

distributor cap, making a sketch if necessary so that they can be reconnected to the same terminals. Remove the leads.

6 On V6 models, remove the distributor screening can (see illustration).

7 Release the two clips or screws which secure the distributor cap. Remove the cap (see illustration).

8 Note that if the distributor cap is secured by clips, the engine must not be cranked with the cap removed. This is because it is possible for a spring clip to foul the rotating parts of the distributor and cause damage.

9 Remove the rotor arm. It may simply pull off, or it may be secured by two screws (see illustration). The rotor arm tips may be coated with silicone grease - if so, do not rub it off.

10 Clean the HT leads and distributor cap

with a dry cloth. Scrape any corrosion or other deposits from the connectors and terminals. Also clean the coil tower.

11 Renew the HT leads if they are cracked, burnt or otherwise damaged. If a multi-meter is available, measure the resistance of the leads. The desired value is given in the Specifications of Chapter 5.

12 Renew the distributor cap if it is cracked or badly burnt inside, or if there is evidence of "tracking" (black lines marking the path of HT leakage). If there is a carbon brush at the centre of the cap, make sure that it moves freely, and is not excessively worn.

13 Clean the metal track of the rotor arm with abrasive paper (but see paragraph 9 first). Renew the arm if it is cracked or badly burnt.

14 Commence reassembly by fitting the rotor

arm to the distributor. It is positively located by a notch or shaped pegs so it cannot be fitted the wrong way round. Tighten the securing screws, when applicable.

15 Refit the distributor cap and secure it with the clips or screws.

16 On V6 models, refit the screening can.

17 Reconnect the HT leads to the distributor cap, making sure that they are correctly fitted. The No 1 connector on the cap is marked (see illustration).

18 On V6 models, refit the screening can lid.

19 Reconnect the HT leads to the spark plugs and coil.

20 Reconnect the battery and run the engine.

DOHC engines

21 Unclip the lower section of the distributor shield from the upper section, then unscrew the two securing nuts, and withdraw the upper section of the shield from the studs on the upper timing chain cover (see illustrations).

22 Disconnect the HT leads from the spark plugs by pulling on the connectors, not the leads. Similarly, disconnect the HT lead from the coil, and release it from the clip on the timing chain cover.

23 Using a suitable Torx key or socket, unscrew the two distributor cap securing screws, then lift off the cap.

24 The rotor arm is a push-fit on the end of the rotor shaft (see illustration).

25 If desired, the rotor housing can be pulled from the timing chain cover.

26 Inspect all components as described in

39.9 Removing a rotor arm

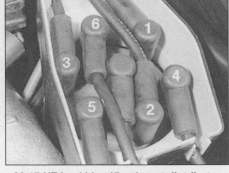

39.17 HT lead identification at distributor cap - V6 engine

39.21a Unclipping the lower section . . .

39.21b . . . and the upper section of the distributor shield - DOHC engine

39.24 Removing the distributor cap and rotor arm - DOHC engine

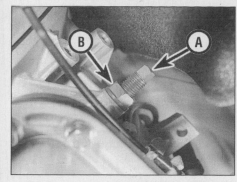

40.3 Brake band adjuster screw (A) and locknut (B)

41.4 Fuel filter outlet union (arrowed) - OHC engine

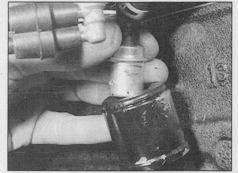

42.1 Pulling the vent valve from the oil separator - SOHC engine

the previous sub Section.

27 Refitting is a reversal of removal, ensuring that the rotor arm is pushed fully home on the rotor shaft. Make sure that the HT leads are fitted to their correct cylinders. Note that the rotor arm will only fit in one position.

40 Automatic transmission brake band adjustment

Note: *A brake band torque wrench - Ford tool No 17-005, or equivalent - will be required for this job.*

1 Raise and support the front of the vehicle.
2 Disconnect the downshift (kickdown) cable from the transmission when so equipped.
3 Release the locknuts on the two brake band adjuster screws. Back off each adjuster screw a couple of turns **(see illustration)**.
4 Using the torque wrench, tighten one adjusting screw to 13 Nm (10 lbf ft). Remove the torque wrench and back off the adjuster screw exactly two full turns from this position, then hold the screw and tighten the locknut.
5 Repeat the operations on the other adjuster.
6 Reconnect the downshift cable, when applicable, then lower the vehicle.

41 Fuel filter renewal

OHC engines

1 Fitted to all fuel-injected models, the filter can be renewed as follows. Disconnect the battery negative lead.
2 Raise and support the rear of the vehicle.
3 Place a drain pan under the fuel filter. Take adequate fire precautions.
4 Wipe clean the area around the filter inlet and outlet unions, then disconnect them **(see Illustration)**. **Caution:** *Fuel under pressure may spray out as the unions are slackened.*
5 Slacken the filter clamp bolt and withdraw the filter from the clamp. Dispose of the filter safely, remember it is full of fuel.
6 Fit the new filter into the clamp, observing the arrows on the filter indicating the direction of fuel flow. If there is a plastic band or sleeve on the filter, position the clamp over the sleeve to prevent chafing. Tighten the clamp bolt.
7 Refit the inlet and outlet unions, using new sealing washers. Tighten the union bolts.
8 Reconnect the battery. Have an assistant

switch the ignition on and off a few times to pressurise the system; watch the filter for leakage as this is done.
9 Lower the vehicle on completion.

V6 engines

10 This operation is essentially the same as described above, noting that the fuel system should first be depressurised, see Chapter 4, Section 28.
11 Once the new filter has been installed, switch the ignition on and off five times, without cranking the engine, to pressurise the system then check the filter unions for leaks.

42 Crankcase ventilation vent valve renewal

Renew the crankcase ventilation vent valve by pulling it from the oil separator and loosening the hose clip **(see illustration)**. Fit the new valve, tighten the clip, and insert it into the oil separator grommet.

Inspect the vent hose for blockage or damage. A blocked hose can cause a build-up of crankcase pressure, which in turn can cause oil leaks.

Every 36 000 miles or 3 years

43 Brake hydraulic system seal and hose renewal

If in doubt as to the condition of any of the brake system seals and hoses, then renew defective items whilst referring to the relevant Sections of Chapter 10.

44 Brake hydraulic fluid renewal

1 An assistant and bleeding equipment will be needed. A considerable quantity of hydraulic fluid will be required - probably about 2 litres (nearly half a gallon).

2 Slacken the front wheel nuts. Raise and support the front of the vehicle and remove the front wheels.
3 Remove the hydraulic fluid reservoir cap.
4 Open both front bleed screws one full turn. Attach one bleed tube to each screw, placing the free end of each tube in a jar.
5 Pump the brake pedal to expel fluid from the bleed screws. Pause after each upstroke to allow the master cylinder to refill.
6 When air emerges from both bleed screws, stop pumping. Detach the left-hand caliper without disconnecting it and remove the inboard brake pad.
7 Depress the caliper piston, using a purpose-made tool or a blunt item such as a tyre lever, to force more fluid out of the caliper. Hold the

piston depressed and have the assistant pump the pedal until air emerges from the bleed screw again.
8 Tighten the bleed screw on the left-hand caliper. Loosely refit the caliper and pad so that the piston is not accidentally ejected.
9 Repeat the purging operation on the right-hand caliper, but do not refit it or tighten the bleed screw yet.
10 Fill the reservoir with fresh hydraulic fluid. Position the bleed jar for the right-hand caliper at least 300 mm (1 foot) above the level of the bleed screw.
11 Have the assistant pump the brake pedal until fluid free of bubbles emerges from the bleed screw. Tighten the bleed screw at the end of a downstroke.

12 Place a piece of wood in the caliper jaws to limit piston travel. Keep your fingers clear of the piston. Have the assistant depress the brake pedal **gently** in order to move the caliper piston out.

13 With the pedal held depressed, slacken the bleed screw on the right-hand caliper and again depress the piston. Tighten the bleed screw when the piston is retracted. The pedal can now be released.

14 Disconnect the bleed tube. Refit the right-hand brake pad and caliper.

15 Remove the left-hand caliper and inboard pad again. Carry out the operations described in paragraphs 10 to 14 on the left-hand caliper.

16 Bleed the rear brakes as described in Chapter 10.

17 Refit the front wheels, lower the vehicle and tighten the wheel nuts.

18 Pump the brake pedal to bring the pads up to the discs, then make a final check of the hydraulic fluid level. Top-up and refit the reservoir cap.

45 Camshaft drivebelt renewal - SOHC engines

Camshaft drivebelt renewal is recommended as a precautionary measure. Refer to Chapter 2, Part A, Sections 13 and 45 for the full renewal procedure.

Every 2 years (regardless of mileage)

46 Engine coolant renewal

1 Before proceeding, note the precautions given in Chapter 3, Section 1.

2 Disconnect the battery negative lead.

3 Remove the expansion tank cap. Take precautions against scalding if the system is hot.

4 Place a drain pan of adequate capacity beneath the radiator drain plug. Unscrew the plug, without removing it, and allow the coolant to drain **(see illustration)**. On OHC engines, release the hose clip and remove the rubber cap from the bleed spigot on top of the thermostat housing **(see illustration)**. On V6 engines, remove the bleed screw (if fitted) from the radiator top hose.

5 Place another drain pan below the cylinder block drain plug, which is located on the right-hand side of the engine (except DOHC engine which has no plug). Remove the drain plug and allow the coolant to drain from the block.

6 Dispose of the old coolant safely, or keep it in a covered container if it is to be re-used.

7 Flushing should not be necessary unless periodic renewal of the coolant has been neglected, or unless plain water has been used as coolant. In either case the coolant will appear rusty and dark in colour. Flushing is then required and should be carried out as follows.

8 Drain the system and disconnect the top hose from the radiator. Insert a garden hose into the radiator and run water into the radiator until it flows clear from the drain plug.

9 Run the hose into the expansion tank (OHC engines) or into the radiator top hose (V6 engines) until clean water comes out of the cylinder block drain plug. On DOHC engines there is no drain plug in the cylinder block, so the engine should be flushed until water runs clear from the radiator bottom hose.

10 If, after a reasonable period the water still does not run clear, the radiator can be flushed with a good proprietary cleaning agent.

11 Flush the heater matrix by disconnecting one of the heater hoses and running the hose into that.

12 In severe cases of contamination the radiator should be removed, inverted and flushed in the reverse direction to normal flow, ie with the water going in at the bottom and out at the top. Shake the radiator gently while doing this to dislodge any deposits.

13 Refit any hoses which were disturbed, making sure that they and their clips are in good condition. Refit the cylinder block drain plug and tighten the radiator drain plug.

14 On OHC engines, make sure that the bleed spigot cap is still removed (not DOHC). On V6 engines, check, if applicable, that the bleed screw is still removed.

15 Pour coolant in through the expansion tank filler hole until the level is up to the MAX line.

16 Refit the bleed spigot cap or screw when coolant starts to emerge from the spigot. Tighten the clip.

17 Squeeze the radiator hoses to help disperse airlocks. Top-up the coolant further if necessary, then refit and tighten the expansion tank cap.

18 Run the engine up to operating temperature, checking for coolant leaks. Stop the engine and allow it to cool, then top-up the coolant again to the MAX mark if necessary.

46.4a Radiator drain plug (arrowed) - OHC engine

46.4b Releasing the bleed spigot cap - OHC engine

Specifications

Engine

Oil filter type (all models) .... Champion C102
Valve clearances (cold):
SOHC:
  Inlet .... 0.20 ± 0.03 mm (0.008 ± 0.001 in)
  Exhaust .... 0.25 ± 0.03 mm (0.010 ± 0.001 in)
V6:
  Inlet .... 0.35 mm (0.014 in)
  Exhaust .... 0.40 mm (0.016 in)

Cooling system

Specific gravity at 45 to 50% antifreeze concentration .... 1.069 to 1.077
Note: *Refer to antifreeze manufacturer for latest recommendations.*

Fuel system

Air filter element type:
1.8 litre (carburettor) .... Champion W118
2.0 litre (carburettor) .... Champion W152
2.0 litre and V6 (injection) .... Champion U507
Fuel filter type:
All models (injection) .... Champion L204

Ignition system

Spark plugs:
1.8 and 2.0 litre SOHC .... Champion RF7YCC or RF7YC
2.0 litre DOHC .... Champion RC7YCC or RC7YC
2.8 litre V6 .... Champion RN7YCC or RN7YC
2.4 and 2.9 litre V6 without catalytic converter .... Champion RC7YCC or RC7YC
2.9 litre V6 with catalytic converter .... Champion RS9YCC or RS9YC
Spark plug electrode gap*:
Champion RF7YCC and RN7YCC .... 0.8 mm
Champion RF7YC and RN7YC .... 0.7 mm
Champion RC7YCC .... 0.8 mm
Champion RC7YC .... 0.7 mm
Champion RS9YCC and RS9YC .... 1.0 mm
Ignition HT lead set:
Resistance .... 30 k ohms maximum per lead
Type:
1.8 and 2.0 litre .... Champion LS-09 boxed set
1.8 and 2.0 litre (Male distributor fitting) .... Champion LS-10 boxed set
The spark plug gap quoted is that recommended by Champion for their specified plugs listed above. If spark plugs of any other type are to be fitted, refer to their manufacturer's recommendations.

Brakes

Brake pad friction material minimum thickness .... 1.5 mm (0.06 in)

Tyres

Tyre sizes .... 175 SR/TR/HR 14, 185/70 HR/TR/VR 14, 195/65 HR 15, 205/60 VR 15

Tyre pressures:	Front	Rear
Normal load	1.8 bar (26 lbf/in²)	1.8 bar (26 lbf/in²)
Full load	2.1 bar (30 lbf/in²)	2.9 bar (42 lbf/in²)

Note: *Pressures apply only to original-equipment tyres, and may vary if any other make or type is fitted; check with the tyre manufacturer or supplier for correct pressures if necessary.*

Torque wrench settings

	Nm	lbf ft
Engine oil drain plug	21 to 28	16 to 21
Engine block coolant drain plug	21 to 25	16 to 18
Spark plugs:		
1.8 and 2.0 litre SOHC	20 to 28	15 to 21
2.0 litre DOHC	15 to 21	11 to 15
2.8 litre V6	30 to 40	22 to 30
2.4 and 2.9 litre V6	15 to 21	11 to 15
Manual gearbox filler/level and drain plugs:		
N9 type	23 to 27	17 to 20
MT75 type	29 to 41	21 to 30
Brake caliper slide bolts:		
Front	20 to 25	15 to 18
Rear	31 to 35	23 to 26
Roadwheel bolts (steel and alloy wheels)	70 to 100	52 to 74

Chapter 2 Part A:
1.8 & 2.0 litre SOHC engines

Contents

2A

Degrees of difficulty

Easy, suitable for novice with little experience	Fairly easy, suitable for beginner with some experience	Fairly difficult, suitable for competent DIY mechanic	Difficult, suitable for experienced DIY mechanic	Very difficult, suitable for expert DIY or professional

Specifications

General

	1.8 HC E	2.0 HC	2.0 HC EFi
Manufacturer's code	REC	NFI	NRA
Bore - mm (in)	86.20 (3.39)	90.82 (3.58)	90.82 (3.58)
Stroke - mm (in)	76.95 (3.03)	76.95 (3.03)	76.95 (3.03)
Cubic capacity - cc (cu in)	1796 (109.6)	1993 (121.6)	1993 (121.6)
Compression ratio	9.5:1	9.2:1	9.2:1
Compression pressure at cranking speed (all models)	11 to 13 bar (160 to 189 lbf/in²)		
Maximum power (DIN, kW @ rpm)	66 @ 5400	77 @ 5200	85 @ 5500
Maximum torque (DIN, Nm @ rpm)	140 @ 3500	157 @ 4000	160 @ 4000

Lubrication system

Oil type	See "Lubricants and fluids"
Oil capacity (drain and refill, including filter)	3.75 litres (6.6 pints) approx
Oil pressure (SAE 10W/30 oil at 80°C/176°F):	
At 750 rpm	2.1 bar
At 2000 rpm	2.5 bar
Oil pressure relief valve opening pressure	4.0 to 4.7 bar
Oil pressure warning light switch setting	0.3 to 0.5 bar

Oil pump

Type	Bi-rotor
Drive	From auxiliary shaft
Operating clearances:	
Outer rotor-to-housing	0.15 to 0.30 mm
Inner-to-outer rotor	0.05 to 0.20 mm
Rotor endfloat	0.04 to 0.10 mm

Cylinder block

	1.8 (REC)	2.0 (NEL and NRA)
Cast identification mark	18S	20S
Bore diameter:		
Standard grade 1	86.180 to 86.190 mm	90.800 to 90.810 mm
Standard grade 2	86.190 to 86.200 mm	90.810 to 90.820 mm
Standard grade 3	86.200 to 86.210 mm	90.820 to 90.830 mm
Standard grade 4	86.210 to 86.220 mm	90.830 to 90.840 mm
Oversize grade 5	86.690 to 86.700 mm	91.310 to 91.320 mm
Oversize grade B	86.700 to 86.710 mm	91.320 to 91.330 mm
Oversize grade C	86.710 to 86.720 mm	91.330 to 91.340 mm
Standard service grade	Not stated	90.830 to 90.840 mm
Oversize 0.5	Not stated	91.330 to 91.340 mm
Oversize 1.0	Not stated	91.830 to 91.840 mm

Crankshaft

Number of main bearings	5
Main bearing journal diameter:	
Standard	56.970 to 56.990 mm
Undersize 0.25	56.720 to 56.740 mm
Undersize 0.50	56.470 to 56.490 mm
Undersize 0.75	56.220 to 56.240 mm
Undersize 1.00	55.970 to 55.990 mm
Main bearing running clearance	0.010 to 0.064 mm
Big-end bearing journal diameter:	
Standard	51.980 to 52.000 mm
Undersize 0.25	51.730 to 51.750 mm
Undersize 0.50	51.480 to 51.500 mm
Undersize 0.75	51.230 to 51.250 mm
Undersize 1.00	50.980 to 51.000 mm
Big-end bearing running clearance	0.006 to 0.060 mm
Thrustwasher thickness:	
Standard	2.30 to 2.35 mm
Oversize	2.50 to 2.55 mm
Crankshaft endfloat	0.08 to 0.28 mm

Connecting rods

Big-end parent bore diameter	55.000 to 55.020 mm
Small-end bush internal diameter	23.964 to 23.976 mm

Pistons

	1.8 (REC)	2.0 (NEL and NRA)
Diameter:		
Standard grade 1	86.145 to 86.155 mm	90.765 to 90.775 mm
Standard grade 2	86.155 to 86.165 mm	90.775 to 90.785 mm
Standard grade 3	86.165 to 86.175 mm	90.785 to 90.795 mm
Standard grade 4	86.175 to 86.185 mm	90.795 to 90.805 mm
Service standard	86.170 to 86.195 mm	90.790 to 90.815 mm
Oversize 0.5	86.670 to 86.695 mm	91.290 to 91.315 mm
Oversize 1.0	87.170 to 87.195 mm	91.790 to 91.815 mm
Clearance in bore	0.015 to 0.050 mm	0.015 to 0.050 mm
Piston ring end gaps:		
Top and centre	0.3 to 0.5 mm	0.4 to 0.6 mm
Bottom	0.4 to 1.4 mm	0.4 to 1.4 mm

Gudgeon pins

Length	68.0 to 68.8 mm
Diameter:	
Red	23.994 to 23.997 mm
Blue	23.997 to 24.000 mm
Yellow	24.000 to 24.003 mm
Clearance in piston	0.008 to 0.014 mm
Interference in connecting rod	0.018 to 0.039 mm

Cylinder head
Identification mark:
  1.8 (REC) 85
  2.0 (NEL and NRA) 0
Valve seat angle .... 44° 30' to 45° 00'
Valve seat width .... 1.5 to 2.0 mm
Valve guide bore:
  Standard .... 8.063 to 8.088 mm
  Oversize 0.2 .... 8.263 to 8.288 mm
  Oversize 0.4 .... 8.463 to 8.488 mm
Camshaft bearing parent bores:
  Front .... 45.072 to 45.102 mm
  Centre .... 47.692 to 47.722 mm
  Rear .... 48.072 to 48.102 mm

Auxiliary shaft
Endfloat .... 0.050 to 0.204 mm

Camshaft
Drive .... Toothed belt
Thrust plate thickness .... 3.98 to 4.01 mm
Endfloat .... 0.104 to 0.204 mm
Cam lift .... 6.3323 mm
Cam length .... 36.26 to 36.60 mm
Valve timing:
  Inlet opens .... 24° BTDC
  Inlet closes .... 64° ABDC
  Exhaust opens .... 70° BBDC
  Exhaust closes .... 18° ATDC
Bearing journal diameter:
  Front .... 41.987 to 42.013 mm
  Centre .... 44.607 to 44.633 mm
  Rear .... 44.987 to 45.013 mm
Bearing bush internal diameter:
  Front .... 42.035 to 42.055 mm
  Centre .... 44.655 to 44.675 mm
  Rear .... 45.035 to 45.055 mm

Valve clearances (cold)
Inlet .... 0.20 ± 0.03 mm (0.008 ± 0.001 in)
Exhaust .... 0.25 ± 0.03 mm (0.010 ± 0.001 in)

Inlet valves
Length:
  1.8 (REC) .... 111.75 to 112.75 mm
  2.0 (NEL and NRA) .... 110.65 to 111.65 mm
Head diameter .... 41.80 to 42.20 mm
Stem diameter:
  Standard .... 8.025 to 8.043 mm
  Oversizes .... +0.2, 0.4, 0.6 and 0.8 mm
Stem-to-guide clearance .... 0.020 to 0.063 mm

Exhaust valves
Length:
  1.8 (REC) .... 111.15 to 112.15 mm
  2.0 (NEL) .... 110.05 to 111.05 mm
  2.0 (NRA) .... 110.75 to 111.75 mm
Head diameter:
  1.8 (REL) .... 34.00 to 34.40 mm
  2.0 (NEL and NRA) .... 35.80 to 36.20 mm
Stem diameter;
  Standard .... 7.999 to 8.017 mm
Oversizes .... +0.2, 0.4, 0.6 and 0.8 mm
Stem-to-guide clearance .... 0.046 to 0.089 mm

Valve springs
Free length .... 47.0 mm
Inside diameter .... 23.45 to 23.95 mm
Wire diameter .... 3.87 to 3.93 mm
Number of turns 4.7

2A

Torque wrench settings

	Nm	lbf ft
Main bearing cap bolts	88 to 102	65 to 75
Big-end bearing cap nuts	40 to 47	30 to 35
Crankshaft pulley bolt:		
1.8 (REC) and 2.0 (NEL)	110 to 115	81 to 85
2.0 (NRA)	115 to 130	85 to 96
Camshaft sprocket bolt	45 to 50	33 to 37
Auxiliary shaft sprocket bolt	45 to 50	33 to 37
Flywheel bolts	64 to 70	47 to 52
Oil pump-to-cylinder block bolts	17 to 21	13 to 16
Oil pump cover bolts	9 to 13	7 to 10
Sump bolts (see text):		
Stage 1	1 to 2	0.7 to 1.5
Stage 2	6 to 8	4 to 6
Stage 3 (after 20 minutes running)	8 to 10	6 to 7
Sump drain plug	21 to 28	16 to 21
Oil pressure switch	12 to 15	9 to 11
Valve adjustment ball-pins	50 to 55	37 to 41
Cylinder head bolts (see text):		
Stage 1	35 to 40	26 to 30
Stage 2	70 to 75	52 to 55
Stage 3 (after 5 minutes)	Tighten further 90°	Tighten further 90°
Rocker cover bolts (see text):		
Bolts 1 to 6 - Stage 1	6 to 8	4 to 6
Bolts 7 and 8 - Stage 2	2 to 3	1.5 to 2
Bolts 9 and 10 - Stage 3	6 to 8	4 to 6
Bolts 7 and 8 - Stage 4	6 to 8	4 to 6
Front cover bolts	13 to 17	10 to 13
Timing belt tensioner bolts	20 to 25	15 to 18
Oil pump pick-up pipe:		
To pump	11 to 14	8 to 10
To block	17 to 21	13 to 16
Engine mounting to crossmember	41 to 51	30 to 38

1 General information

The engine is of four-cylinder, in-line, single overhead camshaft type (see illustration). It is mounted longitudinally at the front of the car. Three versions are available: 1.8 litre carburettor, 2.0 litre carburettor and 2.0 litre fuel-injection.

The crankshaft incorporates five main bearings. Thrustwashers are fitted to the centre main bearing in order to control crankshaft endfloat.

The camshaft is driven by a toothed belt and operates the slightly angled valve via cam followers which pivot on ball-pins.

The auxiliary shaft, which is also driven by the toothed belt, drives the distributor, oil pump and on some models the fuel pump.

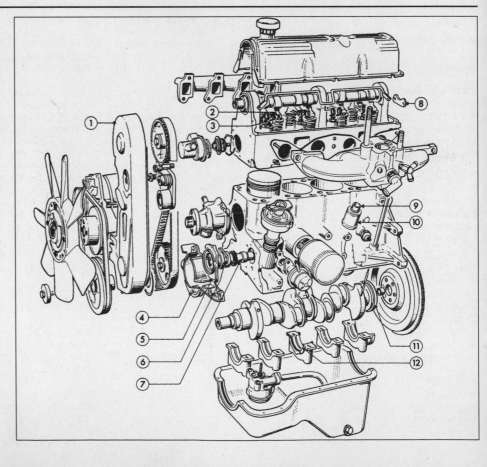

1.1 Exploded view of the SOHC engine

1 Timing cover
2 Cam follower
3 Retaining spring clip
4 Crankshaft front oil seal housing
5 Auxiliary shaft front cover
6 Thrust plate
7 Auxiliary shaft
8 Thrust plate
9 Vent valve
10 Oil separator
11 Crankshaft rear oil seal
12 Thrust washer

The cylinder head is of crossflow design with the inlet manifold mounted on the left-hand side and the exhaust manifold mounted on the right-hand side.

Lubrication is by means of a bi-rotor pump which draws oil through a strainer located inside the sump, and forces it through a full-flow filter into the engine oil galleries where it is distributed to the crankshaft, camshaft and auxiliary shaft. The big-end bearings are supplied with oil via internal drillings in the crankshaft. The undersides of the pistons are supplied with oil from drillings in the big-ends. The distributor shaft is intermittently supplied with oil from the drilled auxiliary shaft. The camshaft and cam followers are supplied with oil via a drilled spray tube from the centre camshaft bearing.

A semi-closed crankcase ventilation system is employed whereby piston blow-by gases are drawn into the inlet manifold via an oil separator and on carburettor models a control valve.

2 Major operations possible with the engine in the vehicle

The following operations can be carried out without removing the engine, although the work may be easier and quicker with the engine removed:

a) Removal and refitting of the cylinder head
b) Removal and refitting of the camshaft (after removing the cylinder head)
c) Removal and refitting of the timing belt and sprockets
d) Removal and refitting of the sump and oil pump
e) Removal and refitting of the pistons, connecting rods and big-end bearings
f) Renewal of the engine mountings
g) Renewal of the crankshaft oil seals
h) Removal and refitting of the auxiliary shaft
j) Removal and refitting of the flywheel

3 Major operations requiring engine removal

The engine must be removed from the vehicle for the following operations:
a) Renewal of the crankshaft main bearings
b) Removal and refitting of the crankshaft

4 Methods of engine removal

The engine may be lifted out either on its own or together with the gearbox. Unless work is also necessary on the gearbox it is recommended that the engine is removed on its own. Where automatic transmission is fitted, the engine should be removed on its own owing to the additional weight. If the engine and gearbox are removed together, they will have to be tilted at a very steep angle; make sure that the range of the lifting tackle is adequate.

5 Engine - removal leaving gearbox/transmission in vehicle

1 Disconnect the battery negative lead.
2 Remove the bonnet.
3 On carburettor models, remove the air cleaner. On fuel injection models, remove the air cleaner cover, vane airflow meter and air inlet trunking.
4 If a splash guard is fitted, remove it.
5 Release the securing clips and bolts and remove the upper half of the fan shroud. On carburettor models remove the lower half of the shroud too.
6 Drain the cooling system.
7 Disconnect the radiator top and bottom hoses from the thermostat housing and water pump. Disconnect the top hose spur from the expansion tank and unclip it.
8 Disconnect the heater hoses from the water pump and from the inlet manifold or automatic choke housing. Unclip the hoses.
9 On models with power steering, remove the steering pump.
10 Disconnect the vacuum pipe(s) from the inlet manifold, labelling them if there is any possibility of confusion.
11 Disconnect the following wiring, as applicable:
a) Alternator
b) Temperature gauge sender
c) Engine management temperature sensor
d) Distributor
e) Oil pressure switch
f) Automatic choke and thermo-switch
g) Carburettor stepper motor
h) Fuel-injection system sub-harness
j) Inlet manifold heater
12 Disconnect the HT lead from the coil.
13 If an oil level sensor is fitted, remove it (see illustration).
14 Unbolt the throttle cable bracket, disconnect the inner cable and move the cable and bracket aside. Also disconnect the downshift cable on automatic transmission models.
15 On carburettor models, disconnect the fuel lines from the fuel pump (mechanised type) and from the carburettor. **Be prepared for fuel spillage.**
16 On fuel-injection models, disconnect the fuel supply union from the injector rail, and the fuel return pipe from the fuel pressure

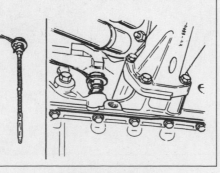

5.13 Oil level sensor

regulator. **Be prepared for fuel spillage, and for some spray if the supply side is still under pressure.**
17 Unbolt the exhaust downpipe from the manifold.
18 On models with air conditioning, unbolt the compressor and move it aside without straining the flexible hoses.
19 Remove the starter motor.
20 Although not specified by the manufacturers, the author advises that either the radiator or the cooling fan be removed, to reduce the risk of damage.
21 Attach the lifting tackle to the two lifting eyes on the engine, so that when suspended the engine will be roughly horizontal. Take the weight of the engine.
22 Remove the single nut on each side which secures each engine bearer to its mounting.
23 Working under the vehicle, remove the bracing strap which connects the engine and transmission. Unbolt the adapter plate from the bottom of the transmission bellhousing.
24 On automatic transmission models, unbolt the torque converter from the driveplate.
25 Remove the engine-to-bellhousing bolts. Note the location of the battery earth strap.
26 Support the transmission, preferably with a trolley jack.
27 Check that nothing has been overlooked, then raise the engine and draw it forwards clear of the transmission input shaft. Do not allow the weight of the engine to hang on the shaft, and do not lift the transmission by it.
28 On automatic transmission models, make sure that the torque converter stays engaged with the oil pump in the transmission as the engine is withdrawn.
29 Lift the engine out of the engine bay and take it to the bench.

6 Engine - removal with manual gearbox

1 Engine removal with automatic transmission is not recommended.
2 Proceed as in the previous Section, paragraphs 1 to 18.
3 Disconnect the wiring from the starter motor, and release the battery earth cable from its bellhousing bolt.
4 Remove the radiator.
5 Remove the propeller shaft.
6 Disconnect and unclip the reversing light switch and speedometer sender unit wiring.
7 Disconnect the clutch cable.
8 Unbolt the anti-roll bar mounting brackets and lower the anti-roll bar as far as possible.
9 From inside the vehicle remove the gear lever.
10 Drain the engine oil.
11 Unhook the exhaust system from its mounting on the gearbox crossmember. Either support the system or remove it completely.
12 Support the gearbox, preferably with a trolley jack, then unbolt and remove the gearbox crossmember. Note the earth strap (if fitted) under one of the crossmember bolts.
13 Attach lifting tackle to the two lifting eyes on the engine so that when suspended it will be at an angle of approximately 45°.

2A

14 Take the weight of the engine and remove the two engine bearer-to-mounting nuts.
15 Lift the engine/transmission, at the same time lowering the trolley jack. Draw the unit forwards and lift it out of the engine bay.
16 Temporarily refit the anti-roll bar if the vehicle is to be moved.

7 Engine - separation from manual gearbox

1 With the engine and gearbox on the bench, remove the starter motor.
2 Remove the bolt from the engine adapter plate.
3 Remove the bracing strap and the remaining engine-to-bellhousing bolts.
4 With the aid of an assistant draw the gearbox off the engine. Do not allow the weight of the gearbox to hang on the input shaft.

8 Engine dismantling - general information

1 It is best to mount the engine on a dismantling stand, but if this is not available, stand the engine on a strong bench at a comfortable working height. Failing this, it will have to be stripped down on the floor.
2 Cleanliness is most important, and if the engine is dirty, it should be cleaned with paraffin while keeping it in an upright position.
3 Avoid working with the engine on a concrete floor, as grit can be a real source of trouble.
4 As parts are removed, clean them in paraffin. However, do not immerse parts with internal oilways in paraffin as it is difficult to remove, usually requiring a high pressure hose.

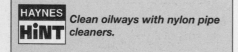

HAYNES HiNT *Clean oilways with nylon pipe cleaners.*

5 It is advisable to have suitable containers to hold small items according to their use, as this will help when reassembling the engine and also prevent possible losses.
6 Always obtain complete sets of gaskets when the engine is being dismantled, but retain the old gaskets with a view of using them as a pattern to make a replacement if a new one is not available.

9.1b Removing an engine bearer arm

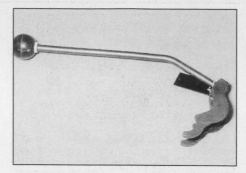
8.10 This valve spring compressor is used by hooking it under the camshaft

7 When possible, refit nuts, bolts and washers in their location after being removed, as this helps protect the threads and will also be helpful when reassembling the engine.
8 Retain unserviceable components in order to compare them with the new parts supplied.
9 A Torx key, size T55, will be needed for dealing with the cylinder head bolts. A 12-spline key (to fit bolt size M8) will be needed for the oil pump bolts. Other Torx and 12-spline bolts may be encountered; sets of the keys required to deal with them are available from most motor accessory shops and tool factors.
10 Another tool which is useful, though by no means essential, is a valve spring compressor of the type which hooks under the camshaft **(see illustration)**. As a Ford tool this bears the number 21-005-A; proprietary versions may also be available.

9 Ancillary components - removal

Before dismantling the engine into its main components, the following ancillary components can be removed. The actual items removed, and the sequence of removal, will depend on the work to be done:
Inlet manifold and associated items
Exhaust manifold
Fuel pump (mechanical type) and pushrod
Alternator
Distributor, HT leads and spark plugs
Fan, water pump and thermostat
Oil pressure switch (see illustration)
Temperature gauge sender

9.1c Removing the alternator bracket

9.1a Engine oil pressure switch (arrowed)

Oil filter and dipstick
Engine bearer arms (see illustration)
Crankcase ventilation components
Clutch
Alternator mounting bracket (see illustration)

10 Cylinder head - removal

1 If the engine is still in the vehicle, carry out the following preliminary operations:
a) *Disconnect the battery negative lead*
b) *Drain the cooling system*
c) *Remove the inlet and exhaust manifolds*
d) *Disconnect the radiator top hose from the thermostat housing, and the spur from the expansion tank*
e) *Disconnect the wiring from the temperature gauge sender*
f) *Remove the distributor cap, HT leads and spark plugs*

2 Unscrew the bolts and withdraw the timing cover **(see illustration)**. Note the location of the cover in the special bolt.
3 Using a socket on the crankshaft pulley bolt. turn the engine clockwise until the TDC (top dead centre) notch on the pulley is aligned with the pointer on the crankshaft front oil seal housing, and the pointer on the camshaft sprocket is aligned with the indentation on the cylinder head **(see illustrations)**. Note the position of the distributor rotor arm, and mark its contact end in relation to the rim of the distributor body.
4 Slacken the timing belt tensioner bolts. Pivot

10.2 Removing the timing cover

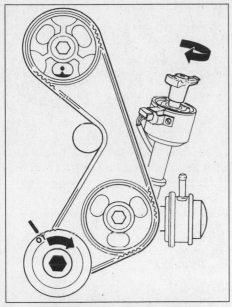

10.3a Alignment of crankshaft and camshaft timing marks, and distributor rotor position, for No 1 firing

the tensioner to release the load on the belt and slip the belt off the camshaft sprocket. Do not kink the belt, or get oil or grease on it.
5 Remove the ten bolts which secure the rocker cover, noting the location of the different shapes of reinforcing plates. Remove the cover and gasket.
6 Using a Torx key, slacken the cylinder head bolts half a turn at a time in the reverse of the tightening sequence.

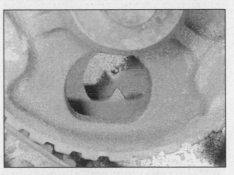

10.3b Camshaft sprocket pointer aligned with the indentation on the cylinder head

7 With the bolts removed, lift the cylinder head from the block. If it is stuck, tap it with a wooden or plastic mallet to free it. **Do not** lever between the head and block, or the mating surfaces may be damaged. **Do not** crank the engine to free the head, as the pistons may contact the valves.
8 Place the cylinder head on a couple of wooden blocks so that the protruding valves are not damaged.

11 Camshaft - removal

1 Remove the cylinder head as described in the previous Section.
2 Hold the camshaft with a spanner on the lug behind the sixth cam. Unscrew and remove the camshaft sprocket bolt **(see illustration)**.

3 Remove the camshaft sprocket using a puller if necessary. Remove the backplate **(see illustration)**.
4 Unscrew the bolts and remove the camshaft oil supply tube **(see illustration)**.
5 Note how the cam follower retaining spring clips are fitted, then unhook them from the cam followers.
6 If the special tool 21-005-A is available, compress the valve springs in turn and remove the cam followers, keeping them identified for location. Alternatively loosen the locknuts and back off the ball-pins until the cam followers can be removed **(see illustration)**.
7 Unscrew the bolts and remove the camshaft thrust plate **(see illustration)**.
8 Carefully withdraw the camshaft from the rear of the cylinder head, taking care not to damage the bearings **(see illustration)**.
9 Prise the oil seal from the front bearing **(see illustration)**.

2A

11.2 Removing the camshaft sprocket bolt and sprocket

11.3 Removing the camshaft sprocket backplate

11.4 Removing the camshaft oil supply tube

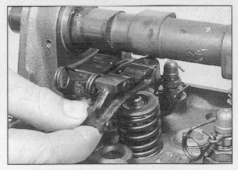

11.6 Removing the cam followers

11.7 Removing the camshaft thrust plate

11.8 Removing the camshaft

11.9 Prise out the camshaft bearing oil seal

12 Cylinder head - dismantling

1 Remove the camshaft as described in the previous Section. (If tool 21-005-A is available, leave the camshaft in place until the valves have been removed).

2 Using a valve spring compressor, compress each valve spring in turn until the split collets can be removed. Release the compressor and remove the cap and spring, keeping them identified for location **(see illustrations)**.

> **HAYNES HiNT** *If the caps are difficult to remove do not continue to tighten the compressor, but gently tap the top of the tool with a hammer. Always ensure that the compressor is held firmly over the cap.*

3 Remove each valve from the cylinder head, but identify them for location **(see illustration)**.

4 Prise the valve stem oil seals from the tops of the valve guides **(see illustration)**.

5 If necessary unscrew the cam follower ball-pins from the cylinder head, keeping them identified for location.

6 If necessary unscrew the bolts and remove the timing belt tensioner.

7 Remove the thermostat and housing.

8 Remove the temperature gauge sender unit.

9 Remove the manifold studs if wished by locking two nuts onto each stud in turn and unscrewing it.

13 Timing belt and sprockets - removal

1 If the engine is still in the vehicle, carry out the following preliminary operations:
a) *Disconnect the battery negative lead*
b) *Remove the radiator and disconnect the hose from the thermostat housing*
c) *Remove the accessory drivebelt(s)*

2 Unscrew the bolts and withdraw the timing cover. Note the location of the cover in the special bolt.

3 Using a socket on the crankshaft pulley bolt, turn the engine clockwise until the TDC (top dead centre) notch on the pulley is aligned

12.2a Compressing a valve spring

12.2b Removing a valve spring and cap

12.3 Removing a valve

12.4 Removing a valve stem oil seal

with the pointer on the crankshaft front oil seal housing, and the pointer on the camshaft sprocket is aligned with the indentation on the cylinder head. Note the position of the distributor rotor arm. Mark the contact end of the rotor in relation to the rim of the distributor body.

4 Slacken the timing belt tensioner retaining bolts then pivot the tensioner pulley away from the belt, to obtain maximum drivebelt free play **(see illustration)**. Hold the tensioner pulley in this position and securely retighten the retaining bolts.

5 Mark the running direction of the belt if it is to be re-used, then slip it off the camshaft sprocket.

6 Slacken the crankshaft pulley bolt. Prevent the crankshaft from turning by engaging 5th

gear (manual gearbox), or by removing the starter motor and jamming the ring gear teeth. Alternatively, if the pulley has peripheral bolt holes, screw in a couple of bolts and use a lever between them to jam it. Do not allow the crankshaft to turn very far, or piston/valve contact may occur.

7 Remove the bolt and washer and withdraw the pulley. If the pulley will not come off easily, refit the bolt part way and use a puller **(see illustration)**. A puller will almost certainly be required on fuel-injection models.

8 Remove the guide washer from in front of the crankshaft sprocket, then remove the timing belt **(see illustration)**. Do not kink it or get oil on it if it is to be re-used.

9 Remove the crankshaft sprocket using a puller if necessary **(see illustration)**.

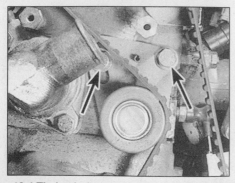

13.4 Timing belt tensioner bolts (arrowed)

13.7 Using a puller to remove the crankshaft pulley

13.8 Remove the guide washer from in front of the crankshaft sprocket

13.9 Removing the crankshaft sprocket

13.11 Removing the auxiliary shaft sprocket

14.4 Removing the auxiliary shaft front cover

10 Unscrew the auxiliary shaft sprocket bolt while holding the sprocket stationary with a screwdriver inserted through one of the holes.

11 Remove the auxiliary shaft sprocket using a puller if necessary **(see illustration)**.

12 Unscrew the camshaft sprocket bolt while holding the sprocket stationary with a screwdriver engaged in one of the grooves. Alternatively remove the rocker cover and use a spanner on the camshaft lug.

13 Remove the camshaft sprocket using a puller if necessary, then remove the backplate. Note that the oil seal can be removed using a special removal tool or by using self-tapping screws and a pair of grips.

14 Auxiliary shaft - removal

1 Remove the timing belt and the auxiliary shaft sprocket (only) (Section 13).

2 Remove the distributor.

3 Remove the fuel pump and pushrod (not applicable to models with an electric pump).

4 Unscrew the bolts and remove the auxiliary shaft front cover **(see illustration)**.

5 Unscrew the cross-head screws, using an impact screwdriver if necessary, remove the thrust plate and withdraw the auxiliary shaft from the block **(see illustrations)**.

6 Cut the front cover gasket along the top of the crankshaft front oil seal housing and scrape off the gasket.

15 Flywheel/driveplate and adapter plate - removal

1 If the engine is still in the vehicle, remove the clutch or automatic transmission.

2 Prevent the flywheel or driveplate rotating by jamming the ring gear tooth, or by bolting a strap to it.

3 Remove the securing bolts and withdraw the flywheel or driveplate. Do not drop it, it is heavy.

4 The engine adapter plate (backplate) may now be withdrawn from the dowels if required **(see illustration)**.

16 Sump - removal

1 If the engine is out of the vehicle, start at paragraph 11. If possible, remove the sump without inverting the engine, so that any sludge in the bottom of the sump stays there.

2 Disconnect the battery negative lead.

3 Raise and support the front of the vehicle.

4 Remove the splash guard, if fitted, and drain the engine oil.

5 Remove the starter motor.

6 Remove the two nuts which secure the engine bearers to the engine mountings.

7 Release the steering shaft universal joint strap bolt to allow for subsequent movement.

8 Free the brake hydraulic pipes from the clips on the front crossmember.

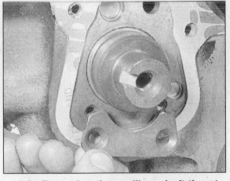

14.5a Removing the auxiliary shaft thrust plate

15.4 Removing the engine adaptor plate (backplate)

9 Support the engine, either with conventional lifting tackle or with a bar positioned across the engine bay and resting on two wooden blocks drilled to fit securely on the suspension turrets. Make sure the support arrangements are satisfactory, as you will be working underneath the suspended engine.

10 Take the weight of the engine. Place a jack under the front crossmember, remove the crossmember mounting bolts and carefully lower the jack. Only lower the crossmember far enough to permit removal of the sump.

11 Remove the 23 bolts retaining the sump.

12 Remove the sump from the cylinder block **(see illustration)**. If it is stuck, hit it with a soft-faced mallet, or prise it sideways (**not** between the mating faces) with a large screwdriver or bar.

13 Recover the gaskets and sealing strips.

2A

14.5b Removing the auxiliary shaft

16.12 Removing the sump

17.3a Removing the crankshaft front oil seal housing

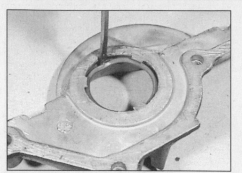

17.3b Driving the oil seal out of the housing

17.4 Using a socket and a hammer to seat the new seal

17.5a Oil seal housing and auxiliary shaft cover gasket in position

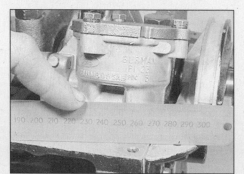

17.5b Checking the alignment of the front oil seal housing

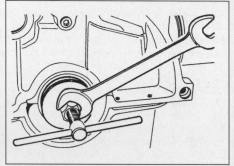

18.2 Using an oil seal removal tool to extract the crankshaft rear oil seal

17 Crankshaft front oil seal - renewal

1 Remove the timing belt and the crankshaft sprocket (only).
2 If an oil seal removal tool is available. the oil seal can be removed at this stage. It may also be possible to remove the oil seal by drilling the outer face and using self-tapping screws and a pair of grips.
3 If the oil seal cannot be removed as described in paragraph 2, remove the sump. Also remove the auxiliary shaft sprocket. Unbolt the oil seal housing and auxiliary shaft front cover and remove the gasket. The oil seal can then be driven out from the inside **(see illustrations)**.
4 Clean the oil seal seating, then drive in a new seal using metal tubing or a suitable socket **(see illustration)**. Make sure that the

sealing lip faces into the engine, and lightly oil the lip.
5 If applicable fit the oil seal housing and auxiliary shaft front cover to the block together with a new gasket and tighten the bolts. Make sure that the bottom face of the housing is aligned with the bottom face of the block **(see illustrations)**. Fit the sump.
6 Refit the timing belt and sprockets.

18 Crankshaft rear oil seal - renewal

1 Remove the flywheel or driveplate and the engine adapter plate (backplate).
2 Using a special removal tool extract the oil seal **(see illustration)**. However it may be possible to remove the oil seal by drilling the outer face and using self-tapping screws and a pair of grips.

3 Clean the oil seal seating, then drive in a new seal using a suitable metal tube. Make sure that the sealing lip faces into the engine, and lightly oil the lip.
4 Refit the adapter plate and the flywheel/driveplate.

19 Oil pump - removal

1 Remove the sump.
2 Unscrew the bolt securing the pick-up tube and strainer to the block **(see illustration)**.
3 Using a special splined key, unscrew the bolts and withdraw the oil pump and strainer **(see illustration)**.
4 Withdraw the hexagon shaped driveshaft which engages the bottom of the distributor, noting which way round it is fitted **(see illustration)**.

19.2 Unbolting the oil pump pick-up strainer from the block

19.3 Removing the splined bolts which secure the oil pump

19.4 Removing the oil pump driveshaft

21.2 Big-end cap and connecting rod identification numbers

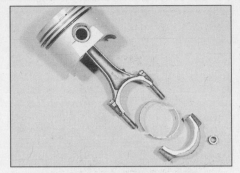

21.4 Piston, connecting rod, cap and bearing shells

22.5 Main bearing cap identification marks
The arrow points to the front of the engine

20 Oil filter - renewal

See Chapter 1, Section 8.

21 Pistons and connecting rods - removal

1 Remove the sump and cylinder head.
2 Check the big-end caps for identification marks and if necessary use a centre-punch to identify the caps and connecting rods **(see illustration)**.
3 Turn the crankshaft so that No 1 crankpin is at its lowest point, then unscrew the nuts and tap off the cap. Keep the bearing shells in the cap and connecting rod.

4 Using the handle of a hammer, push the piston and connecting rod up the bore and withdraw from the top of the cylinder block. Loosely refit the cap to the connecting rod **(see illustration)**.
5 Repeat the procedure in paragraphs 3 and 4 on the No 4 piston and connecting rod, then turn the crankshaft through half a turn and repeat the procedure on Nos 2 and 3 pistons and connecting rods.

22 Crankshaft and main bearings - removal

1 With the engine removed from the vehicle, remove the pistons and connecting rods as described in the previous Section. (In fact it is not necessary to push the pistons out of the bores if no work is to be done on them.)

2 Remove the timing belt and crankshaft sprocket, and the flywheel or driveplate. Also remove the auxiliary shaft sprocket.
3 Unbolt the crankshaft front oil seal housing and auxiliary shaft front cover and remove the gasket.
4 Remove the oil pump and strainer.
5 Check the main bearing caps for identification marks and if necessary use a centre-punch to identify them **(see illustration)**.
6 Before removing the crankshaft check that the endfloat is within the specified limits by inserting a feeler blade between the centre crankshaft web and the thrustwashers **(see illustration)**. This will indicate whether new thrustwashers are required or not.
7 Unscrew the bolts and tap off the main bearing caps complete with bearing shells **(see illustration)**. If the thrustwashers are to be re-used identify them for location.
8 Lift the crankshaft from the crankcase and remove the rear oil seal. Remove the remaining thrustwashers **(see illustrations)**.
9 Extract the bearing shells keeping them identified for location **(see illustration)**.

23 Engine mountings - renewal

1 Unscrew the two nuts which secure the engine bearers to the tops of the mountings. Recover the washers **(see illustration)**.
2 Raise and support the front of the vehicle. Remove the two nuts which secure the

2A

22.6 Checking crankshaft endfloat

22.7 Removing the rear main bearing cap

22.8a Removing the crankshaft

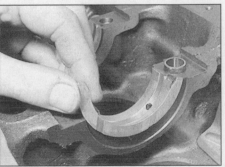

22.8b Removing a thrustwasher from the centre main bearing

22.9 Removing the centre main bearing shell

23.1 An engine mounting

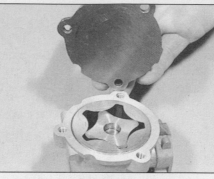

26.1 Removing the oil pump cover

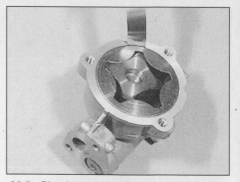

26.2a Checking the outer rotor-to-housing clearance

mountings to the front crossmember. Recover the washers.

3 Raise the engine with a hoist or a suitable protected jack until the mountings are free, then remove them.

4 Fit the new mountings and lower the engine onto them.

5 Fit the nuts and washers and tighten the nuts.

6 Lower the vehicle.

24 Crankcase ventilation system - general information

Carburettor models

The crankcase ventilation system consists of the special oil filter cap (containing a steel wool filter) and an oil separator and vent valve on the left-hand side of the engine. This is connected by hose to the inlet manifold. The system operates according to the vacuum in the inlet manifold. Air is drawn through the filler cap, through the crankcase, and then together with piston blow-by gasses through the oil separator and vent valve to the inlet manifold. The blow-by gases are then drawn into the engine together with the fuel/air mixture. Refer to Chapter 1 for maintenance of the system.

Fuel-injection models

This system is closed, consisting of an oil separator on the left-hand side of the engine and a hose connecting it to the inlet air trunking. Because the trunking is not subject to manifold vacuum, no vent valve is needed.

25 Examination and renovation - general information

1 With the engine completely stripped, clean all the components and examine them for wear. Each part should be checked, and where necessary renewed or renovated as described in the following Sections. Renew main and big end shell bearings as a matter of course, unless you know that they have had little wear and are in perfect condition.

2 If in doubt as to whether to renew a component which is still just serviceable, consider the time and effort which will be incurred should it fail at an early date. Obviously the age and expected life of the vehicle must influence the standards applied.

3 Gaskets, oil seals and O-rings must all be renewed as a matter of routine. Flywheel and cylinder head bolts must be renewed because of the high stresses to which they are subjected.

4 Take the opportunity to renew the engine core plugs while they are easily accessible. Knock out the old plugs with a hammer and chisel or punch. Clean the plug seats, smear the new plugs with sealant and tap them squarely into position.

26 Oil pump - examination and renovation

1 Unscrew the bolts and remove the oil pump cover (see illustration).

2 Using feeler blades check that the rotor clearances are within the limits given in Specifications (see illustrations). If not, unbolt the pick-up tube and strainer and obtain a new unit (see illustration). Fit the pick-up tube and strainer to the new pump using a new gasket, and tighten the bolts.

3 If the oil pump is serviceable refit the cover and tighten the bolts.

27 Crankshaft and bearings - examination and renovation

1 Examine the bearing surfaces of the crankshaft for scratches or scoring and, using a micrometer, check each journal and crankpin for ovality. Where this is found to be in excess of 0.0254 mm (0.001 in) the crankshaft will have to be reground and undersize bearings fitted.

2 Crankshaft regrinding should be carried out by a suitable engineering works, who will normally supply the matching undersize main and big-end shell bearings.

26.2b Checking the inner-to-outer rotor clearance

26.2c Checking the oil pump rotor endfloat

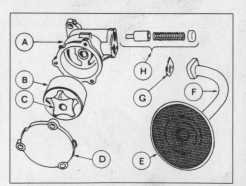

26.2d Exploded view of the oil pump

A Body
B Outer rotor
C Inner rotor
D Cover
E Strainer
F Pick-up tube
G Gasket
H Relief valve

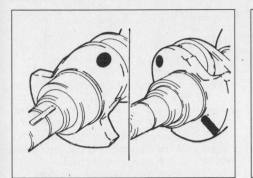

27.3a Undersize crankshaft bearings are indicated by a spot and/or line on the front counterweight

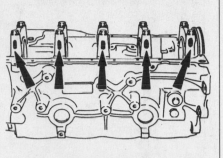

27.3b Main bearing cap marks (arrowed) denote oversize parent bore

27.5 Checking the width of the Plastigage filament against the scale on the packet

3 Note that undersize bearings may already have been fitted, either in production or by a previous repairer. Check the markings on the backs of the old bearing shells, and if in doubt take them along when buying new ones (see illustrations). Production undersizes are also indicated by paint marks as follows:

White line on main bearing cap - parent bore 0.40 mm oversize
Green line on crankshaft front counterweight - main bearing journals 0.25 mm undersize
Green spot on counterweight - big-end bearing journals 0.25 mm undersize

4 If the crankshaft endfloat is more than the maximum specified amount, new thrustwashers should be fitted to the centre main bearings. These are usually supplied together with the main and big-end bearings on a reground crankshaft.

5 An accurate method of determining bearing wear is by the use of Plastigage. The crankshaft is located in the main bearings (and big-end bearings if necessary) and the Plastigage filament located across the journal which must be dry. The cap is then fitted and the bolts/nuts tightened to the specified torque. On removal of the cap the width of the filaments is checked against a scale which shows the bearing running clearance. This clearance is then compared with that given in the Specifications (see illustration).

6 If the spigot bearing in the rear of the crankshaft requires renewal extract it with a suitable puller. Alternatively fill it with heavy grease and use a close fitting metal dowel driven into the centre of the bearing. Drive the new bearing into the crankshaft with a soft metal drift.

28 Cylinder block and bores - examination and renovation

1 The cylinder bores must be examined for taper, ovality, scoring and scratches. Start by examining the top of the bores; if these are worn, a slight ridge will be found which marks the top of the piston ring travel. If the wear is excessive, the engine will have had a high oil consumption rate accompanied by blue smoke from the exhaust.

2 If available, use an inside dial gauge to measure the bore diameter just below the ridge and compare it with the diameter at the bottom of the bore, which is not subject to wear. If the difference is more than 0.152 mm (0.006 in), the cylinders will normally require reboring with new oversize pistons fitted.

3 Proprietary oil control rings can be obtained for fitting to the existing pistons if it is felt that the degree of wear does not justify a rebore. However, any improvement brought about by such rings may be short-lived.

4 If new pistons or piston rings are to be fitted to old bores, deglaze the bores with abrasive paper or a "glaze buster" tool. The object is to produce a light cross-hatch pattern to assist the new rings to bed in.

5 If there is a ridge at the top of the bore and new piston rings are being fitted, either the top piston ring must be stepped ("ridge dodger" pattern) or the ridge must be removed with a ridge reamer. If the ridge is left, the piston ring may hit it and break.

6 Thoroughly examine the crankcase and cylinder block for cracks and damage and use a piece of wire to probe all oilways and waterways to ensure that they are unobstructed.

29 Pistons and connecting rods - examination and renovation

1 Examine the pistons for ovality, scoring and scratches. Check the connecting rods for wear and damage. The connecting rods carry a letter indicating their weight class; all the rods fitted to one engine must be of the same class (see illustration).

2 The gudgeon pins are an interference fit in the connecting rods, and if new pistons are to be fitted to the existing connecting rods the work should be carried out by a Ford garage who will have the necessary tooling. Note that the oil splash hole on the connecting rod must be located on the right-hand side of the piston (the arrow on the piston crown faces forwards) (see illustration).

3 If new rings are to be fitted to the existing pistons, expand the old rings over the top of the pistons. The use of two or three old feeler blades will be helpful in preventing the rings dropping into empty grooves. Note that the oil control ring is in three sections.

4 Before fitting the new rings to the pistons, insert them into the cylinder bore and use a feeler blade to check that the end gaps are within the specified limits (see illustrations).

5 Clean out the piston ring grooves using a piece of old piston ring as a scraper. Be careful not to scratch the aluminium surface of the pistons. Protect your fingers - piston ring edges are sharp. Also probe the groove oil return holes.

6 Fit the oil control ring sections with the spreader ends abutted opposite the front of the piston. The side ring gaps should be 25 mm

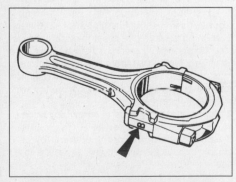

29.1 Weight class mark (arrowed) on connecting rod

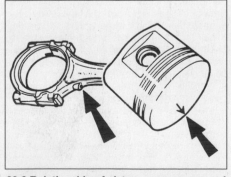

29.2 Relationship of piston crown arrow and connecting rod oil splash hole (arrowed)

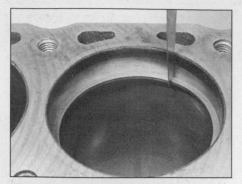

29.4a Checking a piston ring gap at the top of the cylinder

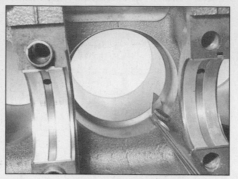

29.4b Checking a ring gap at the bottom of the cylinder

(1.0 in) either side of the spreader gap. Fit the tapered lower compression ring with the TOP mark towards the top of the piston and the gap 150° from the spreader gap, then fit the upper compression ring with the gap 150° on the other side of the spreader gap. Note that the compression rings are coated with a molybdenum skin which must not be damaged.
7 Note that the compression rings are made of cast iron, and will snap if expanded too far.

30 Camshaft and cam followers - examination and renovation

Examine the surface of the camshaft journals and lobes and the cam followers for wear. If excessive, considerable noise would have been noticed from the top of the engine and a new camshaft and followers must be fitted.

Check the camshaft bearings for wear and if necessary have them renewed by a Ford garage.

Check the camshaft lubrication tube for obstructions and make sure that the jet holes are clear. Obstruction of the holes can be due to sludge build-up which occurs when regular oil changes have been neglected.

31 Auxiliary shaft - examination and renovation

Examine the auxiliary shaft for wear and damage and renew it if necessary.

If the auxiliary shaft endfloat is outside the limits given in the Specifications fit a new thrust plate. If this does not bring the endfloat within limits, renew the shaft.

32 Timing belt - examination and renovation

Whenever the timing belt is removed it is worthwhile renewing it, especially if it has covered a high mileage. This is more important on the 2.0 litre engine where stripped teeth on the timing belt can cause the pistons to foul the valves.

33 Flywheel ring gear - examination and renovation

If the ring gear is badly worn or has missing teeth, it should be renewed. The old ring can be removed from the flywheel by cutting a notch between two teeth with a hacksaw and then splitting it with a cold chisel. Wear eye protection when doing this.

To fit a new ring gear requires heating the ring to 204°C (400°F). This can be done by polishing four equal sections of the gear, laying it on a suitable heat resistant surface (such as fire bricks) and heating it evenly with a blow lamp or torch until the polished areas turn a light yellow tinge. Do not overheat or the hard wearing properties will be lost. The gear has a chamfered inner edge which should go against the shoulder when put on the flywheel. When hot enough place the gear in position quickly, tapping it home if necessary and let it cool naturally, without quenching.

34 Cylinder head - decarbonising, valve grinding and renovation

1 This operation will normally only be required at comparatively high mileages. However, if persistent pinking occurs and performance has deteriorated even though the engine adjustments are correct, decarbonising and valve grinding may be required.
2 With the cylinder head removed, use a scraper to remove the carbon from the combustion chambers and ports. Remove all traces of gasket from the cylinder head surface, then wash it thoroughly with paraffin.
3 Use a straight-edge and feeler blade to check that the cylinder head surface is not distorted. If it is, it must be resurfaced by a suitably equipped engineering works.
4 If the engine is still in the car, clean the piston crowns and cylinder bore upper edges, but make sure that no carbon drops between the pistons and bores. To do this, locate two of the pistons at the top of their bores and seal off the remaining bores with paper and masking tape. Press a little grease between the two pistons and their bores to collect any carbon dust; this can be wiped away when the piston is lowered.

> **HAYNES HiNT** *To prevent carbon build-up, polish the piston crown with metal polish, but remove all traces of the polish after.*

5 Examine the heads of the valves for pitting and burning, especially the exhaust valve heads. Renew any valve which is badly burnt. Examine the valve seats at the same time. If the pitting is very slight, it can be removed by grinding the valve heads and seats together with coarse, then fine, grinding paste.
6 Where excessive pitting has occurred, the valve seats must be recut or renewed by a suitably equipped engineering works.
7 Valve grinding is carried out as follows. Place the cylinder head upside down on a bench on blocks of wood.
8 Smear a trace of coarse carborundum paste on the seat face and press a suction grinding tool onto the valve head. With a semi-rotary action, grind the valve head to its seat, lifting the valve occasionally to redistribute the grinding paste. When a dull matt even surface is produced on both the valve seat and the valve, wipe off the paste and repeat the process with fine carborundum paste as before. A light spring placed under the valve head will greatly ease this operation. When a smooth unbroken ring of light grey matt finish is produced on both the valve and seat, the grinding operation is complete.
9 Scrape away all carbon from the valve head and stem, and clean away all traces of grinding compound. Clean the valves and seats with a paraffin soaked rag, then wipe with a clean rag.
10 If the guides are worn they will need reboring for oversize valves or for fitting guide inserts. The valve seats will also need recutting to ensure that they are concentric with the stems. This work should be given to your Ford dealer or local engineering works.
11 If the valve springs have been in use for 20 000 miles (32 000 km) or more, renew them. Always renew the valve stem oil seals when the valves are removed.

35 Engine reassembly - general information

1 To ensure maximum life with minimum trouble from a rebuilt engine, not only must everything be correctly assembled, but it must also be spotlessly clean. All oilways must be clear, and locking washers and spring washers must be fitted where indicated. Oil all bearings and other working surfaces thoroughly with engine oil during assembly.
2 Before assembly begins, renew any bolts or studs with damaged threads.
3 Gather together a torque wrench, oil can, clean rag, and a set of engine gaskets and oil seals, together with a new oil filter.
4 If they have been removed, new cylinder head bolts and flywheel bolts will also be required.

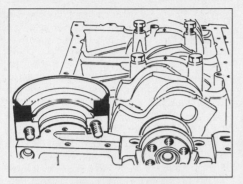

36.12 Apply sealant to the rear main bearing cap areas shown darkened

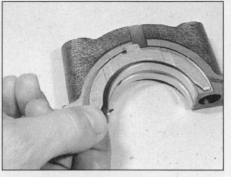

36.14 Fitting a thrust washer to the centre main bearing cap

36.19 Fitting a sealing wedge to the rear main bearing cap

36 Crankshaft and main bearings - refitting

1 Wipe the bearing shell locations in the crankcase with a soft, non-fluffy rag.
2 Wipe the crankshaft journals with a soft, non-fluffy rag.
3 Fit the five upper half main bearing shells to their locations in the crankcase. If the old shells are being re-used, make sure they are refitted to their old locations.
4 Identify each main bearing cap and place in order. The number is cast onto the cap and on intermediate caps an arrow is also marked which should point towards front of engine.
5 Wipe the cap bearing shell location with a soft non-fluffy rag.
6 Fit the bearing half shell onto each main bearing cap.
7 Apply a little grease to each side of the centre main bearing so as to retain the thrustwasher.
8 Fit the upper halves of the thrustwashers into their grooves either side of the main bearing. The slots must face outwards.
9 Lubricate the crankshaft journals and the upper and lower main bearing shells with engine oil and locate the rear oil seal (with lip lubricated) on the rear of the crankshaft.
10 Carefully lower the crankshaft into the crankcase.
11 Lubricate the crankshaft main bearing journals again and then fit No 1 bearing cap. Fit the two securing bolts but do not tighten yet.

12 Make sure that the mating faces are clean, then apply sealant (Loctite 518 or equivalent) to the areas on the rear main bearing cap (see illustration).
13 Fit the rear main bearing cap. Fit the two securing bolts, but as before do not tighten yet.
14 Apply a little grease to either side of the centre main bearing cap so as to retain the thrustwashers. Fit the thrustwashers with the tag located in the groove and the slots facing outwards (see illustration).
15 Fit the centre main bearing cap and the two securing bolts, then refit the intermediate main bearing caps. Make sure that the arrows point towards the front of the engine.
16 Lightly tighten all main cap securing bolts and then fully tighten in a progressive manner to the specified torque wrench setting.
17 Check that the crankshaft rotates freely. Some stiffness is to be expected with new components, but there must be no tight spots or binding.
18 Check that the crankshaft endfloat is within the specified limits by inserting a feeler blade between the centre crankshaft web and the thrustwashers.
19 Make sure that the rear oil seal is fully located onto its seating. Coat the rear main bearing cap wedges with sealing compound, then press them into position with the rounded red face towards the cap (see illustration).
20 Refit the oil pump and strainer.
21 Refit the crankshaft front oil seal housing, and auxiliary shaft front cover, if applicable, together with a new gasket and tighten the bolts.

Make sure that the bottom face of the housing is aligned with the bottom face of the block.
22 Refit the flywheel or driveplate and the pistons and connecting rods.
23 Refit the timing belt and sprockets.

37 Pistons and connecting rods - refitting

1 Clean the backs of the bearing shells and the recesses in the connecting rods and big-end caps.
2 Press the bearing shells into the connecting rods and caps in their correct positions and oil them liberally. Note that the lugs must be adjacent to each other (see illustration).
3 Lubricate the cylinder bores with engine oil.
4 Fit a ring compressor to No 1 piston, then insert the piston and connecting rod into No 1 cylinder. With No 1 crankpin at its lowest point, drive the piston carefully into the cylinder with the wooden handle of a hammer, and at the same time guide the connecting rod onto the crankpin. Make sure that the arrow on the piston crown is facing the front of the engine (see illustrations).
5 Oil the crankpin, then fit the big-end bearing cap in its previously noted position. Oil the big-end bearing cap nuts, fit the nuts and tighten them to the specified torque.
6 Check that the crankshaft turns freely.
7 Repeat the procedure given in paragraphs 4 to 6 inclusive on the remaining pistons.
8 Refit the cylinder head and sump.

2A

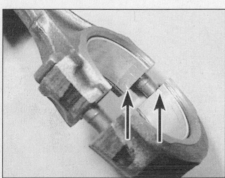

37.2 Big-end bearing shell lugs (arrowed) are adjacent

37.4a Fitting a piston ring compressor

37.4b Piston crown markings
Arrow points to front of engine

38 Oil pump - refitting

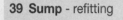

1 Insert the oil pump driveshaft into the block in its previously noted position.
2 Prime the pump by injecting oil into it and turning it by hand (see illustration).
3 Fit the pump. insert the bolts and tighten them to the specified torque with the splined key.
4 Insert the pick-up tube securing bolt and tighten it.
5 Where applicable refit the crankshaft front oil seal housing together with a new gasket and tighten the bolts. Make sure that the bottom face of the housing is aligned with the bottom face of the block.
6 Refit the sump.

39 Sump - refitting

1 Apply sealing compound to the corners of the front and rear rubber sealing strap locations, then press the strips into the grooves of the rear main bearing cap and crankshaft front oil seal housing (see illustrations)
2 Apply a little sealing compound to the bottom face of the cylinder block, then fit the sump gaskets in position and locate the end tabs beneath the rubber sealing strips (see illustration).

38.2 Priming the oil pump

3 Locate the sump on the gaskets and insert the bolts loosely.
4 Tighten the bolts to the specified torques in the two stages given in the Specifications (see illustration). Tighten to the first stage in circular sequence starting at point A, then tighten to the second stage starting at point B. Tighten to the third stage after the engine has been running for twenty minutes.
5 If the engine is in the vehicle, reverse the steps taken to gain access to the sump.

40 Flywheel/driveplate and adapter plate - refitting

1 If it was removed, refit the adapter plate (backplate) over the dowels on the rear of the block.

2 Wipe the mating faces, then locate the flywheel/driveplate on the rear of the crankshaft.
3 Coat the threads of the bolts with a liquid locking agent before fitting. Note that the manufacturers recommend using new bolts.
4 Using a piece of angle iron, hold the flywheel/driveplate stationary, then tighten the bolts evenly to the specified torque in diagonal sequence (see illustrations).
5 If the engine is in the car, refit the automatic transmission or the clutch.

41 Auxiliary shaft - refitting

1 Oil the auxiliary shaft journals, then insert the shaft into the cylinder block.
2 Locate the thrust plate in the shaft groove, then insert the crosshead screws and tighten them with an impact screwdriver.
3 Support the front cover on blocks of wood and drive out the old oil seal. Drive in the new seal using a metal tube or socket (see illustrations). Make sure that the sealing lip faces toward the engine. Smear a little oil on the lip.
4 If applicable cut the unwanted top half of a new gasket and locate it on the cylinder block, then fit the front cover and tighten the bolts.
5 Refit the fuel pump and operating rod (when applicable).
6 Refit the distributor.
7 Refit the auxiliary shaft sprocket and timing belt.

39.1a Applying sealing compound to a rubber strip location

39.1b Fitting the rubber strip into its groove

39.2 Locate the gasket tabs beneath the sealing strips

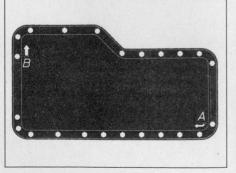

39.4 Sump bolt tightening sequence
For A and B see text

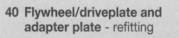

40.4a Method of holding the flywheel when tightening the bolts

40.4b Tightening a flywheel bolt

41.3a Driving out the auxiliary shaft cover oil seal

41.3b Fitting a new oil seal in the auxiliary shaft cover

42.3 Cam follower ball-pins and spring clips fitted

42 Cylinder head - reassembly

1 Refit the thermostat and housing.
2 Refit the timing belt tensioner if it was removed, but do not tighten the bolts yet.
3 If applicable, screw the cam follower ball-pins in their correct locations (see illustration).
4 Oil the valve stems and insert the valves in their correct guides.
5 Wrap some adhesive tape over the collet groove of each valve, then oil the oil seals and slide them over the valve onto the guides. Use a suitable metal tube if necessary to press them onto the guides. Remove the adhesive tape.
6 Working on each valve in turn, fit the valve spring and cap, then compress the spring with the compressor and insert the split collets. Release the compressor and remove it. Tap the end of the valve stem with a non-metallic mallet to settle the collets. If tool 21-005-A is being used, first locate the camshaft in its bearings.

> **HAYNES HINT** *A dab of grease on the collets will keep them in position on the valve stem*

7 Refit the camshaft.

43 Camshaft - refitting

1 Drive the new oil seal into the camshaft front bearing location on the cylinder head using a suitable metal tube or socket (see illustration). Smear the lip with engine oil.
2 Lubricate the bearings with hypoid SAE 80/90 oil, then carefully insert the camshaft.
3 Locate the thrust plate in the camshaft groove, then insert and tighten the bolts.
4 Using feeler blades check that the endfloat is as given in the Specifications.
5 Lubricate the ball-pins with hypoid SAE 80/90 oil, then fit the cam followers in their correct locations and retain with the spring clips. It will be necessary to rotate the camshaft during this operation.
6 Fit the oil supply tube and tighten the bolts.
7 Fit the camshaft sprocket backplate and sprocket. Insert and tighten the bolt while holding the camshaft stationary with a spanner on the lug (see illustration).
8 Refit the cylinder head.

44 Cylinder head - refitting

1 Adjust the valve clearances. This work is easier to carry out on the bench rather than in the car.
2 Turn the engine so that No 1 piston is approximately 2 cm (0.8 in) before top dead centre. This precaution will prevent any damage to open valves.
3 Make sure that the faces of the cylinder block and cylinder head are perfectly clean, then locate the new gasket on the block making sure that all the internal holes are aligned (see illustration). *Do not use jointing compound.*
4 Turn the camshaft so that the TDC pointer is aligned with the indentation on the front of the cylinder head.
5 Lower the cylinder head onto the gasket. The help of an assistant will ensure that the gasket is not dislodged. Alternatively, make a couple of guide studs by sawing the heads off two old cylinder head bolts; remove the studs when the head is in position.
6 Lightly oil the heads and threads of the new head bolts and insert them into their holes.
7 Using the Torx key, tighten the bolts progressively to the Stage 1 specified torque in the indicated sequence (see illustration).
8 In the same sequence tighten the bolts to the Stage 2 specified torque.
9 Wait five minutes, then tighten the bolts through the angle specified for Stage 3, still following the same sequence. (If the engine is on the bench, it may be preferable to leave this final stage until after refitting the engine, when the problem of holding it still will not arise.)
10 Refit the rocker cover, using a new gasket. Make sure that the dovetail sections of the gasket engage correctly (see illustration).
11 Fit the rocker cover bolts and reinforcing plates. Tighten the bolts as follows, referring to

2A

43.1 Fitting the camshaft front bearing oil seal

43.7 Fitting the camshaft sprocket backplate

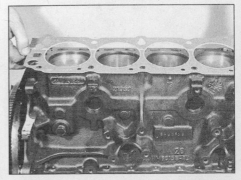

44.3 Fitting a new cylinder head gasket

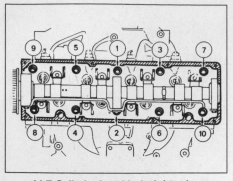

44.7 Cylinder head bolt tightening sequence

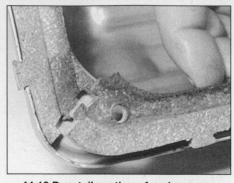

44.10 Dovetail section of rocker cover gasket

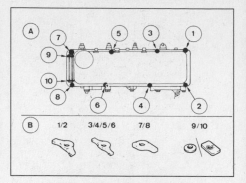

44.11 Rocker cover bolts (A) and reinforcing plates (B)
For tightening sequence see text

the Specifications and to illustration 44.11:
  Stage 1 - Bolts 1 to 6
  Stage 2 - Bolts 7 and 8
  Stage 3 - Bolts 9 and 10
  Stage 4 - Bolts 7 and 8 (again)
12 No further tightening of the cylinder head bolts is required.
13 Refit and tension the timing belt as described in the next Section.

45 Timing belt and sprockets - refitting

1 Fit the camshaft sprocket backplate and sprocket. Insert the bolt, hold the camshaft or sprocket and tighten the bolt to the specified torque.

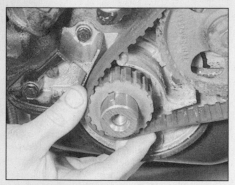

45.4 Fitting the timing belt over the crankshaft sprocket

45.5a Refitting the crankshaft pulley

2 Fit the auxiliary shaft sprocket with the ribs towards the engine. Fit the sprocket bolt and tighten it to the specified torque, counterholding the sprocket with a bar through one of the holes.
3 Fit the crankshaft sprocket, chamfered side inwards.
4 Fit the timing belt over the camshaft sprocket, but do not engage it with the other sprockets yet. Be careful not to kink the belt. If the old belt is being refitted, observe the previously noted running direction **(see illustration)**.
5 Refit the guide washer and the crankshaft pulley. Fit the bolt and washer and tighten just enough to seat the pulley, being careful not to turn the crankshaft **(see illustrations)**.
6 Make sure that the TDC pointer on the camshaft sprocket backplate is still aligned with the indentation on the cylinder head.
7 Turn the crankshaft by the shortest route to align the TDC notch in the pulley with the pointer on the oil seal housing.
8 If the distributor is fitted, turn the auxiliary shaft sprocket so that the rotor arm points to the No 1 HT segment position.
9 Fit the timing belt over the sprockets and round the tensioner. Move the tensioner to tension the belt roughly and nip up the tensioner bolts.
10 Turn the crankshaft through two full turns clockwise, then 60° anti-clockwise (so it is now at 60° BTDC)
11 The belt tension should now ideally be checked by applying Ford tension gauge 21-113

45.5b Crankshaft pulley bolt and washer

to the longest run. Desired gauge readings are:
  Used belt - 4 to 5
  New belt - 10 to 11
12 If the tension gauge is not available, a rough guide is that belt tension is correct when the belt can be twisted 90° in the middle of the longest run with the fingers **(see illustration)**.
13 If adjustment of belt tension is necessary, turn the crankshaft clockwise to bring No 1 cylinder to TDC **(see illustration)** then slacken the tensioner bolts and move the tensioner to increase or decrease belt tension. Tighten the tensioner bolts.
14 Turn the crankshaft 90° clockwise past TDC, then anti-clockwise back to the 60° BTDC position. Check the belt tension again.
15 Repeat the above procedure until the belt tension is correct.
16 Tighten the tensioner bolts and the crankshaft pulley bolt to the specified torques **(see illustration)**.
17 Refit the belt cover and tighten its bolts.
18 If the engine is in the vehicle, reverse the preliminary steps given in Section 13.
19 Check the ignition timing when the engine is next run.

46 Ancillary components - refitting

Refer to Section 9 and refit the components listed. Delicate items such as the alternator and distributor may be left until after the engine has been refitted, if preferred.

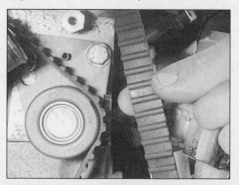

45.12 Twisting the timing belt to assess its tension

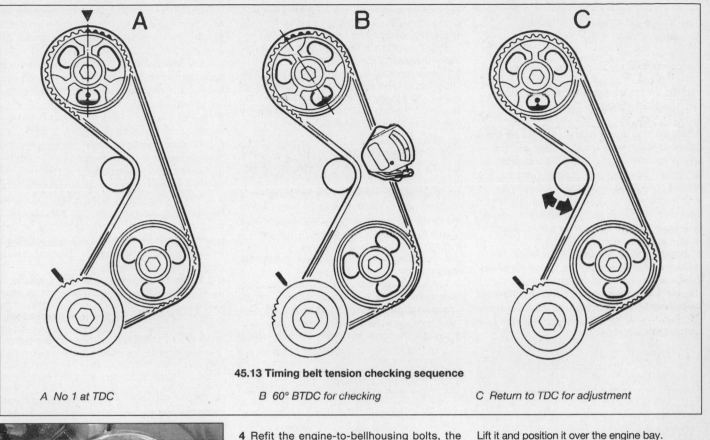

45.13 Timing belt tension checking sequence

A No 1 at TDC   *B 60° BTDC for checking*   *C Return to TDC for adjustment*

2A

45.16 Holding the crankshaft pulley with two bolts and a lever while tightening the central bolt

If the crankcase ventilation oil separator was removed, apply a liquid locking agent to its tube before pressing it into the cylinder block.

47 Engine and gearbox - reconnection

1 Make sure that the clutch is centred.
2 Apply a smear of grease or anti-seize compound to the gearbox input shaft splines.
3 With the aid of an assistant, offer the gearbox to the engine. If the input shaft is reluctant to enter the clutch, rock the gearbox slightly or turn the crankshaft back and forth. Support the gearbox until it is engaged with the dowels on the engine - do not leave it hanging on the input shaft.

4 Refit the engine-to-bellhousing bolts, the bracing strap and the starter motor.

48 Engine - refitting with manual gearbox

1 Sling the engine/gearbox unit so that it hangs at an angle of approximately 45°.
2 Lower the unit into the engine bay, at the same time moving it towards the rear of the vehicle. Have an assistant watch as the unit is lowered to check that no pipes, wires etc are fouled or trapped.
3 Raise the gearbox as the engine is lowered until the unit takes up its correct position. Secure the engine bearers to the mountings and refit the gearbox crossmember.
4 The remainder of refitting is a reversal of the removal procedure. Refer to Section 6. Also refer to Section 49, paragraph 9.
5 Before starting the engine, refer to Section 51.

49 Engine - refitting without gearbox/transmission

1 On manual gearbox models, check that the clutch is centred correctly. Apply a smear of grease or anti-seize compound to the gearbox input shaft.
2 On automatic transmission models, check that the torque converter is fully engaged with the transmission oil pump.
3 Sling the engine so that it is roughly horizontal.

Lift it and position it over the engine bay.
4 Lower the engine into place. Have an assistant watch as the unit is lowered to check that no pipes, wires etc are fouled or trapped.
5 Guide the engine onto the transmission, raising or lowering the transmission slightly if necessary. Do not place any weight on the transmission input shaft. With manual gearbox models, rock the engine gently from side to side to encourage the input shaft to enter the clutch.
6 When the engine and transmission are fully engaged, refit the engine-to-bellhousing bolts. Do not overlook the earth strap.
7 Lower the engine so that the engine bearers engage with the mountings. Fit the mounting nuts and remove the lifting tackle.
8 On automatic transmission models, bolt the torque converter to the driveplate.
9 The remainder of refitting is a reversal of the removal procedure. Note the following additional points:
a) Refill the engine with oil
b) Check the transmission oil level if necessary
c) Adjust the tension of the accessory drivebelts
d) Adjust the throttle cable
e) Adjust the downshift cable when applicable
f) Refill the cooling system
10 Before starting the engine, see Section 51

50 Valve clearances - checking and adjustment

See Chapter 1, Section 23.

51 Initial start-up after overhaul or major repair

1 Make a final check to ensure that everything has been reconnected to the engine and that no rags or tools have been left in the engine bay.
2 Check that oil and coolant levels are correct.
3 Start the engine. This may take a little longer than usual as fuel is pumped up to the engine.
4 Check that the oil pressure light goes out when the engine starts.
5 Run the engine at a fast tickover and check for leaks of oil, fuel and coolant. Also check power steering and transmission fluid cooler unions, when applicable. Some smoke and odd smells may be experienced as assembly lubricant burns off the exhaust manifold and other components.

6 Bring the engine to operating temperature. Check the ignition timing then adjust the idle speed (if applicable) and mixture.
7 Stop the engine and allow it to cool, then re-check the oil and coolant levels.
8 If new bearings, pistons etc have been fitted, the engine should be run in at reduced speeds and loads for the first 500 miles (800 km) or so. It is beneficial to change the engine oil and filter after this mileage.

52 Compression test - description and interpretation

1 When engine performance is down, or if misfiring occurs which cannot be attributed to the ignition or fuel system, a compression test can provide diagnostic clues. If the test is performed regularly it can give warning of trouble before any other symptoms become apparent.
2 The engine must be at operating temperature, the battery must be fully charged and the spark plugs must be removed. The services of an assistant will also be required.
3 Disable the ignition system by dismantling the coil LT feed. Fit the compression tester to No 1 spark plug hole. (The type of tester which screws into the spark plug hole is to be preferred.)
4 Have the assistant hold the throttle wide open and crank the engine on the starter. Record the highest reading obtained on the compression tester.
5 Repeat the test on the remaining cylinders, recording the pressure developed in each.
6 Desired pressures are given in the Specifications. If the pressure in any cylinder is low, introduce a teaspoonful of clean engine oil into the spark plug hole and repeat the test.
7 If the addition of oil temporarily improves the compression pressure, this indicates that bore or piston wear was responsible for the pressure loss. No improvement suggests that leaking or burnt valves, or a blown head gasket, may be to blame.
8 A low reading from two adjacent cylinders is almost certainly due to the head gasket between them having blown.
9 On completion of the test, refit the spark plugs and reconnect the coil LT feed.

Chapter 2 Part B:
2.0 litre DOHC engine

Unless otherwise stated, procedures are as described for the SOHC engines in Part A of this Chapter

Contents

Degrees of difficulty

Easy, suitable for novice with little experience	**Fairly easy,** suitable for beginner with some experience	**Fairly difficult,** suitable for competent DIY mechanic	**Difficult,** suitable for experienced DIY mechanic	**Very difficult,** suitable for expert DIY or professional

Specifications

General

Manufacturer's code:
Carburettor engine N8B
Fuel-injection engine without catalyst N9B
Fuel-injection engine with catalyst N9D
Bore - mm (in) 86.00 (3.386)
Stroke - mm (in) 86.00 (3.386)
Cubic capacity - cc (cu in) 1998 (121.9)
Compression ratio 10.3:1
Compression pressure at cranking speed . . . . 11 to 13 bar (160 to 189 lbf/in^2)
Maximum power (DIN, kW @ rpm):
    N8B engine . . . . 80 @ 5600
    N9B engine . . . . 92 @ 5500
    N9D engine . . . . 88 @ 5500
Maximum torque (DIN, Nm @ rpm):
    N8B engine . . . . 174 @ 3000
    N0D engine . . . . 174 @ 2500
    N9D engine . . . . 171 @ 2500

Lubrication system

Oil type . . . . See *"Lubricants and fluids"*
Oil capacity:
    With filter . . . . 4.5 litres (7.92 pints)
    Without filter . . . . 4.0 litres (7.04 pints)

Cylinder block

Bore diameter:
Standard grade 1	86.000 to 86.010 mm
Standard grade 2	86.010 to 86.020 mm
Oversize 0.15 grade A	86.150 to 86.160 mm
Oversize 0.15 grade B	86.160 to 86.170 mm
Oversize 0.5	86.500 to 86.510 mm

Crankshaft

Endfloat	0.090 to 0.300 mm
Main bearing running clearance	0.011 to 0.048 mm
Main bearing journal diameter:	
Standard (yellow)	54.980 to 54.990 mm
Standard (red)	54.990 to 55.000 mm
Undersize 0.25 (green)	54.730 to 54.750 mm
Main bearing thrustwasher thickness:	
Standard	2.301 to 2.351 mm
Oversize 0.38 (yellow)	2.491 to 2.541 mm
Big-end bearing running clearance	0.006 to 0.060 mm
Big-end bearing journal diameter:	
Standard	50.890 to 50.910 mm
Undersize 0.25 (green)	50.640 to 50.660 mm

Pistons and piston rings

Piston diameter:
Standard 1	85.970 to 85.980 mm
Standard 2	85.980 to 85.990 mm
Standard service	85.980 to 86.000 mm
Oversize 0.15	86.130 to 86.150 mm
Oversize 0.50	86.470 to 86.490 mm

Piston ring end gap:
Top	0.300 to 0.600 mm
Centre	0.500 to 0.800 mm
Bottom (oil control)	0.400 to 1.500 mm

Cylinder head

Valve guide bore	7.063 to 7.094 mm
Camshaft bearing parent bore diameter	26.000 to 26.030 mm

Camshafts

Endfloat	0.020 to 0.260 mm

Valves and valve springs - general

Valve timing:
Carburettor engine:	
Inlet opens	13°BTDC
Inlet closes	39°ABDC
Exhaust opens	43°BBDC
Exhaust closes	13°ATDC
Fuel-injection engines:	
Inlet opens	13°BTDC
Inlet closes	51°ABDC
Exhaust opens	43°BBDC
Exhaust closes	13°ATDC

Valve spring free length:
Inner spring	48.200 mm
Outer spring	46.800 mm

Inlet valve stem diameter:
Standard	7.025 to 7.043 mm
Oversize 0.2	7.225 to 7.243 mm
Oversize 0.4	7.425 to 7.443 mm
Oversize 0.6	7.625 to 7.643 mm
Oversize 0.8	7.825 to 7.843 mm

Exhaust valve stem diameter:
Standard	6.999 to 7.017 mm
Oversize 0.2	7.199 to 7.217 mm
Oversize 0.4	7.399 to 7.417 mm
Oversize 0.6	7.599 to 7.617 mm
Oversize 0.8	7.799 to 7.817 mm

Torque wrench settings

	Nm	lbf ft
Main bearing cap bolts	90 to 104	66 to 77
Big-end bearing cap bolts:		
Stage 1	6 to 8	4 to 6
Stage 2	15 to 17	11 to 13
Stage 3	Tighten further 85° to 95°	Tighten further 85° to 95°
Crankshaft pulley bolt:		
Stage 1	45 to 58	33 to 43
Stage 2	Tighten further 80° to 90°	Tighten further 80° to 90°
Camshaft sprocket bolts	55 to 63	41 to 46
Flywheel bolts	82 to 92	61 to 68
Oil pump bolts	9 to 12	7 to 9
Oil pump sprocket bolt	16 to 19	12 to 14
Oil pump chain tensioner bolt	10 to 13	7 to 10
Sump bolts and nuts	8 to 10	6 to 7
Sump studs	6 to 8	4 to 6
Sump drain plug	21 to 28	15 to 21
Sump front mounting plate	23 to 28	17 to 21
Oil baffle nuts	17 to 21	13 to 15
Oil pick-up pipe-to-cylinder block bolts	9 to 13	7 to 10
Oil pressure warning lamp switch	18 to 22	13 to 16
Cylinder head bolts:		
M11 bolts:		
Stage 1	25	18
Stage 2	55	41
Stage 3	Tighten further 90°	Tighten further 90°
Stage 4	Tighten further 90°	Tighten further 90°
M8 bolts	36 to 39	27 to 29
Camshaft cover bolts	6 to 8	4 to 6
Camshaft bearing cap nuts	22 to 26	16 to 19
Lower timing chain guide:		
Upper bolt	10 to 13	7 to 10
Lower bolt	24 to 28	18 to 21
Upper and lower timing chain cover bolts	7 to 10	5 to 7
Crankshaft rear oil seal housing bolts	8 to 11	6 to 8
Engine-to-gearbox/transmission bolts	29 to 41	21 to 30

2B

1 General information

The 2.0 litre DOHC (Double OverHead Camshaft) engine was introduced in June 1989 to replace the 2.0 litre SOHC engine used previously in the Granada range, at the same time a 2.0 litre version of the Scorpio model was also introduced. The engine is of four-cylinder, in-line type.

The crankshaft incorporates five main bearings. Thrustwashers are fitted to the centre main bearing in order to control crankshaft endfloat.

The camshafts are driven by a chain from the crankshaft and operate the angled valves via hydraulic cam followers. One camshaft operates the inlet valves, and the other operates the exhaust valves.

The distributor is driven directly from the front of the inlet camshaft, and the oil pump is driven by a chain from the crankshaft. An electric fuel pump is mounted in the fuel tank.

Lubrication is by means of a bi-rotor pump which draws oil through a strainer located inside the sump, and forces it through a full-flow filter into the engine oil galleries, from where it is distributed to the crankshaft and camshafts. The big-end bearings are supplied with oil via internal drillings in the crankshaft. The undersides of the pistons are supplied with oil from drillings in the connecting rods. The hydraulic cam followers are supplied with oil from passages in the cylinder head. The camshafts are lubricated by oil from spray tubes mounted above the camshaft bearing caps.

A closed crankcase ventilation system is employed, whereby piston blow-by gases are drawn from the crankcase, through a breather pipe into the inlet manifold where they are burnt with fresh air/fuel mixture.

2 Crankcase ventilation system - general information

The crankcase ventilation system (see illustration) consists of an oil separator and vent valve fitted to the cylinder block on the left-hand side of the engine. This is connected by a pipe to the inlet manifold. The system operates according to the vacuum in the inlet

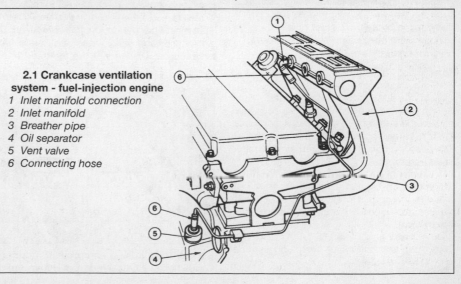

2.1 Crankcase ventilation system - fuel-injection engine

1 Inlet manifold connection
2 Inlet manifold
3 Breather pipe
4 Oil separator
5 Vent valve
6 Connecting hose

manifold. Piston blow-by gases are drawn through the oil separator and the vent valve to the inlet manifold. The blow-by gases are then drawn into the engine together with the fuel/air mixture. Refer to Chapter 1 for maintenance of the system.

3 Major operations possible with the engine in the vehicle

The following operations can be carried out without removing the engine from the vehicle.
a) Removal of the camshafts.
b) Removal and servicing of the cylinder head.
c) Removal of the timing chain and sprockets.
d) Removal of the oil pump.
e) Removal of the sump.
f) Removal of the pistons and connecting rods.
g) Removal of the big-end bearings.
h) Removal of the engine mountings.
i) Removal of the clutch and flywheel.
j) Removal of the crankshaft front and rear oil seals.

4 Major operations requiring engine removal

The following operations can only be carried out after removing the engine from the vehicle.
a) Removal of the crankshaft main bearings.
b) Removal of the crankshaft.

5 Engine - removal leaving manual gearbox in vehicle

⚠️ *Warning: Vehicles equipped with air conditioning: Components of the air conditioning system may obstruct work being undertaken on the engine, and it is not always possible to unbolt and move them aside sufficiently, within the limits of their flexible pipes. In such a case, the system should be discharged by a Ford dealer or air conditioning specialist. Refer also to the precautions given in Chapter 3.*

Note: *A hoist and lifting tackle will be required to lift the engine out of the vehicle.*
1 Disconnect the battery negative lead.
2 Remove the bonnet.
3 On carburettor models, remove the air cleaner.
4 On fuel-injection models, remove the air inlet hose, plenum chamber and air cleaner lid as an assembly.
5 Disconnect the breather hose from the camshaft cover, and unscrew the bolt securing the hose support bracket to the left-hand side of the cylinder head (see illustration).
6 Drain the cooling system.
7 To provide additional working space, remove the radiator.

5.5 Removing the hose support bracket bolt from the cylinder head

8 Disconnect the coolant hoses from the water pump housing on the left-hand side of the engine and the cylinder head **(see illustration)**.
9 Disconnect the coolant hoses from the thermostat housing.
10 Disconnect the heater coolant hose from the inlet manifold.
11 Where applicable, release the coolant hose from the bracket under the carburettor automatic choke housing.
12 Disconnect the throttle cable and (where necessary) speed control cable from the throttle linkage.
13 On carburettor models, disconnect the vacuum pipe from the engine management module.
14 Disconnect the brake servo vacuum hose (where necessary) from the inlet manifold.
15 On fuel-injection models, disconnect the vacuum pipes from the MAP sensor (located on the suspension turret on the right-hand side of the engine compartment) and, where applicable, the air conditioning system.
16 On carburettor models, disconnect the fuel supply and return hoses at the carburettor, and plug the ends of the hoses to minimise petrol spillage. Take adequate fire precautions.
17 On fuel-injection models, slowly loosen the fuel feed union at the fuel rail to relieve the pressure in the fuel system before disconnecting the union. Be prepared for petrol spillage and take adequate fire precautions. Disconnect the fuel feed hose,

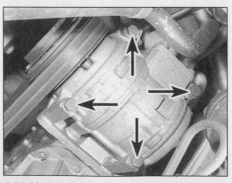

5.21 Air conditioning compressor mounting bolts (arrowed) (viewed from underneath)

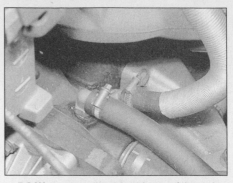

5.8 Water pump coolant hoses (viewed from above)

and disconnect the fuel return hose from the fuel pressure regulator. Plug the ends of the hoses to minimise petrol spillage.
18 Disconnect the HT lead from the ignition coil, and unclip it from the timing chain cover.
19 Disconnect the wiring from the following components as applicable, depending on model. Then free the wiring loom from any necessary retaining clips or ties and position it clear of the engine.
a) Alternator.
b) Starter motor.
c) Oil pressure warning lamp switch.
d) Temperature gauge sender.
e) Cooling fan switch.
f) Anti-dieselling valve (carburettor models).
g) Automatic choke heater (carburettor models).
h) Engine coolant temperature sensor.
i) Crankshaft speed/position sensor.
j) Air charge temperature sensor.
k) Throttle position sensor.
l) Fuel temperature sensor.
m) Fuel injectors.
20 Remove the water pump/alternator drivebelt, then unbolt the power steering pump from the mounting bracket and move it clear of the engine. Note that there is no need to disconnect the fluid hoses, but make sure that the pump is adequately supported to avoid straining them.
21 On models fitted with air conditioning, unbolt the air conditioning compressor from the mounting bracket, and move it clear of the engine **(see illustration)**. **Do not** disconnect the hoses, but make sure that the compressor is adequately supported to avoid straining them.
22 Unscrew and remove the top engine-to-gearbox bolts which are accessible from the engine compartment. Note the location of the bolts, and the positions of the earth strap and any wiring clips attached to the bolts.
23 Unscrew the securing bolt, and disconnect the earth lead from the rear left-hand side of the cylinder head.
24 Unscrew the nuts securing the engine mountings to the engine mounting brackets.
25 Apply the handbrake, jack up the front of the vehicle and support it securely on axle stands (see "Jacking").
26 Drain the engine oil into a container.

5.29 Intermediate shaft lower clamp bolt (arrowed)

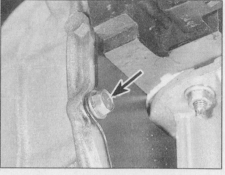

5.33 Engine adaptor plate bolt (arrowed)

5.36 Remove the engine mounting brackets to improve clearance

5.37 Removing a brake line securing clip from the suspension crossmember

5.38 Removing a suspension crossmember securing bolt

2B

27 Remove the starter motor.
28 Remove the exhaust downpipe.
29 Ensure that the steering wheel is positioned in the straight-ahead position then, using a dab of paint or a suitable marker pen, make alignment marks between the intermediate shaft lower clamp and steering gear pinion. Slacken and remove the lower clamp bolt then disconnect the intermediate shaft from the steering gear (see illustration).
30 Working inside the vehicle, place a wooden block under the clutch pedal to raise it fully against the stop, so holding the automatic adjuster pawl clear of the toothed quadrant.
31 Disconnect the clutch cable from the clutch release arm, and pass the cable through the bellhousing.
32 Support the gearbox with a trolley jack, using a block of wood between the jack and the gearbox to spread the load.
33 Unscrew and remove the remaining engine-to-gearbox bolts, and remove the bolt from the engine adapter plate (see illustration). Recover any shims fitted between the sump and the gearbox when removing the lower engine-to-gearbox bolts.
34 Make a final check to ensure that all relevant wires, pipes and hoses have been disconnected and positioned clear of the engine to facilitate engine removal.
35 Attach a suitable hoist to the engine lifting brackets located at the front and rear of the cylinder head, and carefully take the weight of the engine.
36 To improve clearance in the engine compartment when lifting the engine, unbolt the engine mounting brackets from the cylinder block, and remove them (see illustration).
37 Detach the brake lines from the front suspension crossmember (see illustration).
38 Support the crossmember with a jack (do not remove the jack from under the gearbox), then loosen the bolts securing the crossmember to the underbody. Remove the bolts from one side, and carefully lower the crossmember to allow sufficient room for the sump to clear the steering rack and crossmember when pulling the engine forwards from the gearbox (see illustration).

39 Gently raise the engine, then pull it forwards to disconnect it from the gearbox. Ensure that the gearbox is adequately supported, and take care not to strain the gearbox input shaft.

HAYNES HiNT *It may be necessary to rock the engine a little to release it from the gearbox.*

40 Once clear of the gearbox, lift the engine from the vehicle, taking care not to damage the components in the engine compartment.

6 Engine - removal leaving automatic transmission in vehicle

Note: *Refer to Part A, Section 4 of this Chapter and to the warning that appears at the start of Section 5 before proceeding. A suitable hoist and lifting tackle will be required for this operation.*
1 Proceed as described in paragraphs 1 to 21 of Section 5.
2 Unscrew and remove the top engine-to-transmission bolts which are accessible from the engine compartment. Note the location of the earth strap, vacuum pipe bracket, and transmission dipstick tube bracket, as applicable.
3 Proceed as described in paragraphs 23 to 29 of Section 5.

4 Where applicable, remove the bolt securing the transmission fluid dipstick tube to the left-hand side of the cylinder block.
5 Working through the starter motor aperture, unscrew the four torque converter-to-driveplate nuts. It will be necessary to turn the crankshaft, using a suitable spanner on the crankshaft pulley bolt, in order to gain access to each bolt in turn through the aperture.
6 Support the transmission with a trolley jack, using a block of wood between the jack and the transmission to spread the load.
7 Unscrew and remove the remaining engine-to-transmission bolts, and remove the bolt from the engine adapter plate. Recover any shims fitted between the sump and the transmission when removing the lower engine-to transmission bolts. Where applicable, pull the blanking plug from the adapter plate.
8 Proceed as described in paragraphs 34 to 38 of Section 5.
9 Gently raise the engine, then pull the engine forwards to disconnect it from the transmission. Ensure that the torque converter is held firmly in place in the transmission housing, otherwise it could fall out resulting in fluid spillage and possible damage. It may be necessary to rock the engine a little to release it from the transmission.
10 Once clear of the transmission, lift the engine from the vehicle, taking care not to damage the components in the engine compartment.

7 Engine/manual gearbox assembly - removal and separation

Note: *Refer to Part A, Section 4 of this Chapter and to the warning that appears at the start of Section 5 before proceeding. A hoist and lifting tackle will be required for this operation.*

1 Proceed as described in paragraphs 1 to 21 of Section 5.

2 Unscrew the securing bolt, and disconnect the earth lead from the rear left-hand side of the cylinder head.

3 Unscrew the nuts securing the engine mountings to the engine mounting brackets.

4 Jack up the vehicle and support it securely on axle stands (see "*Jacking*"). Ensure that there is enough working room beneath the vehicle.

5 To improve access, disconnect the exhaust downpipe from the manifold and remove the exhaust system.

6 Drain the engine oil into a suitable container.

7 On models fitted with a catalytic converter, release the securing clips and withdraw the exhaust heat shield from under the vehicle for access to the propeller shaft.

8 Remove the propeller shaft.

9 Where applicable, bend back the locktabs, then unscrew the two bolts in each case securing the two anti-roll bar mounting clamps to the vehicle underbody. Lower the anti-roll bar as far as possible.

10 Proceed as described in paragraphs 30 and 31 of Section 5.

11 Support the gearbox with a trolley jack, using a block of wood between the jack and the gearbox to spread the load.

12 Unscrew the four nuts securing the gearbox crossmember to the vehicle underbody. Unscrew the central bolt securing the crossmember to the gearbox, and remove the crossmember. Note the position of the earth strap, where applicable. Recover the mounting cup, and the exhaust mounting bracket and heat shield (as applicable).

13 Lower the gearbox slightly on the jack, then remove the circlip, and disconnect the speedometer drive cable from the gearbox.

14 Disconnect the wiring from the reversing lamp switch, and on models with fuel-injection, disconnect the wiring from the vehicle speed sensor mounted in the side of the gearbox.

15 Slacken and remove the two bolts and washers (one either side) securing the gear linkage support bracket to the gearbox.

16 Using a pin punch, drive out the roll pin securing the gearchange rod to the gear linkage.

17 Attach a hoist to the engine lifting brackets located at the front and rear of the cylinder head, and slowly take the weight of the engine. Arrange the lifting tackle so that the engine/gearbox assembly will assume a steep angle of approximately 40° to 45° as it is being removed.

18 To improve clearance in the engine compartment when lifting the engine, unbolt the engine mounting brackets from the cylinder block, and remove them.

19 Ensure that the steering wheel is positioned in the straight-ahead position then, using a dab of paint or a marker pen, make alignment marks between the intermediate shaft lower clamp and steering gear pinion. Slacken and remove the lower clamp bolt then disconnect the intermediate shaft from the steering gear.

20 Detach the brake lines from the front suspension crossmember.

21 Support the crossmember with a jack (do not remove the jack from under the gearbox), then loosen the bolts securing the crossmember to the underbody. Remove the crossmember securing bolts, and carefully lower the crossmember to allow sufficient room for the engine sump to clear the steering rack and crossmember as the engine/gearbox assembly is removed.

22 Make a final check to ensure that all relevant wires, pipes and hoses have been disconnected to facilitate removal of the engine/gearbox assembly.

23 Raise the engine/gearbox, at the same time lowering the trolley jack which is supporting the gearbox.

24 Place a suitable rod across the vehicle underbody to support the gear linkage support bracket whilst the gearbox is removed.

25 Tilt the engine/gearbox assembly using the hoist and the trolley jack, until the assembly can be lifted from the vehicle. Take care not to damage surrounding components.

26 If the vehicle is to be moved, with the engine/gearbox assembly removed, temporarily refit the suspension crossmember and the anti-roll bar to the underbody, and reconnect the steering column to the intermediate shaft.

27 To separate the engine from the gearbox, proceed as follows.

28 Remove the starter motor.

29 Support the engine and gearbox horizontally on blocks of wood.

30 Unscrew the engine-to-gearbox bolts, noting the locations of the bolts, and the positions of the earth strap and any wiring clips attached to the bolts. Recover any shims fitted between the sump and the gearbox when removing the lower engine-to-gearbox bolts.

31 Unscrew the bolt from the engine adapter plate.

32 Pull the engine and gearbox apart, taking care not to strain the gearbox input shaft. It may be necessary to rock the units slightly to separate them.

8 Engine/automatic transmission assembly - removal and separation

Note: *Refer to Part A, Section 4 of this Chapter and to the warning that appears at the start of Section 5 before proceeding. A suitable hoist and lifting tackle will be required for this operation. Any suspected faults in the automatic transmission should be referred to a Ford dealer or automatic transmission specialist before removal of unit, as the specialist fault diagnosis equipment is designed to operate with the transmission in the vehicle.*

1 Proceed as described in paragraphs 1 to 21 of Section 5.

2 Unscrew the securing bolt, and disconnect the earth lead from the rear left-hand side of the cylinder head.

3 Unscrew the nuts securing the engine mountings to the engine mounting brackets.

4 Jack up the vehicle and support it securely on axle stands (see "*Jacking*"). Ensure that there is enough working room beneath the vehicle.

5 To improve access, disconnect the exhaust downpipe from the manifold and remove the exhaust system .

6 Drain the engine oil into a suitable container.

7 On models fitted with a catalytic converter, release the securing clips and withdraw the exhaust heat shield from under the vehicle for access to the propeller shaft.

8 Remove the propeller shaft.

9 Where applicable, bend back the locktabs, then unscrew the two bolts in each case securing the two anti-roll bar mounting clamps to the vehicle underbody. Lower the anti-roll bar as far as possible.

10 Support the transmission with a trolley jack, using a block of wood between the jack and the transmission to spread the load.

11 Unscrew the four bolts securing the transmission crossmember to the vehicle underbody. Unscrew the central bolt securing the crossmember to the transmission, and remove the crossmember. Note the position of the earth strap, where applicable. Recover the mounting cup, and the exhaust mounting bracket and heat shield (as applicable).

12 Lower the transmission slightly on the jack.

13 Unscrew the unions and disconnect the fluid cooler pipes from the transmission. Plug the open ends of the pipes and the transmission to prevent dirt ingress and fluid leakage. Where applicable, detach the fluid cooler pipe bracket from the engine mounting bracket, and move it to one side.

14 Remove the two clips securing the selector rod, and detach the selector rod from the manual selector lever, and the selector lever on the transmission.

15 Disconnect the wiring from the starter inhibitor switch, downshift solenoid, lock-up clutch, reversing lamp switch, and where applicable, the 3rd/4th gearchange solenoid.

16 Remove the securing screw, and disconnect the speedometer cable (where fitted) from the transmission extension housing. Plug the opening in the transmission to prevent dirt ingress.

17 Proceed as described in paragraphs 17 to 26 of Section 7, substituting transmission for gearbox and ignoring paragraph 24.

18 To separate the engine from the transmission, proceed as follows.

19 Remove the starter motor.

20 Support the engine and transmission horizontally on blocks of wood.

21 Working through the starter motor aperture, unscrew the four torque converter-to-driveplate nuts. It will be necessary to turn the crankshaft using a spanner on the crankshaft pulley bolt in order to gain access to each nut in turn through the aperture.

22 Where applicable, remove the bolt securing the transmission fluid dipstick tube to the left-hand side of the cylinder block.

23 Unscrew the engine-to-transmission bolts, noting the locations of the bolts, and the positions of the earth strap and any wiring clips attached to the bolts. Recover any shims fitted between the sump and the transmission when removing the lower engine-to-transmission bolts.

24 Unscrew the bolt from the engine adapter plate and, where applicable, pull the blanking plug from the adapter plate.

25 Pull the engine and the transmission apart, ensuring that the torque converter is held firmly in place in the transmission housing, otherwise it could fall out resulting in fluid spillage and possible damage. It may be necessary to rock the units slightly to separate them.

9 Engine - refitting (manual gearbox in vehicle)

1 Reverse the procedure described in paragraphs 1 to 40 of Section 5, noting the following points.

2 Before attempting to refit the engine, check that the clutch friction disc is centralised.

3 Check that the clutch release arm and bearing are correctly fitted, and lightly grease the input shaft splines.

4 Check that the engine adapter plate is correctly positioned on the locating dowels. If necessary, a cable-tie can be used to temporarily secure the adapter plate in position on the cylinder block using one of the engine-to-gearbox bolt holes.

5 If shims were fitted between the sump and the gearbox, refit them in their original locations when mating the engine to the gearbox. If the engine has been overhauled, where applicable fit the relevant shims as calculated during engine reassembly .

6 Reconnect the clutch cable to the release arm, ensuring that it is routed as noted during removal.

7 Ensure that the roadwheels and the steering wheel are in the straight-ahead position then align the marks made on removal and reconnect the intermediate shaft to the steering gearing. Tighten the clamp bolt to the specified torque.

8 Refit the exhaust downpipe.

9 Fill the engine with the correct grade and quantity of oil.

10 Check the throttle cable adjustment. Where necessary, also adjust the speed control cable in the same way so that there is only a small amount of slack present in the cable.

11 Reconnect the coolant hoses to the water pump housing.

12 Fill the cooling system .

13 Tighten all fixings to the specified torque, where applicable.

10 Engine - refitting (automatic transmission in vehicle)

1 Reverse the procedure described in Section 6, noting the following points.

2 Check that the engine adapter plate is correctly positioned on the locating dowels. If necessary, a cable-tie can be used to temporarily secure the adapter plate in position on the cylinder block using one of the engine-to-transmission bolt holes.

3 As the torque converter is only loosely engaged in the transmission, care must be taken to prevent the torque converter from falling out forwards. When the torque converter hub is fully engaged with the fluid pump drivegear in the transmission, distance A **(see illustration 2.20 in Chapter 7B)** must be as specified. Incorrect installation of the torque converter will result in damage to the transmission.

4 If shims were fitted between the sump and the transmission, refit them in their original locations when mating the engine to the transmission. If the engine has been overhauled, where applicable fit the relevant shims as calculated during engine reassembly.

5 As the engine is installed, guide the torque converter studs through the holes in the driveplate. When the engine is positioned flush with the engine adapter plate and the transmission housing, check that the torque converter is free to move axially a small amount before refitting and tightening the engine-to-transmission bolts.

6 Do not tighten the torque converter-to-driveplate nuts until the lower engine-to-transmission bolts have been fitted and tightened.

7 Ensure that the roadwheels and the steering wheel are in the straight-ahead position then align the marks made on removal and reconnect the intermediate shaft to the steering gearing. Tighten the clamp bolt to the specified torque.

8 Refit the exhaust downpipe.

9 Fill the engine with the correct grade and quantity of oil.

10 Check the throttle cable adjustment. Where necessary, also adjust the speed control cable in the same way so that there is only a small amount of slack present in the cable.

11 Reconnect the coolant hoses to the water pump housing.

12 Fill the cooling system.

13 Tighten all fixings to the specified torque, where applicable.

11 Engine/manual gearbox assembly - reconnection and refitting

1 Reverse the procedure described in Section 7, noting the following points.

2 Before attempting to reconnect the engine to the gearbox, check that the clutch friction disc is centralised.

3 Check that the clutch release arm and

bearing are correctly fitted, and lightly grease the input shaft splines.

4 Check that the engine adapter plate is correctly positioned on the locating dowels. If necessary, a cable-tie can be used to temporarily secure the adapter plate in position on the cylinder block using one of the engine-to-gearbox bolt holes.

5 If shims were fitted between the sump and the gearbox, refit them in their original locations when mating the engine to the gearbox. If the engine has been overhauled, where applicable fit the relevant shims as calculated during engine reassembly.

6 Ensure that the roadwheels and the steering wheel are in the straight-ahead position then align the marks made on removal and reconnect the intermediate shaft to the steering gearing. Tighten the clamp bolt to the specified torque.

7 Reconnect the clutch cable to the release arm, ensuring that it is routed as noted during removal.

8 Refit the propeller shaft.

9 Refit the exhaust system.

10 Fill the engine with the correct grade and quantity of oil.

11 Check the throttle cable adjustment. Where necessary, also adjust the speed control cable in the same way so that there is only a small amount of slack present in the cable.

12 Reconnect the coolant hoses to the water pump housing.

13 Fill the cooling system.

14 Check and if necessary top-up the gearbox oil level.

15 Tighten all fixings to the specified torque, where applicable.

12 Engine/automatic transmission assembly - reconnection and refitting

1 Reverse the procedure described in Section 8, noting the following points.

2 Check that the engine adapter plate is correctly positioned on the locating dowels. If necessary, a cable-tie can be used to temporarily secure the adapter plate in position on the cylinder block using one of the engine-to-transmission bolt holes.

3 As the torque converter is only loosely engaged in the transmission, care must be taken to prevent the torque converter from falling out forwards. When the torque converter hub is fully engaged with the fluid pump drivegear in the transmission, distance A **(see illustration 2.20 in Chapter 7B)** must be as specified. Incorrect installation of the torque converter will result in damage to the transmission.

4 If shims were fitted between the sump and the transmission, refit them in their original locations when mating the engine to the transmission. If the engine has been overhauled, where applicable fit the relevant shims as calculated during engine reassembly.

5 As the engine and transmission are mated

2B

together, guide the torque converter studs through the holes in the driveplate. When the engine is positioned flush with the engine adapter plate and the transmission housing, check that the torque converter is free to move axially a small amount before refitting and tightening the engine-to-transmission bolts.

6 Do not tighten the torque converter-to-driveplate nuts until the lower engine-to-transmission bolts have been fitted and tightened.

7 Ensure that the roadwheels and the steering wheel are in the straight-ahead position then align the marks made on removal and reconnect the intermediate shaft to the steering gearing. Tighten the clamp bolt to the specified torque.

8 Reconnect the selector rod and adjust as described in Chapter 7, Part B.

9 Refit the propeller shaft.

10 Refit the exhaust system.

11 Fill the engine with the correct grade and quantity of oil.

12 Check the throttle cable adjustment. Where necessary, also adjust the speed control cable in the same way so that there is only a small amount of slack present in the cable.

13 Reconnect the coolant hoses to the water pump housing.

14 Fill the cooling system.

15 Check and if necessary top-up the transmission fluid level.

16 Tighten all fixings to the specified torque, where applicable.

13 Engine mountings - renewal

Proceed as described in Part A, Section 23 of this Chapter but note that on certain models, it may be necessary to unbolt the engine mounting brackets from the cylinder block to allow sufficient clearance to remove the mountings.

14 Engine dismantling - general information

1 Refer to Part A, Section 8 of this Chapter, paragraphs 1 to 8 inclusive.

2 A selection of splined and Torx sockets will be required to remove many of the bolts when dismantling the engine.

3 Before dismantling the main engine components, the following externally mounted ancillary components can be removed.

a) Inlet manifold (and carburettor, where applicable).
b) Exhaust manifold.
c) Alternator.
d) Water pump, and thermostat.
e) Water pump/alternator drivebelt tensioner.
f) Distributor cap, HT leads and spark plugs.
g) Oil pressure warning lamp switch.
h) Crankshaft speed/position sensor.
i) Oil filter.
j) Dipstick.
k) Engine mounting brackets (if not already done).
l) Crankcase ventilation pipe and hoses.

m) Clutch.
n) Alternator mounting bracket.
o) Air conditioning compressor mounting bracket (where applicable).
p) Engine lifting brackets.

15 Timing chain and sprockets - removal and refitting

Note: A puller will be required to remove the crankshaft pulley. A new crankshaft pulley bolt, a new timing chain tensioner plunger assembly, new upper and lower timing chain cover gaskets and a new camshaft cover gasket and reinforcing sleeve sealing rings must be used on refitting.

1 If the engine is in the car, carry out the following operations.

a) Disconnect the battery negative lead.
b) To improve access, remove the radiator. It will be difficult to remove the crankshaft pulley with the radiator in place.
c) On carburettor models, remove the air cleaner.
d) On fuel-injection models, remove the air inlet hose, plenum chamber and air cleaner lid as an assembly.
e) Disconnect the breather hose from the camshaft cover.
f) Remove the distributor cap and HT leads, and the rotor arm and housing.

2 Proceed as described in paragraphs 2 to 11 inclusive of Section 18 **(see illustration).**

3 Remove the water pump/alternator drivebelt.

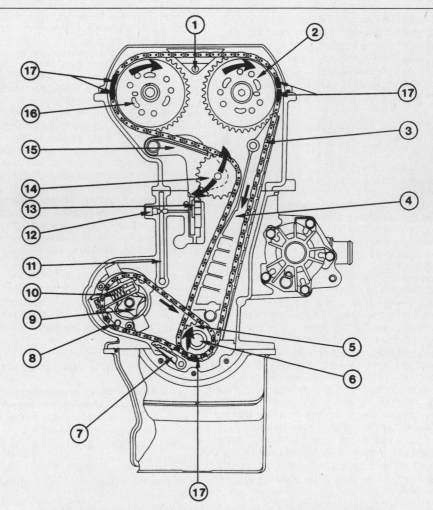

15.2 Timing chain, oil pump drive chain and associated components

1 Upper timing chain guide	10 Oil pressure relief valve
2 Exhaust camshaft sprocket	11 Oil passage to timing chain tensioner plunger
3 Timing chain	12 Plug
4 Lower timing chain guide	13 Timing chain tensioner plunger
5 Crankshaft sprocket (double)	14 Timing chain tensioner sprocket
6 Crankshaft	15 Timing chain tensioner arm
7 Oil pump chain tensioner	16 Inlet camshaft sprocket
8 Oil pump drive chain	17 Copper chain links
9 Oil pump	

15.5a Using a puller to remove the crankshaft pulley (viewed from underneath vehicle)

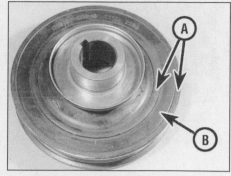

15.5b Position the legs of the puller on the metal surfaces of the pulley (A), not the rubber surface (B)

15.9 Oil pump chain tensioner securing screw (arrowed)

4 Slacken the crankshaft pulley bolt. Prevent the crankshaft from turning by engaging top gear (manual gearbox only) and having an assistant press the brake pedal hard, or by removing the starter motor and jamming the ring gear teeth with a lever.

5 Unscrew the bolt part way, and use a suitable legged-puller to draw the crankshaft pulley off the crankshaft. The legs of the puller must be suitably shaped to enable them to rest on the metal surfaces of the pulley. *Note: Do not attempt to remove the pulley with a puller whose legs contact the rubber surface of the pulley* **(see illustrations)**. Note that a new crankshaft pulley retaining bolt will be required for refitting.

6 Loosen the alternator lower mounting

through-bolt, then remove the alternator upper mounting bolt, and swing the alternator away from the engine.

7 Unscrew the central securing bolt, and withdraw the drivebelt tensioner assembly.

8 Unscrew the eleven securing bolts, and remove the lower timing chain cover. Remove the rubber gasket and discard it; a new one must be used on refitting.

9 Using a suitable Torx socket, unscrew the securing screw, and carefully withdraw the oil pump chain tensioner **(see illustration)**.

10 Unscrew the Torx type securing bolt, and withdraw the oil pump sprocket, complete with the oil pump drive chain.

11 Unscrew the two Torx bolts securing the lower timing chain guide, noting their

locations, and withdraw the timing chain guide through the top of the timing case **(see illustrations)**.

12 Remove the Woodruff key from the end of the crankshaft, prising it free with a screwdriver if necessary, then slide the double chain sprocket from the end of the crankshaft, and lift the chain from the sprocket **(see illustration)**.

13 Withdraw the timing chain through the top of the timing case and, where applicable, remove the cable-tie from the chain **(see illustration)**.

14 The timing chain, sprockets and tensioner can now be examined for wear and damage.

15 Commence refitting as follows. Note that coppered links are provided in the timing chain to assist with refitting, but these can be difficult to see on a chain which has already been in service. If possible, position the coppered links as described during the following procedure. If the coppered links are not visible, the chain should still be refitted as described, but ignore the references to the coppered links.

16 Make sure that the slot for the Woodruff key in the end of the crankshaft is pointing vertically downwards. If necessary, temporarily refit the crankshaft pulley bolt in order to turn the crankshaft to the required position.

17 Lower the timing chain into the timing case from above, with the single coppered link at the bottom. If desired, use a cable-tie to

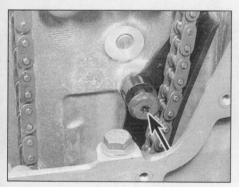

15.11a Lower timing chain guide upper securing bolt (arrowed)

15.11b Lower timing chain guide lower securing bolt (arrowed)

2B

15.11c Withdrawing the lower timing chain guide

15.12 Sliding the double chain sprocket from the end of the crankshaft

15.13 Withdrawing the timing chain through the top of the timing case

15.19 Coppered link in timing chain aligned with crankshaft sprocket timing mark (arrowed)

15.31 Fitting a new lower timing chain cover oil seal

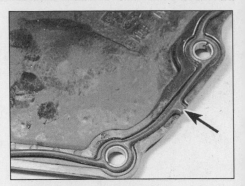

15.32 Lower timing chain cover gasket in position. Ensure that lug on gasket engages with notch in cover (arrowed)

prevent the chain from dropping into the timing case, as during removal.

18 Locate the double chain sprocket loosely over the end of the crankshaft (larger sprocket nearest the crankcase), with the timing mark pointing vertically down.

19 Fit the chain over the inner, larger sprocket, aligning the coppered link in the chain with the timing mark on the sprocket **(see illustration)**.

20 Coat the threads of the lower timing chain guide lower securing bolt with a suitable thread-locking compound.

21 Introduce the lower timing chain guide through the top of the timing case, manipulating the chain around the guide as necessary, then fit the chain guide lower securing bolt and tighten it finger-tight.

22 Push the double chain sprocket onto the crankshaft, engaging the notch in the sprocket with the groove in the end of the crankshaft.

23 Proceed as described in paragraphs 34 to 42 of Section 18, but when fitting the chain over the camshaft sprockets, align the timing mark on each sprocket between the two corresponding coppered links in the chain.

24 Coat the threads of the lower timing chain guide upper securing bolt with a suitable thread-locking compound, then fit the bolt and tighten it finger-tight.

25 Proceed as described in paragraphs 43 to 46 of Section 18.

26 Tighten the two chain guide securing bolts to the specified torque.

27 Proceed as described in paragraphs 47 to 55 of Section 18.

28 Fit the oil pump drive chain around the outer crankshaft sprocket and the oil pump sprocket, then refit the oil pump sprocket, and tighten the securing bolt to the specified torque. If necessary, a screwdriver can be inserted through one of the holes in the sprocket to prevent it from turning as the securing bolt is tightened.

29 Refit the oil pump drive chain tensioner, and tighten the securing bolt to the specified torque.

30 Refit the Woodruff key to the end of the crankshaft.

31 Inspect the oil seal in the lower timing chain cover. If the oil seal is in good condition,

the cover can be refitted as follows, but if the seal is damaged, or has been leaking, a new seal should be fitted to the cover. If necessary, carefully prise the old oil seal from the cover using a screwdriver, and drive in the new seal using a suitable metal tube. Make sure that the seal lip faces into the engine. Note that the oil seal should be fitted dry. Take care not to damage the timing chain cover **(see illustration)**.

32 Fit the lower timing chain cover using a new rubber gasket **(see illustration)**.

33 Loosely refit the timing chain cover securing bolts.

34 Refit the crankshaft pulley to the end of the crankshaft, and draw the pulley onto the crankshaft using the original securing bolt, at the same time centering the lower timing chain cover.

35 With the lower timing chain cover centralised, and the pulley fully home on the crankshaft, remove the old securing bolt, then fit a new bolt.

36 Tighten the new crankshaft pulley bolt to the specified torque, in the two stages given in the Specifications at the beginning of this Chapter. Prevent the crankshaft from turning as during removal.

37 Tighten the lower timing chain cover securing bolts to the specified torque.

38 Refit the drivebelt tensioner assembly, ensuring that the lug on the rear of the tensioner bracket engages with the corresponding hole in the cylinder block, and tighten the securing bolt.

17.5 Disconnecting the heater coolant hose from the inlet manifold

39 Swing the alternator into position to align the upper mounting bolt hole with the corresponding hole in the drivebelt tensioner assembly, then refit the upper mounting bolt, and tighten the upper bolt and the lower through-bolt.

40 Refit the water pump/alternator drivebelt.

41 If the engine is in the vehicle, reverse the operations described in paragraph 1 of Section 15.

42 Where applicable, refill the cooling system.

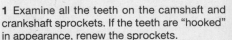

16 Timing chain, sprockets and tensioner - examination and renovation

1 Examine all the teeth on the camshaft and crankshaft sprockets. If the teeth are "hooked" in appearance, renew the sprockets.

2 Examine the chain tensioner plastic sprocket for wear. If excessive wear is evident, the complete tensioner assembly must be renewed as the sprocket cannot be renewed independently. Note that the tensioner plunger assembly must be renewed whenever the timing chain is removed.

3 Examine the timing chain for wear. If the chain has been in operation for a considerable time, or if when held horizontally (rollers vertical) it takes on a deeply bowed appearance, renew it.

17 Cylinder head - removal and refitting (engine in vehicle)

Note: *The cylinder head must not be removed when the engine is warm. Refer to the note at the beginning of the following Section before proceeding.*

1 Disconnect the battery negative lead.

2 On carburettor models, remove the air cleaner.

3 On fuel-injection models, remove the air inlet hose, plenum chamber, and air cleaner lid as an assembly.

4 Drain the cooling system.

5 Disconnect the heater coolant hose from the inlet manifold **(see illustration)**.

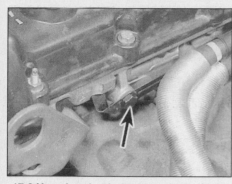

17.6 Hose bracket bolted to cylinder head (arrowed)

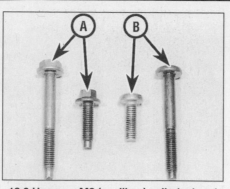

18.0 Use new M8 (auxiliary) cylinder head bolts with hexagonal heads (A), not the earlier Torx type bolts (B)

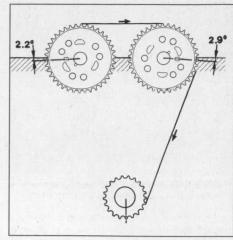

18.4 Timing mark positions with No 1 cylinder at TDC

6 Disconnect the breather hose from the camshaft cover, and unbolt the hose bracket from the left-hand side of the cylinder head **(see illustration)**.

7 Unscrew the securing bolt and disconnect the earth lead from the left-hand rear of the cylinder head.

8 Remove the distributor cap and HT leads, and the rotor arm and housing, as applicable. If necessary, mark the HT leads to aid refitting.

9 The cylinder head can be removed either with or without the manifolds and fuel rail, where applicable (it is easiest to remove the head complete with the manifolds and fuel rail). If desired, the inlet manifold and the fuel rail can be unbolted and moved to one side, leaving the wires, hoses, pipes and cables connected, but care must be taken not to place any strain on them.

10 Unscrew the three securing nuts and disconnect the exhaust downpipe from the manifold. It may be necessary to jack up the front of the vehicle to gain access to the nuts (in which case apply the handbrake and support the front of the vehicle securely on axle stands) (see "Jacking"). Discard the gasket.

11 If the inlet manifold and the fuel rail (where applicable) are to be removed with the cylinder head, disconnect all relevant wires, hoses, pipes and cables, otherwise, unbolt the manifold and the fuel rail, and move them to one side, ensuring that they are adequately supported. If the fuel rail is unbolted, be prepared for fuel spillage, and take adequate fire precautions.

12 Refer to the procedure described in paragraphs 2 to 19 of Section 18 to complete cylinder head removal.

13 Commence refitting by referring to paragraphs 20 to 55 of Section 18, then reverse the procedure described in paragraphs 1 to 11 of this Section, noting the following points.

a) Use a new gasket when reconnecting the exhaust downpipe to the manifold.
b) Ensure that the HT leads are reconnected correctly.
c) Fill the cooling system.

18 Cylinder head - removal and refitting (engine removed)

Note: *New cylinder head bolts, a new cylinder head gasket, a new timing chain tensioner plunger assembly, a new upper timing chain cover gasket, and a new camshaft cover gasket and reinforcing sleeve sealing rings must be used on refitting. It is essential that the three smaller M8 bolts are of the latest type with hexagonal heads, not the earlier Torx type (see illustration).*

1 With the manifolds removed, proceed as follows.

2 Unscrew the eleven bolts and four nuts, and remove the camshaft cover. Recover the gasket.

3 Unscrew the four securing bolts and three studs, and remove the upper timing chain cover. Note the locations of the studs to aid refitting.

4 Using a spanner on the crankshaft pulley, turn the crankshaft to bring No 1 piston to the firing point (TDC). With No 1 piston at the firing point, the timing marks on the camshaft sprockets should be pointing away from each other, and should be approximately level with the top edge of the cylinder head. Timing notches are provided in the camshaft sprockets, and corresponding paint marks are provided on the outside edges of the sprockets **(see illustration)**.

5 Hold the inlet camshaft sprocket stationary using a peg spanner which engages with the

spokes of the camshaft sprocket. Unscrew the camshaft sprocket bolt, and remove the distributor rotor shaft **(see illustration)**.

> **HAYNES HiNT** *If a peg spanner is not available, a tool can be made from two lengths of steel strip (one long, the other short) and three nuts and bolts; one nut and bolt forming the pivot of a forked tool with the remaining two nuts and bolts at the tips of the "forks" to engage with the sprocket spokes.*

6 Repeat the procedure given in paragraph 5 for the exhaust camshaft, but note that a spacer is fitted in place of the distributor rotor shaft.

7 Squeeze the upper timing chain guide securing lugs together, using pliers if necessary, and withdraw the guide from the plate at the front of the cylinder head **(see illustration)**.

8 Mark the position of the timing chain in relation to the camshaft sprockets, so that the chain can be refitted in precisely its original position (ie, make alignment marks between each sprocket and a corresponding link in the chain), then slide the camshaft sprockets from the camshafts. Withdraw the sprockets and lay the timing chain over the exhaust side of the timing case, having eliminated the slack in

18.5 Removing the inlet camshaft sprocket bolt and the distributor rotor shaft

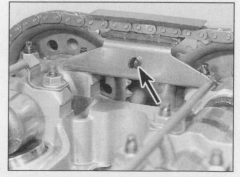

18.7 Upper timing chain guide securing lugs (arrowed)

2B

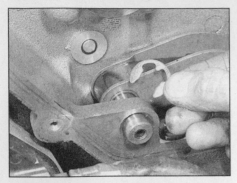

18.9 Removing the chain tensioner arm pivot pin circlip

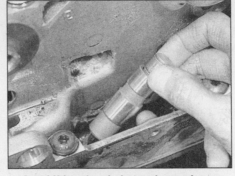

18.11 Lifting the chain tensioner plunger assembly from the cylinder head

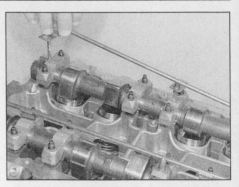

18.13 Lifting off a camshaft oil spray bar

the chain. Secure the chain using a cable-tie through two of the chain links to prevent it from dropping off the crankshaft sprocket.

9 Using a suitable pair of pliers, extract the circlip from the chain tensioner arm pivot pin, taking care not to drop it into the timing case, then withdraw the pivot pin from the tensioner arm. If the pivot pin proves difficult to withdraw, an M6 bolt can be screwed into the end to facilitate removal **(see illustration)**.

10 Lift the tensioner arm from the timing case.

11 Lift the tensioner plunger assembly from the cylinder head, and discard it **(see illustration)**.

 Warning: Take care when removing the plunger assembly; injury could result if the piston flies out. A new timing chain tensioner plunger assembly should be installed on refitting.

12 Take note of the markings on the camshaft bearing caps, then progressively unscrew the bearing cap securing nuts.

13 Remove the bearing cap securing nuts, then lift off the camshaft oil spray bars, and the timing chain guide plate **(see illustration)**.

14 Lift off the bearing caps, and then lift out the two camshafts **(see illustrations)**.

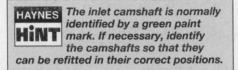 *The inlet camshaft is normally identified by a green paint mark. If necessary, identify the camshafts so that they can be refitted in their correct positions.*

15 Withdraw the cam followers from their locations in the cylinder head, keeping them in order so that they can be refitted in their

original locations **(see illustration)**. It is advisable to store the cam followers upright in an oil bath until they are to be refitted. Ensure that the depth of oil is sufficient to fully cover the cam followers.

16 Working at the front of the cylinder head, unscrew the three small M8 cylinder head bolts which are accessible through the timing case **(see illustration)**.

17 Working in the reverse order to that shown for tightening the cylinder head bolts **(see illustration)**, progressively loosen the remaining cylinder head bolts, and withdraw them from the cylinder head.

18 Lift the cylinder head from the block. If the cylinder head is stuck, tap it free with a soft-faced mallet. Do not insert a lever into the joint between the cylinder head and block, as this may result in damage to the mating faces. Place the cylinder head on blocks of wood to prevent damage to the valves.

19 Recover the gasket, and the locating dowels if they are loose, noting the positions of the locating dowels.

20 Commence refitting as follows.

21 Turn the crankshaft so that No 1 piston is approximately 20.0 mm (0.8 in) before TDC. This precaution will prevent possible contact between the valves and pistons.

22 Make sure that the mating faces of the cylinder block and cylinder head are perfectly clean, then refit the locating dowels (where applicable) and locate a new gasket over the

18.14a Lifting off a camshaft bearing cap

18.14b Lifting out the exhaust camshaft

18.15 Withdrawing a cam follower

18.16 M8 cylinder head bolts (arrowed) located at front of cylinder head

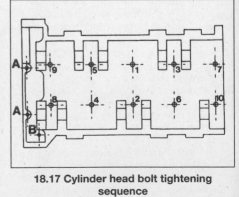

18.17 Cylinder head bolt tightening sequence

A Long M8 bolts   *B Short M8 bolt*

18.22 Fitting a new cylinder head gasket

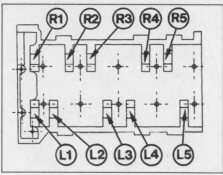

18.30a Camshaft bearing cap tightening sequence

18.30b Camshaft oil spray bars correctly fitted

dowels. Note that the gasket can only fit in one position **(see illustration)**. Do not use jointing compound.

23 Lower the cylinder head onto the gasket, making sure that the locating dowels engage.

24 Oil the threads of the new main cylinder head bolts, and insert them into their locations in the cylinder head.

25 Tighten the bolts in the order shown **(see illustration)** and in the four stages given in the Specifications.

26 Insert the three smaller M8 cylinder head bolts through the top of the timing case **(see illustration)** and tighten them to the specified torque. Note that new bolts must be used, and that they should be of the latest type with hexagonal heads.

27 Lubricate the cam follower bores in the cylinder head, and the cam followers themselves, then insert the cam followers into their original locations in the cylinder head.

28 Lubricate the camshaft bearing surfaces in the cylinder head and the bearing caps.

29 Lubricate the surfaces of the camshafts, then carefully lay the camshafts in their original positions in the cylinder head. Position the camshafts with the slots in their front ends pointing away from each other.

30 Fit the bearing caps L1, L3, L5, R1, R3, and R5 **(see illustration)**, then lay the camshaft oil spray bars and the timing chain guide plate in position over the studs **(see illustrations)**.

31 Carefully tighten the bearing cap securing nuts by hand in the following stages to lower the camshafts into position.

Tighten the nuts for bearing caps L1 and R1 by half-a-turn (180°)

Tighten the nuts for bearing caps L5 and R5 by half-a-turn (180°)

Tighten the nuts for bearing caps L3 and R3 by half-a-turn (180°)

Continue to tighten the nuts in the small stages given until the bearing caps contact the cylinder head.

32 Fit bearing caps L2, L4, R2 and R4, and tap them into position on the cylinder head using light taps from a soft-faced mallet. Tighten the securing nuts evenly by hand.

33 Tighten all the bearing cap nuts to the specified torque in half turn stages, using the following sequence.

L1 and R1
L5 and R5
L3 and R3
L2 and L4
R2 and R4

34 Fit a **new** chain tensioner plunger assembly to the housing in the cylinder head with the piston uppermost. Before fitting the new plunger assembly, take note of the position of the piston **(see illustration)**. The assembly is normally supplied with the piston protruding slightly from the cylinder, or slightly

below the top surface of the cylinder (A). If the new assembly is supplied with the piston partially unlatched (B), or fully unlatched with the latching ring visible (C), it must not be used.

> ⚠ **Warning: Take care when installing the plunger assembly, as there is a risk of injury if the piston flies out.**

35 Locate the chain tensioner arm in position, then insert the pivot pin, and secure it with the circlip. Take care not to drop the circlip into the timing case.

36 Release the cable-tie securing the timing chain, and lay the chain over the exhaust camshaft sprocket, aligning the marks made previously on the chain and sprocket, so that the timing chain is taught on the exhaust side of the engine.

37 Fit the sprocket to the exhaust camshaft, with the camshaft in the TDC position (ie with the exhaust camshaft sprocket timing mark in line with the top edge of the cylinder head, pointing to the exhaust side of the engine, see paragraph 4). If necessary, use a pair of pliers on one of the unmachined sections of the camshaft to turn the camshaft to the TDC position. Take care not to damage the machined surfaces of the camshaft.

38 With the sprocket fitted, fit the spacer to the end of the camshaft, and tighten the securing bolt finger-tight **(see illustration)**.

39 Lay the timing chain over the inlet

18.30c Fitting the timing chain guide plate

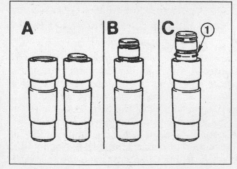

18.34 Timing chain tensioner plunger assembly

A *Piston retracted - plunger assembly useable*
B *Piston partially unlatched - discard plunger assembly*
C *Latching ring (1) visible - discard plunger assembly*

18.38 Spacer and sprocket securing bolt fitted to end of camshaft, with camshaft in TDC position (timing marks arrowed)

2B

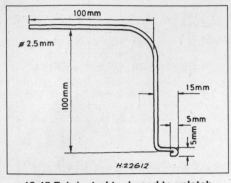

18.45 Fabricated tool used to unlatch tensioner plunger piston

18.53 Upper timing chain cover securing stud locations (arrowed)

18.54 Fitting a camshaft cover reinforcing sleeve and sealing ring

camshaft sprocket, aligning the marks made previously on the chain and the sprocket.

40 Fit the sprocket to the inlet camshaft, with the camshaft in the TDC position (ie with the inlet camshaft sprocket timing mark in line with the top edge of the cylinder head, pointing to the inlet side of the engine see paragraph 4). Again, turn the camshaft if necessary to enable the sprocket to be fitted.

41 With the sprocket fitted, fit the distributor rotor shaft to the end of the camshaft, and tighten the securing bolt finger-tight. Note that it is acceptable for the timing chain to sag slightly between the two pulleys.

42 Fit a new upper timing chain guide to the plate at the front of the cylinder head.

43 Turn the crankshaft clockwise until the inlet camshaft begins to turn.

44 If the chain tensioner plunger piston protrudes from the cylinder, unlatch the piston by pressing the chain tensioner arm down by hand.

45 If the plunger piston is below the top surface of the cylinder, a tool must be fabricated to unlatch the piston **(see illustration)**. It is suggested that 2.5 mm diameter welding rod is used to manufacture the tool. Use the tool to release the piston as follows.

46 Carefully lift the chain tensioner arm with a screwdriver, and insert the tool between the tensioner arm and the piston. Remove the screwdriver, and release the piston by pressing the tensioner arm down by hand. Carefully withdraw the tool once the piston has been released.

47 Tighten the camshaft sprocket securing bolts to the specified torque, holding the sprockets stationary as during removal.

48 Turn the crankshaft clockwise through two complete revolutions, and check that the timing marks on the camshaft sprockets are still aligned with the top face of the cylinder head as described in paragraph 4.

49 Turn the crankshaft clockwise through another complete revolution, and check that the timing marks on the camshaft sprockets are facing each other, directly in line with the top face of the cylinder head.

50 If the timing marks do not align as described, the timing chain has been incorrectly fitted (probably one chain link away

from the correct position on one of the camshaft sprockets), and the chain should be removed from the sprockets and fitted in the correct position.

51 Inspect the oil seal in the upper timing chain cover. If the oil seal is in good condition, the cover can be refitted as follows, but if the seal is damaged, or has been leaking, a new seal should be fitted to the cover. If necessary, carefully prise the old oil seal from the cover using a screwdriver, and drive in the new seal using a suitable metal tube. Make sure that the seal lip faces into the engine. Take care not to damage the timing chain cover.

52 Fit the upper timing chain cover using a new rubber gasket. Great care must be taken to avoid damage to the oil seal when passing the seal over the end of the inlet camshaft. Careful manipulation will be required (possibly using a thin feeler blade) to avoid damage to the oil seal sealing lip. Note that the oil seal should be fitted dry.

53 Refit the timing chain cover securing bolts and studs in their original locations and tighten them to the specified torque **(see illustration)**.

54 Remove the reinforcing sleeves from the camshaft cover, and renew the rubber sealing rings. Note that the four short reinforcing sleeves fit at the front of the cover **(see illustration)**.

55 Refit the camshaft cover using a new gasket, and tighten the securing bolts and studs to the specified torque.

19 Cylinder head - dismantling and reassembly

Note: *A valve spring compressor will be required during this procedure. New valve stem oil seals should be used on reassembly.*

Dismantle the cylinder head as described in paragraphs 2 to 4, Section 12, Part A of this Chapter and reassemble the head as described in paragraphs 4 to 6, Section 42, Part A of this Chapter, noting the following points:

a) *Ignore the references to the special tool.*
b) *Double valve springs are used on all the valves (see illustration).*
c) *Refer to the following Section if the cylinder head is to be inspected and renovated.*

20 Cylinder head - inspection and renovation

Refer to Part A, Section 34 of this Chapter, noting the following points.

a) *Valve and valve seat cutting and regrinding can be carried out using conventional tools.*
b) *The cylinder head cannot be resurfaced, and if the surface distortion exceeds the specified limits, the cylinder head must be renewed.*

21 Camshafts and cam followers - removal, inspection and refitting

Note: *Once the timing chain has been removed from the camshaft sprockets, do not turn the crankshaft until the timing chain has been correctly refitted - this is to prevent contact between the valves and pistons. A new timing chain tensioner plunger assembly, a new upper timing chain cover gasket, and a new camshaft cover and reinforcing sleeve sealing rings must be used on refitting.*

1 If the engine is in the vehicle, carry out the following operations.

a) *Disconnect the battery negative lead.*
b) *On carburettor models, remove the air cleaner.*
c) *On fuel-injection models, remove the air inlet hose, plenum chamber, and air cleaner lid as an assembly.*

19.1 Withdrawing the double valve springs from the cylinder head

d) *Disconnect the breather hose from the camshaft cover.*
e) *Remove the distributor cap and HT leads, and the rotor arm and housing. If necessary, mark the HT leads to aid refitting.*

2 Proceed as described in paragraphs 2 to 15 inclusive of Section 18.
3 Examine the surfaces of the camshaft journals and lobes and the contact surfaces of the cam followers for wear. If wear is excessive, considerable noise will have been noticed from the top of the engine when running, and new camshafts and followers must be fitted. It is unlikely that this level of wear will occur unless a considerable mileage has been covered. Note that the cam followers cannot be dismantled for renewal of individual components.
4 Check the camshaft bearing surfaces in the cylinder head and the bearing caps for wear. If excessive wear is evident, the only course of action available is to renew the cylinder head complete with bearing caps.
5 Check the cam follower bores in the cylinder head for wear. If excessive wear is evident, the cylinder head must be renewed.
6 Check the cam follower oil grooves and the oil ports in the cylinder head for obstructions.
7 Refit the cam followers and the camshafts as described in paragraphs 27 to 55 of Section 18.
8 If the engine is in the vehicle, reverse the operations given in paragraph 1.

22 Flywheel/driveplate - removal inspection and refitting

Refer to Part A, Section 15 of this Chapter, noting the following points.
a) *If the engine is in the car, refer to Chapter 6 when removing and refitting the clutch, where applicable.*
b) *The flywheel/driveplate securing bolts must be renewed on refitting; the new bolts are supplied ready-coated with thread-locking compound (see illustration).*
c) *Check on the availability of new parts before contemplating renewal of the ring gear.*

22.1 Improvised tool used to hold flywheel when tightening securing bolts

23 Crankshaft front oil seal - renewal

Note: *A suitable puller will be required to remove the crankshaft pulley. A new crankshaft pulley bolt and a new lower timing chain cover gasket must be used on refitting.*

1 The crankshaft front oil seal is located in the lower timing chain cover.
2 If the engine is in the car, carry out the following operations.
a) *Disconnect the battery negative lead.*
b) *To improve access, remove the radiator. It will be difficult to remove the crankshaft pulley with the radiator in place.*
c) *On fuel-injection models, remove the air inlet hose, plenum chamber, and air cleaner lid as an assembly.*

3 Proceed as described in paragraphs 3 to 8 of Section 15.
4 With the lower timing chain cover removed, prise the old oil seal from the cover using a screwdriver, and drive in the new seal using a suitable metal tube. Make sure that the seal lip faces into the engine. Take care not to damage the timing chain cover. Note that the seal should be fitted dry.
5 Refit the lower timing chain cover as described in paragraphs 32 to 40 of Section 15.
6 If the engine is in the vehicle, reverse the operations given in paragraph 2.

24 Crankshaft rear oil seal - renewal

Note: *New flywheel/driveplate bolts must be used on refitting.*

1 Remove the flywheel/driveplate and the engine adapter plate.
2 Extract the seal using an oil seal removal tool if available. It may also be possible to remove the oil seal by drilling the outer face and using self-tapping screws and a pair of grips.
3 Clean the oil seal housing, then carefully wind a thin layer of tape around the edge of the crankshaft to protect the oil seal lip as the seal is installed.
4 Install a new oil seal. Make sure that the seal lip faces into the engine **(see illustration)**.

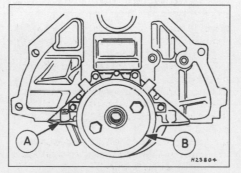

24.4 Tool used to fit the oil seal
A *Rear oil seal housing*
B *Special tool*

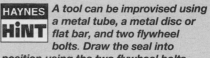

HAYNES HiNT *A tool can be improvised using a metal tube, a metal disc or flat bar, and two flywheel bolts. Draw the seal into position using the two flywheel bolts.*

5 With the oil seal installed, carefully pull the tape from the edge of the crankshaft.
6 Refit the engine adapter plate and the flywheel/driveplate.

25 Sump - removal and refitting

Note: *A new sump gasket will be required on refitting, and suitable sealing compound will be required to coat the sump and cylinder block mating faces. Shims may be required when mating the gearbox/transmission.*

1 Sump removal and refitting is far easier if the engine is removed from the vehicle, however if the engine is in the vehicle, proceed as follows. If the engine has been removed from the vehicle, proceed to paragraph 9.
2 Remove the clutch or automatic transmission, as applicable.
3 Remove the flywheel/driveplate and the engine adapter plate.
4 Drain the engine oil into a suitable container.
5 Ensure that the steering wheel is positioned in the straight-ahead position then, using a dab of paint or a marker pen, make alignment marks between the intermediate shaft lower clamp and steering gear pinion. Slacken and remove the lower clamp bolt then disconnect the intermediate shaft from the steering gear.
6 Attach a suitable hoist to the engine lifting brackets located at the front and rear of the cylinder head, and carefully take the weight of the engine.
7 Detach the brake lines from the front suspension crossmember.
8 Support the crossmember with a jack, then loosen the bolts securing the crossmember to the underbody. Remove the bolts and carefully lower the crossmember sufficiently to allow the sump to be removed.
9 If the engine has been removed, it is preferable to keep it upright until the sump has been removed to prevent sludge from entering the engine internals.
10 Unscrew the sump securing nuts and bolts, and withdraw the sump from the engine. Do not prise between the mating faces of the sump and cylinder block. Discard the old gasket.

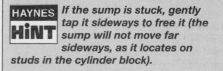

HAYNES HiNT *If the sump is stuck, gently tap it sideways to free it (the sump will not move far sideways, as it locates on studs in the cylinder block).*

11 Thoroughly clean the mating faces of the cylinder block and sump.
12 Commence refitting by locating a new gasket in the grooves in the sump.

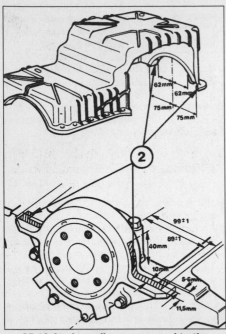

25.13 Apply sealing compound to the sump/cylinder block mating faces at the points indicated (2)
Dimensions are for guidance only

13 Apply a sealing compound to the faces of the cylinder block and sump at the points indicated **(see illustration)**.
14 Apply suitable thread-locking compound to the sump securing studs and bolts, then locate the sump on the cylinder block and fit the securing nuts and bolts, but do not fully tighten them at this stage.
15 Align the sump so that the end faces and the cylinder block are flush. To do this, use a straight-edge. If the sump cannot be positioned so that the faces of the cylinder block and sump are flush, measure the difference in height using a feeler blade as shown **(see illustration)**.
16 Tighten the sump securing nuts and bolts to the specified torque, then repeat the measurement made in paragraph 15. If the end faces of the sump and cylinder block are not flush, suitable shims must be fitted (available from a Ford dealer) between the sump and the gearbox/transmission to eliminate the clearance when mating the engine to the gearbox/transmission. Note that shims should be fitted at both sides of the sump, as required. Select suitable shims from those listed in the following table.

Clearance measured	Shims required
0 to 0.25 mm	No shims required
0.25 to 0.29 mm	0.15 mm (silver)
0.30 to 0.44 mm	0.30 mm (light blue)
0.45 to 0.59 mm	0.45 mm (red)
0.60 to 0.75 mm	0.60 mm (black)

17 If the engine is in the vehicle, reverse the procedure described in paragraphs 3 to 8, noting the following points.
a) *Ensure that the roadwheels and the steering wheel are in the straight-ahead*

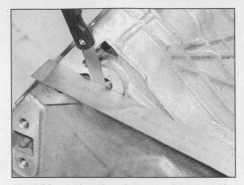

25.15 Measuring the clearance between the cylinder block and sump end faces

position then align the marks made on removal and reconnect the intermediate shaft to the steering gear. Tighten the clamp bolt to the specified torque.
b) *Fill the engine with the correct grade and quantity of oil.*
c) *Refit the engine adapter plate and the flywheel/driveplate.*
d) *Refit the gearbox or automatic transmission, as applicable, ensuring that the required shims are fitted between the sump and the gearbox/transmission.*
e) *Tighten all fixings to the specified torque where applicable.*

26 Oil pump - removal and refitting

Note: *A suitable puller will be required to remove the crankshaft pulley. A new crankshaft pulley bolt, a new lower timing chain cover gasket and a new oil pump gasket must be used on refitting.*

1 If the engine is in the car, carry out the following operations.
a) *Disconnect the battery negative lead.*
b) *To Improve access, remove the radiator. It will be difficult to remove the crankshaft pulley with the radiator in place.*
c) *On fuel-injection models, remove the air inlet hose, plenum chamber and air cleaner lid as an assembly.*

2 Proceed as described in paragraphs 3 to 10 of Section 15.

27.3 Removing the oil pump cover

26.3 Oil pump securing bolts (arrowed)

3 Unscrew the four securing bolts and withdraw the oil pump from the cylinder block **(see illustration)**. Recover the gasket and discard it.
4 If desired, the pump can now be dismantled and inspected.
5 Thoroughly clean the mating faces of the pump and the cylinder block.
6 Prime the pump by injecting clean engine oil into it and turning it by hand.
7 Place a new gasket on the oil pump flange, ensuring that the gasket is correctly located so that the holes align with the oil passages in the pump.
8 Fit the oil pump, and tighten the securing bolts to the specified torque.
9 Proceed as described in paragraphs 28 to 40 of Section 15.
10 If the engine is in the vehicle, reverse the operations described in paragraph 1.

27 Oil pump - dismantling, inspection and reassembly

1 The oil pump can be dismantled for cleaning, but if any of the components are worn, the pump must be renewed as an assembly.
2 To dismantle the pump, proceed as follows.
3 Unscrew the two securing bolts, and remove the pump cover **(see illustration)**.
4 Lift the inner and outer rotors from the pump casing.
5 Unscrew the pressure relief valve plug from

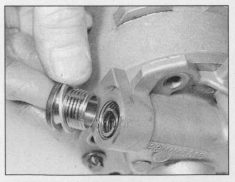

27.5a Unscrew the pressure relief valve plug and washer . . .

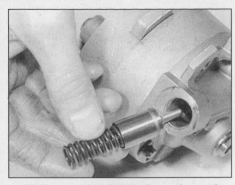

27.5b . . . and withdraw the spring and plunger

27.9 The punch marks (arrowed) on the oil pump rotors must face the pump cover

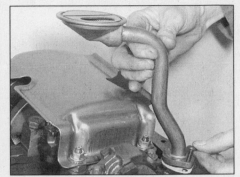

29.2 Removing the oil pick-up pipe

the pump cover, recover the washer, and withdraw the spring and plunger **(see illustrations)**.

6 Thoroughly clean all components in petrol or paraffin, and wipe dry using a non-fluffy rag.

7 Examine the rotors and the pump casing for signs of excessive wear on the machined surfaces. If wear is evident, the complete pump assembly must be renewed, as spare parts are not available individually.

8 Commence reassembly by lubricating the relief valve plunger. Fit the plunger and the spring, and screw the plug into place, ensuring that the washer is in place under the plug.

9 Lubricate the rotors, and fit them to the pump casing with the punch marks facing the pump cover **(see illustration)**.

10 Refit the pump cover and tighten the securing bolts.

11 Prime the pump before refitting.

28 Oil pump drive chain and sprockets - examination and renovation

1 Examine all the teeth on the sprockets. If the teeth are "hooked" in appearance, renew the sprockets.

2 Examine the chain tensioner for wear and renew it if necessary.

3 Examine the chain for wear. If it has been in operation for a considerable time, or if when held horizontally (rollers vertical) it takes on a deeply bowed appearance, renew it.

29 Pistons and connecting rods - removal and refitting

Note: *New connecting rod bolts and a new oil pick-up pipe gasket must be used on refitting.*

1 Remove the sump and the cylinder head.

2 Unscrew the two securing bolts, and remove the oil pick-up pipe **(see illustration)**. Recover the gasket and discard it.

3 Unscrew the four securing nuts and withdraw the oil baffle from the studs on the main bearing caps **(see illustration)**.

4 Removal is as described in Part A, Section 21, paragraphs 2 to 5 of this Chapter, and refitting as described in Part A, Section 37, noting the following additional points:

a) Take note of the orientation of the bearing shells during dismantling, and ensure that they are fitted correctly during reassembly.

b) When fitting the pistons, ensure that the arrow on the piston crown and the letter F on the face of the connecting rod are pointing towards the front of the engine.

c) Use new connecting rod bolts on reassembly; before fitting, oil the threads and the contact faces of the bolts. Tighten the bolts to the three stages given in the Specifications.

d) Refit the oil baffle and tighten the securing nuts.

e) Clean the mating faces of the cylinder block and the oil pick-up pipe, and refit the pick-up pipe using a new gasket.

f) Refit the cylinder head and the sump.

30 Crankshaft and main bearings - removal and refitting

Note: *A new crankshaft rear oil seal and a new rear oil seal housing gasket should be used on reassembly.*

1 With the engine removed from the vehicle, remove the timing chain and crankshaft sprocket, and the flywheel/driveplate.

2 Remove the pistons and connecting rods. If no work is to be done on the pistons and connecting rods, there is no need to push the pistons out of the cylinder bores.

3 Unbolt the crankshaft rear oil seal housing and remove it from the rear of the cylinder block. Recover the gasket and discard it.

4 Unscrew the two securing bolts and remove the sump mounting plate from the front of the cylinder block **(see illustration)**.

5 Check the main bearing caps for identification marks, and if necessary use a centre punch to identify them **(see illustration)**.

6 Before removing the crankshaft, check that the endfloat is within the specified limits by inserting a feeler blade between the centre crankshaft web and one of the thrustwashers (the thrustwashers are fitted to the crankcase, not the bearing cap). This will indicate whether or not new thrustwashers are required.

7 Unscrew the bolts and tap off the main bearing caps complete with bearing shells.

8 Lift the crankshaft from the cylinder block, and remove the rear oil seal if it is still in place on the crankshaft.

29.3 Withdrawing the oil baffle

30.4 Unscrewing a sump mounting plate securing bolt

30.5 Main bearing cap identification mark (arrowed)

2B

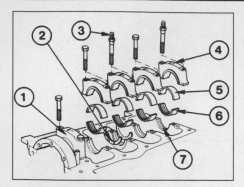

30.11 Crankshaft main bearings and associated components

1 Bearing cap
2 Thrustwasher
3 Stud for oil baffle
4 Identification markings
5 Bearing shell without oil groove
6 Bearing shell with oil groove
7 Bearing seat in cylinder block

9 Extract the bearing shells, and recover the thrustwashers, keeping them identified for location.
10 The crankshaft and bearings can be examined and if necessary renovated.
11 Commence refitting as follows **(see illustration).**
12 Wipe the bearing shell locations in the crankcase, and the crankshaft journals with a soft non-fluffy rag.
13 If the old main bearing shells are to be renewed (not to do so is a false economy, unless they are virtually new) fit the five upper halves of the main bearing shells to their locations in the crankcase.
14 Fit the thrustwashers to the centre main bearing location, using a little grease to retain them if necessary. The oil grooves in the thrustwashers must face outwards (ie facing the crankshaft webs). Note that where standard thrustwashers have been fitted in production, the centre main bearing is unmarked, but if oversize (0.38 mm) thrustwashers have been fitted, the centre main bearing will carry a yellow paint mark.
15 Lubricate the crankshaft journals and the upper and lower main bearing shells with clean engine oil, then carefully lower the crankshaft into the crankcase.
16 Lubricate the crankshaft main bearing journals again, and then fit the main bearing caps in their correct locations, with the arrows on the caps pointing towards the front of the engine.
17 Fit the main bearing cap bolts, noting that the studded bolts secure bearing caps Nos 3 and 5.
18 Lightly tighten all the securing bolts, then progressively tighten all bolts to the specified torque.
19 Check that the crankshaft rotates freely. Some stiffness is to be expected with new

components, but there must be no tight spots or binding.
20 Check that the crankshaft endfloat is within the specified limits by inserting a feeler blade between the centre crankshaft web and the thrustwashers.
21 Refit the sump mounting plate to the front of the cylinder block, and tighten the securing bolts to the specified torque.
22 Carefully wind a thin layer of tape around the rear edge of the crankshaft to protect the oil seal lips as the rear oil seal is installed.
23 Refit the crankshaft rear oil seal housing, using a new gasket, and tighten the securing bolts to the specified torque.
24 Install the new oil seal with reference to Section 24.
25 With the oil seal installed, carefully pull the tape from the edge of the crankshaft.
26 Refit the pistons and connecting rods as described previously in this Chapter.
27 Refit the flywheel/driveplate, and the timing chain and crankshaft sprocket.

31 Crankshaft and bearings - examination and renovation

Proceed as described in Part A, Section 27 of this Chapter, noting that the production bearing undersizes are indicated as follows.
Yellow or red paint marks on crankshaft — standard diameter main bearing journals.
Green line on crankshaft front counterweight — main bearing journals 0.25 mm undersize.
Green spot on counterweight — big-end bearing journals 0.25 mm undersize.

32 Examination and renovation - general information

Refer to Part A, Section 25 of this Chapter, but note that the connecting rod bolts should be renewed on reassembly, and when renewing the cylinder head bolts, the latest type bolts with hexagonal heads should always be used.

33 Engine reassembly - general information

Proceed as described in Part A, Section 35 of this Chapter, noting the following points.
a) *If the cylinder head has been removed, pay particular attention to the note at the beginning of Section 18.*
b) *If removed during any dismantling operations, new flywheel driveplate bolts and connecting rod bolts must be used.*
c) *After reassembling the main engine components, refer to paragraph 3 of Section 14 and refit the ancillary components listed.*

34 Initial start-up after overhaul or major repair

Refer to Part A, Section 51 of this Chapter, but note that when the engine is first started, a metallic tapping noise may be heard. This is due to the timing chain tensioner plunger assembly taking time to pressurize with oil, resulting in a temporarily slack chain. The noise should stop after a short time, once oil pressure has built up.

35 Compression test - description and interpretation

1 When engine performance is down, or if misfiring occurs which cannot be attributed to the ignition or fuel system, a compression test can provide diagnostic clues. If the test is performed regularly it can give warning of trouble before any other symptoms become apparent.
2 The engine must be at operating temperature, the battery must be fully charged and the spark plugs must be removed. The services of an assistant will also be required.
3 Disable the ignition system by dismantling the coil LT feed. Fit the compression tester to No 1 spark plug hole. (The type of tester which screws into the spark plug hole is to be preferred.)
4 Have the assistant hold the throttle wide open and crank the engine on the starter. Record the highest reading obtained on the compression tester.
5 Repeat the test on the remaining cylinders, recording the pressure developed in each.
6 Desired pressures are given in the Specifications. If the pressure in any cylinder is low, introduce a teaspoonful of clean engine oil into the spark plug hole and repeat the test.
7 If the addition of oil temporarily improves the compression pressure, this indicates that bore or piston wear was responsible for the pressure loss. No improvement suggests that leaking or burnt valves, or a blown head gasket, may be to blame.
8 A low reading from two adjacent cylinders is almost certainly due to the head gasket between them having blown.
9 On completion of the test, refit the spark plugs and reconnect the coil LT feed.

Chapter 2 Part C:
2.4, 2.8 and 2.9 litre V6 engines

Contents

Degrees of difficulty

Easy, suitable for novice with little experience	Fairly easy, suitable for beginner with some experience	Fairly difficult, suitable for competent DIY mechanic	Difficult, suitable for experienced DIY mechanic	Very difficult, suitable for expert DIY or professional

Specifications

2.8 litre engine

General

Manufacturer's code	PRE
Bore - mm (in)	93.0 (3.66)
Stroke - mm (in)	68.5 (2.70)
Cubic capacity - cc (cu in)	2792 (170)
Compression ratio	9.2:1
Compression pressure at cranking speed	11.5 to 12.5 bar (167 to 181 lbf/in²)
Maximum power (DIN, kW @ rpm)	110 @ 5800
Maximum torque (DIN, Nm @ rpm)	216 @ 3000

Lubrication system

Oil type	See "Lubricants and fluids"
Oil capacity (drain and refill, including filter)	4.25 litres (7.5 pints) approx
Oil pressure (SAE 10W/30 oil at 80°C/176°F):	
At 750 rpm	1.0 bar
At 2000 rpm	2.5 bar
Oil pressure relief valve opening pressure	4.0 to 4.7 bar
Oil pressure warning light switch setting	0.3 to 0.5 bar

Oil pump

Type	Bi-rotor
Drive	From camshaft
Operating clearances:	
Outer rotor-to-housing	0.15 to 0.30 mm
Inner-to-outer rotor	0.05 to 0.20 mm
Rotor endfloat	0.03 to 0.10 mm

Cylinder block

Cast identification mark	E
Bore diameter:	
Standard grade 1	93.010 to 93.020 mm
Standard grade 2	93.020 to 93.030 mm
Standard grade 3	93.030 to 93.040 mm
Standard grade 4	93.040 to 93.050 mm
Oversize grade A	93.520 to 93.530 mm
Oversize grade B	93.530 to 93.540 mm
Oversize grade C	93.540 to 93.550 mm
Standard service grade	93.040 to 93.050 mm
Oversize 0.5	93.540 to 93.550 mm
Oversize 1.0	94.040 to 94.050 mm
Main bearing parent bore:	
Standard	60.620 to 60.640 mm
Oversize	61.000 to 61.020 mm
Camshaft bearing bore (without bushes):	
Front	47.025 to 47.060 mm
Front centre	46.645 to 46.680 mm
Rear centre	46.265 to 46.300 mm
Rear	45.885 to 45.920 mm

Crankshaft

Number of main bearings	4
Main bearing journal diameter (standard)	56.980 to 57.000 mm
Main bearing running clearance	0.008 to 0.062 mm
No 3 (thrust) bearing shoulder width (standard)	26.390 to 26.440 mm
No 3 (thrust) flanged bearing shell width (standard)	26.240 to 26.290 mm
Crankshaft endfloat	0.08 to 0.20 mm
Big-end bearing journal diameter (standard)	53.980 to 54.000 mm
Big-end bearing running clearance	0.006 to 0.064 mm

Pistons

Diameter:	
Standard grade 1	92.972 to 92.982 mm
Standard grade 2	92.982 to 92.992 mm
Standard grade 3	92.992 to 93.002 mm
Standard grade 4	93.002 to 93.012 mm
Service standard	93.000 to 93.020 mm
Oversize 0.5	93.500 to 93.520 mm)
Oversize 1.0	94.000 to 94.020 mm
Clearance in bore	0.020 to 0.050 mm
Piston ring end gaps:	
Top and centre	0.38 to 0.58 mm
Bottom	0.40 to 1.40 mm

Gudgeon pins

Diameter:	
Red	23.994 to 23.997 mm
Blue	23.997 to 24.000 mm
Clearance in piston	0.008 to 0.014 mm
Interference in connecting rod	0.018 to 0.042 mm

Connecting rods

Big-end parent bore diameter	56.820 to 56.840 mm
Small-end bush internal diameter	23.958 to 23.976 mm

Cylinder heads

Cast identification mark	EN
Valve seat angle	44° 30' to 45° 00'
Valve seat width	1.61 to 2.33 mm
Valve guide bore:	
Standard	8.063 to 8.088 mm
Oversizes	+0.2, 0.4, 0.6 and 0.8 mm

Camshaft

Drive	Gear
Gear backlash	0.17 to 0.27 mm
Valve timing:	
Inlet opens	26° 30' BTDC
Inlet closes	69° 30' ABDC
Exhaust opens	75° 30' BBDC
Exhaust closes	22° 30' ATDC
Cam lift:	
Inlet	6.7 mm
Exhaust	6.6 mm
Cam length:	
Inlet	35.995 to 36.165 mm
Exhaust	35.895 to 36.065 mm
Thrust plate thickness:	
Red	3.960 to 3.985 mm
Blue	3.986 to 4.011 mm
Spacer thickness:	
Red	4.075 to 4.100 mm
Blue	4.101 to 4.125 mm
Camshaft endfloat	0.02 to 0.10 mm
Bearing journal diameter:	
Front	43.903 to 43.923 mm
Front centre	43.522 to 43.542 mm
Rear centre	43.141 to 43.161 mm
Rear	42.760 to 42.780 mm
Bearing bush internal diameter:	
Front	43.948 to 43.968 mm
Front centre	43.567 to 43.587 mm
Rear centre	43.186 to 43.206 mm
Rear	42.805 to 42.825 mm

Valve clearances (cold)

Inlet	0.35 mm (0.014 in)
Exhaust	0.40 mm (0.016 in)

Inlet valves

Head diameter	41.85 to 42.24 mm
Length	105.25 to 106.95 mm
Stem diameter:	
Standard	8.025 to 8.043 mm
Oversizes	+0.2, 0.4, 0.6 and 0.8 mm
Stem-to-guide clearance	0.020 to 0.063 mm
Valve stem oil seal type	Rubber, one size

Exhaust valves

Head diameter	35.83 to 36.21 mm
Length	105.20 to 106.20 mm
Stem diameter:	
Standard	7.999 to 8.017 mm
Oversizes	+0.2, 0.4, 0.6 and 0.8 mm
Stem-to-guide clearance	0.046 to 0.089 mm
Valve stem oil seal:	
Type	Nylon, selective sizes
Identification:	
Standard size	White
+ 0.2	Red
+ 0.4	Blue
+ 0.6	Green
+ 0.8	Black

Torque wrench settings

	Nm	lbf ft
Main bearing cap bolts	90 to 104	66 to 77
Big-end cap nuts	26 to 33	19 to 24
Crankshaft pulley/damper central bolt	115 to 130	85 to 96
Camshaft gear bolt	42 to 50	31 to 37
Camshaft thrust plate bolts	17 to 21	13 to 16
Timing cover to cylinder block	17 to 21	13 to 16

2C

Torque wrench settings (continued)

	Nm	lbf ft
Timing cover to intermediate plate	13 to 17	10 to 13
Intermediate plate to cylinder block	17 to 21	13 to 16
Oil pump to cylinder block	14 to 17	10 to 13
Oil pump cover bolts	9 to 13	7 to 10
Rocker shaft securing bolts	62 to 70	46 to 52
Sump bolts:		
Stage 1	4 to 7	3 to 5
Stage 2	7 to 10	5 to 7
Sump drain plug	21 to 28	16 to 21
Oil pressure switch	12 to 15	9 to 11
Oil cooler threaded sleeve	20 to 40	15 to 30
Cylinder head hexagon bolts:		
Stage 1	40 to 45	30 to 33
Stage 2	55 to 70	41 to 52
Stage 3 (after 10 to 20 minutes)	95 to 115	70 to 85
Stage 4 (after warm-up)	95 to 115	70 to 85
Cylinder head - Torx bolts:		
Stage 1	35 to 40	26 to 30
Stage 2	70 to 75	52 to 55
Stage 3 (after 5 minutes)	Tighten further 90°	Tighten further 90°
Rocker cover bolts	6 to 8	4 to 6
Fuel pump blanking plate	16 to 18	12 to 13
Flywheel bolts	64 to 70	47 to 52
Bellhousing-to-engine bolts	27 to 30	20 to 22

2.4 litre engine

Note: *Unless otherwise stated, the specifications and torque wrench settings for the 2.4 litre engine are as given for the 2.8 litre engine.*

General

Manufacturer's code	ARC
Bore - mm (in)	84.0 (3.307)
Stroke - mm (in)	72.0 (2.865)
Cubic capacity - cc (cu in)	2394 (146.1)
Compression ratio	9.5:1
Maximum power (DIN, kW @ rpm)	96 @ 5800
Maximum torque (DIN, Nm @ rpm)	193 @ 3000

Cylinder block

Identification mark	D
Bore diameter:	
Standard grade 1	84.000 to 84.010 mm
Standard grade 2	84.010 to 84.020 mm
Standard grade 3	84.020 to 84.030 mm
Standard grade 4	84.030 to 84.040 mm
Oversize grade A	84.510 to 84.520 mm
Oversize grade B	84.520 to 84.530 mm
Oversize grade C	84.530 to 84.540 mm
Standard service grade	84.030 to 84.040 mm
Oversize 0.5	84.530 to 84.540 mm
Oversize 1.0	85.030 to 85.040 mm

Pistons

Diameter:	
Standard grade 1	83.962 to 83.972 mm
Standard grade 2	83.972 to 83.982 mm
Standard grade 3	83.982 to 83.992 mm
Standard grade 4	83.992 to 84.002 mm
Standard service grade	83.978 to 84.002 mm
Oversize 0.5	84.478 to 84.502 mm
Oversize 1.0	84.978 to 85.002 mm
Clearance in bore	0.028 to 0.048 mm
Piston ring end gap:	
Top and centre	0.30 to 0.50 mm
Bottom (oil control)	0.40 to 1.40 mm

Cylinder head

Identification mark	H

Crankshaft

Thrustwasher thickness:	
Standard	2.28 to 2.33 mm
Oversize	2.48 to 2.53 mm
Crankshaft endfloat	0.08 to 0.32 mm
Permitted undersize for main and big-end bearing journals	0.254 mm

Camshaft

Camshaft drive	Chain
Cam lift (inlet and exhaust)	6.72 mm
Cam lobe height (inlet and exhaust)	36.08 to 36.25 mm
Camshaft endfloat	0.065 to 0.165 mm
Thrust plate thickness	4.02 to 4.05 mm

Valves

Valve timing:	
Inlet opens	24°BTDC
Inlet closes	64°ABDC
Exhaust opens	66°BBDC
Exhaust closes	22°ATDC
Head diameter:	
Inlet valve	39.67 to 40.06 mm
Exhaust valve	33.83 to 34.21 mm
Length:	
Inlet valve	106.2 to 106.9 mm
Exhaust valve	106.1 to 107.1 mm
Valve spring free length	55.12 mm

Torque wrench settings

	Nm	lbf ft
Camshaft sprocket bolt	60 to 68	44 to 50
Camshaft thrust plate	9 to 13	7 to 10
Timing chain guide to block bolts	10 to 12	7 to 9
Timing chain tensioner to block	9 to 11	7 to 8
Oil inlet pipe to oil pump bolts	9 to 13	7 to 10
Oil pump to block bolts	17 to 21	13 to 15
Sump drain plug	21 to 28	15 to 21
Crankshaft pulley to vibration damper bolts	27 to 33	20 to 24
Crankshaft vibration damper bolt:		
Stage 1	40 to 50	30 to 37
Stage 2	Tighten further 80° to 90°	Tighten further 80° to 90°

2.9 litre engine

Note: *Unless otherwise stated, the specifications and torque wrench settings for the 2.9 litre engine are as given for the 2.8 litre engine.*

General

Manufacturer's code:	
Models without catalytic converter	BRC
Models equipped with type N manual gearbox or automatic transmission and a catalytic converter	BRD
Models equipped with MT75 manual gearbox and catalytic converter	BRE
Stroke - mm (in)	72.0 (2.835)
Cubic capacity - cc (cu in)	2936 (179.2)
Compression ratio:	
BRC engine	9.5:1
BRD and BRE engine	9.0:1
Maximum power (DIN, kW @ rpm):	
BRC engine	110 @ 5700
BRD and BRE engines	107 @ 5500
Maximum torque (DIN, Nm @ rpm):	
BRC engine	233 @ 3000
BRD engine	222 @ 3000
BRE engine	226 @ 3000

Cylinder block

Identification mark	F

Pistons

Clearance in bore	0.028 to 0.048 mm
Piston ring end gaps:	
Top and centre	0.30 to 0.50 mm

Cylinder head

Identification mark:
    BRC engine . . . .   F
    BRD and BRE engines . . . .   K

Crankshaft

Crankshaft endfloat . . . .   0.08 to 0.24 mm
Permitted undersize for main and big-end bearing journals . . . .   0.254 mm

Camshaft

Cam lift (inlet and exhaust):
    BRC engine . . . .   6.72 mm
    BRD and BRE engine . . . .   6.54 mm
Cam lobe height (inlet and exhaust):
    BRC engine . . . .   36.08 to 36.25 mm
    BRD and BRE engine . . . .   36.22 to 36.41 mm
Camshaft endfloat . . . .   0.065 to 0.165 mm
Thrust plate thickness . . . .   4.02 to 4.05 mm

Valves

Valve timing:
    BRC engine . . . .   As 2.4 litre V6
    BRD and BRE engines:
        Inlet opens . . . .   30°BTDC
        Inlet closes . . . .   66°ABDC
        Exhaust opens . . . .   76°BBDC
        Exhaust closes . . . .   20°ATDC
Length:
    BRC engine:
        Inlet . . . .   106.2 to 106.9 mm
        Exhaust . . . .   106.8 to 107.8 mm
    BRD and BRE engine:
        Inlet . . . .   104.7 to 105.4 mm
        Exhaust . . . .   104.6 to 105.6 mm
Valve spring free length:
    BRC engine . . . .   55.12 mm
    BRD and BRE engines . . . .   53.00 mm

1 General information

The V6 engine fitted to the Granada is only available in fuel-injected form. Mechanically, the design of the engine is well-established, and it is improved by the latest fuel, ignition and engine management systems **(see illustration)**.

The combined crankcase and cylinder block is made of cast iron, and houses the pistons, crankshaft and camshaft. The sump is attached to the bottom of the crankcase and the cylinder heads to the top.

The cylinder heads are of the crossflow design, the inlet manifold being located between them and the exhaust manifolds being on the outboard sides. The overhead valves are operated by tappets, pushrods and rockers from the centrally located camshaft. Camshaft drive is by gears (2.8 litre) or chain (2.4 & 2.9 litre).

The crankshaft runs in four main bearings. Endfloat is controlled by thrust flanges on the No 3 bearing shells. The connecting rods are selected so that all are in the same weight class.

Aluminium alloy pistons are used. The gudgeon pins are an interference fit in their connecting rods.

The lubrication system is of the usual wet sump, pressure fed type, with a full-flow disposable canister oil filter. The oil pump is driven by a shaft which engages in the bottom of the distributor drivegear.

2 Major operations possible with the engine in the vehicle

The following operations can be carried out without removing the engine, although some work will be easier and quicker with the engine removed.

a) *Removal and refitting of the cylinder heads*
b) *Removal and refitting of the sump and oil pump*
c) *Removal and refitting of the timing gears*
d) *Removal and refitting of the pistons, connecting rods and big-end bearings*
e) *Renewal of the engine mountings*
f) *Removal and refitting of the flywheel*
g) *Renewal of the crankshaft front and rear oil seals*
h) *Removal and refitting of the camshaft (after removal of the cylinder heads, tappets and timing gears)*

3 Major operations requiring engine removal

The engine must be removed for the following operations:

a) *Renewal of the crankshaft main bearings*
b) *Removal and refitting of the crankshaft*

4 Methods of engine removal

The engine is removed from above, without the transmission. Removal with the transmission is not recommended because of the weight and unwieldiness of the combined units.

5 Engine - removal

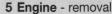

2.8 litre engine

1 Disconnect the battery negative lead.
2 Remove the bonnet.
3 Remove the throttle valve cover, which is retained by three screws.
4 Remove the air cleaner cover, valve airflow

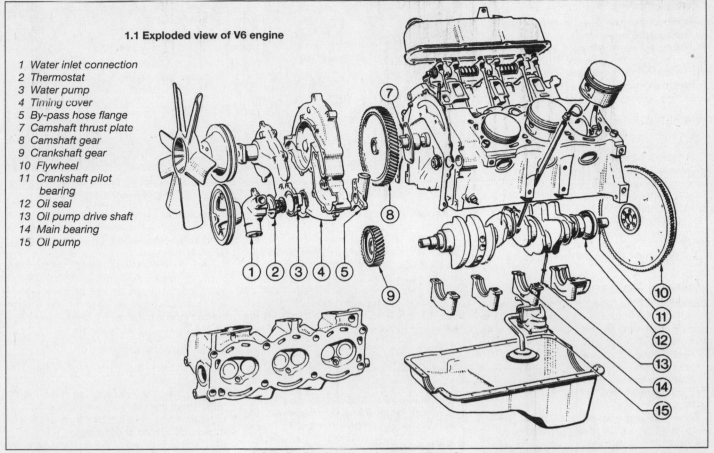

1.1 Exploded view of V6 engine

1 Water inlet connection
2 Thermostat
3 Water pump
4 Timing cover
5 By-pass hose flange
7 Camshaft thrust plate
8 Camshaft gear
9 Crankshaft gear
10 Flywheel
11 Crankshaft pilot
     bearing
12 Oil seal
13 Oil pump drive shaft
14 Main bearing
15 Oil pump

2C

meters and air inlet trunking. Also remove the oil filler cap, which is connected to the trunking by a crankcase ventilation hose.
5 Release the securing clips and bolts and remove the upper half of the fan shroud.
6 Drain the cooling system and remove the radiator.
7 Disconnect the heater hoses from the heater matrix and from the coolant outlet. Unclip the hoses.
8 Remove the fan and viscous clutch (where fitted).
9 Disconnect the following wiring:
a) Alternator
b) Temperature gauge sender
c) Engine management temperature sensor
d) Oil pressure switch
e) Idle speed control valve
f) Throttle position sensor
g) Injector nut-harness
h) Distributor multi-plug
i) Distributor-to-coil HT lead
10 Disconnect the throttle cable. When applicable, also disconnect the downshaft cable or switch.
11 Depressurise the fuel system and disconnect the fuel supply and return lines (see Chapter 4).
12 Remove the steering pump and air conditioning compressor drivebelts (as applicable). Unbolt the steering pump and compressor, move them aside within the limits

of their flexible hoses and support them by wiring them to adjacent components.
13 Remove the distributor cap and rotor.
14 Remove the starter motor.
15 Drain the engine oil. Unscrew the oil filter with a strap or chain wrench and remove it; be prepared for oil spillage.
16 On manual gearbox models, disconnect the clutch cable from the release lever.
17 Unbolt the exhaust pipes from the manifolds.
18 On automatic transmission models, unbolt the torque converter from the driveplate.
19 Attach lifting tackle to the engine. If no lifting eyes are fitted, pass ropes or chains round the exhaust manifolds.
20 Take the weight of the engine, then remove the single nut on each side which holds engine bearer to its mountings.
21 From under the vehicle unbolt the engine adapter plate from the bellhousing.
22 Remove the engine-to-bellhousing bolts. Also disconnect or unclip the battery negative lead, the starter motor lead and the heat shield.
23 Support the transmission, preferably with a trolley jack.
24 Check that nothing has been overlooked, then raise the engine and draw it forwards clear of the transmission input shaft. Do not allow the weight of the engine to hang on the shaft, and do not lift the transmission by it.

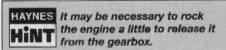

HAYNES HiNT *It may be necessary to rock the engine a little to release it from the gearbox.*

25 With automatic transmission, make sure that the torque converter stays engaged with the oil pump in the transmission as the engine is withdrawn.
26 Lift the engine out of the engine bay and take it to the bench.

2.4 & 2.9 litre engines

27 The removal operations for these engines are essentially as described for the 2.8 litre version. Note the following points.

Coolant hoses

28 Remove the hoses which run between the thermostat housing and the water pump, and the cooling system expansion tank.
29 Remove the heater hoses which run between the thermostat housing or coolant distribution pipe and oil cooler (where fitted).

Vacuum hoses

30 Disconnect the hose from the fuel pressure regulator.
31 Disconnect the hose from the plenum chamber.
32 Disconnect the hose from the throttle valve.
33 Disconnect the hose from the T-piece connector.

Other items

34 Disconnect the throttle cable from the operating lever and bracket.

35 Disconnect the right-hand exhaust downpipe from the manifold then remove the starter motor, the oil filter, and disconnect the left-hand exhaust downpipe, in that order.

6 Engine dismantling - general

Refer to Part A, Section 8, paragraphs 1 to 8 of this Chapter.

Cylinder head bolts on the V6 engine may be conventional (hexagon-headed) or Torx type. The appropriate Torx key will be needed to deal with the latter.

7 Ancillary components - removal

Before dismantling the engine into its main components, the following ancillaries can be removed. The actual items removed, and the sequence of removal, will depend on the work to be done.

Distributor and bracket
Spark plugs
Inlet manifold and associated items
Exhaust manifolds
Clutch
Alternator and bracket
Oil pressure switch (see illustration)

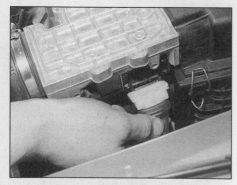

8.14a Front airflow sensor wiring plug

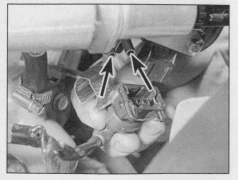

8.14b Throttle position sensor wiring plug
Vacuum nozzles arrowed

7.1 The oil pressure switch is on the left-hand side of the block

Temperature gauge sender
Engine bearer arms
Dipstick

If an oil cooler is fitted between the oil filter and the block, remove it by disconnecting the coolant hoses and unscrewing the central sleeve. The cooler and seal can now be removed. If the threaded bush is removed from the block (it may come out with the sleeve) it must be renewed.

8 Cylinder heads - removal

The procedure is described for the engine in the vehicle. With the engine removed, the preliminary steps can be ignored.

2.8 litre engine

1 Disconnect the battery negative lead.
2 Remove the inlet manifold and associated components.
3 Unbolt the power steering pump, remove the drivebelts and move the pump aside. Support it by wiring it to adjacent components.
4 Remove the alternator and its bracket.
5 Remove the three bolts which secure each rocker shaft. Remove the shafts and pushrods, keeping them in order so that they can be refitted in the same locations.
6 Unbolt the exhaust pipes from the manifolds.
7 Remove the spark plugs.

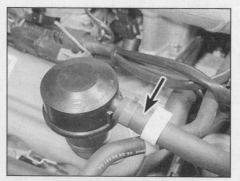

8.15 Oil filler breather hose (arrowed)

8.13 Disconnecting the air hoses from the throttle valve housing

8 Slacken the cylinder head bolts half a turn at a time, following the reverse sequence to that used when tightening (see illustration 38.5). Remove the bolts.
9 Remove the cylinder heads. If they are stuck, try to rock them free, or tap them with a soft-faced hammer. **Do not** hit them directly with a metal hammer, and **do not** lever in between the joint faces.
10 Recover the head gaskets.

2.4 & 2.9 litre engines

11 Disconnect the battery and drain the cooling system.
12 Disconnect the radiator top hose and the heater hose from the thermostat housing.
13 Disconnect the air hoses from the throttle valve housing **(see illustration)**.
14 Detach the two wiring plugs from the airflow sensors **(see illustrations)**.
15 Pull the breather hose from the oil filler cap **(see illustration)**.
16 Unclip the air cleaner cover and remove it together with the airflow sensors and air hoses.
17 Disconnect the hoses from the coolant expansion tank.
18 Disconnect the wiring from the following components:

a) *Alternator (right-hand cylinder head removal only).*
b) *Coolant temperature sensors (see illustration).*
c) *Idle speed control valve (see illustration).*
d) *Throttle valve potentiometer.*
e) *The fuel-injector wiring loom.*

8.18a Coolant temperature sensor location

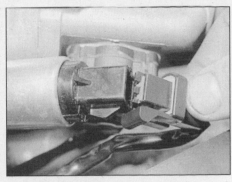

8.18b Disconnecting the idle speed control valve wiring plug

8.19a Disconnecting the distributor wiring plug

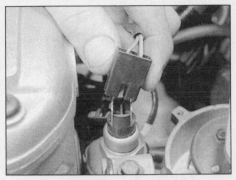

8.19b Disconnecting the fuel temperature sensor wiring plug

19 Disconnect the wiring connectors from the ignition distributor and the fuel temperature sensor **(see illustrations)**.
20 Release the pressure in the fuel distributor pipe by depressing the pin in the vent valve. Cover the valve with a rag during this operation to prevent fuel being sprayed out **(see illustration)**.
21 Disconnect the fuel lines **(see illustration)**.
22 Disconnect the vacuum hoses from the following components:
a) *Fuel pressure regulator.*
b) *Throttle valve assembly.*
c) *T-piece connector* **(see illustration)**.
23 Disconnect the rocker cover breather hose **(see illustration)**.
24 Unbolt the plenum chamber and place it to one side with the throttle cable attached.

25 Disconnect the HT leads from the spark plugs and the ignition coil noting their correct fitted locations. Undo the two retaining screws then remove the distributor cap and HT leads as an assembly.
26 Using a 19 mm socket on the crankshaft damper centre bolt, set No 1 piston to its firing point (12° BTDC) and remove the distributor.
27 If the right-hand cylinder head is to be removed, remove the drivebelts, unbolt the alternator and power steering pump and tie them to one side of the engine compartment.
28 Unbolt and remove the rocker cover(s).
29 Unbolt and remove the rocker shaft(s) **(see illustration)**.
30 Withdraw the pushrods and keep them in their originally fitted sequence.
31 Disconnect the inlet manifold to timing

cover coolant hose from the manifold.
32 Unbolt and remove the inlet manifold complete with fuel rail and injectors. Discard the gasket.
33 Disconnect the exhaust downpipe(s) from the manifold(s).
34 Disconnect the earth straps from the rear of the left-hand cylinder head and release the cable retaining clamp.
35 Unscrew and remove the spark plugs.
36 Unscrew the cylinder head bolts using the reverse of the tightening sequence (see illustration 38.5). Obtain new bolts for refitting. Remove the cylinder head(s) and discard the gasket(s).

2C

9 Sump - removal

Proceed as described in Part A, Section 16 of this Chapter but note that there are 24 bolts retaining the sump, not 23.

10 Timing cover and drive - removal

The procedure is described for the engine in the vehicle. With the engine removed, the preliminary steps can be ignored.

2.8 litre engine

1 Disconnect the battery negative lead.
2 Drain the engine oil.
3 Drain the coolant and remove the radiator.

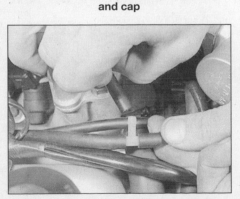

8.20 Fuel rail vent (depressurising) valve and cap

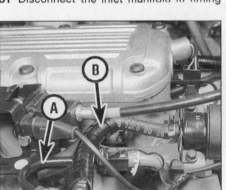
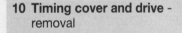

8.21 Fuel feed (A) and return (B) hoses

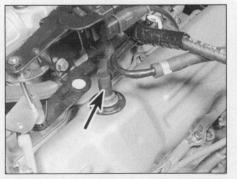

8.22 Vacuum hose T-piece connector

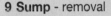

8.23 Rocker cover breather hose (arrowed)

8.29 Removing rocker shaft and pedestal

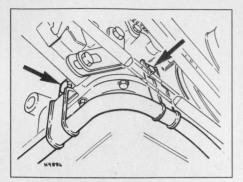

10.9 Heater connecting pipe clip bolts (arrowed)

10.13 Camshaft and crankshaft gear marks in alignment (engine inverted)
Disregard the other mark on the crankshaft gear

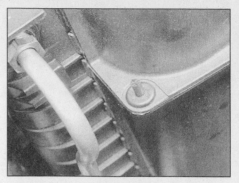

10.22a Radiator upper shroud plastic clip and centre pin

4 Remove the auxiliary drivebelts.

5 Remove the fan and viscous clutch if fitted).

6 Jam the crankshaft, either by engaging 5th gear and applying the handbrake, or by removing the starter motor and having an assistant jam a screwdriver in the starter ring gear teeth. Unbolt the crankshaft pulley. When the pulley is secured to a vibration damper, also remove the damper central bolt.

7 Remove the pulley or damper, using a puller if necessary.

8 Disconnect the coolant hoses from the front of the engine, including the water pump bypass hose.

9 Disconnect the heater connecting pipe from the timing cover and unbolt the two clips which secure the pipe to the cover of the cylinder block **(see illustration)**.

10 If not already done, remove the starter motor.

11 Remove the sump.

12 Remove the nine securing bolts and remove the timing cover complete with water pump and thermostat.

13 Turn the crankshaft to bring the marks on the timing gears into alignment as shown **(see illustration)**. *Note that there are two marks on the crankshaft gear - do not get them confused.*

14 Remove the bolt which secures the camshaft gear. It should now be possible to remove the camshaft gear by hand.

15 Draw off the crankshaft gear using a puller. Recover the Woodruff keys if they are loose.

16 Clean the old gasket off the timing cover and the cylinder block. Remove the oil seal from the timing cover.

2.4 & 2.9 litre engines

17 Using the crankshaft damper centre bolt, turn the engine until No 1 piston is at its firing point (12° BTDC). This can be verified by removing the distributor cap and checking that the rotor arm is aligned with the No 1 HT lead contact.

18 Disconnect the battery negative terminal.

19 Unclip the air cleaner cover and remove it complete with air flow sensors and air hoses. Remove the oil filler cap.

20 Drain the cooling system, disconnect the radiator upper hose from the thermostat housing.

21 Disconnect the hose which runs between the water pump and the expansion tank.

22 Remove the radiator upper shroud, then the radiator **(see illustrations)**.

23 Remove the fan from the water pump hub noting that it has a left-hand thread.

24 Disconnect the coolant hoses from the timing cover/water pump hose stubs.

25 Remove the alternator and power steering pump drivebelts (as applicable)

26 Unscrew the four bolts and remove the crankshaft pulley.

27 Lock the crankshaft by jamming the starter ring gear teeth, and unscrew the vibration damper centre bolt. Withdraw the damper from the front of the crankshaft. A puller will be required for this, preferably one which has two screws for the tapped holes provided **(see illustrations)**.

28 Using an engine support bar or hoist, take the weight of the engine then unscrew the nuts

10.22b Removing radiator upper shroud

10.22c Manoeuvre the radiator out from under the vehicle

10.27a Unscrewing the vibration damper centre bolt

10.27b Using a puller to withdraw the vibration damper

10.28a Using an engine support bar to support the engine

10.28b Engine mounting top nut

10.30 Coolant distribution pipe bracket

10.32 Steering shaft coupling pinch bolt

from the top of the engine mounting brackets **(see illustrations)**.

29 Drain the engine oil, retaining it for further use only if it is not contaminated or due for renewal.

30 Unbolt the coolant distribution pipe bracket from the timing cover **(see illustration)**.

31 Disconnect the leads and remove the starter motor.

32 Ensure that the front roadwheels and the steering wheels are in the straight-ahead position, then remove the pinch-bolt from the steering shaft coupling and slide the coupling down the shaft **(see illustration)**.

33 Unscrew the sump retaining nuts and bolts. The rear bolts can only be unscrewed using a box spanner or thin-walled socket.

34 Release the brake hydraulic lines from their support brackets by pulling out their retaining clips.

35 Unscrew the two bolts from each of the crossmember side brackets. Lower the crossmember just enough to be able to remove the sump. In practice, as the car is standing on its roadwheels, the car body should be raised by placing two axle stands under the front jacking points **(see illustration)**.

36 Extract the nine bolts and remove the timing cover complete with water pump **(see illustration)**. Removal of the radiator grille will provide better access to the cover bolts.

37 Check that the crankshaft and camshaft sprocket timing marks are aligned at the nearest point to each other **(see illustration)**.

If not, turn the crankshaft as necessary.

38 Unbolt and remove the timing chain tensioner. Take care not to allow the spring-loaded tensioner plunger to eject **(see illustration)**.

39 Lock the camshaft sprocket by passing a rod through one of the holes and unscrew the sprocket retaining bolt **(see illustration)**.

40 Remove the camshaft sprocket then release the chain from the crankshaft sprocket and remove the camshaft sprocket and chain from the engine.

41 If required, the crankshaft sprocket, Woodruff key and chain guide can now be also removed.

42 Clean away all old pieces of gasket from the cylinder block and timing cover flanges.

43 Remove and discard the sump gasket. The gasket rear tabs may break off, so pick

10.35 Unscrewing crossmember side bracket mounting bolts

them out of the recesses in the rear main bearing cap using a sharp, pointed knife.

11 Flywheel/driveplate and adapter plate - removal

Refer to Part A, Section 15 of this Chapter.

12 Oil pump - removal

2.8 litre engine

1 Remove the sump.

2 Remove the two securing bolts and remove the oil pump complete with pick-up and strainer.

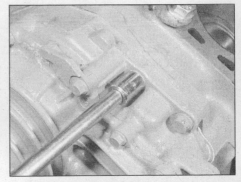

10.36 Removing a timing cover retaining bolt

10.37 Timing sprocket alignment marks (arrowed)

10.38 Timing chain tensioner assembly

10.39 Slackening camshaft sprocket retaining bolt

2C

12.6 Removing the oil pump and driveshaft

3 Recover the oil pump driveshaft, noting which way round it is fitted.
4 Recover the oil pump-to-block gasket.

2.4 & 2.9 litre engines

5 Remove the sump.
6 Unbolt the oil pump/inlet pipe assembly and remove it then extract the driveshaft, which is splined into the distributor shaft **(see illustration)**.

13 Pistons and connecting rods - removal

1 Remove the cylinder heads, the sump and the oil pump.
2 Check that the big-end bearing caps and connecting rods have identification marks. This is to ensure that the correct caps are fitted to the correct connecting rods and at reassembly are fitted in their correct cylinder bores. Note that the pistons have an arrow (or notch) marked on the crown to indicate the forward facing side.
3 Remove the big-end nuts and place to one side in the order in which they are removed.
4 Pull off the big-end caps, taking care to keep them in the right order and the correct way round. Also ensure that the shell bearings are kept with their respective connecting rods unless they are being renewed.

 If the big-end caps are difficult to remove they can be tapped lightly with a soft faced hammer.

14.2 Using a piece of wire to remove the tappets

5 To remove the shell bearings, press the bearing on the side opposite the groove in both the connecting rod and the cap, and the bearing will slide out.
6 Withdraw the pistons and connecting rods upwards out of the cylinder bores.

14 Camshaft and intermediate plate - removal

1 Remove the cylinder heads and pushrods.
2 Remove the tappets from their bores, using a pencil magnet or by inserting a piece of bent brass wire through the lubrication holes **(see illustration)**.
3 Remove the timing cover and the camshaft gear.
4 Remove the two bolts which secure the camshaft thrust plate. Withdraw the camshaft, thrust plate and spacer ring.
5 The intermediate plate may now be removed after removing the retaining bolts. Note the oil seals on the timing cover locating dowels, which must also be removed.

15 Crankshaft and main bearings - removal

1 The engine must be removed from the vehicle for this task.
2 Remove the flywheel/driveplate, timing cover and crankshaft gear, and the pistons and connecting rods, as described in the preceding Sections. (If no work is to be done on the pistons, they need not actually be pushed out of their bores.)
3 Make sure that the main bearing caps carry identification marks, then remove the bolts and lift off the caps. Tap the caps with a soft-faced mallet if necessary to free them.

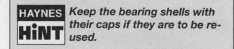 *Keep the bearing shells with their caps if they are to be re-used.*

4 Note that the rear main bearing cap also retains the crankshaft rear oil seal, and that the shells for No 3 main bearing have thrust flanges to control crankshaft endfloat.
5 Lift out the crankshaft. Do not drop it, it is heavy.
6 Recover the upper half main bearing shells from their seats in the crankcase, again keeping them in order if they are to be re-used.
7 Remove the old oil seal from the rear of the crankshaft.

16 Engine mountings - renewal

Refer to Part A, Section 23 of this Chapter.

17 Crankshaft front oil seal - renewal

1 Disconnect the battery negative lead.
2 Remove the crankshaft pulley (and damper, when fitted).
3 Extract the old oil seal by levering it out with a hooked tool.
4 Clean out the seal seat in the timing cover. Lubricate the new seal and fit it, lips inwards. Seat the seal with a piece of tube or a large socket. (If available, Ford tool 21-063 and a non-damper type pulley may be used to seat the seal.)
5 Lubricate the sealing surface of the pulley or damper and refit it.
6 The remainder of refitting is a reversal of the removal procedure. Check the engine oil level on completion.

18 Crankshaft rear oil seal - renewal

Refer to Part A, Section 18 of this Chapter.

19 Examination and renovation - general information

Refer to Part A, Section 25 of this Chapter. New cylinder head bolts are not required if they are of the hexagon head type. Torx type bolts must be renewed. The two types of cylinder head bolt must not be mixed on the same engine.

20 Rocker shaft - dismantling, examination and reassembly

1 Tap out the roll pin from one end of the rocker shaft and remove the spring washer **(see illustration)**.
2 Slide the rocker arms, rocker supports and springs off the rocker shaft. Keep them in the correct order so that they can be reassembled in the same position **(see illustration)**.

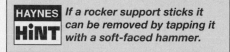 *If a rocker support sticks it can be removed by tapping it with a soft-faced hammer.*

20.1 Rocker shaft roll pin (arrowed)

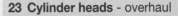

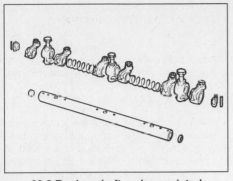

20.2 Rocker shaft and associated components

3 Examine the rocker shaft and rocker arms for wear. If the rocker arm surface that contacts the valve stem is considerably worn, renew the rocker arm. If it is worn slightly step-shaped it may be cleaned up with a fine oil stone.

4 Oil the parts and reassemble them on their shafts in the original order. With both rocker shafts fitted the oil holes must face downwards to the cylinder heads. This position is indicated by a notch on one end face of the rocker shaft **(see illustration)**.

21 Tappets and pushrods - examination

Inspect the tappets for scuffing, surface wear or other damage. Renew them if necessary. It is good practice to renew the tappets if a new camshaft is being fitted.

23.2a Compressing a valve spring to expose the collets

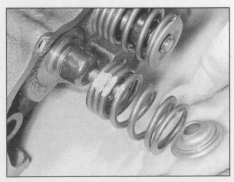

23.2b Removing the spring retainer and spring

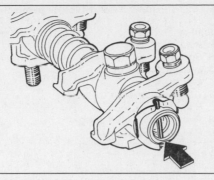

20.4 Notch (arrowed) shows position of oil holes

Check the pushrods for bending by rolling them on a flat surface. Straighten or renew as necessary. Also check the pushrod ends for wear or damage.

22 Camshaft and bearings - examination and renovation

1 If there is excessive wear in the camshaft bearings they will have to be renewed. As the fitting of new bearings requires special tools this should be left to your local Ford dealer.

2 The camshaft may show signs of wear on the bearing journals or cam lobes. The main decision to take is what degree of wear necessitates renewing the camshaft, which is expensive. Scoring or damage to the bearing journals cannot be removed by regrinding; renewal of the camshaft is the only solution.

3 The cam lobes may show signs of ridging or pitting on the high points. If ridging is slight then it may be possible to remove it with a fine oil stone or emery cloth. The cam lobes, however, are surface hardened and once the hard skin is penetrated wear will be very rapid.

4 Excessive endfloat of the camshaft may be remedied by fitting a thicker spacer and/or thrust plate - see Specifications.

5 Excessive backlash in the camshaft drive gears (timing gears), which will have been noticed before dismantling by virtue of the characteristic growling noise, can only be remedied by renewing the gears.

23.2c Removing an inlet valve

23 Cylinder heads - overhaul

1 Clean the dirt and oil off the cylinder heads. Remove the carbon deposits from the combustion chambers and valve heads with a scraper or rotary wire brush.

2 Remove the valves by compressing the valve springs with a suitable valve spring compressor and lifting out the collets. Release the valve spring compressor and remove the valve spring retainer, spring and valve **(see illustrations)**. **Note**: *When removing and refitting the valve spring take care not to damage the valve stem when pressing down the valve spring retainer to remove or refit the collets. If the stem gets damaged the sealing will be ineffective and result in excessive oil consumption and wear of the valve guides.*

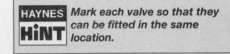

Mark each valve so that they can be fitted in the same location.

3 Remove the valve stem oil seals from the valve guides and discard them.

4 With the valves removed clean out the carbon from the ports.

5 Examine the heads of the valves and the valve seats for pitting and burning. If the pitting on valve and seat is slight it can be removed by grinding the valves and seats together with coarse, and then fine, valve grinding paste.

6 Severe pitting or burning of the valves probably means that they must be renewed. Badly burnt valve seats can be recut, or inserts can be fitted, by a Ford dealer or other specialist.

7 Check the valve guides for wear by inserting the valve into its guide until the valve stem is flush with the end of the guide, then checking the play at the valve head **(see illustration)**. Movement in excess of 0.6 mm (0.024 in) means that the clearance between guide and stem is excessive.

8 Valve guide wear is dealt with by reaming the guides to a known oversize and fitting new valves with oversize stems. Again, this is a dealer or specialist task.

23.7 Checking valve guide wear using a valve and a dial test indicator

2C

9 Inspect the valve springs, if possible comparing their free length with new springs. Renew the springs anyway if they have been in use for 20 000 miles (32 000 km) or more.

10 Use a straight-edge and feeler blades to check that the cylinder head mating faces are not distorted. If they are, have the heads resurfaced by an engineering works.

11 Commence reassembly by oiling a valve stem and inserting the valve into its guide. Cover the collet grooves with adhesive tape and press the new valve stem oil seal down the stem, using a suitable tube to press the seals home. Note that the inlet valve seals are rubber and the exhaust seals nylon. On the 2.8 litre engine, oversize exhaust valve seals must be used when valves with oversize stems are fitted. Remove the adhesive tape.

12 Fit the valve spring and spring retainer. Compress the spring and fit the collets, using a dab of grease to hold them in position. Carefully release the compressor.

13 Tap the valve stem smartly with a mallet to seat the components.

14 Repeat the process on the remaining valves.

24 Cylinder bores - examination and renovation

Refer to Part A, Section 28 of this Chapter. The main bearing caps should be fitted, and their bolts tightened to the specified torque, when making bore measurements.

25 Pistons and connecting rods - examination and renovation

Refer to Part A, Section 29 of this Chapter.

26 Crankshaft and bearings - examination

1 Refer to Part A, Section 27 of this Chapter for the examination procedure. Note that regrinding of this crankshaft is not permitted, so if significant journal wear is present, a new crankshaft (and new bearing shells) must be fitted.

2 As with the SOHC engine, oversize main bearing parent bores may be encountered. These are marked with paint stripes on the bearing caps, corresponding paint marks on the bearing shells and identification codes on the backs of the bearing shells.

3 On the 2.4 litre engine, separate thrustwashers are used to control crankshaft endfloat. On the 2.9 litre engine, No 3 main bearing shells have integral thrust flanges.

27 Oil pump - dismantling, examination and reassembly

2.8 litre engine

1 If oil pump wear is suspected, check the cost and availability of new parts and the cost of a new pump. Examine the pump and then decide whether renewal or repair is the best course of action **(see illustration)**.

27.1 Exploded view of the oil pump

1 Body
2 Bolt
3 Bolts
4 Lockwasher
5 Driveshaft
6 Toothed washer
7 Rotor set
8 Pressure relief valve plunger
9 Pressure relief valve spring
10 Pressure relief valve plug
11 Cover
12 Pick-up pipe and strainer

2 Remove the pick-up pipe and strainer.

3 Note the position of the oil pump cover relative to the body, then remove the bolts and spring washers. Lift off the cover.

4 Mark the rotor faces so that they can be refitted the same way round, then remove them from the body.

5 Remove the pressure relief valve plug by piercing it with a punch and levering it out. Withdraw the spring and plunger.

6 Thoroughly clean all parts in petrol or paraffin and wipe dry using a non-fluffy rag. The necessary clearances may now be checked using a machined straight-edge (a good steel rule) and a set of feeler blades. The critical clearances are between the lobes of the centre rotor and convex faces of the outer rotor; between the rotor and pump body; and between both rotors and the end cover plate (endfloat). The clearances are given in the Specifications.

7 Endfloat may be measured by refitting the rotors, placing the straight-edge across the bottom of the pump and measuring the clearance between the two rotors and the straight-edge.

8 New rotors are only available as a pair. If the rotor-to-body clearance is excessive, a complete new pump should be fitted.

9 Commence reassembly by lubricating the relief valve plunger. Fit the plunger and spring.

10 Fit a new relief valve plug, flat side outwards and seat it with a drift, until it is flush with the pick-up pipe mating face.

11 Lubricate the rotors and fit them, observing the marks made when dismantling if applicable.

12 Fit the cover and secure it with the bolts and spring washers. Tighten the bolts to the specified torque.

13 Fit the pick-up pipe and strainer, using a new gasket.

14 Temporarily insert the driveshaft into the pump and make sure that the rotors turn freely.

15 A new or overhauled pump must be primed before fitting.

2.4 & 2.9 litre engines

16 Oil pump overhaul is essentially as described for the 2.8 litre engine, noting the differences in design of the components **(see illustrations)**.

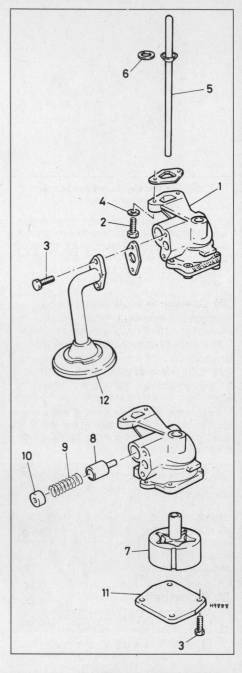

27.16a Removing the pick-up from the oil pump

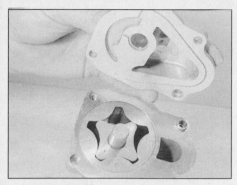

27.16b Removing the oil pump cover

31.1 Rear main bearing shell in the crankcase

31.6 Placing the crankshaft in position

28 Flywheel ring gear - examination and renovation

Refer to Part A, Section 33 of this Chapter.

29 Crankcase ventilation system - general information

The crankcase ventilation system is very simple. One hose joins the rear air inlet trunking to the oil filler cap, and another hose joins the left-hand rocker cover to the plenum chamber. Filtered (and metered) air passes through the oil filler cap into the engine, and is extracted, along with any other fumes, via the second hose. Refer to Chapter 1 for maintenance of the system.

30 Engine reassembly - general information

Refer to Part A, Section 35 of this Chapter but disregard the reference to new cylinder head bolts when these are of the conventional (hexagon-headed) type. Only Torx type bolts need to be renewed.

31 Crankshaft and main bearings - refitting

1 Wipe the bearing shell locations in the crankcase with a clean rag and fit the main

bearing upper half shells in position (see illustration).
2 Clean the main bearing shell locations and fit the half shells in the caps.

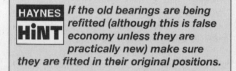

HAYNES HiNT *If the old bearings are being refitted (although this is false economy unless they are practically new) make sure they are fitted in their original positions.*

3 Fit the flanged shells to No 3 bearing.
4 Lubricate the shells and the main bearing journals with engine oil.
5 Lubricate a new rear oil seal and fit it to the end of the crankshaft, lips facing inwards.
6 Carefully place the crankshaft in position (see illustration).
7 Make sure that the surfaces are clean, then apply a film of sealant (Ford No A-70SX-19554-BA, or equivalent) to the mating faces of the crankcase and the rear main bearing cap.
8 Fit the bearing caps, with the arrows on the caps pointing to the front of the engine (see illustration).
9 Insert the main bearing cap bolts. The bolts for bearing caps No 2 and 3 have rounded heads, and are 14 mm (0.55 in) longer than those for caps 1 and 4.
10 Tighten the main bearing cap bolts progressively to the specified torque.
11 Make sure that the crankshaft is free to rotate. Some stiffness is to be expected with

new components, but there should be no tight spots or binding.
12 Press the crankshaft rear oil seal firmly against the rear main bearing.
13 Check the crankshaft endfloat, levering the crankshaft back and forth and inserting feeler blades between the crankshaft and No 3 main bearing (see illustration). Excessive endfloat can only be due to wear of the crankshaft or bearing shell flanges.
14 Coat the rear main bearing cap sealing wedges with sealant and press into position with a blunt screwdriver (see illustration). The rounded end of each wedge carries a red paint mark, which must face the bearing cap.

2C

32 Camshaft and intermediate plate - refitting

1 Slide the spacer ring onto the camshaft, chamfered side first. Refit the Woodruff key if it was removed.
2 Lubricate the camshaft bearings, the camshaft and thrust plate.
3 Carefully insert the camshaft from the front and fit the thrust plate and self-locking securing bolts. Tighten the bolts to the specified torque (see illustrations).
4 Fit the timing cover dowels and O-ring seals onto the crankcase. The chamfered end of the dowels must face outwards towards the timing cover (see illustration).
5 Ensure that the mating faces of the crankcase and front intermediate plate are

31.8 Main bearing cap markings - arrow points to front of engine

31.13 Checking crankshaft endfloat

31.14 Fitting the rear main bearing cap sealing wedges

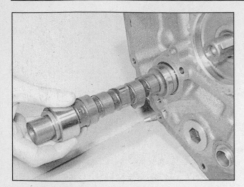

32.3a Fitting the camshaft into the cylinder block

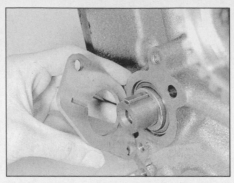

32.3b Fitting the camshaft thrust plate

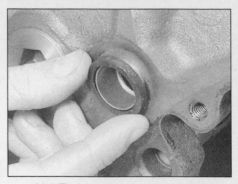

32.4 Timing cover dowel and seal

clean and then apply sealing compound to both faces. Position the gasket on the crankcase and then fit the intermediate plate **(see illustration)**.

6 Fit the two centre bolts finger-tight, then fit another two bolts temporarily for locating purposes. Tighten the centre securing bolts, then remove the temporarily fitted locating bolts.

7 If the engine is in the vehicle, reverse the steps taken to gain access to the camshaft.

33 Pistons and connecting rods - refitting

1 Wipe clean the bearing seats in the connecting rod and cap, and clean the backs of the bearing shells. Fit the shells to each rod

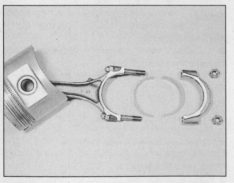

33.1 Piston, connecting rod and shells ready for assembly

and cap with the locating torques engaged in the corresponding cut-outs **(see illustration)**.

2 If the old bearings are nearly new and are being refitted, then ensure that they are refitted in their correct locations on the correct rods.

3 The pistons, complete with connecting rods, are fitted to their bores from the top of the block.

4 Locate the piston ring gaps in the following manner:

Top: 150° from one side of the oil control ring helical expander gap

Centre: 150° from the opposite side of the oil control ring helical expander gap

Bottom: oil control ring helical expander, opposite the marked piston front side

Oil control ring, intermediate rings, 25 mm (1 in) each side of the helical expander gap

5 Lubricate the piston and rings well with engine oil.

6 Fit a universal ring compressor and prepare to insert the first piston into the bore. Make sure it is the correct piston-connecting rod assembly for that particular bore, that the connecting rod is the correct way round and that the front of the piston (marked with an arrow or a notch) is to the front of the engine **(see illustrations)**.

7 Again lubricate the piston and the piston skirt, and insert the connecting rod and piston assembly into the cylinder bore up to the bottom of the piston ring compressor.

8 Gently but firmly tap the piston through the piston ring compressor and into the cylinder

32.5 Intermediate plate in position

bore, using the shaft of a hammer **(see illustration)**.

9 Generously lubricate the crankpin journals with engine oil and turn the crankshaft so that the crankpin is in the most advantageous position for the connecting rods to be drawn onto it.

10 Lubricate the bearing shell in the connecting rod cap. Fit the cap to the rod.

11 Lubricate the threads and contact faces of the big-end cap nuts. Fit the nuts and tighten them to the specified torque.

12 Check the crankshaft for freedom of rotation.

13 Repeat the operations for the other five pistons.

14 Refit the oil pump, the sump and the cylinder heads.

33.6a Piston with ring compressor fitted

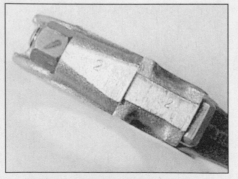

33.6b Connecting rod and cap carry cylinder numbers

33.8 Tapping a piston into the bore

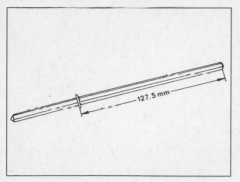

34.2 Oil pump driveshaft washer location

34.4 Fitting the oil pump driveshaft

34.5 Oil pump in position

34 Oil pump - refitting

1 Make sure that the oil pump and crankcase mating faces are clean.
2 Check that the washer on the oil pump driveshaft is located correctly (see illustration).
3 If a new or overhauled pump is being fitted, prime it by injecting oil into it and turning it by hand.
4 Insert the oil pump driveshaft into the block with the pointed end towards the distributor (see illustration).
5 Fit the assembled oil pump, using a new gasket. Insert the pump-to-block bolts and tighten them to the specified torque (see illustration).
6 Refit the sump.

35 Flywheel/driveplate and adapter plate - refitting

Refer to Part A, Section 40 of this Chapter.

36 Timing cover and drive - refitting

2.8 litre engines

1 Lubricate a new oil seal and fit it to the timing cover (see illustration).
2 If the Woodruff keys were removed from the camshaft and crankshaft, refit them.
3 Refit the crankshaft gear, if removed, using a length of tube to drive it home.
4 Position the camshaft and crankshaft so that their keyways are facing each other (see

illustration). Slide the camshaft gear onto the camshaft, rotating the shafts slightly if necessary so that the marks on the two gears are aligned. Remember that there are two marks on the crankshaft gear.
5 Fit the camshaft gear retaining bolt and washer (see illustration). Tighten the bolt to the specified torque.
6 Apply sealant to the mating faces of the timing cover and the intermediate plate.
7 Position a new gasket on the intermediate plate and fit the timing cover to the cylinder block (see illustrations).
8 Fit the timing cover bolts, but do not tighten them yet.
9 Oil the sealing face of the crankshaft pulley or damper. Fit the pulley/damper and the central bolt and washer, applying sealant to the inboard face of the washer (see illustration). Draw the pulley/damper into

2C

36.1 Timing cover oil seal

36.4 Crankshaft and camshaft gears correctly aligned

36.5 Camshaft gear washer and bolt

36.7a Timing cover gasket in position

36.7b Fitting the timing cover

36.9 Fitting the crankshaft pulley

36.15 Crankshaft and camshaft key and slot alignment

36.18 Fitting timing chain and sprockets

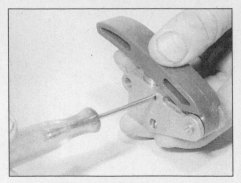

36.20 Releasing timing chain tensioner pawl

place by tightening the bolt; this will centralise the timing cover.

10 Tighten the timing cover bolts evenly to the specified torque.

11 Jam the crankshaft and tighten the pulley/ damper central bolt to the specified torque.

12 Refit the sump.

13 If the water pump was removed from the timing cover, refit it using a new gasket.

14 If the engine is still in the vehicle, reverse the steps taken to gain access.

2.4 & 2.9 litre engines

15 If the crankshaft sprocket was removed, check that the key slots in the end of the crankshaft and camshaft are in alignment at the closest point to each other **(see illustration)**.

16 Fit the crankshaft sprocket and chain guide.

17 Engage the chain around the teeth of the crankshaft sprocket.

18 Engage the camshaft sprocket in the upper loop of the chain in such a way so that the camshaft sprocket will slip onto the key slot when the timing mark is aligned with that on the crankshaft sprocket **(see illustration)**. Some trial and error may be involved in achieving this.

19 Lock the camshaft sprocket and tighten the retaining bolt to the specified torque.

20 Retract the chain tensioner. To do this, insert the plunger (bevelled side entering), then release the pawl with a small screwdriver pushed into the hole in the tensioner body **(see illustration)**.

21 Compress the plunger/slipper and retain it in the retracted position using a cable-tie or similar. New chain tensioners are supplied complete with a retainer **(see illustration)**.

22 Bolt the tensioner in position, at the same time removing the plunger retainer. Tighten the bolts to the specified torque.

23 Locate a new gasket on the front face of the engine.

24 Renew the timing cover oil seal and apply grease to the lips.

25 Fit the timing cover, centre it and align it with the sump mounting flange.

26 Although a special tool (21-137) is available for centring the cover, a piece of plastic pipe, or a socket of suitable thickness, will serve as an adequate substitute. Alternatively measure the space between the crankshaft nose and the timing cover damper recess at several different points and adjust the position of the cover until all the measurements are equal. A strip of metal 14.0 mm wide will serve as a gauge if calipers are not available **(see illustrations)**.

27 Tighten the timing cover bolts **(see illustration)** and fit the Woodruff key (where removed) for the vibration damper.

28 Apply jointing compound to the front and rear sump flange areas on the timing cover/cylinder block and rear main bearing cap. Make sure that the bearing surfaces are perfectly clean. Checking that the rear tabs of the gasket enter the recesses in the main bearing cap, locate a new sump gasket on the crankcase **(see illustration)**.

36.21 Timing chain tensioner retracted using a cable-tie

36.26a Measuring the crankshaft to timing cover gap

36.26b Using a socket to check the crankshaft to timing cover gap

36.27 Timing cover retaining bolts (arrowed)

36.28 Sump gasket at rear main bearing cap

36.39a Alternator drivebelt tensioner strap bolt

36.39b Power steering pump drivebelt tensioner bolt

37.3 Slide the sump gasket tab into the seal cut-out

29 Fit the sump and the retaining nuts and bolts. Tighten them progressively in two stages.
30 Oil the lip of the timing cover oil seal and the contact surface of the crankshaft damper.
31 Fit the damper to the crankshaft, being careful not to dislodge the Woodruff key. Draw the damper into position using the retaining bolt and washer.
32 Remove the bolt and apply sealant to the faces of the washer. Refit the bolt and washer then jam the starter gear ring teeth and tighten the bolt to the specified torque.
33 Refit the crankshaft pulley and tighten the retaining bolts to the specified torque.
34 Refit the crossmember side brackets and brake pipes.
35 Reconnect the engine mountings and remove the engine hoist or axle stands (see "Jacking").

36 Connect the steering shaft coupling with the steering wheel and front roadwheels in the straight-ahead position. Fit the pinch-bolt and tighten it to the specified torque.
37 Fit the starter motor and connect the leads.
38 Bolt the coolant distributor pipe to the timing cover.
39 Refit the alternator and power steering pump drivebelts and tension them **(see illustrations)**.
40 Fit the fan and radiator, connect all coolant hoses, and fit the radiator upper shroud.
41 Fit the air cleaner cover with attachments.
42 Fill the engine with oil and coolant and connect the battery.

37 Sump - refitting

2.8 litre engine

1 Clean the mating faces of the crankcase and sump. Ensure that the grooves in the seal carriers are clean.
2 Fit the rubber seals in the grooves.
3 Apply sealing compound on the crankcase and slide the tabs of the gasket under the cut-outs in the rubber seals **(see illustration)**.
4 Ensure that the gasket hole lines up with the holes in the gasket crankcase and fit the sump. Take care not to dislodge the gasket.
5 Fit the 24 securing bolts. Tighten them in the sequence shown to the Stage 1 specified torque starting at point A **(see illustration)**,

then to the Stage 2 torque starting at point B.
6 Fit the sump drain plug, using a new washer, and tighten it to the specified torque.
7 If the engine is in the vehicle, reverse the steps taken to gain access.

2.4 & 2.9 litre engines

8 Refer to paragraphs 28 to 29, Section 36.

38 Cylinder heads - refitting

2.8 litre engine

1 Lubricate the valve tappets with clean engine oil and insert them in the cylinder block. Ensure that they are fitted in their original locations **(see illustration)**.
2 Ensure that the mating faces of the cylinder block and the cylinder heads are clean.
3 Position the new cylinder head gaskets over the guide bushes on the cylinder block. Check that they are correctly located. The right and left-hand gaskets are different. The gaskets are marked FRONT TOP **(see illustration)**.
4 Carefully lower the cylinder heads onto the cylinder block. Oil the threads and contact faces of the cylinder head bolts and insert them into their holes.
5 Tighten the cylinder head bolts, in the correct order **(see illustration)**, to the Stage 1 specified torque. Repeat in the same order for Stages 2 and 3. Final tightening, when required, is done after warm-up.

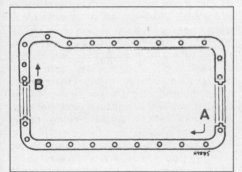
37.5 Sump bolt tightening sequence
For A and B see text

38.1 Fitting a tappet in the block

38.3 Cylinder head gasket markings

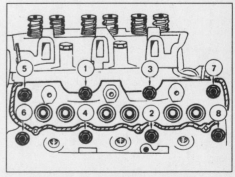
38.5 Cylinder head bolt tightening sequence

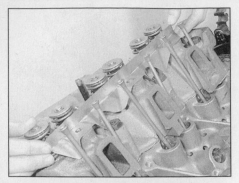

38.7a Fitting the pushrods and oil splash shields

38.7b Fitting an assembled rocker shaft

38.16 Tightening a cylinder head bolt using an angular tightening disc

6 Lubricate the pushrods with engine oil and insert them in the cylinder block.

7 Place the oil splash shields in position on the cylinder heads and fit the rocker shaft assemblies. Guide the rocker arm adjusting screws into the pushrod sockets **(see illustrations)**.

8 Tighten the rocker shaft securing bolts progressively to the specified torque.

9 Refit the inlet manifold, using a new gasket. Do not refit the rocker covers yet.

10 Adjust the valve clearances (Section 39).

11 Refit the spark plugs.

12 Refit the rocker covers, using new gaskets. The adhesive side of the gaskets should face the rocker cover.

13 If the engine is in the vehicle, reverse the preliminary steps.

2.4 & 2.9 litre engines

14 Refitting the cylinder heads to these engines is essentially a reversal of the removal procedure but also refer to information given for the 2.8 litre engine whilst noting the following points.

15 Always use new Torx type cylinder head bolts. Oil them and allow them to drain. When fitted the word OBEN should be visible on the new gaskets.

16 Tighten the bolts in the specified sequence (as for the 2.8 litre engine) to the correct torque. The final stage in the tightening procedure is by the angular method. Use a disc similar to the one shown or make a paint mark at the same point on each bolt head to ensure that each bolt is turned through exactly the same number of degrees **(see illustration)**.

17 As a result of the bolt tightening torque used and the elasticity of the bolts, no further tightening is required after the initial running-in period.

18 Apply jointing compound to the areas where the inlet manifold and cylinder heads meet and locate a new gasket in position. Make sure that it is the correct way around. Tighten the inlet manifold bolts to the specified torque and in the sequence shown **(see illustrations)**.

19 Check that No 1 piston is still at the firing point (12° BTDC) and fit the distributor.

20 Adjust the valve clearances.

21 Fit new rocker cover gaskets, peeling off the self-adhesive shield before sticking the gaskets to the covers. Note the aluminium spacers in the gaskets to prevent overtightening **(see illustration)**.

22 Use a new gasket at the plenum chamber and tighten the fixing bolts to the specified torque **(see illustration)**.

23 Refit the alternator and power steering pump (where removed) and tension the drivebelts.

24 Reconnect the fuel lines and secure them in position with new clips. Reconnect all coolant and vacuum hoses and electrical connectors. Refill the engine with coolant and reconnect the battery.

25 Switch on the ignition and bleed the fuel system by operating the vent valve on the fuel rail.

26 Run the engine up to normal operating temperature and then check the ignition timing.

38.18a Inlet manifold gasket correctly located

38.18b Fitting inlet manifold complete with fuel rail and injectors

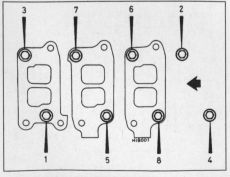

38.18c Inlet manifold tightening sequence
Arrow indicates the front of the engine

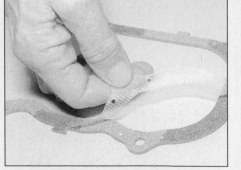

38.21 Peeling off rocker cover gasket protective shield

38.22 Lowering the plenum chamber into position

27 The inlet manifold bolts should be retightened to the specified torque in the correct sequence. This will mean disconnecting the air hoses from the throttle valve housing, the vacuum hose from the left-hand rocker cover, and the wiring connector from the idle speed control valve and throttle valve potentiometer. Remove the plenum chamber, place it to one side, then release the fuel rail bolts but **do not** disconnect the fuel pipes. It may also be necessary to remove the distributor again to gain access to one of the bolts.

39 Valve clearances - checking and adjustment

See Chapter 1, Section 23.

40 Ancillary components - refitting

1 Refer to Section 7 and refit the items listed.
2 If the oil cooler and its threaded bush were removed, refit them as follows **(see illustration)**.
3 Screw the new bush into the cylinder block. Apply Omnifit Activator "Rapid" (to Ford specification SSM-99B-9000-AA) to the exposed threads of the bush and to the inside of the threaded sleeve.
4 Apply one drop of Omnifit Sealant "300 Rapid" (to Ford specification SSM-4G-9003-AA) to the leading threads of the bush. **Do not** use more than one drop, otherwise sealant may get into the lubrication circuit.
5 Fit the cooler, using a new gasket, and secure with the threaded bush. Make sure that the coolant pipes are positioned at the correct angle **(see illustration)**, then tighten the threaded sleeve to the specified torque.
6 Fit a new oil filter element, oiling its sealing ring prior to installation. Tighten the filter approximately three-quarters of a turn beyond the point where the seal contacts the cooler face. Do not use any tool to tighten the filter.

41 Engine - refitting

Refer to Part A, Section 49, paragraphs 1 to 9 of this Chapter. Before starting the engine, refer to the following Section.

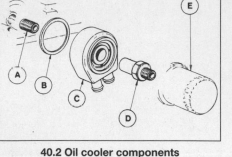

40.2 Oil cooler components

A Threaded bush   D Sleeve
B Seal   E Oil filter
C Cooler

42 Initial start-up after overhaul or major repair

1 Refer to Part A, Section 51 of this Chapter.
2 When conventional (hexagon-headed) cylinder head bolts are fitted, they must be re-tightened after the engine has warmed up. Proceed as follows.
3 Stop the engine and remove the rocker covers.
4 Working in the sequence used for tightening, slacken one cylinder head bolt a quarter turn, then re-tighten it to the Stage 4 specified torque. Repeat in sequence for all the cylinder head bolts.
5 Tighten the inlet manifold bolts.
6 Check the valve clearances.
7 Refit the rocker covers and other disturbed components.

43 Compression test - description and interpretation

1 When engine performance is down, or if misfiring occurs which cannot be attributed to the ignition or fuel system, a compression test can provide diagnostic clues. If the test is performed regularly it can give warning of trouble before any other symptoms become apparent.
2 The engine must be at operating temperature, the battery must be fully charged and the spark plugs must be removed. The services of an assistant will also be required.

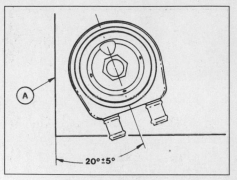

40.5 Oil cooler installation angle
A Rear face of cylinder block

3 Disable the ignition system by dismantling the coil LT feed. Fit the compression tester to No 1 spark plug hole. (The type of tester which screws into the spark plug hole is to be preferred.)
4 Have the assistant hold the throttle wide open and crank the engine on the starter. Record the highest reading obtained on the compression tester.
5 Repeat the test on the remaining cylinders, recording the pressure developed in each.
6 Desired pressures are given in the Specifications. If the pressure in any cylinder is low, introduce a teaspoonful of clean engine oil into the spark plug hole and repeat the test.
7 If the addition of oil temporarily improves the compression pressure, this indicates that bore or piston wear was responsible for the pressure loss. No improvement suggests that leaking or burnt valves, or a blown head gasket, may be to blame.
8 A low reading from two adjacent cylinders is almost certainly due to the head gasket between them having blown.
9 On completion of the test, refit the spark plugs and reconnect the coil LT feed.

2C

Notes

Chapter 3
Cooling, heating and ventilation systems

Contents

Degrees of difficulty

| **Easy,** suitable for novice with little experience | 🔧 | **Fairly easy,** suitable for beginner with some experience | 🔧 | **Fairly difficult,** suitable for competent DIY mechanic | 🔧 | **Difficult,** suitable for experienced DIY mechanic | 🔧 | **Very difficult,** suitable for expert DIY or professional | 🔧 |

3

Specifications

General

System type	Sealed, pressurised, thermostatically controlled
Fan type	Mechanical temperature-sensitive viscous clutch, or electric (DOHC)

Coolant

Type	See "Lubricants and fluids"
Capacity:	
SOHC	8.0 litres (14.1 pints) approx
DOHC:	
Carburettor models	7.9 litres (13.9 pints) approx
Fuel injection models	7.3 litres (12.8 pints) approx
V6	8.5 litres (15.0 pints) approx
Specific gravity at 45 to 50% antifreeze concentration	1.069 to 1.077

Expansion tank cap

Opening pressure:	
SOHC and V6	0.85 to 1.10 bar
DOHC	1.0 to 1.4 bar

Thermostat

Nominal rating:.	
SOHC	88°C (190°F)
DOHC	102°C (216°F)
V6	82°C (180°F)
Actual opening temperature:	
SOHC and DOHC	85° to 89°C (185° to 192°F)
V6	79° to 83°C (174° to 181°F)

Water pump drivebelt

Deflection	10 mm (0.4 in) approx under normal fingertip pressure at mid-point of longest run

Torque wrench settings

	Nm	lbf ft
Radiator lower mountings	8 to 12	6 to 9
Thermostat housing bolts:		
SOHC, DOHC and 2.8 litre V6	17 to 20	13 to 15
2.4 & 2.9 litre V6	7 to 10	5 to 7
Water pump bolts:		
SOHC, M8 bolts	17 to 21	13 to 16
SOHC, M10 bolts	35 to 42	26 to 31
DOHC	21 to 28	16 to 21
2.8 litre V6	9 to 13	7 to 10
2.4 & 2.9 litre V6	7 to 10	5 to 7
Water pump pulley bolts	21 to 26	16 to 19
Water pump/alternator drivebelt tensioner bolt (DOHC)	70 to 97	52 to 72
Fan-to-viscous clutch bolts:		
SOHC	8 to 10	6 to 7
V6	17 to 23	13 to 17
Fan shroud bolts	8 to 11	6 to 8
Cylinder block drain plug	21 to 25	16 to 18

1 General information and precautions

Cooling system

The cooling system is of pressurised type and includes a front mounted crossflow radiator, belt-driven water pump, temperature-sensitive thermo-viscous fan (on DOHC models, an electrically-operated cooling fan is fitted, operated by a switch in the thermostat housing), wax type thermostat, and an expansion and degas tank.

The radiator matrix is of copper and brass construction and the end tanks are of plastic. On automatic transmission models the right-hand side end tank incorporates the transmission oil cooler.

The thermostat is located behind the water outlet elbow at the front of the cylinder head on OHC models, and on the front of the water pump on V6 models. Its purpose is to ensure rapid engine warm-up by restricting the flow of coolant in the engine when cold, and also to assist in regulating the normal operating temperature of the engine.

The expansion tank incorporates a pressure cap which effectively pressurises the cooling system as the coolant temperature rises, thereby increasing the boiling point of the coolant. The tank also has a further degas function. Any accumulation of air bubbles in the coolant, in particular in the thermostat housing and the radiator, is returned to the tank and released in the air space thus maintaining the efficiency of the coolant.

On models fitted with the auxiliary warning system, the expansion tank contains a level sensor which operates a warning light if the coolant level falls significantly.

When the engine is started from cold, the water pump circulates coolant around the cylinder block, cylinder head(s) and inlet manifold. The warm coolant passes through the automatic choke housing (when applicable) and through the heater matrix before returning to the engine. As the coolant expands, the level in the expansion tank rises.

Circulation of coolant through the radiator is prevented while the thermostat is shut. When the coolant reaches the predetermined temperature the thermostat opens and hot water passes through the top hose to the top of the radiator. As the water circulates down through the radiator, it is cooled by the passage of air past the radiator when the car is in forward motion, supplemented by the action of the thermo-viscous fan when necessary. Having reached the bottom of the radiator, the water is now cool and the cycle is repeated. Circulation of water continues through the expansion tank, inlet manifold and heater at all times; the heater temperature control being by an air flap.

The thermo-viscous fan is controlled by the temperature of air behind the radiator. When the air temperature reaches a predetermined level, a bi-metallic coil commences to open a valve within the unit and silicon fluid is fed through a system of vanes. Half of the vanes are driven directly by the water pump and the remaining half are connected to the fan blades. The vanes are arranged so that drive is transmitted to the fan blades in relation to the drag or viscosity of the fluid, and this in turn depends on ambient temperature and engine speed. The fan is therefore only operated when required, and compared with direct drive type fan represents a considerable improvement in fuel economy, drivebelt wear and fan noise.

Air conditioning

Air conditioning is fitted as standard on Scorpio models and is optionally available on some other models. In conjunction with the heater, the system enables any reasonable air temperature to be achieved inside the car, it also reduces the humidity of the incoming air, aiding demisting even when cooling is not required.

The refrigeration side of the air conditioning system functions in a similar way to a domestic refrigerator. A compressor, belt-driven from the crankshaft pulley, draws refrigerant in its gaseous phase from an evaporator. The compressed refrigerant passes through a condenser where it loses heat and enters its liquid phase. After dehydration the refrigerant returns to the evaporator where it absorbs heat from air passing over the evaporator fins. The refrigerant becomes a gas again and the cycle is repeated.

Various subsidiary controls and sensors protect the system against excessive temperature and pressures. Additionally, engine idle speed is increased when the system is in use to compensate for the additional load imposed by the compressor.

Precautions

Antifreeze mixture

Antifreeze mixture is poisonous. Keep it out of reach of children and pets. Wash splashes off skin and clothing with plenty of water. Wash splashes off vehicle paintwork to avoid discolouration.

Antifreeze/water mixture must be renewed every two years to preserve its anti-corrosive properties. In climates where antifreeze protection is unnecessary, a corrosion inhibitor may be used instead - consult a Ford dealer. Never run the engine for long periods with plain water as coolant. Only use the specified antifreeze, as inferior brands may not contain the necessary corrosion inhibitors, or may break down at high temperatures. Antifreeze containing methanol is particularly to be avoided, as the methanol evaporates.

The specified mixture is 45 to 50% antifreeze and 50 to 55% clean soft water (by volume). Mix the required quantity in a clean container.

Air conditioning refrigerant

Although the refrigerant is not itself toxic, in the presence of a naked flame (or a lighted cigarette) it forms a highly toxic gas. Liquid refrigerant spilled on the skin will cause frostbite. If refrigerant enters the eyes, rinse them with a dilute solution of boric acid and seek medical advice immediately.

In view of the above points, and of the need for specialised equipment for evacuating and recharging the system, any work which requires the disconnection of a refrigerant line must be left to a specialist.

Do not allow refrigerant lines to be exposed to temperatures above 110°C (230°F) - eg during welding or paint drying operations and do not operate the air conditioning system if it is known to be short of refrigerant, or further damage may result.

5.2a Radiator top hose

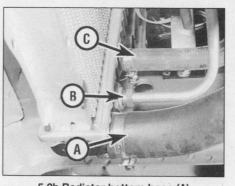

5.2b Radiator bottom hose (A)
Also shown are automatic transmission fluid cooler lower union (B) and hose to expansion tank (C)

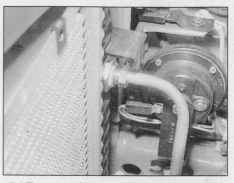

5.4 Transmission fluid cooler upper union

2 Cooling system - draining

See Chapter 1, Section 46.

3 Cooling system - flushing

See Chapter 1, Section 46.

4 Cooling system - filling

See Chapter 1, Section 46.

5 Radiator - removal and refitting

1 Drain the radiator. There is no need to drain the cylinder block. On DOHC engines the electric cooling fan assembly must be removed to gain the clearance to remove the radiator.
2 Disconnect the top and bottom hoses from the radiator by slackening the hose clips and pulling off the hoses with a twisting motion **(see illustrations)**. Do not use excessive force - the radiator side tanks are made of plastic.
3 On OHC models, disconnect the small hose running from the expansion tank to the radiator.
4 On automatic transmission models, clean around the transmission fluid cooler unions on the radiator and disconnect them **(see**

illustration**)**. Be prepared for fluid spillage; plug or cap the cooler lines to keep dirt out.
5 On models with air conditioning, disconnect the auxiliary fan thermo-switch. If the thermo-switch is mounted in the radiator, remove it.
6 Remove the upper half of the fan shroud by removing the two bolts and four clips **(see illustration)**.
7 Release the two radiator top mounting clips by pulling out the plastic plugs **(see illustration)**.
8 Raise and support the front of the vehicle. Support the radiator and remove the two bottom mounting bolts **(see illustration)**.
9 Carefully lower the radiator slightly to free the top mountings, then remove it from under the vehicle.
10 If a new radiator is being fitted, transfer the fan shrouds and mountings from the old one.
11 Refit by reversing the removal operations, then refill the cooling system.
12 On automatic transmission models, check the transmission fluid level.

6 Radiator - inspection and repair

1 If the radiator has been removed because of suspected blockage, reverse-flush it.
2 Clean dirt and debris from the radiator fins, using an air jet, or water and a soft brush. Be careful not to damage the fins, or cut your fingers.

3 A radiator specialist can perform a "flow test" on the radiator to establish whether an internal blockage exists.
4 A leaking radiator must be referred to a specialist for permanent repair. Do not attempt to weld or solder a leaking radiator, as damage to the plastic parts may result.
5 In an emergency, minor leaks from the radiator can be cured by using a radiator sealant while the radiator is *in situ*.

7 Thermostat - removal and refitting

SOHC engines

1 Disconnect the battery negative lead.
2 Drain the cooling system. As it is not necessary to completely drain the radiator, the bottom hose can be disconnected from the water pump.
3 Disconnect the top hose from the thermostat housing at the front of the cylinder head (see illustration).
4 Unscrew the bolts and remove the housing and gasket **(see illustration)**.
5 Using a screwdriver, prise the retaining clip from the housing, and extract the thermostat and sealing ring **(see illustrations)**.
6 Clean the thermostat housing and cylinder head mating surfaces. Obtain a new gasket for reassembly, and if necessary a new sealing ring too.
7 Refit by reversing the removal operations.

3

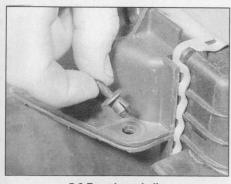

5.6 Fan shroud clip

5.7 Pull out the plug to release the radiator top mounting

5.8 One of the radiator bottom mounting bolts (arrowed)

7.3 Top hose attachment to the thermostat housing

7.4 Removing the thermostat housing

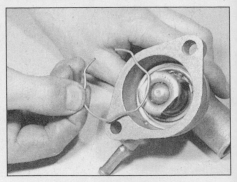

7.5a Remove the retaining clip . . .

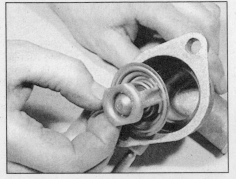

7.5b . . . extract the thermostat . . .

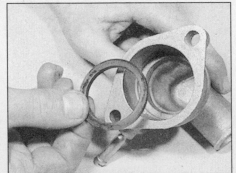

7.5c . . . and the sealing ring

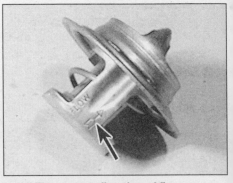

7.7 Thermostat direction of flow arrow

7.12a Disconnecting the coolant hoses . . .

Make sure that the thermostat is the right way round - the wax capsule fits into the cylinder head, with the direction of flow arrow facing forwards **(see illustration)**.
8 Refill the cooling system.

DOHC engines

9 Disconnect the battery negative lead.
10 Drain the cooling system.
11 On fuel-injection models, for access to the thermostat housing, loosen the clips and remove the air inlet tube which connects the plenum chamber to the inlet manifold.
12 Disconnect the coolant hoses from the thermostat housing **(see illustrations)**.
13 Disconnect the wiring plug from the cooling fan switch mounted in the thermostat housing **(see illustration)**.
14 Unscrew the three securing bolts, and

withdraw the thermostat housing **(see illustration)**.
15 Manoeuvre the thermostat away from the inlet manifold and recover the O-ring. If it is necessary to prise the thermostat out, take care not to damage the surface of the housing in the inlet manifold.
16 Refitting is a reversal of removal, bearing in mind the following points:
a) Ensure that the O-ring seal is correctly fitted around the edge of the thermostat.
b) When fitting the thermostat to the inlet manifold ensure that the relief valve is located in the 12 o'clock position **(see illustration)**.
c) Tighten the thermostat housing bolts to the specified torque.
d) Refill the cooling system.

7.12b . . . from the thermostat housing

7.13 Disconnect the cooling fan switch wiring plug . . .

7.14 . . . and remove the thermostat housing

7.16 Thermostat relief valve (arrowed) positioned in the 12 o'clock position

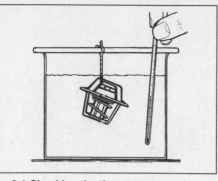

8.1 Checking the thermostat opening temperature

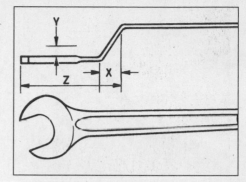

9.3a Dimensions of spanner for undoing fan clutch nut. Spanner thickness must not exceed 5 mm (0.2 in)

X = 10 mm (0.4 in)   Z = 50 mm (2.0 in)
Y = 10 mm (0.4 in)

V6 engines

17 The thermostat is removed in the course of water pump removal.

8 Thermostat - testing

1 A rough test of the thermostat may be made by suspending it with a piece of string in a saucepan full of water (see illustration). Bring the water to the boil. The thermostat most open by the time the water boils. If not, renew it.
2 If a thermometer is available, the precise opening temperature of the thermostat may be determined and compared with that given in the Specifications.
3 A thermostat which fails to close as the water cools must also be renewed.

9 Viscous-coupled fan - removal and refitting

1 Disconnect the battery negative lead.
2 Remove the upper half of the fan shroud (two bolts, four clips).
3 Undo the nut which secures the fan clutch to the water pump. **This nut has a left-hand thread,** ie it is undone in a clockwise direction. A thin cranked spanner, 32 mm (OHC) or 36 mm (V6) AF is needed (see illustration); alternatively, if two of the pulley bolts are removed, a normal thickness or even an

adjustable spanner can be used (see illustrations). Tap the spanner with a mallet if need be to release the nut.

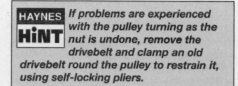

HAYNES HINT *If problems are experienced with the pulley turning as the nut is undone, remove the drivebelt and clamp an old drivebelt round the pulley to restrain it, using self-locking pliers.*

4 The fan can now be unbolted from the viscous clutch if required. Do not overtighten the bolts when refitting.
5 Refit by reversing the removal operations.

10 Electric cooling fan(s) - removal and refitting

1 Disconnect the battery negative lead.
2 To provide additional clearance when removing the cooling fan shroud assembly (which is removed from below the vehicle), apply the handbrake, then jack up the front of the vehicle and support it securely on axle stands (see "Jacking").
3 Disconnect the wiring plug(s) from the motor(s), and where applicable, unclip the wiring from the fan shroud.
4 Unclip the expansion tank hose from the fan shroud.
5 Unscrew the two nuts securing the fan shroud to the top of the radiator, then tilt the top of the

shroud away from the radiator, and lift the shroud to release the lower securing clips. Withdraw the assembly from below the vehicle.
6 To remove the fan blades, prise the securing clip from the end of the motor shaft.
7 The motor can be separated from the fan shroud by unscrewing the three securing nuts and bolts.
8 Note that two cooling fans may be fitted, depending on model. Both fans are secured to the shroud in the same manner.
9 Refitting is a reversal of removal, but when fitting the fan blades, ensure that the drive dog on the motor shaft engages with the slot in the rear of the fan blades.

11 Water pump - removal and refitting

SOHC engines

1 Disconnect the battery negative lead.
2 Drain the cooling system.
3 Remove the fan and viscous coupling.
4 If not already done, remove the pump drivebelt(s), then unbolt and remove the water pump pulley (see illustration).
5 Disconnect the radiator bottom hose and the heater return hose from the pump.
6 Remove the timing belt cover, which is secured by three bolts.

3

9.3b Undoing the viscous fan clutch nut

9.3c Removing the fan and clutch

11.4 Undoing a water pump pulley bolt

11.7a This water pump bolt also secures the alternator strap

11.7b Water pump removed

11.9 Fitting a new gasket to the water pump

7 Remove the three securing bolts and withdraw the water pump (see illustrations).
8 A leaking, noisy or otherwise defective pump must be renewed.
9 Clean the mating faces and obtain a new gasket for reassembly (see illustration).
10 Refit by reversing the removal operation, tightening all fastenings to the correct torque (where specified).
11 Refill the cooling system.

DOHC engines

12 Disconnect the battery negative lead.
13 On fuel-injection models, for access to the water pump, remove the air inlet hose, plenum chamber, and air cleaner lid as an assembly.
14 Drain the cooling system.
15 Remove the water pump/alternator drivebelt.

11.17 Withdrawing the water pump from the cylinder block (engine removed)

11.18 On refitting, renew the water pump O-ring (arrowed)

16 If the pump pulley is to be removed, it is easiest to do this with the pump in position as follows. Prevent the pulley from rotating using a strap wrench (which can be improvised using an old drivebelt and a large socket and wrench), and unscrew the four pulley securing bolts. Withdraw the pulley.
17 Position a suitable container beneath the water pump to catch the coolant which will be released as the pump is removed, then unscrew the five securing bolts and withdraw the pump from the housing in the cylinder block (see illustration). Recover the O-ring seal and discard it; a new one must be used on refitting.
18 Refitting is a reversal of removal, bearing in mind the following points:
a) Ensure that the mating faces of the water pump and cylinder block are clean and fit a new O-ring to the pump (see illustration).
b) Tighten the water pump bolts and where applicable the pump pulley bolts to the specified torque.
c) On completion refill the cooling system.
19 Note that on models up to May 1990, the coolant hoses were connected to the water pump housing as shown (see illustration).
20 On models from May 1990, the heater hose (A) and the expansion tank hose (B) connections were swapped over.

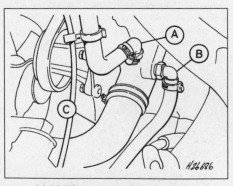

11.19 Water pump housing hose connections
A Heater hose connection - up to May 1990
B Expansion tank hose connection - up to May 1990
C Bottom radiator hose

21 If the hoses are disconnected on earlier models, such as during engine removal, they should be reconnected as on later models, ie connect the heater hose to connection B and connect the expansion tank hose to connection A. This will reduce the possibility of noises from the heater matrix due to air in the system.

V6 engines

22 Disconnect the battery negative lead.
23 Drain the cooling system.
24 Remove the fan and viscous coupling.
25 If not already done, remove the pump drivebelt(s), then unbolt and remove the water pump pulley.
26 Disconnect the radiator bottom hose and the heater return hose from the thermostat housing.
27 Remove the three bolts which secure the thermostat housing to the water pump. Remove the housing and the thermostat.
28 Remove the twelve securing bolts and withdraw the water pump. Note that on some models it will be necessary to remove the crankshaft pulley and damper to gain access to the lower water pump bolts (see illustration).
29 A leaking, noisy or otherwise defective pump must be renewed.
30 Clean the mating faces and obtain a new gasket for reassembly. Use a new thermostat housing gasket also.
31 Refit by reversing the removal operation, tightening all fastenings to the correct torque (where specified).
32 Refill the cooling system.

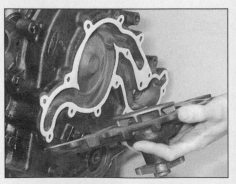

11.28 Removing the water pump

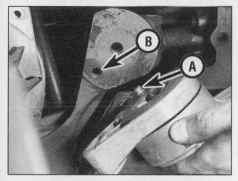

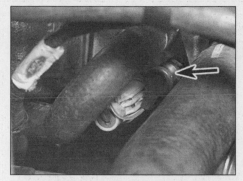

13.4 On refitting, ensure the drivebelt tensioner lug (A) engages with hole in the mounting bracket (B)

15.1a Temperature gauge sender (manifold removed)

15.1b Temperature gauge sender unit location (arrowed)

12 Water pump/alternator drivebelt(s) - inspection, renewal and adjustment

See Chapter 1, Section 21.

13 Water pump/alternator drivebelt tensioner - removal and refitting

1 On 2.0 litre DOHC engines only, remove the water pump/alternator drivebelt as described in the previous Section.
2 Loosen the alternator lower mounting through-bolt, then remove the alternator upper mounting bolt, and swing the alternator away from the engine.
3 Unscrew the central securing bolt, and withdraw the drivebelt tensioner assembly.
4 Commence refitting by positioning the tensioner on the cylinder block, ensuring that the lug on the rear of the tensioner bracket engages with the corresponding hole in the cylinder block (see illustration). Tighten the securing bolt.
5 Swing the alternator into position to align the upper mounting bolt hole with the corresponding hole in the drivebelt tensioner assembly, then refit and tighten the upper mounting bolt, then the lower throughbolt.
6 Check the full length of the drivebelt for cracks and deterioration and renew if necessary.
7 Fit the drivebelt using a reversal of the removal procedure, and release the tensioner to tension the drivebelt.

14 Expansion tank - removal and refitting

1 Disconnect the battery negative lead.
2 Depressurize the cooling system by unscrewing the expansion tank cap. **Take precautions against scalding if the system is hot.**
3 Slacken the hose clips on all the hoses which are connected to the tank. Pull off and plug those hoses which are above the waterline.

4 Remove the two screws which secure the tank. Tilt the tank so that the coolant lies away from the outlets, then disconnect and plug the remaining hose.
5 Disconnect the coolant level sensor, when fitted, and remove the tank.
6 Refit by reversing the removal operations. Top-up the cooling system on completion.

15 Temperature gauge sender - removal and refitting

1 The temperature gauge sender is located towards the front of the engine. On SOHC models it is just below the inlet manifold (see illustration); on V6 models it is just below the top hose connection on the front of the left-hand cylinder head, and on DOHC models it is located at the front of the inlet manifold (see illustration).
2 Slacken the expansion tank cap to release pressure in the cooling system, **taking precautions against scalding if the system is hot.** Tighten the cap again to minimise coolant loss.
3 Disconnect the wiring from the sender unit. Unscrew and remove it, being prepared for some coolant spillage.
4 Smear sealant on the sender unit threads before refitting, then insert and tighten it. Reconnect the wiring.
5 Top-up the cooling system if necessary, then run the engine and check the operation of the temperature gauge.

17.4 Heater control cable clip (arrowed) viewed through windscreen

16 Cooling fan switch - removal and refitting

The cooling fan switch is located in the end of the thermostat housing.
Removal and refitting of the switch is as described for the temperature gauge sender in the previous Section.

17 Heater controls - removal and refitting

Models before April 1992

Front

1 Disconnect the battery negative lead.
2 Remove the instrument cluster (Chapter 13).
3 Remove the facia top (Chapter 12).
4 Unclip the two control cables from the control levers (see illustration).
5 On air conditioned models, disconnect the hoses from the vacuum switch.
6 Remove the four screws which secure the heater control assembly. Withdraw the assembly from the facia.
7 When refitting, secure the control assembly with the four screws. Reconnect the vacuum switch (when applicable) and the control cables. Adjust the control cables if necessary by altering the positions of the cable clips.
8 When satisfied with the operation of the cables, refit the other disturbed components.

Rear

9 Remove the centre console (Chapter 12).
10 Unclip the control cables and remove the control unit.
11 Refit in the reverse order to removal.

Models from April 1992

12 Undo the two instrument panel surround retaining screws, then carefully release the retaining clips and remove the surround from the facia.
13 Pull off the three knobs from the heater and ventilation controls to gain access to the two hidden central vent panel retaining screws. Slacken and remove the four panel retaining screws and partially withdraw the

3

17.14 Heater control panel retaining screws (arrowed)

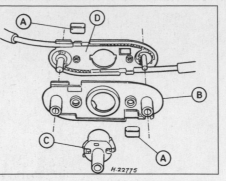

17.15 Exploded view of the heater control panel

A Control cable retaining clips
B Cover
C Fan switch
D Base plate

18.14 Rear heater control cable at nozzle

panel. Disconnect the wiring connectors from the heated window switches and fuel computer (where fitted) and remove the panel from the car.

14 Undo the two retaining screws then manoeuvre the control panel out of the facia and disconnect the wiring connector **(see illustration)**.

15 Unclip the central fan switch from the panel then, using a small flat-bladed screwdriver, bend back the retaining tabs and remove the cover from the panel base plate **(see illustration)**.

16 Cut the cable retaining clips then release the cables from the toothed guides and remove the base plate.

17 Refitting is a reversal of the removal procedure securing the cables to the base plate using new retaining clips.

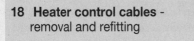

18 Heater control cables - removal and refitting

Models before April 1992

Front

1 Remove the heater controls as described in the previous Section.

2 Remove the centre console as described in Chapter 12. Also remove the console bracket and the gear lever inner gaiter.

3 Unclip the under-dash trim on both sides. Remove the glovebox lid.

4 Remove the radio (Chapter 13).

5 Remove the ABS and (when applicable) the EEC IV modules (Chapters 10 and 13).

6 Remove the remaining lower trim on the passenger side to expose the heater casing.

7 Remove the two securing screws and release the cables from the heater.

8 When refitting, place the air distribution and temperature control valve levers in their uppermost positions, then connect the cables.

9 The remainder of refitting is a reversal of the removal procedure.

Rear

10 Remove the centre console (Chapter 12).

11 Remove the front seat on the side concerned. Also remove the rear seat cushion.

12 Remove the front seat belt lower anchor bolt.

13 Remove the front scuff plate, which is secured by three screws. Remove the front screw from the rear scuff plate.

14 Roll back the front carpet from the scuff plates to expose the heater cable. Release the cable from its ties and disconnect it from the control unit and the nozzle **(see illustration)**.

15 Refit by reversing the removal operations.

Models from April 1992

16 Remove the facia undercovers, the right-hand lower facia panel and the glovebox.

17 Undo the two retaining nuts, then release the retaining clips and remove the trim panel from the glovebox aperture.

18 Remove the heater control panel.

19 Slacken and remove the control cable retaining screws then release the retaining clips (one screw and one clip for each cable). Detach the cables from the heater assembly and withdraw them from the facia whilst noting the correct routing **(see illustration)**.

20 Refitting is a reverse of the removal procedure noting the following points.

a) Ensure that the cables are correctly routed prior to connecting them to the heater housing.

b) Prior to refitting the glovebox aperture trim panel, check that the panel controls function correctly and that the cables move the relevant operating lever smoothly from the fully open to the fully closed position without any trace of undue friction.

19 Heater assembly - removal and refitting

Models before April 1992

1 Disconnect the battery negative lead.

2 Depressurise the cooling system by slackening the expansion tank cap. Take precautions against scalding if the system is hot.

3 Disconnect the two heater hoses from the stubs on the bulkhead. Be prepared for some coolant spillage: catch the coolant in a clean container if it is fit for re-use. Plug the hoses, or tie them up with their open ends raised.

4 Expel as much coolant as possible from the heater matrix by blowing through it.

5 Remove the matrix connector plate and gasket from the bulkhead.

6 Working inside the vehicle, remove the centre console and other trim as described for access to the heater control cables.

7 Remove the instrument cluster surround, which is secured by four screws. Also pull out the heater louvre panel.

8 Remove the facia panel top, which is secured by five screws and four clips.

9 Detach the air trunking from the heater casing. Release the trunking from the bulkhead when necessary.

10 Remove the two nuts which secure the heater unit. Pull the unit into the vehicle until the pipe stubs are clear of the bulkhead, then remove it sideways. Be prepared for coolant spillage.

11 Check the condition of the foam gasket on the bulkhead and renew it if necessary.

12 Refit by reversing the removal operations.

13 Top-up the cooling system on completion, and check the level again after the engine has been run.

Models from April 1992

14 Disconnect the battery negative terminal.

15 Drain the cooling system.

18.19 Heater control cable retaining screw and clip (arrowed)

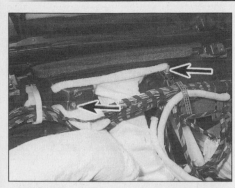

19.19 Release the facia wiring loom from the bulkhead to gain access to the demister nozzle retaining nut and screw (arrowed)

16 Locate the heater matrix feed and return hoses on the engine compartment bulkhead. Slacken the retaining clips and disconnect both hoses from the matrix unions. Be prepared for some coolant spillage. Plug the matrix unions to prevent residual coolant being spilt as the assembly is removed.
17 Slacken and remove the two retaining screws then remove the matrix cover plate and gasket from the bulkhead; discard the gasket as a new one should be used on refitting.
18 Remove the facia panel.
19 Release the facia wiring loom from the bulkhead to gain access to the demister nozzle fasteners **(see illustration)**.
20 Remove the retaining nut and screw then detach each windscreen demister nozzle from the heater assembly. Undo the two retaining nuts and detach the centre face level nozzle from the heater.
21 Slacken and remove the two retaining nuts then detach the right-hand face level nozzle from the heater and remove it from the vehicle. Repeat the procedure for the left-hand nozzle.
22 To detach each rear footwell nozzle from the heater unit, remove the pin from the nozzle retaining clip whilst supporting the outer part of the retaining clip from the rear **(see illustration)**. Note: *If the rear of the clip is not supported when the pin is removed it will drop down into the nozzle. To retrieve the clip will require the removal of the vent which first requires the front seat to be removed and carpet lifted.*
23 Disconnect the wiring connector from the heater control panel.
24 Undo the two nuts securing the heater assembly to the bulkhead then carefully manoeuvre the assembly out of the vehicle whilst being prepared for the possibility of coolant spillage from the matrix unions.
25 Refitting is a reverse of the removal procedure noting the following points.
a) *Tighten all retaining nuts and screws securely and ensure that all nozzles are securely connected to the heater assembly so that there are no air gaps or leaks.*

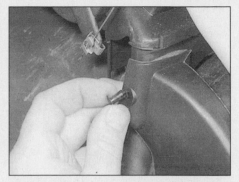

19.22 Detach the rear footwell nozzles from the heater assembly

b) *Check the operation of all heater cables before refitting the facia, ensuring that the relevant component moves smoothly from the fully open to the fully closed position.*
c) *Ensure that the heater hoses are correctly reconnected and are securely held by the retaining clips.*
d) *Use a new gasket when refitting the matrix cover plate.*
e) *Refill the cooling system.*

20 Heater matrix - dismantling and reassembly

1 Remove the heater assembly as described in the previous Section.
2 Remove the two screws which secure the heater matrix. Withdraw the matrix.
3 If the matrix is leaking it is best to obtain a new or reconditioned unit; home repairs are seldom successful.

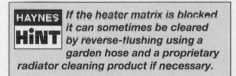

HAYNES HINT *If the heater matrix is blocked it can sometimes be cleared by reverse-flushing using a garden hose and a proprietary radiator cleaning product if necessary.*

4 To dismantle, release the clips which secure the casing halves together by using a screwdriver. Carefully prise the halves apart and separate them.
5 Remove the flap valves and operating levers from the casing halves, noting how they are fitted for reference when reassembling.
6 Flush the matrix with clean water to remove any debris.
7 Reassembly is a reversal of dismantling. Additional clips may be needed to secure the casing halves once they have been separated.

21 Heater coolant valve - removal and refitting

1 Drain the cooling system.
2 Noting the correct fitted positions, slacken the retaining clips and disconnect the coolant hoses from the valve.
3 Disconnect the vacuum pipe from the top of the valve then unclip the valve and remove it from the retaining bracket.
4 Refitting is a reverse of the removal procedure ensuring that the coolant hoses are reconnected to their original unions on the valve and are securely held in position with the retaining clips.

22 Air conditioning system - component renewal

1 Only those items which can be renewed without discharging the system are described here. Other items must be dealt with by a Ford dealer or air conditioning specialist **(see illustration)**.

Compressor drivebelt

2 Disconnect the battery earth lead.
3 On OHC engines, remove the radiator cooling fan.
4 Slacken the compressor strap and pivot bolts **(see illustration)**, move the compressor

3

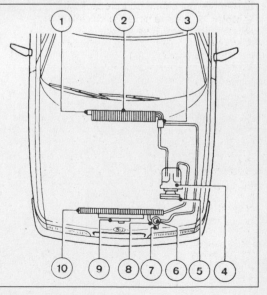

22.1 Air conditioning system component locations

1 De-ice thermostat
2 Evaporator
3 Expansion valve
4 Compressor
5 Compressor clutch
6 Pressure switch
7 Sight glass
8 Dehydrator
9 Cooling fan
10 Condenser

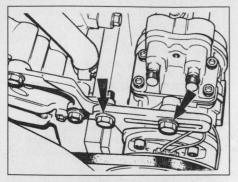

22.4 Air conditioning compressor adjuster strap bolts (arrowed)

towards the engine and remove the old drivebelt.

5 Fit the new drivebelt, position the compressor to achieve the correct belt tension and tighten the strap and pivot bolts.

6 Refit and secure the fan, when applicable, and reconnect the battery.

7 Recheck the belt tension after it has run for at least 10 minutes under load.

Condenser fan and motor

8 Disconnect the battery earth lead and remove the radiator grille.

9 Disconnect the fan wiring connector at the right-hand side of the condenser.

10 Remove the three securing bolts and remove the fan and motor **(see illustration)**. Turn the frame to position the fan wiring on the dehydrator side to avoid damaging the wiring. Take care also not to damage the condenser fins or tube.

11 Unclip the fan guard from the top of the frame.

12 To remove the fan blades from the motor, remove the retaining nut and circlip. **The nut has a left-hand thread** ie it is undone **clockwise**.

13 With the blades removed, the motor can be unscrewed from the frame.

14 Reassemble and refit in the reverse order of dismantling and removal.

De-ice thermostat

15 Disconnect the battery negative lead.

16 Disconnect the vacuum hoses from the plenum chamber cover. Pull off the rubber seal and remove the plenum chamber cover; it is secured by four screws and one nut.

17 Disconnect the thermostat from the evaporator casing and remove it. Also remove the thermostat probe.

18 Refit by reversing the removal operations.

Heater water valve

19 The heater water valve used with air conditioning is vacuum-operated. It is located on the right-hand side of the engine bay, near the bulkhead.

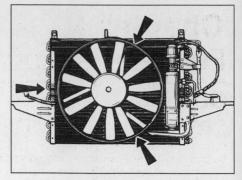

22.10 Condenser fan securing bolts (arrowed)

20 Drain the cooling system.

21 Slacken the hose clips and detach the coolant hoses from the valve, noting how they are connected.

22 Disconnect the vacuum hose from the top of the valve.

23 Unclip the valve from its bracket and remove it.

24 Refit by reversing the removal operations. Refill the cooling system.

Chapter 4
Fuel and exhaust systems

Contents

4

Degrees of difficulty

Easy, suitable for novice with little experience	**Fairly easy,** suitable for beginner with some experience	**Fairly difficult,** suitable for competent DIY mechanic	**Difficult,** suitable for experienced DIY mechanic	**Very difficult,** suitable for expert DIY or professional

Specifications

General

System type:
1.8 litre	Twin choke Pierburg carburettor
2.0 litre carburettor:	
SOHC	Twin choke Weber 2V carburettor
DOHC	Twin choke Weber 2V TLD carburettor
All models with fuel injection	Multi-point fuel-injection system controlled by EEC IV engine management system
Fuel tank capacity	70 litres (15.4 gallons) approx
Fuel grade*:	
Leaded	97 octane RON (UK 4-star)
Unleaded	95 octane RON (Premium)

* Models fitted with a catalytic converter must be operated on unleaded fuel at all times. **Do not** use leaded fuel as the catalyst will be destroyed.

Idle speed:	
1.8 litre	800 ± 20 rpm
2.0 litre carburettor:	
SOHC*	800 or 875 rpm
DOHC:	
Manual gearbox*	850 ± 25 rpm
Automatic transmission*	875 ± 25 rpm
2.0 litre fuel-injection:	
SOHC*	800 or 875 rpm
DOHC*	875 ± 50 rpm

Idle speed (continued):
2.4 litre*	850 ± 50 rpm
2.8 litre*	850 rpm
2.9 litre*	850 ± 50 rpm

Idle mixture (CO) level:
1.8 litre	1.3%
2.0 litre carburettor:	
SOHC	0.75 to 1.50%
DOHC	1.0 ± 0.25%
2.0 litre fuel-injection:	
SOHC	0.5 to 1.0%
DOHC - models without catalytic converter	1.0 to 1.5%
2.4 litre - models without a catalytic converter	0.5 to 1.0 %
2.8 litre	0.5 to 1.0%
2.9 litre - models without a catalytic converter	0.5 to 1.0 %

Electronically controlled

Pierburg 2V carburettor

Venturi diameter:
Primary	23 mm
Secondary	26 mm

Jet sizes:
Idle (fuel)	45
Idle (air bleed)	115
Primary main	107.5
Secondary main	130

Adjustments:
Fast idle speed (engine warm)	1800 ± 100 rpm (on second highest step of cam)
Choke pull-down	3 mm (0.12 in)
Throttle damper setting	2 ± 0.5 mm (0.08 ± 0.02 in)
Float level	Not adjustable
Automatic choke setting	Index

Weber 2V carburettor

	Primary	Secondary
Barrel diameter	30 mm	34 mm
Venturi diameter:		
85HFCA and -DA	25 mm	27 mm
85HFGA, -HA, -MA and -NA	23 mm	25 mm
Jet sizes - 85HFCA:		
Main jet	112	135
Air correction jet	165	150
Emulsion tube	F22	F22
Idle jet	45	45
Jet sizes - 85HFDA:		
Main jet	110	135
Air correction jet	160	150
Emulsion tube	F22	F22
Idle jet	45	45
Jet sizes - 85HFGA and -HA:		
Main jet	107	125
Air correction jet	180	160
Emulsion tube	F59	F59
Idle jet	45	50
Jet sizes - 85HFMA:		
Main jet	105	130
Air correction jet	200	160
Emulsion tube	F59	F59
Idle jet	45	50
Jet sizes - 85HFNA:		
Main jet	110	125
Air correction jet	180	160
Emulsion tube	F59	F59
Idle jet	45	50
Adjustments:		
Choke pull-down (maximum):		
85HFCA	9.0 mm (0.35 in)	
85HFDA	8.0 mm (0.32 in)	
All others	7.5 mm (0.30 in)	
Bi-metal housing setting:		
85 HFCA, -DA, -HA and -MA	Index	
85HFGA and -NA	3 mm (0.12 in) lean	
Float level	7.5 to 8.5 mm (0.30 to 0.34 in)	

Weber 2V TLD carburettor	Primary	Secondary
Venturi diameter	23.0 mm	25.0 mm
Main jet:		
Manual gearbox	115	157
Automatic transmission	112	157
Air correction jet:		
Manual gearbox	175	145
Automatic transmission	210	145
Emulsion tube:		
Manual gearbox	F114	F3
Automatic transmission	210	145
Fast Idle speed	1800 ± 50 rpm	
Float level (with gasket)	29.0 ± 0.5 mm	
Automatic choke vacuum pull-down	5.0 ± 0.5 mm	
Throttle kicker speed (see text):		
Manual gearbox	2000 ± 50 rpm	
Automatic transmission	2200 ± 50 rpm	

Fuel-injection system

Make	Bosch
Fuel pump type	Roller cell, electric
Fuel pump output pressure	Greater than 5 bar at 12 volts, no flow
System control pressure	2.5 bar

Torque wrench settings

	Nm	lbf ft
Inlet manifold:		
SOHC	17 to 21	13 to 16
DOHC	20 to 24	15 to 18
V6:		
Stage 1	4 to 8	3 to 6
Stage 2	8 to 15	6 to 11
Stage 3	15 to 21	11 to 16
Stage 4	21 to 25	16 to 18
Stage 5 (after warm-up)	21 to 25	16 to 18
Exhaust manifold:		
OHC	21 to 25	16 to 18
V6	25 to 30	18 to 22
Plenum chamber to inlet manifold:		
2.8 litre	7 to 10	5 to 7
2.4 & 2.9 litre	20 to 25	15 to 18
Carburettor bolts (DOHC)	8 to 10	6 to 7
Fuel pump bolts (mechanical pump)	14 to 18	10 to 13
Fuel pipe to fuel-injection pressure regulator:		
SOHC	15 to 20	11 to 15
2.8 litre	10 to 12	7 to 9
Pressure regulator base nut/bolt:		
SOHC	20 to 25	15 to 18
DOHC	9 to 12	7 to 9
V6:		
2.8 litre	15 to 20	11 to 15
2.4 & 2.9 litre	9 to 11	7 to 8
Fuel rail bolts:		
SOHC	9 to 11	7 to 8
DOHC	21 to 26	15 to 19
Exhaust downpipe flange nuts	35 to 40	26 to 30
Exhaust clamps and U-bolts	38 to 45	28 to 33
Exhaust gas oxygen sensor	50 to 70	37 to 52
Throttle body bolts	9 to 11	7 to 8
Idle speed control valve bolts	9 to 11	7 to 8
Fuel filter unions	14 to 20	10 to 15
Fuel rail temperature sensor (DOHC)	8 to 11	6 to 8
Fuel rail temperature switch (2.4 & 2.9 litre)	20 to 25	15 to 18
HEGO sensor	50 to 70	37 to 52

1 General information and precautions

All models are fitted with a rear-mounted fuel tank. Fuel is conveyed from the tank by a mechanical or electrical fuel pump, according to model and equipment, to the carburettor or fuel-injection system. The delivery capacity of the fuel pump exceeds the maximum demands of the system, so excess fuel is constantly returned to the tank. This helps to avoid the problems of vapour locks in the fuel lines.

Carburettor models have a twin venturi downdraught carburettor of Pierburg manufacture on 1.8 litre models and Weber on 2.0 litre models. Both makes of carburettor have an automatic choke.

Fuel-injection, when fitted, is of the Bosch L-Jetronic type. This system is under the control of the EEC IV module.

The exhaust system fitted in production is made of aluminised steel, with stainless steel used in the endplates and baffles of the rear silencer. Individual sections of the system are easily renewed in service.

Emission control for the UK market is achieved largely by the inherent efficiency of the fuel, ignition and engine management systems. A welcome spin-off from such efficiency is remarkably good fuel economy for a vehicle of such size and weight.

Precautions

Fuel

Many of the procedures in this Chapter require the removal of fuel lines and connections which may result in some fuel spillage. Residual pressure in fuel-injection systems will remain in the fuel lines long after the vehicle was last used, therefore extra care must be taken when disconnecting a fuel line hose. Loosen any fuel hose slowly to avoid a sudden release of pressure which may cause fuel spray. As an added precaution place a rag over each union as it is disconnected to catch any fuel which is forcibly expelled. Before carrying out any operation on the fuel system refer to the precautions given in "Safety first!" at the beginning of this Manual and follow them implicitly. Petrol is a highly dangerous and volatile liquid and the precautions necessary when handling it cannot be overstressed

Tamperproof adjustment screws

Certain adjustment points in the fuel system (and elsewhere) are protected by tamperproof caps, plugs or seals. The purpose of such tamperproofing is to discourage, and to deter, adjustment by unqualified operators.

In some EU countries (though not yet in the UK) it is an offence to drive a vehicle with missing or broken tamperproof seals. Before disturbing a tamperproof seal, satisfy yourself that you will not be breaking local or national anti-pollution regulations by doing so. Fit a new seal when adjustment is complete when this is required by law.

Do not break tamperproof seals on a vehicle which is still under warranty.

Catalytic converter

The catalytic converter is a reliable and simple device which needs no maintenance in itself, but there are some facts of which an owner should be aware if the converter is to function properly for the full service life.

a) *DO NOT use leaded petrol in a car equipped with a catalytic converter the lead will coat the precious metals, reducing their converting efficiency and will eventually destroy the converter.*

b) *Always keep the ignition and fuel systems well-maintained in accordance with the manufacturer's schedule - particularly, ensure that the air cleaner filter element, the fuel filter and the spark plugs are renewed at the correct interval - if the inlet*

air/fuel mixture is allowed to become too rich due to neglect, the unburned surplus will enter and burn in the catalytic converter, overheating the element and eventually destroying the converter.

c) *If the engine develops a misfire, do not drive the car at all (or at least as little as possible) until the fault is cured - the misfire will allow unburned fuel to enter the converter, which will result in overheating, as noted above.*

d) *DO NOT push- or tow-start the car - this will soak the catalytic converter in unburned fuel, causing it to overheat when the engine does start - see b) above.*

e) *DO NOT switch off the ignition at high engine speeds - if the ignition is switched off at anything above idle speed, unburned fuel will enter the (very hot) catalytic converter, with the possible risk of igniting on the element and damaging the converter.*

f) *DO NOT use fuel or engine oil additives - these may contain substances harmful to the catalytic converter.*

g) *DO NOT continue to use the car if the engine burns oil to the extent of leaving a visible trail of blue smoke - the unburned carbon deposits will clog the converter passages and reduce the efficiency; in severe cases the element will overheat.*

h) *Remember that the catalytic converter operates at very high temperatures - hence the heat shields on the car's underbody and the casing will become hot enough to ignite combustible materials which brush against it - DO NOT, therefore, park the car in dry undergrowth, over long grass or piles of dead leaves.*

i) *Remember that the catalytic converter is FRAGILE, do not strike it with tools during servicing work, take great care when working on the exhaust system, ensure that the converter is well clear of any jacks or other lifting gear used to raise the car and do not drive the car over rough ground, road humps, etc, in such a way as to "ground" the exhaust system.*

j) *In some cases, particularly when the car is new and/or is used for stop/start driving, a sulphurous smell (like that of rotten eggs)*

may be noticed from the exhaust. This is common to many catalytic converter-equipped cars and seems to be due to the small amount of sulphur found in some petrols reacting with hydrogen in the exhaust to produce hydrogen sulphide (H_2S) gas; while this gas is toxic, it is not produced in sufficient amounts to be a problem. Once the car has covered a few thousand miles the problem should disappear - in the meanwhile a change of driving style or of the brand of petrol used may effect a solution.

k) *The catalytic converter, used on a well-maintained and well-driven car, should last for between 50 000 and 100 000 miles - from this point on, careful checks should be made at all specified service intervals of the CO level to ensure that the converter is still operating efficiently - if the converter is no longer effective it must be renewed.*

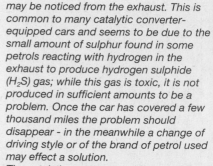

2 Air cleaner and element - removal and refitting

See Chapter 1, Section 38.

3 Air cleaner temperature control - description and testing

1 On carburettor models only, the air cleaner can take in both hot and cold air. Hot air is obtained from a shroud bolted to the exhaust manifold.

2 A flap valve in the air cleaner spout determines the mix of hot and cold air. The valve is operated by a vacuum diaphragm. Vacuum is obtained from the inlet manifold and is applied via a heat-sensing valve, which cuts off the vacuum as the temperature of the incoming air rises. Thus the air cleaner takes in only hot air on starting from cold, changing progressively to cold air as the engine warms up **(see illustrations)**.

3 If the system fails, either the engine will take a long time to warm up (flap stuck in "cold" position), or it may run roughly and not develop full power when warm (flap stuck in "hot" position). Check it as follows.

3.2a Air cleaner vacuum diaphragm unit

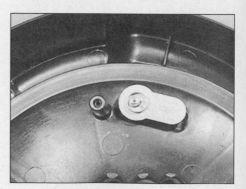

3.2b Air cleaner heat sensor

4.6a Removing the mechanical fuel pump

4.6b Fuel pump pushrod

4 With the engine cold, disconnect the cold air inlet trunking from the spout. Look into the spout and check that the flap valve is covering the hot air inlet.
5 Start the engine and allow it to idle. Check that the flap moves to cover the cold air inlet. If the flap does not move, check the diaphragm and heat sensor as follows.
6 Stop the engine. Disconnect the diaphragm vacuum pipe from the heat sensor. Apply vacuum to the diaphragm, using a vacuum head pump or by connecting the pipe directly to manifold vacuum. If the flap now moves, the heat sensor or vacuum line was faulty. If the flap still does not move, the diaphragm is faulty or the flap is jammed.
7 On completion reconnect the vacuum pipe and the cold air trunking.

4 Fuel pump - testing, removal and refitting

Mechanical

1 Carburettor models without air conditioning are fitted with a mechanical fuel pump, located on the left-hand side of the engine block.
2 To test the pump, disconnect the ignition coil LT lead. Disconnect the outlet hose from the pump and place a wad of rag next to the pump outlet. Take appropriate fire precautions.
3 Have an assistant crank the engine on the starter. Well-defined spurts of fuel must be

ejected from the pump outlet - if not, the pump is probably faulty (or the tank is empty). Dispose of the fuel-soaked rag safely.
4 To remove the fuel pump, first disconnect the battery negative lead.
5 Disconnect and plug the pump inlet and outlet hoses. Be prepared for fuel spillage.
6 Unscrew the two bolts and withdraw the pump from the cylinder block. Remove the gasket. If necessary extract the pushrod (**see illustrations**).
7 Clean the exterior of the pump in paraffin and wipe dry. Clean all traces of gasket from the cylinder block and pump flange.
8 If the fuel pump has a removable cover, remove the screw and withdraw the cover and nylon mesh filter with seal (**see illustrations**). Clean the filter, cover and pump in fuel. Locate the filter in the cover and fit the cover to the pump so that the pipe and indentation are aligned. Tighten the screw.
9 Refitting is a reversal of removal, but fit a new gasket and tighten the bolts to the specified torque. If necessary discard the crimped type hose clips and fit screw type clips.

Electrical

SOHC and 2.8 litre V6 engines

10 All fuel-injection models, and carburettor models when fitted with air conditioning, have an electric fuel pump. The two types of pump are not the same, although both are mounted under the vehicle next to the fuel tank.

11 If the fuel pump appears to have failed completely, check the appropriate fuse and relay. On fuel-injection models, also check the inertia switch (when fitted).
12 To test the carburettor type pump, disconnect the fuel supply hose from the pressure regulator or vapour separator in the engine compartment. Lead the hose into a measuring cylinder.
13 Take appropriate fire precautions. Switch on the ignition for 30 seconds and measure the quantity of fuel delivered: it should be at least 400 cc (0.7 pint).
14 To test the fuel-injection type pump, special equipment is required. Consult a Ford dealer or other fuel-injection specialist. The problem may be due to a clogged filter.
15 To remove a pump, first disconnect the battery negative lead. Take appropriate fire precautions.
16 Raise and support the rear of the vehicle. Clean the fuel pump and its surroundings.
17 Clamp the tank-to-pump hose, or make arrangements to collect the contents of the fuel tank which will otherwise be released.
18 Place a drain pan beneath the pump. Disconnect the inlet and outlet hoses; be prepared for fuel spillage. **Caution:** *Fuel under pressure may spray out of the outlet hose union as it is slackened.*
19 Disconnect the wiring plug from the pump.
20 Slacken the pump bracket clamp bolt and slide the pump out of the bracket.
21 Refit by reversing the removal operations. Make sure that all hoses and unions are in good condition.
22 On 2.4 & 2.9 litre V6 engines up to mid-1990, switch the ignition on and off five times, without cranking the engine, to pressurise the fuel system then check the pump unions for signs of leakage.
23 Run the engine and check for leaks.

DOHC engine

24 On these models the fuel pump is mounted in the fuel tank, on the same mounting as the fuel level sender unit (**see illustration**). To test the pump specialist equipment is required, therefore this task must be entrusted to a Ford dealer.

4.8a Removing the fuel pump cover - note alignment indentations

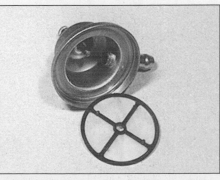

4.8b Fuel pump cover and filter screen

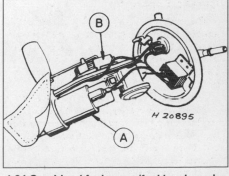

4.24 Combined fuel pump/fuel level sender unit

A Fuel pump *B Fuel level sender unit*

5.7 Fuel tank supply (left) and return hoses

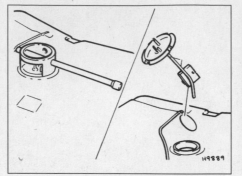

6.3 Removing the fuel gauge sender unit

7.3 Fuel cut-off inertia switch location - Estate models

25 To remove the pump, first remove the fuel tank.

26 Unscrew the fuel pump/fuel level sender unit by engaging two crossed screwdrivers in the slots on either side of the unit mounting flange. Recover the seal.

27 Refitting is a reversal of removal. It is necessary to fit a new seal.

5 Fuel tank - removal and refitting

1 Run the fuel level as low as possible before removing the tank.

2 Disconnect the battery negative lead.

3 Remove the fuel filler cap. Siphon or pump the remaining fuel out of the tank. Store the fuel in a suitable sealed container.

4 Remove the two screws on either side of the filler neck.

5 Raise and support the rear of the vehicle.

6 Remove the shield from the right-hand rear inner wheel arch. Also remove the rear bumper undershield. which is secured by six screws.

7 Disconnect the fuel supply and return lines from the tank (see illustration). Drain the fuel in the lines into a suitable container and remove it.

8 Support the fuel tank. Remove the two bolts which secure the rear ends of the fuel tank supporting straps.

9 Lower the tank and supporting straps,

unhooking the front ends of the straps from their locations. Disconnect the wiring and the vent hose from the tank. Remove the tank with filler pipe attached.

10 Fuel tank repairs including soldering or welding must be left to specialists. Even when empty, the tank may contain explosive vapour. Proprietary compounds are available for making temporary "cold" repairs.

11 Refit the fuel tank in the reverse order to removal. Check for leaks on completion.

6 Fuel gauge sender unit - removal and refitting

1 Remove the fuel tank.

2 Unscrew the sender unit from the tank. There is a Ford tool (No 23-014) which engages with the lugs on the unit, but with patience a pair of crossed screwdrivers or similar items can be used instead.

3 Remove the sender unit, taking care not to damage the float or bend the float arm (see illustration). Recover the seal.

4 A defective sender unit must be renewed; spares are not available. Renew the seal in any case.

5 Refit by reversing the removal operations.

7 Fuel cut-off inertia switch - removal and refitting

1 Fitted to DOHC and 2.4 & 2.9 litre V6 engined models, this device is designed to cut

off pressurised fuel to the fuel-injection system in the event of an accident. It does this by interrupting the electrical supply to the fuel pump.

2 To remove the switch, first disconnect the battery negative lead.

3 Open up the tailgate and locate the switch which is mounted near the tailgate lock striker. On Estate models the switch is located behind a trim panel in the rear right-hand corner of the luggage compartment (see illustration).

4 Remove the trim panel and disconnect the switch wiring connector (see illustrations).

5 Extract the two retaining screws and remove the switch.

6 Refitting is a reverse of the removal procedure. On completion, depress the switch button to ensure that the switch has been reset.

8 Throttle pedal - removal and refitting

1 Disconnect the battery negative lead.

2 Unclip the under-dash insulation on the driver's side.

3 Disconnect the cable from the pedal. The cable may be secured by a clip, or it may slot into a "keyhole" fitting (see illustration).

4 Remove the two nuts which secure the throttle pedal bracket to the bulkhead. Remove the pedal and bracket.

5 Refit by reversing the removal operations.

7.4a On early models it will be necessary to remove the luggage compartment rear trim panel to gain access to the fuel cut-off inertia switch . . .

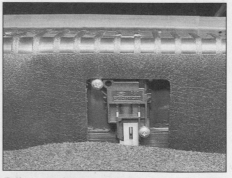

7.4b . . . on later models an access cover in the trim panel is provided

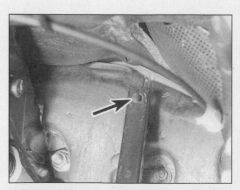

8.3 Throttle pedal showing "keyhole" cable fitting (arrowed)

9.5a Three screws (arrowed) secure the throttle linkage cover

9.5b Throttle linkage with cover removed

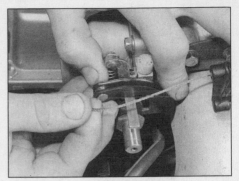

9.6 Removing a throttle cable inner - barrel and slot type

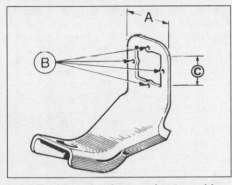

9.7 Tool for releasing accelerator cable lugs

A 25 mm (1 in)   C 16 mm (0.63 in)
B Centrepunch indents

9 Throttle cable - removal and refitting

1 Disconnect the battery negative lead.
2 Disconnect the cable from the pedal.
3 Working under the bonnet, free the cable outer from the bulkhead and pull the cable into the engine bay.
4 On carburettor models, remove the air cleaner.

5 On V6 models, remove the throttle linkage cover, which is secured by three screws (see illustrations).
6 Disconnect the cable inner from the throttle lever on the carburettor or fuel-injection linkage. The cable may be secured by a spring clip, or by a simple barrel and slot arrangement (see illustration).
7 Disconnect the cable outer from its bracket. It may be secured by a spring clip, or by four plastic lugs. The lugs are most easily released with a tool (see illustration).
8 Refit by reversing the removal operations. Adjust the threaded sleeve on the cable outer so that there is a small amount of slack with the pedal released; have an assistant operate the throttle pedal and check that the throttle lever moves over its full range of travel.
9 On automatic transmission models, check the adjustment of the kickdown cable.

10 Vapour separator - removal and refitting

1 All carburettor models are fitted with a vapour separator, mounted on the left-hand inner wing. On 1.8 litre models the separator incorporates a pressure regulator (see illustrations).

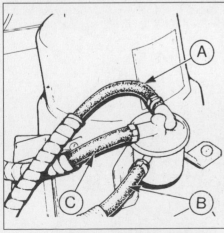

10.1a Fuel vapour separator without pressure regulator

A Fuel return   C Carburettor supply
B Fuel supply

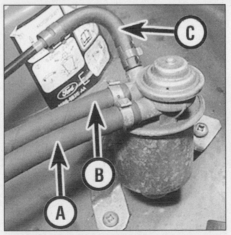

10.1b Fuel vapour separator and pressure regulator

A Fuel supply   C Fuel return
B Carburettor supply

2 Disconnect the battery negative lead.
3 Identify the three hoses connected to the separator. Disconnect the hoses, cutting off the hose clips if they are of the crimped type.
4 Remove the two securing screws and lift out the separator. Remember it is full of fuel.
5 Refit by reversing the removal operations. Make sure that the different hoses are connected to the correct stubs on the regulator. Use new hose clips when necessary.

11 Pierburg 2V carburettor - idle speed and mixture adjustments

See Chapter 1, Sections 15 and 16.

12 Pierburg 2V carburettor - removal and refitting

1 Disconnect the battery negative lead.
2 Remove the air cleaner.
3 Disconnect the automatic choke electrical lead from the manifold thermo-switch.
4 Unclip the throttle arm from the throttle lever (see illustration).
5 Disconnect the fuel hose from the carburettor and plug it. If a crimped hose clip is fitted, cut it off and use a worm drive clip when refitting (see illustration).
6 Depressurise the cooling system by removing the expansion tank filler cap. Take precautions against scalding if the system is hot.

12.4 Throttle arm-to-lever clip (arrowed)

12.5 Crimped hose clip (arrowed) must be renewed

12.7 Disconnecting a coolant hose from the automatic choke

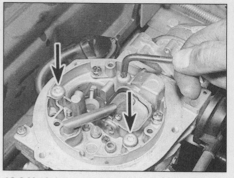

12.8 Undoing a carburettor securing screw. Other two screws are arrowed

7 Disconnect and plug the automatic choke coolant hoses (see illustration). Be prepared for coolant spillage.
8 Remove the three Torx screws which secure the carburettor to the manifold (see illustration).
9 Check that no attachments have been overlooked, then lift the carburettor off the manifold. Recover the gasket.
10 Clean the carburettor and manifold mating

surfaces, being careful not to get dirt into the manifold.
11 Refit by reversing the removal operations. Top-up the cooling system if necessary on completion, then check the idle speed and mixture.
12 On engines from September 1986, a modified carburettor was fitted which incorporates a secondary choke pull-down diaphragm that assists in reducing fuel consumption (see illustration). If such a replacement carburettor is to be fitted to earlier models, always use a new mounting

gasket and also carry out the following operations.
a) Obtain the special wiring loom and connect the wiring connector (see illustration).
b) Disconnect the positive feed wire from the ignition coil and then connect the leads of the new loom to the positive terminal of the coil and the end of the disconnected positive feed wire.
c) Connect the loom earth eyelet to one of the ignition coil retaining screws.
d) After fitting the air cleaner, check the carburettor settings (Section 11).

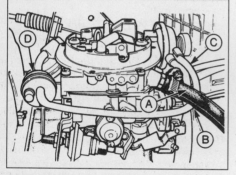

12.12 Pierburg 2V carburettor fitted to later 1.8 litre engines
A Fuel inlet hose
B Swivel clip location
C Diaphragm hose
D Diaphragm (secondary choke pulldown)

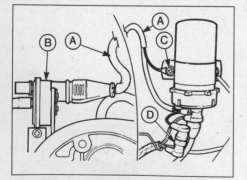

12.13 Wiring connections to Pierburg 2V carburettor fitted to later 1.8 litre engines
A Loom
B Secondary choke pulldown diaphragm
C Earth
D Original coil connector

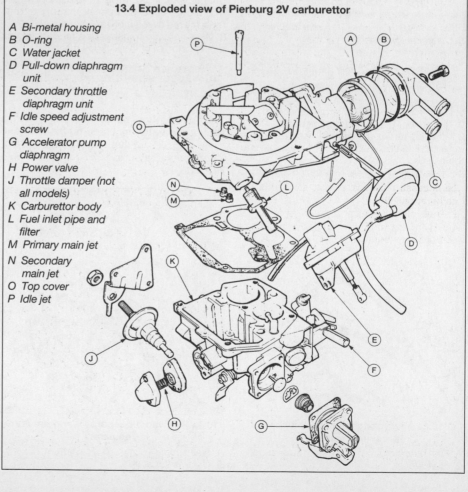

13.4 Exploded view of Pierburg 2V carburettor
A Bi-metal housing
B O-ring
C Water jacket
D Pull-down diaphragm unit
E Secondary throttle diaphragm unit
F Idle speed adjustment screw
G Accelerator pump diaphragm
H Power valve
J Throttle damper (not all models)
K Carburettor body
L Fuel inlet pipe and filter
M Primary main jet
N Secondary main jet
O Top cover
P Idle jet

13 Pierburg 2V carburettor - dismantling and reassembly

1 Check the cost and availability of spare parts before deciding to dismantle the carburettor. If the unit has seen much service, fitting a new or reconditioned carburettor may prove more satisfactory than any attempt at overhaul.
2 Obtain a carburettor repair kit, which will contain the necessary gaskets, diaphragms and other renewable items.
3 With the carburettor removed from the vehicle, clean it thoroughly externally and place it on a clean worksurface.
4 Referring to the exploded view of the carburettor (see illustration), remove each component part whilst making a note of its fitted position. Make alignment marks on linkages etc.
5 Reassemble in the reverse order to dismantling, using new gaskets, O-rings etc.
6 To check the choke pull-down after reassembly, position the fast idle screw on the highest step of the cam. Press the pull-down adjusting screw towards the pull-down diaphragm and measure the choke valve opening with a twist drill or gauge rod of the specified diameter. Adjust if necessary using a 2 mm Allen key (see illustration).
7 After refitting the throttle damper, adjust its position in the bracket so that with a 2 mm (0.08 in) feeler blade inserted between the idle speed adjusting screw and the throttle lever, the damper plunger is just touching the actuating lever (see illustration).
8 Adjust the idle speed and mixture, and if necessary the fast idle speed, after refitting the carburettor.
9 Recheck the throttle damper adjustment, when applicable.

14 Pierburg 2V carburettor - fast idle adjustment

1 This is not a routine operation. It should only be necessary after overhaul, or when a new carburettor is fitted.
2 The idle speed and mixture must be correctly set and the engine must be at operating temperature.

13.6 Choke pull-down adjustment

3 Remove the air cleaner and plug the manifold vacuum connection.
4 With the engine running, position the fast idle screw on the second highest step of the fast idle cam (see illustration). Measure the engine speed and compare it with that given in the Specifications.
5 If adjustment is necessary, remove the tamperproof plug from the fast idle screw by crushing it with pliers. Stop the engine and open the throttle to gain access to the screw with a small screwdriver. Turn the screw a small amount clockwise to increase the speed, anti-clockwise to reduce it, then reseat the screw on the second highest step of the cam and recheck the engine speed. Repeat as necessary.
6 Fit a new tamperproof cap where this is required by law, then refit the air cleaner.

15 Weber 2V carburettor - idle speed and mixture adjustments

Idle speed cannot be adjusted in the usual way on this carburettor, as it is controlled by the ESC II module.
If mixture adjustment is required, proceed as described in Chapter 1, Section 16.

16 Weber 2V carburettor - removal and refitting

1 Disconnect the battery negative lead.
2 Remove the air cleaner.

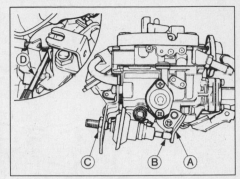
13.7 Throttle damper adjustment - Pierburg 2V carburettor

A Actuating lever   C Damper locknut
B Damper plunger   D Feeler blade

3 Disconnect the choke and stepper motor wiring. The stepper motor multi-plug locking device must be depressed to release the plug (see illustration).
4 Unclip the throttle arm from the throttle lever and remove the throttle cable bracket.
5 Disconnect the fuel hose from the carburettor and plug it. If a crimped type hose clip is fitted, cut it off and use a worm drive clip when refitting.
6 Disconnect the vacuum pipe(s) from the carburettor, noting their connecting points if there is any possibility of confusion.
7 Remove the four carburettor-to-manifold nuts. Check that nothing has been overlooked, then lift off the carburettor. Recover the gasket.
8 Clean the carburettor and manifold mating faces, being careful not to sweep dirt into the manifold.
9 Refit by reversing the removal operations. If the stepper motor has been disturbed, refer to Chapter 5, Section 19 for the initial adjustment.

17 Weber 2V carburettor - dismantling and reassembly

1 Check the cost and availability of spare parts before deciding to dismantle the carburettor. If the unit has seen much service, fitting a new or reconditioned carburettor may prove more satisfactory than any attempt at overhaul.
2 Obtain a carburettor repair kit, which will contain the necessary gaskets, diaphragms and other renewable items.
3 With the carburettor removed from the vehicle, clean it thoroughly externally and place it on a clean worksurface.
4 Referring to the exploded view of the carburettor (see illustration), remove each component part whilst making a note of its fitted position. Make alignment marks on linkages etc.
5 Reassemble in the reverse order to dismantling, using new gaskets, O-rings etc. Be careful not to kink the diaphragms.

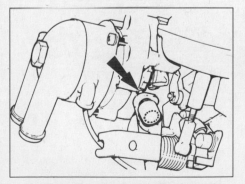
14.4 Fast idle adjustment - Pierburg 2V
Tip of fast idle screw is arrowed

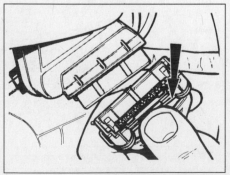
16.3 Depress locking clip (arrowed) when disconnecting stepper motor multi-plug

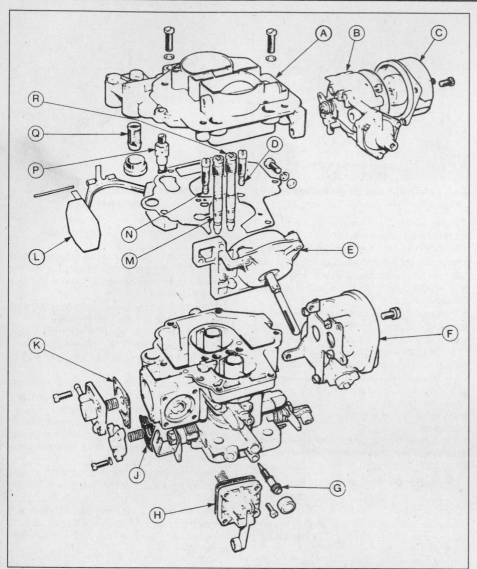

17.4 Exploded view of Weber 2V carburettor

A Top cover
B Choke lever housing
C Choke bi-metal housing
D Secondary idle jet
E Secondary throttle vacuum unit
F Stepper motor
G Idle mixture adjustment screw
H Accelerator pump diaphragm
J Power valve diaphragm
K Low vacuum enrichment diaphragm
L Float
M Primary emulsion tube
N Primary idle jet
P Needle valve
Q Fuel inlet filter
R Secondary emulsion tube

18 Weber 2V carburettor - automatic choke adjustment

1 Disconnect the battery negative lead.
2 Remove the air cleaner.
3 Disconnect the feed wire from the choke bi-metal housing.
4 Make alignment marks if necessary, then remove the three screws which secure the bi-metal housing. Detach the housing and recover the heat shield.
5 Fit a rubber band over the choke valve lever and tension the rubber band to hold the choke valve closed **(see illustration)**.
6 Using a small screwdriver, press the vacuum pull-down rod into the pull-down housing as far as it will go. Hold the rod in this position and use a drill shank or similar item to measure the clearance between the choke valve and the wall of the primary venturi. Measure the clearance on the down side of the valve. The desired pull-down clearance is given in the Specifications.
7 If adjustment is necessary, remove the end plug from the pull-down diaphragm cover. Turn the adjusting screw located under the plug **(see illustration)**. Refit the plug when adjustment is correct.

6 Check the float level as follows. Hold the top cover vertically so that the needle valve is closed by the float. Measure the dimension from the gasket face of the cover (with the gasket fitted) to the top rib on the float **(see illustration)**. The correct value is given in the Specifications. Correct if necessary by bending the tag on the float arm.
7 For adjustment of the automatic choke, refer to the next Section.

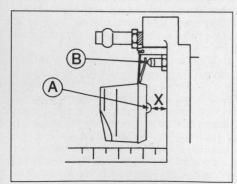

17.6 Float level adjustment - Weber 2V carburettor

A Rib on float   X Level measurement
B Adjusting tag

18.5 Choke vacuum pull-down check - Weber 2V carburettor

A Pull-down   B Rubber band
   diaphragm rod   C Screwdriver

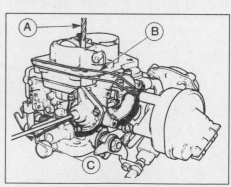

18.7 Adjusting the vacuum pull-down - Weber 2V carburettor

A Twist drill   C Screwdriver
B Rubber band

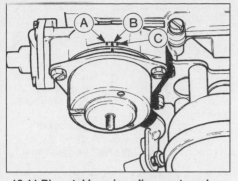

18.11 Bi-metal housing alignment marks -
Weber 2V carburettor

A Rich   C Lean
B Index

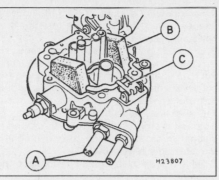

21.4 Float and needle valve locations in
carburettor top cover - Weber 2V TLD
carburettor

A Fuel hose   B Float
   connections   C Needle valve

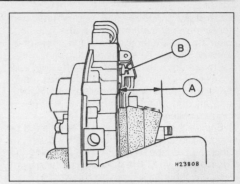

21.15 Float level adjustment - Weber 2V
TLD carburettor

A Check dimension   B Adjustment tag

8 Remove the drill and the rubber band.
9 Refit the heat shield, making sure it is properly located.
10 Refit the bi-metal housing, engaging the end of the spring with the choke valve lever. Fit the three screws, position the housing in its original alignment (paragraph 4) and tighten the screws.
11 If the bi-metal housing alignment has been lost, refer to the Specifications (see illustration). Small deviations from the specified setting may be made to correct over or under-choking.
12 Reconnect the choke feed wire, refit the air cleaner and reconnect the battery.
13 Check the idle mixture adjustment.

19 Weber 2V TLD carburettor - idle speed and mixture adjustments

To adjust idle speed, refer to Chapter 1, Section 15.
To adjust idle mixture, refer to Chapter 1, Section 16.

20 Weber 2V TLD carburettor - removal and refitting

1 Disconnect the battery negative lead.
2 Remove the air cleaner.
3 Disconnect the wiring from the anti-dieselling (anti-run-on) valve.
4 Disconnect the wiring from the automatic choke heater.
5 Disconnect the fuel supply and return hoses, noting their locations to aid refitting. Plug the ends of the hoses to minimise petrol spillage and prevent the ingress of dirt into the fuel system.
6 Disconnect the link arm from the throttle linkage.
7 Disconnect the vacuum pipe.
8 Release the coolant hose from the bracket under the automatic choke housing.
9 Unscrew the four Torx screws, and lift the carburettor from the inlet manifold. Recover the gasket.

10 Refitting is a reversal of removal, bearing in mind the following points.
a) Ensure that the mating faces of the inlet manifold and the carburettor are clean, and use a new gasket.
b) Ensure that all hoses, pipes and wiring are correctly routed, and free from restrictions. If any of the hoses were originally secured with crimped-type clips, discard these and replace them with standard worm drive hose clips.
c) On completion check and if necessary, adjust the idle speed and mixture settings.

21 Weber 2V TLD carburettor - needle valve and float removal, refitting and adjustment

1 Disconnect the battery negative lead.
2 Remove the air cleaner.
3 Thoroughly clean all external dirt from the carburettor.
4 Disconnect the fuel supply and return hoses from the carburettor, noting their locations to aid refitting, and plug their ends to minimise petrol spillage (see illustration).
5 Disconnect the wiring from the automatic choke.
6 Disconnect the wiring from the anti-dieselling (anti-run-on) valve.
7 Remove the four Torx screws securing the carburettor to the inlet manifold.
8 Remove the two securing screws, and lift off the carburettor top cover, leaving the carburettor main body in place on the inlet manifold.
9 Slide the float retaining pin from the carburettor top cover, tapping it gently if necessary, then lift out the float and needle valve.
10 If desired, the needle valve housing can be unscrewed from the top cover. Recover the washer and discard it; a new one must be fitted on reassembly.
11 Inspect the components for damage, and renew as necessary. Check the needle valve for wear, and check the float assembly for leaks by shaking it to see if it contains petrol.

12 Refitting is a reversal of removal, bearing in mind the following points.
a) Use a new washer when refitting the needle valve housing.
b) When refitting the float and needle valve, ensure that the tag on the float locates under the spring clip on the needle valve. Check that the float and needle valve operate smoothly.
c) Check and, if necessary, adjust the float level as described below.
d) Ensure that the carburettor mating surfaces are clean then fit a new gasket onto the main body and refit the carburettor top cover.
e) If the fuel hoses were originally secured with crimped clips, discard these and secure the hoses in position with new worm drive hose clips.
f) On completion, check and if necessary adjust the idle speed and mixture.
13 With the carburettor top cover removed as described above, proceed as follows.
14 Fit a new gasket to the top cover, then hold the carburettor top cover in a vertical position, with the needle valve uppermost and shut.
15 Measure the distance between the top cover gasket and the bottom of the float (see illustration).
16 If the distance is not as specified, adjust by bending the tag on the float assembly.
17 Refit the carburettor top cover by reversing the removal operations.

22 Weber 2V TLD carburettor - secondary throttle valve vacuum diaphragm renewal

1 Disconnect the battery negative terminal.
2 Remove the air cleaner assembly.
3 Disconnect the diaphragm operating rod from the throttle linkage by pulling the lower section of the rod downwards and twist the end of the rod from the socket.
4 Remove the four cover retaining screws then remove the cover and withdraw the spring (see illustration).

5 Carefully remove the diaphragm and operating rod assembly from the housing. Examine the diaphragm for signs of splits or holes and renew if necessary.
6 Ensure that the diaphragm housing and cover mating surfaces are clean, then insert the diaphragm into the housing, aligning the hole in the diaphragm with the housing vacuum gallery.
7 Ensure that the diaphragm is not kinked or distorted in any way then locate the spring in diaphragm centre. Refit the cover, aligning the cover port with the housing gallery, and securely tighten the retaining screws.
8 Reconnect the operating rod to the throttle linkage, then refit the air cleaner and reconnect the battery negative terminal.

23 Weber 2V TLD carburettor - power valve diaphragm renewal

1 Disconnect the battery negative terminal.
2 For improved access, remove the air cleaner.
3 Thoroughly clean all external dirt from around the power valve housing.
4 Remove the three retaining screws then lift off the power valve cover and remove the spring.

5 Withdraw the diaphragm from the housing flange. Inspect the diaphragm for cracks or holes and renew if necessary.
6 Ensure that the diaphragm and housing flange mating surfaces are clean then insert the diaphragm into the housing, aligning the hole in the diaphragm with the corresponding hole in the housing flange.
7 Ensure that the diaphragm is not kinked or distorted in any way, then locate the spring in diaphragm centre. Refit the cover and tighten the retaining screws securely.
8 Refit the air cleaner and reconnect the battery.

24 Weber 2V TLD carburettor - low vacuum enrichment diaphragm renewal

1 This procedure is as described for the power valve. Note the following points.
a) If necessary disconnect the vacuum pipe from the diaphragm cover, and ensure it is securely reconnected on completion.
b) The diaphragm cover is retained by four screws.

25 Weber 2V TLD carburettor - accelerator pump diaphragm renewal

1 This procedure is as described for the power valve. Note the following points.
a) The accelerator pump cover is secured by four screws.
b) The diaphragm return spring is fitted between the pump housing and the diaphragm, not between the diaphragm and the cover.
c) When removing the return spring, the supply valve should come out on the end of the spring, complete with the O-ring seal. Check the valve and the O-ring for damage, and renew them if necessary. When refitting, ensure that the O-ring seal is correctly fitted to the end of the valve.

26 Weber 2V TLD carburettor - automatic choke unit removal, refitting and adjustment

1 Remove the carburettor top cover.
2 Note the position of the alignment marks on the choke housing and bi-metal housing and, if necessary, make additional alignment marks to aid refitting. Remove the three screws and lift off the bi-metal housing and retaining plate.
3 Remove the internal heat shield.
4 Remove the three choke housing screws, noting that it may be necessary to disconnect the fast idle cam return spring to access one of the screws, then disconnect the choke link from the operating lever and remove the automatic choke unit. Recover the O-ring from the rear of the unit.
5 Undo the three retaining screws then remove the vacuum pulldown diaphragm cover and withdraw the diaphragm. Examine the diaphragm for signs of splits or holes and renew if necessary.

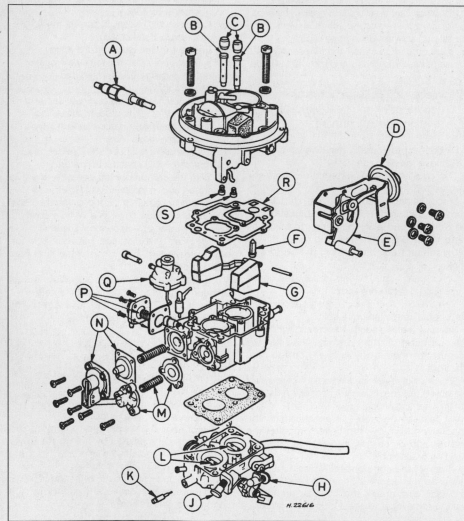

22.4 Exploded view of Weber 2V TLD carburettor

A Anti-dieselling valve
B Emulsion tubes
C Air correction jets
D Choke pull-down diaphragm assembly
E Choke linkage
F Needle valve
G Float
H Fast idle adjustment screw
J Idle speed adjustment screw
K Idle mixture adjustment screw
L Throttle valves
M Power valve assembly
N Accelerator pump assembly
P Low vacuum enrichment drive
Q Throttle kicker
R Gasket
S Main jet

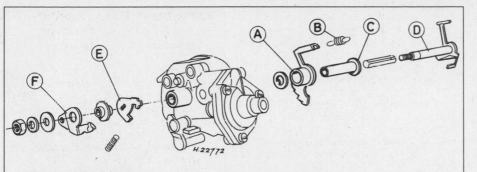

26.6 Exploded view of the automatic choke mechanism - Weber 2V TLD carburettor

A Upper choke operating link
B Fast idle cam return spring
C Spindle sleeve

D Connecting rod and lever assembly
E Pulldown link
F Actuating lever

6 If necessary, dismantle the automatic choke unit **(see illustration).**
7 Refitting is a reverse of the removal procedure noting the following points.
a) *Ensure that the pull-down diaphragm is correctly seated prior to refitting the cover.*
b) *Ensure that the O-ring is correctly seated in the choke housing prior to refitting.*
c) *With the choke housing installed check and, if necessary, adjust the vacuum pull-down diaphragm.*
d) *Refit the heat shield ensuring that the hole in the shield engages with choke housing peg.*
e) *Engage the bi-metal spring with the choke lever and refit the bi-metal housing. Align the marks made, or noted, on removal and securely tighten the housing retaining screws.*
f) *On completion check and, if necessary, adjust the fast idle speed.*

Vacuum pull-down adjustment

8 This procedure is as described in Section 18, referring to the Specifications at the start of this Chapter for the specified pull-down setting.

Fast idle speed adjustment

9 Check the idle speed and mixture adjustment as described earlier in this Chapter and leave the tachometer connected. Note that the idle speed must be correct before attempting to check or adjust the fast idle speed.
10 Warm the engine up to normal operating temperature and remove the air cleaner.
11 Partially open the throttle valve then close the choke valve until the fast idle adjustment screw is positioned on the third (middle) step of the fast idle cam **(see illustration)** and release the throttle valve.
12 Start the engine without touching the throttle pedal and check that the engine speed is within the speed range given in the Specifications at the start of this Chapter.
13 If this is not the case, adjust the engine speed by rotating the fast idle adjusting screw until the speed is within the specified range. Operate the throttle pedal and check that the engine returns to the specified idle speed.
14 Stop the engine then disconnect the tachometer and refit the air cleaner.

27 Weber 2V TLD carburettor - throttle kicker removal, refitting and adjustment

1 Disconnect the battery negative lead.
2 Remove the air cleaner assembly.
3 Disconnect the throttle kicker vacuum hose.
4 Withdraw the plastic shield from the throttle kicker **(see illustration).**
5 Remove the two securing screws, then disconnect the operating rod from the throttle linkage, and withdraw the assembly from the carburettor.
6 The assembly can be dismantled by removing the four securing screws and lifting off the diaphragm cover. Recover the spring.
7 Carefully withdraw the diaphragm and the operating rod assembly from the housing. Examine the condition of the diaphragm, and renew it if necessary.
8 Clean the mating faces of the housing and the diaphragm cover.

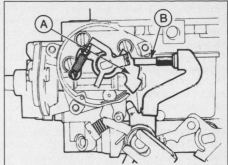

26.11 Fast idle speed adjustment - Weber 2V TLD carburettor

A Fast idle cam
B Fast idle screw shown on middle step of cam

9 Commence reassembly by inserting the diaphragm and operating rod assembly into the housing.
10 Refit the spring, and the cover, ensuring that the spring is correctly located, and tighten the securing screws progressively to avoid distorting the diaphragm.
11 Further refitting is a reversal of removal, but before refitting the plastic shield, check the throttle kicker adjustment as described in the following paragraphs.

Adjustment

12 Warm the engine up to normal operating temperature, and check the idle speed and mixture settings as described earlier in this Chapter.
13 Remove the air cleaner assembly.
14 Withdraw the plastic shield from the throttle kicker, if not already done.
15 Disconnect the throttle kicker vacuum hose, and connect the throttle kicker directly to the inlet manifold using a length of tubing.

4

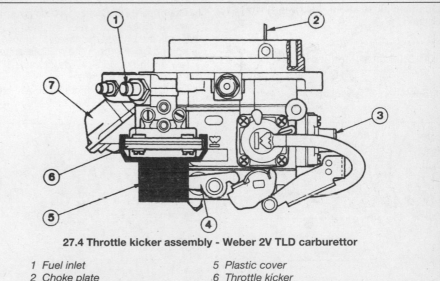

27.4 Throttle kicker assembly - Weber 2V TLD carburettor

1 Fuel inlet
2 Choke plate
3 Accelerator pump cover
4 Throttle kicker pivot lever

5 Plastic cover
6 Throttle kicker
7 Secondary throttle valve vacuum diaphragm

16 Start the engine and note the engine speed (rpm). The engine speed should increase above the normal idle speed, and should be as given in the Specifications.

17 If the engine speed is not as specified, remove the tamperproof plug from the top of the throttle kicker housing, and turn the adjustment screw to give the specified speed.

18 On completion of adjustment, fit a new tamperproof cap.

19 Disconnect the tubing from the inlet manifold, and reconnect the throttle kicker vacuum hose.

20 Refit the plastic shield and the air cleaner.

28 Fuel-injection system - depressurisation

On 2.4 & 2.9 litre V6 models especially, residual pressure will remain in the fuel lines long after the vehicle was last used therefore the fuel system must be depressurised before any hose is disconnected; the system is depressurised via the vent valve on the fuel rail, noting that it may be necessary to depress the valve several times before the pressure is fully released. As an added precaution place a rag over the valve as it is depressed to catch any fuel which is forcibly expelled. Before carrying out any operation on the fuel system refer to the precautions given in *Safety first!* at the beginning of this Manual and follow them implicitly. Petrol is a highly dangerous and volatile liquid and the precautions necessary when handling it cannot be overstressed.

29 Fuel-injection system relays - location

Access to the relays is obtained by removing the facia top cover (crash pad).

The relays are located on the passenger side **(see illustration)**. Also see Chapter 13, Section 16.

30 Fuel filter - renewal

See Chapter 1, Section 41.

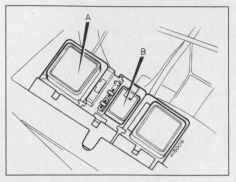

29.2 Fuel injection system relays - 2.4 and 2.9 litre V6 engines

A Power relay   *B Fuel pump relay*

31 Fuel-injection system - idle speed and mixture adjustment

SOHC and 2.8 litre V6 engines

1 Idle speed is controlled by the EEC IV module and no direct adjustment is possible.

2 Idle mixture adjustment should not be necessary on a routine basis. After component renewal or a similar circumstance it may be checked and adjusted as follows.

3 The engine must be at operating temperature. The valve clearances must be correct, the air cleaner element must be clean and the ignition system must be in good condition.

4 Connect an exhaust gas analyser (CO meter) and a tachometer (rev. counter) to the engine as instructed by their makers.

5 Run the engine at 3000 rpm for 15 seconds, then allow it to idle. Repeat the procedure every 60 seconds until adjustment is complete.

6 With the engine idling after the 3000 rpm burst, record the CO level when the reading has stabilised. The desired value is given in the Specifications.

7 If adjustment is necessary, remove the tamperproof plug from the mixture adjusting screw on the underside of the vane airflow meter **(see illustration)**.

8 On V6 models, note that adjustment should first be carried out on the front airflow meter.

31.7 Tamperproof plug (arrowed) covering mixture adjusting screw

Airflow meter is inverted for photo

The rear meter should only be adjusted if the range of adjustment on the front meter is insufficient.

9 Turn the mixture adjusting screw with a hexagon key until the CO level is correct **(see illustration)**.

10 Stop the engine and disconnect the test gear.

11 Fit a new tamperproof plug if required.

DOHC engine

Note: *Before carrying out any adjustments ensure that the ignition timing and spark plug gaps are as specified. To carry out the adjustments, an accurate tachometer and an exhaust gas analyser (CO meter) will be required.*

12 Idle speed is controlled by the EEC IV module, and manual adjustment is not possible, although the "base" idle speed can be adjusted by a Ford dealer using special equipment.

13 On models with a catalytic converter, the mixture is controlled by the EEC IV module, and no manual adjustment is possible.

14 On models without a catalytic converter, the idle mixture can be adjusted as follows.

15 Run the engine until it is at normal operating temperature.

16 Stop the engine and connect a tachometer and an exhaust gas analyser in accordance with the manufacturer's instructions.

17 Start the engine and run it at 3000 rpm for 15 seconds, ensuring that all electrical loads (headlamps, heater blower, etc) are switched off, then allow the engine to idle, and check the CO content. Note that the reading will initially rise, then fall and finally stabilise.

18 If adjustment is necessary, remove the cover from the mixture adjustment potentiometer (located on the right-hand side of the engine compartment, behind the MAP sensor), and turn the screw to give the specified CO content **(see illustration)**.

19 If adjustment does not produce a change in reading, the potentiometer may be at the extreme of the adjustment range. To centralise the potentiometer, turn the adjustment screw 20 turns clockwise followed by 10 turns anti-clockwise, then repeat the adjustment procedure.

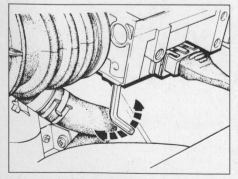

31.9 Idle mixture adjustment - fuel-injection models

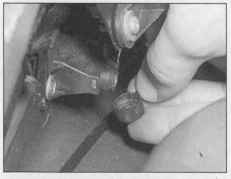

31.18 Remove the cover from the mixture adjustment potentiometer

20 Checking and adjustment should be completed within 30 seconds of the meter readings stabilising. If this has not been possible, run the engine at 3000 rpm for 15 seconds, then allow the engine to idle. Re-check the CO content and carry out further adjustments if necessary.

21 On completion of adjustment, stop the engine and disconnect the tachometer and the exhaust gas analyser. Refit the cover to the adjustment screw.

2.4 & 2.9 litre V6 engines

22 As with the 2.8 V6, idle speed is electronically controlled. Basic idle speed adjustment can only be carried out by a Ford dealer using special equipment.

23 On models not equipped with a catalytic converter, mixture adjustment can be carried out as described above.

24 On models equipped with a catalytic converter, the mixture is controlled by the EEC IV module and no manual adjustment is possible.

32 Throttle position sensor - removal and refitting

SOHC and V6 engines

1 Disconnect the battery negative lead.

2 Free the throttle position sensor multi-plug from its clip. On the OHC models this is below the idle speed control valve, on the underside of the inlet manifold; on V6 engines it is located below the throttle valve housing.

3 Relieve the locktabs and unbolt the throttle position sensor **(see illustration)**. Pull the sensor off the throttle valve shaft, disconnect the multi-plug and remove the sensor.

4 Do not rotate the centre part of the sensor beyond its normal range of movement, or damage may result.

5 When refitting, line up the flat on the throttle valve shaft with the flat on the centre of the sensor. Make sure that the sensor is the right way round and fit it over the shaft.

6 Fit and tighten the two bolts and secure it with the locktabs.

7 Reconnect and secure the multi-plug, then reconnect the battery.

DOHC engine

8 Disconnect the battery negative lead.

9 Free the throttle position sensor wiring plug from the retaining clip located on the underside of the throttle body. Disconnect the wiring plug halves by releasing the locktabs and pulling on the plug halves, not the wiring **(see illustration)**.

10 Unscrew the two sensor securing screws, and withdraw the sensor from the throttle shaft.

11 Refitting is a reversal of removal, noting that the sensor fits with the wiring at the bottom, and ensuring that the sensor actuating arm engages correctly with the throttle spindle.

32.3 Throttle position sensor retaining bolts (arrowed)

33 Throttle body - removal and refitting

1 On DOHC models, disconnect the battery negative lead.

2 Free the throttle position sensor wiring plug from the retaining clip located on the underside of the throttle body. Disconnect the wiring plug halves by releasing the locktabs and pulling on the plug halves, not the wiring.

3 Disconnect the throttle cable and (where necessary) the speed control cable from the throttle linkage.

4 Loosen the securing clip, and disconnect the air inlet hose from the throttle body.

5 Unscrew the four securing bolts and withdraw the throttle body from the inlet manifold along with the gasket.

6 Refitting is a reversal of removal, bearing in mind the following points.

a) Ensure that the mating faces of the throttle body and the inlet manifold are clean, and fit a new gasket.

b) On completion, adjust the throttle cable and where necessary, adjust the speed control cable so that there is only a small amount of slack in the cable.

c) Where applicable, check and if necessary adjust the idle mixture.

34.2 Disconnecting the idle speed control valve

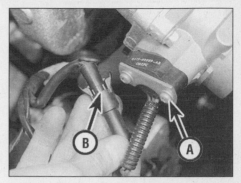

32.9 Throttle position sensor (A) and wiring plug (B)

34 Idle speed control valve - removal and refitting

SOHC and all V6 engines

1 Disconnect the battery negative lead.

2 Disconnect the multi-plug from the idle speed control valve by prising up the retaining lug and pulling the plug, not the wires **(see illustration)**.

3 Remove the two securing nuts (OHC) or bolts (V6) and withdraw the valve **(see illustration)**. Recover the gasket.

4 If necessary, the solenoid can be separated from the valve block by removing the two screws to enable the parts to be cleaned. Contamination or air leaks in this area will cause unstable idling. After careful cleaning, the parts can be reassembled.

5 Refit the valve, using a new gasket, and tighten the retaining nuts or bolts. Reconnect the multi-plug and the battery.

6 Start the engine and check that the idle is steady. Bring the engine to operating temperature, then switch on all possible electrical loads (headlights, heated screens, heater blower etc) and check that the idle remains steady. This confirms that the valve is working.

DOHC engine

7 Disconnect the battery negative lead.

8 Loosen the securing clip, and disconnect the air inlet hose from the throttle body.

34.3 Removing the idle speed control valve

4

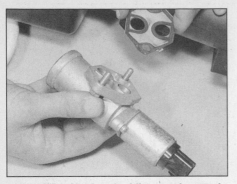

34.12 Withdrawing the idle speed control valve

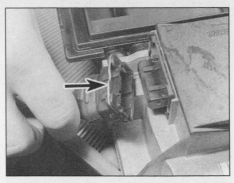

35.2 Disconnecting the airflow meter multi-plug. Meter is inverted to show locking clip (arrowed)

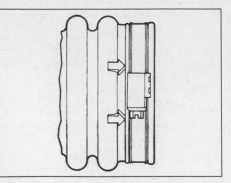

35.6 Correct alignment of air inlet trunking and hose clip

9 Unscrew the securing nut, and release the air inlet tube from the bracket on the engine compartment front panel.

10 Disconnect the wiring plug from the idle speed control valve.

11 Release the air cleaner lid securing clips, then remove the air inlet tube, plenum chamber, and air cleaner lid as an assembly, disconnecting the breather hose from the air inlet tube.

12 Unscrew the two securing bolts, and withdraw the valve from the air inlet tube **(see illustration)**. Recover the gasket.

13 Clean the valve and air inlet tube mating faces before refitting, taking care not to allow dirt to enter the air inlet tube.

14 Refitting is a reversal of removal, using a new gasket.

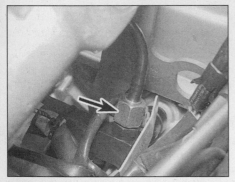

36.7 Fuel feed union (arrowed) on fuel rail

15 On completion, start the engine and check that the idle speed is stable - if not, check for air leaks around the valve. Switch on all available electrical loads and check that the idle speed is maintained - if not, suspect a faulty valve.

35 Vane airflow meter(s) - removal and refitting

OHC engines

1 Disconnect the battery negative lead.

2 Release the locking clip and disconnect the multi-plug from the meter **(see illustration)**.

3 Release the hose clip and disconnect the air trunking from the meter.

4 Unclip the air cleaner cover and remove it with the meter. Do not drop or jar it.

5 To separate the meter from the cover, remove the four retaining bolts.

6 Refit by reversing the removal operations. Make sure that the seal in the air cleaner cover is correctly located and align the hose clip **(see illustration)**.

7 Check the exhaust CO level on completion.

V6 engines

8 Proceed as described above, noting that there are two meters instead of one.

36 Fuel-injectors - removal and refitting

SOHC and 2.8 litre V6 engines

1 Disconnect the battery negative lead.

2 On V6 models, remove the throttle linkage cover, which is secured by three screws.

3 Remove the trunking which connects the airflow meter(s) to the inlet manifold.

4 On OHC models, release the distributor cap and place it clear of the fuel rail. It will be necessary to disconnect the cap-to-coil HT lead at the coil.

5 Disconnect the multi-plugs from the idle speed control valve, the throttle position sensor and the coolant temperature sensor.

6 On V6 models, unclip the HT leads from the fuel pressure regulator bracket.

7 Disconnect the vacuum and fuel pipes from the fuel pressure regulator, and the fuel feed union from the fuel rail **(see illustration)**. Be prepared for fuel spillage.

8 On V6 models, disconnect the throttle cable(s). Remove the plenum chamber and throttle body.

9 Disconnect the injector wiring harness.

10 Unbolt the fuel rail and remove it with the injectors **(see illustrations)**. It will be necessary to pull on the rail in order to free the injectors from the manifold.

11 Disconnect the multi-plugs from the injectors **(see illustration)**.

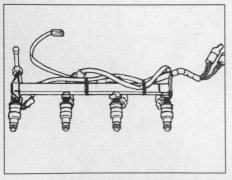

36.10a Fuel rail and injectors

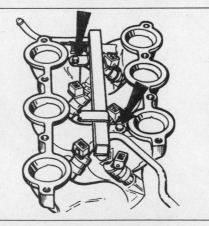

36.10b Fuel rail retaining bolts (arrowed) on V6 inlet manifold

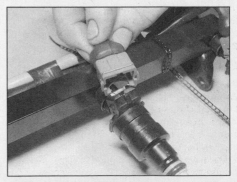

36.11 Disconnecting a fuel injector multi-plug

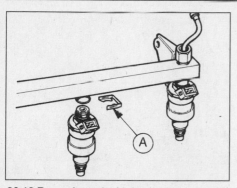

36.12 Removing a fuel injector from the rail
A Retaining clip

36.13 Injector with seals removed

36.31 Disconnecting the fuel feed hose from the fuel rail

12 Extract the retaining clips and pull the injectors out of the fuel rail **(see illustration).**

13 The sealing rings and retaining clips on all injectors must be renewed, even if only one injector has been removed from the rail. The lower seal fits between the thick and thin washers at the tip of the injector **(see illustration)**.

14 Commence refitting by coating the injector sealing rings with silicone grease to Ford spec ESEM 1C171A.

15 Press the injectors into the fuel rail and secure them with the new retaining clips. Press the clips home.

16 Reconnect the multi-plugs to the injectors.

17 Place the assembled fuel rail on the inlet manifold and press the injectors into their holes.

18 On V6 models, fit and tighten the fuel rail bolts. Refit the plenum chamber, using new gaskets, and tighten the bolts to the specified torque. Reconnect the throttle cable(s).

19 On OHC models, fit the fuel rail bolts but do not tighten them yet.

20 On all models, reconnect the fuel and vacuum pipes. Tighten the fuel pipe unions.

21 On OHC models, tighten the fuel rail bolts to the specified torque.

22 Reconnect the multi-plugs which were displaced during removal. On V6 models, secure the HT leads to the pressure regulator bracket.

23 On OHC models, refit the distributor cap.

24 Refit the air inlet trunking.

25 On V6 models, refit the throttle linkage cover.

26 Reconnect the battery. Run the engine and check that there are no fuel leaks.

27 Check the exhaust CO level.

DOHC engine

28 Disconnect the battery negative lead.

29 If desired, to improve access, disconnect the wiring from the inlet air temperature sensor in the inlet manifold. Similarly, the throttle cable can be moved to one side by disconnecting the cable from the throttle linkage and the spark plug HT leads can be disconnected and moved to one side, noting their locations and routing to aid refitting.

30 Slowly loosen the fuel rail fuel feed union

to relieve the pressure in the system. Be prepared for fuel spillage, and take adequate fire precautions.

31 Disconnect the fuel feed hose from the fuel rail **(see illustration)**.

32 Disconnect the fuel return hose from the fuel pressure regulator. Again, be prepared for fuel spillage.

33 Disconnect the vacuum pipe from the top of the fuel pressure regulator.

34 Disconnect the wiring plugs from the fuel temperature sensor and the fuel-injectors, noting their locations to assist with refitting.

35 Unscrew the two securing bolts, and withdraw the fuel rail.

36 Lift the fuel-injectors from their locations in the cylinder head **(see illustration)**.

37 Overhaul of the fuel-injectors is not possible, as no spares are available. If faulty, an injector must be renewed.

38 Commence refitting by fitting new seals to both ends of each fuel-injector. It is advisable to fit new seals to all the injectors, even if only one has been removed. Lubricate the seals with clean engine oil.

39 Further refitting is a reversal of removal, ensuring that all hoses, pipes and wiring plugs are correctly connected.

40 On completion, where applicable, check and if necessary adjust the idle mixture.

2.4 & 2.9 litre V6 engines

41 Disconnect the battery.

42 Remove the air inlet pipes from the throttle housing

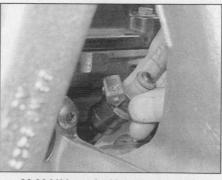

36.36 Lifting a fuel injector from the cylinder head

43 Disconnect the link arm from the throttle housing and unscrew the two bolts which retain the throttle cable bracket.

44 Disconnect the vacuum pipes from the throttle housing, crankcase vent valve and the fuel pressure regulator.

45 Disconnect the wiring connectors from the throttle position sensor, engine and coolant temperature sensors and the idle speed control valve.

46 Extract the six Torx bolts which hold the air inlet chamber in position.

47 Carefully disconnect the fuel-injector wiring connectors **(see illustration)**.

48 Depressurise the fuel system.

49 Disconnect the fuel rail feed pipe and the fuel return pipe. This is best done at the wing valance and will require cutting the crimped hose clips.

50 The crimped-type clips must then be replaced with standard worm drive hose clips on refitting.

51 Unscrew the fuel rail retaining bolts and remove the fuel rail.

52 Extract the retaining clips and remove the injectors from the fuel rail.

53 Refitting is a reverse of the removal procedure bearing in mind the following.

54 Renew all the upper and lower injector seals, even if only one injector has been disturbed. Lubricate all new seals with clean engine oil.

55 On models fitted with an early level fuel pressure regulator, it is necessary to fit a new fuel inlet pipe to the fuel rail, the new

4

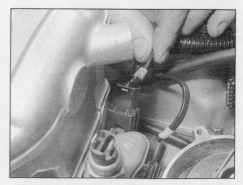

36.47 Disconnecting a fuel injector wiring connector

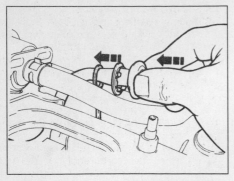

36.55a Pressing connector together to eject "tell-tale" ring

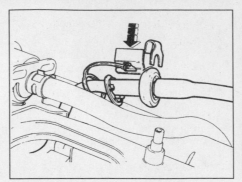

36.55b Fitting fuel rail connector clip

37.3 Disconnecting the fuel return pipe from the fuel pressure regulator

connector is supplied with a captive "tell-tale" ring, the purpose being to hold the connector teeth retracted. When the two halves of the connector are pressed together, the ring is ejected to show that the connection has been successfully made. Fit the fuel pipe connector clip **(see illustrations)**.

56 As soon as the injectors and fuel rail are installed and the fuel pipes are connected, connect the battery and switch the ignition on and off twice, without cranking the engine, to pressurise the fuel system. With the system pressurised check all disturbed fuel unions for leaks.

57 Refit and reconnect all other removed and disconnected components.

58 Reconnect the battery.

37.4 Disconnecting the vacuum pipe from the fuel pressure regulator

37 Fuel pressure regulator - removal and refitting

SOHC and 2.8 litre V6 engines

1 Disconnect the battery negative lead.
2 On V6 models, unclip the HT leads from the fuel pressure regulator bracket.
3 Place a drain pan or plenty of rags beneath the regulator, then disconnect the fuel return pipe **(see illustration)**. Be prepared for fuel spillage.
4 Disconnect the vacuum pipe from the regulator **(see illustration)**.
5 Slacken the fuel feed union nut **(see illustration)**. Wait until any residual fuel pressure has decayed, then unscrew the nut.
6 Unscrew the nut from the base of the regulator. Remove the regulator.
7 When refitting, only tighten the regulator base nut lightly at first. Secure the fuel feed union and tighten its nut, then fully tighten the base nut.
8 Reconnect the vacuum and fuel return pipes.
9 Remove the drain pan or rags. On V6 models, secure the HT leads to their clip.
10 Reconnect the battery. Switch the ignition on and off five times (without cranking the engine) and check that there are no fuel leaks from the regulator.

DOHC engine

11 Disconnect the battery negative lead.
12 Slowly loosen the fuel rail feed union to relieve the pressure in the system. Be

prepared for fuel spillage, and take adequate fire precautions.
13 Disconnect the fuel return hose from the pressure regulator **(see illustration)**. Again, be prepared for fuel spillage.
14 Disconnect the vacuum pipe from the top of the pressure regulator.
15 Unscrew the two securing bolts, and withdraw the regulator from the fuel rail along with the O-ring seal. Discard the O-ring.
16 Fit a new O-ring to the regulator, and lubricate it with a smear of clean engine oil.
17 Fit both the securing bolts to the regulator, then position the regulator on the fuel rail, and tighten the securing bolts.
18 Further refitting is a reversal of removal, but if the fuel return line was originally secured with a crimped-type clip, discard this and use a new worm drive hose clip.
19 On completion, check the fuel line connections for leaks, pressurising the system by switching the ignition on and off several times.

2.4 & 2.9 litre V6 engines

20 Disconnect the battery negative lead.
21 Depressurise the fuel system.
22 On models equipped with an aluminium fuel rail and late level fuel pressure regulator, remove the fuel return pipe retaining collar from the top of the regulator.
23 On all models, place a suitable container below the engine to catch any spilt fuel, then disconnect the fuel return pipe and the vacuum pipe from the fuel pressure regulator **(see illustration)**.

37.5 Slackening the fuel pressure regulator feed union nut

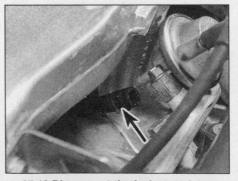

37.13 Disconnect the fuel return hose (arrowed) from the fuel pressure regulator

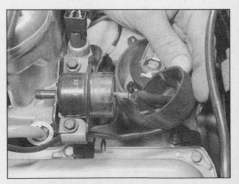

37.23 Disconnecting the vacuum hose from the fuel pressure regulator

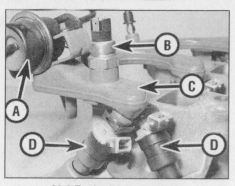

39.3 Fuel rail components
A *Fuel pressure regulator*
B *Fuel temperature switch*
C *Fuel rail*
D *Fuel injectors*

24 Unbolt and remove the regulator from the fuel rail. Remove the sealing O-ring and discard it; a new one must be used on refitting.

25 Refitting is a reverse of the removal procedure applying a smear of clean engine oil to the new regulator O-ring. On models equipped with a late level regulator, ensure that the return pipe is securely held in position by the retaining collar.

26 On completion, switch the ignition on and off five times without cranking the engine to pressurise the fuel system.

27 With the system pressurised check all disturbed fuel unions for signs of leakage.

38 Mixture adjustment potentiometer - removal and refitting

1 The potentiometer is located on the right-hand side of the engine compartment, behind the MAP sensor.

2 Disconnect the battery negative lead.

3 Remove the securing screw, then withdraw the potentiometer and disconnect the wiring plug.

4 Refitting is a reversal of removal. On completion adjust the idle mixture.

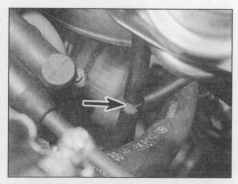

40.29 Manifold vacuum pipe T-piece (arrowed)

39 Fuel rail temperature switch - removal and refitting

1 On 2.4 & 2.9 litre V6 engines, disconnect the battery.

2 Disconnect the switch wiring connector.

3 Slacken and remove the switch from the fuel rail (see illustration).

4 Refitting is a reverse of removal, tightening the switch to the specified torque setting.

40 Inlet manifold - removal and refitting

Carburettor models

All engines except DOHC

1 Remove the carburettor or, if preferred, the final removal of the carburettor from the manifold can be left until the manifold has been removed).

2 Drain the cooling system.

3 Disconnect the coolant and vacuum pipes from the manifold, noting their positions if there is any possibility of confusion.

4 Disconnect the wires from the manifold heater and the coolant temperature sender unit.

5 Disconnect the crankcase ventilation hose from the manifold.

6 Unscrew the six nuts and bolts which secure the manifold and withdraw it. Recover the gasket.

7 Before refitting the manifold, make sure that the mating surfaces are perfectly clean.

8 Apply a bead of sealant at least 5 mm (0.2 in) wide around the central coolant aperture on both sides of a new gasket.

9 Place the gasket over the studs, then fit the manifold and secure it with the six nuts and bolts. Tighten the nuts and bolts evenly to the specified torque.

10 The remainder of refitting is a reversal of the removal procedure. Refill the cooling system on completion.

DOHC engine

11 Disconnect the battery negative lead.

12 Drain the cooling system.

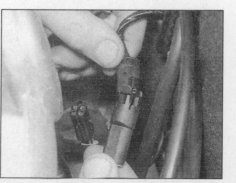

40.30 Fuel-injection wiring harness plugs

13 Remove the air cleaner.

14 Disconnect the coolant hoses from the thermostat housing and the inlet manifold, noting the locations to assist with refitting.

15 Disconnect the fuel supply and return hoses from the carburettor. Plug their ends to minimise petrol spillage.

16 Release the coolant hose from the bracket under the automatic choke housing.

17 Disconnect the HT leads from the spark plugs, and move them to one side.

18 Disconnect all relevant wiring and vacuum pipes from the carburettor, thermostat housing and inlet manifold, noting the locations as an aid to refitting.

19 Disconnect the crankcase breather hose from the inlet manifold.

20 Disconnect the throttle cable from the throttle linkage.

21 Make a final check to ensure that all relevant wires, pipes and hoses have been disconnected to facilitate removal of the manifold.

22 Unscrew the ten bolts and two nuts securing the manifold to the cylinder head.

23 Lift the manifold clear of the cylinder head and recover the gasket.

24 Recover the two plastic spark plug spacers from the recesses in the cylinder head.

25 If desired, the carburettor can be removed from the manifold by unscrewing the securing screws.

26 Refitting is a reversal of removal, bearing in mind the following points.
a) *Ensure that all mating faces are clean and renew all gaskets.*
b) *Ensure that the spark plug spacers are in position in the cylinder head recesses before refitting the manifold.*
c) *Tighten all manifold securing nuts and bolts progressively to the specified torque.*
d) *Make sure that all hoses, pipes and wires are securely reconnected in their original positions. Replace all crimp-type hose clips (where fitted) with standard worm drive hose clips.*
e) *On completion, refill the cooling system, check the adjustment of the throttle cable, then check, and if necessary adjust the idle speed and mixture.*

Fuel-injection models

SOHC engine

27 Disconnect the battery negative lead.

28 Drain the cooling system.

29 Disconnect the vacuum pipe(s) from the manifold. The number of pipes varies according to equipment. Label the pipes if necessary (see illustration).

30 Disconnect the fuel-injection harness multi-plugs at the bulkhead end of the manifold (see illustration).

31 Disconnect the oil pressure warning light sender wire from below the manifold.

32 Release the hose clips and move the airflow meter-to-manifold trunking clear of the manifold.

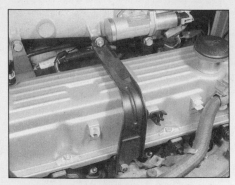

40.34 Inlet manifold-to-cylinder head bracing strut

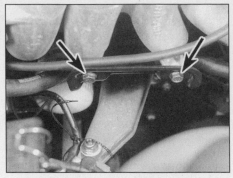

40.35 Two bolts (arrowed) secure the bracket to the manifold; the bolts securing it to the block are hidden

40.36 Unbolting the throttle cable bracket

33 Remove the distributor cap, unclip the HT leads and move the cap out of the way.
34 Remove the strut which runs from the manifold to the right-hand side of the cylinder head. It is secured by two nuts (see illustration).
35 Remove the bracket which joins the base of the manifold to the left-hand side of the block. It is secured by four bolts (see illustration).
36 Unbolt the throttle cable bracket. Unhook the cable inner and move the bracket and cable(s) aside (see illustration).
37 Disconnect the fuel feed pipe from the injector rail, and the return pipe from the fuel pressure regulator. Be prepared for fuel spillage.
38 Disconnect the coolant pipe from the base

of the manifold. Be prepared for coolant spillage.
39 Remove the six nuts and bolts which secure the manifold to the cylinder head. There may be an earth strap attached to one of the studs by an extra nut.
40 Carefully withdraw the manifold from the cylinder head, complete with its associated fuel-injection components (see illustration). If the distributor obstructs removal, extract the manifold front stud by locking two nuts together on it and thus unscrewing the stud (see illustration). Alternatively, remove the distributor.
41 Recover the gasket from the cylinder head.
42 With the manifold removed, items such as

the fuel-injector rail and the throttle body housing can be removed if required (see illustrations).
43 Clean the mating faces of the manifold and cylinder head. Keep dirt out of the ports and other orifices.
44 Commence refitting by applying a bead of sealant at least 5 mm (0.2 in) wide around the central coolant aperture on both sides of a new gasket.
45 Fit the gasket over the studs, refit the manifold and secure with the six nuts and bolts. Tighten them evenly to the specified torque.
46 The remainder of refitting is a reversal of the removal procedure. Refill the cooling system on completion.

DOHC engine

47 Disconnect the battery negative lead.
48 Drain the cooling system.
49 Disconnect the coolant hoses from the thermostat housing and the inlet manifold.
50 Disconnect the air inlet hose from the front of the inlet manifold.
51 Disconnect the breather hoses and the vacuum hoses from the inlet manifold.
52 Disconnect the throttle cable and (where necessary) the speed control cable from the throttle linkage (see illustration).
53 Disconnect the HT leads from the spark plugs, noting the locations to aid refitting, and move them to one side.
54 Disconnect the wiring from the cooling fan switch, the engine coolant temperature sensor, and the temperature gauge sender.

40.40a Removing the inlet manifold

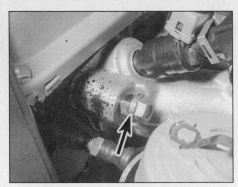

40.40b Use two nuts locked together (arrowed) to remove the stud

40.42a Removing the fuel rail and injectors from the manifold

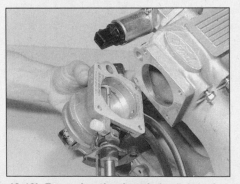

40.42b Removing the throttle body housing

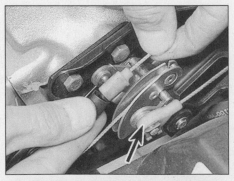

40.52 Disconnect the throttle cable from the linkage. Speed control cable (arrowed)

40.59 Removing a spark plug spacer from the cylinder head recess

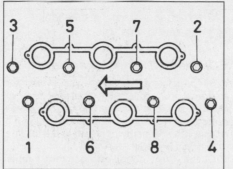

40.79 Inlet manifold bolt tightening sequence
Arrow points to front of engine

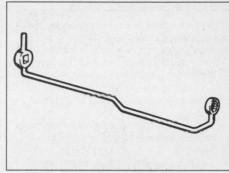

40.87 Cranked spanner needed for tightening V6 inlet manifold bolt with distributor fitted

55 Release the throttle position sensor wiring connector from the clip under the throttle body, and separate the two halves of the connector.
56 Remove the fuel-injectors.
57 Check that all relevant wiring, hoses and pipes have been disconnected to facilitate removal of the manifold.
58 Unscrew the ten bolts and two nuts securing the inlet manifold to the cylinder head, and carefully withdraw the manifold. Recover the gasket.
59 Recover the two plastic spark plug spacers from the recesses in the cylinder head **(see illustration)**.
60 If desired, the manifold can be dismantled with reference to the relevant paragraphs of this Chapter.
61 Refitting is a reversal of removal, bearing in mind the following points.
a) *Ensure that the spark plug spacers are in position in the cylinder head recesses before refitting the manifold.*
b) *Ensure manifold and cylinder head mating surfaces are clean and dry and fit a new gasket.*
c) *Tighten the manifold retaining nuts and bolts evenly and progressively to the specified torque.*
d) *Refit the fuel-injectors.*
e) *Make sure that all hoses, pipes and wires are securely reconnected in their original positions.*
f) *On completion, refill the cooling system.*
g) *Check the adjustment of the throttle cable and where necessary, adjust the speed control cable so that only a small amount of slack is present in the cable.*
h) *Where applicable, check and if necessary adjust the idle speed and mixture.*

V6 engines

62 Disconnect the battery negative lead.
63 Drain the cooling system.
64 Remove the throttle linkage cover.
65 Release the hose clips and move the airflow meter-to-manifold trunking aside. Unclip or remove the crankcase ventilation hose.
66 Disconnect the radiator top hose and the heater hose from the outlet at the front of the manifold. Be prepared for some coolant spillage.

67 Disconnect the multi-plugs from the idle speed control valve, the temperature gauge sender unit; the coolant temperature sensor and the throttle position sensor. Also disconnect the injector wiring harness.
68 Disconnect the throttle cable from the linkage, unclip it and move it aside. On automatic transmission models, also disconnect the downshift cable or multi-plug, as applicable.
69 Disconnect the fuel feed and return pipes. Be prepared for fuel spillage.
70 Remove the HT leads and the distributor.
71 Remove the plenum chamber, which is secured by eight bolts.
72 Remove the rocker covers, which are each secured by seven bolts.
73 Disconnect the water pump bypass hose from the inlet manifold.
74 Remove the eight bolts which secure the inlet manifold to the cylinder heads.
75 Lift off the manifold complete with fuel pressure regulator, fuel rail, throttle body housing etc. If it is stuck, carefully lever it free. **Do not apply leverage at the mating faces.** Recover the gasket.
76 Clean all mating faces, being careful to keep dirt out of ports and other orifices. Obtain new gaskets for both the cylinder head and plenum chamber sides of the manifold, and for the rocker covers.
77 Commence refitting by applying sealant (Ford part No A70X-19554-BA, or equivalent) around the ports and coolant passages on the cylinder head.
78 Apply sealant around the apertures on both sides of the gasket, then fit the gasket to the cylinder heads.
79 Refit the manifold and insert the securing bolts. Tighten the bolts, in the order shown **(see illustration),** through the first four stages given in the Specifications.
80 Refit the water pump bypass hose.
81 Refit the rocker covers, using new gaskets. The adhesive sides of the gaskets must face the covers.
82 Reverse the remaining removal operations, but do not refit the throttle linkage cover yet.
83 When the cooling system has been

refilled, reconnect the battery and start the engine. Check for fuel and other leaks.
84 Bring the engine to operating temperature, then stop it and carry out the final tightening of the inlet manifold bolts as follows.
85 Release the air inlet trunking. Unplug the idle speed control valve and the throttle position sensor. Unbolt the plenum chamber and move it aside, disconnecting vacuum and breather hoses as necessary.
86 Slacken, but do not remove, the two bolts which secure the fuel rail to the manifold.
87 Tighten the inlet manifold bolts to the Stage 5 specified torque, again following the sequence shown. A special cranked spanner (Ford tool No 21-079, or equivalent) **(see illustration)** will be needed to tighten No 4 bolt when the distributor is fitted. In the absence of such a spanner, remove the distributor again.
88 Tighten the fuel rail securing bolts.
89 Refit the disturbed components. Run the engine again and check the ignition timing and the exhaust CO level.
90 Refit the throttle linkage cover.

41 Exhaust manifold(s) - removal and refitting

SOHC and all V6 engines

1 Disconnect the battery negative lead.
2 Apply copious quantities of penetrating oil to the manifold and exhaust pipe flange nuts and bolts.
3 On carburettor models, remove the air cleaner and the hot air pick-up pipe.
4 Unbolt any heat shields or shrouds from the manifold.
5 Unbolt the exhaust pipe(s) from the manifold flange. Support the exhaust system if necessary.
6 Unbolt the manifold from the cylinder head and remove it. Recover the gasket.
7 Refit by reversing the removal operations. Use a new gasket, and apply anti-seize compound to the various nuts and bolts. Tighten the manifold fastenings to the specified torque.

DOHC carburettor engine

8 This procedure is essentially as described above, noting the following points:
a) *Note the plastic bush which is fitted to the rear manifold stud. This must be removed before the gasket can be withdrawn.*
b) *On refitting ensure that the mating surfaces are clean and dry and fit new gaskets.*
c) *Apply a thin coat of anti-seize compound to the manifold studs to aid future removal.*
d) *Tighten the manifold nuts to the specified torque settings.*

DOHC fuel-injection engine

9 Disconnect the battery negative lead.
10 Disconnect the wiring plug from the idle speed control valve at the front of the plenum chamber.
11 Loosen the clamp, and detach the air inlet hose from the air inlet tubing.
12 Unscrew the securing nut, and release the air inlet tube from the bracket on the engine compartment front panel.
13 Release the air cleaner lid securing clips, then lift away the air inlet tube, plenum chamber and air cleaner lid as an assembly, disconnecting the breather hose from the air inlet tube.
14 On models fitted with a catalytic converter, disconnect the exhaust gas oxygen sensor wiring plug.
15 Unscrew the securing nuts and disconnect the exhaust downpipe from the manifold. Recover the gasket. Support the exhaust downpipe from underneath the vehicle (eg with an axle stand) to avoid placing unnecessary strain on the exhaust system.
16 Unscrew the six securing nuts, and lift the manifold from the cylinder head. Recover the gasket.
17 Refitting is a reversal of removal, bearing in mind the following points.
a) *Ensure that all mating faces are clean, and use a new gasket.*
b) *Tighten the manifold securing nuts and the downpipe securing nuts progressively to the specified torque (where given).*

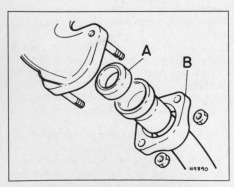

42.11 Exhaust pipe flanged joint
A *Sealing ring*
B *Flange*

42 Exhaust system - inspection, repair and renewal

SOHC and 2.8 litre V6 engines

1 Periodically inspect the exhaust system for freedom from corrosion and security of mountings. Large holes will be obvious; small holes may be found more easily by letting the engine idle and partly obstructing the tailpipe with a wad of cloth.
2 Check the condition of the rubber mountings by applying downward pressure on the exhaust system and observing the mountings for splits or cracks. Renew deteriorated mountings.
3 The exhaust systems fitted in production have fewer sections than those available for repair. Repair sections may be fitted to production systems by cutting at the appropriate point.
4 The production exhaust systems are made of aluminised and stainless steel. Repair systems are available to the same standard, or in standard quality (SQ) painted mild steel.
5 It is recommended that the whole exhaust system be removed even if only part requires renewal, since separation of old joints, cutting pipes etc is much easier away from the vehicle. Proceed as follows.
6 Disconnect the battery negative lead. Raise and support the vehicle.
7 Unbolt the manifold-to-downpipe flanged joint(s).
8 On V6 models, unbolt the left-hand front silencer mounting.
9 Release any earth straps.
10 With the help of an assistant, unhook the system from its mountings and remove it.
11 Renew sections as necessary. Apply exhaust jointing compound to sliding and flanged joints, but do not tighten their clamps yet. Use new sealing rings where necessary **(see illustration)**.
12 Offer the system to the vehicle and hook it onto the mountings.
13 Refit any earth straps. On V6 models, also refit the left-hand front silencer mounting.
14 Loosely fit the manifold flange nuts. Correct the alignment of the system, then tighten all clamp nuts and bolts, starting at the manifold flange(s) and working rearwards.
15 Check that the system alignment is still satisfactory then reconnect the battery. Run the engine and check for leaks.
16 When the system has warmed up, stop the engine and carefully check the tightness of the clamp nuts and bolts.

DOHC and 2.4 & 2.9 litre V6 engines

17 Follow the above procedure, noting that flanged joints incorporating gaskets may be used to join exhaust sections on these models. Where applicable, renew the gaskets on refitting.
18 On models fitted with a catalytic converter, disconnect the battery negative terminal and disconnect the exhaust gas oxygen (HEGO) sensor wiring plug before removing the downpipe.

43 Exhaust gas oxygen (HEGO) sensor (models with catalytic converter) - removal and refitting

DOHC engine

Note: *The exhaust gas oxygen (HEGO) sensor is delicate and will not work if it is dropped or knocked, if the power supply is disrupted, or if any cleaning materials are used on it.* **Never touch the tip of the sensor as this can also damage it.**

1 Ensure that the engine and the exhaust system are cold.
2 Disconnect the battery negative lead.
3 Apply the handbrake, then jack up the front of the vehicle, and support it securely on axle stands (see "*Jacking*").
4 Disconnect the sensor wiring plug halves by releasing the locktabs and pulling on the plug halves, not the wiring.
5 Slide the heat shield (where fitted) from the sensor.
6 Bearing in mind the note made at the start of this operation, unscrew the sensor from the exhaust downpipe, and recover the sealing ring **(see illustration)**.
7 Commence refitting by ensuring that the sensor threads and the corresponding threads in the downpipe are clean.
8 Refit the sensor using a new sealing ring, and tighten it to the specified torque.
9 Further refitting is a reversal of removal, but on completion start the engine, and check for leaks around the sensor sealing ring.

V6 engines

10 The sensors fitted to these models can be removed and refitted using the information given above, noting that on early models there was only one sensor, which was fitted at the point where the two downpipes meet below the engine, and on some later models there are two sensors, one in each downpipe.

43.6 Exhaust gas oxygen (HEGO) sensor (viewed from underneath)

44 Carbon canister (models with catalytic converter) - removal and refitting

Models up to July 1990

1 The carbon canister is situated in the engine compartment where it is mounted onto the right-hand valance next to the suspension strut mounting.

2 To remove the canister first disconnect the battery negative terminal. If necessary, undo the two coolant expansion tank retaining screws and position the tank clear of the canister to improve access.

3 Disconnect the vacuum hose from the top of the canister.

4 Slacken and remove the mounting bolt and withdraw the canister from the engine compartment.

5 Refitting is a reverse of the removal procedure.

Models from July 1990

6 The carbon canister is situated behind the right-hand rear wheel where it is mounted onto the vehicle underbody **(see illustration)**.

7 To gain access to the canister, chock the front wheels then jack up the rear of the vehicle and support it securely on axle stands (see "*Jacking*").

8 Disconnect the battery negative terminal.

9 Disconnect the vacuum hose from the top of the canister and remove the canister retaining screw.

10 Lift the canister upwards to disengage it from the mounting bracket and remove it from under the car.

11 Refitting is a reversal of the removal procedure ensuring that the canister retaining clip is correctly located in the mounting bracket.

45 Carbon canister purge solenoid (models with catalytic converter) - removal and refitting

1 The purge solenoid is located on the right-hand side of the engine compartment next to the suspension strut mounting **(see illustration)**.

2 Disconnect the battery negative lead.

3 Disconnect the solenoid wiring plug halves by releasing the locktabs and pulling on the plug halves, not the wiring.

4 Note the locations of the two solenoid pipes, and the orientation of the solenoid to assist with refitting.

5 Disconnect the two pipes from the solenoid, and withdraw the solenoid from the location.

6 Refitting is a reversal of removal, ensuring that the solenoid pipes are correctly reconnected, and that the solenoid is correctly orientated as noted before removal.

46 Unleaded fuel - general

SOHC and 2.8 litre V6 engines

1 It is generally believed that continuous use of unleaded fuel can cause rapid wear of conventional valve seats. Valve seat inserts which can tolerate unleaded fuel are fitted to some engines. These engines are identified as follows:

1.8 litre - S stamped adjacent to No 4 spark plug
2.0 litre - A, L, P, PP or R stamped adjacent to No 4 spark plug
2.8 litre - D or E stamped in centre of cylinder head exhaust flange

2 Engines which are marked as above can be run entirely on unleaded fuel.

3 Engines which are not fitted with the special valve seat inserts can still be run on unleaded fuel, but one tankful of leaded fuel should be used for every three tankfuls of unleaded. This will protect the valve seats.

4 On all models, the ignition timing may have to be retarded when unleaded fuel is used. For up to date information consult a Ford dealer.

DOHC engines

5 All models can be operated on unleaded petrol without the need for any adjustments. Note that models fitted with a catalytic converter must only be operated on unleaded petrol, and leaded petrol **must not** be used.

2.4 & 2.9 litre V6 engines

6 All engines can be run on 95 octane unleaded fuel (ie Premium grade unleaded).

7 On 2.9 litre models equipped with a manual gearbox produced after approximately December 1988 and models equipped with automatic transmission which were produced after approximately July 1988, there is no need to adjust the ignition timing to run on unleaded petrol. These models can be identified by their ignition module number suffixes; on manual gearbox models the module should have a JA suffix and on models equipped with automatic transmission the module should have a BD suffix. Refer to your Ford dealer for further information.

8 On all other earlier models, the ignition timing must be adjusted before the engine can be run on unleaded petrol. On these models the timing must be adjusted by the fitment of an octane adjustment lead, described in Chapter 5, Section 23. On both the 2.4 & 2.9 litre engines, the lead should be fitted and the red terminal earthed; this retards the ignition timing by 4° from the initial setting of 12° BTDC, to the correct setting of 8° BTDC.

9 Models which are equipped with a catalytic converter **must** be run on unleaded fuel **only**.

44.6 Carbon canister location (arrowed) - models from July 1990

45.1 Carbon canister purge valve

Chapter 5
Engine electrical systems

Contents

Degrees of difficulty

Easy, suitable for novice with little experience	Fairly easy, suitable for beginner with some experience	Fairly difficult, suitable for competent DIY mechanic	Difficult, suitable for experienced DIY mechanic	Very difficult, suitable for expert DIY or professional

Specifications

General

Electrical system type	12 volt, negative earth
Ignition system type:	Breakerless, Hall effect, with electronic control of advance
Carburettor models	ESC II system
Fuel-injection models	EEC IV system
Firing order:	
OHC	1-3-4-2 (No 1 at pulley end)
V6	1-4-2-5-3-6 (No 1 at front of right-hand bank)

Alternator

Make and type	Bosch KI-55A, NI-70A or NI-90A
Rated output at 13.5 volts and 6000 engine rpm	55, 70 or 90 amps
Rotor winding resistance at 20°C (68°F):	
KI-55A	3.4 to 3.7 ohms
NI-70A and NI-90A	2.8 to 3.1 ohms
Brush wear limit	5 mm (0.2 in)
Regulated voltage at 4000 engine rpm and 3 to 7 amp load	13.7 to 14.6 volts
Voltage regulator type	Solid state, integral

Starter motor

Make and type	Bosch short frame, long frame or reduction gear
Rating:	
Short frame	0.85 or 0.95 kW
Long frame	1.1 kW
Reduction gear	1.4 kW
Brush wear limit:	
Short frame and reduction gear	8 mm (0.32 in)
Long frame	10 mm (0.39 in)
Commutator minimum diameter	32.8 mm (1.29 in)
Armature endfloat	0.3 mm (0.012 in)

5

Ignition coil

Make	Bosch, Femsa or Polmot
Primary resistance	0.72 to 0.86 ohm
Secondary resistance:	
All except DOHC fuel-injection	4.5 to 7.0 k ohms
DOHC fuel-injection	4.5 to 8.6 k ohms
Output voltage (open-circuit):	
All except DOHC fuel-injection	25 kV minimum
DOHC fuel-injection	30 kV minimum

HT leads

Maximum resistance per lead	30 k ohms

Distributor

Make	Bosch or Motorcraft
Rotation	Clockwise (viewed from above)
Automatic advance	Controlled by module
Dwell angle	Controlled by module

Ignition timing (see text)

SOHC and 2.8 litre V6 engines:	
Leaded fuel (97 octane):	
Carburettor models	10° BTDC
Fuel-injection models	12°BTDC
Unleaded fuel (95 octane):	
Carburettor models	6°BTDC
Fuel-injection models:	
2.0 litre	8°BTDC
2.8 litre	12°BTDC (no change)
2.4 & 2.9 litre V6 engines:	
Models with catalytic converter	15° BTDC
Models without catalytic converter	12° BTDC*

* Standard setting for 97 octane leaded fuel.

Torque wrench settings

	Nm	lbf ft
Alternator adjusting strap:		
To steering pump bracket (OHC)	21 to 26	16 to 19
To front cover (V6)	41 to 51	30 to 38
Spark plugs:		
All models except 2.8 litre V6	20 to 28	15 to 21
2.8 litre V6	30 to 40	22 to 30
Air charge temperature sensor	20 to 25	15 to 18
Engine coolant temperature sensor	20 to 25	15 to 18
Fuel rail temperature sensor (DOHC)	8 to 11	6 to 8
Crankshaft speed/position sensor screw (DOHC)	3 to 5	2 to 4

1 General information and precautions

The ignition system is responsible for igniting the fuel/air charge in each cylinder at the correct moment. The components of the system are the spark plugs, ignition coil, distributor and connecting leads. Overall control of the system is one of the functions of the engine management module. Fuel-injection models have a subsidiary ignition module mounted on the distributor.

There are no contact breaker points in the distributor. A square wave signal is generated by the distributor electro-magnetically; this signal is used by the engine management module as a basis for switching the coil LT current. Speed-related (centrifugal) advance is also handled by the module. On carburettor models, ignition timing is also advanced under conditions of high inlet manifold vacuum.

The engine management models are "black boxes" which regulate both the fuel and the ignition systems to obtain the best power, economy and emission levels. The module fitted to carburettor models is known as the ESC II (Electronic Spark Control Mk II) module. On fuel-injection models the more powerful EEC IV (Electronic Engine Control Mk IV) module is used.

Both types of module receive inputs from sensors monitoring coolant temperature, distributor rotor position and (on some models) manifold vacuum. Outputs from the module control ignition timing, inlet manifold heating and (except on 1.8 litre models) idle speed. The EEC IV module also has overall control of the fuel-injection system, from which it receives information.

Provision is made for the ignition timing to be retarded to allow the use of low octane fuel if necessary. On all except 1.8 litre models there is also a facility for raising the idle speed.

The EEC IV module contains self-test circuitry which enables a technician with the appropriate test equipment to diagnose faults in a very short time. A Limited Operation Strategy (LOS) means that the car is still driveable, albeit at reduced power and efficiency, in the event of a failure in the module or its sensors.

Due to the complexity and expense of the test equipment dedicated to the engine management system, suspected faults should be investigated by a Ford dealer, or other competent specialist. This Chapter deals with component removal and refitting, and with some simple checks and adjustments.

On DOHC carburettor engines, the basic operating principles of the ignition system are as described above. A development of the ESC II (Electronic Spark Control II) system is used to control the operation of the engine. The ESC II module receives information from a crankshaft speed/position sensor and an engine coolant temperature sensor. The crankshaft speed/position sensor is activated by a toothed disc on the rear of the crankshaft, inside the cylinder block. The disc has 35 equally spaced teeth (one every 10°), with a gap in the 36th position. The gap is used by the sensor to determine the crankshaft position relative to Top Dead Centre (TDC) of No 1 piston.

The ignition advance is a function of the ESC II module, and is controlled by vacuum. The module is connected to the carburettor by a vacuum pipe, and a transducer in the module translates the vacuum signal into an electrical voltage. From the vacuum signal, the module determines engine load; engine speed and temperature are determined from the crankshaft speed/position sensor and the engine coolant temperature sensor. The module has a range of spark advance settings stored in the memory, and a suitable setting is selected for the relevant engine speed, load and temperature. The degree of advance can thus be constantly varied to suit the prevailing engine speed and load conditions.

On DOHC fuel-injected engines, a development of the EEC IV (Electronic Engine Control IV) engine management system is used to control both the ignition and fuel-injection systems. The EEC IV module receives information from a crankshaft speed/position sensor (the same as that fitted to the carburettor models), a throttle position sensor, an engine coolant temperature sensor, a fuel temperature sensor, an air charge temperature sensor, a Manifold Absolute Pressure (MAP) sensor, and a vehicle speed sensor (mounted on the gearbox). Additionally, on models with a catalytic converter, an additional input is supplied to the EEC IV module from an exhaust gas oxygen (HEGO) sensor. On models with automatic transmission, additional sensors are fitted to the transmission to inform the EEC IV module when the transmission is in neutral, and when the downshift is being operated.

The module provides outputs to control the fuel pump, fuel-injectors, idle speed, ignition system and automatic transmission . Additionally, on models with air conditioning, the EEC IV module disengages the air conditioning compressor clutch when starting the engine or when the engine is suddenly accelerated. On models fitted with a catalytic converter, the EEC IV module also controls the carbon canister purge solenoid valve.

Using the inputs from the various sensors, the EEC IV module computes the optimum ignition advance, and fuel-injector pulse duration to suit the prevailing engine conditions.

On 2.4 & 2.9 litre V6 engines, the system operates in much the same way as that fitted to the DOHC fuel-injected engine, noting the following points.
a) There is no crankshaft speed/position sensor.
b) The vehicle speed sensor is only fitted to models equipped with a catalytic converter.

Precautions

ESC II module

Although it will tolerate all normal under-bonnet conditions, the ESC II module may be adversely affected by water entry during steam cleaning or pressure washing of the engine bay.

If cleaning the engine bay, therefore, take care not to direct jets of water or steam at the ESC II module. If this cannot be avoided, remove the module completely, and protect its multi-plug with a plastic bag.

Ignition system HT voltage

Take care to avoid receiving electric shocks from the HT side of the ignition system. Do not handle HT leads, or touch the distributor or coil, when the engine is running. When tracing faults in the HT system, use well insulated tools to manipulate live leads. **Electronic ignition HT voltage could prove fatal.**

Electronic ignition systems

⚠️ *Warning. The voltages produced by the electronic ignition system are considerably higher than those produced by conventional systems. Extreme care must be taken when working on the system with the ignition switched on. Persons with surgically-implanted cardiac pacemaker devices should keep well clear of the ignition circuits, components and test equipment.*

General

Further details of the various systems are given in the relevant Sections of this Chapter. While some repair procedures are given, the usual course of action is to renew the component concerned. The owner whose interest extends beyond mere component renewal should obtain a copy of the *Automobile Electrical & Electronic Systems Manual*, available from the publishers of this manual.

It is necessary to take extra care when working on the electrical system, to avoid damage to semi-conductor devices (diodes and transistors), and to avoid the risk of personal injury. In addition to the precautions given in *Safety first!* at the beginning of this manual, observe the following when working on the system:

Always remove rings, watches, etc before working on the electrical system. Even with the battery disconnected, capacitive discharge could occur if a component's live terminal is earthed through a metal object. This could cause a shock or nasty burn.

Do not reverse the battery connections. Components such as the alternator, electronic control units, or any other components having semi-conductor circuitry, could be irreparably damaged.

If the engine is being started using jump leads and a slave battery, connect the batteries *positive-to-positive* and *negative-to-negative* (see *"Jump starting"*). This also applies when connecting a battery charger.

Never disconnect the battery terminals, the alternator, any electrical wiring, or any test instruments, when the engine is running.

Do not allow the engine to turn the alternator when the alternator is not connected.

Never test for alternator output by "flashing" the output lead to earth.

Never use an ohmmeter of the type incorporating a hand-cranked generator for circuit or continuity testing.

Always ensure that the battery negative lead is disconnected when working on the electrical system.

Before using electric-arc welding equipment on the car, disconnect the battery, alternator, and components such as the fuel-injection/ignition electronic control unit, to protect them from the risk of damage.

2 Electrical fault-finding - general information

Refer to Chapter 13

3 Battery - charging

1 In normal use the battery should not require charging from an external source, unless the vehicle is laid up for long periods, when it should be recharged every six weeks or so. If vehicle use consists entirely of short runs in darkness it is also possible for the battery to become discharged. Otherwise, a regular need for recharging points to a fault in the battery or elsewhere in the charging system.
2 There is no need to disconnect the battery from the vehicle wiring when using a battery charger, but switch off the ignition and leave the bonnet open.
3 Domestic battery chargers (up to about 6 amps output) may safely be used overnight without special precautions. Make sure that the charger is set to deliver 12 volts before connecting it. Connect the leads (red or positive to the positive terminal, black or negative to the negative terminal) **before** switching the charger on at the mains.
4 When charging is complete, switch off at the mains **before** disconnecting the charger from the battery. Remember that the battery will be giving off hydrogen gas, which is potentially explosive.
5 Charging at a higher rate should only be carried out under carefully controlled conditions. Very rapid or "boost" charging should be avoided if possible, as it is liable to cause permanent damage to the battery through overheating.
6 During any sort of charging, battery electrolyte temperature should never exceed 38°C (100°F). If the battery becomes hot, or the electrolyte is effervescing vigorously, charging should be stopped.

4 Battery - removal and refitting

1 Disconnect the battery negative (earth) lead.
2 Disconnect the battery positive leads. These may be protected by a plastic cover. Do not allow the spanner to bridge the positive and negative terminals.
3 Release the battery hold-down clamp. Lift out the battery. Keep it upright and be careful not to drop it - it is heavy.
4 Commence by placing the battery in its tray, making sure it is the right way round. Secure it with the hold-down clamp.
5 Clean the battery terminals if necessary then reconnect them. Connect the positive lead first, then the negative lead.

5 Alternator - testing on the vehicle

1 Should it appear that the alternator is not charging the battery, check first that the drivebelt is intact and in good condition and that its tension is correct. Also check the condition and security of the alternator electrical connections and the battery leads.
2 Accurate assessment of alternator output requires special equipment and a degree of skill. A rough idea of whether output is adequate can be gained by using a voltmeter (range 0 to 15 or 0 to 20 volts) as follows.
3 Connect the voltmeter across the battery terminals. Switch on the headlights and note the voltage reading: it should be between 12 and 13 volts.
4 Start the engine and run it at a fast idle (approx 1500 rpm). Read the voltmeter: it should indicate 13 to 14 volts.
5 With the engine still running at a fast idle, switch on as many electrical consumers as possible (heated rear window, heater blower etc). The voltage at the battery should be maintained at 13 to 14 volts. Increase the engine speed slightly if necessary to keep the voltage up.
6 If alternator output is low or zero, check the brushes. If the brushes are OK, seek expert advice.

7 Occasionally the condition may arise where the alternator output is excessive. Clues to this condition are constantly blowing bulbs; brightness of lights vary considerably with engine speed; overheating of alternator and battery, possible with steam or fumes coming from the battery. This condition is almost certainly due to a defective voltage regulator, but expert advice should be sought.
8 Note that the alternator voltage regulator can be renewed without removing the alternator from the vehicle. The procedure is part of brush renewal.

6 Alternator - removal and refitting

1 Disconnect the battery negative lead.
2 Disconnect the multi-plug from the rear of the alternator. It may be secured by a wire clip.
3 Slacken the alternator adjusting and pivot nut(s), bolt(s) and washer(s) (see illustration). Swing the alternator towards the engine and slip the drivebelt(s) off the pulley.
4 Support the alternator. Remove the adjusting and pivot nuts, bolts and washers, noting the fitted positions of the washers. Lift out the alternator. Do not drop it, it is fragile.
5 Refit by reversing the removal operations. Tension the drivebelt(s) then tighten the adjustment strap bolt followed by the pivot nut and bolt. If there are two pivot bolts, tighten the front one first.
6 Refit the multi-plug and reconnect the battery.

7 Alternator - brush renewal

1 The alternator brushes can be inspected or renewed without removing the alternator from the vehicle, but disconnect the battery negative lead first.
2 From the rear of the alternator remove the two screws which secure the voltage regulator/brush carrier assembly. Withdraw the assembly (see illustration).
3 Measure the length of each brush protruding from the carrier (see illustration). If they are worn down to, or below, the minimum

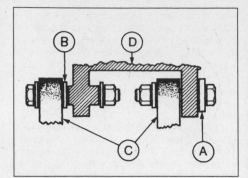

6.3 Alternator mounting details
A Large washer
B Small washer (not always fitted)
C Mounting bracket
D Alternator
Some models have a single pivot bolt

specified, the old brushes will have to be unsoldered and new ones soldered into place. Some skill with a soldering iron will be required; excess heat from the soldering iron could damage the voltage regulator. When fitted, the new brushes must move freely in their holders.
4 Clean the slip rings with a cloth moistened with methylated spirit (see illustration). If they are badly burnt or damaged, seek expert advice.
5 Refit the assembled brush carrier/voltage regulator and secure it with the two screws. If the alternator is on the vehicle, reconnect the battery negative lead.

8 Starter motor - testing on the vehicle

1 If the starter motor fails to operate, first check that the battery is charged by switching on the headlights. If the headlights do not come on, or rapidly become dim, the battery or its connections are at fault.
2 Check the security and condition of the battery and starter solenoid connections. Remember that the heavy lead to the solenoid is always "live" - disconnect the battery negative lead before using tools on the solenoid connections.

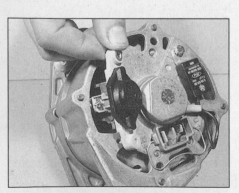

7.2 Removing the voltage regulator/brush carrier

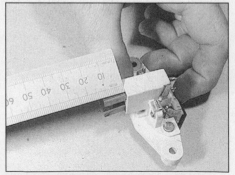

7.3 Measuring brush protrusion

7.4 Clean the slip rings (arrowed)

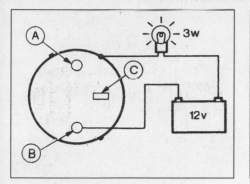

8.4 Solenoid winding check

A Battery terminal   C Spade terminal
B Motor terminal

Solenoid check

3 Disconnect the battery negative lead, and all leads from the solenoid.

4 Connect a battery and a 3 watt test lamp between the solenoid body and the solenoid motor terminal **(see illustration)**. The test lamp should light: if not, the solenoid windings are open-circuit.

5 Connect a battery and an 18 to 21 watt test lamp across the solenoid motor and battery terminals. Connect a further lead from the battery positive terminal to the solenoid spade terminal **(see illustration)**. The solenoid should be heard to operate and the test lamp should light: if not, the solenoid contacts are defective.

On load voltage check

6 Remake the original connections to the solenoid and reconnect the battery negative lead. Connect a voltmeter across the battery terminals, then disconnect the low tension lead from the coil positive terminal and operate the starter by turning the ignition switch. Note the reading on the voltmeter which should not be less than 10.5 volts.

7 Now connect the voltmeter between the starter motor terminal on the solenoid and the starter motor body. With the coil low tension lead still disconnected, operate the starter and check that the recorded voltage is not more than 1 volt lower than that previously noted. If the voltage drop is more than 1 volt a fault exists in the wiring from the battery to the starter.

8 Connect the voltmeter between the battery positive terminal and the terminal on the starter motor. With the coil low tension lead disconnected operate the starter for two or three seconds. Battery voltage should be indicated initially, then dropping to less than 1 volt. If the reading is more than 1 volt there is a high resistance in the wiring from the battery to the starter and the check in paragraph 9 should be made. If the reading is less than 1 volt proceed to paragraph 10.

9 Connect the voltmeter between the two main solenoid terminals and operate the starter for two or three seconds. Battery

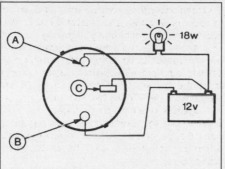

8.5 Solenoid contact check

A Battery terminal   C Spade terminal
B Motor terminal

voltage should be indicated initially then dropping to less than 0.5 volt. If the reading is more than 0.5 volt, the solenoid and connections may be faulty.

10 Connect the voltmeter between the battery negative terminal and the starter motor body, and operate the starter for two or three seconds. A reading of less than 0.5 volt should be recorded; however, if the reading is more, the earth circuit is faulty and the earth connections to the battery and body should be checked.

9 Starter motor - removal and refitting

1 Disconnect the battery negative lead. Raise and support the front of the vehicle.

2 From underneath the vehicle, disconnect the feed (heavy) cable from the solenoid.

3 Disconnect the command lead from the solenoid spade terminal.

4 Undo the starter motor securing bolts and (where fitted) the support bracket fastenings. Withdraw the starter motor from the vehicle.

5 Refit by reversing the removal operations. Check for correct operation on completion.

10 Starter motor - brush renewal

1 Disconnect the motor lead from the solenoid terminal.

2 Remove the two screws which secure the armature end cap. Remove the cap, the C-washer and the plain washer(s).

3 Remove the two through-bolts or studs.

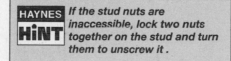

HAYNES HiNT *If the stud nuts are inaccessible, lock two nuts together on the stud and turn them to unscrew it.*

4 Remove the commutator end cover to expose the brushgear. Carefully withdraw the brushplate from the commutator. Be careful to avoid damage to the brushes as they are released.

5 Examine the brushes: they should not be

excessively worn (see Specifications) and must slide freely in their holders. Brush renewal varies according to motor type as follows:

Short frame - the brush lead must be removed from the stand-off connector on the brushplate, and the clip on the new brush lead soldered to the connector.

Long frame - the old brush leads must be cut and the new leads attached by soldering

Reduction gear - the brushplate must be renewed complete with brushes, holders and springs

6 Reassembly is the reverse of dismantling whilst noting the following:

7 Clean the commutator with a rag moistened with methylated spirit, then refit the brushplate.

8 Either clip the brushes in place after fitting the plate, or use a tube of suitable diameter to keep the brushes retracted during fitting.

9 Make sure that the brushplate is correctly positioned to allow the passage of through-bolts or studs.

11 Spark plugs - removal, inspection and refitting

See Chapter 1, Section 20.

12 HT leads, distributor cap and rotor arm - removal, inspection and refitting

See Chapter 1, Section 39.

13 Distributor - removal and refitting

All engines except 2.4 & 2.9 litre V6

Note: *The distributor should not be removed without good cause, since the accuracy of ignition timing achieved in production is unlikely to be regained*

1 Disconnect the battery negative lead.

2 Remove the distributor cap as described in the previous Section. Depending on model, it may be possible to move the cap aside without disconnecting the HT leads.

3 Using a spanner on the crankshaft pulley bolt, turn the engine to bring No 1 cylinder to firing point. (If the distributor cap is secured by clips, make sure the clips stay clear of the distributor moving parts.) No 1 cylinder is at firing point when:

a) The timing marks are in alignment.

b) The tip of the rotor arm is pointing to the place occupied by the No 1 HT lead connector in the distributor cap **(see illustration)**.

4 With No 1 cylinder at firing point, the tip of the rotor arm should also be aligned with a notch in the distributor body. Mark the notch for reference when refitting.

5 Depress the locking tab on the distributor

5

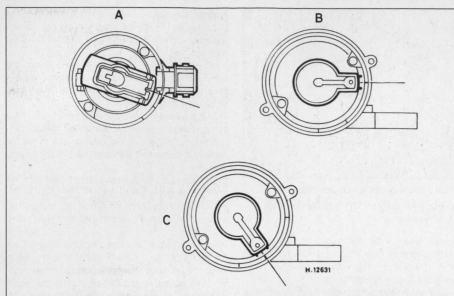

13.3 Distributor rotor arm positions before removal - No 1 firing point

A Carburettor models   B OHC fuel-injection models   C V6 models

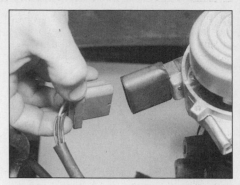

13.5 Disconnecting a distributor multi-plug

13.6 Distributor clamp bolt (arrowed)

multi-plug. Disconnect the plug, pulling on the plug itself, not the wires **(see illustration)**.

6 Make alignment marks between the distributor body and the engine, then remove the distributor clamp bolt and clamp plate **(see illustration)**. On V6 models access is poor, and a crow's-foot spanner will be needed. The clamp bolt may be covered in

13.7 Removing the distributor

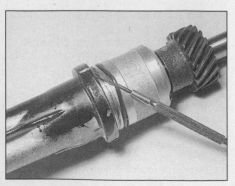

13.8 Distributor shaft O-ring

sealant to discourage tampering - if so, scrape it off. Unbolt the support bracket, when fitted.

7 Lift out the distributor **(see illustration)**. Mark the position taken up by the rotor arm after removal.

8 If the distributor is mechanically or electrically defective, it must be renewed. The only spares available are the cap, rotor arm, module (when applicable) and the shaft O-ring **(see illustration)**.

9 Commence refitting by positioning the rotor arm to the point noted in paragraph 7. This will be approximately 20° clockwise from the No 1 firing point (paragraph 4) **(see illustration)**.

10 Make sure that the engine is still

positioned at the firing point for No1 cylinder.

11 Offer the distributor to the engine, observing the distributor body-to-engine alignment marks. As the drivegear meshes, the distributor shaft will turn anti-clockwise. The rotor arm should end up in the correct position for No1 firing - if not, withdraw the distributor, re-position the shaft and try again.

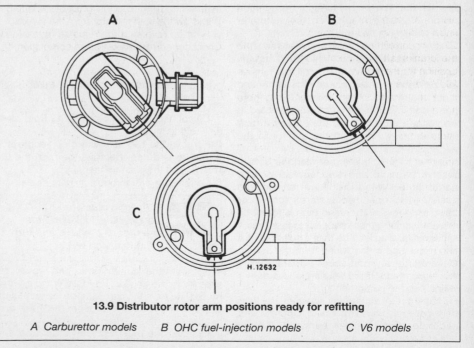

13.9 Distributor rotor arm positions ready for refitting

A Carburettor models   B OHC fuel-injection models   C V6 models

12 When the distributor is at the firing point, the leading edge of one of the vanes should be in line with the rib on the sensor **(see illustration)**. Turn the distributor body slightly if necessary to achieve this.

13 Refit the clamp plate and bolt. Just nip up the bolt for the time being. Tighten it finally after checking the timing. Also secure the support bracket, when fitted.

14 Refit the rotor arm, distributor cap and HT leads.

15 Reconnect the distributor multi-plug.

16 Reconnect the battery. Run the engine and check the ignition timing as described in the next Section.

2.4 & 2.9 litre V6 engines

Note: *The distributor should not be removed or disturbed without good cause, since the accuracy of timing achieved in production is unlikely to be regained. If difficulty is experienced in setting the timing after refitting, or if a new distributor has been fitted, the timing should be set by a Ford dealer using a STAR (Self Test Automatic Readout) tester.*

17 Disconnect the battery negative lead.

18 Disconnect the HT leads from the spark plugs noting the correct fitted locations.

19 Release the distributor cap and place it to one side, complete with the HT leads.

20 Turn the engine by means of the vibration damper centre bolt until No 1 piston is at its firing point (12° BTDC) **(see illustration)**.

21 If there is no mark visible, mark the rim of the distributor body to indicate the point of alignment of the contact end of the rotor.

22 Mark the position of the distributor mounting plate in relation to the cylinder block.

23 Disconnect the distributor wiring connector.

24 Scrape the sealant from around the distributor clamp bolt then unscrew the bolt and withdraw the distributor.

25 Prior to refitting the distributor check that the crankshaft is still set in the 12° BTDC position for the No 1 piston.

26 Hold the distributor over the hole so that the mounting plinth and cylinder head marks are aligned then align the rotor arm contact end with the mark on the distributor rim **(see illustration)**.

27 As the distributor is inserted, the rotor will turn due to the meshing of the drive gears. When the distributor is fully inserted, rotate the distributor body until the rotor arm aligns with mark C on the distributor rim.

28 Once the rotor arm, cylinder head and distributor alignment marks are all correctly aligned, fit the clamp bolt and tighten it securely.

29 Refit the distributor cap then connect the HT leads, reconnect the vacuum pipe and wiring plug.

30 Run the engine to normal operating temperature and check the ignition timing, bearing in mind the note made at the start of this sub-Section.

13.12 Vane leading edge and sensor rib (arrowed) are aligned at firing point

13.20 Crankshaft pulley notch set to the 12° BTDC position

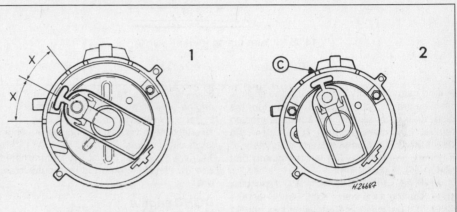
13.26 Rotor arm position before (1) and after (2) refitting the distributor

X = X   C Notch

14 Ignition timing - checking

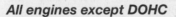

All engines except DOHC

1 Ignition timing is set very accurately in production. It does not need to be checked or adjusted on a routine basis. Adjustment will only be necessary if the distributor, or an associated component such as the timing belt, has been disturbed.

2 Before checking the timing, the following conditions must be met:
  a) *The engine must be warmed up*
  b) *On carburettor models, the vacuum pipe must be disconnected from the manifold and the manifold hole be plugged*
  c) *Idle speed must be below 900 rpm*
  d) *Any earthed "octane adjustment" wires must be temporarily isolated*

3 Locate the timing marks. On SOHC engines the timing scale is on the crankshaft pulley, and a pointer on the timing cover must be aligned with the appropriate mark on the pulley **(see illustration)**. Note that two alternative types of pulley may be fitted **(see illustration)**. On V6 engines there is a single notch on the pulley and the timing scale is on the timing cover **(see illustration)**. The desired values are given in the Specifications. Highlight the appropriate marks with white paint.

4 Connect a timing light (strobe) to No 1 HT lead, following the maker's instructions. Some lights require additional power connections to be made, either to the mains or to the battery.

5 Run the engine at idle and shine the timing light onto the marks. Take care not to get the timing light leads, clothing etc tangled in the fan blades or other moving parts. The timing marks will appear stationary and (if the timing is correct) in alignment.

14.3a Timing marks and pointer
Cast pulley shown

5

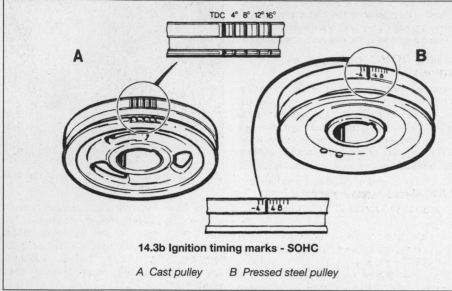

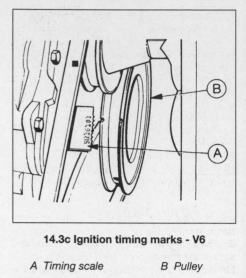

14.3b Ignition timing marks - SOHC

A Cast pulley   *B Pressed steel pulley*

14.3c Ignition timing marks - V6

A Timing scale   *B Pulley*

6 If adjustment is necessary, stop the engine. Slacken the distributor clamp bolt and turn the distributor body slightly. To retard the ignition (move the mark nearer TDC) turn the distributor body clockwise, and *vice versa* to advance the ignition. Tighten the clamp bolt and re-check the timing.

7 When adjustment is correct, stop the engine and disconnect the timing light. Reconnect the vacuum pipe, when applicable, and reconnect any "octane adjustment" wires.

DOHC engine

8 The ignition timing for this engine is controlled by the ESC II or EEC IV module and no adjustment is possible.

15 Ignition module (fuel-injection models) - removal and refitting

SOHC and 2.8 litre V6 engines

1 Disconnect the battery negative lead.

2 Disconnect the distributor multi-plug.

3 On V6 models only, make alignment marks between the distributor body and the engine. Slacken the distributor clamp bolt and swivel the distributor to make the module securing screws accessible.

4 Remove the two screws which secure the module **(see illustration)**. These screws are deeply recessed. The screws seen here have Torx heads; ordinary hexagon heads have also been encountered, and to undo these a thin socket or box spanner will be required.

5 Pull the module downwards and remove it.

6 When refitting, coat the rear face of the module with heat sink compound to Ford spec 815F-12103-AA. This is extremely expensive, so it may be worthwhile trying to obtain a smear from a friendly dealer or auto electrician.

7 Plug the module into the distributor and secure it with the two screws.

8 On V6 models, return the distributor to its original position and nip up the clamp bolt.

9 Reconnect the distributor multi-plug.

10 Reconnect the battery and run the engine to check for correct function.

11 On V6 models, check the ignition timing and then finally tighten the distributor clamp bolt.

DOHC engine

12 The ignition module is located in the left-hand front corner of the engine compartment, beside the air cleaner housing.

13 To remove the module, first disconnect the battery negative lead.

14 To improve access remove the air cleaner housing.

15 Release the locking lug and disconnect the ignition module wiring plug **(see illustration)**. Pull on the plug, not on the wiring.

16 Remove the two securing screws, and remove the module from the engine compartment.

17 Refitting is a reversal of removal, ensuring that the underside of the module and the corresponding area of the body panel are clean.

2.4 & 2.9 litre V6 engines

Note: *Removal of the ignition module requires the distributor to be disturbed.*

18 The ignition module is mounted onto the side of the distributor.

19 To remove the module first disconnect the battery negative terminal.

20 Carefully disconnect the distributor wiring connector.

21 Make alignment marks between the distributor mounting and cylinder block then scrape the sealant from around the distributor clamp bolt and slacken but **do not** remove the bolt.

22 Rotate the distributor to gain access to the ignition module retaining bolts.

23 Slacken and remove the two retaining bolts and carefully slide the module downwards to disengage it from the distributor, taking great care not to damage the module wiring pins.

24 Apply a coating of the special Ford heat-sink compound (Part number 815F-12103-AA, available from a Ford dealer This is extremely expensive, so it may be worthwhile trying to obtain a smear from a friendly dealer or auto electrician) to the rear of the ignition module and carefully slide the module into position on the distributor. **Note:** Do not force the module

15.4 Two screws (arrowed) which secure the ignition module

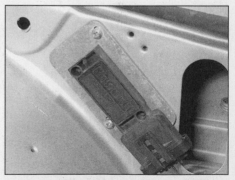

15.15 Ignition module (viewed with air cleaner removed)

16.1 Ignition coil location

into position or the wiring pins will be damaged.
25 Refit the module retaining bolts and tighten them securely.
26 Rotate the distributor until the marks made on removal are aligned then securely tighten the clamp bolt.
27 Reconnect the distributor wiring connector and the battery negative terminal.
28 Run the engine to normal operating temperature and check the ignition timing.

16 Ignition coil - testing, removal and refitting

All engines except DOHC fuel-injection

1 The ignition coil is mounted on the left-hand side of the engine compartment (see illustration). If it fails, there will be no spark and the engine will stop.
2 To test the coil an ohmmeter will be required. Disconnect the LT and HT leads from the coil and measure the resistance between the two LT terminals (primary resistance), then between the HT terminal and either LT terminal (secondary resistance). Desired values are given in the Specifications. In fact most test gear will not be able to distinguish between a normal primary resistance (which is very low) and a short-circuit.
3 In the absence of an ohmmeter, test the coil by substitution of a known good unit.

4 To remove the coil, disconnect the LT and HT leads, then remove the two screws which secure the coil clamp. Lift out the coil.
5 Refit by reversing the removal operations.

2.0 litre DOHC fuel-injection engines

6 Refer to the above paragraphs but note that on some models the coil heat shield must be removed for access to the coil securing bolts. The heat shield is secured by two screws. An earthing lead and/or a suppressor may also be secured by one of the coil retaining screws (see illustration).

17 Fuel trap (carburettor models) - removal and refitting

1 On carburettor models, a fuel trap is fitted in the vacuum pipe between the inlet manifold and the ESC II module.
2 Disconnect the battery negative lead.
3 Disconnect the vacuum pipes from the trap and remove it. Dispose of it carefully, it may contain fuel.
4 When refitting, note that the end of the trap marked CARB goes towards the manifold, and the end marked DIST towards the module.
5 Reconnect the battery.

18 Engine management control module - removal and refitting

ESC II module (carburettor models)

SOHC engines

1 Disconnect the battery negative lead.
2 Disconnect the vacuum pipe from the module (see illustration).
3 Release the locking catch and disconnect the multi-plug from the module (see illustration).
4 Remove the three securing screws and detach the module and bracket from the left-hand inner wing.
5 Refit by reversing the removal operations. Make sure that the multi-plug is securely fitted and the locking catch engaged.

16.6 Suppresser secured by one of the coil retaining screws

Note: From January 1987, a new type of module was fitted to the 1.8 litre engine. The new module is smaller than the old unit and is in the engine compartment mounted onto the left-hand wing valance. The new module is known as the ESC Hybrid Module. (see illustration)

DOHC engine

6 Removal and refitting is as above.
7 The module is located on the left-hand side of the engine compartment and is secured by two screws.

EEC IV module (fuel-injection models)

SOHC and 2.8 litre V6 engines

8 Disconnect the battery negative lead.
9 Remove the under-dash trim on the passenger side.
10 Unclip the module and lower it onto the vehicle floor.
11 Remove the control bolt from the multi-plug and disconnect the plug from the module.
12 Refit by reversing the removal operations.

DOHC and 2.4 & 2.9 litre V6 engines

13 The module is situated behind the passenger side of the facia and is accessible from underneath the glovebox.
14 To remove the module first disconnect the battery negative terminal.
15 Reach up behind the glovebox and unclip the module from the mounting bracket (see illustration).

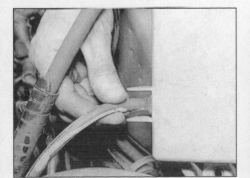

18.2 Disconnecting the ESC II module vacuum pipe

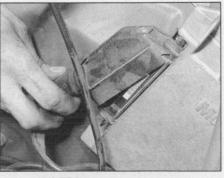

18.3 ESC II module multi-plug

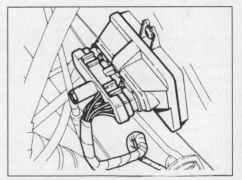

18.5 Engine management module - 1.8 litre engine from January 1987

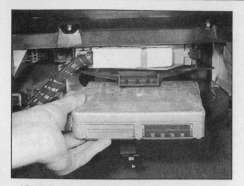

18.15 Removing the engine management modules (glovebox removed for clarity)

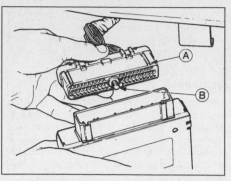

18.16 Disconnecting the EEC IV module

A Multi-plug   *B Securing bolt*

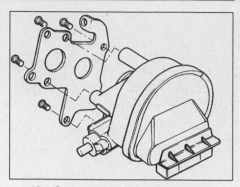

19.4 Carburettor stepper motor and mounting bracket

16 Undo the wiring connector retaining bolt then carefully disconnect the wiring plug and remove the module from the car **(see illustration)**.

17 Refitting is a reverse of the removal procedure ensuring that the wiring plug bolt is securely tightened. On completion start the engine and check that it runs correctly.

19 Carburettor stepper motor (2.0 litre models) - removal, refitting and adjustment

Note: *Irregular idle is not necessarily caused by a faulty or badly adjusted stepper motor. Good electrical contact between the stepper motor plunger and the adjusting screw is essential. Before attempting adjustment or renewal of the motor, try the effect of cleaning the plunger and adjusting screw contact faces with abrasive paper followed by switch cleaning fluid. Switch cleaning fluid is available from electronic component shops.*

1 Disconnect the battery negative lead.

2 Remove the air cleaner.

3 Disconnect the multi-plug from the stepper motor. Release the locking clip and pull on the plug, not on the wires.

4 Remove the four screws which secure the stepper motor bracket to the carburettor.

Remove the motor and bracket and separate them **(see illustration)**.

5 Refit the motor and bracket to the carburettor and secure with the four screws. Reconnect the multi-plug.

6 Make an initial adjustment to the throttle lever adjusting screw if necessary so that it protrudes from the lever by dimension X **(see illustration)**.

7 Reconnect the air cleaner vacuum hose. Position the air cleaner to one side so that there is still access to the carburettor and stepper motor.

8 Connect a tachometer (rev. counter) to the engine as instructed by the manufacturers. Reconnect the battery.

9 Run the engine. Check the idle mixture (CO level) as described in Chapter 4 and adjust if necessary.

10 Switch off all electrical loads (headlights, heater blower etc). If the idle speed adjustment lead is earthed, temporarily isolate it. Make sure that the automatic transmission selector is in the N or P position (where applicable).

11 Accelerate the engine to a speed greater then 2500 rpm, allow it to return to idle, then repeat. Insert a feeler blade of thickness 1.0 mm (0.04 in) between the stepper motor plunger and the adjusting screw **(see illustration)**. With the feeler blade in place, engine speed should be 875 ± 25 rpm.

12 If adjustment is necessary, remove the tamperproof cap from the adjusting screw locknut. Release the locknut, turn the adjusting screw to achieve the correct speed and tighten the locknut.

13 Repeat paragraph 11 and check that the speed is still correct. Readjust if necessary.

14 Remove the feeler blade. Stop and restart the engine, observing the stepper motor plunger. Immediately after switching off, the plunger should move to the "anti-dieseling" position; after a few seconds it should extend to the "vent manifold/start" position **(see illustration)**.

15 Disconnect the test gear and refit the air cleaner.

16 Recheck the idle mixture.

17 Fit new tamperproof plugs or caps if necessary - see Chapter 4,

18 Reconnect the idle speed adjustment lead if it was earthed.

20 Coolant temperature sensor - removal and refitting

1 The engine management system temperature sensor is located on the underside of the inlet manifold (SOHC engines), the side of the manifold (DOHC engines) or on the front face of the cylinder block (V6 engines).

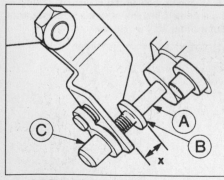

19.6 Throttle lever initial adjustment

A Plunger	X 7.5 ±1.0 mm
B Adjusting screw	(0.30 ± 0.04 in)
C Cap	

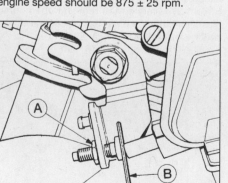

19.11 Stepper motor adjustment

A Locknut   *B Feeler blade*

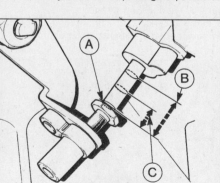

19.14 Stepper motor plunger positions

| A Vent manifold/start | C Idle |
| B Anti-dieseling | |

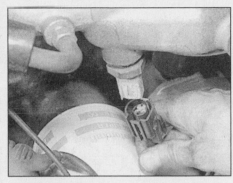

20.4 Coolant temperature sensor multi-plug

21.5 Removing the manifold heater

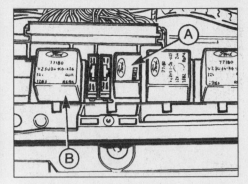

22.1 Engine management system relays

A Power hold   B Manifold heater

2 Disconnect the battery negative lead.
3 Drain the cooling system (Chapter 3). Save the coolant if it is fit for re-use.
4 Disconnect the multi-plug from the sensor. Pull on the plug, not on the wiring **(see illustration)**.
5 Unscrew the sensor and remove it.
6 Refit by reversing the removal operations. Refill the cooling system.

21 Manifold heater (carburettor models) - removal and refitting

Note: *The manifold heater must not be removed while it is hot.*
1 Disconnect the battery negative lead.

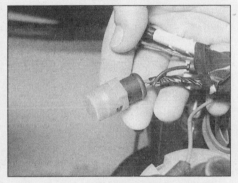

23.2a Octane adjustment lead multi-plug

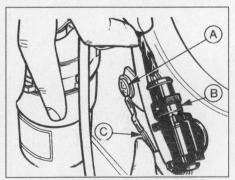

23.2b Service adjustment lead for timing and idle adjustment

A Earthing point (coil   C Cut wires not to be
*   screw)   earthed*
B Multi-plug

2 Remove the air cleaner to improve access.
3 Remove the three bolts which secure the heater to the underside of the manifold.
4 Disconnect the electrical feed from the heater.
5 Remove the heater. Recover the gasket and O-ring **(see illustration)**.
6 Use a new gasket and O-ring when refitting. Offer the heater to the manifold, insert the three bolts and tighten them evenly, making sure that the heater does not tip or jam.
7 Reconnect the electrical feed.
8 Refit the air cleaner and reconnect the battery.

22 Engine management system relays - testing

All relays are located behind the facia panel. Access is gained by removing the facia top **(see illustration).**
Testing of a suspect relay is by substitution of a known good unit.

23 Ignition timing and idle speed adjustments

1 All models have a facility for retarding the ignition timing by up to six degrees without physically disturbing the distributor. The adjustment is intended for use when the correct grade of fuel is not available.
2 Adjustment is made by earthing one or two leads (sometimes called "octane adjustment" leads) which terminate in a multi-plug next to the ignition coil **(see illustrations)**. Ideally a service adjustment lead, available from a Ford dealer, should be used. Cut and insulate the wires in the adjustment lead which are not to be earthed.
3 The amount of ignition retardation is as follows:

Wire(s) earthed	Degrees retard		
	Carb.	Injection	V6
Blue	2	4	6
Red	4	2	3
Blue and red	6	6	Forbidden

4 Performance and efficiency will suffer as a result of this adjustment. Normal timing should be restored (by isolating the adjustment leads) when the correct grade of fuel is available.
5 If the yellow adjustment lead is earthed, this

will raise the idle speed by 75 rpm (OHC) or 50 rpm (V6). It may be found that the yellow lead has already been earthed in production, in which case disconnecting it will lower the idle speed by the same amount. This adjustment does not apply to 1.8 litre carburettor models.

1.8 models from January 1987

6 The effect of the "octane adjustment" leads on these models fitted with the ESC Hybrid Module is as follows.

Red lead earthed	2° retarded
Blue lead earthed	4° retarded
Red and blue leads earthed	6° retarded

24 Crankshaft speed/position sensor - removal and refitting

1 Fitted to DOHC engines, the sensor is located at the right-hand rear of the cylinder block, behind the oil filter **(see illustration)**.
2 To remove the sensor, first disconnect the battery negative lead.
3 Access is most easily obtained from underneath the vehicle. To improve access, apply the handbrake, then jack up the front of the vehicle and support it securely on axle stands (see "*Jacking*").
4 Disconnect the wiring plug from the sensor.
5 Remove the securing screw and withdraw the sensor from the location in the cylinder block.
6 Refitting is a reversal of removal, using a new sensor O-ring and tightening the retaining screw to the specified torque setting.

24.1 Crankshaft speed/position sensor (viewed from underneath)

5

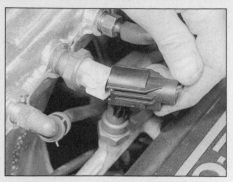

25.3 Disconnecting the air charge temperature sensor wiring plug

26.3 Disconnecting the fuel temperature sensor wiring plug

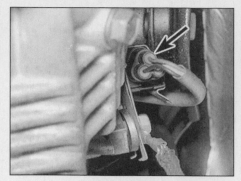

27.4 Vehicle speed sensor wiring plug (arrowed)

25 Air charge temperature sensor - removal and refitting

1 The sensor is located in the upper section of the inlet manifold (DOHC fuel-injection engines) or the side of the plenum chamber (V6 engines).
2 To remove the sensor, first disconnect the battery negative lead.
3 Disconnect the sensor wiring plug by pulling on the plug, not the wiring **(see illustration)**.
4 Unscrew the sensor from the inlet manifold and remove it.
5 Refitting is a reversal of removal, applying a smear of sealant to the threads of the sensor and tightening it to the specified torque.

26 Fuel temperature sensor - removal and refitting

1 Fitted to 2.0 litre DOHC fuel-injected engines, this sensor is located in the top of the fuel rail.
2 To remove the sensor, first disconnect the battery negative lead, and to improve access, disconnect the wiring plug from the air charge temperature sensor (in the inlet manifold). Disconnect the sensor wiring plug by pulling on the plug, not the wiring.
3 Disconnect the fuel temperature sensor wiring plug, again pulling on the plug **(see illustration)**.
4 Unscrew the sensor from the fuel rail and remove it.
5 Refitting is a reversal of removal, tightening the sensor to the specified torque.

27 Vehicle speed sensor - removal and refitting

1 Fitted to DOHC fuel-injected engines and to V6 engines with catalytic converters, this sensor is located in the left-hand side of the gearbox/transmission.
2 To remove the sensor first disconnect the battery negative lead.
3 Firmly apply the handbrake then jack up the vehicle and support it securely on axle stands (see "*Jacking*").
4 Detach the sensor wiring connector from the bracket, and separate the two halves of the connector **(see illustration)**.
5 Unscrew the securing bolt, and withdraw the wiring connector bracket, noting the orientation.
6 Withdraw the sensor from the gearbox/transmission casing.
7 Before refitting the sensor, examine the O-ring, and renew if damaged or worn.
8 Refitting is a reversal of removal, ensuring that the wiring connector bracket is correctly located.

28 Manifold absolute pressure (MAP) sensor - removal and refitting

1 On DOHC fuel-injected engines, this sensor is located on the right-hand side of the engine compartment where it is mounted either on the suspension turret or on the bulkhead **(see illustration)**. V6 engines have the sensor

28.1 Manifold Absolute Pressure (MAP) sensor location - models equipped with a catalytic converter

mounted on the centre of the engine compartment bulkhead.
2 To remove the sensor first disconnect the battery negative terminal.
3 Remove the two sensor retaining screws and carefully withdraw the sensor, taking care not to strain the wiring.
4 Disconnect the wiring plug from the sensor, pulling on the plug not the wiring, then disconnect the vacuum hose and remove the sensor.
5 Refitting is a reversal of removal.

Chapter 6
Clutch

Contents

6

Degrees of difficulty

Easy, suitable for novice with little experience	Fairly easy, suitable for beginner with some experience	Fairly difficult, suitable for competent DIY mechanic	Difficult, suitable for experienced DIY mechanic	Very difficult, suitable for expert DIY or professional

Specifications

General
Clutch type . . . . Single dry plate, diaphragm spring, cable actuation
Adjustment . . . . Automatic in use

Driven plate
Nominal diameter:
   1.8 litre and 2.0 litre . . . . 216 mm (8.5 in)
   V6 . . . . 241 mm (9.5 in)
Lining thickness (new):
   1.8 litre and 2.0 litre . . . . 3.85 mm (0.152 in)
   V6 . . . . 3.81 mm (0.150 in)

Torque wrench setting	Nm	lbf ft
Clutch pressure plate	22 to 33	16 to 24

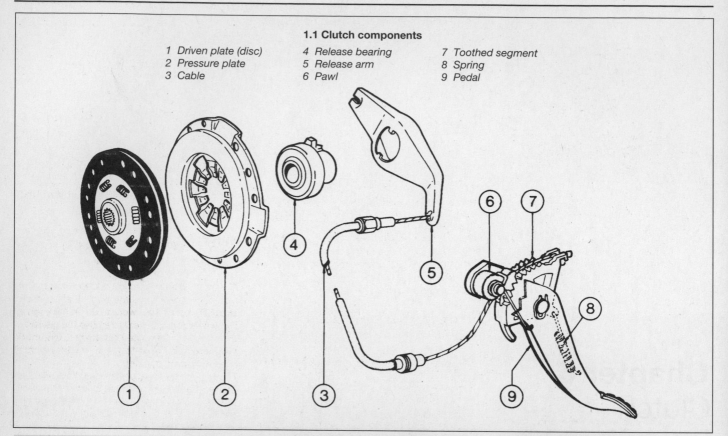

1.1 Clutch components

1 Driven plate (disc)   4 Release bearing   7 Toothed segment
2 Pressure plate   5 Release arm   8 Spring
3 Cable   6 Pawl   9 Pedal

1 General information

The clutch is of single dry plate type with a diaphragm spring pressure plate **(see illustration)**. The unit is dowelled and bolted to the rear face of the flywheel.

The clutch plate (or disc) is free to slide along the splines of the gearbox input shaft and is held in position between the flywheel and the pressure plate by the pressure of the pressure plate spring. Friction lining material is riveted to the clutch plate and it has a spring cushioned hub to absorb transmission shocks and to help ensure a smooth take off.

The circular diaphragm spring is mounted on shoulder pins and held in place in the cover by two fulcrum rings which are riveted in position.

The clutch plate is actuated by a cable controlled by the clutch pedal. Wear of the friction linings is compensated for by an automatic pawl and quadrant adjuster on the top of the clutch pedal. The clutch release mechanism consists of a ball bearing which slides on a guide sleeve at the front of the gearbox, and a release arm which pivots inside the clutch bellhousing.

Depressing the clutch pedal actuates the clutch release arm by means of the cable. The release arm pushes the release bearing forwards to bear against the release fingers so moving the centre of the diaphragm spring inwards. The spring is sandwiched between

two annular rings which act as fulcrum points. As the centre of the spring is pushed in, the outside of the spring is pushed out, so moving the pressure plate backwards and disengaging the pressure plate from the clutch plate.

When the clutch pedal is released the diaphragm spring forces the pressure plate into contact with the friction linings on the clutch plate and at the same time pushes the clutch plate a fraction of an inch forwards on its splines so engaging the clutch plate with the flywheel. The clutch plate is now firmly sandwiched between the pressure plate and the flywheel so the drive is taken up.

From approximately mid-1989 onwards, a "low-lift" clutch assembly was fitted to some models in production. The modified clutch assembly was designed so that less pressure was required to operate the clutch.

Overhaul procedures for the low-lift clutch assembly remain unchanged from those described in this Chapter. However, it must be noted that the modified low-lift clutch assembly is not interchangeable with the standard assembly. If the vehicle was originally fitted with a standard clutch then the replacement clutch must also be of the standard type. The same applies to vehicles originally equipped with a low-lift clutch assembly on which the replacement clutch must be of the low-lift type.

On low-lift clutches, the driven plate and pressure plate are stamped **Low-lift** for identification.

2 Clutch pedal - removal, overhaul and refitting

1 Disconnect the clutch cable from the release arm and clutch pedal as described in Section 3, but do not remove the cable.
2 Disconnect the wiring from the stop light switch. On models with cruise control, also disconnect the brake and clutch vacuum dump switches.
3 Disconnect the brake hydraulic unit pushrod from the brake pedal.
4 Remove the two nuts and one bolt which secure the pedal bracket to the bulkhead.
5 Remove the spring clip from the pedal shaft. Push the shaft through the brake and clutch pedals and remove the clutch pedal, complete with adjuster components.
6 Prise the bushes from each side of the pedal and extract the toothed segment. Unhook the spring.
7 Prise one of the clips from the pawl pin, withdraw the pin and remove the pawl and spring.
8 Clean all the components and examine them for wear and damage. Renew them as necessary.
9 Lubricate the bores of the pawl and segment with graphite grease.
10 Assemble the pawl, spring and pin to the pedal then refit the clip **(see illustration)**.
11 Attach the spring to the toothed segment, then insert the segment into the pedal and press in the two pivot bushes.

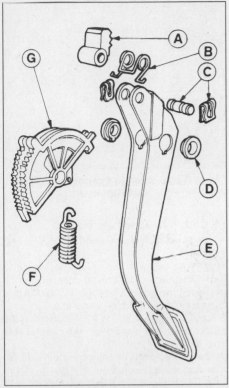

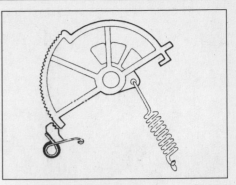

2.10 Clutch pedal and automatic adjuster components

A *Pawl*
B *Spring*
C *Pawl pin and clip*
D *Bush*
E *Clutch pedal*
F *Toothed segment tension spring*
G *Toothed segment*

2.12 Clutch pedal toothed segment at initial setting

14 Lubricate the pedal shaft with a molybdenum-based grease. Pass the shaft through the pedals and secure it with the spring clip.

15 Secure the pedal bracket to the bulkhead, then reconnect the brake unit pushrod, the stop-light switch and (when applicable) the cruise control switches.

16 Reconnect the clutch cable.

3 Clutch cable - removal and refitting

1 Raise and securely support the front of the vehicle.

2 Inside the vehicle, lift up the clutch pedal as far as possible and jam it in this position with a piece of wood.

3 Underneath the vehicle, unclip the rubber gaiter which protects the end of the clutch cable and the release arm. Pull the cable down in front of the release arm and unhook the cable inner from the release arm with pliers. Remove the rubber insulator **(see illustrations)**.

4 Pull the gaiter off the cable and free the cable at the gearbox end.

5 Inside the vehicle, unclip the under-dash insulation on the driver's side. Unhook the cable inner from the toothed segment **(see illustration)**.

6 Pull the cable into the engine compartment and remove it.

7 Refit by reversing the removal operations. Make sure that the release arm gaiter is securely in position.

8 Remove the piece of wood and operate the clutch pedal a few times to settle the adjustment mechanism.

4 Clutch assembly - removal, inspection and refitting

1 For access to the clutch components it is necessary to remove the engine or gearbox. Unless there is other work to do on the engine, it is easier and quicker to remove the gearbox.

2 If the pressure plate may be re-used, mark its position relative to the flywheel, using a scriber or dabs of paint.

3 Slacken the six bolts which secure the pressure plate to the flywheel. Undo each bolt a little at a time, in a criss-cross sequence, until the spring pressure is released. Remove the bolts and washers.

4 Lift the pressure plate off the dowels on the flywheel. Note which way round the driven plate is fitted and lift it from the pressure plate or flywheel **(see illustration)**.

5 Clean off dust and dirt using a damp cloth or an old damp paintbrush. **Do not disperse the dust into the air, and take care not to inhale it, as it may contain asbestos.**

6 Examine the friction surfaces of the flywheel and the pressure plate for scoring or cracks. Light scoring may be ignored. Excessive scoring or cracks can sometimes be machined off the flywheel face - consult a specialist. The pressure plate must be renewed if it is badly scored.

7 Inspect the pressure plate cover and the diaphragm spring for damage, or blue discolouration suggesting overheating. Renew the pressure plate if in doubt.

HAYNES HINT *Pay attention to the tips of the spring fingers where the release bearing operates.*

8 Renew the driven plate if the friction linings are worn down to, or approaching, the rivets. If the linings are oil-soaked or have a hard black glaze, the source of oil contamination - the crankshaft rear oil seal or gearbox input shaft oil seal - must be dealt with before the plate is renewed. Also inspect the driven plate springs, hub and splines.

9 Note that if the driven plate only is renewed, problems may be experienced related to the

12 Lift the pawl and turn the segment so that the pawl rests on the smooth curved surface at the end of the teeth **(see illustration)**.

13 Attach the segment spring to the pedal.

3.3a Clutch cable attachment to release arm

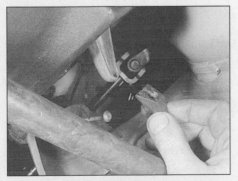

3.3b Removing the clutch cable rubber insulator

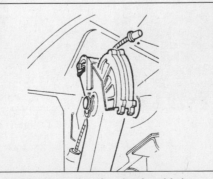

3.5 Disconnecting the clutch cable inner from the toothed segment

6

4.4 Removing the pressure plate and the driven plate from the flywheel

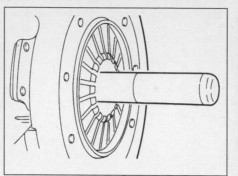

4.14 Centralising the clutch driven plate

4.15 Clutch fitted to flywheel and driven plate centred

bedding-in of the driven plate and old pressure plate. It is certainly better practice to renew the driven plate and pressure plate together, if finances permit.

10 Spin the release bearing in the clutch bellhousing and feel for roughness or shake. The bearing should be renewed without question unless it is known to be in perfect condition.

11 It is important that no oil or grease gets on the clutch plate friction linings, or the pressure plate and flywheel faces. It is advisable to refit the clutch with clean hands and to wipe down the pressure plate and flywheel faces with a clean rag before assembly begins.

12 Place the driven plate against the flywheel, making sure it is the right way round. The flatter side of the plate (marked FLYWHEEL SIDE) must go towards the flywheel.

13 Fit the pressure plate loosely on the flywheel dowels, aligning the previously made marks if the original plate is being refitted. Insert the six bolts and spring washers.

Tighten the bolts finger tight, so that the driven plate is just gripped but can still be moved.

14 The driven plate must now be centralised so that when the engine and gearbox are mated, the gearbox input shaft splines will pass through the splines in the centre of the plate. Ideally a universal clutch centralising tool should be used, or if available an old gearbox input shaft. Alternatively a wooden mandrel can be made **(see illustration)**.

15 Make sure that the centralising tool is located correctly in the driven plate and in the crankshaft pilot bearing, then tighten the pressure plate bolts progressively to the specified torque. Remove the tool and check the centralisation of the driven plate visually **(see illustration)**.

16 Make sure that the release bearing and arm have been refitted, then refit the engine or gearbox with reference to Chapters 2 or 7.

17 If a new driven plate has been fitted, it may take 30 or 40 starts before the new plate beds in and operates satisfactorily.

5 Clutch release bearing and arm - removal and refitting

1 With the gearbox and engine separated to provide access to the clutch, attention can be given to the release bearing located in the clutch housing, over the input shaft.

2 If the gearbox is still in the car, remove the rubber boot and disconnect the clutch cable from the release arm.

3 Free the release bearing from the release arm and withdraw it from the guide sleeve **(see illustration)**. On models equipped with an MT75 gearbox, the release bearing may be secured to the arm using a circlip instead of spring clips.

4 Pull the release arm from the fulcrum pin, then withdraw the arm over the input shaft **(see illustration)**.

5 Check the release bearing. If there are any signs of grease leakage, renew the bearing.

6 Refitting is a reversal of removal.

5.3 Removing the clutch release bearing

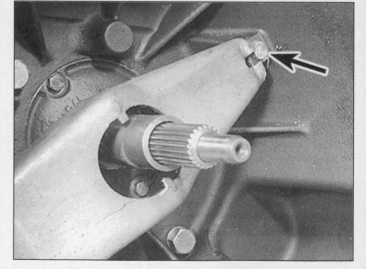

5.4 Clutch release arm, showing fulcrum pin (arrowed)

Chapter 7 Part A:
Manual gearbox

Contents

Degrees of difficulty

Easy, suitable for novice with little experience	Fairly easy, suitable for beginner with some experience	Fairly difficult, suitable for competent DIY mechanic	Difficult, suitable for experienced DIY mechanic	Very difficult, suitable for expert DIY or professional

Specifications

General

Gearbox type . . . .   5 forward speeds and 1 reverse. Synchro on all foward gears
Maker's designation . . . .   N and MT75

Ratios

N type:	1.8/2.0/2.4 litre	2.8/2.9 litre
1st	3.650 : 1	3.360 : 1
2nd	1.970 : 1	1.810 : 1
3rd	1.370 : 1	1.260 : 1
4th	1.000 : 1	1.000 : 1 .
5th	0.816 : 1	0.825 : 1
Reverse	3.660 : 1	3.365 : 1
MT75 type:		
1st	3.89 : 1	
2nd	2.08 : 1	
3rd	1.34 : 1	
4th	1.00 : 1	
5th	0.82 : 1	
Reverse	3.51 : 1	

Lubrication

Lubricant type:
  N type . . . .   Semi-synthetic gear oil to Ford spec ESD M2C175-A (80EP)
  MT75 type . . . .   ATF to Ford spec ESD-M2C186-A (Automatic transmission fluid)
Lubricant capacity . . . .   1.25 litres (2.2 pints) approx

7A

Torque wrench settings

	Nm	lbf ft
N type		
Clutch housing to gear housing	70 to 90	52 to 66
Clutch housing to engine	40 to 51	30 to 38
Clutch release bearing guide sleeve.	9 to 11	7 to 8
Extension housing to gear housing	45 to 49	33 to 36
Crossmember to floor	20 to 25	15 to 18
Crossmember to mounting	16 to 20	12 to 15
Mounting to gearbox	50 to 57	37 to 42
Reversing light switch	1 to 2	0.7 to 1.5
Oil filler plug	23 to 27	17 to 20
Gear lever to extension housing	20 to 27	15 to 20
Air deflector plate nut	21 to 26	16 to 19
Gearbox top cover bolts	9 to 11	7 to 8
MT75 type (where different to N type)		
Crossmember to underbody	30 to 40	22 to 30
Crossmember to gearbox	52 to 71	38 to 52
Gear linkage support bracket to gearbox	21 to 29	15 to 21
Engine to gearbox	29 to 41	21 to 30
Oil level\filler plug	29 to 41	21 to 30
Oil drain plug	29 to 41	21 to 30

1 General information

Five-speed gearboxes are fitted to these models. The earlier type N gearbox is essentially the same as that fitted to some Sierra, Capri and "old" Granada models and follows conventional rear-wheel drive practice. Drive from the clutch is picked up by the input shaft, which runs in line with the mainshaft. The input shaft gear and mainshaft gears are in constant mesh with the layshaft gear cluster. Selection of gears is by sliding synchromesh hubs, which lock the appropriate mainshaft gear to the mainshaft. Drive in 4th gear is direct, ie the input shaft is locked to the mainshaft.

Reverse gear is obtained by sliding an idler gear into mesh with two straight-cut gears on the mainshaft and layshaft. All the forward gear teeth are helically cut to reduce noise and improve wear characteristics. Drive from the gearbox is picked up by the propeller shaft, which mates with the mainshaft tail.

The MT75 gearbox introduced in October 1988, is a completely new design and is lighter, more compact and more robust than its predecessor. It comprises front and rear housings of aluminium alloy with the 5th gear components accommodated in the main casing. The floor-mounted gear lever operates the selector shaft via an external rod which protrudes from the front casing.

2 Removal and refitting

N type

1 Disconnect the battery negative lead.
2 On V6 models only, remove the distributor screening can, cap and rotor.

3 On all models, unscrew the gear lever knob and remove the outer gaiter.
4 Remove the centre console and its bracket. Refer to Chapter 12 if necessary.
5 Remove the gear lever inner gaiter, frame and sound insulation. These items are secured by four screws.
6 Unbolt the gear lever from the extension housing and remove it.
7 Raise the vehicle both front and rear and support it securely, or position it over a pit.
8 Unbolt the front anti-roll bar brackets.
9 Unbolt the exhaust heat shield, when fitted (V6 only).
10 Unhook the exhaust system rear mountings and tie the system out of the way. It may be preferable to remove the system completely. On V6 models, remove the left-hand exhaust hanger bracket.
11 Remove the propeller shaft (Chapter 8).
12 Support the engine, either with a hoist or bar from above, or with a jack and a block of wood from below. The support should be adjustable to enable the best position to be assumed, especially when refitting.
13 Remove the gearbox crossmember. This is secured by five bolts two on each side and one in the centre.
14 Disconnect the reversing light switch and the speedometer sender multi-plugs.
15 Remove the starter motor (Chapter 5).
16 Disconnect the clutch cable from the release arm. Also unbolt the clutch housing adapter plate.
17 On OHC models only, unbolt the engine/gearbox bracing strap.
18 Remove the six bolts which secure the clutch housing to the engine. On V6 models, also remove the air deflector plate, if fitted.
19 The services of an assistant may now be required. Alternatively, a home-made gearbox cradle mounted on a trolley jack may be used.
20 Take the weight of the gearbox and carefully draw it rearwards off the engine.

Once the locating dowels have been cleared, the gearbox will try to drop - *do not let the weight of the gearbox hang on the input shaft, or damage to the shaft and clutch may occur.*
21 When the input shaft is clear of the clutch, lower the gearbox and remove it from under the vehicle.
22 Commence refitting by making sure that the clutch driven plate is accurately centred (Chapter 6). Apply a smear of grease or anti-seize compound to the input shaft splines, and secure the clutch release arm with wire or string to stop the release bearing falling forwards during refitting.
23 Offer the gearbox to the engine, making sure that the input shaft is entering the clutch driven plate and that the gearbox is well supported. Some adjustment of the engine or gearbox position may be needed to get the two units aligned correctly.

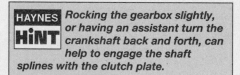

HAYNES HiNT *Rocking the gearbox slightly, or having an assistant turn the crankshaft back and forth, can help to engage the shaft splines with the clutch plate.*

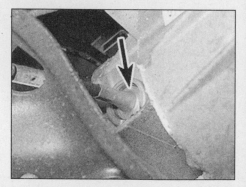

2.36 Speedometer drive cable retaining circlip (arrowed)

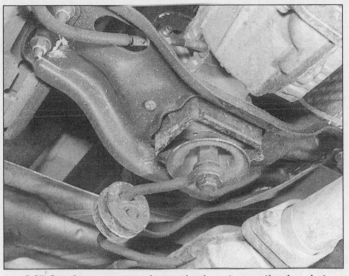

2.37 Gearbox crossmember and exhaust mounting bracket

2.39 Gear linkage support bracket securing bolt (arrowed)

24 When the gearbox is snug against the engine, refit the engine-to-clutch housing bolts and tighten them to the specified torque.

25 The remainder of refitting is a reversal of the removal procedure. Tighten fastenings to the correct torque, when specified. Before lowering the vehicle, check the gearbox oil level and top-up if necessary.

MT75 type

26 Removal of the engine and gearbox as an assembly is described in Chapter 2. To remove the gearbox alone proceed as follows.

27 Disconnect the battery negative lead.

28 Unscrew and remove the top engine-to-gearbox bolts which are accessible from the engine compartment. Note the location of the bolts, and the positions of the earth strap and any wiring clips attached to the bolts; on V6 engines it may be necessary to remove the distributor cap and rotor arm to gain access to the bolts.

29 Jack up the vehicle and support it on axle stands (see "Jacking").

30 To improve access, disconnect the exhaust downpipe from the manifold and remove the exhaust system as described in Chapter 4.

31 On models fitted with a catalytic converter, release the securing clips and withdraw the exhaust heat shield from under the vehicle for access to the propeller shaft.

32 Remove the propeller shaft (Chapter 8).

33 Where applicable, bend back the locktabs, then unscrew the two bolts securing each of the two anti-roll bar mounting clamps to the vehicle underbody. Lower the anti-roll bar as far as possible.

34 Disconnect the wiring from the starter motor, and remove the starter motor.

35 Support the gearbox with a trolley jack, and interposed block of wood to spread the load.

36 Remove the securing circlip and, where necessary, disconnect the speedometer drive cable from the gearbox **(see illustration)**.

37 Unscrew the four nuts securing the gearbox crossmember to the vehicle underbody. Unscrew the central bolt securing the crossmember to the gearbox, and remove the crossmember. Note the position of the earth strap, where applicable. Recover the mounting cup, and where applicable the exhaust mounting bracket and heat shield **(see illustration)**.

38 Lower the gearbox slightly on the jack, then disconnect the wiring from the reversing lamp switch, and on models with fuel-injection, disconnect the wiring from the vehicle speed sensor mounted in the side of the gearbox.

39 Unscrew the two securing bolts (one either side), and disconnect the gear linkage support bracket from the gearbox **(see illustration)**.

40 Using a suitable pin punch, drive out the roll-pin securing the gearchange rod to the gear linkage.

41 Place a suitable rod across the vehicle underbody to support the gear linkage support bracket whilst the gearbox is removed.

42 Working inside the vehicle, place a wooden block under the clutch pedal to raise it fully against the stop, so holding the automatic adjuster pawl clear of the toothed quadrant.

43 Disconnect the clutch cable from the clutch release arm, and pass the cable through the bellhousing, with reference to Chapter 6 if necessary. Take note of the routing of the cable to aid refitting.

44 Unscrew and remove the remaining engine-to-gearbox bolts, and remove the bolt from the engine adapter plate. On DOHC engines recover any shims fitted between the sump and the gearbox when removing the lower engine-to-gearbox bolts.

45 With the aid of an assistant, lift the gearbox from the engine, using the trolley jack to take the weight. Do not allow the weight of the gearbox to hang on the input shaft. It may be necessary to rock the gearbox a little to release it from the engine.

46 With the gearbox removed, temporarily reconnect the anti-roll bar to the underbody if the vehicle is to be moved.

47 Refitting is a reversal of removal, taking note of the following points.

a) *Before attempting to refit the gearbox, check that the clutch friction disc is centralised as described in Chapter 6.*

b) *Check that the clutch release arm and bearing are correctly fitted, and lightly grease the input shaft splines.*

c) *Check that the engine adapter plate is correctly positioned on the dowels. If necessary, a cable-tie can be used to temporarily secure the adapter plate in position on the cylinder block using one of the engine-to-gearbox bolt holes.*

d) *On DOHC engines, if shims were fitted between the sump and the gearbox, refit them in their original locations when mating the engine to the gearbox. If the engine has been overhauled, where applicable fit the relevant shims as calculated during engine reassembly (see Sump - removal and refitting - Chapter 2).*

e) *Reconnect the clutch cable to the release arm with reference to Chapter 6, ensuring that it is routed as noted during removal.*

f) *Refit the propeller shaft with reference to Chapter 8.*

g) *Refit the exhaust system with reference to Chapter 4.*

h) *Tighten all fixings to the specified torque, where applicable.*

j) *On completion, check the gearbox oil level, and top-up if necessary.*

7A

3 Gear linkage (MT75 type) - removal and refitting

1 Working inside the vehicle, pull the gear lever knob off the gear lever, noting that it may be a very tight fit.

2 Carefully prise the gearchange lever trim panel out from the centre console, then turn the outer gaiter inside out and unclip the trim panel from the gaiter.

3 Detach the gear lever inner gaiter, together with the retaining frame, and turn it inside out.

4 Proceed as described in paragraphs 29 to 43 of Section 2, ignoring paragraph 41.

5 Manipulate the rubber gaiter from the gear linkage support bracket for access to the base of the gear lever.

6 Remove the circlip and the pivot pin, then disconnect the gear shift rod from the base of the gear lever. Withdraw the gear shift rod.

7 Remove the circlip securing the base of the gear lever to the gear linkage support bracket, and withdraw the gear lever assembly through the floor from inside the vehicle, and the gear linkage support bracket from under the vehicle.

8 The gear lever assembly cannot be dismantled, and must be renewed as a unit if faulty.

9 Refitting is a reversal of removal, bearing in mind the following points.

a) *Reconnect the clutch cable to the release arm with reference to Chapter 6, ensuring that it is routed as noted during removal.*

b) *Refit the propeller shaft with reference to Chapter 8.*

c) *Refit the exhaust system with reference to Chapter 4.*

d) *Tighten all fixings to the specified torque, where applicable.*

4 Overhaul - general information

Overhauling a gearbox is a difficult and involved job for the DIY home mechanic. In addition to dismantling and reassembling many small parts, clearances must be precisely measured and, if necessary, changed by selecting shims and spacers. Gearbox internal components are also often difficult to obtain and in many instances extremely expensive. Because of this, if the gearbox developes a fault or becomes noisy, the best course of action is to have the unit overhauled by a specialist or to obtain an exchange reconditioned unit.

Nevertheless, it is not impossible for the more experienced mechanic to overhaul a gearbox provided that the special tools are available and the job is done in a deliberate step-by-step manner so that nothing is overlooked.

The tools necessary for overhaul include internal and external circlip pliers, bearing pullers, a slide-hammer, a set of pin punches, a dial test indicator and possibly an hydraulic press. In addition, a large sturdy workbench and a vice will be required.

All work should be done in conditions of extreme cleanliness. When dismantling, make careful notes of how each component is fitted. This will facilitate accurate and straightfoward reassembly.

Before dismantling the gearbox, it will help to have some idea of which component is malfunctioning. Certain problems can be related to specific areas in the gearbox which can in turn make component examination and replacement more straightfoward. Refer to the Fault Finding Section at the end of this Manual for more information.

Chapter 7 Part B:
Automatic transmission

Contents

Degrees of difficulty

Easy, suitable for novice with little experience	Fairly easy, suitable for beginner with some experience	Fairly difficult, suitable for competent DIY mechanic	Difficult, suitable for experienced DIY mechanic	Very difficult, suitable for expert DIY or professional

Specifications

General

Transmission type . . . . A4LD type with 4 forward speeds and 1 reverse
Torque converter type . . . . Trilock (hydraulic, with lock-up facility)

Torque wrench settings

	Nm	lbf ft
Converter housing to transmission housing	40 to 48	30 to 35
Extension housing to transmission housing	40 to 48	30 to 35
Driveplate to torque converter	32 to 38	24 to 28
Sump bolts:		
Polyacrylic gasket	8 to 11	6 to 8
Cork gasket	15 to 18	11 to 13
Downshift cable bracket	18 to 22	13 to 16
Selector lever nut	11 to 14	8 to 10
Downshift lever nut	45 to 50	33 to 37
Starter inhibitor switch	10 to 14	7 to 10
Brake band adjusting screw locknut	50 to 58	37 to 43
Oil cooler unions:		
Pipe to connector	22 to 24	16 to 18
Connector to transmission housing	24 to 30	18 to 22
Converter housing to engine	30 to 36	22 to 27
Centre carrier bolt	9 to 12	7 to 9

7B

1 General information

The early A4LD transmission has four forward gears and one reverse. The torque converter locks up in 3rd and 4th gears, so avoiding losses due to converter slip. 4th gear is an overdrive, maximum speed and acceleration being obtained in 3rd.

The gear selector has seven positions: P, R, N, D, 3, 2 and 1. (On early models positions D and 3 are labelled DE and D, but their functions are the same). The engine can only be started in positions P and N. In position D the transmission will change automatically through all four forward gears, according to speed, load and throttle position. In position 3, top (overdrive) gear will not be engaged. Position 2 allows selection of 1st and 2nd gears only, position 1 engages 1st gear only, but if these positions are selected while travelling at speed, the transmission will not change down until speed has reduced sufficiently to avoid damage.

Engine braking in the lower gears is only obtained in positions 1 and 2; in position 3 and D there is a freewheel effect in the first three gears.

A "kickdown" facility causes the transmission to change down a gear (subject to speed) if the throttle is depressed fully and held down. This is useful when rapid acceleration is required, for example when overtaking. Kickdown is controlled either by a cable linked to the transmission and the throttle cable, or by a throttle-operated switch and a solenoid actuator on the transmission (see illustrations).

An A4LD type automatic transmission with partial electronic control is fitted to 2.0 litre

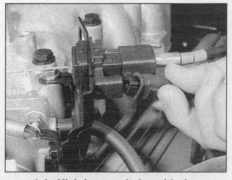
1.4a Kickdown switch multi-plug

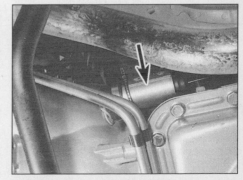
1.4b Kickdown solenoid actuator (arrowed)

DOHC models and later V6 engines. The transmission with partial electronic control can be identified by looking at the lock-up clutch solenoid wiring plug, which has three wires instead of the previous two.

The later type transmission behaves in exactly the same way as the earlier type for gearchanges up and down between 1st and 2nd, and 2nd and 3rd gears, but the changes up from 3rd to 4th, and down from 4th to 3rd, and the torque converter lock-up clutch are controlled by the engine management module. This provides more accurate control of the transmission according to the prevailing engine operating conditions.

On models from late 1989, a modified downshift solenoid with a shorter operating cable is fitted.

The removal, refitting and adjustment procedures are as described in this Chapter but note the clearance between the downshift lever and the stop given in Section 5.

The automatic transmission is a complex unit, but if it is not abused it is reliable and long-lasting. Repair or overhaul operations are beyond the scope of many dealers, let alone the home mechanic; specialist advice should be sought if problems arise which cannot be solved by the procedures given in this Chapter.

2 Removal and refitting

Note: *If the transmission is being removed for repair by a specialist, make sure that the specialist does not wish to test the transmission while it is still in the vehicle.*

All engines except DOHC

1 Disconnect the battery negative lead.
2 Raise and securely support the vehicle at front and rear, or drive it over a pit.
3 Remove the exhaust system as described in Chapter 4. On SOHC models, also unbolt the exhaust mounting bracket from the transmission crossmember.
4 Remove the propeller shaft as described in Chapter 8. Plug or cap the transmission rear extension to minimise fluid loss.
5 Unbolt the front anti-roll bar clamps.
6 Remove the starter motor as described in Chapter 5.
7 On V6 models, remove the distributor cap to avoid damage when the engine is fitted.
8 Unbolt the transmission crossmember from the side rails (four bolts) and from the transmission (one bolt, which may also secure an exhaust hanger). The transmission will drop as the crossmember is unbolted. Although not specified by the makers, it would be prudent to support the engine with a hoist, bar or jack to reduce the strain on the engine mountings. The support must be adjustable.
9 Disconnect the oil cooler unions at the transmission. Be prepared for fluid spillage. Plug or cap the open unions to keep fluid in

and dirt out. If a new transmission is being fitted, flush the oil cooler by pumping some clean transmission fluid through it.
10 Unbolt the transmission oil filler/dipstick tube from the engine. Remove the dipstick and pull the tube out of the transmission. Be prepared for further fluid spillage; plug the hole.
11 Remove the transmission selector rod by releasing the bayonet clips which secure each end of it.
12 Disconnect the downshift (kickdown) cable from the lever on the transmission. On models where kickdown is electrically-operated, disconnect the kickdown solenoid wiring.
13 Disconnect the multi-plug from the starter inhibitor/reversing light switch.
14 Remove the speedometer sender unit and move it aside. Plug the hole to keep dirt out.
15 Disconnect the pipe from the vacuum diaphragm. Unclip the pipe and move it aside.
16 Unbolt the adapter plate from the bottom of the engine. On SOHC models, also unbolt the engine/transmission bracing strap.
17 Working through the starter motor aperture, remove the four nuts which secure the driveplate to the torque converter **(see illustration)**. Turn the crankshaft to bring each nut into view, using a spanner on the crankshaft pulley or by prising on the starter ring gear.
18 Remove the remaining bolts which secure the torque converter housing to the engine. The transmission is now hanging on the dowels.
19 With the help of an assistant, or using a cradle and a trolley jack, take the weight of the transmission and withdraw it from the engine. As the transmission comes clear, push the torque converter rearwards and hold it secure as the transmission is removed.
20 Commence refitting by checking that the torque converter is fully engaged in the transmission oil pump. Correct engagement is indicated when the nose of the converter is positioned distance A from the converter housing flange **(see illustration)**. Rotate the converter and push it into mesh with the oil pump if necessary. **Damage will result if the transmission is refitted with the converter improperly engaged.**

21 Make sure that the adapter plate is located on the dowels at the rear of the engine.
22 Offer the transmission to the engine. Do not allow the torque converter to fall forwards. The studs on the torque converter must pass through the holes in the driveplate. Support the transmission until it is engaged with the dowels.
23 Insert the torque converter housing-to-engine bolts, omitting the one which secures the dipstick/filler tube. Before tightening the bolts, make sure that the torque converter has perceptible endfloat - if not, it is not properly engaged. When satisfied, tighten the bolts evenly to the specified torque.
24 Fit the driveplate-to-torque converter nuts, rotating the crankshaft to bring them into position. Just nip each nut up at first, then go round again and tighten them to the specified torque.
25 Secure the adapter plate and (on SOHC models) the bracing strap.
26 Reconnect the vacuum pipe.
27 Refit the speedometer sender unit.
28 Reconnect the starter inhibitor/reversing light switch.
29 Reconnect the downshift cable to the operating lever, or reconnect the solenoid, as appropriate.
30 Refit the selector rod and secure it with the clips. If adjustment is necessary, refer to Section 6.
31 Reconnect the oil cooler pipes to the transmission.
32 Insert the dipstick/oil filler tube into the transmission and secure it to the engine with the remaining converter housing-to-engine bolt.
33 Refit the transmission crossmember.
34 Refit the propeller shaft as described in Chapter 8.
35 Refit the starter motor as described in Chapter 5.
36 Secure the front anti-roll bar clamps, tightening the bolts to the specified torque.
37 Refit the exhaust system.
38 Lower the vehicle to the ground. Refit the distributor cap if it was removed, then reconnect the battery negative lead.
39 Fill the transmission with fluid up to the MIN mark on the dipstick.

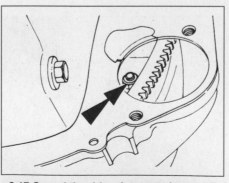

2.17 One of the driveplate nuts (arrowed) seen through the starter motor aperture

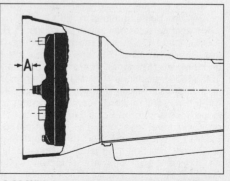

2.20 With torque converter correctly fitted, dimension A must be at least 8 mm (0.32 in)

40 Road test the vehicle to check for correct operation of the selector and kickdown mechanism and adjust if necessary .

41 With the transmission warmed up, recheck the fluid level and top-up if necessary. Also check for leaks at the fluid cooler unions, the bottom of the dipstick/filler tube and at any other disturbed components.

DOHC engine

42 Removal of the engine and automatic transmission as an assembly is described in Chapter 2.

43 To remove and refit the transmission separately, refer to the above procedure whilst noting the following points.

a) *Ignore the references to the downshift cable, and on models fitted with a transmission having partial electronic control, ignore the references to the vacuum pipe.*

b) *Remove and refit the exhaust system with reference to Chapter 4.*

3 Brake band adjustment

See Chapter 1, Section 40.

4 Starter inhibitor/reversing light switch - removal and refitting

1 Raise and support the front of the vehicle.

2 Disconnect the multi-plug from the switch (on the left-end side of the transmission, towards the front) **(see illustration)**.

3 Unscrew the switch from the transmission. Recover the O-ring.

4 Use a new O-ring when refitting. Screw in the switch and tighten it to the specified torque.

5 Reconnect the multi-plug and check the operation of the switch. The starter motor must only operate in positions P and N, and the reversing lights must only come on in position R. Any adjustment can only be to the selector linkage, the switch itself is not adjustable.

6 Lower the vehicle.

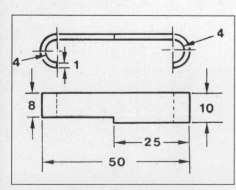

5.3 Downshift cable setting gauge - dimensions in mm

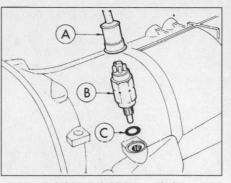

4.2 Starter inhibitor switch

A Multi-plug   C O-ring
B Switch

5 Downshift mechanism adjustment

1 On models built up to mid-1986, the downshift (kickdown) linkage is by mechanical cable. On later models a throttle switch and a solenoid actuator are used.

Cable adjustment

2 Adjustment takes place at the throttle cable bracket under the bonnet **(see illustration)**.

3 Make up a setting gauge to the dimensions shown **(see illustration)**.

4 Release the downshift cable adjusting nut and locknut and unscrew them to the end of their thread.

5 Have an assistant depress the throttle pedal as far as it will go. Make sure that the pedal travel is not restricted by mats or carpets.

6 Turn the throttle cable adjusting nut to achieve a dimension X **(see illustration)** of 10 mm (0.39 in). Use the 10 mm end of the setting gauge to check this gap. Make sure that the spring and the spring cup do not turn when turning the adjusting nut.

7 Remove the setting gauge and re-insert it with the 8 mm end in gap X. Have the assistant release the throttle pedal: the gauge will be clamped in position.

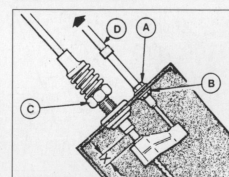

5.6 Downshaft cable adjustment

A *Downshift cable adjusting nut*
B *Downshift cable locknut*
C *Throttle cable adjusting nut*
D *Downshift cable*
X *See text*

5.2 Throttle cable and downshift cable bracket and adjusters

8 Pull the downshift cable outer sleeve in the direction arrowed to take up any slack. Hold the sleeve in this position and secure it with the downshift cable adjusting nut and locknut. Tighten the nuts.

9 Remove the setting gauge. Adjustment is now complete.

Solenoid adjustment

10 Raise and support the vehicle.

11 Slacken the two screws which secure the solenoid bracket **(see illustration)**.

12 Have an assistant switch on the ignition and press the throttle pedal to the floor. Do not start the engine.

13 Move the downshift lever on the transmission anti-clockwise as far as possible, and position the solenoid so that its cable is under slight tension.

14 Tighten the bracket screws, bottom one first, to retain the solenoid in this position.

15 Have the assistant release and reapply the throttle several times. Each time that the pedal is fully depressed, the downshift lever should be drawn anti-clockwise to within 0.2 mm (0.008 in) of its stop. On models from late 1989, the downshift lever-to-stop clearance should be between 0.5 and 1.0 mm (0.02 and 0.04 in). Do not try to adjust the solenoid to eliminate this very small amount of free play.

16 Switch off the ignition and lower the vehicle.

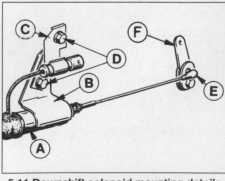

5.11 Downshift solenoid mounting details

A *Solenoid*
B *Bracket*
C *Multi-plug clip*
D *Bracket screws*
E *Cable end*
F *Downshift lever*

7B

6 Selector rod - removal, refitting and adjustment

1 Raise and support the front of the vehicle.
2 Remove the selector rod by releasing the bayonet clip at each end of it. The rod bushes can now be renewed if necessary.
3 Commence refitting by moving the gear selector to position DE (or D on later models). Move the selector lever on the transmission to the same position.
4 Connect the rod to the selector lever on the transmission and secure it with the clip.
5 Offer the other end of the rod to the gear selector. If it will fit without strain, and without disturbing the gear selector or the selector lever, adjustment is correct.
6 If adjustment is necessary, slacken the selector rod locknut (see illustration). Rotate the rod end-piece to lengthen or shorten the rod until it is a comfortable fit in the selector, then tighten the locknut.
7 Secure the selector rod to the gear selector with the spring clip.
8 Lower the vehicle. Check that the gear selector accurately engages each function.

6.6 Selector rod locknut (arrowed)

Pay particular attention to the engagement of the parking pawl in position P, and the correct operation of the starter inhibitor/reversing light switch. Readjust the selector rod if necessary.

7 Vacuum line modification - 2.4 litre V6 models

1 To overcome the problem of a jerky change down from 3rd to 2nd gear at approximately 15 mph, Ford introduced a vacuum holding system which is fitted into the vacuum line between the inlet manifold and transmission.
2 The holding system consists of an electrically-operated solenoid valve and a vacuum sustain valve along with the various vacuum pipes, connectors and wiring required to install the system on the vehicle. Refer to your Ford dealer for further information.
3 The solenoid valve and vacuum sustain valve are connected into the existing vacuum line (see illustrations). Note that the blue side of the sustain valve, marked DIST, must face towards the transmission and the black side of the valve, marked CARB, must face towards the inlet manifold. The solenoid wires are then connected to the two outer wires of the brake light switch via two suitable lengths of wire and a couple of "Scotch-lock" type connectors (see illustration). With the solenoid connected in this way, the valve should be closed when the brake pedal is depressed and open when the pedal is released.

8 Fluid contamination after component failure

1 Failure of the torque converter, or of the automatic transmission itself, can result in the contamination of the transmission fluid with friction lining and/or metallic particles. If these particles enter new or previously undamaged components, further damage may occur.
2 If the torque converter is renewed, the transmission sump must be removed, the oil strainer renewed and the valve block cleared of debris. This work should be entrusted to a Ford dealer or suitable transmission specialist. In severe cases of contamination the transmission will have to be dismantled for cleaning.
3 At the same time as the above work, or if the transmission itself is renewed, the fluid cooler lines and fluid cooler/radiator assembly must be flushed.

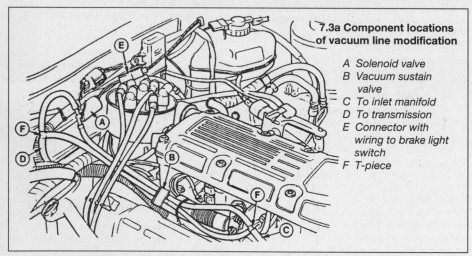

7.3a Component locations of vacuum line modification

A Solenoid valve
B Vacuum sustain valve
C To inlet manifold
D To transmission
E Connector with wiring to brake light switch
F T-piece

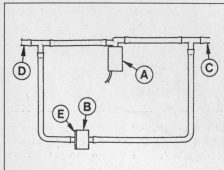

7.3b Vacuum line modification

A Solenoid valve
B Vacuum sustain valve
C To inlet manifold
D To transmission
E Blue side of vacuum sustain valve

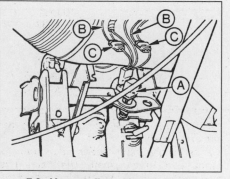

7.3c Vacuum line solenoid wiring connections

A Brake light switch
B Wiring from solenoid valve
C "Scotch-lock" connectors

Chapter 8
Propeller shaft

Contents

Degrees of difficulty

Easy, suitable for novice with little experience		Fairly easy, suitable for beginner with some experience		Fairly difficult, suitable for competent DIY mechanic		Difficult, suitable for experienced DIY mechanic		Very difficult, suitable for expert DIY or professional	

Specifications

General

Shaft type	Tubular, three-piece, with centre bearing and rubber coupling

Torque wrench settings

	Nm	lbf ft
N type gearbox		
Pinion flange bolts	57 to 75	42 to 55
Centre bearing carrier to floor	18 to 23	13 to 17
Universal joint bolt	34 to 39	25 to 29
MT75 type gearbox		
Gearbox output flange studs:		
GAF30 rubber coupling	70 to 90	52 to 66
GAF 41 rubber coupling	100 to 120	74 to 89
Front rubber coupling-to-vibration damper nuts	67 to 83	49 to 61

1 General Information

The propeller shaft is in three parts. The front part is splined and mates with the gearbox output shaft. It is joined to the centre part by a rubber "doughnut" coupling. The centre part of the shaft joins the rear part by means of a universal joint. Another universal joint, which carries the flange which bolts to the final drive pinion flange, terminates the rear part of the shaft.

A self-aligning ball bearing supports the centre part of the shaft. The bearing is mounted in a carrier which is bolted to the vehicle floor.

The parts of the shaft are carefully balanced during manufacture. If it is necessary to separate the parts - as when renewing the centre bearing - it is important that alignment marks be made so that the original balance can be maintained. Attempts to repair worn universal joints are likely to upset the balance of the shaft; in any case, spares are not supplied by the manufacturers.

A modified propeller shaft is used in conjunction with the later MT75 type gearbox. Instead of the splined spigot on the end of the propeller shaft which fits into the gearbox on earlier models, a vibration damper is fitted between the front end of the propeller shaft and the output flange on the gearbox.

2 Propeller shaft - removal and refitting

N type gearbox

1 Chock the front wheels. Raise and support the rear of the vehicle.

2 Make alignment marks between the propeller shaft and final drive pinion flanges.

3 Remove the four bolts which hold the flanges together **(see illustration)**.

4 Remove the two bolts which hold the centre bearing carrier to the floor. Lower the shaft and bearing carrier, noting the number and location of any shims and washers.

5 Pull the shaft rearwards and out of the transmission extension. Be prepared for oil spillage; insert a chamfered plastic cap into the extension, or cover it with a plastic bag secured with a rubber band.

6 Withdraw the propeller shaft from under the vehicle.

7 Commence refitting by removing the plastic bag or cap from the transmission extension.

8 Clean and lubricate the front section of the propeller shaft. Enter the front section into the transmission, being careful not to damage the oil seal.

9 Refit the centre bearing carrier to the floor, remembering the shims and washers. Fit the bolts but do not tighten them yet.

10 Align the flange mating marks, when applicable, then insert the flange bolts and tighten them to the specified torque.

11 Tighten the bearing carrier bolts to the specified torque.

12 Check the transmission oil or fluid level and top-up if necessary.

13 Lower the vehicle.

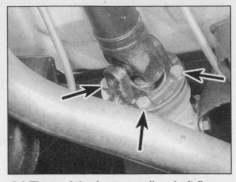

2.3 Three of the four propeller shaft flange bolts (arrowed)

MT75 type gearbox

14 The removal and refitting procedure is as described for the N type gearbox but note that on models fitted with a catalytic converter, the exhaust heat shield must be removed from the underbody for access to the propeller shaft. Also note that instead of pulling the propeller shaft from the rear of the gearbox, carry out the following procedure.

15 Counterhold the gearbox output flange studs using a suitable socket, ensuring that the studs cannot turn in the output flange, and unscrew the three nuts securing the propeller shaft rubber coupling to the vibration damper.

16 The propeller shaft can now be disconnected from the gearbox.

17 Two types of rubber coupling may be fitted to the propeller shaft, and both carry identifying marks - either GAF 30 or GAF 41.

18 When reconnecting the propeller shaft to the gearbox, proceed as follows, depending on the type of rubber coupling used.

GAF 30 coupling

19 Check that the studs are seated securely in the gearbox output flange by applying a torque of 80 Nm (59 lbf ft) to the stud heads using a torque wrench and suitable socket. Note that only Torx type studs must be used (studs with hexagonal collars must not be used). If a stud turns, it must be removed and refitted as follows.

20 Clean the stud threads at the gearbox flange end.

21 Apply two drops of thread-locking fluid to the threads at 180° to one another.

22 Insert the stud and tighten it to a torque of 80 Nm (59 lbf ft). The stud must be fitted and tightened within 5 minutes of applying the thread-locking fluid.

23 Allow the thread-locking fluid to harden for 30 minutes, then reconnect the propeller shaft to the gearbox.

24 Before reconnecting the propeller shaft to the gearbox, the washers on both sides of the coupling must be greased, and the condition of the rubber coupling must be checked as follows.

25 Examine the rubber "spokes" for cracks **(see illustration)**. If cracks are visible, the complete propeller shaft and coupling assembly must be renewed with one of the later GAF 41 type (the propeller shaft is balanced with the rubber coupling as an assembly, and therefore the coupling **must not** be removed from the propeller shaft). Cracks in the rubber skin (area C) are insignificant.

26 Secure the propeller shaft rubber coupling to the vibration damper using new nuts.

27 Further refitting is a reversal of removal.

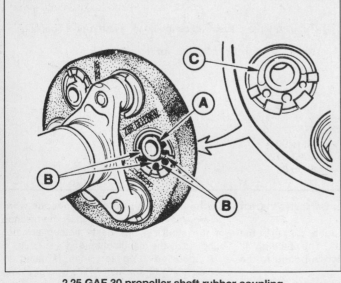

2.25 GAF 30 propeller shaft rubber coupling

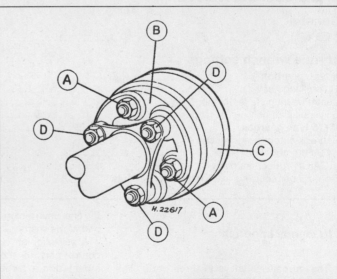

2.29 GAF 41 propeller shaft rubber coupling

A Metal bush
B Rubber "spokes"
C Rubber skin (front side only)

A Coupling-vibration-damper nuts
B GAF 41 type coupling
C Vibration damper
D Propeller shaft-to-coupling nuts

4.3 Propeller shaft centre bearing
Retaining bolt is arrowed

GAF 41 coupling

28 Check that the studs are seated securely in the gearbox output flange by applying a torque of 110 Nm (81 lbf ft) to the stud heads using a torque wrench. If a stud turns, it must be renewed, and the new stud must be tightened to the same torque. Note that only studs with hexagonal collars must be used (Torx type studs must not be used).

29 Secure the propeller shaft rubber coupling to the vibration damper using new nuts **(see illustration)**.

30 Further refitting is a reversal of removal.

3 Rubber coupling (MT75 type gearbox) - renewal

Note that the rubber coupling cannot be, as it is balanced as an assembly with the propeller shaft at the factory. The rubber coupling is not available as a spare part, and if worn or damaged, the complete propeller shaft must be renewed. If the propeller shaft is renewed, always fit a new item with the latest GAF 41 type coupling as a replacement.

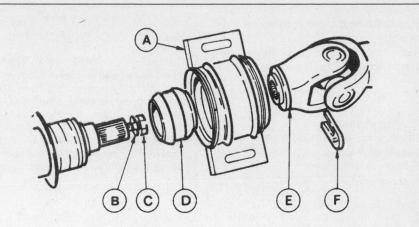

4.5 Centre bearing components

A *Mounting bracket with rubber insulator* D *Ball bearing and dust caps*
B *Locking plate* E *Splined universal joint yoke*
C *Bolt* F *U-shaped washer*

4 Centre bearing - renewal

1 Remove the propeller shaft.

2 Mark the front and rear sections of the propeller shaft in relation to each other and the exact position of the U-shaped washer beneath the bolt located in the central universal joint.

3 Bend back the locking plate and loosen the bolt in the central universal joint so that the U-shaped washer can be removed **(see illustration)**.

4 With the U-shaped washer removed, slide the rear section from the front section.

5 Pull the centre bearing bracket together with the insulator rubber from the centre bearing **(see illustration)**.

6 Remove the outer protective dust cap then, using a puller, pull the centre bearing and inner dust cap from the front propeller shaft section **(see illustration)**.

7 Wipe clean the centre bearing components. Fit the inner protective dust cap to the new bearing and pack the cavity between the cap and bearing with grease.

8 Using a suitable metal tube on the inner race, push the centre bearing and inner cap onto the front propeller shaft section. Note that the red double seal end of the bearing must face forward.

9 Fit the outer dust cap and pack the cavity between the cap and bearing with grease.

10 Ease the bracket together with the insulator rubber over the centre bearing.

11 Screw the bolt and locking plate into the

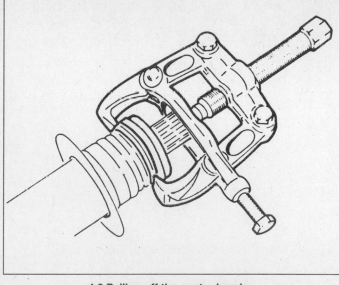

4.6 Pulling off the centre bearing

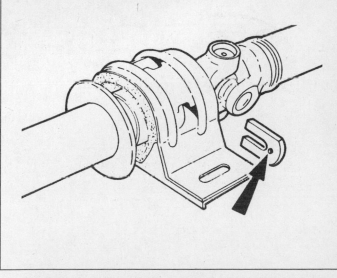

4.13 Correct position of peg (arrowed) when refitting the U-shaped washer

8

end of the front propeller shaft section leaving a sufficient gap for the U-shaped washer to be inserted.

12 Slide the rear section onto the front section, making sure that the previously made marks are aligned.

13 Refit the U-shaped washer in its previously noted position with the small peg towards the splines **(see illustration).**

14 Tighten the bolts and bend over the locking plate to secure.

15 Refit the propeller shaft.

5 Vibration damper (MT75 type gearbox) - removal and refitting

1 The propeller shaft vibration damper is attached to the gearbox output flange.

2 Two alternative types of vibration damper may be used, depending on whether a GAF 30 or GAF 41 type rubber coupling is used.

3 To remove the vibration damper, detach the propeller shaft rubber coupling from the damper then unscrew and remove the studs securing the damper to the gearbox output flange.

4 For models fitted with a GAF 30 type rubber coupling, proceed as described in paragraphs 19 to 27 of Section 2 .

5 On models fitted with a GAF 41 type rubber coupling, new studs must be used to secure the vibration damper to the gearbox output flange, and new nuts must be used to secure the rubber coupling to the vibration damper.

6 Further refitting is a reversal of removal, ensuring that all fixings are tightened to the specified torque.

Chapter 9
Final drive and driveshafts

Contents

Degrees of difficulty

Easy, suitable for novice with little experience	Fairly easy, suitable for beginner with some experience	Fairly difficult, suitable for competent DIY mechanic	Difficult, suitable for experienced DIY mechanic	Very difficult, suitable for expert DIY or professional

Specifications

General

Final drive type	Hypoid, bolted to rear underbody and to rear axle beam
Driveshaft type	Open, tubular, constant velocity (CV) joint at each end

Final drive lubrication

Lubricant type	Gear oil SAE 90EP to API GL5
Lubricant capacity:	
7 inch crownwheel	0.9 litres (1.6 pints) approx
7.5 inch crownwheel	1.3 litres (2.3 pints) approx

Adjustment data

Crownwheel and pinion backlash	0.08 to 0.15 mm (0.003 to 0.006 in)
Pinion turning torque:	
All models except 2.4 & 2.9 litre	1.6 to 2.1 Nm (1.2 to 1.6 lbf ft)
2.4 and 2.9 litre	1.8 to 2.4 Nm (1.3 to 1.8 lbf ft)

Torque wrench settings

	Nm	lbf ft
Pinion flange nut:		
All models except 2.4 & 2.9 litre	110 to 130	81 to 96
2.4 and 2.9 litre	100 to 120	74 to 89
Final drive mountings:		
To crossmember	70 to 90	52 to 66
Rear mounting to casing	40 to 50	30 to 37
Rear mounting to floor	20 to 25	15 to 18
Final drive cover screws	45 to 60	33 to 44
Final drive oil filler/level plug	35 to 45	26 to 33
Driveshaft flange screws	38 to 43	28 to 32

9

1 General information

The final drive assembly is bolted to the floor and to the rear axle crossmember, so reducing unsprung weight. It is enclosed in a light alloy housing. Oil seals protect the pinion and output shafts.

A conventional crownwheel end pinion set-up is used. A two-pinion differential is standard, with both the differential and the pinion running in taper roller bearings. Preload of the differential bearings is by means of adjustable cups, whilst that for the pinion bearings is determined by a collapsible spacer. A shim under the head of the pinion controls its depth of mesh with the crownwheel.

A viscous-coupled limited slip differential is available on some models. This type of differential is unlike earlier friction plate limited slip units, which had inherent problems of increased tyre wear, noise and adverse effects on handling. The viscous-coupled unit is silent, causes no extra tyre wear and needs no special lubricant. It operates by virtue of the shear force set up between the viscous coupling plates when one rear wheel is turning faster than the other.

Drive from the differential is taken to the wheels by two open driveshafts with a constant velocity (CV) joint at each end. Connection to the final drive unit and hubs is by bolted flanges.

Overhaul of the final drive unit is not covered in this book, because of the need for various specified tools and fixtures not normally available to the home mechanic. Overhaul should therefore be referred to a Ford dealer.

2 Final drive unit - removal and refitting

1 Chock the front wheels. Raise and support the rear of the vehicle.
2 Unhook the exhaust system rear mountings and move the system aside. Tie it up to support it.
3 Remove the propeller shaft (Chapter 8).

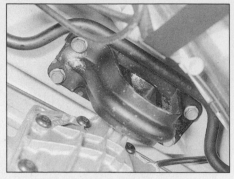

2.6 Final drive unit rear mounting

4 Disconnect the driveshafts from the final drive output flanges. Each driveshaft is secured by six Torx screws and three double lockwashers. Support the driveshafts.
5 Unbolt the anti-roll bar left-hand bracket from the floor. This will improve access to the final drive rear mounting.
6 Support the final drive unit with a jack. Unbolt the rear mounting from the floor **(see illustration)**.
7 Lower the final drive unit and unbolt the rear mounting from it. Remove the mountings.
8 Unbolt the final drive unit from the rear axle crossmember. It is secured by two through-bolts and two short bolts **(see illustration)**.
9 Lower the final drive unit and remove it from the vehicle.
10 Refit by reversing the removal operations. When offering the unit to the crossmember, fit the bottom through-bolt first.
11 Tighten all fastenings to the correct torque, when specified.
12 Check the final drive oil level and top-up if necessary.

3 Final drive pinion oil seal - renewal

1 Chock the front wheels. Raise and securely support the rear of the vehicle.
2 Unhook the exhaust system rear mountings. Move the system aside and tie it up to support it.
3 Remove the propeller shaft (Chapter 8).

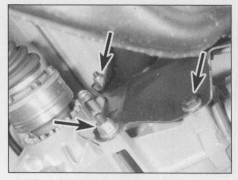

2.8 The two through-bolts and one of the shaft bolts (all arrowed) which secure the final drive unit to the rear axle crossmember

4 Hold the final drive flange stationary by bolting a long bar to it or by fitting two long bolts to it and inserting a long bar between them **(see illustration)**.
5 Unscrew the self-locking pinion flange nut.
6 Using a suitable puller pull the drive flange from the pinion **(see illustration)**. As there may be some loss of oil, place a suitable container beneath the final drive unit.
7 Using a screwdriver, lever the oil seal from the final drive unit **(see illustration)**.
8 Clean the oil seal seating within the housing, the drive flange, and the end of the pinion.
9 Pack the lips of the new oil seal with grease. (The seal may be supplied already greased, in which case do not disturb it.) Fit the seal to the housing, lips inwards, and drive it in until flush using a tube or a wooden block with a hole in it.
10 Slide the drive flange onto the pinion splines, taking care not to damage the oil seal.
11 Fit the self-locking nut and tighten it to the specified torque while holding the drive flange stationary using the method described in paragraph 4. Ideally a new self-locking nut should be used, and it should not be unscrewed and tightened more than three times otherwise it will lose its self-locking characteristic.
12 Refit the propeller shaft (Chapter 8).
13 Top-up the final drive oil (Chapter 1).

3.4 Holding the final drive flange

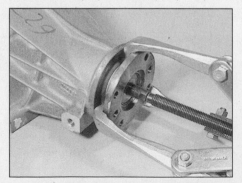
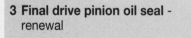

3.6 Using a puller to remove the flange

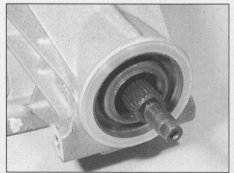

3.7 Pinion oil seal is now accessible

5.2 Undoing a driveshaft flange screw

4 Final drive output flange oil seals - renewal

1 Remove the final drive unit.
2 Remove the rear cover from the final drive unit. This is secured by nine Torx screws. Any oil left inside the unit will be released when the cover is removed.
3 Clean old sealant from the cover mating faces, taking care to keep it out of the interior of the unit.
4 Remove the circlips which secure the output flanges inside the differential. *Do not get the circlips mixed up,* as their thickness is selected and may differ from left to right.
5 Withdraw the output flanges and stubs. Clean the seal rubbing faces.
6 Measure the fitted depths of the old oil seals, then prise them from their locations. Clean the seal seats.
7 Pack the lips of the new seals with grease (if they are not supplied ready-greased). Fit the seals, lips inwards, and drive them in to the depth previously noted, using a piece of tube.
8 Refit the output flanges and stubs, being careful not to damage the seal lips. Secure them with the same circlips.
9 Apply liquid sealant (to Ford spec. SQM 4G 9523 A) to the mating faces of the final drive unit and the rear cover.
10 Fit the rear cover. Insert the cover screws and tighten them evenly to the specified torque.
11 Refit the final drive unit, remembering to refill it with oil on completion.

5 Driveshaft - removal and refitting

1 Chock the front wheels. Raise and support the rear of the vehicle.
2 Remove the six Torx screws which secure the inboard flange to the final drive unit **(see illustration)**. Recover the three double lockwashers. Support the driveshaft.
3 Similarly remove the six screws which secure the outboard flange to the rear hub. Remove the driveshaft.
4 At all times, avoid bending the CV joints to excessive angles, and do not allow the shaft to hang down from one end.
5 Refit by reversing the removal operations. Tighten the flange screws to the specified torque.

6 Driveshaft - overhaul

1 The CV joints cannot be overhauled, but they can be renewed separately, as can the rubber gaiters. Check when purchasing gaiters whether the grease required for the CV joints is included.
2 Remove the driveshaft as described in the previous Section.
3 Undo or cut the clips which secure the rubber gaiters. Peel the gaiters back from the CV joints.
4 Release the CV joints by removing the outer circlips (one per joint) which secure them to the shaft. Pull off the joints and remove the inner circlips.
5 The gaiters can now be removed from the shaft.
6 Renew components as necessary. The gaiter clips must be renewed in any case.
7 Pack the CV joints with the specified type and quantity of grease.
8 Fit the gaiters and the CV joint inner covers to the shaft. Fit the inner circlips. Apply sealant to the protective cover face where it will meet the CV joint **(see illustration)**. Clean any grease off the corresponding face of the joint.

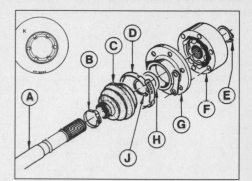

6.8 Driveshaft CV joint assembly

A Shaft
B Wire clip
C Gaiter
D Clip
E Outer circlip
F Constant velocity joint
G Protective cover
H Dished washer (if fitted)
J Inner circlip
K Sealant application

6.9 Correct fitting of CV joints with grooves (arrowed) outermost

9 Fit the CV joints, grooves outermost, and secure them with the outer circlips **(see illustration)**.
10 Secure the gaiters with the new clips.
11 Refit the driveshaft.

9

Chapter 10
Braking system

Contents

Degrees of difficulty

Easy, suitable for novice with little experience | Fairly easy, suitable for beginner with some experience | Fairly difficult, suitable for competent DIY mechanic | Difficult, suitable for experienced DIY mechanic | Very difficult, suitable for expert DIY or professional

Specifications

General
System type: .... Discs all round, hydraulic operation, anti-lock braking system (ABS). Handbrake by mechanical operation of rear calipers

System make:
  Models up to April 1992 .... Teves MK II ABS
  Models from April 1992 .... Teves MK IV ABS

Hydraulic system
Fluid type .... Hydraulic fluid to Ford spec SAM-6C9103-A
Operating pressure .... 130 to 190 bar (1885 to 2755 lbf/in^2)
Pressure warning switch operates at .... 100 to 110 bar (1450 to 1595 lbf/in^2)

Brake pads
Lining minimum thickness .... 1.5 mm (0.06 in)

Brake discs
Run-out .... 0.15 mm (0.006 in) maximum
Thickness variation .... 0.015 mm (0.0006 in) maximum
Minimum thickness:
  Front .... 22 mm (0.87 in)
  Rear .... Cast into outer rim (typically 8.9 mm/0.35 in)
  Rear - Estate models .... 18 mm (0.71 in)

10

Torque wrench settings

	Nm	lbf ft
Front caliper:		
To stub axle carrier	51 to 61	38 to 45
Slide bolts	20 to 25	15 to 18
Rear caliper:		
Bracket to carrier plate	51 to 61	38 to 45
Slide bolts	31 to 35	23 to 26
Hydraulic unit to bulkhead	41 to 51	30 to 38
Accumulator to pump body	35 to 45	26 to 33
Pump mounting bolts	7 to 9	5 to 7
High pressure hose banjo bolts	16 to 24	12 to 18
Reservoir mounting bolts	4 to 6	3 to 4
Wheel sensor fixing bolts	8 to 11	6 to 8
Vacuum servo unit retaining nuts (Teves MK IV)	35 to 45	26 to 33
Master cylinder retaining nuts (Teves MK IV)	20 to 25	15 to 18
Valve block and pump assembly mounting nuts (Teves MK IV)	21 to 28	15 to 21

1 General information

Models covered in this Manual have disc brakes fitted all round. The footbrake operates hydraulically on all four wheels, and the handbrake operates mechanically on the rear wheels. Both footbrake and handbrake are self-adjusting in use.

Ford's anti-lock braking system (ABS) is fitted to all models. The system monitors the rotational speed of each roadwheel. When a wheel begins to lock under heavy braking, the ABS reduces the hydraulic pressure to that wheel, so preventing it from locking. When this happens a pulsating effect will be noticed at the brake pedal. On some road surfaces the tyres may squeal when braking hard even though the wheels are not locked.

The main components of the system are the hydraulic unit, the calipers, pads and discs, the wheel sensors and the "brain" or control module. The hydraulic unit contains the elements of a traditional master cylinder, plus an electric motor and pump, a pressure accumulator and control valves. The pump is the source of pressure for the system and does away with the need for a vacuum servo.

The hydraulic circuit is split front and rear, as is normal practice with rear-wheel drive vehicles. In the event that the hydraulic pump fails, unassisted braking effort is still available on the front calipers only.

Warning lights inform the driver of low brake fluid level, ABS failure and (on some models) brake pad wear. The low fluid level light doubles as a "handbrake on" light; if it illuminates at the same time as the ABS warning light, it warns of low hydraulic pressure.

ABS cannot overturn the laws of physics: stopping distances will inevitably be greater on loose or slippery surfaces. However, the system should allow even inexperienced drivers to retain directional control under panic braking.

From August 1986 the following modifications were made to the braking system.

a) *The relays differ from earlier versions.*

b) *The hydraulic pump is constructed of iron rather than alloy.*

c) *A new pressure warning switch is used.*

d) *The earlier high pressure rubber hose is replaced by a steel pipe.*

To overcome the problem of excessive rear brake pad wear, Ford introduced a differential valve which is screwed into the ABS valve block. The valve limits the pressure applied to the rear brake calipers and so reduces brake pad wear. From 1988 onwards, the valve has been fitted during production. The differential valve can also be fitted to earlier models. Refer to your Ford dealer for further information.

From April 1992 onwards, the models covered in this Manual were equipped with a new Teves MK IV anti-lock braking system instead of the Teves MK II system fitted to the earlier models.

The Teves MK IV system differs from the earlier MK II system in the following ways.

a) *The source of hydraulic pressure for the system is a conventional master cylinder and vacuum servo assembly.*

b) *A valve block and pump assembly is used instead of the hydraulic control unit. The block contains the inlet and outlet solenoid valves that control the hydraulic system. There are three pairs of valves, one for each brake circuit (paragraph c).*

c) *The hydraulic braking system consists of three separate circuits; one for each front brake (which are totally independent of each other), and a joint circuit which operates both rear brakes.*

d) *A G (gravity) switch is incorporated in the system. This is an inertia type switch and informs the control module when the vehicle is decelerating rapidly.*

e) *A Pedal Travel Sensor (PTS) is fitted to the vacuum servo unit. The PTS informs the control module of the position of the brake pedal when the anti-lock sequence starts and ensures that a constant pedal height is maintained during the sequence.*

The MK IV system operates as follows.

During normal operation the system functions in the same way as a non-ABS system would. During this time the three inlet valves in the valve block are open and the outlet valves are closed, allowing full hydraulic pressure present in the master cylinder to act on the main braking circuit. If the control module receives a signal from one of the wheel sensors and senses that a wheel is about to lock, it closes the relevant inlet valve in the valve block which then isolates the brake caliper on the wheel which is about to lock from the master cylinder, effectively sealing in the hydraulic pressure. If the speed of rotation of the wheel continues to decrease at an abnormal rate, the control module will then open the relevant outlet valve in the valve block; this allows the fluid from the relevant hydraulic circuit to return to the master cylinder reservoir, releasing pressure on the brake caliper so that the brake is released. The pump in the valve block also operates to assist in the quick release of pressure. Once the speed of rotation of the wheel returns to an acceptable rate the pump stops, the outlet valve closes and the inlet valve is opened, allowing the hydraulic master cylinder pressure to return to the caliper which then reapplies the brake. This cycle can be carried many times a second. The solenoid valves connected to the front calipers operate independently, but the valve connected to the rear calipers operates both calipers simultaneously.

The operation of the ABS system is entirely dependent on electrical signals. To prevent the system responding to any inaccurate signals, a built-in safety circuit monitors all signals received by the control module. If an inaccurate signal or low battery voltage is detected, the ABS system is automatically shut down and the warning lamp on the instrument cluster is illuminated to inform the driver that the ABS system is not operational. Whilst in this state the system functions in the same way as a non-ABS system would. If a fault does develop in the ABS system, the car must be taken to a Ford dealer for fault diagnosis and repair. The system is equipped with a diagnostic plug into which a special diagnostic (STAR) tester can be plugged. This allows faults to be easily traced.

2 Brake hydraulic system - bleeding

Note: *Hydraulic fluid is poisonous; wash off immediately and thoroughly in the case of skin contact and seek immediate medical advice if any fluid is swallowed or gets into the eyes. Certain types of hydraulic fluid are inflammable and may ignite when allowed into contact with hot components; when servicing any hydraulic system it is safest to assume that the fluid is inflammable and to take precautions against the risk of fire as though it is petrol that is being handled. Finally, it is hygroscopic (it absorbs moisture from the air) old fluid may be contaminated and unfit for further use. When topping-up or renewing the fluid, always use the recommended type and ensure that it comes from a freshly-opened sealed container*

> **HAYNES HiNT**
> *Hydraulic fluid is an effective paint stripper and will attack plastics; if any is spilt, it should be washed off immediately using copious quantities of fresh water.*

1 Bleeding is necessary whenever air has entered the hydraulic system - for instance after component renewal. Because the hydraulic circuits are split, if only the front or rear circuit has been disturbed it will normally only be necessary to bleed the front or rear calipers. If the hydraulic unit has been disturbed or the fluid level has been allowed to fall so low that air has entered the system, both front and rear circuits must be bled, starting with the front

2 The services of an assistant will be required. As far as is known, pressure bleeding or other "one-man" equipment cannot be used. In addition a supply of fresh brake fluid of the correct type will be needed, together with a length of flexible tube to fit the bleed screws and a clean glass or plastic container.

3 Do not allow the hydraulic unit pump motor to run for more than two minutes at a time. The motor must be allowed to cool (with the ignition off) for at least ten minutes after each two minute spell of running.

4 Remember that brake fluid is poisonous and that the rear brake hydraulic system may be under considerable pressure. Take care not to allow hydraulic fluid to spray into the face or eyes.

5 Keep the reservoir topped up to the MAX mark during bleeding.

6 Discard the fluid bled out of the system as it is unfit for re-use.

Models before April 1992

Front brakes

7 Remove the dust cap (if fitted) from the left-hand caliper bleed screw. Slacken the bleed screw, then nip it up again. Make sure that the ignition is off.

8 Fit the bleed tube over the bleed screw. Place the other end of the tube in the bleed jar (glass or plastic container). Pour sufficient brake fluid into the jar to cover the end of the tube.

9 Open the bleed screw one full turn. Have the assistant depress the brake pedal as far as it will go, and hold it depressed. Tighten the bleed screw, then tell the assistant to release the pedal.

10 Repeat paragraph 9 until clean fluid, free of air bubbles, flows from the bleed screw during the downstrokes. Remember to keep the fluid reservoir topped up.

11 Repeat the operations on the right-hand caliper. Refit the bleed screw dust caps (if applicable) on completion.

Rear brakes

12 Remove the dust cap (if fitted) from the rear left-hand caliper bleed screw. Open the bleed screw one full turn.

13 Fit the bleed tube over the bleed screw. Place the other end of the tube in the bleed jar **(see illustration)**.

14 Have the assistant depress the brake pedal as far as it will go and hold it down. Switch on the ignition: the hydraulic unit pump will start and fluid will flow from the bleed screw.

15 When clean fluid, free of air bubbles, emerges from the bleed screw, tighten the bleed screw and have the assistant release the pedal.

16 Wait for the hydraulic unit pump to stop, then top-up the reservoir and repeat the procedure on the right-hand caliper. This time the brake pedal should only be depressed half-way.

17 Switch off the ignition, top-up the reservoir again and refit the reservoir cap. Refit the bleed screw dust caps (if applicable).

Models from April 1992

18 This operation can be carried out using the information given above in paragraphs 1 to 10, ignoring the reference to the hydraulic unit pump and bearing in mind the following.

19 Note that if only one circuit is disturbed it will only be necessary to bleed that relevant circuit on completion.

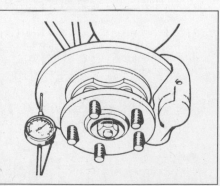

4.3 Measuring brake disc run-out

2.13 Bleeding a rear brake caliper

20 If the complete system is to be bled, it should be done in the following order.
a) Left-hand front caliper.
b) Right-hand front brake caliper.
c) Left-hand rear caliper.
d) Right-hand rear caliper.

3 Brake hydraulic system - fluid renewal

See Chapter 1, Section 44.

4 Brake discs - inspection

1 Whenever the brake pads are inspected, also inspect the brake discs for deep scratches, scores or cracks. Light scoring is normal and may be ignored. A cracked disc must be renewed; scratches and scores can sometimes be machined out, provided that the thickness of the disc is not reduced below the specified minimum.

2 When the brake pads are renewed, or if brake judder or snatch is noticed, check the discs for run-out and thickness variation. (Note that wheel bearing wear can cause disc run-out.)

3 Position a dial test indicator probe against the disc wear face, approximately 15 mm (0.6 in) in from the outer circumference. Zero the indicator, rotate the disc and read the run-out from the indicator **(see illustration)**. Maximum run-out is given in the Specifications. If a dial test indicator is not available, use a fixed pointer and feeler blades.

4 Measure the thickness of the disc, using a micrometer, in eight evenly spaced positions around the disc. Maximum thickness variation is given in the Specifications. Renew the disc if the variation is out of limits.

5 Front brake disc - removal and refitting

1 Slacken the front wheel nuts, raise and support the vehicle and remove the relevant front wheel.

2 Remove the two bolts which hold the caliper bracket to the stub axle carrier. Lift the caliper

 10

5.3 Disc-securing spring clip

7.2 Spring clip fitted to outboard face of front caliper

7.3 Pad wear warning multi-plug (arrowed) on front caliper

7.4 Undoing a caliper slide bolt

and bracket off the disc and tie them up out of the way. Do not allow the caliper to hang on the flexible hose.

3 Remove the spring clip which secures the disc (see illustration).

4 Mark the relationship of the disc to the hub if it is to be re-used, then remove the disc.

5 Refit by reversing the removal operations. Tighten the caliper bracket bolts to the specified torque, and check that the brake flexible hose is not kinked or fouling in any position of the steering wheel.

6 Pump the brake pedal to bring the pads up to the disc.

6 Rear brake disc - removal and refitting

1 Chock the front wheels and release the handbrake. Slacken the rear wheel nuts, raise and support the vehicle and remove the relevant rear wheel.

2 Free the handbrake cable from its clip in the suspension lower arm.

3 Remove the two bolts which secure the caliper bracket to the hub. Lift the caliper and bracket off the disc and suspend it without straining the flexible hose.

4 Remove the spring clip from the wheel stud. Mark the disc-to-hub relationship and remove the disc.

5 Refit by reversing the removal operations.

6 Pump the brake pedal to bring the pads up to the disc.

7 Front brake pads - inspection and renewal

1 Disc pads can be inspected without removing the front wheels, using a mirror and a torch through the aperture in the rear face of the caliper. If any one pad is worn down to the minimum specified, all four pads (on both front wheels) must be renewed.

2 To renew the pads, first remove the front wheels, then prise free the spring clip from the outboard face of a caliper (see illustration).

3 Disconnect the pad wear warning wires, when fitted (see illustration).

4 Unscrew the two caliper slide bolts, using a 7 mm hexagon key, until the caliper is free of the bracket (see illustration).

5 Lift the caliper off the disc and remove the pads (see illustration). Support the caliper so that the flexible hose is not strained. Do not press the brake pedal with the caliper removed.

6 Clean the dust and dirt from the caliper, bracket and disc, using a damp cloth or old paintbrush which can be thrown away afterwards. **Take care not to disperse the dust into the air, or to inhale it, since it may contain asbestos.** Scrape any scale or rust from the disc. Investigate any hydraulic fluid leaks.

7 Push the caliper piston back into its housing, using the fingers or a blunt instrument, to accommodate the extra thickness of the new pads.

8 Fit the new pads to the caliper, being careful not to contaminate the friction surfaces with oil

or grease. The inboard pad has a spring clip which fits into the piston recess; the outboard pad must have its backing paper peeled off, after which the pad should be stuck to the other side of the caliper (see illustrations).

9 Fit the caliper and pads over the disc and onto the caliper bracket. Tighten the slide bolts to the specified torque.

10 Reconnect the wear warning wires, if fitted.

11 Refit the spring clip to the caliper.

12 Repeat the operations on the other caliper, then refit the wheels and lower the vehicle. Tighten the wheel nuts.

13 Pump the brake pedal several times to bring the pads up to the disc, then check the brake fluid level.

14 Avoid heavy braking as far as possible for the first hundred miles or so to allow the new pads to bed in.

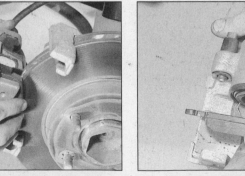

7.5 Lifting a front caliper off the disc

7.8a Clipping the inboard front pad into the piston

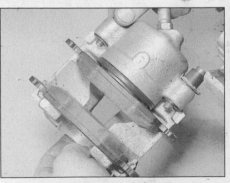

7.8b Both pads fitted to a front caliper

8.3 Undoing a rear caliper front slide bolt

8.4 Pad wear warning multi-plug (arrowed) on rear caliper

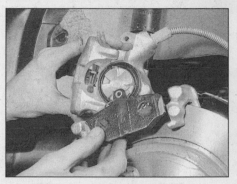

8.5 Removing a rear brake pad

8 Rear brake pads - inspection and renewal

1 It is necessary to remove the rear wheels in order to inspect the rear pads. The pads can be viewed through the top of the caliper after removing the spring clip. If any one pad is worn down to the minimum specified, all four pads (on both rear wheels) must be renewed.

2 Free the handbrake cable from its clip on the suspension lower arm. Release the handbrake.

3 Remove the caliper slide bolt nearest the front, counter-holding the slide pin with another spanner (see illustration).

4 Disconnect the pad wear warning wires, when fitted (see illustration).

5 Swing the caliper rearwards and remove the pads (see illustration). Do not press the brake pedal with the caliper removed.

6 Clean the dust and dirt from the caliper, bracket and disc, using a damp cloth or old paintbrush which can be thrown away afterwards. Take care not to disperse the dust into the air, or to inhale it, since it may contain asbestos. Scrape any scale or rust from the disc. Investigate any hydraulic fluid leaks.

7 Retract the caliper piston, by turning it clockwise, to accommodate the extra thickness of the new pads. There is a Ford tool (No 12-006) for this purpose, but a pair of circlip pliers or any similar tool can be used instead (see illustration).

8 Remove any backing paper from the new

pads, then fit them to the caliper bracket. Be careful not to contaminate the friction surfaces with oil or grease.

9 Swing the caliper over the pads. Refit and tighten the slide bolt.

10 Reconnect the wear warning wires, if fitted.

11 Repeat the operations on the other rear caliper.

12 Secure the handbrake cable, refit the wheels and lower the vehicle. Tighten the wheel nuts.

13 Switch on the ignition and pump the brake pedal several times to bring the pads up to the discs. Switch off the ignition and check the operation of the handbrake.

14 Avoid heavy braking as far as possible for the first hundred miles or so to allow the new pads to bed in.

9 Front caliper - removal and refitting

1 With the ignition off, pump the brake pedal at least 20 times (or until it becomes hard) to depressurise the hydraulic system.

2 Slacken the front wheel nuts, raise and support the vehicle and remove the relevant front wheel.

3 Slacken the flexible hose hydraulic union at the caliper by no more than a quarter turn.

4 Remove the brake pads (Section 7).

5 The caliper can now be removed by holding the flexible hose stationary and rotating the caliper to unscrew it. Be prepared for hydraulic fluid spillage: plug or cap the caliper and hose.

A brake hose clamp may be used if available (see illustration). Take great care to keep dirt out of the hydraulic system.

6 The caliper bracket may be unbolted from the stub axle carrier if wished.

7 Refit by reversing the removal operations, but before refitting the wheel, check the positioning of the flexible hose. It must not be kinked, nor foul adjacent components, in any position of the steering wheel. Release the other end of the hose from its bracket if necessary and reposition it.

8 Bleed both front brake calipers as described in Section 2.

10 Front caliper - overhaul

1 It is possible to carry out these operations without disconnecting the caliper hydraulic hose, but this is not recommended because of the risk of introducing dirt into the hydraulic system. Scrupulous cleanliness is essential.

2 Obtain a caliper repair kit, which will contain a piston seal and a dust boot. (The piston itself can also be renewed if necessary.)

3 Remove the piston from the caliper. This is best done with low air pressure (eg from a foot pump) applied to the hydraulic inlet union. Place a piece of wood opposite the piston to prevent damage, and keep your fingers clear as the piston may be ejected with some force.

4 With the piston removed, pull off the dust boot (see illustration).

8.7 Rotating the caliper piston to retract it

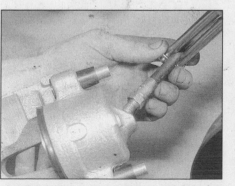

9.5 Removing a front caliper - note clamp on brake hose

10.4 Removing the dust boot from a front caliper

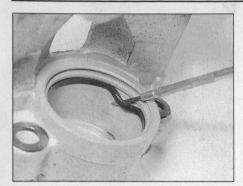

10.5 Removing the piston seal

10.9 Pressing the piston into the bore

11.5a Unhook the handbrake cable . . .

5 Extract the piston seal from the groove in the bore, using a blunt instrument **(see illustration)**. Discard the seal and dust boot.
6 Clean the piston and bore with methylated spirit and inspect them for scuffs, scores or other damage. If the piston is corroded it must be renewed. Slight imperfections in the bore can be polished out with wire wool.
7 Place the clean component on a clean surface ready for reassembly. Lubricate the caliper hose with clean hydraulic fluid.
8 Fit the new piston seal to the groove in the bore, using fingers only to work it into position.
9 Lubricate the piston with clean hydraulic fluid and fit the dust boot over the piston, making sure it is the right way up. Insert the piston into the bore and press it home, engaging the dust boot lip with the groove on the caliper **(see illustration)**.
10 This completes the overhaul of the hydraulic components. Items such as slide bolts and bracket can also be renewed if necessary.
11 Remove the bleed screw while the caliper is on the bench and apply a little anti-seize compound to its threads, to avoid trouble in undoing it later.

11 Rear caliper - removal and refitting

1 With the ignition off, pump the brake pedal at least 20 times (or until it becomes hard) to depressurise the system.
2 Chock the front wheels and release the handbrake. Slacken the rear wheel nuts, raise

and support the vehicle and remove the relevant wheel.
3 Disconnect the pad wear warning wires, when fitted.
4 Disconnect the flexible hose from the brake pipe. Plug or cap the open unions to reduce spillage and to keep dirt out. Unscrew the flexible hose from the caliper and remove it.
5 Remove the two slide bolts. Lift the caliper off the pads and bracket, at the same time unhooking the handbrake cable **(see illustrations)**. Alternatively, the two bracket-to-hub bolts can be removed and the caliper and bracket separated on the bench.
6 Refit by reversing the removal operations, but before refitting the wheel, bleed both rear calipers as described in Section 2.
7 When bleeding is complete, pump the brake pedal several times to bring the pads up to the disc, then check the operation of the handbrake.

12 Rear caliper - overhaul

Note: *Complete dismantling of the rear caliper should not be attempted unless Ford spring compressor (tool No 12-007) is available. or unless the problems likely to arise in the absence of the tool are understood. Renewal of the piston seal and dust boot requires no special tools.*
1 Clean the caliper externally and mount it in a soft-jawed vice.
2 Rotate the piston anti-clockwise until it is

11.5b . . . and remove the rear caliper

protruding from the bore by about 20 mm (0.8 in). Free the dust boot from the groove in the piston, then carry on unscrewing the piston and remove it. Remove and discard the dust boot.
3 The piston and bore may now be cleaned and examined, and the piston seal and dust boot renewed, as described for the front caliper (Section 10).
4 The piston adjuster nut seal should also be renewed. Remove the circlip from the piston, then extract the thrustwashers, wave washer and thrust bearing. Note the fitted sequence of these components. Finally remove the nut **(see illustrations)**.
5 Remove the seal from the nut, noting which way round it is fitted. Clean the nut with methylated spirit. Lubricate the new seal with clean hydraulic fluid and fit it to the nut.

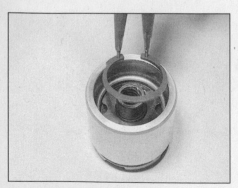

12.4a Removing the circlip from a rear caliper piston . . .

12.4b . . . followed by a thrustwasher . . .

12.4c . . . a wave washer and (not shown) another thrustwasher . . .

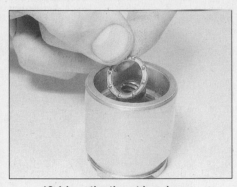

12.4d . . . the thrust bearing . . .

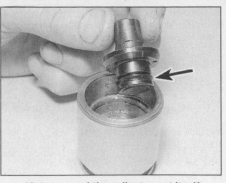

12.4e . . . and the adjuster nut itself
Note seal (arrowed) on nut

12.6 Using the adjuster nut to compress the caliper spring

6 For further dismantling it is virtually essential to have Ford tool 12-007. This tool appears to be a cut-down adjuster nut with a handle for turning it. In the workshop it was found that the piston adjuster nut could be used to compress the spring if it were turned with circlip pliers **(see illustration)**. This works well enough for dismantling, but reassembly proved extremely difficult because of the limited clearance between the skirt of the nut and the caliper bore.

7 Having compressed the adjuster spring just enough to take the load off the circlip, release the circlip inside the caliper bore. Remove the spring compressor, then extract the circlip, spring cover, spring and washer **(see illustrations)**.

8 A long thin pair of circlip pliers will now be needed to release the key plate retaining circlip from the caliper bore **(see illustration)**. With the circlip removed, the pushrod and key plate can be pulled out.

9 Remove the handbrake strut from the caliper bore.

10 Remove the handbrake lever return spring and stop bolt. Pull the lever and shaft nut out of the caliper. Prise out the shaft seal.

11 Clean up the handbrake shaft using wire wool; renew the shaft if it is badly corroded. The shaft bush in the caliper can also be renewed if necessary. Pull out the old bush with an internal puller or slide hammer; press in the new bush to 7.5 mm (0.30 in) below the shaft seal lip **(see illustration)**. The slot in the side of the bush must line up with the pushrod bore in the caliper.

12 Having renewed components as necessary, commence reassembly by smearing a little brake grease or anti-seize compound on the handbrake shaft and bush.

13 Fit a new handbrake shaft seal to the caliper. Pass the shaft through the seal and into the caliper, being careful not to damage the seal lips.

14 Refit the handbrake lever stop bolt and return spring.

15 Refit the handbrake strut, lubricating it with brake grease.

16 Fit a new O-ring to the base of the pushrod. Refit the pushrod and the key plate, engaging the pip on the key plate with the recess in the caliper. Secure the key plate with the circlip.

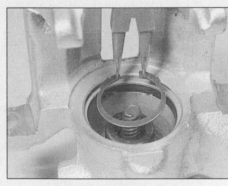

12.7a Extract the circlip . . .

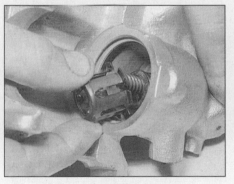

12.7b . . . the spring cover . . .

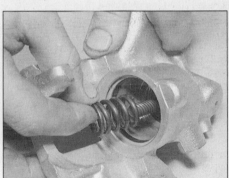

12.7c . . . the spring itself . . .

12.7d . . . and the washer

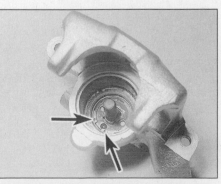

12.8 Remove the circlip (ends arrowed) to release the pushrod and key plate

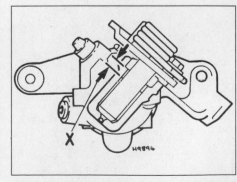

12.11 Handbrake shaft bush correctly fitted
X = 7.5 mm (0.30 in)

10

12.21 Dust boot fitted to caliper and piston

17 Refit the washer, spring and spring cover. Compress the spring and refit the circlip, then release the spring compressor.
18 Lubricate the caliper bore with clean hydraulic fluid and fit a new piston seal.
19 Reassemble the piston components. Lubricate the contact face of the adjuster nut with a little brake grease, then fit the adjuster nut (with new seal), thrust bearing, thrustwasher, wave washer and the second thrustwasher. Secure with the circlip.
20 Fit a new dust boot. The manufacturers recommend that it be fitted to the caliper groove and the piston fitted afterwards; it is also possible to fit the boot to the piston first and engage it in the caliper groove afterwards. Either way it is a fiddly business.
21 Refit the piston and screw it into the caliper, then fit whichever lip of the dust boot was left free **(see illustration)**.

22 Renew the slide pin gaiters and apply a little anti-seize compound to the slide pins when reassembling the caliper to the bracket.

13 Rear disc splash shield - removal and refitting

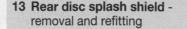

The splash shield is retained by the rear hub bolts. Proceed as described in Chapter 11 for removal and refitting of the rear hub.

14 Brake pedal - removal and refitting

1 Disconnect the battery negative lead.
2 Depressurise the hydraulic system by pumping the brake pedal at least 20 times, or until it becomes hard.
3 Remove the under-dash trim on the driver's side.
4 Remove the spring clip which secures the hydraulic unit pushrod to the brake pedal. Also remove the clip from the brake pedal shaft **(see illustration)**.
5 Withdraw the brake pedal shaft towards the left of the vehicle - through the clutch pedal, when applicable - until the brake pedal is free.
6 Remove the pedal, noting the fitted sequence of bushes, spacers and washers.
7 Refit by reversing the removal operations. Check the correct functioning of the stop-light and (if applicable) cruise control switches before refitting the trim. See Chapter 13.

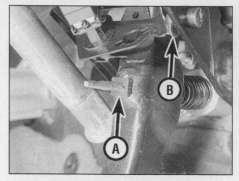

14.4 Pushrod spring clip (A) and brake pedal shaft clip (B)

15 Hydraulic unit - removal and refitting

1 Disconnect the battery negative lead.
2 Depressurise the hydraulic system by pumping the brake pedal at least 20 times, or until it becomes hard.
3 Disconnect the six multi-plugs from the hydraulic unit. They are all different, so there is no need to label them. When a plug has a spring clip retainer, lift the clip before pulling out the plug. To release the pump plug, pull back the rubber boot and the plug sleeve **(see illustrations)**.
4 Unbolt the earth strap from the unit **(see illustration)**.
5 Make arrangements to catch spilt hydraulic

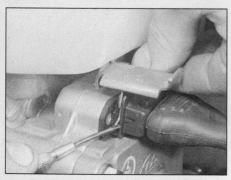

15.3a Disconnect the valve block multi-plug. Lift the clip and pull off the plug

15.3b Disconnecting a fluid level sensor plug

15.3c Disconnecting the main valve plug

15.3d Disconnecting the pressure switch multi-plug

15.3e Disconnecting the pump motor plug

15.4 Earth strap (arrowed) bolted to hydraulic unit

15.7 Four nuts (arrowed) which hold the hydraulic unit to the bulkhead

fluid. Identify the hydraulic pipes and disconnect them from the base of the unit. Hint: Plug or cap the open unions to keep fluid in and dirt out.

6 Remove the under-dash trim on the driver's side. Disconnect the spring clip which secures the hydraulic unit pushrod to the brake pedal.

7 Have an assistant support the hydraulic unit. Remove the four nuts which hold the unit to the bulkhead **(see illustration)**. Withdraw the unit from under the bonnet.

8 Recover the sealing compound from the unit and the bulkhead.

9 Drain the hydraulic fluid from the reservoir. *Do not actuate the pushrod with the unit removed.*

10 Dismantling of the hydraulic unit should be limited to the operations described in the following Sections. These operations can all be carried out without removing the unit from the vehicle if wished.

11 Refit by reversing the removal operations, noting the following points:

a) *Do not refill the reservoir until the end of refitting*
b) *Use new sealing compound between the unit and the bulkhead*
c) *Make sure that the hydraulic pipes are reconnected to the correct unions*
d) *Bleed the complete hydraulic system on completion - see Section 2*

16 Hydraulic unit fluid reservoir - removal and refitting

1 Disconnect the battery negative lead.

2 Depressurise the hydraulic system by pumping the brake pedal at least 20 times, or until it becomes hard.

3 Disconnect the multi-plugs and remove the reservoir cap.

4 Remove the reservoir securing screw, which is located just above the valve block multi-plug **(see illustration)**.

5 Make arrangements to catch spilt fluid, then disconnect the low pressure hose from its connections to the pump. The hose is secured by a spring clip **(see illustrations)**. Allow the brake fluid to drain out of the hose.

6 Pull the reservoir out of the seals on the hydraulic unit and remove it **(see illustration)**.

7 Note the spigot locating bush on the rear inlet union, which may stay in the hydraulic unit or may come out with the reservoir **(see illustration)**.

8 Refit by reversing the removal operations. Use new seals between the hydraulic unit and the reservoir.

9 Bleed the complete hydraulic system on completion (Section 2). Check for leaks around the disturbed components.

17 Hydraulic unit accumulator - removal and refitting

1 Disconnect the battery negative lead.

2 Depressurise the hydraulic system by pumping the brake pedal at least 20 times, or until it becomes hard.

3 Wrap a clean rag round the base of the accumulator to catch any spilt fluid.

4 Unscrew the accumulator using a hexagon key. Remove the accumulator, being prepared for fluid spillage **(see illustration)**.

5 When refitting, fit a new O-ring to the base of the accumulator. Fit the accumulator and tighten it.

6 Reconnect the battery. Switch on the ignition and check that the hydraulic unit pump stops within 60 seconds. If not, there may be something wrong with the accumulator.

7 Bleed the complete hydraulic system as described in Section 2.

16.4 Undoing the reservoir securing screw

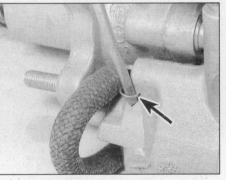

16.5a Extract the spring clip . . .

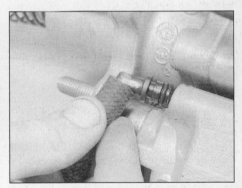

16.5b . . . and disconnect the hose

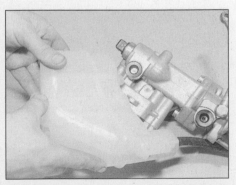

16.6 Removing the hydraulic fluid reservoir

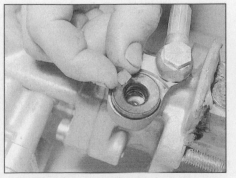

16.7 The spigot locating bush fits into this union

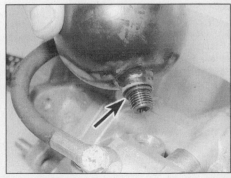

17.4 Removing the accumulator
Note O-ring (arrowed)

10

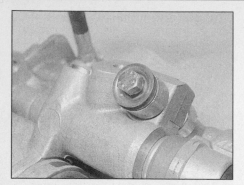

18.5 Hydraulic unit pump mounting bolt

19.4 Refitting the pressure switch
Hole (arrowed) in sleeve must face pump motor

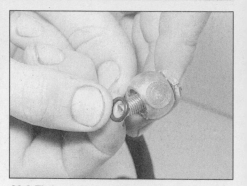

20.9 Fitting new sealing washers to a banjo union

18 Hydraulic unit pump and motor - removal and refitting

1 Remove the accumulator (Section 17).
2 Disconnect the high pressure hose from the pump. Be prepared for fluid spillage.
3 Disconnect the low pressure hose from the pump. Allow the fluid to drain out of the reservoir through the hose.
4 Disconnect the multi-plugs from the pressure switch and the pump motor.
5 Remove the pump mounting bolt **(see illustration)**.
6 Pull the pump and motor assembly off the mounting spigot and remove it.
7 Recover the mounting bushes and renew them if necessary.
8 If a new pump is to be fitted, transfer the pressure switch to it, using a new O-ring.
9 Commence refitting by offering the pump to the spigot, then reconnecting the low pressure hose.
10 Refit and tighten the pump mounting bolt.
11 Reconnect the high pressure hose, using new sealing washers on the banjo union.
12 Refit the accumulator, using a new O-ring.
13 Reconnect the multi-plugs and the battery.
14 Refill the reservoir, then switch on the ignition and allow the pump to prime itself. Do not let the pump run for more than two minutes - see Section 3. Check for leaks around the disturbed components.
15 Bleed the complete system (Section 2).

19 Hydraulic unit pressure switch - removal and refitting

Note: *To remove the pressure switch from the hydraulic unit in situ, Ford tool No 12-008, or equivalent, will be required. The switch may be removed without special tools after removing the hydraulic unit complete (Section 16) or the pump (Section 18).*
1 Disconnect the battery negative lead.
2 Depressurise the hydraulic system by pumping the brake pedal at least 20 times, or until it becomes hard.
3 Disconnect the multi-plug from the switch, then unscrew and remove it.

4 When refitting, use a new O-ring on the switch. Position the plastic sleeve so that the hole in the sleeve is facing the pump motor **(see illustration)**. Tighten the switch.
5 Reconnect the multi-plug and the battery.
6 Bleed the complete system (Section 2).

20 Hydraulic unit hoses - removal and refitting

1 There are two hoses on the hydraulic unit. The low pressure hose connects the reservoir to the pump inlet; the high pressure hose connects the pump outlet to the booster and valve block.
2 To remove either hose, first disconnect the battery. Depressurise the hydraulic system by pumping the brake pedal at least 20 times, or until it becomes hard.

Low pressure hose

3 Have ready a container to catch spilt fluid. Remove the spring clip and pull the hose off the pump inlet. Allow the contents of the reservoir to drain out of the hose and into the container.
4 Pull the hose off the reservoir and remove it.
5 Refit by connecting the hose to the reservoir and pump inlet. Secure the hose to the pump with the spring clip.
6 Refill the reservoir, reconnect the battery and bleed the complete system (Section 2). Check for leaks.

High pressure hose

7 Remove the banjo bolts which secure the hose. Be prepared for fluid spillage.
8 Remove the hose and recover the sealing washers.
9 Refit by reversing the removal operations, using new sealing washers on both sides of each union **(see illustration)**.
10 Reconnect the battery and bleed the complete system (Section 2). Check for leaks.

21 Brake pipes and hoses - inspection, removal and refitting

1 Periodically inspect the rigid brake pipes for rust and other damage, and the flexible hoses for cracks, splits or "ballooning". Have an assistant depress the brake pedal (ignition on) and inspect the hose and pipe unions for leaks. Renew defective items without delay.
2 Before removing any pipe or hose, depressurise the hydraulic system by switching off the ignition and pumping the brake pedal 20 times, or until it becomes hard.
3 To remove a flexible hose, first undo the union nut which secures the rigid pipe to it. The use of a split ring spanner, sold for this purpose, is recommended **(see illustration)**. Be prepared for hydraulic fluid spillage, and take precautions to keep dirt out.
4 Having disconnected the rigid pipe, release the hose from the bracket by removing the locknut and washer **(see illustration)**.

21.3 Undoing a rigid pipe union nut
Flexible hose locknut is just above

21.4 Removing a flexible hose from its bracket

21.5 Disconnecting the hose from the caliper

21.7 Brake pipe union T-piece (arrowed)

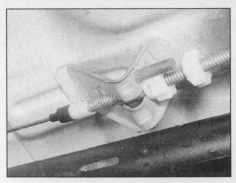

22.3 Handbrake cable adjuster
Locknut previously backed off adjuster nut

5 Unscrew the hose from its union on the caliper and remove it **(see illustration)**.

6 Refit by reversing the removal operations, then bleed the appropriate part of the hydraulic system (Section 2). In the case of the front hoses, check that they are not kinked or twisted, and that they do not contact other components when the steering is moved from lock to lock. Reposition the hose in the bracket if necessary.

7 To remove a rigid pipe, simply undo the union nuts at the hydraulic unit, hose bracket or T-piece **(see illustration)**. Free the pipe from any retaining clips and remove it.

8 New pipes can be bought ready-made, with the unions attached. Some garages and motor factors will make up pipes to order, using the old pipe as a pattern. If purchasing proprietary pipes made of copper alloy or similar material, follow the manufacturer's instructions carefully concerning bending, provision of extra clips etc.

9 Fit and secure the new pipe and tighten the union nuts, bleed the appropriate part of the hydraulic system (Section 2).

22 Handbrake cable - adjustment

1 The handbrake is normally self-adjusting in use. Adjustment may be required to compensate for cable stretch over a long period, and is also necessary after fitting a new cable.

2 Chock the front wheels, release the handbrake and raise and support the rear of the vehicle.

3 Release the adjuster locknut from the adjuster nut. Back off the adjuster nut, slackening the cable until both handbrake levers on the calipers are resting against their stops **(see illustration)**.

4 Paint alignment marks between each handbrake lever and the caliper body **(see illustration)**.

5 Tighten the adjuster nut until either handbrake lever just starts to move - as shown by the alignment marks.

6 Apply the handbrake and release it a few times to equalise the cable runs.

7 Tighten the locknut onto the adjuster nut finger tight, then tighten a further three to six clicks using self-locking pliers or a peg spanner.

23 Handbrake cable - removal and refitting

1 Slacken the rear wheel nuts and chock the front wheels. Raise and support the rear of the vehicle and remove both rear wheels. Release the handbrake.

2 Slacken off the handbrake cable adjuster locknut and adjuster nut.

3 Free the cable from the equaliser yoke by removing the circlip and clevis pin **(see illustration)**. Beware of self-tapping screws protruding through the floor in this area.

4 Unhook the cable inner from the handbrake levers on the calipers. Free the cable outer from the caliper brackets **(see illustration)**.

5 Free the cable from the lower arm and underbody brackets and remove it.

6 Refit by reversing the removal operations, but before refitting the rear wheels, adjust the cable as described in the previous Section.

24 Handbrake control lever - removal and refitting

1 Chock the front wheels and release the handbrake. Raise and support the rear of the vehicle.

2 Disconnect the battery negative lead.

3 Disconnect the handbrake cable equaliser yoke by removing the circlip and clevis pin.

4 Remove the centre console (Chapter 12).

5 Remove the handbrake control lever boot.

6 Disconnect the wiring from the handbrake warning switch.

7 Unbolt the handbrake lever and remove it, complete with switch. Remove the switch if necessary.

8 Refit by reversing the removal operations.

25 ABS module - removal and refitting

1 Remove the under-dash trim on the passenger's side.

2 Push the module upwards and then swing it forwards to release it from its clip.

22.4 Alignment marks painted on lever and body

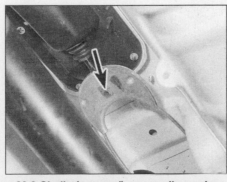

23.3 Circlip (arrowed) on equaliser yoke
Note protruding screws in transmission tunnel

23.4 Handbrake cable outer attached to caliper bracket

10

26.3 Removing a front sensor

26.4 Unclipping the sensor wire from the strut

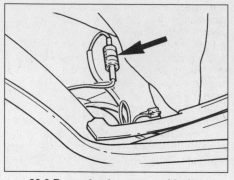

26.9 Rear wheel sensor multi-plug (arrowed)

3 Press the multi-plug locking lever, disconnect the multi-plug and unhook it from the module. Remove the module.

4 Refit by reversing the removal operations. Make sure that the multi-plug is properly engaged before refitting the module.

26 Wheel sensors - removal and refitting

Front

1 Ensure that the handbrake is applied. Raise and support the front of the vehicle.

2 From under the bonnet disconnect the wheel sensor wiring multi-plug. Unclip the wiring, working towards the sensor.

3 Remove the securing bolt and withdraw the sensor from the stub axle carrier **(see illustration)**.

4 Unclip the wire from the bracket on the strut. Remove the sensor and its wiring **(see illustration)**.

5 Clean any rust or debris from the sensor bore in the stub axle carrier. Pack the bore with clean wheel bearing grease.

6 Renew the O-ring on the sensor and smear it with grease.

7 Refit by reversing the removal operations.

Rear

8 Chock the front wheels and release the handbrake. Slacken the rear wheel nuts, raise

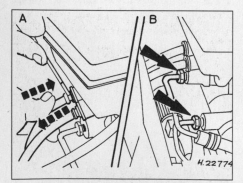

27.4 Disconnecting the master cylinder low pressure hoses (A) and brake pipes (B) - models from April 1992

and support the rear of the vehicle and remove the rear wheel.

9 Fold the rear seat cushion forwards, remove the side kick panel and roll back the carpet to gain access to the sensor multi-plug **(see illustration)**.

10 Disconnect the multi-plug, release the floor grommet and pass the cable through the floor.

11 Unclip the handbrake cable from the suspension lower arm.

12 Remove the caliper front slide bolt and pivot the caliper rearwards to gain access to the sensor.

13 Remove the sensor securing bolt and withdraw the sensor.

14 Clean up the sensor bore, pack it with grease and renew the sensor O-ring.

15 Refit by reversing the removal operations.

27 Master cylinder (April 1992 on) - removal and refitting

1 Disconnect the battery negative terminal.

2 Disconnect the wiring plug then remove the master cylinder reservoir cap; do not invert the cap as hydraulic fluid could enter and damage the reservoir level switch. Syphon the hydraulic fluid from the reservoir. **Note:** *Do not syphon the fluid by mouth, as it is poisonous; use a syringe or an old poultry baster.* Alternatively, open any convenient bleed screw in the system and gently pump the brake pedal to expel the fluid through a plastic tube connected to the screw.

3 Wipe clean the area around the brake pipe unions on the right-hand side of the master cylinder and place absorbent rags beneath the pipe unions to catch any surplus fluid.

4 To disconnect the plastic low pressure hoses, use a small flat bladed screwdriver to carefully press the flange of the collet into the master cylinder then pull the hoses out from the reservoir **(see illustration)**. Unscrew the two union nuts and disconnect the brake pipes from master cylinder. Plug or tape over the pipe/hose ends and master cylinder orifices to minimise the loss of brake fluid and to prevent the entry of dirt into the system. Wash off any spilt fluid immediately with cold water.

5 Slacken and remove the two nuts securing the master cylinder to the vacuum servo unit then withdraw the unit from the engine compartment. Remove the O-ring from the rear of master cylinder and discard it.

6 If necessary remove the reservoir from the master cylinder and withdraw the mounting bush seals and O-rings. Note that the master cylinder is a sealed unit with no spare parts available separately. Therefore if it is faulty it must be renewed as a unit.

7 Fit new mounting bush seals and O-rings to the master cylinder and refit the reservoir (if removed). Remove all traces of dirt from the master cylinder and servo unit mating surfaces and fit a new O-ring onto the master cylinder body.

8 Fit the master cylinder to the servo unit ensuring that the pushrod enters the servo unit bore centrally. Refit the master cylinder mounting nuts and tighten them to the specified torque.

9 Wipe clean the brake pipe/hose unions and the master cylinder ports. Refit the pipes to the master cylinder ports and tighten them securely. Push the low pressure hoses into position and check they are securely held by their retaining collets.

10 Refill the master cylinder reservoir with new fluid and bleed the hydraulic system

28 Vacuum servo unit (April 1992 on) - testing, removal and refitting

1 To test the operation of the servo unit depress the footbrake several times to exhaust the vacuum then start the engine whilst keeping the pedal firmly depressed. As the engine starts there should be a noticeable "give" in the brake pedal as the vacuum builds up. Allow the engine to run for at least two minutes then switch it off. If the brake pedal is now depressed it should feel normal, but further applications should result in the pedal feeling firmer, with the pedal stroke decreasing with each application.

2 If the servo does not operate as described, inspect the servo unit check valve as described in paragraph 3 of Section 29.

3 If the servo unit still fails to operate satisfactorily the fault lies within the unit itself. Repairs to the unit are not possible.

4 Remove the master cylinder (Section 27).

5 Disconnect the vacuum hose from the servo unit taking care not to displace the rubber sealing grommet. Disconnect the wiring plug from the Pedal Travel Sensor (PTS) which is situated on the front of the servo.

6 Working from inside the vehicle, remove the servo pushrod retaining clip from the brake pedal. If necessary, to improve access to the brake pedal remove the right-hand lower facia panel .

7 Slacken and remove the four nuts securing the servo unit to the bulkhead, then return to the engine compartment and remove the servo unit from the vehicle. Remove the gasket from the rear of the unit and discard it.

8 Note that the vacuum servo unit is a sealed assembly with no spare parts available separately. Therefore if it is faulty it must be renewed as a unit. Inspect the vacuum servo vacuum hose sealing grommet for damage or deterioration and renew if necessary.

9 Remove all traces of dirt from the servo unit and bulkhead mating surfaces and fit a new gasket onto the rear of the servo.

10 Manoeuvre the servo unit into position, ensuring that the servo unit pushrod is correctly located with the hole in the pedal. Refit the servo unit retaining nuts and tighten them to the specified torque setting. Secure the pushrod in position with the retaining clip

11 Carefully refit the vacuum hose to the servo unit taking great care not to damage or displace the sealing grommet. Reconnect the wiring connector to the Pedal Travel Sensor (PTS).

12 Refit the master cylinder as described above. On completion start the engine and check the operation of the servo unit.

29 Vacuum servo unit check valve (April 1992 on) - removal, testing and refitting

1 Disconnect the vacuum hose from the servo unit taking care not to displace the rubber sealing grommet.

2 To disconnect the hose from the inlet manifold, use a small flat-bladed screwdriver to carefully press the flange of the collet into the manifold then pull the hose out and remove it from the vehicle **(see illustration)**.

3 Examine the vacuum hose and sealing grommet for damage, splits, cracks or general deterioration and renew as necessary. Make sure that the check valve is working correctly by blowing through the hose from the servo unit end. Air should flow in this direction, but not when blown through from the inlet manifold hose end. Renew the check valve if it is at all suspect.

4 Ensure that the check valve is fitted the correct way around then push the connector into the manifold and check that it is securely held by the retaining collet.

5 Carefully refit the vacuum hose to the servo unit taking great care not to damage or displace the sealing grommet.

6 On completion start the engine and check the operation of the servo unit.

30 Valve block and pump assembly (April 1992 on) - removal and refitting

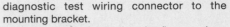

1 Disconnect the battery negative terminal.

2 Carry out the operations described in paragraphs 2 to 4 of Section 27.

3 Remove all traces of dirt from the exterior of the block then disconnect the motor and valve block wiring plugs and free the diagnostic test wiring plug from the mounting bracket.

4 Position some absorbent rag beneath the valve block then unscrew the three brake pipe outlet unions whilst avoiding getting surplus brake fluid in the wiring plugs. Plug the block ports and pipe ends to minimise the loss of fluid and prevent the entry of dirt into the system. Wash off any spilt fluid immediately with cold water.

5 Slacken and remove the three valve block and pump assembly mounting nuts and remove the unit from the engine compartment.

6 Note that the valve block and pump assembly is a sealed unit and cannot be overhauled. If it is faulty it must be renewed. Note that if the low pressure hoses are disconnected from the assembly, great care must be taken when reconnecting them to ensure that the valve block filter is not damaged.

7 Manoeuvre the assembly into position then refit the mounting nuts and tighten them by hand only. Taking into account the amount of movement in the mounting rubbers, position the assembly so that it will not contact the mounting bracket then tighten the mounting nuts to the specified torque setting.

8 Remove the plugs then reconnect the outlet pipes to the assembly and tighten the union nuts securely.

9 Ensure that the wiring is correctly routed and reconnect the wiring plugs to the valve block and pump assembly. Refit the diagnostic test wiring connector to the mounting bracket.

10 Wipe clean the brake pipe/hose unions and the master cylinder ports. Refit the pipes to the master cylinder ports and securely tighten the union nuts. Push the low pressure hoses into position and check they are securely held by their retaining collets.

11 Reconnect the battery negative terminal, then fill the master cylinder and bleed the complete hydraulic system using the information given earlier in this Section.

31 Control module (April 1992 on) - removal and refitting

1 The anti-lock braking control module is located behind the glovebox. To remove the module first disconnect the battery negative terminal.

2 Open up the glovebox then, using a small flat-bladed screwdriver, carefully prise up the retaining clip and disconnect the glovebox hinge arms. Withdraw the glovebox assembly from the facia noting the plastic bushes which are fitted to the glovebox pivot points.

3 Lift the wiring plug retaining clip and disconnect the plug to the control module. The ABS module is the upper of the two control modules mounted horizontally.

4 Release the retaining clips and slide the module out of the mounting bracket **(see illustration)**.

5 Commence refitting by sliding the module into the mounting bracket until it clips into position.

6 Connect the wiring connector to the module, ensuring that the wiring is correctly routed, and secure it in position with the retaining clip

7 Ensure that the plastic bushes are correctly fitted to the glovebox then refit the glovebox assembly, locating the pivots in the correct locations on the facia panel. Clip the hinge arms onto the glovebox and check that it opens and closes smoothly.

8 Reconnect the battery negative terminal.

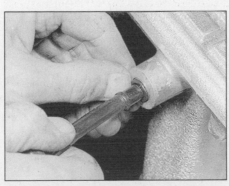

29.2 Disconnecting brake servo vacuum hose from the inlet manifold (DOHC engine shown)

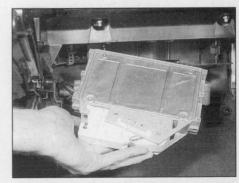

31.4 Removing the ABS control module - models from April 1992

10

32 Pedal Travel Sensor (PTS) (April 1992 on) - removal and refitting

1 Disconnect the battery negative terminal then deplete the vacuum in the braking system servo unit by depressing the footbrake several times.

2 Disconnect the wiring plug from the sensor which is situated on the front of the vacuum servo unit.

3 Using a small flat-bladed screwdriver, prise off the retaining circlip, then carefully withdraw the sensor from the servo unit taking great care not to displace the sealing O-ring (see illustration). Note: *If the O-ring becomes displaced and falls into the servo unit it* **must** *be recovered before the sensor is refitted.*

4 If the sensor is to be renewed, ensure that the tip of the new sensor pushrod is the same colour as that of the original.

5 Fit a new O-ring to the sensor and apply a

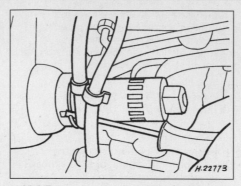

32.3 Removing the Pedal Travel Sensor (PTS) circlip - models from April 1992

smear of clean engine oil to it to ease installation.

6 Ease the sensor into position in the servo unit, taking care not to displace the O-ring, and secure it in position with the circlip.

7 Reconnect the sensor wiring connector and the battery negative terminal.

33 G (gravity) switch (April 1992 on) - removal and refitting

1 Remove the driver's seat as described in Chapter 12.

2 Carefully peel back the carpet from immediately behind the crossmember to reveal the G switch.

3 Disconnect the wiring connector then undo the two retaining screws and remove the switch from the vehicle.

4 Refitting is a reversal of the removal procedure.

Chapter 11
Steering and suspension

Contents

Degrees of difficulty

Easy, suitable for novice with little experience	Fairly easy, suitable for beginner with some experience	Fairly difficult, suitable for competent DIY mechanic	Difficult, suitable for experienced DIY mechanic	Very difficult, suitable for expert DIY or professional

Specifications

General

Suspension type:

Front . . . . Independent, MacPherson struts and anti-roll bar

Rear . . . . Independent, semi-trailing arms and anti-roll bar; ride height control optionally available

Steering type . . . . Rack and pinion, power-assisted on some models

Front wheel alignment

Toe:

Setting value . . . . 2 ± 1 mm (0.08 ± 0.04 in) toe-in

Tolerance in service . . . . 0.5 mm (0.02 in) toe-out to 4.5 mm (0.18 in) toe-in

Castor :

SOHC and 2.8 litre models:

Standard, without ride height control . . . . + 1°51' ± 1°00'

Standard, with ride height control . . . . + 1°58' ± 1°00'

Heavy duty . . . . + 1°46' ± 1°00'

DOHC carburettor and low series fuel-injection models . . . . + 2°27' ± 1°00'

DOHC high series models . . . . + 2°26' ± 1°00'

2.4 litre:

low series models . . . . + 2°17' ± 1°00'

high series models . . . . + 2°50' ± 1°00'

2.9 litre models . . . . + 2°22' ± 1°00'

11

Front wheel alignment (continued)

Camber :
SOHC and 2.8 litre models:
  Standard .... 0°23' ± 1°00'
  Heavy duty .... 0°00' ± 1°00'
DOHC models .... -0°17'
2.4 litre low series models .... -0°27'
2.4 litre high series and 2.9 litre models .... -0°21'
Tolerance:
  DOHC, 2.4 and 2.9 litre models: .... 1°00' to + 0°60'
Difference between left-hand and right-hand sides:
SOHC and 2.8 litre models:
  Castor .... 1°00' maximum
  Camber .... 1°15' maximum
DOHC, 2.4 and 2.9 litre models:
  Castor .... 1°00'
  Camber .... 1°15'

Steering gear

Make:
  Manual .... Cam Gears
  Power-assisted .... Cam Gears or ZF
Power steering fluid type .... ATF to Ford spec SQM-2C9010-A (Automatic Transmission Fluid)

Tyres

Tyre sizes .... 175 SR/TR/HR 14, 185/70 HR/TR/VR 14, 195/65 HR 15, 205/60 VR 15

Tyre pressures:	Front	Rear
Normal load	1.8 bar (26 lbf/in²)	1.8 bar (26 lbf/in²)
Full load	2.1 bar (30 lbf/in²)	2.9 bar (42 lbf/in²)

Torque wrench settings

	Nm	lbf ft
Steering		
Steering gear-to-crossmember bolts:		
Stage 1 (clamping)	45	33
Slacken, then Stage 2 (snug)	15	11
Stage 3	Tighten further 90°	Tighten further 90°
Track rod end balljoint nut	25 to 30	18 to 22
Track rod end locknut	57 to 68	42 to 50
Track rod inner balljoint nut	75	55
Intermediate shaft coupling pinch-bolts	20	15
Pinion retaining nut (manual steering)	70 to 100	52 to 74
Pinion shaft nut (power steering)	37 to 47	27 to 34
Slipper yoke plug (see text):		
Manual steering	4 to 5	3 to 4
Power steering	3 to 4	2 to 3
Steering wheel nut	45 to 55	33 to 41
Steering column mounting nuts	17 to 24	13 to 18
Steering column adjuster pivot nut	10 to 13	7 to 10
Steering pump bracket to block	52 to 64	38 to 47
Steering pump pulley hub bolt	10 to 12	7 to 9
Pressure hose to steering pump	26 to 31	19 to 23
Steering pump bracket-to-engine mounting	41 to 58	30 to 43
Steering pump to bracket (V6)	22 to 29	16 to 21
Front suspension		
Hub nut	390 to 450	288 to 332
Lower arm balljoint nut	65 to 85	48 to 63
Top mount retaining nuts	20 to 24	15 to 18
Stub axle carrier pinch-bolt	80 to 90	59 to 66
Anti-roll bar clamps	70 to 90	52 to 66
Anti-roll bar to lower arms	70 to 110	52 to 81
Crossmember to frame	70 to 90	52 to 66
Suspension strut to turret	40 to 52	30 to 38
Lower arm pivot:		
Stage 1 (clamping)	45	33
Slacken. then Stage 2 (snug)	15	11
Stage 3	Tighten further 90°	Tighten further 90°

Torque wrench settings (continued)

	Nm	lbf ft
Rear suspension		
Driveshaft stub axle nut	250 to 290	180 to 210
Final drive mounting to floor	20 to 25	15 to 18
Final drive mounting to rear cover	40 to 50	30 to 37
Guide plate-to-floor bolts	41 to 51	30 to 38
Guide plate insulator bolt	69 to 88	51 to 65
Lower arm to crossmember	80 to 95	59 to 70
Brake anchor plate to lower arm	52 to 64	38 to 47
Anti-roll bar bracket bolts	20 to 25	15 to 18
Shock absorber mountings:		
Top	73 to 97	54 to 72
Bottom	68 to 92	50 to 68
Rear hub bolts	80 to 100	59 to 74
Wheels		
Wheel nuts (steel or alloy wheels)	70 to 100	52 to 74

1 General information

The steering gear is of rack-and-pinion type. Power assistance is standard on V6 models and optional on others. The power-assisted steering gear has a "variable ratio" effect which increases the steering ratio about the straight-ahead position: this provides quick lock-to-lock action without the penalty of over-responsiveness in open road driving.

The steering wheel is adjustable both up-and-down and fore-and-aft. Both steering column and shaft are designed to collapse under impact. The steering shaft is connected to the pinion by an intermediate shaft, which has a universal joint at its upper end and a flexible coupling at the lower end.

Front suspension is independent, of the MacPherson strut type, with coil springs and concentric telescopic shock absorbers. The struts are attached to the tops of the stub axle carriers, which are located at their lower ends by balljoints incorporated in the lower suspension arms. The lower suspension arms pivot at their inner ends, where they are attached to a central crossmember. The anti-roll bar is attached to the rear of the arms and serves to control fore-and-aft movement as well as reducing roll.

Suspension geometry has been designed to give good steering "feel", resistance to pulling caused by uneven braking effort or tyre deflation, and (in the case of manual steering) acceptably low steering wheel effort at parking speeds. Only toe is adjustable in service.

The rear suspension is also independent. It is of the semi-trailing arm type, with coil springs and separate telescopic shock absorbers. An optionally-available ride height control system keeps the rear suspension height constant, regardless of vehicle load.

Both front and rear wheel bearings are of a special taper-roller type and require no periodic adjustment in service.

2 Power steering fluid - level check and bleeding

1 Refer to Chapter 1, Section 35, to check the power steering fluid level.
2 If the fluid level falls so low that air enters the pump, or after component renewal, the system must be bled as follows.
3 Remove the reservoir filler cap. Top-up with clean fluid to the appropriate "cold" level. It is important that the fluid is free of air bubbles, so do not shake the container when topping-up, and pour the fluid slowly.
4 Disconnect the negative LT lead from the ignition coil. Have an assistant crank the engine on the starter in two second bursts, at the same time turning the steering wheel from lock to lock. Keep the reservoir topped up whilst this is going on.
5 When air bubbles no longer appear in the fluid, stop the cranking. Reconnect the coil negative lead and run the engine for a few seconds, then stop it and check the level again. Refit the filler cap.
6 Run the vehicle for a few miles to warm up the fluid and expel any remaining air, then stop the engine and make a final fluid level check.

3 Steering gear - removal and refitting

Manual steering

1 Position the steering in the straight-ahead position, then remove the ignition key so that the steering is locked.
2 Slacken the front wheel nuts. Raise and support the front of the vehicle and remove the front wheels.
3 Remove the pinch-bolt and nut which secure the intermediate shaft flexible coupling to the pinion shaft **(see illustration)**.
4 Slacken the track rod end locknuts by half a turn each **(see illustration)**.
5 Remove the split pin from the track rod balljoint nuts. Unscrew the nuts, break the balljoint tapers using a separator tool and disengage the track rod ends from the steering arms.
6 Remove the two bolts which secure the steering gear to the crossmember. Lift out the steering gear.
7 Mark the positions of the track rod ends on the track rods, using paint or sticky tape, so that they can be refitted in approximately the same positions. Unscrew the track rod ends and locknuts.
8 Commence refitting by screwing on the locknuts and track rod ends, observing previously made position marks when applicable.
9 Bring the rack to the straight-ahead position. Do this by counting the number of turns of the pinion needed to go from lock to lock, then applying half that number of turns from full lock on one side.
10 Offer the steering gear to the vehicle, engaging the flexible coupling and loosely fitting the securing bolts. Note that the master spline on the pinion shaft mates with the corresponding groove in the flexible coupling.
11 Tighten the two steering gear-to-crossmember bolts to the specified Stage 1 torque. Slacken the bolts and retighten to the Stage 2 torque. Finally tighten the bolts through the angle specified for Stage 3.
12 Make sure that the flexible coupling and pinion shaft are properly engaged, then fit the pinch-bolt and nut. Tighten the pinch-bolt to the specified torque.

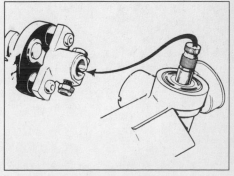

3.3 Master spline and groove on pinion shaft and coupling

11

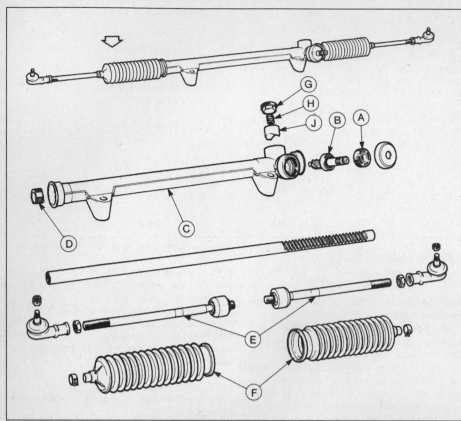

3.4 View of manual steering gear
A Pinion nut
B Pinion
C Rack housing
D Support bush
E Track rods
F Bellows
G Slipper plug
H Spring
J Slipper

13 Refit the track rod ends to the steering arms. Fit the balljoint nuts and tighten them to the specified torque, then secure with new split pins.
14 Nip up the track rod end locknuts, but do not tighten them fully yet.
15 Refit the front wheels and wheel nuts. Lower the vehicle and tighten the wheel nuts to the specified torque.
16 Check the toe setting as described in Section 19. When toe is correct, tighten the track rod end locknuts fully.

Power-assisted steering

17 Proceed as described for manual steering gear, but before removing the steering gear-to-crossmember bolts, remove the clamp plate bolt from the steering gear valve body (see illustration).

18 Pull the fluid pipes out of the valve body. Be prepared for fluid spillage. Plug or cap the open pipes and orifices.
19 The steering gear may now be removed.
20 Refit in the reverse order to removal, using new O-rings on the fluid pipes.
21 Bleed the steering gear hydraulic system on completion.

4 Steering rack bellows - renewal in vehicle

1 Remove the track rod end on the side concerned. Also remove the locknut.
2 Remove the bellows retaining clips and slide the bellows off the track rod (see illustration).
3 On manual steering racks, apply a smear of grease to the track rod

4 Fit the new bellows and secure with new clips. Make sure that the ends of the bellows are located in their grooves. Do not tighten the outer clip yet - leave it slack until toe has been checked after refitting.
5 Refit the track rod end locknut, followed by the track rod end itself.
6 Repeat on the other side of the vehicle if necessary.

5 Steering wheel - removal and refitting

Models before April 1992

1 Disconnect the battery negative lead.
2 Prise off the horn push pad from the centre of the steering wheel.
3 Remove the three screws which secure the horn switch plate. Withdraw the plate, disconnect its wires and remove it.
4 Engage the steering lock, then undo and remove the steering wheel nut. Unlock the steering again.
5 Mark the relationship of the wheel to the shaft, then pull the wheel off the shaft. Use a puller if it cannot be removed by hand. Do not use hammer blows, which may damage the collapsible parts of the column and shaft.
6 Recover the spacer from below the steering wheel (see illustration).
7 Refit by reversing the removal operations. Tighten the steering wheel nut to the specified torque.

Models from April 1992

8 The steering wheel can be removed and refitted as described above whilst ignoring the

3.17 Clamp plate bolt (arrowed) is located between two fluid pipes

4.2 Steering rack bellows retaining clips (arrowed)

5.6 Spacer ring (arrowed) fits below steering wheel

7.8 Two of the three nuts (arrowed) which secure the column height adjuster

reference to horn switch plate retaining screws. Note that the wheel is retained by a bolt, not a nut as on earlier models. To gain access to the bolt, prise out the horn button and disconnect the wiring connectors.

6 Steering wheel - centralising

1 This operation is for correcting small errors in steering wheel centralisation - up to 60°. For larger errors, remove the steering wheel and make a rough correction by repositioning the wheel on refitting.
2 Drive the vehicle in a straight line on a level surface. Note the angle by which the steering wheel deviates from the desired straight-ahead position.
3 Raise the front of the vehicle by driving it onto ramps, or with a jack and axle stands (see "Jacking").
4 Slacken both track rod end locknuts. Also slacken the steering rack bellows outer clips.
5 Make alignment marks between each track rod end and its rod, so that the amount of rotation applied can be accurately determined.
6 Turn both track rods **in the same direction** to correct the steering wheel position. As a rough guide, 19° of track rod rotation will change the steering wheel position by 1°. To correct error at the steering wheel, rotate both track rods anti-clockwise (viewed from the left-hand side of the vehicle), and the reverse to correct as anti-clockwise errors. *Both track rods must be rotated by the same amount.*
7 Tighten the bellows clips and the track rod end locknuts when adjustment is correct. Lower the vehicle.

7 Steering column - removal and refitting

1 Disconnect the battery negative lead.
2 Position the steering in the straight-ahead position.
3 Remove the steering wheel. This is not essential, but will improve access.
4 Working under the bonnet, disconnect the intermediate shaft universal joint from the steering column shaft.

HAYNES HiNT *Make alignment marks between the two shafts for reference when reassembling.*

5 Remove the steering column shrouds and disconnect the switch multi-plugs. Do not forget the ignition/starter switch.
6 Disconnect the bonnet release cable from the operating lever on the underside of the column.
7 Prise out the driver's side air vent. Remove the under-dash insulation and trim panel on the driver's side, unclipping the bulb failure module, where applicable.
8 Remove the three nuts which secure the column height adjuster to the mounting bracket **(see illustration)**. Remove the column assembly by drawing it into the vehicle. Do not drop it or otherwise mistreat it if it is to be re-used.

9 When refitting, have an assistant guide the column shaft into the intermediate shaft universal joint. Secure the column with the three nuts inside the vehicle and adjust it to the minimum length position, then tighten the coupling pinch-bolt.
10 Complete refitting by reversing the removal operations.

8 Steering column lock - removal and refitting

1 Remove the steering column **(see illustration)**.
2 Insert the key into the lock and turn it to position 1. (If the lock has failed so that the key will not enter, destructive methods will have to be used.)

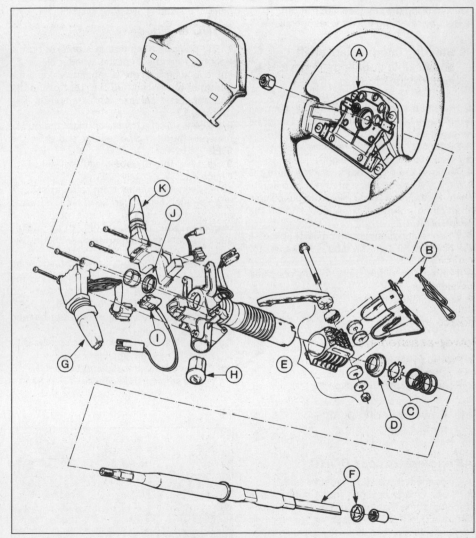

8.1 View of steering wheel and column

A Steering wheel
B Mounting bracket and spring
C Thrust washer and spring
D Lower bearing
E Height adjuster
F Column shaft and spire washer
G Multi-function switch
H Ignition/steering lock
I Horn brush unit
J Upper bearing
K Multi-function switch

11

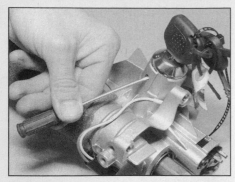

8.3 Depress the column lock locking button

11.4 Steering pump pivot bolt (arrowed) - V6 model shown

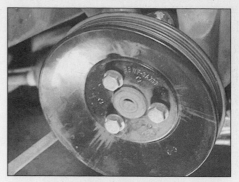

11.10 Unbolt the power steering pump pulley . . .

3 Depress the locking button with a small screwdriver. Draw the lock barrel out of its housing using the key **(see illustration)**.
4 Refit by reversing the removal operations.

9 Steering intermediate shaft and flexible coupling - removal and refitting

1 The intermediate shaft and flexible coupling are not available separately, and so must be renewed as a unit.
2 Disconnect the battery negative lead.
3 Position the steering straight-ahead.
4 Remove the pinch-bolts which secure the upper and lower ends of the intermediate shaft. Free the universal joint from the column shaft, then pull the flexible coupling off the pinion shaft.
5 When refitting, engage the master spline on the pinion shaft with the groove in the flexible coupling.
6 Tighten the pinch-bolts to the specified torque.
7 Reconnect the battery.

10 Power steering pump drivebelt - removal, refitting and tensioning

Refer to Chapter 1, Section 21.

11 Power steering pump - removal and refitting

All engines except DOHC

1 Disconnect the battery negative lead.
2 Wipe clean around the unions, then disconnect the high pressure and return pipes from the pump and the reservoir. Be prepared for fluid spillage; take steps to keep fluid out of the alternator.
3 Remove the pump drivebelt(s).
4 Remove the pump mounting, pivot and adjustment bolts (as applicable) and lift the pump from the engine **(see illustration)**.
5 If a new pump is to be fitted, recover the pulley and mounting plate from the old pump.

6 Refit by reversing the removal operations. Adjust the drivebelt tension on completion and bleed the steering hydraulic system.

DOHC engines

7 The pump is mounted on a bracket on the front right-hand side of the cylinder block. To improve access to the pump, firmly apply the handbrake then jack up the front of the car and support it securely on axle stands (see *"Jacking"*).
8 Place a suitable container under the pump, unscrew the fluid pipe unions, and drain the fluid.
9 Remove the drivebelt with reference to Chapter 1.
10 Prevent the pulley from rotating using a strap wrench (which can be improvised using an old drivebelt and a large socket and wrench), and unscrew the three pulley securing bolts **(see illustration)**. Withdraw the pulley.
11 Unscrew the three pump securing bolts from the front of the pump bracket, and the single bolt from the rear of the bracket, and withdraw the pump **(see illustration)**.
12 Refitting is a reversal of removal, bearing in mind the following points:
a) Reconnect the fluid unions using new O-rings.
b) On completion, top-up and bleed the power steering fluid circuit.

12 Power steering hoses - removal and refitting

1 Disconnect the battery negative lead.
2 Clean around the hose unions on the steering gear. Remove the single securing bolt, withdraw the hoses and catch the fluid which will drain from the reservoir.
3 Clean around the hose unions on the pump. Disconnect the unions and remove the hoses.
4 Refit in the reverse order to removal, using new O-rings.
5 Top-up the steering fluid and bleed the system.

13 Track rod end - removal and refitting

1 Slacken the front wheel nuts, raise and support the vehicle and remove the front wheel on the side concerned.
2 Slacken the track rod end locknut by half a turn.
3 Remove the split pin from the track rod end balljoint nut. Unscrew the nut a few turns **(see illustration)**.
4 Break the balljoint taper with a proprietary balljoint separator **(see illustration)**. Remove the separator and the nut and disengage the track rod end from the steering arm.
5 Unscrew the track rod end from the track rod, being careful not to disturb the locknut.

11.11 . . . for access to the front pump securing bolts (arrowed)

13.3 Track rod end balljoint nut unscrewed

13.4 Using a balljoint separator

6 When refitting, screw the track rod end onto the track rod as far as the locknut, then back it off half a turn.

7 Insert the ball-pin into the steering arm. Tighten the balljoint nut to the specified torque and secure with a new split pin. Nip up the track rod end locknut, but do not tighten it fully yet.

8 Refit the roadwheel, lower the vehicle and tighten the wheel nuts to the specified torque.

9 Check the toe setting as described in the following Section. (This may not be strictly necessary if the same track rod end has been refitted, but is certainly advisable if any components have been renewed.)

10 Tighten the track rod end locknut when toe is correct.

14 Front wheel alignment - checking and adjusting

1 Front wheel alignment is defined by camber, castor, steering axis inclination and toe setting. The first three factors are determined in production; only toe can be adjusted in service. Incorrect toe will cause rapid tyre wear (see illustration).

2 Toe is defined as the amount by which the distance between the front wheels, measured at hub height, differs from the front edges to the rear edges. If the distance between the front edges is less than that at the rear, the wheels are said to toe-in; the opposite case is known as toe-out.

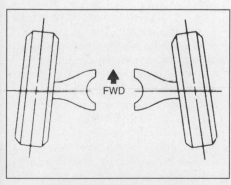

14.1 Front wheel toe-in (greatly exaggerated)

3 To measure toe, it will be necessary to obtain or make a tracking gauge. These are available in motor accessory shops, or one can be made from a length of rigid pipe or bar with some kind of threaded adjustment facility at one end. Many tyre specialists will also check toe free, or for a nominal sum.

4 Before measuring toe, check that all steering and suspension components are undamaged and that tyre pressures are correct. The vehicle must be at approximately kerb weight, with the spare wheel and jack in their normal positions and any abnormal loads removed.

5 Park the vehicle on level ground and bounce it a few times to settle the suspension.

6 Use the tracking gauge to measure the distance between the inside faces of the front wheel rims, at hub height, at the rear of the front wheels. Record this distance; call it measurement A.

7 Push the vehicle forwards or backwards so that the wheels rotate exactly 180°(half a turn). Measure the distance between the front wheel rims again, this time at the front of the wheels. Record this distance; call it measurement B.

8 Subtract measurement B from measurement A. If the answer is positive it is the amount of toe-in; if negative it is the amount of toe-out. Permissible values are given in the Specifications.

9 If adjustment is necessary loosen the track rod end locknuts and the outer bellows clips, then rotate each track rod by equal amounts until the setting is correct. Hold the track rod ends in their horizontal position with a spanner while making the adjustment.

10 Tighten the locknuts and outer bellows clips.

11 Provided the track rods have been adjusted by equal amounts the steering wheel should be central when moving straight-ahead. The amount of visible thread on each track rod should also be equal.

15 Front suspension crossmember - removal and refitting

1 Disconnect the battery negative lead.

2 Raise and securely support the front of the vehicle.

3 Remove the suspension lower arm pivot nuts and bolts (see illustration). Disengage the arms from the crossmember.

4 Disconnect the steering column shaft from the intermediate shaft universal joint.

5 Remove the two bolts which secure the steering gear to the crossmember. Draw the steering gear forwards so that it is clear of the crossmember and support it by wiring it to the frame rails.

6 It is now necessary to support the engine, preferably from above, using a hoist or an adjustable support bar resting on the wings or suspension turrets. Alternatively a jack and some wooden blocks may be used from

below, but this is bound to obstruct access to some extent.

7 Remove the engine mounting lower securing nuts. Raise the engine until the mountings are just clear of the crossmember.

8 Release the brake pipe clips from the crossmember and slide the brake pipes from their slots. Be careful not to strain the pipes.

9 Support the crossmember and remove its four securing bolts. Lower the crossmember and remove it from the vehicle.

10 Commence refitting by offering the crossmember to the frame rails. Insert the four securing bolts and tighten them to the specified torque.

11 Secure the brake pipes to the crossmember.

12 Refit the steering gear to the crossmember. Tighten its securing bolts to the specified torque.

13 Insert the suspension arms into the crossmember and secure them with the pivot bolts and nuts. Do not tighten the nuts and bolts yet, just nip them up.

14 Lower the engine onto the crossmember. Make sure that the engine mountings locate correctly into the holes in the crossmember. Tighten the engine mounting nuts. The engine support bar or hoist can now be removed.

15 Reconnect the steering column shaft to the intermediate shaft. Tighten the pinch-bolt to the specified torque.

16 Lower the vehicle onto its wheels, then tighten the lower arm pivot bolts to the specified torque.

17 Reconnect the battery.

16 Front stub axle carrier - removal and refitting

1 Slacken the front wheel nuts. Raise and support the front of the vehicle and remove the front wheel.

2 Separate the track rod end from the steering arm.

3 Unbolt the brake caliper, pull it off the disc and tie it up out of the way. Do not allow it to hang by its hose.

4 Remove the split pin from the suspension lower arm balljoint nut. Slacken the nut a few

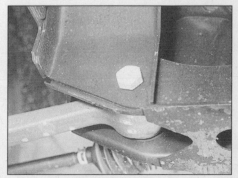

15.3 Front suspension lower arm pivot bolt

11

times, then use a proprietary balljoint separator to break the taper **(see illustration)**.

5 Use a stout piece of wood to lever the lower arm downwards and free the balljoint from the stub axle carrier.

6 Remove the ABS wheel sensor from its hole.

7 Remove the spring clip from one of the wheel studs and pull the brake disc off the hub.

8 Remove the stub axle carrier pinch-bolt. Spread the stub axle carrier by carefully introducing a chisel or blunt instrument into its slot. Draw the stub axle carrier off the suspension strut and remove it.

9 Refit by reversing the removal operations, noting the following points:

a) *Tighten all fastenings to the specified torque*

b) *Use new split pins, when applicable*

c) *Renew the wheel sensor O-ring if necessary; clean the sensor and its bore, and smear them with wheel bearing grease*

17 Front wheel bearings - renewal

Models before August 1989

1 Remove the stub axle carrier as described in the previous Section.

2 Screw the wheel nuts onto the studs to protect the threads. Clamp the stub axle carrier in a vice by means of the studs and nuts; do not overtighten.

3 Remove the dust cap from the hub nut, carefully levering it free **(see illustration)**. A new cap and a new hub nut will be required for reassembly.

4 Undo the hub nut. This nut is very tight. The right-hand hub nut has a **left-hand** thread, therefore it is undone in a **clockwise** direction.

5 Remove the ABS rotor from below the hub nut.

6 Lift the carrier off the stub axle, tapping it with a mallet if necessary to free it. Remove the bearing inner race from the carrier.

7 Prise the oil seal out of the carrier and recover the bearing outer race.

16.4 Slackening the front suspension lower arm balljoint nut

8 Drive the bearing tracks out of the stub axle carrier using a blunt drift and a hammer. Be careful not to mark the bearing seats.

9 Clean all old grease and debris from the stub axle carrier.

10 New bearing components are matched in production and must only be fitted as a set. Only the manufacturer's approved components should be used in order to obtain the required long service life and freedom from adjustment.

11 Drive the new bearing tracks into the carrier, preferably using a suitable diameter tube to seat them. Make sure the tracks are fully seated.

12 Work some clean grease into the bearing races. Use high melting-point lithium-based grease (to Ford spec. SAMIC-9111A or equivalent). Make sure all the spaces between the rollers are filled; do not pack grease into the space between the inner and outer bearings however.

13 Fit the bearing outer race. Grease the lips of a new oil seal and fit it to the stub axle carrier, lips facing inwards. Seat the seal with a pipe or large socket and a mallet.

14 Offer the carrier to the stub axle, tapping it home if necessary. Fit the bearing inner race over the stub axle.

15 Refit the ABS rotor, dished face uppermost.

16 Fit a new hub nut (left-hand thread on the right-hand hub) and tighten it to the specified torque.

17.3 Removing the dust cap from the stub axle carrier to expose the hub nut

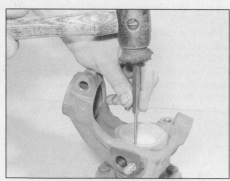

17.17 Seating the new dust cap

17 Fit a new dust cap and seat it by tapping round the rim **(see illustration)**.

18 Refit the stub axle carrier.

Models from August 1989

19 Modified front wheel bearing assemblies were fitted to all models after 1989. The modified bearings are of similar design, but are interference fit type bearings. This was to reduce the amount of endfloat present at the wheel hub and to improve bearing preload tolerances. This was achieved by increasing the diameter of the stub axle, thus causing the axle to be an interference fit in the bearing. Note that the modified bearings can be fitted to earlier models which were originally equipped with non-interference fit front wheel bearings. **Note:** *Due to the design of the interference fit bearings, a suitable heavy duty bearing puller and a hydraulic press and several suitable mandrels will be required to remove the original bearing and install the new one.*

20 Interference fit front wheel bearings can be removed and refitted as described above, noting the following points.

a) *It will be necessary to press or draw the stub axle out of the carrier using a hydraulic press or a suitable bearing puller.*

b) *Draw the outer bearing off the stub axle using a suitable bearing puller.*

c) *Press new bearing tracks into the hub carrier using a suitable tubular spacer which bears only on the tracks outer edge.*

d) *Pack the new outer bearing with Ford grease (SAM-1C9111-A) and press the bearing into the carrier.*

e) *Press a new seal into position in the carrier and pack all cavities with the specified grease.*

f) *Position the hub carrier over the stub axle and press the carrier onto the axle using a suitable tubular spacer which bears only on the bearing track outer edge.*

g) *Pack the new inner bearing with the specified grease then press the bearing onto the stub axle, using a suitable tubular spacer, whilst rotating the hub carrier to ensure that the bearing is correctly seated.*

h) *Whilst tightening the hub nut to the specified torque, rotate the hub carrier to ensure that the bearing preload is correct and bearings are correctly seated. Once the nut is tightened to the specified torque, rotate the hub carrier 20 times to settle the bearings in position then recheck that the hub nut is tightened to the specified torque. Pack the inner bearing with the specified grease and fit a new dust cap.*

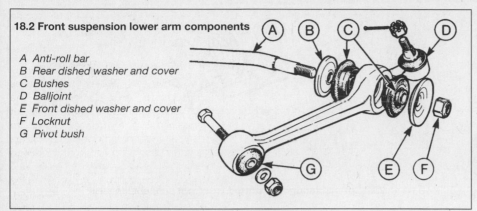

18.2 Front suspension lower arm components

A Anti-roll bar
B Rear dished washer and cover
C Bushes
D Balljoint
E Front dished washer and cover
F Locknut
G Pivot bush

19.2 A front anti-roll bar clamp

18 Front suspension lower arm - removal, overhaul and refitting

1 Raise the vehicle on ramps or on a hoist, so that the weight is still on the wheels.
2 Remove the lower arm pivot nut and bolt (see illustration).
3 Remove the anti-roll bar end nut, dished washer and plastic cover. Note which way round these components are fitted.
4 Now raise and support the vehicle so that the front wheels are off the ground.
5 Remove the split pin from the lower arm balljoint nut. Back off the nut a few turns, break the taper with a balljoint separator, then remove the nut and free the balljoint from the stub axle carrier.
6 Pull the lower arm off the anti-roll bar and remove it.
7 If the balljoint is defective, the whole arm must be renewed. The dust boot can be renewed separately if required.
8 The anti-roll bar bushes (compliance bushes) can be removed by cutting off their flanges with a chisel, then pressing or tapping out the remains. Fit new bushes by tapping them home with a tube or socket.
9 The pivot bush can be pressed out using a bench vice and a couple of large sockets or suitable pieces of tube. The new pivot bush should be lubricated with soap or glycerine (not oil or grease) before being fitted in a similar fashion. Do not keep the new bush compressed in the tube for longer than necessary, in case it becomes permanently distorted.
10 Commence refitting by offering the arm to the anti-roll bar. Make sure that the shallow dished washer and the plastic cover are fitted on the inboard side of the bar (furthest from the nut).
11 Refit the balljoint to the stub axle carrier. Tighten the castellated nut to the specified torque and secure it with a new split pin.
12 Fit the pivot end of the arm into the crossmember and secure it with the pivot nut and bolt. Jacking the vehicle up or down to vary the loading on the wheels may help to get the holes lined up. Do not tighten the pivot nut and bolt yet.
13 Lower the vehicle back onto its wheels.

14 Fit the deep dished washer and the plastic cover over the end of the anti-roll bar. Fit the nut and tighten it to the specified torque.
15 Tighten the lower arm pivot nut and bolt to the specified torque.

19 Front anti-roll bar - removal and refitting

1 Raise the vehicle on ramps or a hoist, so that the weight is still on the wheels.
2 Unbolt the two anti-roll bar clamps (see illustration).
3 Now raise and support the vehicle with the wheels free.
4 Remove the two nuts which hold the ends of the anti-roll bar to the lower arms. Recover the plastic covers and deep dished washers.
5 Remove one lower arm pivot nut and bolt. Prise the lower arm out of the crossmember and work the anti-roll bar free from it.
6 Pull the anti-roll bar out of the other lower arm and remove it. Recover the other compliance bush covers and washers.
7 Refit by reversing the removal operations, but do not finally tighten any fastenings until the weight of the vehicle is back on the wheels. Tighten in the following order:
a) Anti-roll bar clamps
b) Anti-roll bar-to lower arm nuts
c) Lower arm pivot nut and bolt
8 Make sure that the anti-roll bar clamp bushes are not twisted on completion.

20 Front anti-roll bar bushes - renewal

Compliance bushes

1 These are described in Section 18. It is not strictly necessary to remove the lower arms to renew these bushes, though obviously access is not good with the arms installed.

Clamp bushes

2 Although it is possible to remove and refit the clamp bushes without removing the anti-roll bar, since the bushes are split, this is not recommended by the makers.
3 Remove the anti-roll bar as described in the previous Section.

4 Slide the clamp bushes off the anti-roll bar, if necessary prising them open a little first.
5 Lubricate the new bushes with glycerine or soap and slide them into position with the split facing forwards.
6 Refit the anti-roll bar.

21 Front suspension strut - removal and refitting

1 Slacken the front wheel nuts, raise and support the vehicle and remove the front wheel.
2 Disconnect the battery negative lead.
3 Unbolt the brake caliper and suspend it nearby so that the flexible hose is not strained.
4 Remove the ABS sensor from the stub axle carrier.
5 Separate the track rod end and suspension lower arm balljoints from the stub axle carrier.
6 Unclip the ABS/brake pad wear wiring from the strut.
7 Remove the dust cover from the top of the strut.
8 Have an assistant support the strut. Remove the three nuts which secure the strut to the turret (see illustration). Do not undo the centre nut.
9 Lower the strut out of the turret and remove it.
10 Refit by reversing the removal operations. Do not fully tighten the strut-to-turret nuts until the weight of the vehicle is back on its wheels.

21.8 Two of the three nuts (arrowed) securing the suspension strut to the turret

11

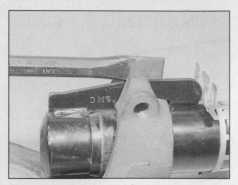

22.2 Spreading the stub axle carrier clamp

22 Front suspension strut - dismantling and reassembly

⚠️ *Warning: Spring compressors of adequate rating must be used for this job. The use of makeshift or inadequate equipment may result in damage and personal injury.*

1 With the strut removed, clamp it in a vice with protected jaws.

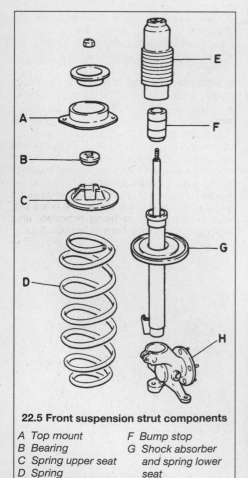

22.5 Front suspension strut components

A Top mount
B Bearing
C Spring upper seat
D Spring
E Gaiter
F Bump stop
G Shock absorber and spring lower seat
H Stub axle

22.3 Spring compressors fitted to a front suspension strut

2 Remove the stub axle carrier pinch-bolts. Spread the carrier by carefully introducing a chisel or blunt screwdriver into the crack, then slide it off the strut **(see illustration)**.
3 Fit spring compressors to the strut. Compress the spring until it is no longer tensioning the strut. Make sure that the compressors are secure **(see illustration)**.
4 Hold the piston rod with a hexagon key and remove the piston rod nut. Also remove the dished retainer.
5 Remove the top mount, the bearing and the spring upper seat **(see illustration)**.
6 Carefully lift off the compressed spring. Place it where it will not be knocked or jarred.
7 Remove the shock absorber gaiter and bump stop.
8 Examine all components for wear and damage and renew as necessary. The shock absorber must be renewed if it is leaking, or if it shows uneven resistance when "worked" with its lower end clamped in a vice. In theory springs and shock absorbers should be renewed in pairs in order to maintain balanced handling characteristics.
9 Commence reassembly by sliding the bump stop onto the shock absorber piston rod. Refit the gaiter.
10 Make sure that the spring seats are clean, then fit the compressed spring to the lower seat.
11 Refit the spring upper seat, the bearing (small hole upwards) and the top mount.
12 Refit the dished retainer and the piston rod nut. Hold the piston rod and tighten the nut.

23.10a One of the rear suspension guide plates

13 Carefully release the spring compressors. Make sure that the ends of the spring are correctly located in the spring seats.
14 Spread the stub axle carrier again. Slide it onto the strut, remove the spreader and refit the pinch-bolt. Tighten the pinch-bolt to the specified torque.
15 Refit the strut to the vehicle.

23 Rear suspension and final drive assembly - removal and refitting

Models before 1987

1 Raise the rear of the vehicle and support it securely under the frame rails.
2 Remove the exhaust system.
3 Remove the propeller shaft.
4 Release the handbrake cable from the equaliser yoke by removing the circlip from the handbrake lever pin. Release the cable from its floor brackets.
5 Disconnect the brake flexible hoses from the rear brake pipes.
6 Disconnect the ABS and brake pad wear sensor wires (as applicable). Free the wires from the suspension lower arms.
7 Unbolt the two anti-roll bar brackets from the floors.
8 Disconnect the ride height control sensor and the shock absorber air lines, when so equipped.
9 Lower the vehicle onto its wheels in order to load the rear springs a little. Place a jack under the final drive unit and support it.
10 Unbolt and remove the two guide plates **(see illustrations)**. The centre bolt on each plate is retained by a lockwasher which must be released first.
11 Unbolt the final drive unit rear mounting from the floor.
12 Remove the luggage area side trim, then remove the rear shock absorber upper mounting bolts.
13 Raise and support the rear of the vehicle again. Withdraw the rear suspension and final drive assembly.
14 Refit by reversing the removal operations. Tighten all fastenings to the specified torque, when known. When applicable use new O-rings on the ride height control line unions.

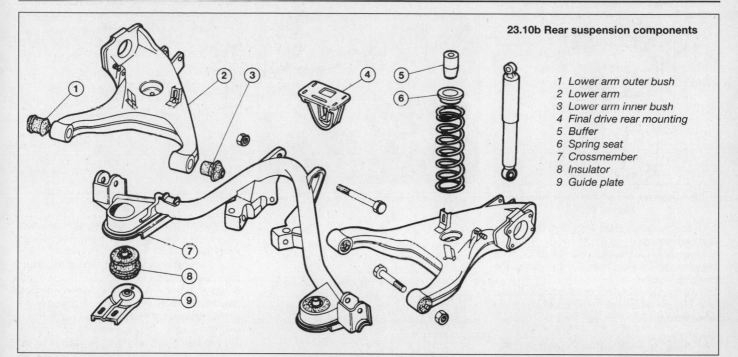

23.10b Rear suspension components

1 Lower arm outer bush
2 Lower arm
3 Lower arm inner bush
4 Final drive rear mounting
5 Buffer
6 Spring seat
7 Crossmember
8 Insulator
9 Guide plate

15 Bleed the brake hydraulic system and adjust the handbrake on completion.

Models from 1987

16 From 1987, the tab washer which secures the guide plate centre bolt on each side has been deleted. A self-locking bolt and plain washer are used instead.
17 The new bolt and washer should be fitted to earlier models if the old bolt has been removed for any reason. The tab washer should be discarded.
18 The tightening torque for the new bolt remains the same as that given for the original.

24 Rear hub - removal and refitting

1 Remove the wheel trim. Apply the handbrake and chock the front wheels.
2 Slacken the driveshaft stub axle. This nut is very tight. The left-hand nut has a **left-hand** thread, therefore it is undone **clockwise**.
3 Remove the brake disc.
4 Remove the driveshaft stub axle.
5 Remove the four bolts which secure the hub. Pull the hub off the driveshaft stub, leaving the disc splash shield loose.
6 Refit by reversing the removal operations. Carry out the final tightening of the driveshaft stub nut with the wheels on the ground.

25 Rear wheel bearings - renewal

1 Remove the rear hub as described in the previous Section (**see illustration**).
2 Prise out both oil seals from the hub. Recover the bearing races.
3 Drive the bearing tracks out of the hub with a hammer and a blunt drift.

4 Clean grease and debris from the hub and clean up any burrs or nicks.
5 Fit the new bearing tracks, pressing them in squarely with the help of a piece of pipe or tube.
6 Thoroughly grease the bearing races and pack the lips of the oil seals with grease.
7 Fit the races and the oil seals, lips inwards. Seat the oil seals with a mallet and the pipe or tube.
8 Refit the rear hub.

26 Wheel stud - renewal

1 This procedure is only specified by the manufacturers as applying to the rear wheels, but there is no reason to believe that it will not work on the front.
2 Remove the rear wheel, brake caliper and brake disc.
3 Drive the wheel stud out of the hub flange.

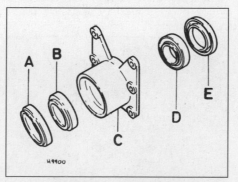

25.1 Rear hub components

A Outer oil seal
B Outer bearing
C Hub
D Inner bearing
E Inner oil seal

4 Insert the new stud from the inboard side of the flange. Engage the splines by hand pressure, then draw the stud into place with a wheel nut and progressively thicker spacers (**see illustration**).
5 Refit the brake disc, caliper and wheel.

27 Rear spring - removal and refitting

1 Raise and support the rear of the vehicle.
2 Unbolt the driveshaft outboard flange from the stub. It is secured by six Torx screws.
3 Disconnect the anti-roll bar from the link rod by prising it free. On models with ride height control, also disconnect the height sensor from the anti-roll bar link rod.
4 Free the brake pipe and flexible hose from the brackets next to the spring. If it is the left-hand spring which is being removed, also unbolt the brake pipe T-piece from the floor.
5 Raise a jack under the rear suspension lower arm to load the spring.
6 Unbolt the shock absorber from the lower arm.

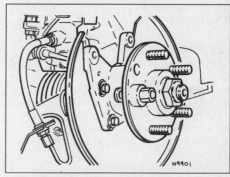

26.4 Fitting a new wheel stud using a nut and spacer

11

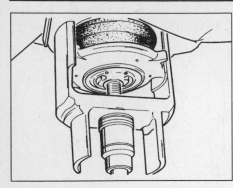

28.4 Drawing out an insulator with the special tool

30.2 Rear anti-roll bar link rod

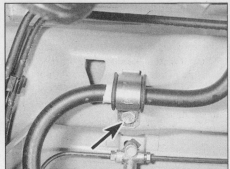

30.3 A rear anti-roll bar bracket - bolt arrowed

7 Unbolt the guide plate from the body on the side concerned.
8 Carefully lower the jack until the spring is no longer under tension. Remove the spring and the rubber buffer.
9 Refit by reversing the removal operations, tightening all fastenings to the specified torque when known.

28 Rear crossmember insulator - removal and refitting

Note: *Ford tool No 15-014, or locally made equivalent, will be required for this job.*
1 Raise and support the rear of the vehicle.
2 Flatten the lockwasher which secures the guide plate centre bolt. Remove the centre bolt and the two bolts which hold the guide plate to the floor; remove the guide plate.
3 Wedge a piece of wood between the crossmember and the floor.
4 Draw the insulator out with the special tool **(see illustration).**
5 Smear the new insulator with glycerine or liquid soap, then press it in as follows.
6 Use the special tool spindle or other long M12 bolt. Screw a nut up to the bolt head, then fit a plain washer and the insulator onto the bolt. Pass the bolt through the hole in the crossmember and screw it into the floor, then press the insulator home by winding the nut and washer up the bolt.
7 Remove the installation tool and the wood.
8 Refit the guide plate, tightening the bolts to the specified torque. Secure the centre bolt with the lockwasher.
9 Lower the vehicle.

29 Rear suspension lower arm - removal and refitting

1 Remove the rear hub.
2 Disconnect both rear brake flexible hoses from the brake pipes. Free the brake pipes from the brackets on the lower arms.
3 Unclip the handbrake cable from the lower arm.
4 Remove the rear spring.
5 Remove the lower arm-to-crossmember bolts. Withdraw the lower arm.

6 Renew the rubber bushes if wished, using lengths of tube or sockets and a vice, or large nuts and bolts. Lubricate the new bushes with glycerine or liquid soap.
7 Refit by reversing the removal operations, tightening the lower arm-to-crossmember bolts with the weight of the vehicle back on its wheels. Bleed the brake hydraulic system on completion.

30 Rear anti-roll bar - removal and refitting

1 Raise and support the rear of the vehicle.
2 Separate the anti-roll bar from the link rods on each side by prising them free **(see illustration).**
3 Unbolt the two anti-roll bar brackets. Remove the bar, brackets and bushes **(see illustration).**
4 Refit by reversing the removal operations. Tighten the bracket bolts to the specified torque.

31 Rear shock absorber - removal and refitting

1 Working inside the vehicle, remove the luggage area side trim to gain access to the shock absorber top mounting.
2 Raise and support the rear of the vehicle. Raise a jack under the rear suspension lower arm to take the load off the shock absorber.

31.4 Undoing a rear shock absorber top mounting

3 On models with ride height control, disconnect the air line from the shock absorber.
4 Unbolt the shock absorber top mounting **(see illustration).**
5 Unbolt the shock absorber lower mounting **(see illustration).** Pull the shock absorber out of the lower mounting bracket and remove it.
6 Refit by reversing the removal operations. Tighten the shock absorber mountings to the specified torque. On models with ride height control, use new O-rings on the air line union.

32 Ride height control system - general information

The ride height control system is an optional extra, designed to keep the rear suspension height constant regardless of vehicle load. This is obviously useful if heavy loads are often carried, or if the vehicle is used for towing.

The main components of the system are a height sensor, a compressor and two special rear shock absorbers. The compressor supplies air to the shock absorbers, so "pumping up" the rear suspension, when so commanded by the height sensor. Other components include the connecting pipes, electrical wiring and a compressor relay. The relay is mounted behind the glovebox.

Variations in vehicle height are not recognised by the system for approximately 20 seconds, in order to prevent responses to temporary changes such as those induced by

31.5 Undoing a rear shock absorber lower mounting

cornering or braking. Control circuitry also prevents the compressor being energised for more than five minutes continuously, as could otherwise happen if the system sprang a leak.

No repairs to individual components are possible. Apparent control faults should be referred to a Ford dealer before embarking on an expensive programme of testing by substitution. Always use new O-rings on the pipe unions once they have been disturbed.

33 Ride height control compressor - removal and refitting

1 Disconnect the battery negative lead.
2 Raise and support the front of the vehicle.
3 Remove the compressor cover (front left-hand side of engine) which is secured by four screws.
4 Disconnect the air pipe and the power supply leads from the compressor (see illustration).
5 Remove the three bolts which secure the compressor to the bracket. Withdraw the compressor, at the same time disconnecting the suction line and the control multi-plug.
6 Refit by reversing the removal operations; use new O-rings on the air pipe union (see illustration).

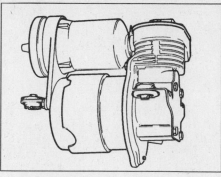
33.4 Ride height control compressor

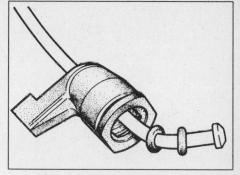
33.6 Detail of ride height control pipe union

34 Ride height control sensor - removal and refitting

1 Disconnect the battery negative lead.
2 Raise and support the rear of the vehicle to gain access to the sensor, located to the right of the rear crossmember (see illustration).
3 Unclip the linkage balljoint from the sensor.
4 Disconnect the sensor multi-plug.
5 Unbolt the sensor from the floor and remove it.
6 Do not attempt to adjust the sensor by altering the position of the control arm.
7 Refit by reversing the removal operations.

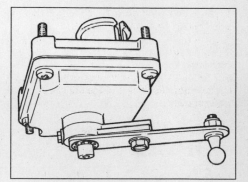
34.2 Ride height control height sensor

Notes

Chapter 12
Bodywork and fittings

Contents

Degrees of difficulty

Easy, suitable for novice with little experience	Fairly easy, suitable for beginner with some experience	Fairly difficult, suitable for competent DIY mechanic	Difficult, suitable for experienced DIY mechanic	Very difficult, suitable for expert DIY or professional

Specifications

Torque wrench settings

	Nm	lbf ft
Front seat belt buckle to seat frame	51 to 64	38 to 47
Seat belt retractor bolts (front and rear)	25 to 45	18 to 33
Other seat belt anchorages	25 to 45	18 to 33
Rear seat back hinge to body	21 to 25	16 to 18
Rear seat back latch striker	40 to 60	30 to 44
Front seat retaining bolts	25 to 32	18 to 24
Front seat frame-to-slide bolts	25 to 32	18 to 24
Rear bumper mountings	21	16
Front bumper adjuster lockbolt	21	16

12

1 General information

The bodyshell and floorpan are of pressed steel, and form an integral part of the vehicle's structure. Various reinforcing and mounting components beneath the floorpan are made of HSLA (High Strength Low Alloy) and REPHOS (rephosphorised) steels, which have superior strength-to-weight characteristics when compared with conventional steels.

Extensive use is made of plastic for peripheral components such as the radiator grille, bumpers and wheel trims, and for much of the interior trim.

Interior fittings are to the high standard expected in a vehicle of this class, with even the basic level models well equipped. A wide range of options is available, including air conditioning and leather upholstery.

2 Maintenance - bodywork and underframe

The general condition of a vehicle's bodywork is the one thing that significantly affects its value. Maintenance is easy, but needs to be regular. Neglect, particularly after minor damage, can lead quickly to further deterioration and costly repair bills. It is important also to keep watch on those parts of the vehicle not immediately visible, for instance the underside, inside all the wheel arches, and the lower part of the engine compartment.

The basic maintenance routine for the bodywork is washing - preferably with a lot of water, from a hose. This will remove all the loose solids which may have stuck to the vehicle. It is important to flush these off in such a way as to prevent grit from scratching the finish. The wheel arches and underframe need washing in the same way, to remove any accumulated mud, which will retain moisture and tend to encourage rust. Paradoxically enough, the best time to clean the underframe and wheel arches is in wet weather, when the mud is thoroughly wet and soft. In very wet weather, the underframe is usually cleaned of large accumulations automatically, and this is a good time for inspection.

Periodically, except on vehicles with a wax-based underbody protective coating, it is a good idea to have the whole of the underframe of the vehicle steam-cleaned, engine compartment included, so that a thorough inspection can be carried out to see what minor repairs and renovations are necessary. Steam-cleaning is available at many garages, and is necessary for the removal of the accumulation of oily grime, which sometimes is allowed to become thick in certain areas. If steam-cleaning facilities are not available, there are some excellent grease solvents available which can be brush-applied; the dirt can then be simply hosed off. Note that these methods should not be used on vehicles with wax-based underbody protective coating, or the coating will be removed. Such vehicles should be inspected annually, preferably just prior to Winter, when the underbody should be washed down, and any damage to the wax coating repaired. Ideally, a completely fresh coat should be applied. It would also be worth considering the use of such wax-based protection for injection into door panels, sills, box sections, etc, as an additional safeguard against rust damage, where such protection is not provided by the vehicle manufacturer.

After washing paintwork, wipe off with a chamois leather to give an unspotted clear finish. A coat of clear protective wax polish will give added protection against chemical pollutants in the air. If the paintwork sheen has dulled or oxidised, use a cleaner/polisher combination to restore the brilliance of the shine. This requires a little effort, but such dulling is usually caused because regular washing has been neglected. Care needs to be taken with metallic paintwork, as special non-abrasive cleaner/polisher is required to avoid damage to the finish. Always check that the door and ventilator opening drain holes and pipes are completely clear, so that water can be drained out. Brightwork should be treated in the same way as paintwork. Windscreens and windows can be kept clear of the smeary film which often appears, by the use of proprietary glass cleaner. Never use any form of wax or other body or chromium polish on glass.

3 Maintenance - upholstery and carpets

Mats and carpets should be brushed or vacuum-cleaned regularly, to keep them free of grit. If they are badly stained, remove them from the vehicle for scrubbing or sponging, and make quite sure they are dry before refitting. Seats and interior trim panels can be kept clean by wiping with a damp cloth. If they do become stained (which can be more apparent on light-coloured upholstery), use a little liquid detergent and a soft nail brush to scour the grime out of the grain of the material. Do not forget to keep the headlining clean in the same way as the upholstery. When using liquid cleaners inside the vehicle, do not over-wet the surfaces being cleaned. Excessive damp could get into the seams and padded interior, causing stains, offensive odours or even rot. If the inside of the vehicle gets wet accidentally, it is worthwhile taking some trouble to dry it out properly, particularly where carpets are involved. Do not leave oil or electric heaters inside the vehicle for this purpose.

4 Minor body damage - repair

Repairs of minor scratches in bodywork

If the scratch is very superficial, and does not penetrate to the metal of the bodywork, repair is very simple. Lightly rub the area of the scratch with a paintwork renovator, or a very fine cutting paste, to remove loose paint from the scratch, and to clear the surrounding bodywork of wax polish. Rinse the area with clean water.

Apply touch-up paint to the scratch using a fine paint brush; continue to apply fine layers of paint until the surface of the paint in the scratch is level with the surrounding paintwork. Allow the new paint at least two weeks to harden, then blend it into the surrounding paintwork by rubbing the scratch area with a paintwork renovator or a very fine cutting paste. Finally, apply wax polish.

Where the scratch has penetrated right through to the metal of the bodywork, causing the metal to rust, a different repair technique is required. Remove any loose rust from the bottom of the scratch with a penknife, then apply rust-inhibiting paint to prevent the formation of rust in the future. Using a rubber or nylon applicator, fill the scratch with bodystopper paste. If required, this paste can be mixed with cellulose thinners to provide a very thin paste which is ideal for filling narrow scratches. Before the stopper-paste in the scratch hardens, wrap a piece of smooth cotton rag around the top of a finger. Dip the finger in cellulose thinners, and quickly sweep it across the surface of the stopper-paste in the scratch; this will ensure that the surface of the stopper-paste is slightly hollowed. The scratch can now be painted over as described earlier in this Section.

Repairs of dents in bodywork

When deep denting of the vehicle's bodywork has taken place, the first task is to pull the dent out, until the affected bodywork almost attains its original shape. There is little point in trying to restore the original shape completely, as the metal in the damaged area will have stretched on impact, and cannot be reshaped fully to its original contour. It is better to bring the level of the dent up to a point which is about 3 mm below the level of the surrounding bodywork. In cases where the dent is very shallow anyway, it is not worth trying to pull it out at all. If the underside of the dent is accessible, it can be hammered out gently from behind, using a mallet with a wooden or plastic head. Whilst doing this, hold a suitable block of wood firmly against the outside of the panel, to absorb the impact from the hammer blows and thus prevent a large area of the bodywork from being "belled-out".

Should the dent be in a section of the bodywork which has a double skin, or some other factor making it inaccessible from behind, a different technique is called for. Drill several small holes through the metal inside the area - particularly in the deeper section. Then screw long self-tapping screws into the holes, just sufficiently for them to gain a good purchase in the metal. Now the dent can be pulled out by pulling on the protruding heads of the screws with a pair of pliers.

The next stage of the repair is the removal of the paint from the damaged area, and from an inch or so of the surrounding "sound" bodywork. This is accomplished most easily by using a wire brush or abrasive pad on a power drill, although it can be done just as effectively by hand, using sheets of abrasive paper. To complete the preparation for filling, score the surface of the bare metal with a screwdriver or the tang of a file, or alternatively, drill small holes in the affected area. This will provide a really good "key" for the filler paste.

To complete the repair, see the Section on filling and respraying.

Repairs of rust holes or gashes in bodywork

Remove all paint from the affected area, and from an inch or so of the surrounding "sound" bodywork, using an abrasive pad or a wire brush on a power drill. If these are not available, a few sheets of abrasive paper will do the job most effectively. With the paint removed, you will be able to judge the severity of the corrosion, and therefore decide whether to renew the whole panel (if this is possible) or to repair the affected area. New body panels are not as expensive as most people think, and it is often quicker and more satisfactory to fit a new panel than to attempt to repair large areas of corrosion.

Remove all fittings from the affected area, except those which will act as a guide to the original shape of the damaged bodywork (eg headlight shells etc). Then, using tin snips or a hacksaw blade, remove all loose metal and any other metal badly affected by corrosion. Hammer the edges of the hole inwards, in order to create a slight depression for the filler paste.

Wire-brush the affected area to remove the powdery rust from the surface of the remaining metal. Paint the affected area with rust-inhibiting paint, if the back of the rusted area is accessible, treat this also.

Before filling can take place, it will be necessary to block the hole in some way. This can be achieved by the use of aluminium or plastic mesh, or aluminium tape.

Aluminium or plastic mesh, or glass-fibre matting, is probably the best material to use for a large hole. Cut a piece to the approximate size and shape of the hole to be filled, then position it in the hole so that its edges are below the level of the surrounding bodywork. It can be retained in position by several blobs of filler paste around its periphery.

Aluminium tape should be used for small or very narrow holes. Pull a piece off the roll, trim it to the approximate size and shape required, then pull off the backing paper (if used) and stick the tape over the hole; it can be overlapped if the thickness of one piece is insufficient. Burnish down the edges of the tape with the handle of a screwdriver or similar, to ensure that the tape is securely attached to the metal underneath.

Bodywork repairs - filling and respraying

Before using this Section, see the Sections on dent, deep scratch, rust holes and gash repairs.

Many types of bodyfiller are available, but generally speaking, those proprietary kits which contain a tin of filler paste and a tube of resin hardener are best for this type of repair. A wide, flexible plastic or nylon applicator will be found invaluable for imparting a smooth and well-contoured finish to the surface of the filler.

Mix up a little filler on a clean piece of card or board - measure the hardener carefully (follow the maker's instructions on the pack), otherwise the filler will set too rapidly or too slowly. Using the applicator, apply the filler paste to the prepared area; draw the applicator across the surface of the filler to achieve the correct contour and to level the surface. As soon as a contour that approximates to the correct one is achieved, stop working the paste - if you carry on too long, the paste will become sticky and begin to "pick-up" on the applicator. Continue to add thin layers of filler paste at 20-minute

intervals, until the level of the filler is just proud of the surrounding bodywork.

Once the filler has hardened, the excess can be removed using a metal plane or file. From then on, progressively-finer grades of abrasive paper should be used, starting with a 40-grade production paper, and finishing with a 400-grade wet-and-dry paper. Always wrap the abrasive paper around a flat rubber, cork, or wooden block - otherwise the surface of the filler will not be completely flat. During the smoothing of the filler surface, the wet-and-dry paper should be periodically rinsed in water. This will ensure that a very smooth finish is imparted to the filler at the final stage.

At this stage, the "dent" should be surrounded by a ring of bare metal, which in turn should be encircled by the finely "feathered" edge of the good paintwork. Rinse the repair area with clean water, until all of the dust produced by the rubbing-down operation has gone.

Spray the whole area with a light coat of primer - this will show up any imperfections in the surface of the filler. Repair these imperfections with fresh filler paste or bodystopper, and once more smooth the surface with abrasive paper. Repeat this spray-and-repair procedure until you are satisfied that the surface of the filler, and the feathered edge of the paintwork, are perfect. Clean the repair area with clean water, and allow to dry fully.

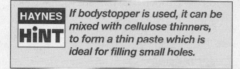
If bodystopper is used, it can be mixed with cellulose thinners, to form a thin paste which is ideal for filling small holes.

The repair area is now ready for final spraying. Paint spraying must be carried out in a warm, dry, windless and dust-free atmosphere. This condition can be created artificially if you have access to a large indoor working area, but if you are forced to work in the open, you will have to pick your day very carefully. If you are working indoors, dousing the floor in the work area with water will help to settle the dust which would otherwise be in the atmosphere. If the repair area is confined to one body panel, mask off the surrounding panels; this will help to minimise the effects of a slight mis-match in paint colours. Bodywork fittings (eg chrome strips, door handles etc) will also need to be masked off. Use genuine masking tape, and several thicknesses of newspaper, for the masking operations.

Before commencing to spray, agitate the aerosol can thoroughly, then spray a test area (an old tin, or similar) until the technique is mastered. Cover the repair area with a thick coat of primer; the thickness should be built up using several thin layers of paint, rather than one thick one. Using 400-grade wet-and-dry paper, rub down the surface of the primer until it is really smooth. While doing this, the work area should be thoroughly doused with water, and the wet-and-dry paper periodically rinsed in water. Allow to dry before spraying on more paint.

Spray on the top coat, again building up the

thickness by using several thin layers of paint. Start spraying at one edge of the repair area, and then, using a side-to-side motion, work until the whole repair area and about 2 inches of the surrounding original paintwork is covered. Remove all masking material 10 to 15 minutes after spraying on the final coat of paint.

Allow the new paint at least two weeks to harden, then, using a paintwork renovator, or a very fine cutting paste, blend the edges of the paint into the existing paintwork. Finally, apply wax polish.

Plastic components

With the use of more and more plastic body components by the vehicle manufacturers (eg bumpers, spoilers, and in some cases major body panels), rectification of more serious damage to such items has become a matter of either entrusting repair work to a specialist in this field, or renewing complete components. Repair of such damage by the DIY owner is not really feasible, owing to the cost of the equipment and materials required for effecting such repairs. The basic technique involves making a groove along the line of the crack in the plastic, using a rotary burr in a power drill. The damaged part is then welded back together, using a hot-air gun to heat up and fuse a plastic filler rod into the groove. Any excess plastic is then removed, and the area rubbed down to a smooth finish. It is important that a filler rod of the correct plastic is used, as body components can be made of a variety of different types (eg polycarbonate, ABS, polypropylene).

Damage of a less serious nature (abrasions, minor cracks etc) can be repaired by the DIY owner using a two-part epoxy filler repair material. Once mixed in equal proportions, this is used in similar fashion to the bodywork filler used on metal panels. The filler is usually cured in twenty to thirty minutes, ready for sanding and painting.

If the owner is renewing a complete component himself, or if he has repaired it with epoxy filler, he will be left with the problem of finding a suitable paint for finishing which is compatible with the type of plastic used. At one time, the use of a universal paint was not possible, owing to the complex range of plastics encountered in body component applications. Standard paints, generally speaking, will not bond to plastic or rubber satisfactorily. However, it is now possible to obtain a plastic body parts finishing kit which consists of a pre-primer treatment, a primer and coloured top coat. Full instructions are normally supplied with a kit, but basically, the method of use is to first apply the pre-primer to the component concerned, and allow it to dry for up to 30 minutes. Then the primer is applied, and left to dry for about an hour before finally applying the special-coloured top coat. The result is a correctly-coloured component, where the paint will flex with the plastic or rubber, a property that standard paint does not normally posses.

12

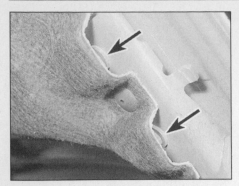

6.2 Left-hand hinge bolts (arrowed) are obscured by insulation

6.7 Bonnet lock striker and safety catch

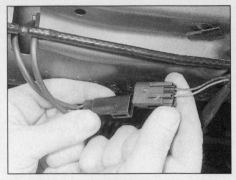

6.8 On later models disconnect the washer nozzle heater wiring plugs before removing the bonnet

5 Major body damage - repair

Where serious damage has occurred or large areas need renewal due to neglect, it means certainly that completely new sections or panels will need welding in and this is best left to professionals. If the damage is due to impact, it will also be necessary to completely check the alignment of the bodyshell structure. Due to the principle of construction, the strength and shape of the whole car can be affected by damage to one part. In such instances the services of a Ford agent with specialist checking jigs are essential. If a body is left misaligned, it is first of all dangerous as the car will not handle properly, and secondly uneven stresses will be imposed on the steering, engine and transmission, causing abnormal wear or complete failure. Tyre wear may also be excessive.

6 Bonnet - removal and refitting

1 Open and prop the bonnet.
2 Mark around the bonnet hinge bolts, using soft pencil or a washable marker pen, to provide a guide when refitting (see illustration).
3 Disconnect the windscreen washer hose at

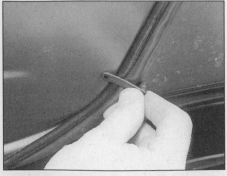

6.10 On refitting ensure the wiring and hoses are correctly routed and secured by all necessary retaining clips

the non-return valve or washer pump. Be prepared for fluid spillage.
4 Disconnect the under-bonnet light (when fitted).
5 Free the insulation from around the left-hand hinge bolts. With the help of an assistant, support the bonnet and remove the hinge bolts. Unhook the bonnet from the pump and remove it.
6 Refit by reversing the removal operations. Make sure that the gap between the bonnet and the wings is equal on both sides when the bonnet is shut; adjust if necessary at the hinge bolts.
7 Adjust the bump stops and bonnet lock striker if necessary to obtain satisfactory opening and closing of the bonnet (see illustration).

Later models

8 The operation for later models is essentially as described above, noting that it will be necessary to unclip the insulation panel from the underside of the bonnet to gain access to the windscreen washer hose and washer nozzle heater wiring plugs (see illustration).
9 Disconnect the wiring plugs and hose and free them from the retaining clips on the right-hand side of the bonnet before removal.
10 On refitting ensure that the hose and wiring are correctly routed and retained by all the necessary clips before refitting the insulation panel (see illustrations).

7.1 Door wiring multi-plug

7 Door - removal and refitting

1 Open the door and disconnect the wiring multi-plug from the door pillar (see illustration).
2 Unbolt the door check strap.
3 Slacken, but do not remove, the hinge cotter pin nuts (see illustration).
4 Open the door to approximately 60° from the vehicle body and lift it off the hinges. If the door is reluctant to move, make sure that it is opened to the correct angle and that the cotter pin nuts are adequately slackened.
5 Refit by reversing the removal operations. Adjust the door striker plate if necessary as described in Section 12.
6 If a new door is to be fitted, new hinges will have to be welded to it after trial fitting. Consult a Ford dealer for details.

8 Tailgate - removal and refitting

Hatchback models

1 Open the tailgate and remove the interior trim panel, which is retained by eleven screws.
2 Disconnect the wiring from the heated rear window, aerial pre-amplifier and lock solenoid.
3 Repeat paragraph 2 for the rear wiper motor and the rear washer tube, and any other electrical equipment.

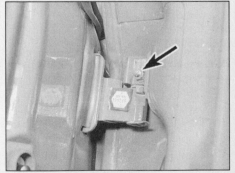

7.3 One of the hinge cotter pins (arrowed)

8.6 Tailgate hinge nuts are accessible through headlining

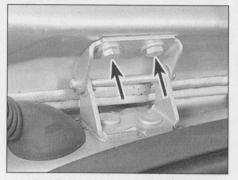

8.14 Tailgate hinge retaining bolts (arrowed) - Estate models

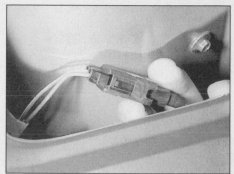

9.2 On Saloon models remove the trim panel to gain access to the lock and warning switch wiring connectors

---

HAYNES HiNT *Tie some string to each piece of wiring, then free the grommet and draw the wiring out of the tailgate. Untie the string and leave it in the tailgate for use when refitting.*

---

4 Have an assistant support the tailgate. Disconnect the struts from the tailgate.

5 Jam the tailgate latch with a piece of wood or cardboard so that the tailgate cannot shut. Lower the tailgate.

6 Working inside the vehicle, prise out the hinge covers from the headlining. Remove the hinge nuts and recover the washers **(see illustration)**.

7 With the aid of an assistant, lift the tailgate away from the vehicle.

8 Commence refitting by offering the tailgate to its aperture, aligning the hinges and reconnecting the struts. Do not allow the struts alone to support the tailgate until the hinge nuts have been fitted.

9 Fit the hinge nuts and washers. Do not fully tighten the nuts yet.

10 Secure any wiring looms and the washer tube to the pieces of string used during removal. (It is to be hoped that a new tailgate will be supplied with wiring or string in place.) Draw the wires and tube into position. Tape up the connectors if necessary to prevent them snagging.

11 Reconnect the wires and the washer tube and refit the grommets.

12 Close and latch the tailgate and adjust its position so that an even gap exists all round it, then tighten the hinge nuts.

13 Refit the hinge covers and the interior trim panel.

Estate models

14 On Estate models the tailgate can be removed and refitted as described above, noting the following points:

a) *Prior to removing the interior trim panel, it will be necessary to remove the upper rear windscreen trim panel which is retained by eight screws.*

b) *When removing the interior trim panel note that it is retained by fourteen screws; two are situated behind each of the*

access covers in the centre of the panel.

c) *To gain access to the tailgate hinge retaining nuts it will be necessary to carefully peel the headlining away from the rear trim panel. Therefore if hinge removal is not strictly necessary, it is recommended that the hinges are left in place on the vehicle and the tailgate is unbolted from the hinges* **(see illustration).**

9 Boot lid - removal, refitting and adjustment

1 On saloon models, open the boot lid and using a suitable marker pen, mark the outline of the hinges on the inside of the lid.

2 Unclip the trim panel from the inside of the lid to gain access to the boot lid lock and warning switch wiring connectors **(see illustration)**. Release the wiring loom from the retaining clips and tie a suitable length of string to each of the wiring connectors. Withdraw the wiring loom from the boot lid until the connectors emerge then untie the string and leave it in position in the lid; the string can then be used to draw the wiring loom back into position on refitting.

3 Support the lid with the aid of an assistant then slacken and remove the four hinge retaining bolts (accessed from inside the lid) and remove the boot lid from the car **(see illustration)**.

4 Offer up the boot lid, aligning the hinges with the marks made on removal, and tighten

the hinge bolts securely. Tie the piece of string to the wiring loom and use the string to draw the loom through the boot lid. If a new boot lid is being installed it will be necessary to centralise the boot lid on the hinges and feed the wiring loom through the boot lid, ensuring that it is correctly routed.

5 Reconnect the wiring connectors to the lock and warning switch.

6 Refit the trim panel and check it is securely held in position by the retaining clips.

7 Close the boot lid and check that is correctly aligned with all surrounding bodywork with an equal clearance all around. If necessary, adjustment can be made by slackening the hinge bolts and repositioning the boot lid. Once correctly positioned, tighten the hinge bolts securely.

8 Once the boot lid is correctly aligned ensure that it closes without slamming and is securely retained. If not, slacken the boot lid striker retaining bolts and reposition the striker. Once the boot lid operation is satisfactory tighten the striker retaining bolts securely.

10 Sliding roof - removal and refitting

1 This procedure applies to the manually-operated roof. For removal of the electrically-operated roof motor, see Chapter 13.

2 Open the roof. Remove the four setscrews and ten self-tapping screws which secure the sliding roof frame.

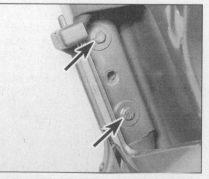

9.3 Boot lid retaining bolts (arrowed) - Saloon models

10.4 Removing the sliding roof operating handle

12

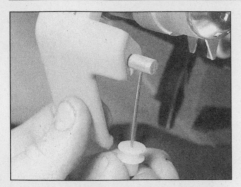

11.3 Unhooking the cable inner from the release lever

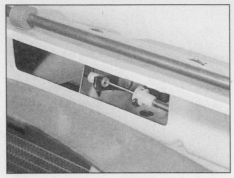

11.5 Bonnet release cable connected to catch

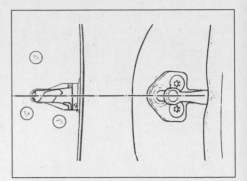

12.2 Door latch striker in line with centre of opening

3 Apply masking tape to the front and sides of the roof aperture to protect the paintwork.
4 Close the roof. Remove the Torx screw which secures the operating handle, counterholding the handle whilst slackening the screw **(see illustration)**. Remove the operating handle.
5 With the aid of an assistant, remove the sliding roof assembly by pushing it up from inside and drawing it forwards from outside. Support the rear of the roof as it is removed.
6 Refit by reversing the removal operations.

11 Bonnet release cable - removal and refitting

1 If the release cable has broken, the bonnet catch can be released from below with the aid of a long screwdriver. It will be necessary to raise and support the front of the vehicle for access. With the bonnet open, proceed as follows.
2 Remove the steering column lower shroud.
3 Disconnect the cable from the release lever by pulling the cable outer from the bracket, then unhooking the inner from the lever **(see illustration)**.
4 Pull the cable through the bulkhead grommet into the engine bay. Release the cable from any clips or ties.
5 Disengage the inner and outer cables from the bonnet catch **(see illustration)**. Remove the cable.
6 Refit by reversing the removal operations, being careful not to kink or bend the cable. Check that operation of the release lever causes the catch to move before closing the bonnet.

12 Door striker plate - adjustment

1 Open the door and slacken the two Torx screws which secure the striker plate. The screws should be loosened until the plate can be moved by tapping, but not by hand pressure.
2 Move the striker plate if necessary until it is aligned with the centre of the latch opening **(see illustration)**.
3 Open and close the door a few times until the locking action is smooth and the door position when shut is satisfactory. Then open the door again and tighten the striker plate screws.

13 Door exterior handle - removal and refitting

1 Remove the door interior trim panel.
2 Carefully peel away the foam rubber sheet in the area of the door handle operating rod. Disconnect the rod from the handle.
3 Remove the two screws which secure the handle to the door, then remove the handle.
4 Refit by reversing the removal operations.

14 Door lock barrel - removal and refitting

1 Remove the door interior trim panel.
2 Carefully peel away the foam rubber sheet in the area of the lock barrel. Unhook the operating rod from the lock barrel lever **(see illustration)**.
3 When so equipped, unclip the switch from the lock barrel and disconnect its wiring.
4 Remove the large U-clip which secures the lock barrel to the door. Remove the barrel.
5 Refit by reversing the removal operations. Check the lock for correct operation before refitting the door trim.

15 Door latch assembly - removal and refitting

1 Remove the door interior trim panel.
2 Carefully peel away the foam rubber sheet in the area of the door latch. Unhook the lock barrel operating rod from the latch. Also unhook the exterior handle operating rod.
3 Disconnect the lock motor multi-plug (when fitted). Remove the two screws to release the lock motor. Pivot the motor to release the operating rod from it.
4 Remove the door interior handle securing screw **(see illustration)**. Slide the handle rearwards to release it from the door. Unhook the rods from the handle and release them from their bushes.
5 When door latch switches are fitted, disconnect the switch multi-plug.
6 Remove the three screws which secure the door latch **(see illustration)**. Manoeuvre the latch behind the window channel and out of

14.2 Unhook the operating rod (arrowed) from the lock barrel lever

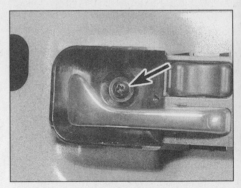

15.4 Door interior handle securing screw (arrowed)

15.6 Door latch securing screws

the door through the large cut-out. Further displacement or removal of the foam rubber sheet may be necessary.
7 Refit in the reverse order to removal, noting the following points:
 a) Apply a little grease to the interior handle rods where they pass through the plastic bushes
 b) When securing the interior handle, have the locking lever in the "unlocked" position, hold the assembly forwards as far as it will go and tighten the securing screw
 c) Check all functions before refitting the trim panel.

16 Door weatherstrip - removal and refitting

Door weatherstrip

1 Open the door and remove the weatherstrip securing screw from the latch end. In the case of the rear door, also remove the screw from the hinge end.
2 Carefully lift the latch end of the weatherstrip and pull it off the door.
3 Refit by reversing the removal operations, using your palm to seat the weatherstrip.

Aperture weatherstrip

4 Open the door. Remove the scuff plate securing screws from the bottom of the door aperture.
5 Pull the old weatherstrip out of the door aperture.
6 Fit the new weatherstrip, starting at the right-angled corner at the top. Fit the weatherstrip to the other corners and bends, leaving the straight sections until last.
7 Refit the scuff, plate securing screws.

17 Tailgate lock barrel - removal and refitting

All models except Estate

1 Disconnect the battery negative lead.
2 Remove the tailgate interior trim panel, which is secured by eleven screws.
3 Remove the six nuts which secure the tailgate handle. Remove the handle and recover the gasket.
4 Disconnect the tailgate lock switch multi-plug. Release the switch locking tab and remove the switch.
5 Disconnect the operating rod from the lock lever (see illustration). Extract the U-clip and remove the lock barrel.
6 Refit by reversing the removal operations.

Estate models

7 The tailgate lock barrel can be removed and refitted as described above, bearing in mind the notes made in Section 8 when removing the interior trim panels and noting that the lock assembly is retained by two Torx bolts.

17.5 Operating rod (arrowed) connected to tailgate lock lever

18 Boot lid lock barrel - removal and refitting

1 Open up the boot lid and remove the trim panel from the inside of the lid.
2 Unscrew the four boot lid exterior trim retaining panel bolts (two situated on each side of the lock) then carefully prise out the nine panel retaining clips and remove the panel from the boot lid.
3 Undo the two lock barrel retaining nuts then partially withdraw the barrel and disconnect the wiring connector and lock operating rod from the barrel. Remove the lock barrel from the lid.
4 Undo the four lid lock retaining bolts then withdraw the lock assembly from the boot lid, disconnecting the central locking and warning switch wiring plugs (see illustration).
5 Refitting is a reversal of the removal procedure tightening all retaining bolts securely. On completion check the operation of the boot lid lock and lock barrel before refitting the trim panel.

19 Tailgate latch assembly - removal and refitting

1 Disconnect the battery negative lead.
2 Remove the tailgate interior trim panel, which is secured by eleven screws.
3 Unhook the operating rod from the tailgate latch. Also disconnect the lock switch and solenoid multi-plugs.

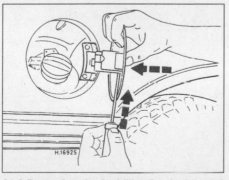
21.2 Removing the fuel filler flap lock barrel

18.4 Boot lid lock retaining bolts (arrowed) - Saloon models

4 Remove the three bolts which secure the tailgate latch. Remove the latch.
5 Refit by reversing the removal operations.

20 Tailgate strut - removal and refitting

1 Open the tailgate and support it with a piece of wood.
2 Release the strut from its mountings by raising the spring clips with a small screwdriver, then pulling the strut off the ball-stands. Do not raise the clips more than 4 mm (0.16 in) if the strut is to be re-used.
3 Do not attempt to dismantle a strut, and dispose of it safely. It contains gas under pressure.
4 To refit a strut, position it over the ball-studs. Push on each end in turn until it snaps home.

21 Fuel filler lock barrel - removal and refitting

1 Open the fuel filler flap. Remove the key.
2 Apply pressure to the lock barrel at the key slot, using the thumb of one hand. With the other hand insert a screwdriver into the cut-out in the filler flap to release the lock barrel retaining spring. As the spring is released, thumb pressure will eject the lock barrel into the petrol tank (see illustration).
3 To refit, push the lock barrel into the flap until the retaining spring clicks home.

22 Door interior trim panel - removal and refitting

Front door

1 Open the door and remove the screws which secure the front and rear edges of the trim panel (see illustration).
2 Remove the two screws from under the covers on the door pocket. Unclip and remove the pocket.
3 On models with electrically-operated windows and mirrors, prise out and disconnect the window and mirror switches. The window switch multi-plugs on the driver's side are

12

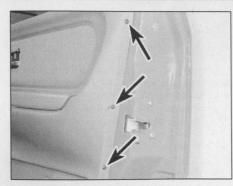

22.1 Three screws (arrowed) secure the rear edge of the front door trim panel

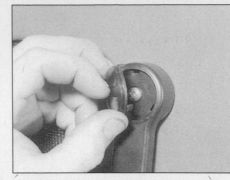

22.3 Prise the cap off the window winder handle to expose the screw

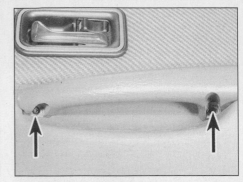

22.4a The two armrest screws (arrowed) - low level trim

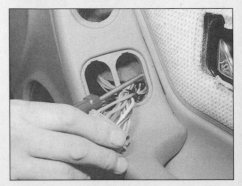

22.4b Access to the screw is through the window switch aperture

colour-coded: the blue plug is outermost. On models with manually-operated windows, remove the window winder handle, which is secured by a single screw **(see illustration)**.

4 Remove the two screws located under the arm-rest. One of these screws will be accessible through the window switch aperture (on higher level trim models) when applicable **(see illustrations)**.

5 Remove the door interior handle surround, which is retained by a single screw **(see illustration)**.

6 Remove the triangular trim panel which covers the door mirror mountings. This trim panel is secured by a single screw concealed under a cover **(see illustration)**.

7 Pull the trim panel away from the door at the top to free the push-in clips, then lift it to free it from the lower mountings. A certain amount of

jerking and thumping may be necessary to release the clips and mountings.

8 To gain access to the components within the door it will be necessary to peel back the foam rubber sheet. This sheet is secured by a bead of powerful adhesive around its edge, and some of the door hardware may be riveted through it. To remove the sheet from around a riveted fitting, carefully cut it free with a sharp knife, then glue it back in place afterwards **(see illustrations)**.

9 Refit by reversing the removal operations.

Rear door

10 Operations are similar to those just described for the front door. Note that the interior handle surround is secured by two screws, one of which is accessible after removing the ashtray.

23 Door window glass - removal and refitting

1 Remove the door interior trim panel as described in the previous Section. Peel back the foam rubber sheet.
2 Remove the door weather strip.

Front door

3 Raise and support the window. Undo the two screws which secure the glass to the regulator mechanism and lower the glass into the door.
4 Remove the three screws (one front, two rear) which secure the window channels **(see illustration)**.

22.5 Removing the door handle surround screw

22.6 Removing the mirror mounting trim screw

22.8a Peeling back the rubber sheet

22.8b Front door with rubber sheet peeled back

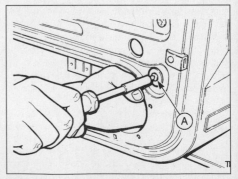

23.4 One of the front door window channel screws (A)

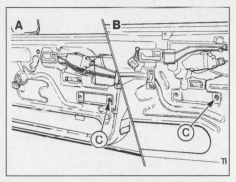

23.6 Window regulator adjustment screws (C)

A Front door   *B Rear door*

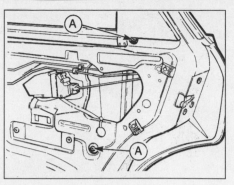

23.7 Rear door window channel screws (A)

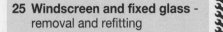

5 Free the glass from the channels. Carefully remove the glass upwards through the window aperture.

6 Refit by reversing the removal operations. Note that the channels are adjustable: wind the window up and down after securing the channels and adjust them if necessary for smooth operation. The regulator mechanism can also be adjusted **(see illustration)**.

Rear door

7 Remove the two screws which secure the window channel **(see illustration)**.

8 Remove the two screws which secure the glass to the regulator mechanism. Free the glass from the channel and carefully lift it out through the window aperture.

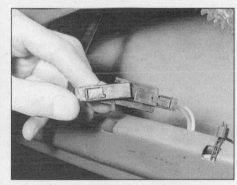

24.4 Window motor multi-plug

9 When refitting, secure the glass and the channel, then make sure that the window can wind up and down smoothly before proceeding further. Adjust the channel or regulator if necessary.

10 Refit the weatherstrip and trim panel.

24 Door window regulator mechanism - removal and refitting

1 The window regulator mechanism is riveted to the door skin. A blind rivet gun will therefore be needed for successful refitting.

2 Remove the door interior trim panel and peel back the foam rubber sheet.

3 Support the glass and remove the two screws which secure it to the regulator mechanism. Wedge or tape the glass in the raised position.

4 When applicable, disconnect the window motor multi-plug **(see illustration)**.

5 Remove the two slide screws and drill out the four rivets which secure the regulator **(see illustrations)**. Remove the regulator through the large lower aperture in the door.

6 When refitting, secure the regulator with the two slide screws, then fit four new rivets in the rivet holes.

7 The remainder of refitting is a reversal of removal.

25 Windscreen and fixed glass - removal and refitting

The windscreen, the rear (tailgate) window and the rear quarter windows are all secured and weatherproofed by special adhesives. The equipment and skills required to remove and refit this type of window are beyond the scope of this book. Consult a Ford dealer or a windscreen specialist.

26 Bonnet insulation panel - removal and refitting

1 Open and prop the bonnet.

2 When an under-bonnet light is fitted, disconnect its wire. Remove the screw which secures the light, pull the wire through the insulation panel and remove it.

3 Remove the centre screws from the plastic fittings which secure the insulation. Prise the outer parts of the fittings out of the bonnet and remove the insulation panel.

4 Refit by reversing the removal operations. Feed the under-bonnet light wire into place before finally securing the insulation panel.

27 Radiator grille - removal and refitting

Early models

1 Open and prop the bonnet.

2 Remove the two screws which secure the centre section of the grille.

3 When fitted, remove the headlight washer jets by pulling them out of their fittings.

4 Release one end of the grille side section from its fixing next to the direction indicator lens **(see illustration)**. Carefully pull the side section away from its mountings until it can be separated from the grille centre section.

5 The centre section can now be released from the other side section by raising the tang on the catch which holds the sections together, then twisting them apart **(see illustration)**.

6 Refit by reversing the removal operations.

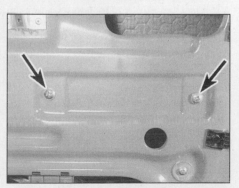

24.5a The two regulator slide screws (arrowed)

24.5b Two of the rivets (arrowed) which secure the regulator

Two other rivets are out of shot to right

27.4 Removing a grille side section

12

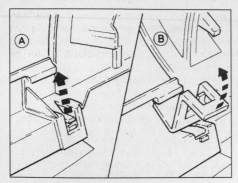

27.5 Removing the radiator grille centre section

A Raise tang   *B Twist apart*

Later models

7 The radiator grille of these models can be removed and refitted as described above, noting that it will also be necessary to remove the headlamp wiper arms (where fitted) before the grille can be removed. To remove a wiper arm, lift the cover to gain access to the retaining nut then undo the nut and pull the arm off the spindle **(see illustration)**. On refitting, position the arm so that it is correctly aligned with the base of the headlamp and locate it on the spindle splines. Refit the spindle nut and tighten it securely.

28 Side mouldings - removal and refitting

1 Prise the centre insert out of the moulding with a screwdriver.
2 Remove the securing screws and pull off the moulding. In the case of the door mouldings, note that the ends are also secured with adhesive tape **(see illustration)**.
3 Refit by reversing the removal operations. Use new adhesive tape when necessary.

29 Windscreen mouldings - removal and refitting

1 A blind rivet gun will be needed for this job.
2 Open the front doors. Remove the gutter weatherstrip, making sure to release the bottom flap which is glued to the A-pillar.
3 Drill out the five rivets which secure the side moulding. The side moulding can now be removed
4 Repeat the operations on the other side of the vehicle, then remove the upper moulding by pulling it upwards.
5 Commence refitting by pushing the upper moulding onto its clips. Make sure it is centrally aligned.
6 Refit the side mouldings and secure them with new blind rivets.
7 Clean and degrease the gutter weatherstrip flaps, then glue them in position and refit the weatherstrips.

27.7 Removing a headlamp wiper arm

30 Tailgate window mouldings - removal and refitting

1 Open the tailgate. From inside remove the two nuts which secure the upper moulding and the two screws which secure the lower moulding. Close the tailgate.
2 Prise off the lower moulding and fittings.
3 Pull off the side mouldings, which are clipped to the edge of the glass.
4 To remove the upper moulding, carefully lift one end. Free the moulding from its clips, working from the lifted end, and remove it.
5 To remove the lower moulding, simply pull it from its clips.
6 Refit by reversing the removal operations. Make sure that the upper and lower mouldings are centred before securing them.

31 Door window frame mouldings - removal and refitting

1 A blind rivet gun will be needed to refit some of these mouldings.
2 Commence by removing the door weatherstrip.

Front door

3 Remove the nut which secures the upper moulding. Carefully prise the upper moulding off the door.
4 Prise the edge moulding out of the window channel, then twist it and remove it.

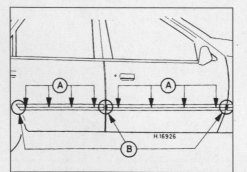

28.2 Door side mouldings

A Screws   *B Adhesive tape*

5 Remove the door mirror.
6 Drill out the rivet which secures the front corner moulding. Remove the moulding.
7 Refit by reversing the removal operations, using a new blind rivet to secure the corner moulding.

Rear door

8 Remove the nut securing the upper moulding to the front top corner of the door. Carefully pull the moulding from the door, separating the stud and bush fitting at the rear end.
9 Drill out the rivet which secures the rear moulding to the top of the door. Separate the rear moulding flange from the door and window channel and remove it by twisting it.
10 Remove the front moulding by separating the weatherstrip from the back of it and lifting the moulding from the door.
11 Refit by reversing the removal operations. Use a new rivet to secure the rear moulding.

32 Rear quarter window moulding - removal and refitting

1 A blind rivet gun will be needed to refit the moulding.
2 Open the rear door. Drill out the rivets which secure the weatherstrip to the mouldings.
3 Drill out the top rivet and remove the upper moulding from its studs.
4 Open the tailgate, drill out the lower moulding rivet and remove the lower moulding from its clips.
5 Drill out the three rivets which secure the side moulding. Remove the side moulding.
6 Refit by reversing the removal operations, using new rivets to secure the mouldings.

33 Motifs and emblems - removal and refitting

1 The bonnet emblem, tailgate motif and other badges are glued in place. They may be removed by using a piece of thin braided nylon cord, making a back-and-forth motion to cut through the adhesive.
2 Clean old adhesive from the bonnet or boot lid using methylated spirit.
3 If a new emblem is to be fitted, warm it (for instance with a hairdryer) until it is warm to the touch. Peel the backing paper off the adhesive surface and press the emblem into position, making sure that it is properly aligned. Hold the emblem in place for at least half a minute to allow the glue to set.

34 Front bumper - height adjustment

1 Front bumper height is easily adjusted by means of the two adjusters incorporated in the front mountings **(see illustration)**. A Torx key to fit the locking bolt and a 24 mm socket will be required.

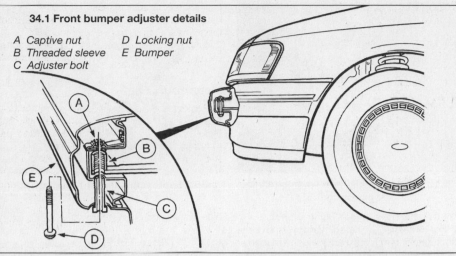

34.1 Front bumper adjuster details

A *Captive nut*   D *Locking nut*
B *Threaded sleeve* E *Bumper*
C *Adjuster bolt*

2 Slacken the locking bolts by half a turn each using the Torx key.

3 Turn the adjuster bolts, using the 24 mm socket, until the bumper height is correct and the same on each side. As a guide, bumper height is correct when the gap between the top of the bumper and the bottom of the radiator grille side extensions is 7 mm (0.28 in).

4 Tighten the locking bolts when adjustment is correct.

35 Bumpers - removal and refitting

1 Raise the front or rear of the vehicle (as applicable) and support it securely.

Front

2 Release the side fasteners by turning them through 90° **(see illustration)**. Release the lateral supports by pulling them off the bumper.

3 Remove the locking bolts completely, using a Torx key, then use a 24 mm socket to remove the adjuster bolts.

4 Pull the bumper away from the front of the vehicle and remove it.

5 Commence refitting by offering the bumper to the vehicle, engaging the side pins and the front mounting brackets in their recesses.

6 Insert the locking bolts into the adjuster

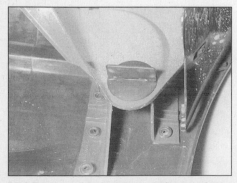

35.2 Bumper side fastener - twist to release

bolts. Screw the adjusters into place, but do not tighten them yet.

7 Refit the lateral supports and side fasteners.

8 Adjust the bumper height as described in the previous Section, then lower the vehicle.

Rear

9 Release the side fasteners by turning them though 90°.

10 Remove the two Torx screws which secure the rear bumper to its mountings.

11 Disconnect the number plate light wiring and free the wiring from the bumper.

12 Pull the bumper away from the rear of the vehicle and remove it.

13 If a new bumper is being fitted, adjust the mounting brackets so that the distance between the bumper and bracket top faces is 111 mm (4.4 in)

14 Refit by reversing the removal operations. Lower the vehicle on completion.

36 Bumper mouldings - removal and refitting

Models before mid 1990

1 Remove the bumper as described in the previous Section

All models except Ghia

2 Prise the old moulding out of the bumper.

3 Scrape all remains of adhesive from the moulding groove in the bumper. Clean the groove with methylated spirit and allow it to dry.

4 Apply adhesive primer (to Ford spec. ESK-M2G-264A) to the bumper groove and allow it to dry. This primer should be obtained with the new moulding from a Ford dealer.

5 Heat the new moulding with (for instance) a hair dryer or fan heater until it is warm to the touch. Do not coil the moulding tighter than 300 mm (11.8 in) in diameter.

6 Peel the backing paper off the moulding. Insert one end into the slot at one end of the groove so that approximately 10 mm (0.4 in) protrudes through the slot. Press the moulding

into the groove, working along the bumper, and tuck the other end of the moulding into the slot at the far end. *Do not cut off the ends of the moulding, they are sealed to prevent water entering.*

7 Seat the moulding by running a hand-held roller along it.

8 Refit the bumper.

Ghia only

9 The procedure is similar to that just described, but with the following differences:

a) The moulding is secured with studs and nuts as well as with adhesive.

b) The adhesive tape is supplied separately from the moulding, and both bumper and moulding must be primed.

10 When purchasing the new moulding, also obtain the correct type of adhesive tape and primer.

Models from mid 1990

11 From approximately mid-1990, the bumper mouldings on all models should be removed and refitted using the information given above for the Ghia models, regardless of their specification.

37 Front spoiler - removal and refitting

1 A blind rivet gun will be needed to refit the spoiler.

2 Raise and support the front of the vehicle.

3 Drill out the two rivets at each end which secure the spoiler to the bumper.

4 Remove the twelve nuts and washers which secure the line of the spoiler to the bumper. Lift off the spoiler; it can be separated into two halves if wished.

5 When refitting, secure the ends of the spoiler first. Use new rivets and make sure that the bumper and spoiler are correctly aligned.

6 Refit and tighten the twelve nuts and washers. Lower the vehicle on completion.

38 Headlining - removal and refitting

1 Open the doors, the tailgate, the sliding roof (when fitted) and the bonnet.

2 Disconnect the battery negative lead.

3 Free the weatherstrips from the tops of the door apertures and from around the pillars.

4 On models with a sliding roof, remove the edge trim from the aperture.

5 Remove the tailgate hinge covers.

6 If a rear interior light is fitted, remove it.

7 Remove the grab handles and the sun visors.

8 Remove the front interior light, the sliding roof handle and the overhead console (as applicable).

9 Unbolt the front seat belt upper anchors. Remove the upper trim from the B-pillars. This trim is secured by a single screw on each side of the vehicle.

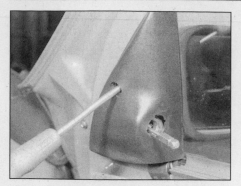

39.1a Removing the mirror mounting trim screw

39.1b Pull out the clip (arrowed) to release the mirror control

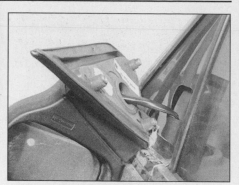

39.3 Removing a mirror from the door

10 Remove the securing screws and detach the C and D-pillar trim panels.

11 Remove the top of the facia panel.

12 Remove the securing screw from the base of the A-pillar trim on each side. Detach the A-pillar trim panels.

13 Remove the headlining through the tailgate, peeling it back from around the sliding roof (when applicable - see paragraph 15).

14 Refitting is essentially a reversal of the removal procedure. The services of an assistant will be required during the initial stages of refitting.

15 When a sliding roof is fitted, the headlining is secured around the aperture with double-sided adhesive tape.

39 Exterior mirror - removal and refitting

1 To remove a manually-adjusted mirror, first pull off the operating lever cover. Remove the triangular trim panel which covers the mirror mounting: this panel is secured by a single screw concealed under a cover. Pull out the

control retaining clip **(see illustrations)**.

2 For electrically-adjusted mirrors, remove the door interior trim panel (including the triangular trim panel) and peel back the top part of the foam sheet for access to the mirror multi-plug. Disconnect the multi-plug.

3 For all mirrors, support the mirror and remove the three securing screws. Lift the mirror off the door, disengaging the base from the rubber seal **(see illustration)**.

4 Refit by reversing the removal operations.

40 Interior mirror - removal and refitting

1 Remove the mirror from the windscreen by "sawing" through the adhesive bond with a piece of nylon cord.

2 Clean the mirror base and the mounting area on the windscreen with methylated spirit. Both items must be perfectly clean, and the windscreen must be at room temperature (20°C/68°F approx).

3 Peel off the backing paper from one side of the special adhesive patch. Press the sticky

side of the patch firmly onto the mirror base.

4 Warm the mirror base and patch to 50° to 70°C (122° to 158°F). Immediately remove the backing paper from the other side of the patch and press the mirror firmly onto the mounting area. Hold it in position for at least two minutes, and do not attempt to adjust the mirror for at least half an hour.

5 Beware of using proprietary adhesives to attach the mirror to the windscreen: not all are suitable and some may leave residues which are difficult to remove.

41 Facia panels and trim - removal and refitting

Models before April 1992

1 Disconnect the battery negative lead.

2 Remove the instrument panel surround, which is secured by four screws. Pull out the heater louvre panel.

3 Remove the facia top (crash pad), which is secured by five screws and four spring clips. With the screws and clip removed, a good tug will free the top from the clips next to the windscreen **(see illustration)**.

4 Remove the carpet and soft trim from below the facia on both sides. It is clipped in place.

5 Remove the driver's side lower trim panel, which is secured by six screws. One of the screws is only accessible after removing the air vent grille. Unclip the AWS bulb failure warning module, when fitted **(see illustration)**.

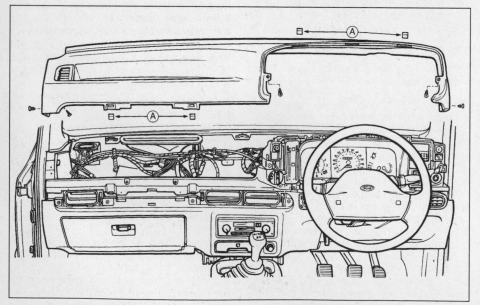

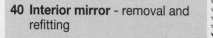

41.3 Facia top retaining screws and spring clips (A)

41.5 Remove the grille for access to the screw (arrowed)

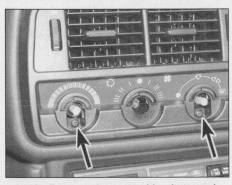

41.18a Remove the control knobs to gain access to the two hidden central vent panel retaining screws (arrowed)

41.18b Withdraw the central vent panel and disconnect the heated window and fuel computer wiring connectors

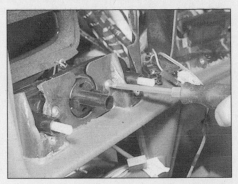

41.19 Undo the heater control panel retaining screws and free the panel from the facia

6 Disconnect the glovebox arms and hinges. Withdraw the hinge pins and remove the lid.

7 Slide the auxiliary fuse panel off its mounting and remove the glovebox light (when fitted).

8 Remove the ABS and ESC/EEC modules (Chapter 13). Remove the two nuts and washers from inside the glovebox.

9 Remove the radio, stowage box or graphic equaliser, ashtray, cigarette lighter panel and (when applicable) the gear lever gaiter.

10 Remove the centre console, disconnecting switches, rear heater controls etc as necessary.

11 Remove the six screws which secure the passenger's side lower panel. Remove the panel.

12 Refit by reversing the removal operations, transferring the brackets, captive nuts or other fittings to any new panels being fitted.

Models from April 1992

13 Disconnect the battery negative terminal.

14 Remove the centre console.

15 Remove the radio, amplifier unit and (where necessary) the CD player.

16 Remove the instrument cluster.

17 Remove the steering wheel and then the steering column direction indicator/headlight flasher switch and windscreen wipe/wash switch.

18 Pull off the three knobs from the heater and ventilation controls to gain access to the two hidden central vent panel retaining

screws. Slacken and remove the four panel retaining screws and partially withdraw the panel. Disconnect the wiring connectors from the heated window switches and fuel computer (where fitted) and remove the panel from the car (see illustrations).

19 Undo the two retaining screws and free the heater and ventilation control panel from the facia panel (see illustration).

20 Depress the retaining tang, situated at the bottom of the control knob, and remove the light switch knob from the switch (see illustration).

21 Withdraw the light switch from right-hand vent panel and disconnect the wiring plug (see illustration).

22 Remove the light switch surround from the vent panel and disconnect the wiring connector (see illustration).

23 Undo the three retaining screws and remove the right-hand vent panel from the facia (see illustration).

24 Remove the ashtray insert, then slacken and remove the three ashtray retaining screws. Remove the ashtray assembly, detaching the illumination lamp as it is removed (see illustration).

25 Undo the retaining screw then disconnect the wiring plugs and remove the cigarette lighter from the facia panel (see illustration).

26 Unclip and remove both the left- and right-hand facia undercover panels.

27 Carefully prise out the bonnet release lever surround to gain access to the lever retaining

41.20 Depress the tang (arrowed) and pull off the light switch control knob

41.21 Withdraw the light switch and disconnect the wiring plug

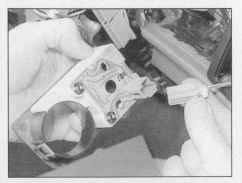

41.22 Withdraw the light switch surround and disconnect the wiring connector

41.23 Undo the three retaining screws (arrowed) to disconnect the right-hand vent

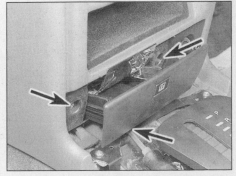

41.24 Ashtray retaining screw locations (arrowed)

12

41.25 Withdraw the cigarette lighter and disconnect the wiring plugs

41.27a Remove the three bonnet release lever retaining screws (arrowed)

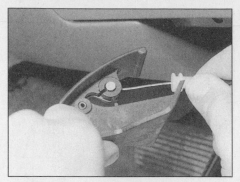

41.27b Withdraw the bonnet release lever and disconnect it from the operating cable

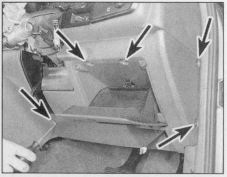

41.28 Undo the five right-hand lower facia panel retaining screws (arrowed)

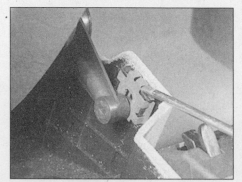

41.29a Lift the glovebox hinge retaining clips and disconnect the hinge arms

41.29b Withdraw the glovebox noting the plastic bushes (arrowed) which are fitted to the pivot bolts

41.29c Withdraw the glovebox illumination light and disconnect the wiring connector

41.30 Removing the passenger side lower kick panel

41.31a A-pillar trim panel retaining clip . . .

41.31b . . . and lower locating tab (viewed through windscreen)

41.32 Disconnect the alarm warning LED wiring connector

41.33 Removing the windscreen vent panel (viewed through the windscreen)

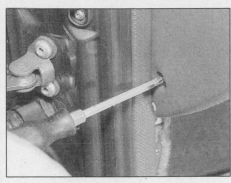

41.34a Facia left-hand mounting screw

41.34b Facia upper mounting screw

41.34c Facia mounting nuts (arrowed) situated in glovebox aperture

screws. Undo the three screws then withdraw the lever. Remove the cable retaining clip and detach the operating lever from the cable (see illustrations).

28 Slacken and remove the five right-hand lower facia panel retaining screws and remove the panel from the vehicle (see illustration).

29 Open up the glovebox then, using a small flat-bladed screwdriver, carefully prise up the retaining clip and disconnect the glovebox hinge arms. Withdraw the glovebox assembly from the facia noting the plastic bushes which are fitted to the glovebox pivot points. Withdraw the glovebox illumination light, disconnect the wiring connector and remove it from the facia (see illustrations).

30 Slacken and remove the three screws securing the passenger side lower kick panel in position and remove the panel (see illustration).

31 Carefully prise the upper end of the left-hand A-pillar trim out of position until all the retaining clips are released. Lift the panel up to disengage the lower tab from the pillar and remove the trim panel (see illustrations). Repeat the procedure for the right-hand panel.

32 Disconnect the alarm warning LED wiring connector which is accessed via the instrument cluster aperture (see illustration).

33 Carefully prise the windscreen vent panel out from the top of the facia to gain access to the upper facia retaining screws (see illustration).

34 Slacken and remove the facia retaining nuts and screws, then partially withdraw the

41.35a Partially withdraw the facia to gain access to left-hand support bracket retaining screws (arrowed) . . .

facia panel (see illustrations).

35 Undo the two screws securing the left-hand side facia support bracket to the body and remove the bracket (see illustrations).

36 Make a final check that all the necessary wiring retaining clips have been released then carefully manoeuvre the facia panel out of position and out from the vehicle.

37 Refitting is a reverse of the removal procedure noting the following points.
a) Manoeuvre the facia panel into position then refit the left-hand facia support bracket.
b) Ensure that all wiring connections are fed through the relevant apertures, then refit the facia retaining nuts and screws.

41.35b . . . then undo the screws and remove the bracket from behind the facia

c) Tighten all fasteners securely.
d) On completion reconnect the battery and check the operation of all switches and electrical components.

42 Centre console - removal and refitting

Models before April 1992

Low series

1 Remove the rubber mat and the two screw cover plugs from the front of the console. Remove the two front screws (see illustration).

2 Remove the gear lever knob by unscrewing it.

3 Remove the central securing screw, which is also concealed by a cover plug (see illustration) and the two rear screws (one each side of the handbrake).

4 Lift off the console, moving the handbrake and gear lever as necessary.

5 Refit by reversing the removal operations.

High series

6 Disconnect the battery negative lead.

7 Open the cassette box. Remove the two screws, accessible from under the lid, which secure the switch panel (see illustration). Raise the rear of the panel, disconnect the multi-plugs and remove it.

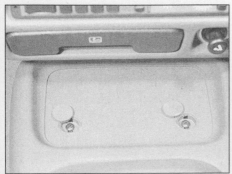

42.1 The two front screws which secure the low series console

42.3 The central console securing screw (low series)

12

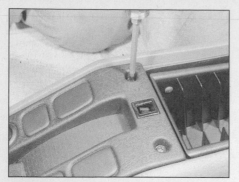

42.7 Removing a switch panel screw (high series)

42.8 Cassette box, showing securing screws (high series)

42.12 Removing a centre console front securing screw (high series)

42.17a On models equipped with automatic transmission remove the outer . . .

8 Remove the cassette box liner and the box itself, which is secured by two screws **(see illustration)**.

9 Remove the rear control panel by undoing the two screws in the top corners and pulling off the heater control knob. Disconnect the cigarette lighter, and other wiring when applicable.

10 Remove the two screws which secure the rear heater control.

11 Remove the gear selector knob by unscrewing it.

12 Remove the four remaining screws (two at the front and one on each side) **(see illustration)**. It may be necessary to cut the carpet to gain access to the side screws.

13 Remove the console, freeing it from the facia lower trim, the gear selector and the handbrake.

14 Refit by reversing the removal operations.

Models from April 1992

15 Disconnect the battery negative terminal.

16 On models equipped with a manual gearbox, carefully prise the gearchange lever trim panel out from the centre console then turn the outer gaiter inside out and unclip the trim panel.

17 On models equipped with automatic transmission carefully prise out the outer and inner selector lever trim panels **(see illustrations)**.

18 Open up the centre console rear compartment lid and remove the cassette storage box (where fitted) from the compartment to gain access to the rear console retaining screws.

42.17b . . . and inner selector lever trim panels

42.19a Slacken and remove the two switch panel retaining screws . . .

42.19b . . . for access to the wiring connectors (arrowed)

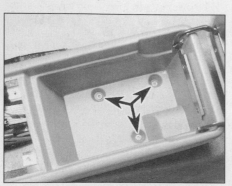

42.20a Centre console rear retaining screws (arrowed)

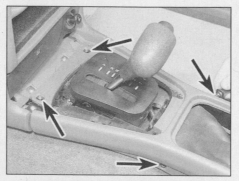

42.20b Centre console front retaining screw - locations (arrowed)

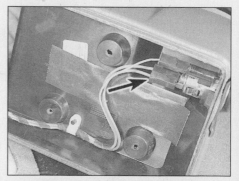

42.20c Disconnect the light wiring (arrowed) as the centre console is removed

43.4a One of the overhead console retaining screws

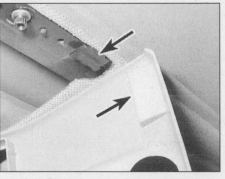

43.4b Slide the console rearwards to release the clips (arrowed)

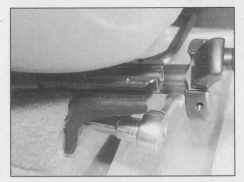

44.1 Removing a front seat retaining bolt

19 Slacken and remove the two switch panel retaining screws then carefully slide the panel up over the handbrake lever until the switch wiring connectors can be accessed **(see illustrations)**. Disconnect the wiring connectors from all the switches, then release the loom from any relevant retaining clips and manoeuvre the switch panel off the handbrake lever.

20 Slacken and remove the seven centre console retaining screws (two at the front, one on each side and three at the rear) then lift up the console and disconnect the wiring connector from the rear cigarette lighter. Remove the console assembly from the car **(see illustrations)**.

21 Refitting is a reverse of the removal procedure.

43 Overhead console - removal and refitting

1 Disconnect the battery negative lead.
2 Remove the interior light by carefully prising it out of the console and disconnecting it.
3 Remove the sliding roof control handle or switches (as applicable).
4 Remove the two retaining screws from the front of the console. Pull the front of the console down and then slide the assembly rearwards to release it from the two clips **(see illustrations)**. These clips may be quite tight. Disconnect the clock.
5 Refit by reversing the removal operations.

44 Front seat - removal and refitting

1 Move the seat rearwards as far as possible, then remove the two front retaining bolts **(see illustration)**.
2 Disconnect the assist spring from under the driver's seat. (Moving the seat forwards will reduce the tension on this spring, but also makes it harder to get at.)
3 When applicable, disconnect the seat heating and/or adjustment motor multi-plugs.
4 Move the seat fully forwards and remove the three rear retaining bolts. These bolts are under plastic covers **(see illustrations)**.
5 Lift out the seat, complete with adjustment mechanism and seat belt buckle.
6 If a new seat is being fitted, transfer the adjustment mechanism and other components to it.
7 Refit by reversing the removal operations. Tighten the seat retaining bolts to the specified torque.

45 Front seat air cushion - removal and refitting

1 Remove the front seat as described in the previous Section.
2 Remove the side trim pieces from the seat. Free the air tube by removing its two securing screws.
3 Separate the backrest from the base of the

seat by removing the four retaining bolts.
4 Remove the backrest cover by unbending its retaining tags and sliding it off.
5 Expose the air cushion by lifting up the foam padding. Cut the hog rings (wire loops) which secure the corners of the cushion and remove it with the air hoses.
6 When refitting, use new hog rings. Position the cut-out in the cushion level with the second spring in the backrest.
7 The remainder of refitting is a reversal of the removal procedure.

46 Seat belts - care and maintenance

1 All models are fitted with inertia reel front seat belts as standard. Rear seat belts are available as an extra.
2 Maintenance is limited to periodic inspection of the belts for fraying or other damage. Also check the operation of the buckles and retractor mechanisms. In case of damage or malfunction the belt must be renewed.
3 If it is wished to clean the belts, use only an approved upholstery cleaner or a weak solution of detergent, followed by rinsing with water. Do not use solvents, strong detergents, dyes or bleaches. Keep the belt extended until it is dry.
4 Belts which have been subjected to impact loads must be renewed.

47 Front seats belts - removal and refitting

1 Remove the cover from the belt top anchor. With the adjustable type of anchor **(see illustration)** the cover is removed by levering out the adjuster button and removing two screws.
2 Remove the anchor bolt or nut and detach the seat belt runner from it. Note the position of any washers or spacers.
3 Carefully pull out the door aperture weatherstrips (front and rear) from the B-pillar **(see illustration)**. Unclip the pillar trim.
4 Remove the screws which secure the retractor cover trim, pull away more of the

12

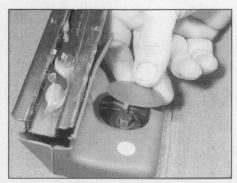

44.4a Front seat outboard rear retaining bolt

44.4b The other two rear retaining bolts are under the cover

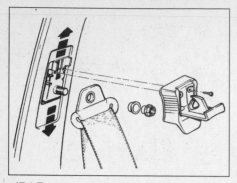

47.1 Front seat belt adjustable top anchor

47.3 Removing the weatherstrip from the B-pillar

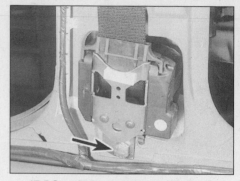

47.5 Seat belt retractor mechanism - securing the bolt arrowed

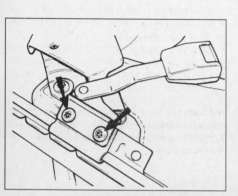

47.6 Front seat belt buckle secured by two Torx screws (arrowed)

weatherstrips and remove the trim. Also remove the webbing guide, which is secured by two screws.

5 Unbolt the lower anchor and the retractor, again noting the position of any washers or spacers. Remove the retractor and webbing **(see illustration)**.

6 The seat belt buckle is secured to the seat frame by two Torx screws **(see illustration)**. There is no need to renew the buckle just because the retractor and webbing are being renewed. If it is wished to remove the buckle, first remove the seat.

7 Refit by reversing the removal operations. Tighten all anchorages to the specified torque, and make sure that the belt is not twisted.

48 Rear seats belts - removal and refitting

1 This Section describes the removal and refitting of factory or dealer-installed rear seat belts. A rear belt kit can be purchased from a Ford dealer and should be found to correspond with the items shown here. If a proprietary kit is purchased, make sure it is suitable for the vehicle in question and follow the manufacturer's instructions.

2 Fold the rear seat cushion forwards.

3 Feed the buckle webbing through the slits in the carpet. Remove the buckle securing bolt, remove the pins from the buckle elastic straps and remove the buckles.

4 Remove the lower anchor bolts, then fold the seat backrests forwards. Fold back the luggage area carpet and remove the backrest hinges.

5 Remove the seat back striker pins (low series) or adjuster mechanism cover (high series) **(see illustration)**.

6 Prise the webbing guides from each side cushion.

7 Remove the side cushions. Each one is retained by a single nut and washer located near the loudspeaker **(see illustration)**. With the nut and washer removed, the cushion is then released by prising open the metal tags which secure its bottom wire. Pull the bottom of the cushion forwards and upwards to free it from the retractor.

8 The retractor can now be unbolted and the

webbing withdrawn through the side cushions.

9 Commence refitting by fitting the retractor. First fit the rear bolt and tighten it by a few turns only, so that the retractor is still free to move. Push the retractor rearwards and then downwards so that it takes up its fitted positions, then fit the front bolt. Tighten both bolts to the specified torque.

10 The remainder of refitting is a reversal of the removal procedure. Tighten the belt and buckle anchor bolts to the specified torque.

49 Rear seat components - removal and refitting

Cushion

1 Fold the seat cushion forwards and remove the hinge retaining screws **(see illustration)**. To remove the hinges as well, unbolt the hinges from the body instead.

2 When refitting, just nip up the hinge screws or bolts and check the fit of the cushions. Tighten the screws or bolts fully when satisfied.

Backrests

3 Fold the backrests forward and peel back the carpet to expose the hinges **(see illustration)**.

4 Remove the hinge screws, free the seat belt webbing clips (when applicable) and remove the backrests.

5 Refit by reversing the removal operations.

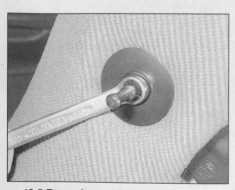

48.5 Removing a seat back striker pin

48.7 Removing a side cushion nut

49.1 Rear seat hinge-to-cushion screws

49.3 Rear seat backrest hinges. One of the backrests has been removed

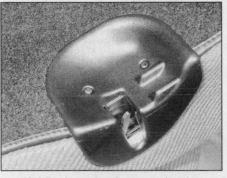

49.6 Backrest catch cover, showing securing screws

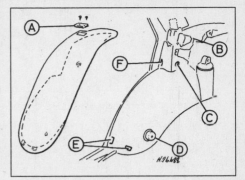

50.1 Rear seat side trim panel fasteners - Saloon models

Backrest catch

6 Fold the backrest forwards. Remove the catch cover, which is secured by two screws **(see illustration)**.

7 Remove the two Torx screws which secure the catch. Unhook the operating rod from the catch and remove it.

8 The operating rod and button can now be withdrawn if wished. When refitting, position the rod with the hooked end facing inwards.

9 Refit the catch, engage it with the operating rod and secure it with the Torx screws.

10 Refit and secure the catch cover. Check the catch for correct operation.

50 Rear parcel shelf - removal and refitting

1 On saloon models, fold the rear seat backs down then release the rear seat side trim panels and remove them from the car **(see illustration)**.

2 Remove the rear speakers.

3 Unclip the seven parcel shelf retaining clips (four situated along the front edge and three in the centre of the panel) then slide the shelf forwards to disengage it from the locating lugs. Manoeuvre the shelf out from the vehicle.

A Seat belt trim
B Retaining stud
C Seat catch fixing
D Seat hinge fixing
E Lower locating tangs
F Upper locating slot

4 Refitting is a reversal of the removal procedure ensuring that the shelf and rear seat side trims are held securely in position with the retaining clips.

12

Chapter 13
Body electrical system

Contents

Degrees of difficulty

Easy, suitable for novice with little experience	Fairly easy, suitable for beginner with some experience	Fairly difficult, suitable for competent DIY mechanic	Difficult, suitable for experienced DIY mechanic	Very difficult, suitable for expert DIY or professional

Specifications

General
System type . . . .   12 volt, negative earth

Light bulbs (typical)

	Fitting	Wattage
Headlights	H4	60/55
Auxiliary driving lights and front foglights	H3	55
Side/parking lights	Glass base	5
Direction indicators, reversing light and rear foglight	Bayonet	21
Stop and tail lights	Bayonet	21/5
Door open/kerb illumination lights, luggage area light	Bayonet	5
Number plate lights, reading light and footwell lights	Glass base	5
Engine bay light	Bayonet	10
Interior lights	Festoon	10
Vanity mirror light	Festoon	3
Glovebox light	Glass base	3
Ashtray light	Glass base	1.2
Instrument illumination, pilot and warning lights	Glass base	1.2/2.5
Heater control light	Glass base	1
Automatic transmission selector light and clock light	Bayonet	1.4

Fuses and circuit breakers- main fuse box

Fuse No	Rating (A)	Circuit(s) protected
1	20	LH main beam, LH auxiliary driving light
2	20	RH main beam, LH auxiliary driving light
3	10	LH dipped beam
4	10	RH dipped beam
5	10	LH side and tail lights
6	10	RH side and tail lights

13

Fuses and circuit breakers- main fuse box (continued)

Fuse No	Rating (A)	Circuit(s) protected
7	15	Instrument illumination, number plate lights
8	10	Control circuits for air conditioning, heated windscreen and ride height control
9	30	Headlight washer pump, tailgate and fuel filler flap release
10	20	Central locking system, interior lights, clock, mirror adjustment
11	20	Fuel pump (with air conditioning), taxi circuits
12	10	Hazard warning flasher
13	30	Heated seats, cigarette lighters
14	30	Horn
15	30	Wiper motors and screen washer pumps
16	30	Heated rear window, heated mirrors
17	20	Front foglights
18	30	Heater blower
19	10	Accessory circuits
20	15	Direction indicators, reversing lights
21	15	Stop-lights
22	10	Instrument and controls
23	C20	Power windows (front) and sliding roof
24	C20	Power windows (rear) and rear seat adjustment

C = Circuit breaker

Fuses and circuit breakers - auxiliary fuse box

Colour	Rating (A)	Circuit(s) protected
Black	20	Fuel-injection pump
Pink	20	Air conditioning cooling fan
Yellow	20	Anti-lock braking system control circuitry
Green	30	Anti-lock braking system pump
Brown	30	Heated windscreen (left-hand side)
Brown	30	Heated windscreen (right-hand side)
Grey	C20	Front seat adjustment
Orange	20	Ride height control

C = Circuit breaker

Relays in main fuse box

Identification	Function
I	Ignition circuit
II	Heated rear window and mirrors
III	Power windows and sliding roof
IV	Seat belt warning
V	Intermittent wipe - front
VI	Intermittent wipe - rear
VII	Headlight washer
VIII	Interior light delay
IX	Rear seat adjustment
X	Headlights (main beam)
XI	Engine auxiliary
XII	Automatic transmission inhibitor
A	Spare
B	Radio
C	Horn
D	Tailgate release
E	Spare
F	Headlights (dipped beam)
G	Seat heaters
H	Front foglights

Other relays and modules

Identification	Function
Behind facia (centre):	
L1	Lights on buzzer
L2	Rear fog light control
L3	Automatic transmission kickdown time
L4	Fuel pump (with air conditioning)
L5	Hydraulic switch
L6	Anti-theft alarm
Behind facia (passenger side):	
M1	Manifold heater (carburettor) or fuel pump (fuel-injection)
M2	Power hold (carburettor) or inspection valve (fuel-injection)
M3	Heated windscreen (power)

Other relays and modules (continued)

Identification	Function
Behind facia (passenger side) (continued):	
M4	Heated windscreen (timer)
M5	Air conditioning cooling fan
M6	ABS pump relay
M7	ABS main relay
M8	ABS control unit
M9	Ride height control
Below instrument panel (driver's side):	
N1	Bulb failure warning unit
Below facia (passenger side):	
P1	ABS module
P2	Fuel-injection system module
Behind facia (passenger side):	
R1	Speed control system module
R2	Auxiliary warning system module
R3	Rear audio console module

Torque wrench settings

	Nm	lbf ft
Alternator adjusting strap:		
To steering pump bracket (SOHC)	21 to 26	16 to 19
To front cover (V6)	41 to 51	30 to 38

1 General information

The electrical system is a 12 volt, negative earth type. Electricity is generated by an alternator, belt-driven from the crankshaft pulley. A lead-acid battery provides a reserve of power for starting and when the demands of the system temporarily exceed the alternator output.

The battery negative terminal is connected to "earth" - vehicle metal - and most electrical system components are wired so that they only receive a positive feed, the current returning via vehicle metal. This means that the component mounting forms part of the circuit. Loose or corroded mountings can therefore cause apparent electrical faults.

Many semiconductor devices are used in the electrical system, both in the "black boxes" which control vehicle functions and in other components. Semiconductors are very sensitive to excessive (or wrong polarity) voltage, and to extremes of heat. Observe the appropriate precautions to avoid damage.

Although some repair procedures are given in this Chapter, sometimes renewal of a well-used item will prove more satisfactory. The reader whose interests extend beyond component renewal should obtain a copy of the "Automobile Electrical Manual", available from the publishers of this book.

Before starting work on the electrical system, read the precautions listed in "Safety first!" at the beginning of the manual.

2 Electrical fault-finding - general information

Note: *Refer to the precautions given in "Safety first!" and in Section 1 of this Chapter before starting work. The following tests relate to testing of the main electrical circuits, and should not be used to test delicate electronic circuits (such as anti-lock braking systems), particularly where an electronic control unit (ECU) is involved.*

General

1 A typical electrical circuit consists of an electrical component, any switches, relays, motors, fuses, fusible links or circuit breakers related to that component, and the wiring and connectors which link the component to both the battery and the chassis. To help to pinpoint a problem in an electrical circuit, wiring diagrams are included at the end of this Chapter.

2 Before attempting to diagnose an electrical fault, first study the appropriate wiring diagram, to obtain a more complete understanding of the components included in the particular circuit concerned. The possible sources of a fault can be narrowed down by noting whether other components related to the circuit are operating properly. If several components or circuits fail at one time, the problem is likely to be related to a shared fuse or earth connection.

3 Electrical problems usually stem from simple causes, such as loose or corroded connections, a faulty earth connection, a blown fuse, a melted fusible link, or a faulty relay. Visually inspect the condition of all fuses, wires and connections in a problem circuit before testing the components. Use the wiring diagrams to determine which terminal connections will need to be checked in order to pinpoint the trouble-spot.

4 The basic tools required for electrical fault-finding include: a circuit tester or voltmeter (a 12-volt bulb with a set of test leads can also be used for certain tests), a self-powered test light (sometimes known as a continuity tester), an ohmmeter (to measure resistance), a battery and set of test leads, and a jumper wire, preferably with a circuit breaker or fuse incorporated, which can be used to bypass suspect wires or electrical components. Before attempting to locate a problem with test instruments, use the wiring diagram to determine where to make the connections.

5 To find the source of an intermittent wiring fault (usually due to a poor or dirty connection, or damaged wiring insulation), an integrity test can be performed on the wiring, which involves moving the wiring by hand, to see if the fault occurs as the wiring is moved. It should be possible to narrow down the source of the fault to a particular section of wiring. This method of testing can be used in conjunction with any of the tests described in the following sub-Sections.

6 Apart from problems due to poor connections, two basic types of fault can occur in an electrical circuit - open-circuit or short-circuit.

7 Open-circuit faults are caused by a break somewhere in the circuit, which prevents current from flowing. An open-circuit fault will prevent a component from working, but will not cause the relevant circuit fuse to blow.

8 Short-circuit faults are caused by a "short" somewhere in the circuit, which allows the current flowing in the circuit to "escape" along an alternative route, usually to earth. Short-circuit faults are normally caused by a breakdown in wiring insulation, which allows a feed wire to touch either another wire, or an earthed component such as the bodyshell. A short-circuit fault will normally cause the relevant circuit fuse to blow. **Note:** *A short-circuit that occurs in the wiring between a circuit's battery supply and its fuse will not cause the fuse in that particular circuit to blow. This part of the circuit is unprotected - bear this in mind when fault-finding on the vehicle's electrical system.*

Finding an open-circuit

9 To check for an open-circuit, connect one lead of a circuit tester or voltmeter to either the negative battery terminal or a known good earth.

10 Connect the other lead to a connector in the circuit being tested, preferably nearest to the battery or fuse.

11 Switch on the circuit, bearing in mind that some circuits are live only when the ignition switch is moved to a particular position.

12 If voltage is present (indicated either by the tester bulb lighting or a voltmeter reading, as applicable), this means that the section of

13

the circuit between the relevant connector and the battery is problem-free.

13 Continue to check the remainder of the circuit in the same fashion.

14 When a point is reached at which no voltage is present, the problem must lie between that point and the previous test point with voltage. Most problems can be traced to a broken, corroded or loose connection.

Finding a short-circuit

15 To check for a short-circuit, first disconnect the load(s) from the circuit (loads are the components which draw current from a circuit, such as bulbs, motors, heating elements, etc).

16 Remove the relevant fuse from the circuit, and connect a circuit tester or voltmeter to the fuse connections.

17 Switch on the circuit, bearing in mind that some circuits are live only when the ignition switch is moved to a particular position.

18 If voltage is present (indicated either by the tester bulb lighting or a voltmeter reading), this means that there is a short-circuit.

19 If no voltage is present, but the fuse still blows with the load(s) connected, this indicates an internal fault in the load(s).

Finding an earth fault

20 The battery negative terminal is connected to "earth" - the metal of the engine/transmission and the car body - and most systems are wired so that they only receive a positive feed, the current returning via the metal of the car body. This means that the component mounting and

the body form part of that circuit. Loose or corroded mountings can therefore cause a range of electrical faults, ranging from total failure of a circuit, to a puzzling partial fault. In particular, lights may shine dimly (especially when another circuit sharing the same earth is in operation), motors (eg wiper motors or the radiator cooling fan motor) may run slowly, and the operation of one circuit may have an apparently-unrelated effect on another. Note that on many vehicles, earth straps are used between certain components, such as the engine/transmission and the body, usually where there is no metal-to-metal contact between components, due to flexible rubber mountings, etc.

21 To check whether a component is properly earthed, disconnect the battery, and connect one lead of an ohmmeter to a known good earth point. Connect the other lead to the wire or earth connection being tested. The resistance reading should be zero; if not, check the connection as follows.

22 If an earth connection is thought to be faulty, dismantle the connection, and clean back to bare metal both the bodyshell and the wire terminal, or the component's earth connection mating surface. Be careful to remove all traces of dirt and corrosion, then use a knife to trim away any paint, so that a clean metal-to-metal joint is made. On reassembly, tighten the joint fasteners securely; if a wire terminal is being refitted, use serrated washers between the terminal and the bodyshell, to ensure a clean and secure connection. When the connection is remade, prevent the onset of corrosion in the future by

applying a coat of petroleum jelly or silicone-based grease, or by spraying on (at regular intervals) a proprietary ignition sealer, or a water-dispersant lubricant.

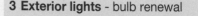

3 Exterior lights - bulb renewal

Headlight

1 Open and prop the bonnet. Remove the cover from the rear of the headlight unit by twisting it anti-clockwise.

2 Disconnect the wiring plug from the headlight bulb. Release the spring clip by squeezing its legs together and move it clear of the bulb (see illustration).

3 Remove the headlight bulb (see illustration). Caution: *If the lights have just been in use, the bulb may be extremely hot.*

4 When handling the new bulb, use a tissue or clean cloth to avoid touching the glass with the fingers. If the glass is accidentally touched, wipe it clean using methylated spirit. Moisture and grease from the skin can cause blackening and rapid failure of the new bulb.

5 Fit the new bulb, making sure that the legs and cut-outs in the bulb base and the reflector match up. Secure with the spring clip.

6 Reconnect the wiring plug. Check the headlight for correct operation, then refit and secure the rear cover.

Front parking light (sidelight)

7 Gain access as for the headlight bulb, then pull the parking light bulbholder from the headlight reflector.

8 Extract the wedge base bulb from the holder (see illustration). Fit the new bulb, refit the bulbholder and check for correct operation.

Auxiliary driving light (when fitted)

9 From above the auxiliary light unit, release the cover spring clip and remove the cover (see illustration).

10 Release the spring clip from the bulb. Withdraw the bulb and unplug its wiring connector (see illustration). Caution: *If the lights have just been in use, the bulb may be extremely hot.*

11 Do not touch the glass of the new bulb with the fingers.

3.2 Squeeze the spring clip legs (arrowed) to remove the headlight bulb

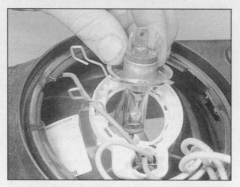

3.3 Removing a headlight bulb

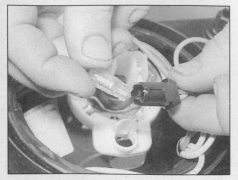

3.8 Removing the front parking light bulb from the holder

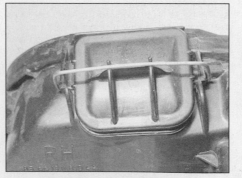

3.9 Auxiliary driving light cover

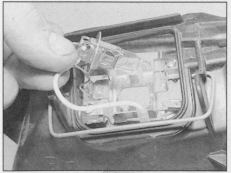

3.10 Removing the auxiliary driving light bulb

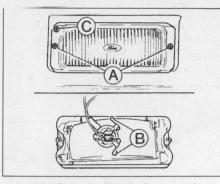

3.14 Front foglight bulb renewal

A Rotating screws   C Alignment screw
B Spring clip

12 Connect the new bulb, fit it and secure it with the spring clip.
13 Check the light for correct operation, then refit and secure the cover.

Front foglight (when fitted)

14 Remove the lens and reflector together by undoing the two retaining screws. Do not disturb the alignment screw **(see illustration)**.
15 Disconnect the wiring from the bulb. Release the spring clip and extract the bulb.
Caution: *If the lights have just been in use, the bulb may be extremely hot.*
16 Do not touch the glass of the new bulb with the fingers.
17 Fit the new bulb and secure it with the spring clip. Reconnect the wiring.

3.24a Removing a direction indicator side repeater

3.27 Rear light cluster bulbholder retaining lugs (arrowed)

3.19 Unhook the spring (arrowed) to release the front indicator light unit

18 Refit the lens and reflector and secure it with the two screws. Check for correct operation.

Front direction indicator

19 From under the bonnet, unhook the spring which secures the direction indicator light unit **(see illustration)**.
20 Withdraw the light unit and free the bulbholder from it by twisting it anti-clockwise **(see illustration)**.
21 Remove the bulb from the holder by pushing and twisting anti-clockwise. Fit the new bulb to the holder, refit the bulb and holder to the light unit and refit and secure the light unit.
22 Check the direction indicators for correct operation.

Direction indicator side repeaters

23 Reach up behind the wing and release the light unit by squeezing the two release tags together.
24 Pull the light unit out of the wing. Twist the bulbholder anti-clockwise to release it. Pull out the old bulb and press in the new one **(see illustrations)**.
25 Refit the bulbholder, then insert the light unit into its hole and press it home.

Rear light cluster

26 Access to rear light cluster bulbs is gained from within the luggage area. First remove the

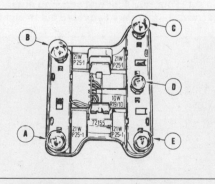

3.28 Identification of rear light bulbs

A Reversing light   D Tail light
B Direction indicator E Rear foglight
C Stop-light

3.20 Removing the bulb and holder from the direction indicator light unit

access cover on the side concerned; on the right-hand side, also remove the jack.
27 Grasp the bulbholder in the apertures provided, squeeze the retaining lugs together and withdraw the bulbholder **(see illustration)**.
28 The appropriate bulb(s) can now be renewed, and the bulbholder refitted **(see illustration)**.

Number plate light

29 Carefully prise the light unit out of the bumper with a screwdriver.
30 Twist the light unit and bulbholder anti-clockwise to separate them **(see illustration)**. Pull out the wedge base bulb and press in the new one.
31 Reassemble the light unit and bulbholder, then push the assembly home.

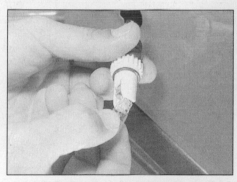

3.24b Fitting a new side repeater bulb

3.30 Separate the unit to gain access to the number plate light bulb

13

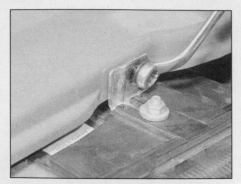

4.6a Headlight top mounting screw

4.6b Headlight bottom mounting screw

4.6c Headlight side mounting nut

4 Exterior light units - removal and refitting

1 For removal and refitting of the front foglights, front direction indicators, direction indicator repeaters and the number plate lights, refer to the previous Section.

Headlight

2 Unhook the direction indicator light unit retaining spring. Withdraw the direction indicator unit and allow it to hang.
3 Pull out the rubber moulding from between the base of the headlight and the bumper. (This moulding may in fact be stuck to the headlight surround.)
4 Release the headlight surround retaining lugs, prising them carefully with a screwdriver. Work from the outside towards the centre of the vehicle. Remove the surround by pulling it forwards and then sideways.
5 Remove the radiator grille, secured by two screws.
6 Disconnect the headlight wiring connector. Remove the two retaining screws, and the nut on the side mounting (see illustrations). Draw the headlight unit forwards and twist it to remove it.
7 Refit by reversing the removal operations. Make sure that the locating pin on the outside of the headlight unit engages in the hole in the apron panel.
8 If the new unit has been fitted, or if the adjusting screws have been disturbed, have the beam alignment checked without delay.

9 Note that the headlight lens can be renewed independently of the rest of the unit, once the securing clips have been removed (see illustration).

Auxiliary driving light

10 This is integral with the headlight unit.

Rear light cluster

Hatchback

11 Remove the rear light cluster bulbholder as described in the previous Section.
12 Remove the six nuts which secure the rear light unit (see illustration).
13 Withdraw the light unit from the vehicle and disconnect the multi-plug and wiring harness from it (see illustration).
14 Fit a new gasket to the light unit if the old one was damaged.
15 Refit by reversing the removal operations.

Saloon

16 Remove the relevant trim panel from the rear corner of the boot, noting that it may be necessary to remove one or more of the rear lower trim panel retaining screws (see illustration).
17 Disconnect the wiring connector from the rear light cluster, then undo the four retaining nuts and withdraw the light unit from the car along with the rubber sealing gasket (see illustration).
18 Refitting is a reverse of removal ensuring that the light unit rubber sealing gasket is in good condition.

4.9 Removing a headlight lens securing clip

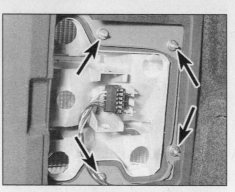

4.12 Four rear light unit securing nuts (arrowed) - there are two more out of sight

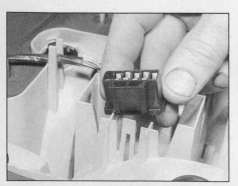

4.13 Disconnecting the multi-plug from the rear light unit

4.16 Remove the trim panel for access to the rear light cluster retaining nuts

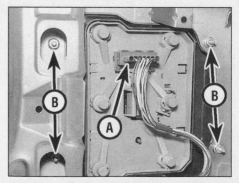

4.17 Rear light cluster wiring connector (A) and retaining nuts (B)

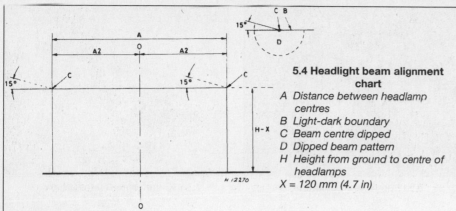

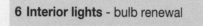

5.4 Headlight beam alignment chart
A Distance between headlamp centres
B Light-dark boundary
C Beam centre dipped
D Dipped beam pattern
H Height from ground to centre of headlamps
X = 120 mm (4.7 in)

5.5 Headlight beam adjustment screws (arrowed)

Estate

19 This procedure is the same as described above for the Saloon models noting that it is necessary to remove the luggage compartment side trim panel to gain access to the light cluster retaining nuts.

5 Headlight beam alignment

1 It is recommended that beam adjustment be carried out by a Ford garage using optical alignment equipment. In an emergency, however, the following procedure will produce acceptable results.
2 The vehicle should be normally laden and the tyre pressures must be correct. Park the vehicle on level ground, approximately 10 metres (33 feet) in front of a flat wall or garage door.
3 Draw a vertical line on the wall or door corresponding to the centre-line of the vehicle. (The position of this line can be determined by marking the centres of the windscreen and rear window with crayon, then viewing the wall or door from the rear of the vehicle.)
4 With the centre-line established, construct the other lines shown **(see illustration)**.
5 Switch the headlights on to dipped beam. Cover one headlight with cloth and adjust the other, using the two screws at the rear of the unit, to bring the centre of the beam to the point C on the appropriate side of the alignment chart **(see illustration)**.

6 Transfer the cloth to the adjusted headlight, and repeat the adjustment on the other headlight.
7 Have the alignment checked professionally at the first opportunity.

6 Interior lights - bulb renewal

1 Always switch the light off, or disconnect the battery negative lead, before changing a bulb.

Courtesy light

2 Carefully prise the light unit from its location. If reading (spot) lights are fitted, prise from the middle; if not, prise from one end **(see illustration)**.
3 Renew the bulb(s), detaching the reflector or contact plate as necessary.
4 Reassemble the light unit and press it home.

Vanity mirror light

5 Carefully prise the frame off the mirror to expose the bulbs **(see illustration)**.
6 Unclip the blown bulb(s) and press in the new ones. Make sure that the spring contacts which secure the bulb are clean and tight; bend them slightly to improve their tension if necessary.
7 Check for correct operation, then snap the mirror frame home.

Door lights

8 The door open warning light can be removed from the edge of the door by prising

the lens from the inside edge **(see illustration)**.
9 Renew the bulb and press the lens home.
10 The kerb illumination light is renewed in a similar way. Prise out the lens using the slot provided, renew the bulb and refit the lens **(see illustration)**.

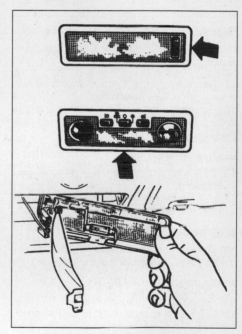

6.2 Courtesy light bulb renewal
Prise at points arrowed

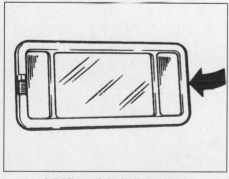

6.5 Mirror light bulb renewal
Prise frame at point arrowed

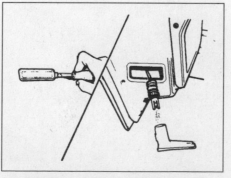

6.8 "Door open" light bulb renewal

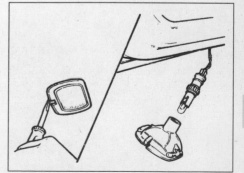

6.10 Kerb illumination light bulb renewal

13

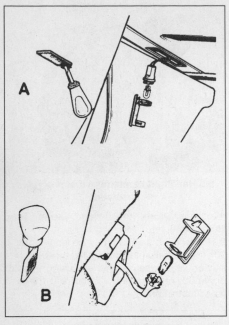

6.11 Footwell light bulb renewal - front (A) and rear (B)

Footwell lights

11 Free the light unit by carefully prising with a screwdriver **(see illustration)**.
12 Extract the bulbholder by twisting and pulling. Renew the bulb, refit the holder and press the light unit home.

Luggage area light

13 Carefully prise free the light unit **(see illustration)**.
14 Pull out the old bulb, press in the new one and refit the light unit.

Engine bay light

15 This light bulb is directly accessible once the bonnet is opened. It is of the bayonet type.

Instrument panel lights

16 Remove the instrument cluster.
17 Extract the appropriate bulb and holder by twisting it 90° anti-clockwise **(see illustration)**.
18 Large bulbs are of the wedge base type

6.13 Luggage area light unit

and can be pulled out of their holders. Small bulbs and holders cannot be separated, but must be renewed complete.
19 Refit the bulbs and holder, then refit the instrument panel.

Switch illumination lights

20 The pilot lights in the minor switches cannot be renewed independently of the switch.
21 The bulbs which illuminate the lighting master switch and the heater blower switch can be renewed after pulling off the switch knob **(see illustration)**.
22 The switch symbols in the instrument panel surround are illuminated by a single bulb. To gain access to the bulb, remove the instrument panel surround, which is secured by four screws. The bulb is of the wedge base type **(see illustration)**.

Glovebox light

23 Open the glovebox. Remove the combined switch/light unit, which is secured by two screws **(see illustration)**.
24 Prise out the switch, renew the bayonet fitting bulb and refit the switch
25 Refit and secure the light unit with the two screws.

Ashtray light

26 Remove the storage box or audio unit from just above the ashtray **(see illustration)**.
27 Free the bulbholder from above the ashtray, either by pulling it outwards (low series trim) or by carefully prising it away from its housing using a screwdriver (high series trim).

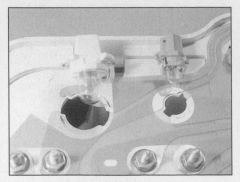

6.17 Instrument panel lights

28 Renew the wedge base bulb. Refit the bulbholder and the other disturbed components.

Radio fader light

29 Carefully prise off the fader surround.
30 Extract the bulbholder by twisting it anti-clockwise. Disconnect its wiring plug and remove it.
31 The bulb and holder cannot be separated. Fit the new bulbholder unit, check for correct operation, then refit the fader surround.

Heater control light

32 Remove the instrument panel surround.
33 Pull off the heater control knobs, then prise the display panel off the heater controls to expose the bulb.

6.21 Pull off the switch knob to expose the bulb

6.22 Removing the switch symbol illumination light

6.23 The glovebox light unit

6.26 Ashtray light bulb seen through radio aperture

6.34 Renewing the heater control light bulb

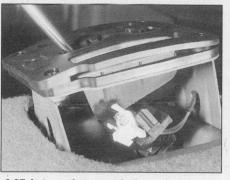

6.37 Automatic transmission selector with bulbholder displaced

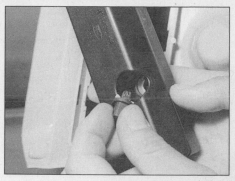

6.51 Renewing the clock bulb

34 Renew the bulb, check for correct operation, then refit the disturbed components (see illustration).

Automatic transmission selector light

35 Carefully pull off the selector housing. Remove the selector knob by unscrewing it.
36 Release the selector indicator plate, which is secured by two clips. Remove the indicator plate by sliding it up the selector stalk.
37 Remove the selector guide plate, which is secured by four screws. Extract the bulbholder and renew the bulb (see illustration).
38 An alternative means of access is by removing the centre console.
39 Refit by reversing the removal operations.

Rear console light

40 Remove the rear heater control lever knob by pulling it off.
41 Remove the rear console panel, which is secured by two screws at the top.
42 Free the bulbholder by twisting it anti-clockwise. Renew the wedge base bulb.
43 Refit the bulbholder and the other disturbed components.

Hazard warning switch light

44 Remove the steering column upper shroud, which is secured by three screws.
45 Make sure that the switch is in the "off" position, then pull off the switch cap.
46 Pull out the wedge base bulb and press in the new one.

47 Refit the switch cap and the steering column upper shroud.

Clock light

48 If the clock is in the instrument panel, renewal is as described for the other instrument panel lights.
49 To renew the light bulb in the overhead type of clock, first remove the overhead console.
50 Remove the back of the clock, which is secured by two screws, for access to the bulb.
51 Renew the bayonet fitting bulb (see illustration). Refit the back of the clock, then refit the overhead console.

7 Instrument cluster - removal and refitting

Models before April 1992

1 Although not essential, it is wise to disconnect the battery negative lead.
2 Remove the instrument panel surround, which is secured by four screws. Disengage the switch symbol illumination light from the surround.
3 Remove the four screws which secure the instrument cluster.
4 Partly withdraw the instrument cluster, disconnect the multi-plugs and remove the cluster (see illustrations). The multi-plugs are colour coded and not interchangeable; when a graphic display module is fitted, its multi-plug

has a red locking mechanism which must be retracted before the plug can be disconnected.
5 Refit by reversing the removal operations.

Models from April 1992

6 For these models, note the following points:
a) *The instrument cluster surround is retained by two screws and two clips. It will also be necessary to disconnect the panel dimmer switch (see illustration).*
b) *When removing the cluster note that it will also be necessary to release the retaining clip and disconnect the speedometer cable (see illustration). On refitting push the cable back into position and check that it is securely held in position with the retaining clip.*

7.4a Instrument cluster viewed through windscreen to show multi-plugs

7.4b Removing the instrument cluster

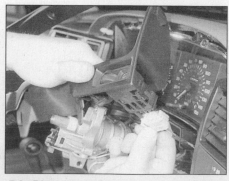

7.6a Disconnect the dimmer switch wiring connector as the surround is removed

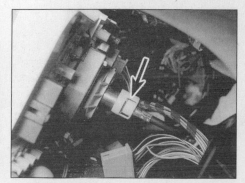

7.6b Release the retaining clip and disconnect the cable from the cluster

13

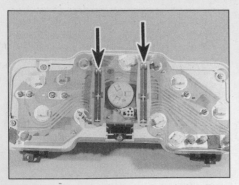

8.3 Instrument cluster printed circuit
Unclip retainers at their top ends (arrowed)

12.3 Three screws (arrowed) secure the horn switch plate

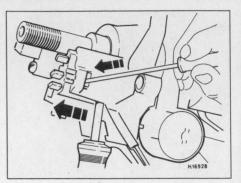

12.10 Removing the horn brush unit

8 Instrument cluster - dismantling and reassembly

1 With the instrument cluster removed, a particular gauge or other component can be renewed by following the appropriate parts of this Section.
2 Remove all the light bulbs and holders from the rear of the panel by twisting them anti-clockwise.
3 To remove the printed circuit, unclip and remove the two multi-plug terminal retainers. Remove all the nuts and washers from the printed circuit terminals, then unclip and remove the printed circuit. Be careful with it, it is fragile **(see illustration)**.
4 To remove the instrument cluster glass, release the two securing clips from the bottom edge of the glass. Swing the glass upwards and remove it.
5 With the glass removed, the speedometer, fuel and temperature gauges can be removed individually after undoing their securing nuts or screws. To remove the clock or tachometer, the printed circuit must be removed as well.
6 When fitted, the low fuel/high temperature warning light bulbs can be renewed after removing the combined gauge unit. Use tweezers to extract the old bulb and to fit the new one.
7 The graphic display module, when fitted, can be removed after undoing its two securing screws.
8 Reassemble the instrument cluster by reversing the dismantling operations.

9 Clock - removal and refitting

1 To remove the clock from the instrument panel, refer to the previous Section.
2 To remove the clock from the overhead console, first remove the console.
3 Remove the clock rear cover, which is secured by two screws.
4 Remove the two screws which secure the clock itself, then withdraw the clock.
5 Refit by reversing the removal operations.

10 Cigarette lighter - removal and refitting

1 Disconnect the battery negative lead.

Front lighter

2 On models with high level trim, pull the centre console surround away from the radio to gain access to the lighter. On models with low level trim, remove the radio/cassette unit.
3 Disconnect the wires from the cigarette lighter and push it out of the illuminated ring.
4 Refit by reversing the removal operations.

Rear lighter

5 Pull off the rear heater control lever knob.
6 Remove the rear console panel, which is secured by two screws.
7 Disconnect the wires from the lighter and push it out of the illuminated ring.
8 Refit by reversing the removal operations.

11 Horn - removal and refitting

1 Two horns are fitted as standard. The high tone horn is located to the right of the radiator and is accessible from under the bonnet. The low tone horn is located below and to the left of the radiator and is accessible from below.
2 Remove the horn securing nut or bolt and recover the shakeproof washer.
3 Disconnect the wiring and remove the horn.

13.3 Seat heating element
Thermostat (arrowed) must face the foam

4 When refitting the horn, make sure it is correctly positioned before tightening the securing nut or bolt.

12 Horn switch plate, slip rings and brushes - removal and refitting

1 Disconnect the battery negative lead.

Switch plate

2 Pull off the steering wheel centre cover.
3 Undo the three screws which retain the switch plate. Disconnect and remove the switch plate **(see illustration)**.
4 Refit by reversing the removal operations.

Slip rings

5 Remove the steering wheel.
6 Release the tangs which secure the slip rings to the underside of the steering wheel. Disconnect the slip rings from the switch plate and remove them.
7 Refit by reversing the removal operations.

Brushes

8 Remove the steering wheel.
9 Remove the steering column upper and lower shrouds.
10 Disconnect the wiring from the horn brushes. Carefully lever out the brush unit, using a thin screwdriver inserted into the bottom edge of the unit **(see illustration)**.
11 Refit by reversing the removal operations.

13 Seat heating elements - removal and refitting

1 Remove the seat.
2 Remove the seat cushion or backrest trim.
3 Note which way round the heating element is facing **(see illustration)**, then remove the wire clips and adhesive tape which secure it to the seat. Retrieve the tie-rod and fit it to the new element.
4 Fit the new element with the thermostat facing the cushion foam. Secure the element with wire clips and tape, ensuring that it is not too tight - it must be able to flex under load.
5 Refit the cushion or backrest trim.
6 Refit the seat and check the heating elements for correct operation.

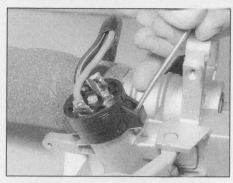

14.3 Ignition/starter switch removal
Depress the retaining tabs to lift off the switch

15.10 Removing the instrument illumination dimmer switch

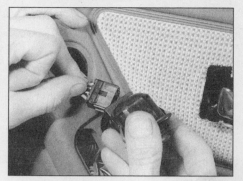

15.15 Removing a mirror control switch

14 Ignition/starter switch - removal and refitting

1 Disconnect the battery negative lead.
2 Remove the steering column upper and lower shrouds.
3 Remove the switch by depressing its two retaining tabs. Unplug the wiring connector and remove the switch **(see illustration)**.
4 When refitting, make sure that the slot in the centre of the switch is aligned with the driver on the lock.
5 Reconnect the switch and push it home until the retaining tabs click into place.
6 Reconnect the battery and check the switch for correct operation, then refit the steering column shrouds.

15 Switches - removal and refitting

1 Disconnect the battery negative lead, or satisfy yourself that there is no risk of a short-circuit, before removing any switch.
2 Except where noted, a switch is refitted by reversing the removal operations.

Lighting master switch

Models before April 1992

3 Pull the knob off the lighting switch.
4 Depress the two retaining lugs and pull the switch out of the instrument panel surround.

5 Disconnect the multi-plug from the switch and remove it.

Models from April 1992

6 Note that there is a retaining lug on the bottom of the switch knob which must be depressed before the knob can be removed.

Heater blower switch

Models before April 1992

7 This is removed in the same way as the lighting master switch.

Models from April 1992

8 The switch can be removed and refitted as described for the heater controls in Chapter 3.

Instrument illumination dimmer switch

9 Remove the instrument panel surround, which is retained by four screws.
10 Pull the dimmer switch from its location and disconnect the multi-plug **(see illustration)**.
11 Although the switch looks as if it can be dismantled, this should not be attempted unless the switch is surplus to requirements, and a new unit is readily available.

Models up to April 1992

12 On these models, remove the four instrument cluster surround retaining screws and remove the surround from the facia. Carefully prise the switch out of the aperture and disconnect the wiring connector.

Models from April 1992

13 On these models, remove the two instrument cluster surround retaining screws and release the two retaining clips. Remove the surround from the facia and disconnect the wiring connector from the dimmer switch. Depress the dimmer switch retaining tangs and slide the switch out of the surround.

Mirror control switch

14 Carefully prise the switch out of the armrest using a thin-bladed screwdriver. Protect the armrest with a piece of cloth or thick card.
15 Disconnect the multi-plug and remove the switch **(see illustration)**.

Direction indicator/headlight flasher switch and unit

Models before April 1992

16 Remove the steering wheel centre cover.
17 Remove the steering column upper and lower shrouds, which are secured by a total of six screws.
18 Unlock the steering and turn the steering wheel to gain access to the two screws which retain the switch **(see illustration)**. Remove the screws.
19 Withdraw the switch from the steering column and disconnect its multi-plug **(see illustration)**. It may be necessary to release some cable-ties in order to free the multi-plug. The flasher unit is plugged into the side of the switch furthest from the wheel **(see illustration)**.

15.18 Two screws (arrowed) secure the switch. Steering wheel removed for clarity

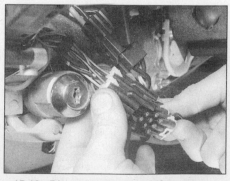

15.19a Disconnecting a steering column switch multi-plug

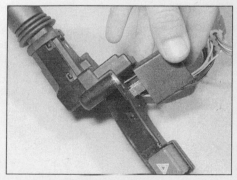

15.19b Unplugging the direction indicator flasher unit

13

15.24 Door pillar switch securing screws (arrowed)

15.31 Removing a window operating switch

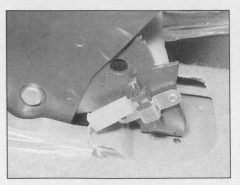

15.39 Handbrake "On" switch

20 When refitting, check the switch for correct operation before refitting the shrouds and steering wheel centre cover. When fitting the shrouds, be careful not to trap the switch rubber gaiter.

Models from April 1992

21 Note that if access to the switch retaining screws cannot be gained with the steering wheel in position, then the steering wheel must first be removed.

Windscreen wipe/wash switch

Models before April 1992

22 Proceed as described in the previous sub-section for the direction indicator switch. Depending on equipment, the wipe/wash switch may have more than one multi-plug connected to it.

Models from April 1992

23 Note that if access to the switch retaining screws cannot be gained with the steering wheel in position, then the steering wheel must first be removed.

Door pillar switch (for courtesy light)

24 Remove the single securing screw and pull the switch from its location (see illustration).
25 Retain the wiring with (for instance) string or a clothes peg, so that it cannot fall into the door pillar, then disconnect the switch.
26 Lubricate the plunger of the switch with a little petroleum jelly when refitting

Reversing light switch (manual gearbox)

27 Raise the front of the vehicle and support it securely.
28 Locate the reversing light switch, which is located on the right-hand side of the gearbox.
29 Disconnect the wiring from the switch, wipe clean around it and unscrew it.
30 When refitting, make sure that the switch wiring is routed sufficiently far from the exhaust system to avoid damage due to heat.

Window operating switch

31 The window operating switch is removed from the armrest or console in the same way as the mirror control switch previously described (see illustration).

Sliding roof switch

32 Carefully prise the switch from the overhead console using a thin-bladed screwdriver.
33 Disconnect the multi-plug and remove the switch.

Tailgate lock switch

34 The tailgate lock switch controls the luggage area lights. When appropriate, it also provides inputs to the auxiliary warning and anti-theft systems.
35 To avoid damage to other components, the battery must be disconnected before the tailgate lock switch is removed.
36 Remove the tailgate interior trim panel, which is secured by eleven screws.

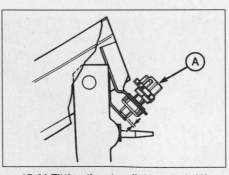

15.44 Fitting the stop-light switch (A)
Plunger protrusion (between arrows) must be at least 2 mm (0.08 in)

37 Release the switch locking tab, pivot the switch away from the lock and disconnect it.
38 When refitting, make sure that the slot on the switch engages with the operating lug on the lock barrel.

Handbrake "ON" switch

39 Gain access to the base of the handbrake lever by removing the rubber gaiter and (if necessary) the centre console or switch panel (see illustration).
40 Disconnect the wiring from the handbrake switch. Undo the two screws and remove the switch, noting how the screws do not pass through holes in the lever but engage in slots.
41 After refitting the switch, check for correct operation before refitting the surrounding trim.

Stop-light switch

42 Remove the under-dash trim on the driver's side. The trim is secured by plastic clips.
43 Disconnect the wiring from the switch. Turn the switch 90° anti-clockwise and remove it from the brake pedal bracket (see illustration).
44 When refitting, hold the pedal in the fully raised position, push in the switch and turn it clockwise to lock it. Release the pedal and check that at least 2 mm (0.08 in) of the switch plunger is visible (see illustration).

Oil pressure warning switch

All engines except DOHC

45 This switch is located on the left-hand side of the cylinder block. Access may be impeded by one of the manifolds and associated equipment.
46 Disconnect the wire from the switch, then unscrew the switch and remove it.
47 Clean the switch and its seat before refitting. Apply a little sealant to the switch threads if wished.
48 Run the engine and check that there are no oil leaks from the switch. Stop the engine and check the oil level.

DOHC engines

49 On these engines the switch is located on the right-hand side of the cylinder block between the core plugs.

15.43 Stop-light switch fitted to brake pedal bracket

Heated rear window switch

Models before April 1992

50 Remove the instrument panel surround, which is secured by four screws.

51 Carefully prise the switch from its location, disconnect the multi-plug and remove it.

Models from April 1992

52 Using a small flat-bladed screwdriver, carefully prise the switch out of the centre facia vent panel and disconnect the wiring connector.

53 On refitting, reconnect the wiring connector and push the switch in until it clicks into position.

Foglight switch(es)

54 These are removed in the same way as the heated rear window switch (see illustration).

Hazard warning switch

55 This is integral with the direction indicator switch.

Front seat adjusting switch

56 Remove the seat trim panel.

57 Prise the operating levers off the switch with a thin-bladed screwdriver (see illustration).

58 Remove the two securing screws, withdraw the switch and unplug it.

Rear seat adjusting switch

59 This is removed in the same way as the mirror control switch already described in paragraphs 10 and 11.

Heated seat control switches

60 These are removed in the same way as the mirror control switch already described in paragraphs 10 and 11.

Starter inhibitor/reversing light switch (automatic transmission)

61 Refer to Chapter 7 part B.

16 Fuses, relays and control units - removal and refitting

Fuses

1 The battery positive (live) lead is protected by a fusible link. If this link melts, a major short-circuit is indicated and expert advice should be sought before repairing it.

2 The main fuse/relay box is located under the bonnet, near the bulkhead on the right-hand side. It contains up to 24 fuses and nearly as many relays (according to equipment). Fuse applications are listed on the underside of the fuse box lid (see illustration).

3 There is an auxiliary fuse box inside the vehicle, accessible after opening the glovebox (see illustration). An in-line fuse for the radio is located under the facia on the left-hand side, near the heater.

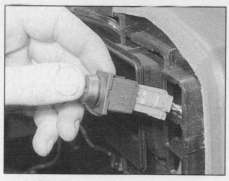

15.54 Removing a foglight switch

4 The "blade" type fuses are colour-coded to show their current rating. A blown fuse can be recognised by the melted wire link in the middle.

5 To renew a blown fuse, first switch off the circuit concerned. Pull the old fuse out of its holder, using tweezers or long-nosed pliers. Press in a new fuse of the same rating and try the circuit again.

6 If the new fuse blows immediately or within a short time, do not carry on renewing fuses but look for a short-circuit in the wiring to the item(s) protected by the fuse. When more than one item is protected by a single fuse, switching on one item at a time until the fuse blows will help to isolate the defect.

7 Never fit a fuse of a higher rating (current capacity) than specified, and do not bypass fuses with silver foil or strands of wire. Serious damage, including fire, could result.

8 In some positions (such as for power window and seat adjustment motors) circuit breakers are fitted instead of fuses. These are normally self-resetting once the cause of the overload has been cleared.

Relays

9 If a circuit or system served by a relay develops a fault, always remember that the problem could be in the relay. Testing is by substitution of a known good unit. Beware of substituting relays which look the same but perform different functions (see illustration).

16.2 Main fuse/relay box under the bonnet

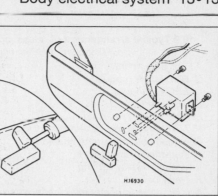

15.57 Removing the front seat adjusting switch

10 To renew a relay, simply unplug it from its holder and plug in the new one. Access to the relays in the main fuse box is as described for the fuses. Access to the relays located behind the facia is achieved by removing the facia top.

11 The sliding roof relay is located in the overhead console.

Control units and modules

12 The two major modules are the EEC IV module (on fuel-injection models) and the ABS control module. These are located below the glovebox on the passenger side, and are accessible after removing the under-dash trim.

13 As with relays, testing by the home mechanic is limited to substitution of known good units. This is likely to be prohibitively expensive on a trial and error basis so in case of problems a Ford dealer or other competent specialist should be consulted at an early stage.

17 Central locking motor - removal and refitting

1 Disconnect the battery negative lead and unlock all the doors before starting work on the central locking system. Make sure that the keys are outside the vehicle before reconnecting the battery on completion.

2 Remove the door interior trim panel.

16.3 Auxiliary fuse box in the glovebox

16.9 Typical arrangement of relays, control units and module
LHD shown - RHD is mirror image

A Taxi equipment
B Bulb failure module
C EEC IV module
D ABS module
E Rear headphone relay
F Auxiliary warning system control unit
G Speed control system module
H Anti-theft alarm module
I Warning display lighting
K Relay bank
1 Inlet manifold heater relay (carburettor)
2 Fuel pump relay (fuel-injection)
3 Power hold relay (carburettor)
4 Injector relay (fuel-injection)
5 Heated windscreen relay
6 Heated windscreen timer
7 Cooling fan relay (air conditioning)
8 ABS pump relay
9 ABS relay
10 ABS diodes
12 Ride height control relay
12 Day running lights relay (not UK)

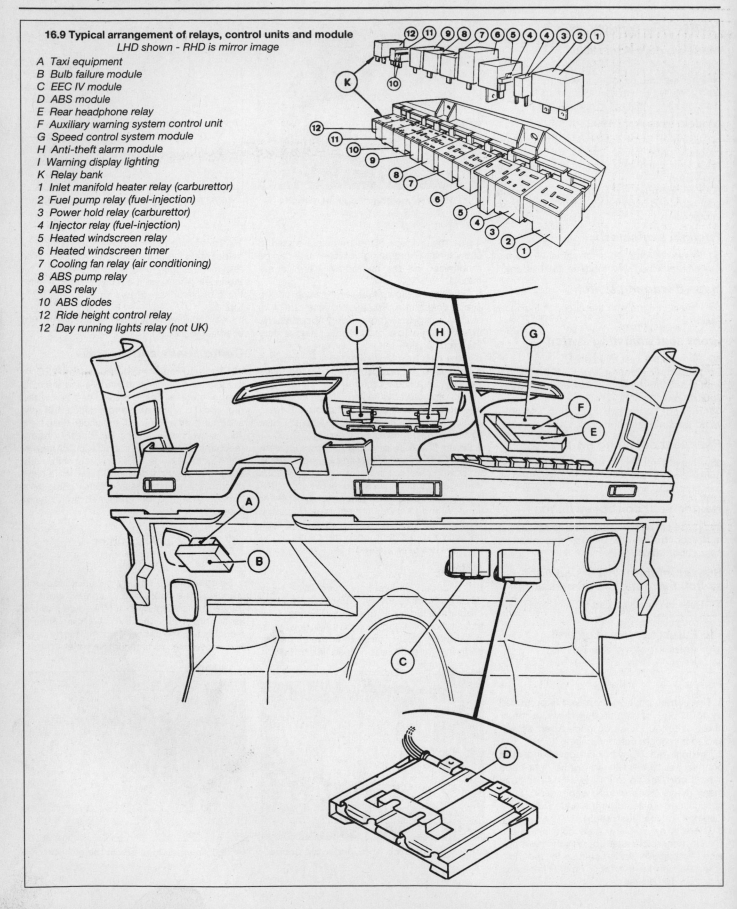

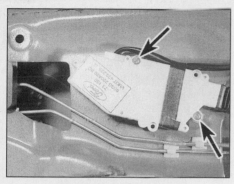

17.4 A door lock motor
Securing screws are arrowed

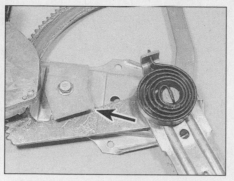

18.2a Make sure that the lever is against the stop (arrowed) . . .

18.2b . . . then remove the three bolts (arrowed) which secure the motor

3 Carefully peel away the foam rubber sheet in the area of the lock motor.

4 Remove the two securing screws, unhook the motor from the lock operating rod and disconnect the multi-plug. Remove the motor **(see illustration)**.

5 A defective lock motor must be renewed. No spare parts are available.

6 Refit by reversing the removal operations, then adjust the lock linkage as follows.

7 Move the locking lever to the "unlocked" position. Slacken the screw which secures the interior handle/lock lever assembly, push the assembly forwards as far as it will go and tighten the screw.

18 Window operating motor - removal and refitting

1 Remove the window operating mechanism, complete with motor.

2 Make sure that the spring is holding the lever against its stop, then remove the three bolts and separate the motor from the operating mechanism **(see illustrations)**. **Caution:** *Uncontrolled release of the spring can cause injury and damage.*

3 Refit by reversing the removal operations. Check the operations of the motor before refitting the door trim panel.

19 Seat adjusting motors - removal and refitting

Front height and fore-and-aft motors

1 Move the front seat rearwards as far as possible to improve access. Remove the two securing bolts from the front of the seat frame and tip the seat backwards.

2 Unbolt and remove the motor(s). Each motor is secured by two bolts **(see illustration)**. Make sure that the drive cables come away from the worm drives without difficulty - if not, disconnect one end of the worm drive too.

3 If only one motor is being removed, free its

spade connectors from the common multi-plug washer removing the plug shell **(see illustration)**. It is probably easier to remove both motors and deal with the connectors on the bench.

4 Refit by reversing the removal operations. Check for correct operation of the motors on completion.

Front recline motor

5 Remove the front seat.

6 Remove the seat cover and cushion.

7 Remove the two securing bolts **(see illustration),** disconnect the multi-plug and withdraw the motor from the reclining mechanism.

8 When refitting, make sure that the motor pinion gear meshes with the reclining mechanism gear. Connect the multi-plug and secure the motor with the two bolts.

9 Refit the seat cover and cushion, then refit the seat to the vehicle.

Rear recline motor

10 Remove the trim panel from the left-hand side of the luggage area.

11 Remove the three Torx screws which secure the motor and reclining mechanism. Disconnect the multi-plug (next to the seat squab) and remove the motor **(see illustration)**.

12 Refit by reversing the removal operations. Check for correct operation before refitting the luggage area trim panel.

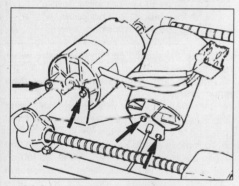

19.2 Seat adjusting motor bolts (arrowed)

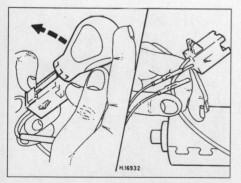

19.3 Removing the spade connectors from the multi-plug

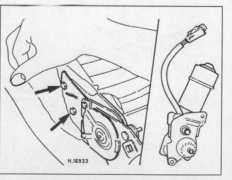

19.7 Front seat recline motor bolts (arrowed)

19.11 Rear seat recline motor

13

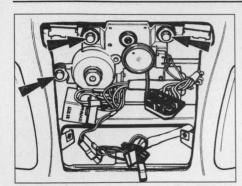

20.2 Sliding roof motor retaining bolts (arrowed)

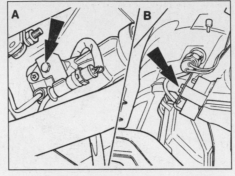

21.3 Speedometer sender unit securing bolt (arrowed)
A Automatic transmission
B Manual gearbox

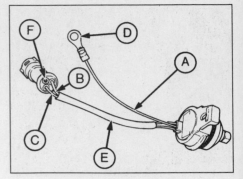

21.5 Latest type speedometer sender unit

A Brown wire   E Sleeve
B Brown/yellow wire   F Cut brown wire
C Brown/black wire   here (see text)
D Earth tag (see text)

20 Sliding roof motor - removal and refitting

1 Remove the overhead console.
2 Remove the three bolts which secure the motor **(see illustration)**. Lower the motor, disconnect the multi-plug and remove it. Recover the relay.
3 When refitting, make sure that the motor drivegear meshes with the roof operating mechanism. Refit the relay, reconnect the multi-plug and secure the motor with the three bolts.
4 Check the operation of the motor, then refit the overhead console.

21 Speedometer sender unit - removal and refitting

1 All vehicles are fitted with an electrical speedometer sender unit instead of a mechanical cable. The sender unit is located on the left-hand side of the transmission extension.
2 Raise and securely support the front of the vehicle. Place a drain pan underneath the speedometer sender unit.
3 Remove the securing bolt, pull the sender unit out of the transmission and disconnect the multi-plug **(see illustration)**. Be prepared for some spillage of gearbox oil or ATF (automatic transmission fluid).
4 If a new sender unit is being fitted, transfer the driven gear and circlip from the old unit. On automatic transmission models, also transfer the O-ring.
5 If the old sender unit had two connecting wires and the new unit has three, the brown wire must be cut at the multi-plug and an earth tag fitted **(see illustration)**. Consult a Ford dealer if in doubt.
6 Fit the new sender unit, using a new bolt (M6 x 25 mm for manual gearbox, M6 x 35 mm for automatic transmission). Besides the sender unit, the bolt also secures the new earth tag (when applicable), the radio earth strap and the multi-plug retaining bracket.
7 Connect the multi-plug and fit it to the bracket.

8 If any spillage of gearbox oil or transmission fluid occurred, top-up the level before the vehicle is next run.

22 Wiper arms and blades - removal and refitting

All models

1 To remove a windscreen wiper arm, first open the bonnet.

> **HAYNES HiNT** *Mark the position of the blade on the windscreen or rear window (as applicable) with a piece of masking tape.*

2 Lift up the plastic cap and undo the wiper arm retaining nut.
3 Pull the arm off the drive spindle **(see illustrations)**.
4 Refit in the reverse order to removal, using the masking tape to indicate the correct fitted position of the arm and blade.
5 To remove a blade alone, hinge the arm and blade away from the screen. Press the tab on the spring clip in the middle of the blade and unhook the blade from the arm **(see illustration)**.
6 Refit the blade by sliding it onto the hook on the arm.

22.3a Lift the cap to expose the nut

22.3b Pull the arm off the spindle

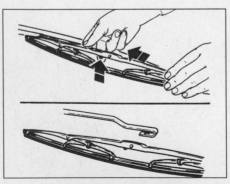

22.5 Removing a wiper blade

22.7 Disconnecting the rear wiper arm washer hose

23.2a Two screws (arrowed) in the front of the motor . . .

23.2b . . . three screws around the right-hand spindle . . .

23.2c . . . and two screws on the left.
Eighth screw is midway between the spindles

Estate

7 Note that when removing the rear window wiper arm, it will be necessary to detach the washer hose from the spindle prior to removing the wiper arm retaining nut **(see illustration)**.

23 Windscreen wiper motor and linkage - removal and refitting

1 Remove the windscreen wiper arms as described in the previous Section.
2 Undo the eight Torx screws which secure the wiper motor and linkage to the bulkhead **(see illustrations)**.

23.3 Disconnecting the wiper motor multi-plug

3 Disconnect the multi-plug and remove the motor and linkage **(see illustration)**.
4 The linkage arms can be removed by levering them off the pivot pins.
5 To remove the motor, undo the crank arm nut and remove the three securing bolts **(see illustration)**. The motor cover can then be removed. A defective motor must be renewed.
6 Refit by reversing the removal operations. Before refitting the wiper arms, switch the wipers on and then off so that the motor takes up the "parked" position.

24 Rear window wiper motor - removal and refitting

1 Remove the rear wiper arm from the spindle.
2 Open the tailgate and remove the interior trim panel, which is secured by eleven screws.
3 Remove the three bolts which secure the wiper motor bracket to the tailgate **(see illustration)**. Also remove the screw which secures the earth tag. Disconnect the wiring plug and remove the motor and bracket.
4 The bracket can be unbolted from the motor if wished. No spare parts for the motor are available.
5 Commence refitting by offering the motor and bracket to the tailgate. Secure the assembly with the three bolts, then reconnect the wiring and secure the earth tag.
6 Switch on the ignition and operate the rear wiper control briefly so that the motor stops in the "parked" position.

7 Refit the wiper arm and blade. Wet the window and operate the rear wiper control again to check the function of the motor.
8 Switch off the ignition and refit the tailgate interior trim panel.

25 Windscreen, rear window and headlight washer components - removal and refitting

Windscreen and rear washer jets are removed simply by prising or pulling them from their locations **(see illustration)**. Headlight washer jets can be unclipped from their holders after disconnection of the high pressure hose from the jet.

To remove a washer pump, first syphon out the contents of the reservoir. Disconnect the wiring and the hose from the pump, then pull the pump out of its grommet in the reservoir. Renew the grommet if necessary when refitting the pump.

26 Fuel computer components - removal and refitting

1 The fuel tank sender unit, EEC IV module and speedometer sender unit are not peculiar to the fuel computer. Their removal and refitting procedures are given in Chapter 4, Chapter 5 and this Chapter respectively.

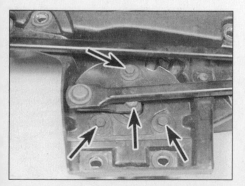

23.5 Undo the crank arm nut and the three bolts (arrowed)

24.3 Three bolts secure the rear wiper motor (two arrowed)

25.1 A windscreen washer jet prised out of its location in the bonnet

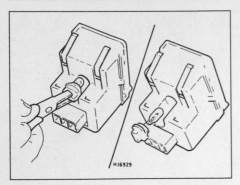

26.4 Renewing the fuel computer module bulb

26.9 Fuel computer retaining screws (arrowed)

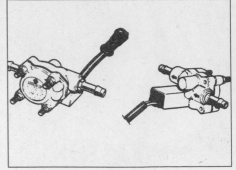

26.11 Fuel flow sensor fitted to carburettor models

Computer module and bulb

Models before April 1992

2 Remove the instrument panel surround, which is secured by four screws.
3 Carefully pull the module from its location. Release the multi-plug by pressing downwards and disconnect it.
4 The module illumination bulbholder may now be extracted by gripping it with pliers and twisting it anti-clockwise (see illustration). Extract the old wedge base bulb, press in the new one and refit the bulb and holder.
5 Reconnect the multi-plug and press the module back into its hole. Check for correct operation, then refit the instrument panel surround.

Models from April 1992

6 Disconnect the battery negative terminal.
7 Undo the two instrument cluster surround retaining screws then release the two retaining clips and remove the surround. Disconnect the instrument cluster dimmer switch as it is removed.
8 Pull off the three knobs from the heater and ventilation controls to gain access to the two hidden central vent panel retaining screws. Slacken and remove the four panel retaining screws and partially withdraw the panel. Disconnect the wiring connectors from the heated window switches and fuel computer and remove the panel from the car.
9 Undo the four fuel computer retaining screws and remove the computer from the vent panel (see illustration).
10 Refitting is a reverse of the removal procedure.

Fuel flow sensor (carburettor models only)

11 The fuel flow sensor is located under the bonnet, on the left-hand inner wing (see illustration).
12 Disconnect the battery negative lead.
13 Disconnect the multi-plug and the fuel pipes from the sensor. Be prepared for fuel spillage; plug or cap the pipes.
14 Remove the three screws which secure the sensor bracket. Remove the sensor and bracket together; they can be separated on the bench if wished.

15 Refit by reversing the removal operations. Use new fuel pipe clips if the old ones were damaged during removal.

27 Auxiliary warning system components - testing, removal and refitting

Note that if a fault develops in the AWS, thorough testing and fault finding should be left to a Ford dealer or other competent specialist. Unskilled or uninformed testing may cause further damage. When checking wires or sensors for continuity, disconnect the control assembly and bulb failure module first, otherwise damage may be caused.

Warning light bulbs

1 Refer to Sections 7 and 8.

Graphic display module

2 Refer to Sections 7 and 8.
3 The bulbs and light emitting diodes (LEDs) can be removed from the module using tweezers or jeweller's pliers. When renewing the fuel filler warning LED, note that the pip on the LED must align with the yellow dot on the circuit board.

Fuel filler switch

4 Open the fuel filler flap and remove the cap.
5 Inside the luggage area, remove the trim on the right-hand side and disconnect the switch multi-plug (see illustration).

6 Remove the screw which secures the switch to the filler neck. Remove the switch and withdraw its wires.
7 Refit by reversing the removal operations.

Air temperature sensor

8 From under the front bumper, unclip and disconnect the sensor multi-plug.
9 Unclip the sensor from its slot by pulling the securing tag inwards. Remove the sensor (see illustration).
10 When refitting, first connect the multi-plug. Fit the hook on the end of the sensor into the slot and press the sensor into place, then secure the multi-plug in its clip.

Door/tailgate switch

11 Remove the door interior or tailgate interior trim panel (eleven screws).
12 Pull the switch to detach it from the lock and disconnect its multi-plug.
13 Refit by reversing the removal operations.

Coolant level switch

14 Remove the cap from the coolant expansion tank, taking precautions against scalding if the coolant is hot.
15 Syphon coolant out of the tank if necessary until the level is below the switch.
16 Disconnect the switch multi-plug. Unscrew the retaining ring and pull the switch out of its grommet. Note how flats on the grommet and switch ensure correct fitting (see illustration).

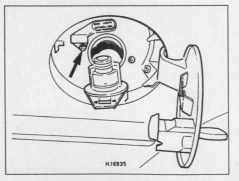

27.5 Fuel filler switch screw (arrowed)

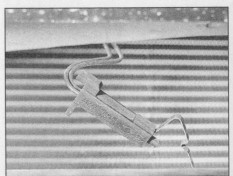

27.9 Removing the air temperature sensor

27.16 Removing the coolant level switch

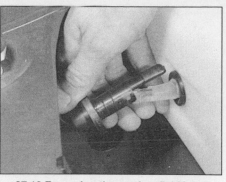

27.19 Removing the washer fluid level switch

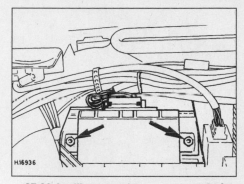

27.22 Auxiliary warning system control assembly - retaining nuts arrowed

17 Refit by inserting the switch into the grommet - use a new grommet if necessary - and screwing on the retaining ring. Reconnect the multi-plug and top-up the cooling system.

Washer fluid level switch

18 Syphon the fluid out of the washer reservoir until the level is below the switch.
19 Disconnect the switch multi-plug. Carefully prise the switch out of its grommet and remove it. Note how flats on the grommet and switch ensure correct fitting (see illustration).
20 When refitting, make sure that the grommet is in good condition (renew if necessary) and is correctly seated. Press the switch home, reconnect the multi-plug and refill the reservoir.

Control assembly

Models before April 1992

21 Remove the instrument panel surround and the facia top.
22 Remove the two nuts which secure the assembly (see illustration). Disconnect the multi-plug by pressing in the locking lever and pulling the plug. Remove the control assembly.
23 Refit by reversing the removal operations. Check the AWS for correct operation before refitting the disturbed trim.

Models from April 1992

24 Unclip and remove the right-hand facia undercover panel.

25 Carefully prise out the bonnet release lever surround to gain access to the lever retaining screws. Undo the three screws then withdraw the lever. Remove the cable retaining clip and detach the operating lever from the cable.
26 Slacken and remove the five right-hand lower facia panel retaining screws and remove the panel from the vehicle.
27 Undo the module retaining screw then disconnect the wiring connectors and remove the control module from the vehicle (see illustration).
28 Refitting is a reverse of the removal procedure.

Bulb failure module

Models before April 1992

29 Remove the under-dash trim on the driver's side. This is secured by six screws, one of which is only accessible after removing the air vent grille.
30 Pull the module from its bracket. Disconnect the multi-plug by pressing in the locking lever and pulling the plug. Remove the module (see illustration).
31 Refit by reversing the removal operations.

Models from April 1992

32 Remove the right-hand facia undercover and lower facia panel.
33 The bulb failure module is the right-hand of the two modules situated directly above the control pedals. Release the module retaining clips then disconnect the wiring connector and remove the module from the vehicle.
34 Refitting is a reverse of removal.

Control switches

1 Remove the steering wheel.
2 Remove the three screws which secure the horn contact plate. Disconnect the spade terminals and remove the contact plate.
3 Carefully prise the switch out of the steering wheel. Disconnect the spade terminals and remove it.
4 Refit by reversing the removal operations.

Vacuum dump valve/switch

5 Remove the under-dash trim on the driver's side.
6 For the brake pedal, slacken the switch top and bottom mounting nuts, then remove the bottom nut completely. Disconnect the wiring plug and vacuum hose from the switch and remove it.
7 The clutch pedal switch is mounted in a spring-loaded bracket to allow for small changes in pedal position with the operation of the self-adjusting mechanism. Disconnect the wiring plug and vacuum hose, then push the switch out of its bracket.
8 Refit by reversing the removal operations. Adjust the switch position so that there is a gap of at least 1.5 mm (0.06 in) between the switch plunger cap and the body of the switch (see illustration).

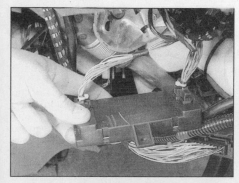

27.27 Removing the auxiliary warning system control module

27.30 The bulb failure module secured to the under-dash trim

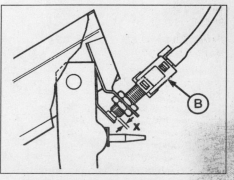

28.8 Vacuum dump valve/switch (B)
X = 1.5 mm (0.06 in) minimum

13

28.10 Removing the speed control module

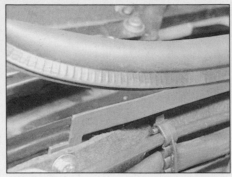

29.2 Pulling off the rubber sealing strip

29.3 Pulling out a wiring harness clip

Speed control module

Models before April 1992

9 Refer to Section 27. The speed control module shares the same mountings as the AWS module; the AWS module is larger.

Models from April 1992

10 The speed control module fitted to these models is situated behind the glovebox on the left-hand side of the facia. To gain access to the module remove the left-hand facia undercover panel. The speed control module is vertically mounted just to the right of the engine management module. Push the module upwards to release the retaining clips then lower it out from under the facia and disconnect the wiring connector **(see illustration)**.

11 Refitting is a reverse of the removal procedure ensuring that the module is securely retained by the retaining clips.

Vacuum pump

12 The vacuum pump is located behind the left-hand headlight on carburettor models, and behind the right-hand headlight on fue-injection models. Start by removing the appropriate headlight unit.

13 Disconnect the multi-plug and the vacuum hose from the pump. The multi-plug is released by squeezing and pulling it at the same time.

14 Prise out the three mountings and remove the pump.

15 When refitting, pull the pump mountings into position with pliers.

16 Reconnect the vacuum hose and the multi-plug, then refit the headlight unit.

Vacuum servo

17 Disconnect the servo-to-throttle linkage cable at one end.

18 Disconnect the vacuum hose from the servo.

19 Undo the servo retaining nut and remove the servo from its bracket.

20 Refit by reversing the removal operations. On all but 2.0 litre carburettor models, adjust the cable so that it is slightly slack when the throttle linkage is in the idle position (pedal released).

21 On 2.0 litre carburettor models, the stepper motor plunger must be withdrawn before the cable is adjusted. Proceed as follows.

22 Observe the stepper motor plunger. Have an assistant switch on the ignition for a few seconds, then switch it off again. When the ignition is switched off, the stepper motor plunger will retract fully ("vent manifold" position). Disconnect the battery negative lead while the stepper motor plunger is retracted.

23 Adjust the servo cable so that it is slightly slack, then reconnect the battery negative lead.

Printed circuit board

24 The printed circuit board is located in the steering wheel. It can be removed after detaching the horn contact plate and disconnecting the switch spade terminals as described at the beginning of this Section.

29 Heater blower motor - removal and refitting

1 Disconnect the battery negative lead.

2 Pull off the rubber sealing strip from the top of the plenum chamber **(see illustration)**.

3 Pull the two wiring harness clips from the front of the plenum chamber **(see illustration)**.

4 Remove the two screws and two clips which secure the plenum chamber cover **(see illustration)**. Lift out the cover.

5 Disconnect the multi-plug from the blower motor resistor. Also disconnect the motor earth cable **(see illustration)**.

6 Remove the two nuts which secure the motor assembly. Lift out the motor, casing and resistor together.

7 The casing halves and the resistor can be separated from the motor after prising open the clamp which holds the casing halves together.

8 Refit by reversing the removal operations.

30 Radio or radio/cassette player (original equipment) - removal and refitting

1 Two DIN standard extraction tools will be needed to remove the radio/cassette unit. These tools are available from vehicle audio equipment specialists.

Radio (only)

2 Pull off the control knobs, remove the spindle nuts and washers and remove the radio face plate.

3 Push the two securing lugs inwards, at the same time pulling the radio from its location. The services of an assistant may be required.

4 Withdraw the radio and disconnect the aerial cable and the other wiring plugs from it.

5 If a new radio is to be fitted, transfer the support brackets and locating plate from the old unit to the new one.

6 Refit by reconnecting the wiring to the radio, then sliding it into its aperture. Press it in until the securing lugs click into position.

7 Refit the face plate, spindle nuts and washers and control knobs. The top of the face plate is marked on the side which faces the radio.

29.4 One of the plenum chamber cover clips

29.5 Blower motor showing wiring connections

30.9 A DIN extraction tool fitted to a radio/cassette unit

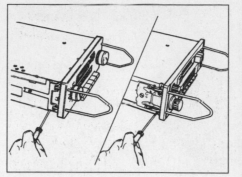

30.11 Releasing a DIN extraction tool

30.18 Carefully prise out the left-hand vent panel . . .

8 If a new unit has been fitted, trim it by tuning in a weak medium wave station (around 1500 kHz/200 m) and turning the trimmer screw in either direction until the best reception is obtained. On the radio originally fitted, the trimmer screw is on the front face of the unit; for other types of radio, consult the manufacturer's instructions. Electronic units are normally self-trimming.

Radio/cassette unit

9 Insert the DIN extraction tools (paragraph 1) into the holes at each end of the unit (see illustration). Push the tools home, then pull them apart and rearwards to remove the unit. Pull evenly on each side, otherwise the unit may jam in its slide.
10 Disconnect the aerial cable and other wiring plugs.
11 To remove the DIN tools from the unit, push the clips into which they engage rearwards with a screwdriver (see illustration).
12 If a new unit is being fitted, transfer the support bracket and locating plate to it.
13 Reconnect the wiring to the unit, engage it in its slide and press it home until the retaining clips engage.
14 Refer to paragraph 8 to trim the new unit.

Radio/cassette unit amplifier

Models before April 1992

15 Remove the facia top crash pad.
16 Disconnect the wiring connectors from the

amplifier unit then undo the four retaining nuts and remove the amplifier from the facia.
17 Refitting is a reverse of removal.

Models from April 1992

18 Using a flat-bladed tool carefully prise the left-hand facia vent panel out from the facia to gain access to the amplifier unit (see illustration).
19 Slacken and remove the two retaining screws then carefully withdraw the amplifier unit, disconnecting the wiring connectors as they become accessible (see illustrations).
20 Refit by reversing the removal procedure ensuring that the vent panel is held securely in position by the retaining clips.

Graphic equaliser

21 When fitted, the graphic equaliser is removed in the same way as the radio/cassette unit.

31 Loudspeakers (original equipment) - removal and refitting

1 Depending on the level of equipment fitted, loudspeakers may be located in the front door panels, below the rear parcel shelf and in the facia. Those in the facia are high frequency units.

Front door speakers

2 Remove the door interior trim panel.
3 Remove the four screws which secure the loudspeaker. Withdraw the speaker, disconnect the wiring and remove it.

4 Refit by reversing the removal operations; observe the TOP marking when fitting the speaker (see illustration).

Rear parcel shelf speakers

Hatchback

5 Remove the speaker cover by twisting it anti-clockwise and pulling it off.
6 Remove the four nuts which secure the speaker, lower the speaker and disconnect the wiring from it. Note that the terminals are different sizes to ensure correct reconnection.
7 Refit by reversing the removal operations.

Saloon

8 From within the boot, slacken and remove the single speaker retaining bolt (see illustration).
9 From inside the car, lift the speaker out of the rear parcel shelf and disconnect the wiring connector.
10 Refitting is the reverse of the removal procedure.

Rear luggage compartment speakers (Estate models)

11 Release the retaining clips and remove the relevant luggage compartment interior side trim panel to gain access to the speaker.
12 Undo the two retaining screws then remove the speaker, disconnecting the wiring connector as it becomes accessible.
13 Refitting is the reverse of the removal procedure.

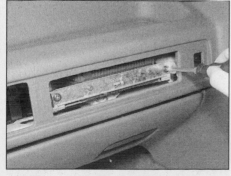

30.19a . . . undo the retaining screws . . .

30.19b . . . then withdraw the amplifier unit and disconnect the wiring connectors

31.4 Front door loudspeaker - note TOP marking

31.8 Removing a rear speaker retaining bolt

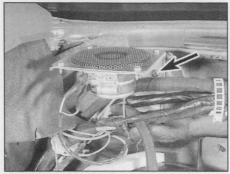

31.15 High frequency loudspeaker located under the facia top. One bracket securing screw (arrowed) is visible

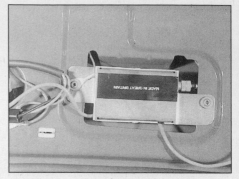

32.3 Radio aerial pre-amplifier mounted in the tailgate

High frequency units

14 Remove the instrument panel surround and the facia top.

15 Remove the two screws which secure the speaker bracket. Disconnect the wiring and withdraw the speaker and bracket together. The screws which secure the speaker to the bracket can then be removed **(see illustration)**.

16 Refit by reversing the removal operations.

32 Radio aerial pre-amplifier (original equipment) - removal and refitting

Hatchback

1 The heated rear window element is used as the radio aerial. To produce a good signal at the radio a pre-amplifier, mounted in the tailgate, is used.

2 Remove the tailgate interior trim panel, which is secured by eleven screws.

3 Remove the two screws which secure the pre-amplifier **(see illustration)**. Disconnect the wiring from the pre-amplifier and remove it.

4 Refit by reversing the removal operations.

Saloon

5 On these models the pre-amplifier unit is located under the rear parcel shelf and can be accessed from within the boot.

6 To remove the unit, from within the boot, slacken and remove the two retaining screws

then lower the pre-amplifier out of position and disconnect the wiring connectors **(see illustration)**.

7 Refitting is the reverse of removal.

Estate

8 On Estate models the pre-amplifier unit is situated in the roof, just in front of the tailgate.

9 To remove the pre-amplifier, open up the tailgate then carefully release the headlining from all the relevant trim panels and peel it back until access to the unit can be gained.

10 Undo the two retaining screws then lower the unit out from the roof and disconnect the wiring connectors.

11 Refitting is a reverse of the removal procedure ensuring that the headlining is neatly fitted and correctly located behind all the relevant trim panels.

33 Joystick fader control - removal and refitting

1 This Section deals with the facia-mounted control. On models with a graphic equaliser, the joystick fader is incorporated in the equaliser.

2 Remove the instrument cluster.

3 Prise out the fader surround and detach the bulbholder **(see illustration)**.

4 Release the fader control by turning its retaining clip anticlockwise. Withdraw it from the facia and disconnect its multi-plug.

5 Refit by reversing the removal operations.

34 Rear entertainment console - removal and refitting

1 Pull the heater control knob off its lever. Remove the two retaining screws from the top corners of the rear console faceplate.

2 Pull off the balance and volume control knobs. Withdraw the console and disconnect the wiring from it.

3 The console may be removed from the face plate if wished by undoing the three retaining screws.

4 To renew the console bulbs, extract the bulbholders by grasping with pliers and turning them anti-clockwise.

5 Refit by reversing the removal operations.

35 Rear headphone relay - removal and refitting

1 The rear headphone relay is located behind the facia, next to the AWS control assembly and the speed control module (when fitted). Its function is to mute the loudspeakers when the headphones are plugged into the rear entertainment console.

2 To remove the relay, first remove the AWS control assembly and (if applicable) the speed control unit.

3 Disconnect the relay multi-plug, undo its securing screw and nut and remove it.

4 Refit by reversing the removal operations.

36 Anti-theft alarm system components - removal and refitting

The alarm system is available as an optional extra. On vehicles so equipped, the alarm is automatically set by locking the driver's or front passenger's door with the key. After a brief delay (approximately 20 seconds), the alarm will be set off if the doors, bonnet or tailgate are opened.

The only way to disarm the alarm system is by unlocking one of the front doors with the key. Even if the key is used to open the tailgate, if the alarm is set it will go off.

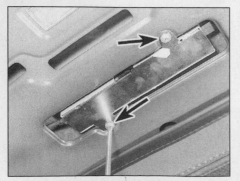

32.6 Radio aerial pre-amplifier retaining screws (arrowed)

33.3 Removing the joystick fader

36.6 Removing the anti-theft alarm control module

36.9 Removing the alarm system warning buzzer

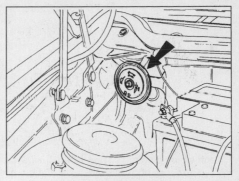

36.11 Alarm horn location

The components of the alarm system are a control module, tripping switches, activating switches, an alarm horn and a signal buzzer.

The control module is located behind the facia. It determines whether the alarm is set or not, monitors the tripping switches and the ignition circuit, and limits the duration of the alarm to 30 seconds. This last item is a legal requirement. The control module also operates the signal buzzer to tell the driver that the alarm is set, and controls the activator delay.

The tripping switches on the doors and tailgate are the same as those used for "open door" warnings in the AWS. The bonnet switch is peculiar to the alarm system.

The activating switches are fitted to the front door lock barrels, where they are activated by a lug on the end of the barrel. They only make contact momentarily as the lock is operated.

The alarm horn is mounted next to the battery. Both the horn and its leads are claimed to be inaccessible without opening the bonnet. The signal buzzer is also mounted under the bonnet.

No service, repair or component renewal procedures have been published for the alarm system components on earlier models. Any problems arising which cannot be dealt with by component substitution should therefore be referred to a Ford dealer.

Ultrasonic sensor

1 Disconnect the battery negative terminal.
2 Prise out the retaining screw trim cap from the centre of the sensor then slacken and remove the retaining screws and lower the sensor away from the headlining, disconnecting the wiring plug as it becomes accessible.
3 Refitting is the reverse of the removal procedure.

Anti-theft alarm module (models from April 1992)

4 On these models the alarm module is located behind the righthand lower facia panel.
5 To remove the module, remove the right-hand facia undercover and lower facia panel.
6 The anti-theft alarm module is the left-hand of the two modules situated directly above the control pedals. Release the module retaining clips then disconnect the wiring connector and remove the module from the vehicle **(see illustration)**.

7 Refitting is the reverse of the removal procedure.

Alarm signal buzzer (models from April 1992)

8 The alarm signal buzzer is situated under the bonnet where it is mounted on the upper right-hand side of the engine compartment bulkhead.
9 To remove the buzzer, open the bonnet then unclip the buzzer from the bulkhead and disconnect the wiring connector **(see illustration)**.
10 Refitting is the reverse of the removal procedure.

Alarm system horn (models from April 1992)

11 On these models the alarm system horn is mounted in the front right-hand corner of the engine compartment **(see illustration)**.
12 To remove the horn, undo the two horn mounting bracket retaining screws then disconnect the wiring connectors and remove the horn from the engine compartment.
13 Refitting is the reverse of the removal procedure.

Explanatory notes for wiring diagrams

Each wiring diagram covers a particular system of the vehicle; as indicated in each caption. When a number is shown on a diagram inside a box with an arrow symbol, this indicates that the circuit concerned starts, or is continued, in the diagram having that number.

Space limitations mean that not all diagrams have been included. Therefore the diagram numbers are not consecutive, neither is it always possible to follow a particular circuit to completion. Some diagrams are out of sequence; this is to ensure that the halves of the larger diagrams appear on opposite pages.

The prefix C indicates a connector or multi-plug, S a soldered joint and G an earthing point (ground). The numbers appearing at the break in each wire indicate the circuit number and wire colour.

```
SYMBOL-EXPLANATION:

⊡▶  POWER DISTRIBUTION FROM
    OR CONTINUATION ON        PAGE 2

⑥Ⓑ  SHOWS SPECIFIC LEGAL
    REQUIREMENT OF THIS COUNTRY.

(?)  CONNECTION DOES NOT EXIST
     IN EVERY VARIATION.
```

Colour code

BL	Blue
BR	Brown
GE	Yellow
GR	Grey
GN	Green
RS	Pink
RT	Red
SW	Black
VI	Violet
WS	White

Subject	Diagram number
ABS	21
Auxiliary warning system	23
Central locking system	14
Charge, start and run	3
Charge, start and run	3A
Engine management (1.8 litre)	4
Engine management (2.0 litre carburettor)	4A
Engine management (2.0 litre fuel-injection)	5
Engine management (2.8 litre)	5C
Exterior lighting	7A
Heater blower	11
Interior lighting	10
Power Operated windows	15
Power distribution	2
Power-operated sliding roof	16
Radio/cassette player and associated circuits	29
Signalling and warning systems	9
Wipers and washers	12

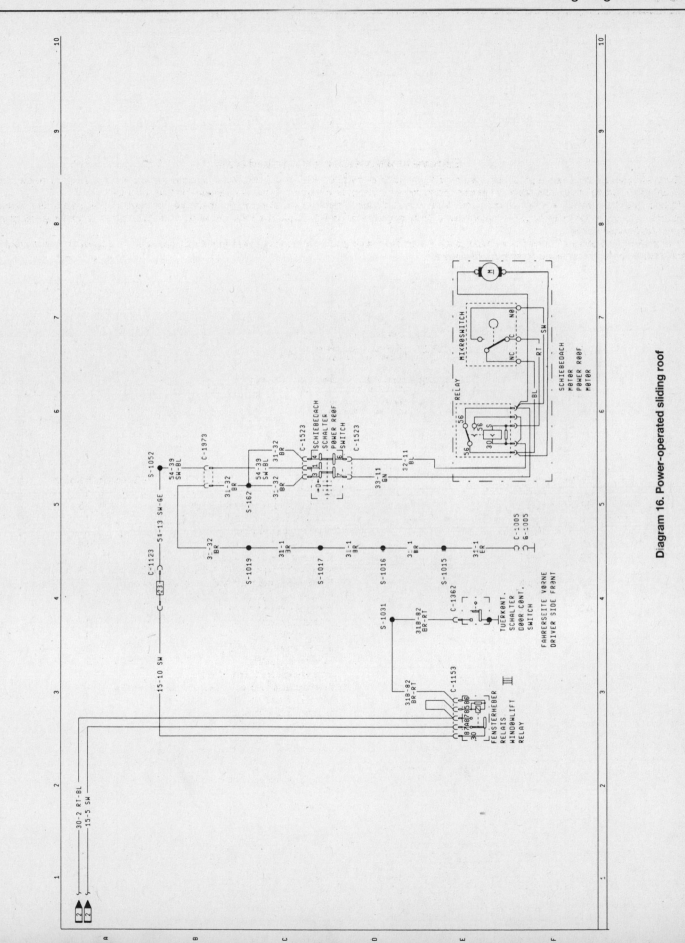

Diagram 16. Power-operated sliding roof

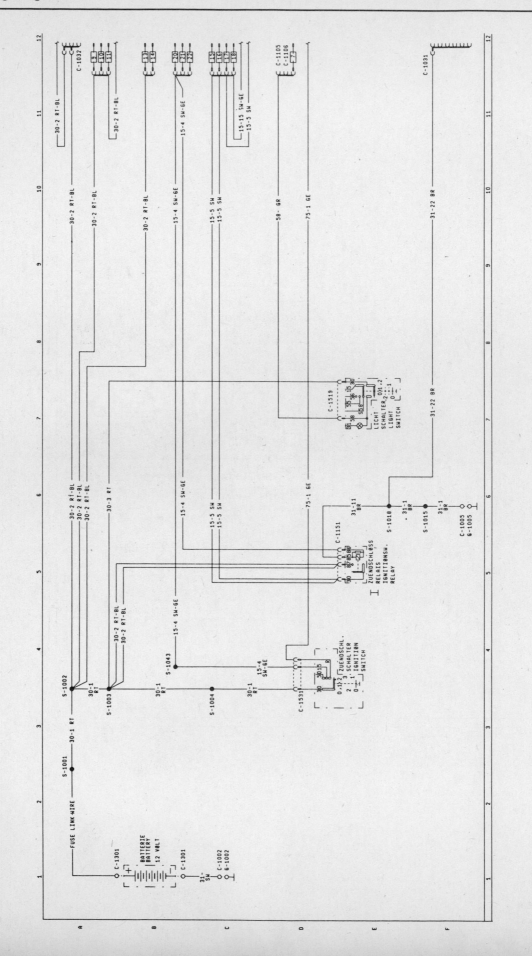

Diagram 2. Power distribution

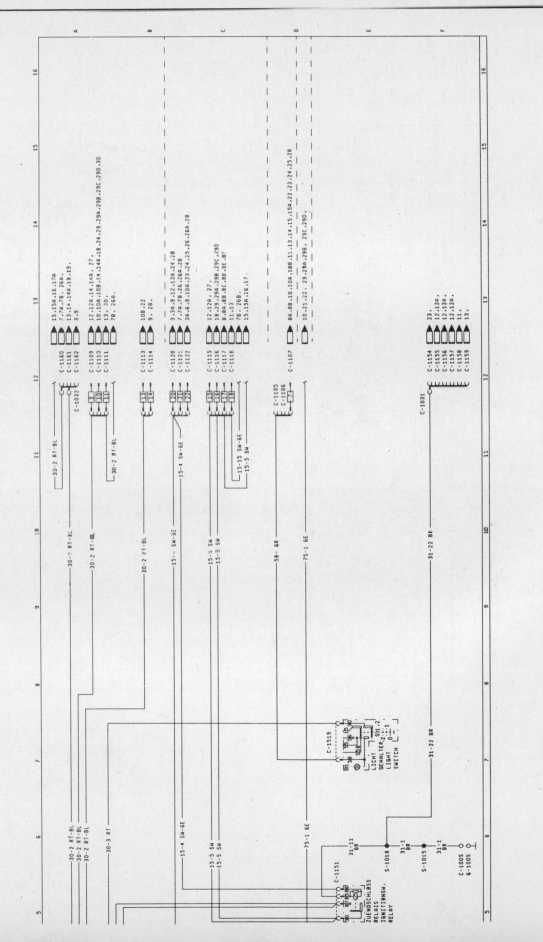

Diagram 2. Power distribution (continued)

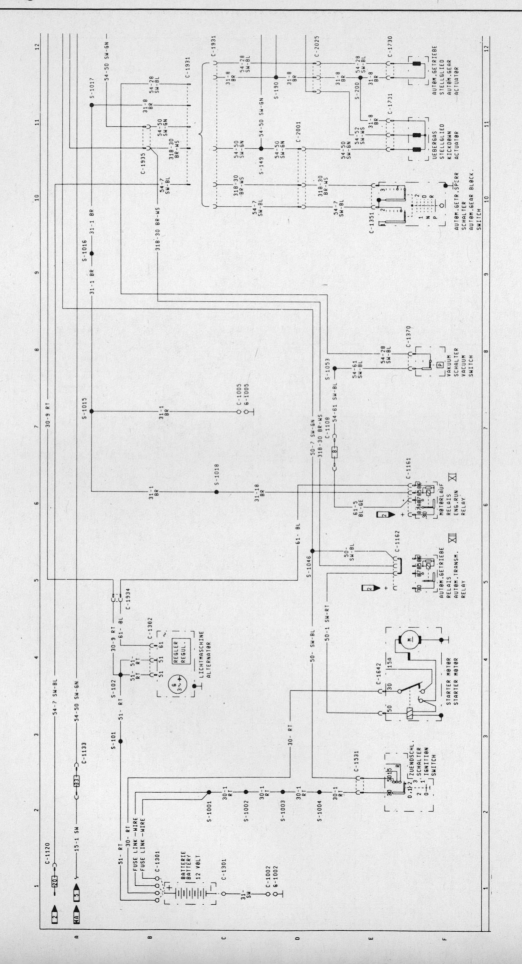

Diagram 3. Charge, start and run (Part 1)

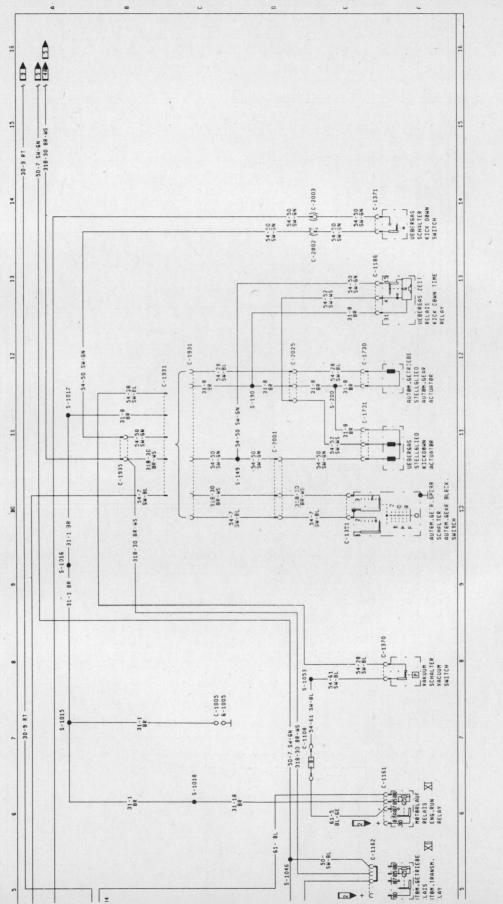

**Diagram 3. Charge, start and run (Part 1)
(continued)**

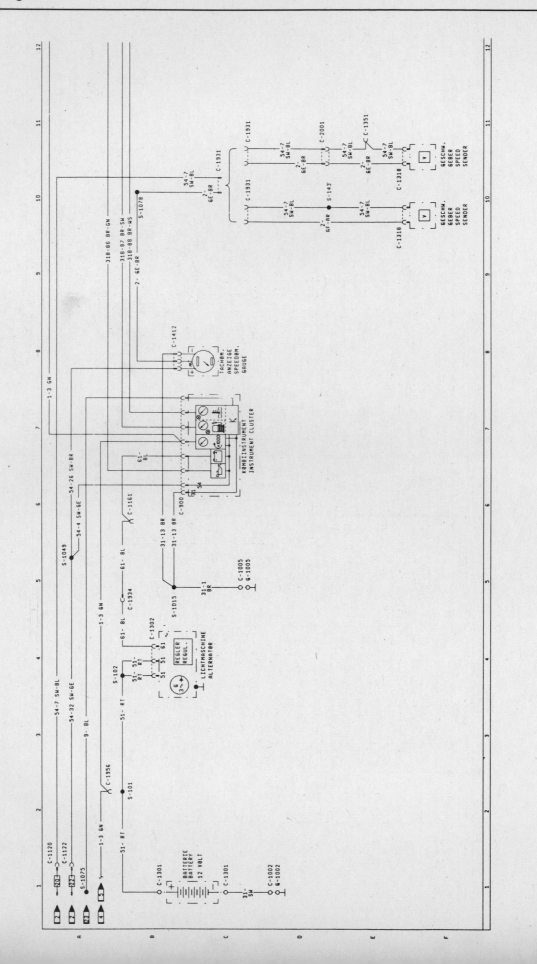

Diagram 3A. Charge, start and run (Part 2)

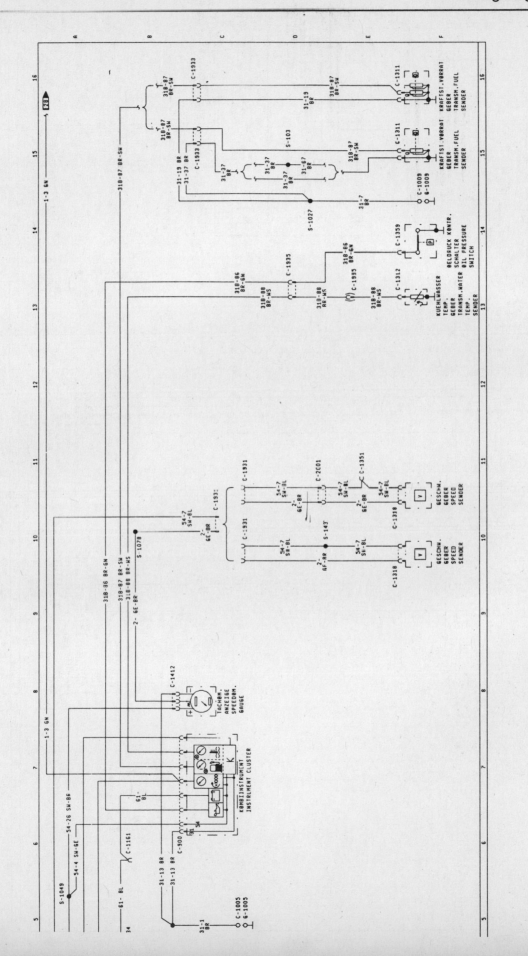
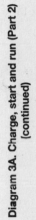

Diagram 3A. Charge, start and run (Part 2) (continued)

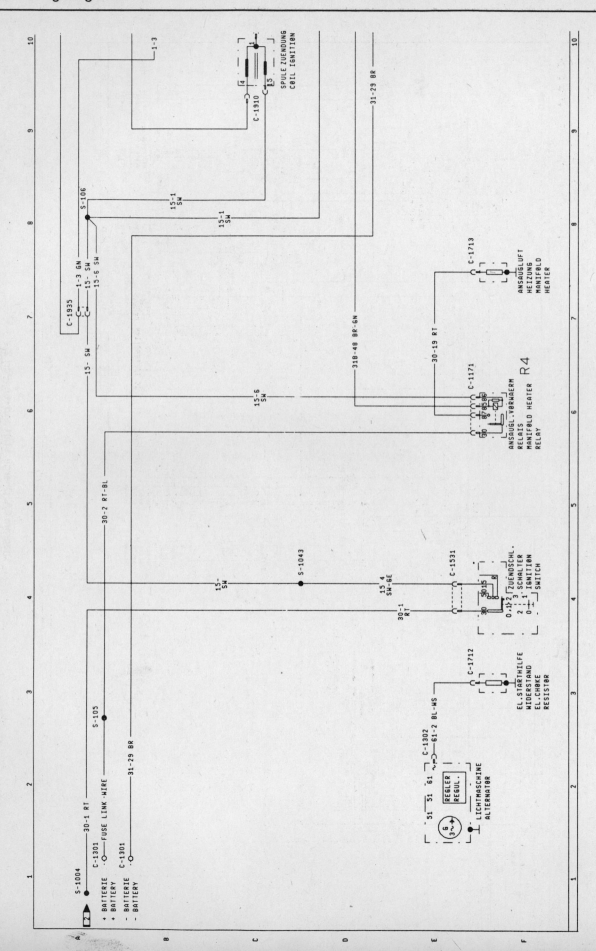

Diagram 4. Engine management (1.8 litre)

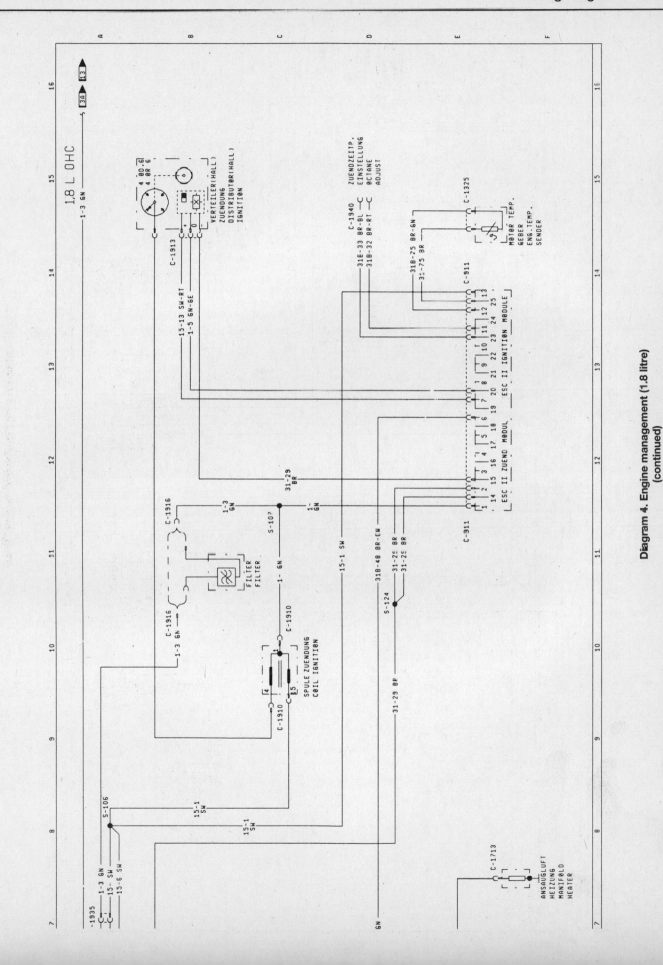

Diagram 4. Engine management (1.8 litre)
(continued)

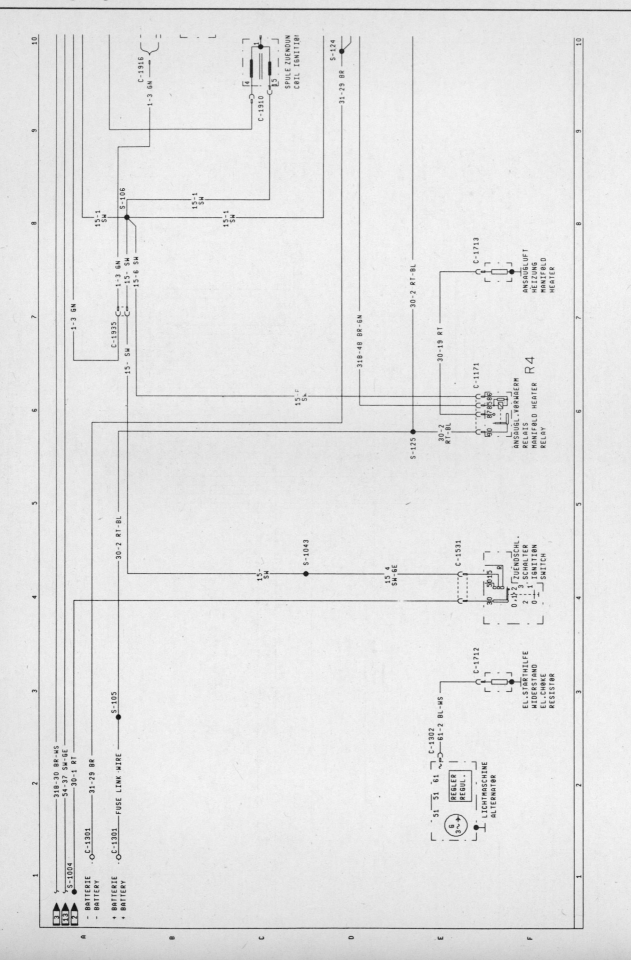

Diagram 4A. Engine management (2.0 litre carburettor)

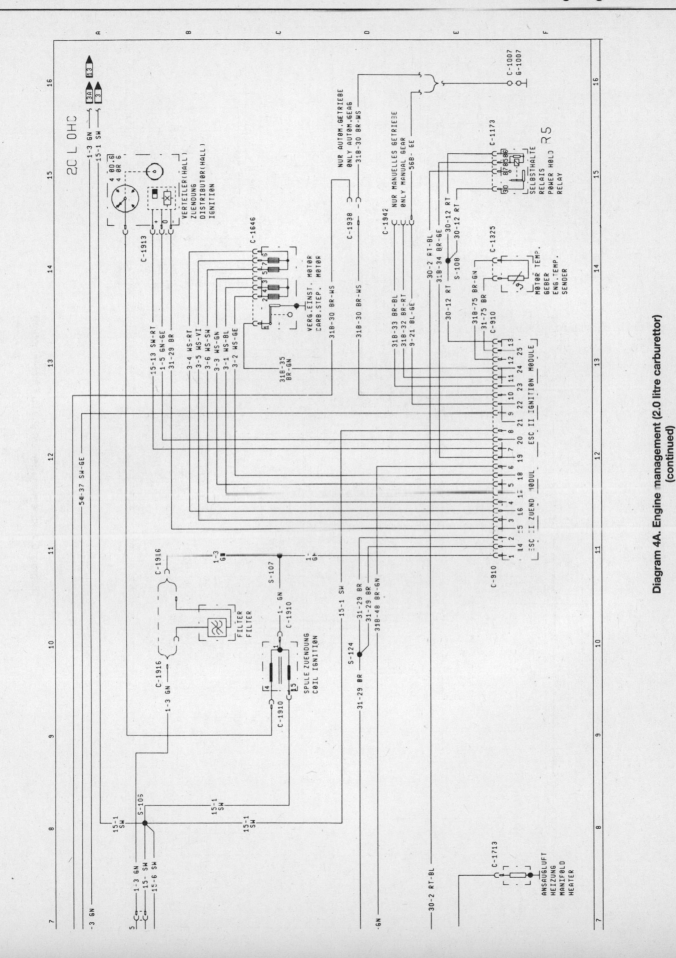

Diagram 4A. Engine management (2.0 litre carburettor) (continued)

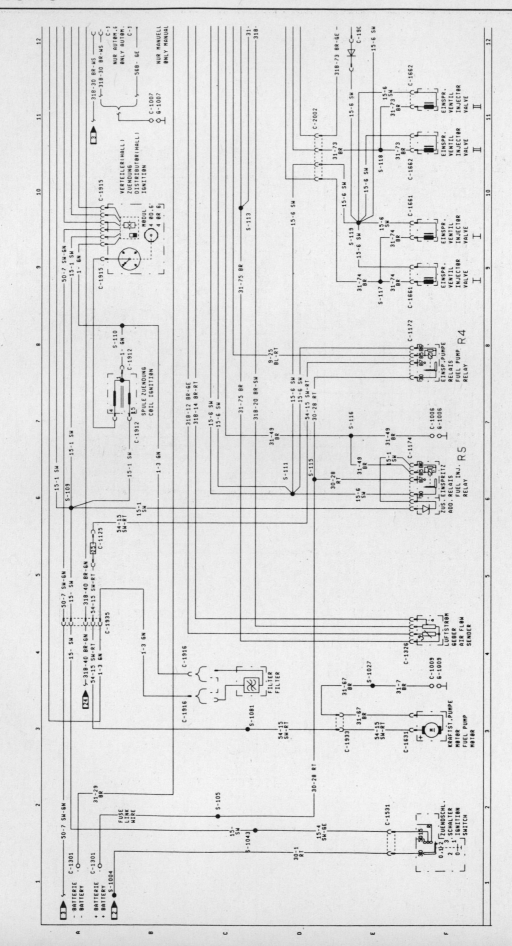

Diagram 5. Engine management (2.0 litre fuel-injection)

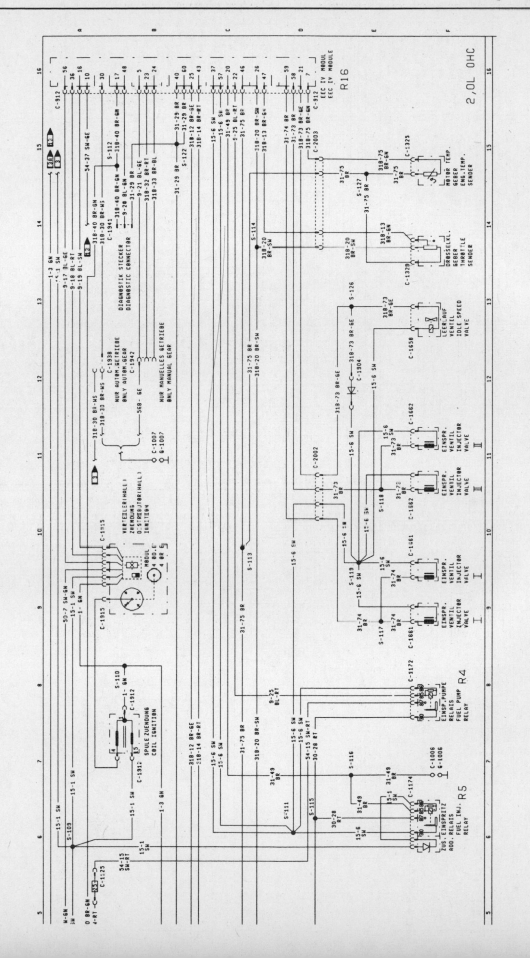

Diagram 5. Engine management (2.0 litre fuel-injection) (continued)

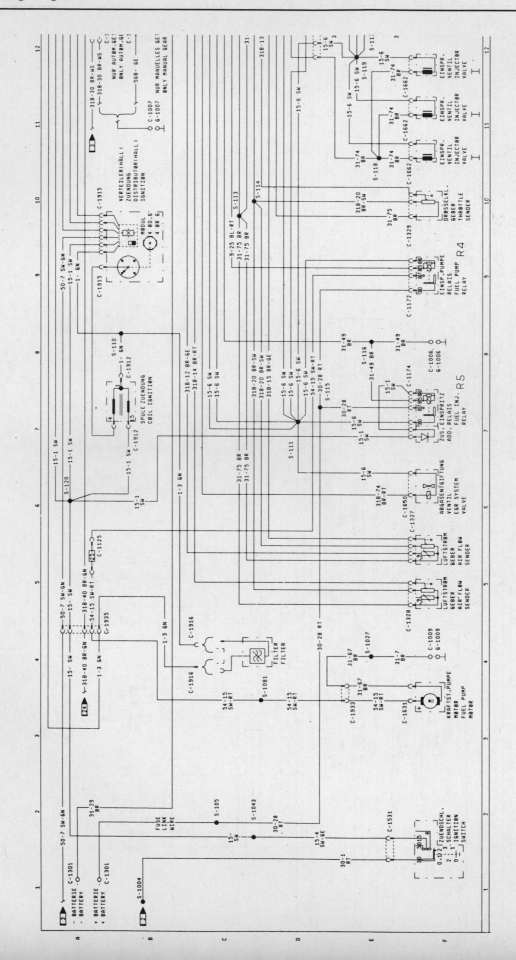

Diagram 5C. Engine management* (2.8 litre)

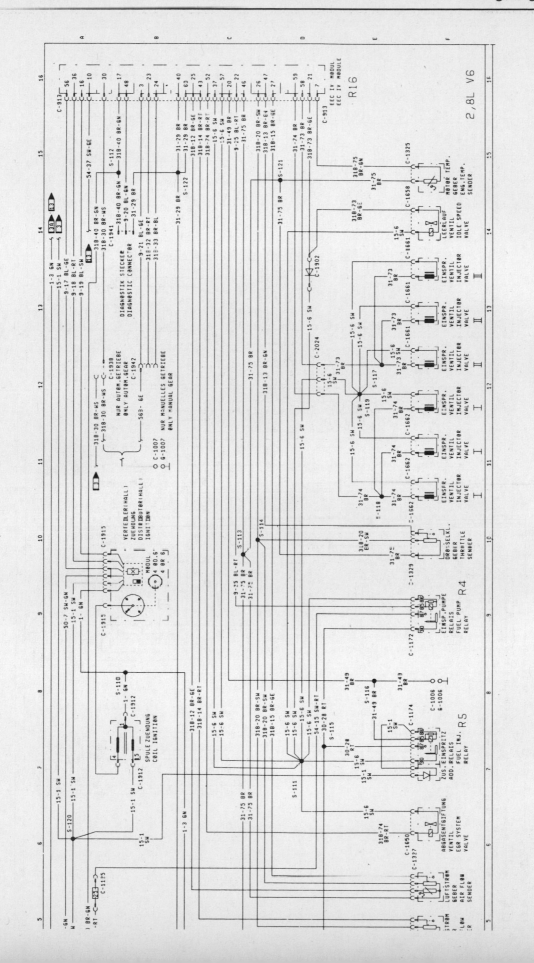

Diagram 5C. Engine management (2.8 litre)
(continued)

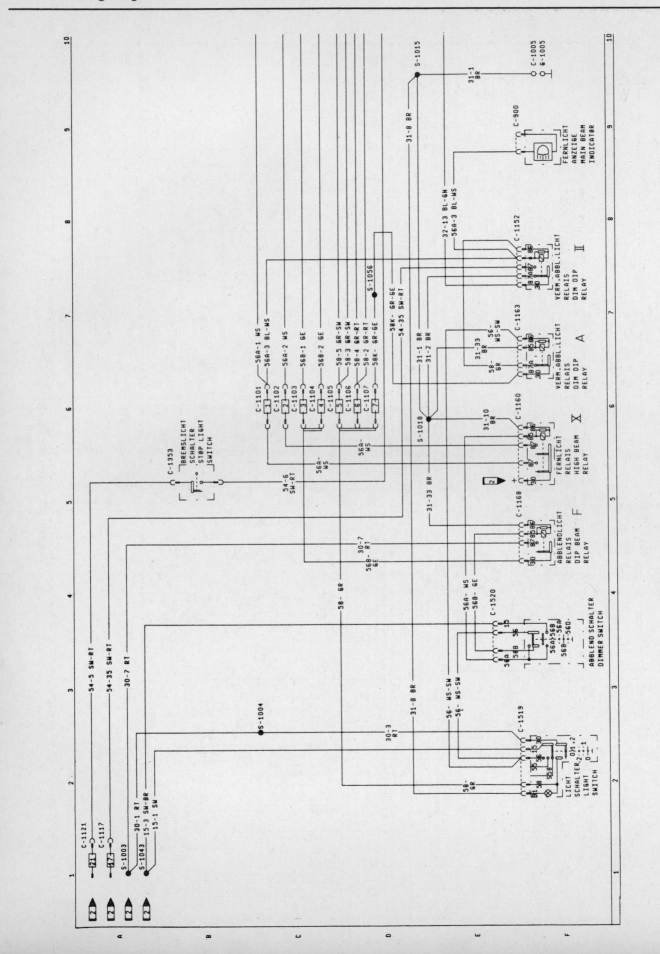

Diagram 7A. Exterior lighting

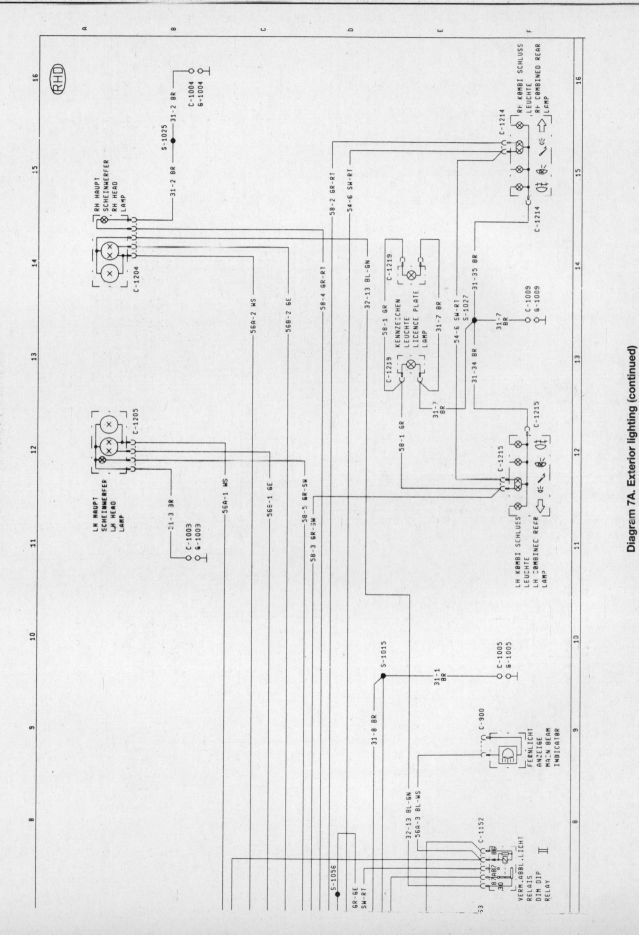

Diagram 7A. Exterior lighting (continued)

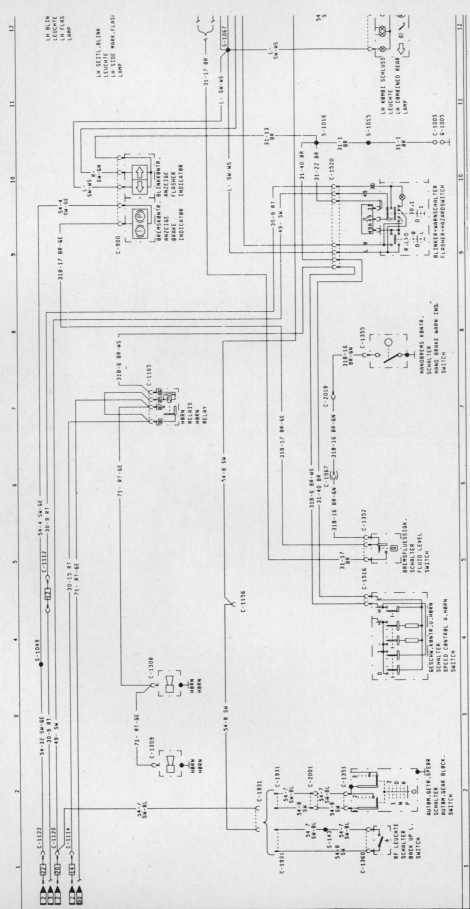

Diagram 9. Signalling and warning systems

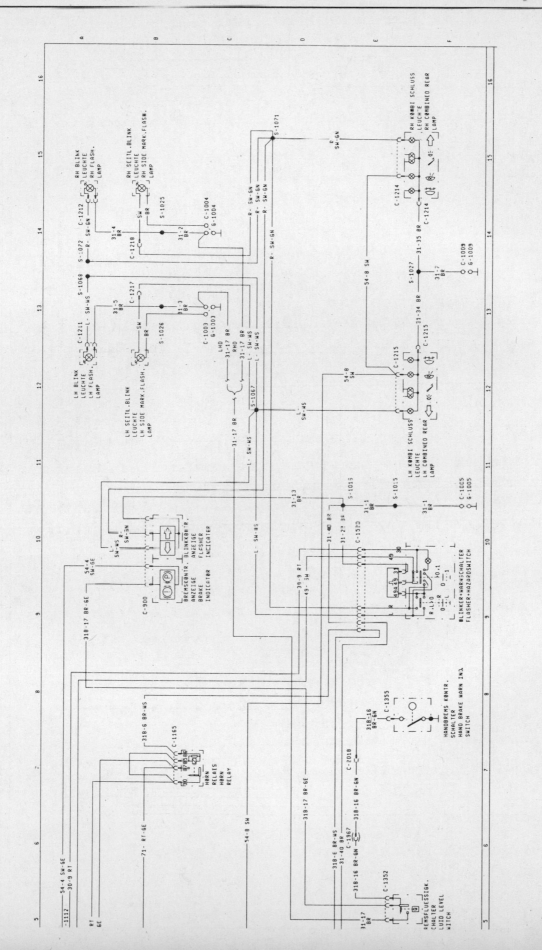

Diagram 9. Signalling and warning systems (continued)

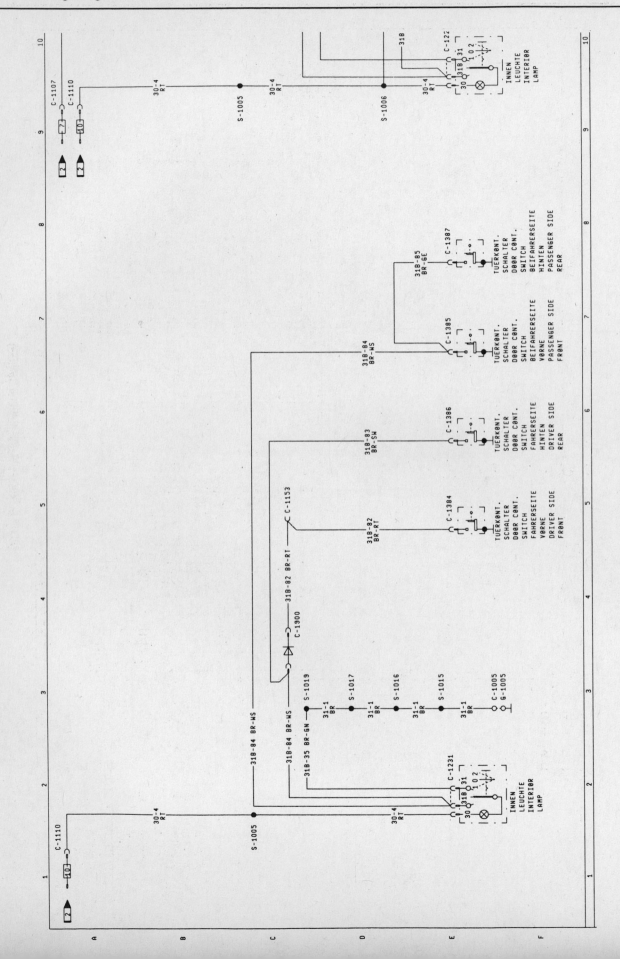

Diagram 10. Interior lighting

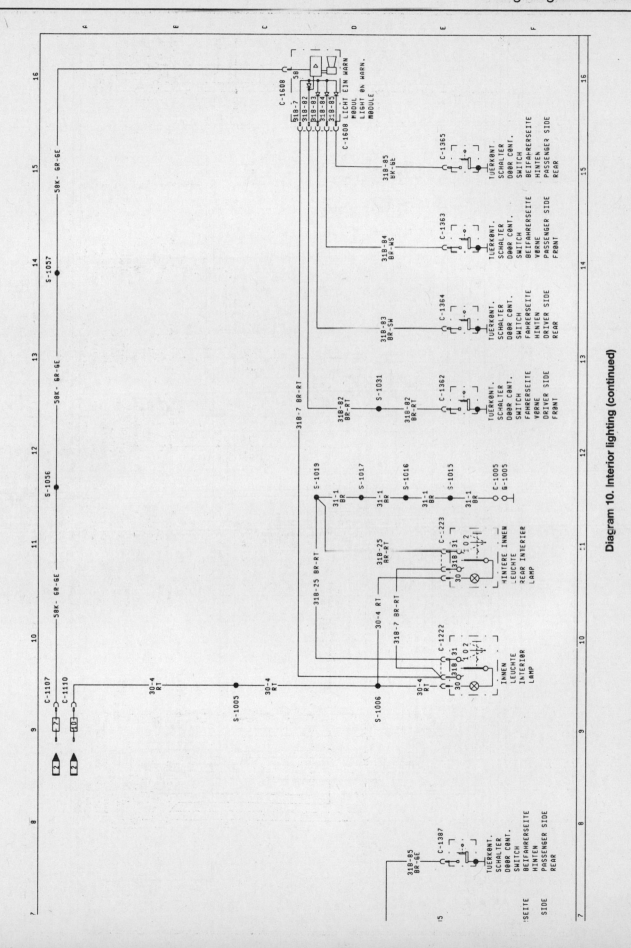

Diagram 10. Interior lighting (continued)

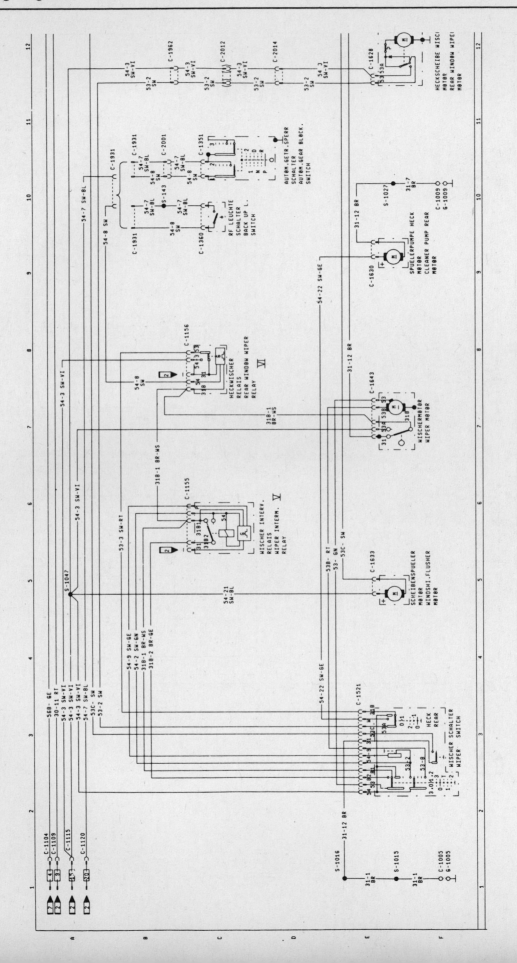

Diagram 12. Wipers and washers

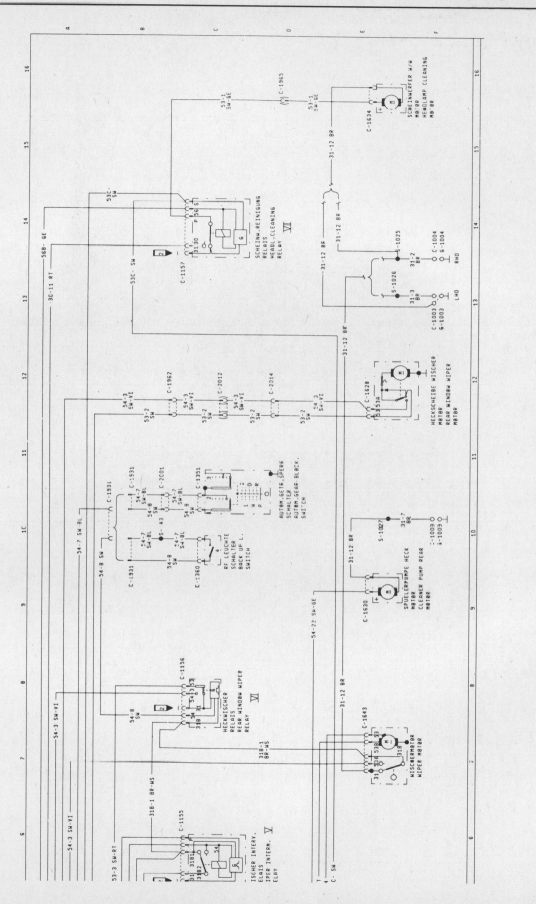

Diagram 12. Wipers and washers (continued)

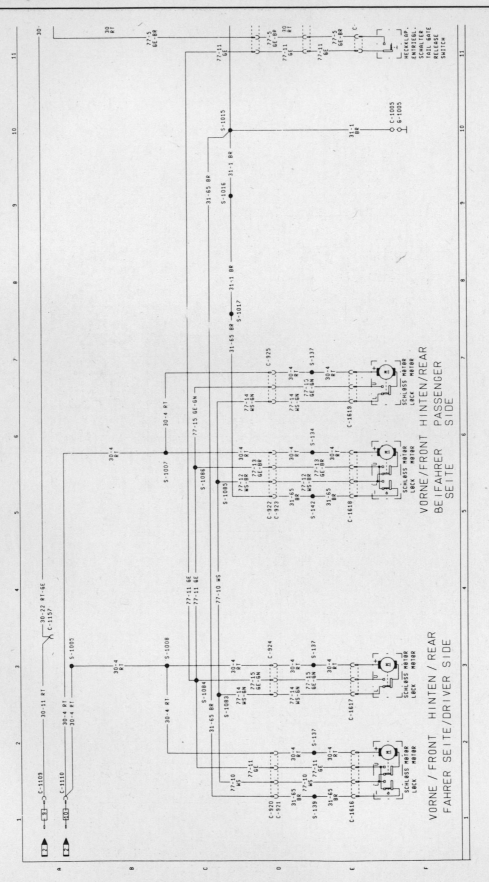

Diagram 14. Central locking system

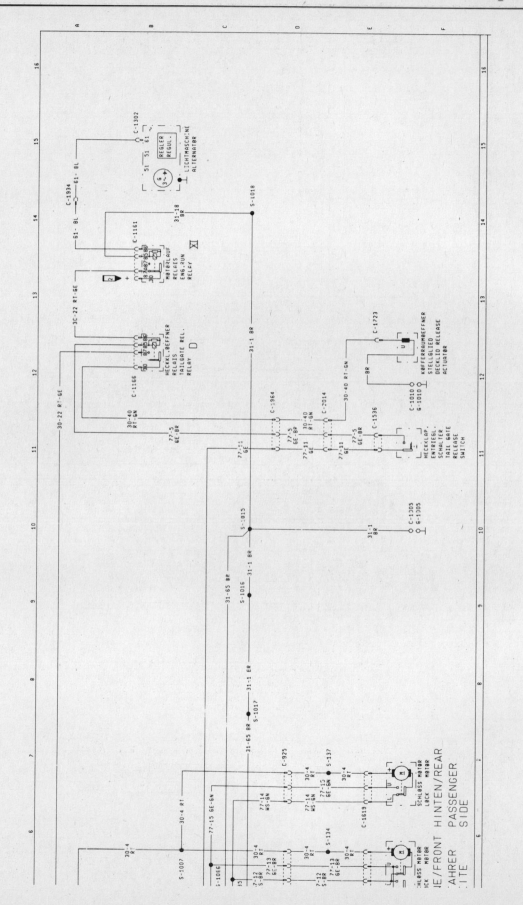

Diagram 14. Central locking system (continued)

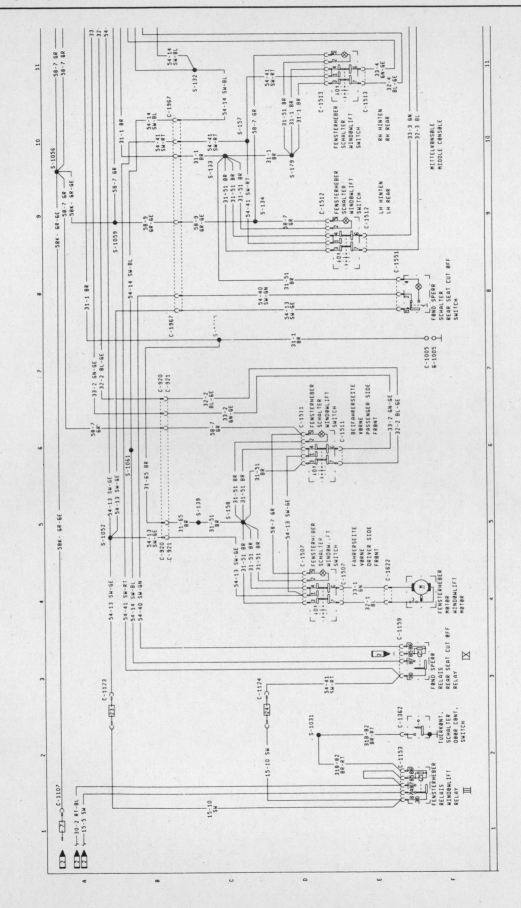

Diagram 15. Power-operated windows

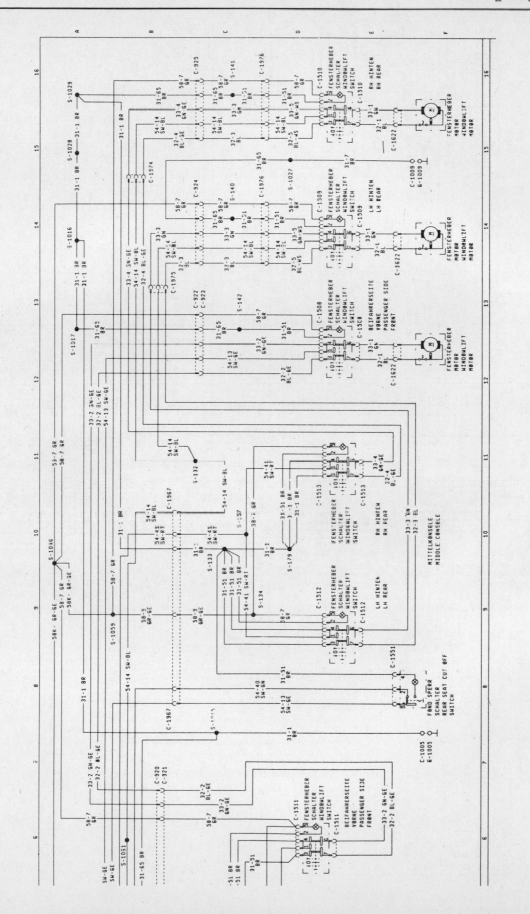

**Diagram 15. Power-operated windows
(continued)**

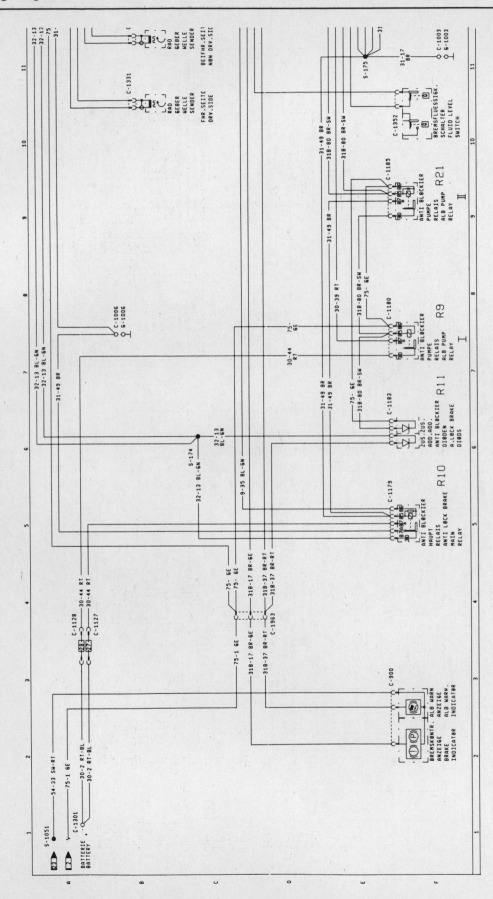

Diagram 21. ABS

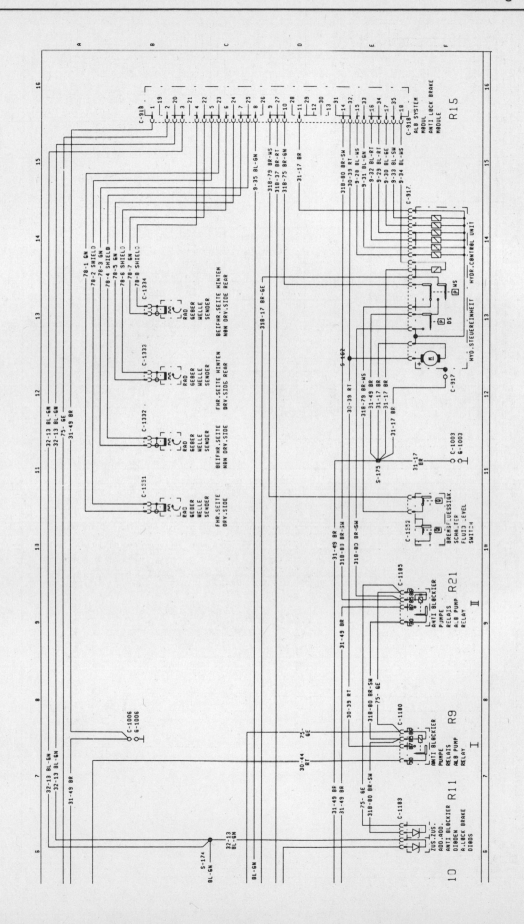

Diagram 21. ABS (continued)

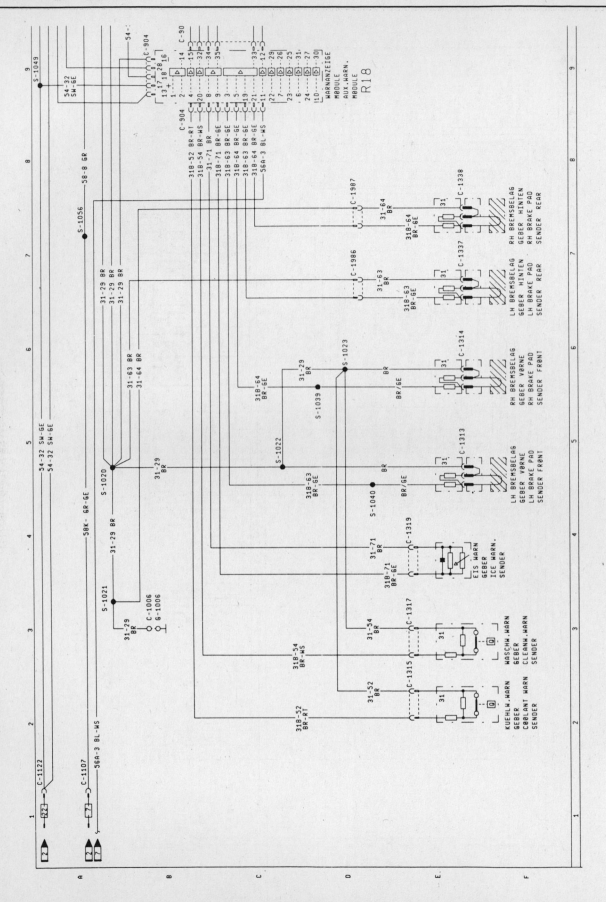

Diagram 23. Auxiliary warning system

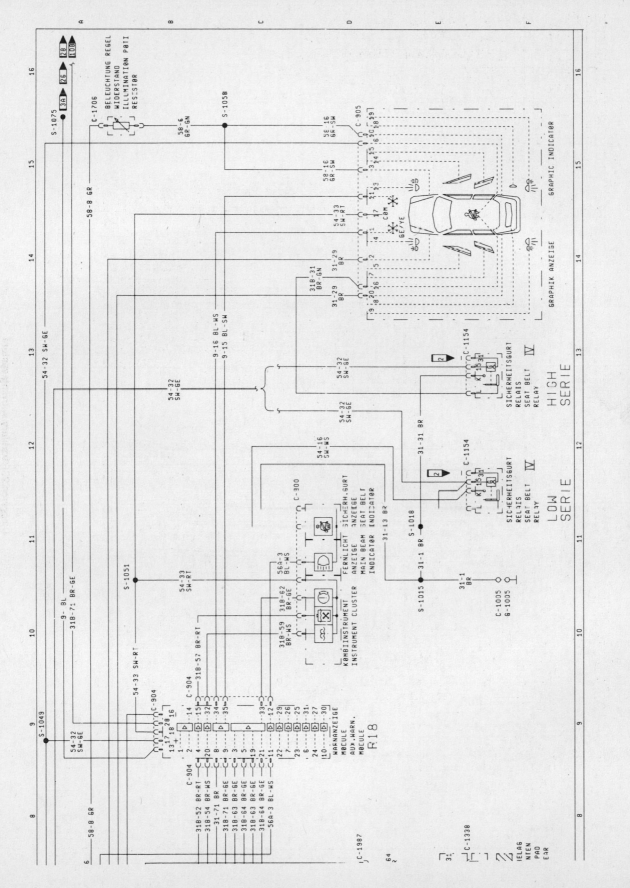

Diagram 23. Auxiliary warning system (continued)

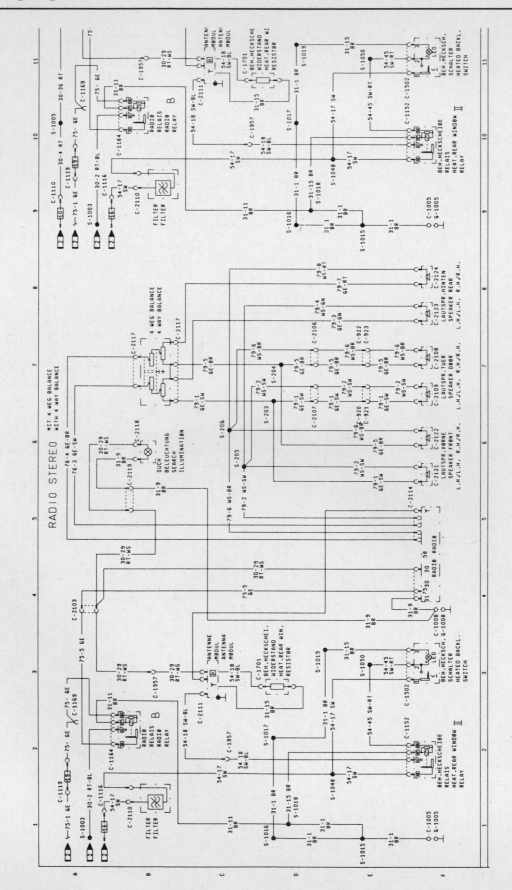

Diagram 29. Radio/cassette player and associated circuits (typical)

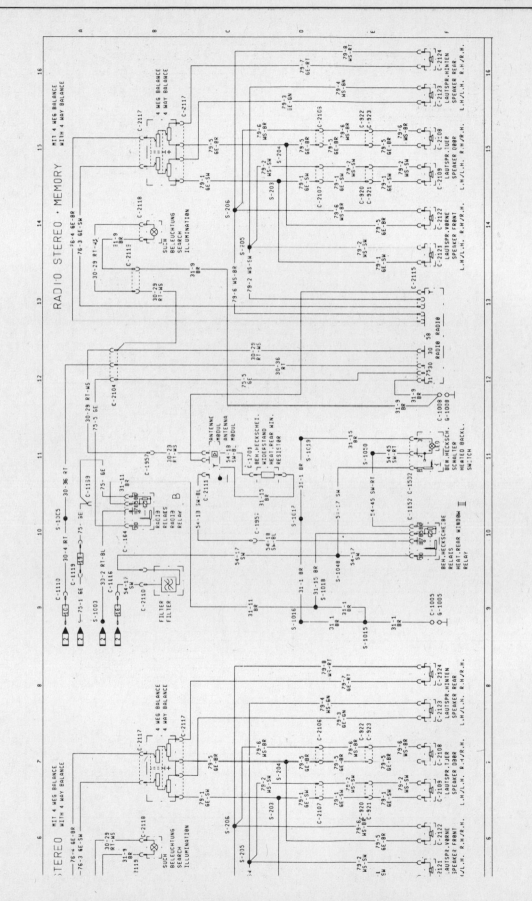

Diagram 29. Radio/cassette player and associated circuits (typical) (continued)

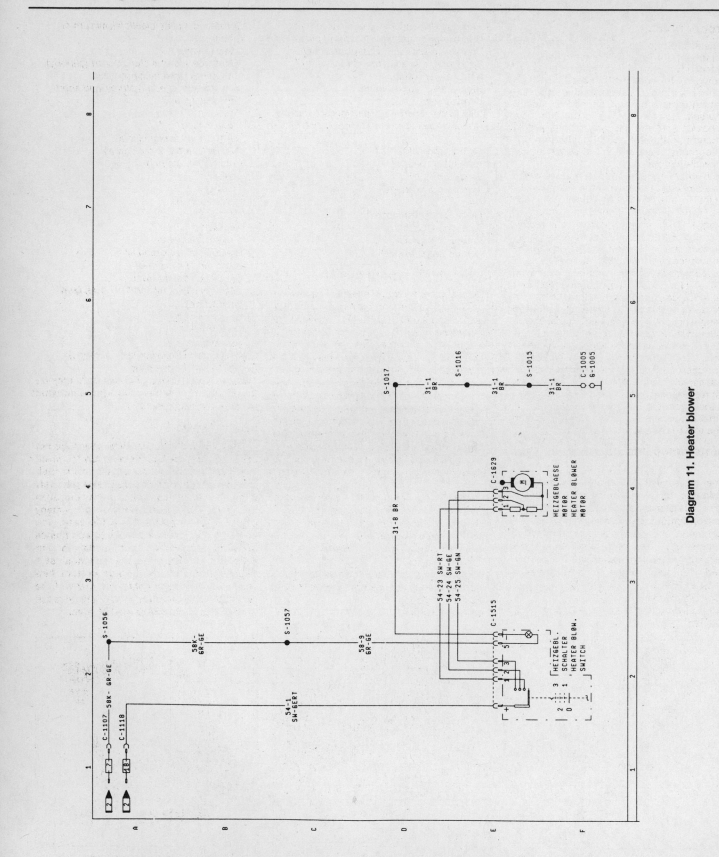

Diagram 11. Heater blower

Introduction

A selection of good tools is a fundamental requirement for anyone contemplating the maintenance and repair of a motor vehicle. For the owner who does not possess any, their purchase will prove a considerable expense, offsetting some of the savings made by doing-it-yourself. However, provided that the tools purchased meet the relevant national safety standards and are of good quality, they will last for many years and prove an extremely worthwhile investment.

To help the average owner to decide which tools are needed to carry out the various tasks detailed in this manual, we have compiled three lists of tools under the following headings: *Maintenance and minor repair*, *Repair and overhaul*, and *Special*. Newcomers to practical mechanics should start off with the *Maintenance and minor repair* tool kit, and confine themselves to the simpler jobs around the vehicle. Then, as confidence and experience grow, more difficult tasks can be undertaken, with extra tools being purchased as, and when, they are needed. In this way, a *Maintenance and minor repair* tool kit can be built up into a *Repair and overhaul* tool kit over a considerable period of time, without any major cash outlays. The experienced do-it-yourselfer will have a tool kit good enough for most repair and overhaul procedures, and will add tools from the *Special* category when it is felt that the expense is justified by the amount of use to which these tools will be put.

Maintenance and minor repair tool kit

The tools given in this list should be considered as a minimum requirement if routine maintenance, servicing and minor repair operations are to be undertaken. We recommend the purchase of combination spanners (ring one end, open-ended the other); although more expensive than open-ended ones, they do give the advantages of both types of spanner.

☐ Combination spanners:
   Metric - 8, 9, 10, 11, 12, 13, 14, 15, 17 & 19 mm
☐ Adjustable spanner - 35 mm jaw (approx)
☐ Gearbox and final drive filler/level plug keys
☐ Spark plug spanner (with rubber insert)
☐ Spark plug gap adjustment tool
☐ Set of feeler blades
☐ Brake bleed nipple spanner
☐ Screwdrivers:
   Flat blade - approx 100 mm long x 6 mm dia
   Cross blade - approx 100 mm long x 6 mm dia
☐ Combination pliers
☐ Hacksaw (junior)
☐ Tyre pump
☐ Tyre pressure gauge
☐ Oil can
☐ Oil filter removal tool
☐ Fine emery cloth
☐ Wire brush (small)
☐ Funnel (medium size)

Repair and overhaul tool kit

These tools are virtually essential for anyone undertaking any major repairs to a motor vehicle, and are additional to those given in the *Maintenance and minor repair* list. Included in this list is a comprehensive set of sockets. Although these are expensive, they will be found invaluable as they are so versatile - particularly if various drives are included in the set. We recommend the half-inch square-drive type, as this can be used with most proprietary torque wrenches. If you cannot afford a socket set, even bought piecemeal, then inexpensive tubular box spanners are a useful alternative.

The tools in this list will occasionally need to be supplemented by tools from the *Special* list:

☐ Sockets (or box spanners) to cover range in previous list (including Torx sockets)*
☐ Reversible ratchet drive (for use with sockets) **(see illustration)**
☐ Extension piece, 250 mm (for use with sockets)
☐ Universal joint (for use with sockets)
☐ Torque wrench (for use with sockets)
☐ Self-locking grips
☐ Ball pein hammer
☐ Soft-faced mallet (plastic/aluminium or rubber)
☐ Screwdrivers:
   Flat blade - long & sturdy, short (chubby), and narrow (electrician's) types
   Cross blade - Long & sturdy, and short (chubby) types
☐ Pliers:
   Long-nosed
   Side cutters (electrician's)
   Circlip (internal and external)
☐ Cold chisel - 25 mm
☐ Scriber
☐ Scraper
☐ Centre-punch
☐ Pin punch
☐ Hacksaw
☐ Brake hose clamp
☐ Brake/clutch bleeding kit
☐ Selection of twist drills
☐ Steel rule/straight-edge
☐ Allen keys (inc. splined/Torx type) **(see illustration)**
☐ Selection of files
☐ Wire brush
☐ Axle stands
☐ Jack (strong trolley or hydraulic type)
☐ Light with extension lead
* Some Imperial sized nuts and bolts may be found on air conditioning and automatic transmission components

Special tools

The tools in this list are those which are not used regularly, are expensive to buy, or which need to be used in accordance with their manufacturer's instructions. Unless relatively difficult mechanical jobs are undertaken frequently, it will not be economic to buy many of these tools. Where this is the case, you could consider clubbing together with friends (or joining a motorists' club) to make a joint purchase, or borrowing the tools against a deposit from a local garage or tool hire specialist. It is worth noting that many of the larger DIY superstores now carry a large range of special tools for hire at modest rates.

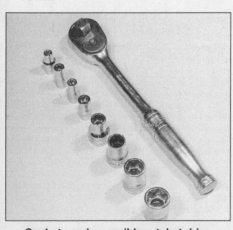

Sockets and reversible ratchet drive

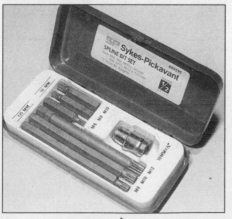

Spline bit set

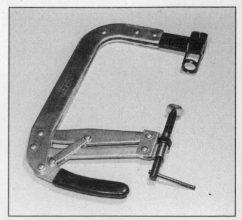

Valve spring compressor

Tools and Working Facilities

Piston ring compressor

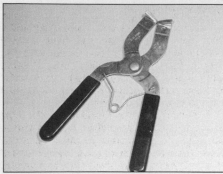

Piston ring removal/installation tool

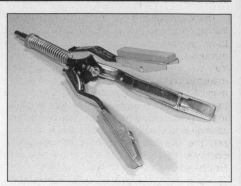

Cylinder bore hone

Three-legged hub and bearing puller

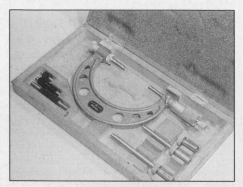

Micrometer set

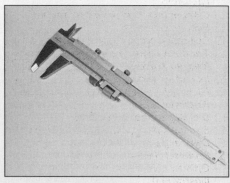

Vernier calipers

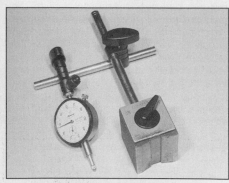

Dial test indicator and magnetic stand

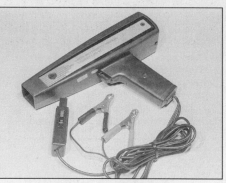

Stroboscopic timing light

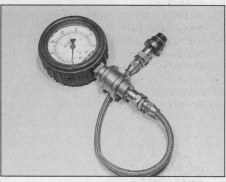

Compression testing gauge

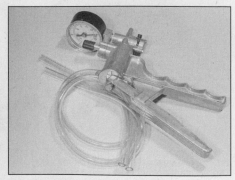

Vacuum pump and gauge

Clutch plate alignment set

Brake shoe steady spring cup removal tool

The following list contains only those tools and instruments freely available to the public, and not those special tools produced by the vehicle manufacturer specifically for its dealer network. You will find occasional references to these manufacturer's special tools in the text of this manual. Generally, an alternative method of doing the job without the vehicle manufacturer's special tool is given. However, sometimes there is no alternative to using them. Where this is the case and the relevant tool cannot be bought or borrowed, you will have to entrust the work to a franchised garage.

- [ ] *Valve spring compressor* **(see illustration)**
- [ ] *Valve grinding tool*
- [ ] *Piston ring compressor* **(see illustration)**
- [ ] *Piston ring removal/installation tool* **(see illustration)**
- [ ] *Cylinder bore hone* **(see illustration)**
- [ ] *Balljoint separator*
- [ ] *Coil spring compressors (where applicable)*
- [ ] *Two/three-legged hub and bearing puller* **(see illustration)**
- [ ] *Impact screwdriver*
- [ ] *Micrometer and/or vernier calipers* **(see illustrations)**
- [ ] *Dial gauge* **(see illustration)**
- [ ] *Stroboscopic timing light* **(see illustration)**
- [ ] *Dwell angle meter/tachometer*
- [ ] *Universal electrical multi-meter*
- [ ] *Cylinder compression gauge* **(see illustration)**
- [ ] *Hand-operated vacuum pump and gauge* **(see illustration)**
- [ ] *Clutch plate alignment set* **(see illustration)**
- [ ] *Brake shoe steady spring cup removal tool* **(see illustration)**
- [ ] *Bush and bearing removal/installation set* **(see illustration)**
- [ ] *Stud extractors* **(see illustration)**
- [ ] *Tap and die set* **(see Illustration)**
- [ ] *Lifting tackle*
- [ ] *Trolley jack*

Buying tools

For practically all tools, a tool factor is the best source, since he will have a very comprehensive range compared with the average garage or accessory shop. Having said that, accessory shops often offer excellent quality tools at discount prices, so it pays to shop around.

Remember, you don't have to buy the most expensive items on the shelf, but it is always advisable to steer clear of the very cheap tools. There are plenty of good tools around at reasonable prices, but always aim to purchase items which meet the relevant national safety standards. If in doubt, ask the proprietor or manager of the shop for advice before making a purchase.

Care and maintenance of tools

Having purchased a reasonable tool kit, it is necessary to keep the tools in a clean and serviceable condition. After use, always wipe off any dirt, grease and metal particles using a clean, dry cloth, before putting the tools away. Never leave them lying around after they have been used. A simple tool rack on the garage or workshop wall, for items such as screwdrivers and pliers, is a good idea. Store all normal spanners and sockets in a metal box. Any measuring instruments, gauges, meters, etc, must be carefully stored where they cannot be damaged or become rusty.

Take a little care when tools are used. Hammer heads inevitably become marked, and screwdrivers lose the keen edge on their blades from time to time. A little timely attention with emery cloth or a file will soon restore items like this to a good serviceable finish.

Working facilities

Not to be forgotten when discussing tools is the workshop itself. If anything more than routine maintenance is to be carried out, some form of suitable working area becomes essential.

It is appreciated that many an owner-mechanic is forced by circumstances to remove an engine or similar item without the benefit of a garage or workshop. Having done this, any repairs should always be done under the cover of a roof.

Wherever possible, any dismantling should be done on a clean, flat workbench or table at a suitable working height.

Any workbench needs a vice; one with a jaw opening of 100 mm is suitable for most jobs. As mentioned previously, some clean dry storage space is also required for tools, as well as for any lubricants, cleaning fluids, touch-up paints and so on, which become necessary.

Another item which may be required, and which has a much more general usage, is an electric drill with a chuck capacity of at least 8 mm. This, together with a good range of twist drills, is virtually essential for fitting accessories.

Lastly, always keep a supply of old newspapers and clean, lint-free rags available, and try to keep any working area as clean as possible.

Bush and bearing removal/installation set

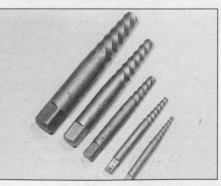

Stud extractor set

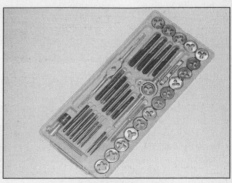

Tap and die set

General Repair Procedures

Whenever servicing, repair or overhaul work is carried out on the car or its components, it is necessary to observe the following procedures and instructions. This will assist in carrying out the operation efficiently and to a professional standard of workmanship.

Joint mating faces and gaskets

When separating components at their mating faces, never insert screwdrivers or similar implements into the joint between the faces in order to prise them apart. This can cause severe damage which results in oil leaks, coolant leaks, etc upon reassembly. Separation is usually achieved by tapping along the joint with a soft-faced hammer in order to break the seal. However, note that this method may not be suitable where dowels are used for component location.

Where a gasket is used between the mating faces of two components, ensure that it is renewed on reassembly, and fit it dry unless otherwise stated in the repair procedure. Make sure that the mating faces are clean and dry, with all traces of old gasket removed. When cleaning a joint face, use a tool which is not likely to score or damage the face, and remove any burrs or nicks with an oilstone or fine file.

Make sure that tapped holes are cleaned with a pipe cleaner, and keep them free of jointing compound, if this is being used, unless specifically instructed otherwise.

Ensure that all orifices, channels or pipes are clear, and blow through them, preferably using compressed air.

Oil seals

Oil seals can be removed by levering them out with a wide flat-bladed screwdriver or similar implement. Alternatively, a number of self-tapping screws may be screwed into the seal, and these used as a purchase for pliers or some similar device in order to pull the seal free.

Whenever an oil seal is removed from its working location, either individually or as part of an assembly, it should be renewed.

The very fine sealing lip of the seal is easily damaged, and will not seal if the surface it contacts is not completely clean and free from scratches, nicks or grooves.

Protect the lips of the seal from any surface which may damage them in the course of fitting. Use tape or a conical sleeve where possible. Lubricate the seal lips with oil before fitting and, on dual-lipped seals, fill the space between the lips with grease.

Unless otherwise stated, oil seals must be fitted with their sealing lips toward the lubricant to be sealed.

Use a tubular drift or block of wood of the appropriate size to install the seal and, if the seal housing is shouldered, drive the seal down to the shoulder. If the seal housing is unshouldered, the seal should be fitted with its face flush with the housing top face (unless otherwise instructed).

Screw threads and fastenings

Seized nuts, bolts and screws are quite a common occurrence where corrosion has set in, and the use of penetrating oil or releasing fluid will often overcome this problem if the offending item is soaked for a while before attempting to release it. The use of an impact driver may also provide a means of releasing such stubborn fastening devices, when used in conjunction with the appropriate screwdriver bit or socket. If none of these methods works, it may be necessary to resort to the careful application of heat, or the use of a hacksaw or nut splitter device.

Studs are usually removed by locking two nuts together on the threaded part, and then using a spanner on the lower nut to unscrew the stud. Studs or bolts which have broken off below the surface of the component in which they are mounted can sometimes be removed using a proprietary stud extractor. Always ensure that a blind tapped hole is completely free from oil, grease, water or other fluid before installing the bolt or stud. Failure to do this could cause the housing to crack due to the hydraulic action of the bolt or stud as it is screwed in.

When tightening a castellated nut to accept a split pin, tighten the nut to the specified torque, where applicable, and then tighten further to the next split pin hole. Never slacken the nut to align the split pin hole, unless stated in the repair procedure.

When checking or retightening a nut or bolt to a specified torque setting, slacken the nut or bolt by a quarter of a turn, and then retighten to the specified setting. However, this should not be attempted where angular tightening has been used.

For some screw fastenings, notably cylinder head bolts or nuts, torque wrench settings are no longer specified for the latter stages of tightening, "angle-tightening" being called up instead. Typically, a fairly low torque wrench setting will be applied to the bolts/nuts in the correct sequence, followed by one or more stages of tightening through specified angles.

Locknuts, locktabs and washers

Any fastening which will rotate against a component or housing in the course of tightening should always have a washer between it and the relevant component or housing.

Spring or split washers should always be renewed when they are used to lock a critical component such as a big-end bearing retaining bolt or nut. Locktabs which are folded over to retain a nut or bolt should always be renewed.

Self-locking nuts can be re-used in non-critical areas, providing resistance can be felt when the locking portion passes over the bolt or stud thread. However, it should be noted that self-locking stiffnuts tend to lose their effectiveness after long periods of use, and in such cases should be renewed as a matter of course.

Split pins must always be replaced with new ones of the correct size for the hole.

When thread-locking compound is found on the threads of a fastener which is to be re-used, it should be cleaned off with a wire brush and solvent, and fresh compound applied on reassembly.

Special tools

Some repair procedures in this manual entail the use of special tools such as a press, two or three-legged pullers, spring compressors, etc. Wherever possible, suitable readily-available alternatives to the manufacturer's special tools are described, and are shown in use. Unless you are highly-skilled and have a thorough understanding of the procedures described, never attempt to bypass the use of any special tool when the procedure described specifies its use. Not only is there a very great risk of personal injury, but expensive damage could be caused to the components involved.

Environmental considerations

When disposing of used engine oil, brake fluid, antifreeze, etc, give due consideration to any detrimental environmental effects. Do not, for instance, pour any of the above liquids down drains into the general sewage system, or onto the ground to soak away. Many local council refuse tips provide a facility for waste oil disposal, as do some garages. If none of these facilities are available, consult your local Environmental Health Department for further advice.

With the universal tightening-up of legislation regarding the emission of environmentally-harmful substances from motor vehicles, most current vehicles have tamperproof devices fitted to the main adjustment points of the fuel system. These devices are primarily designed to prevent unqualified persons from adjusting the fuel/air mixture, with the chance of a consequent increase in toxic emissions. If such devices are encountered during servicing or overhaul, they should, wherever possible, be renewed or refitted in accordance with the vehicle manufacturer's requirements or current legislation.

OIL CARE
FOLLOW THE CODE

OIL BANK LINE
0800 66 33 66

Note: It is antisocial and illegal to dump oil down the drain. To find the location of your local oil recycling bank, call this number free.

Engine   1

- [ ] Engine fails to rotate when attempting to start
- [ ] Starter motor turns engine slowly
- [ ] Engine rotates, but will not start
- [ ] Engine difficult to start when cold
- [ ] Engine difficult to start when hot
- [ ] Starter motor noisy or excessively-rough in engagement
- [ ] Engine starts, but stops immediately
- [ ] Engine idles erratically
- [ ] Engine misfires at idle speed
- [ ] Engine misfires throughout the driving speed range
- [ ] Engine hesitates on acceleration
- [ ] Engine stalls
- [ ] Engine lacks power
- [ ] Engine backfires
- [ ] Oil pressure warning light illuminated with engine running
- [ ] Engine runs-on after switching off
- [ ] Engine noises

Cooling system   2

- [ ] Overheating
- [ ] Overcooling
- [ ] External coolant leakage
- [ ] Internal coolant leakage
- [ ] Corrosion

Fuel and exhaust systems   3

- [ ] Excessive fuel consumption
- [ ] Fuel leakage and/or fuel odour
- [ ] Excessive noise or fumes from exhaust system

Clutch   4

- [ ] Pedal travels to floor - no pressure or very little resistance
- [ ] Clutch fails to disengage (unable to select gears)
- [ ] Clutch slips (engine speed increases, with no increase in vehicle speed)
- [ ] Judder as clutch is engaged
- [ ] Noise when depressing or releasing clutch pedal

Manual gearbox   5

- [ ] Noisy in neutral with engine running
- [ ] Noisy in one particular gear
- [ ] Difficulty engaging gears
- [ ] Jumps out of gear
- [ ] Vibration
- [ ] Lubricant leaks

Automatic transmission   6

- [ ] Fluid leakage
- [ ] Transmission fluid brown, or has burned smell
- [ ] General gear selection problems
- [ ] Transmission will not downshift (kickdown) with accelerator fully depressed
- [ ] Engine will not start in any gear, or starts in gears other than Park or Neutral
- [ ] Transmission slips, shifts roughly, is noisy, or has no drive in forward or reverse gears

Propeller shaft   7

- [ ] Clicking or knocking noise on turns (at slow speed on full-lock)
- [ ] Vibration when accelerating or decelerating

Final drive and driveshafts   8

- [ ] Excessive final drive noise
- [ ] Oil leakage from final drive
- [ ] Grating, knocking or vibration from driveshafts

Braking system   9

- [ ] Vehicle pulls to one side under braking
- [ ] Noise (grinding or high-pitched squeal) when brakes applied
- [ ] Excessive brake pedal travel
- [ ] Brake pedal feels spongy when depressed
- [ ] Excessive brake pedal effort required to stop vehicle
- [ ] Judder felt through brake pedal or steering wheel when braking
- [ ] Pedal pulsates when braking hard
- [ ] Brakes binding
- [ ] Rear wheels locking under normal braking

Suspension and steering systems   10

- [ ] Vehicle pulls to one side
- [ ] Wheel wobble and vibration
- [ ] Excessive pitching and/or rolling around corners, or during braking
- [ ] Wandering or general instability
- [ ] Excessively-stiff steering
- [ ] Excessive play in steering
- [ ] Lack of power assistance
- [ ] Tyre wear excessive

Electrical system   11

- [ ] Lights inoperative
- [ ] Ignition/no charge warning light remains illuminated with engine running
- [ ] Ignition/no-charge warning light fails to come on
- [ ] Battery will not hold a charge for more than a few days
- [ ] Instrument readings inaccurate or erratic
- [ ] Horn inoperative, or unsatisfactory in operation
- [ ] Windscreen/tailgate wipers inoperative, or unsatisfactory in operation
- [ ] Windscreen/tailgate washers inoperative, or unsatisfactory in operation
- [ ] Electric windows inoperative, or unsatisfactory in operation
- [ ] Central locking system inoperative, or unsatisfactory in operation

Introduction

The vehicle owner who does his or her own maintenance according to the recommended service schedules should not have to use this section of the manual very often. Modern component reliability is such that, provided those items subject to wear or deterioration are inspected or renewed at the specified intervals, sudden failure is comparatively rare. Faults do not usually just happen as a result of sudden failure, but develop over a period of time. Major mechanical failures in particular are usually preceded by characteristic symptoms over hundreds or even thousands of miles. Those components which do occasionally fail without warning are often small and easily carried in the vehicle.

With any fault-finding, the first step is to decide where to begin investigations. Sometimes this is obvious, but on other occasions, a little detective work will be necessary. The owner who makes half a dozen haphazard adjustments or replacements may be successful in curing a fault (or its symptoms), but will be none the wiser if the fault recurs, and ultimately may have spent more time and money than was necessary. A calm and logical approach will be found to be more satisfactory in the long run. Always take into account any warning signs or abnormalities that may have been noticed in the period preceding the fault - power loss, high or low gauge readings, unusual smells, etc - and remember that failure of components such as fuses or

Fault Finding

spark plugs may only be pointers to some underlying fault.

The pages which follow provide an easy-reference guide to the more common problems which may occur during the operation of the vehicle. These problems and their possible causes are grouped under headings denoting various components or systems, such as Engine, Cooling system, etc. The Chapter and/or Section which deals with the problem is also shown in brackets. Whatever the fault, certain basic principles apply. These are as follows:

Verify the fault. This is simply a matter of being sure that you know what the symptoms are before starting work. This is particularly important if you are investigating a fault for someone else, who may not have described it very accurately.

Don't overlook the obvious. For example, if the vehicle won't start, is there fuel in the tank? (Don't take anyone else's word on this particular point, and don't trust the fuel gauge either!) If an electrical fault is indicated, look for loose or broken wires before digging out the test gear.

Cure the disease, not the symptom. Substituting a flat battery with a fully-charged one will get you off the hard shoulder, but if the underlying cause is not attended to, the new battery will go the same way. Similarly, changing oil-fouled spark plugs for a new set will get you moving again, but remember that the reason for the fouling (if it wasn't simply an incorrect grade of plug) will have to be established and corrected.

Don't take anything for granted. Particularly, don't forget that a "new" component may itself be defective (especially if it's been rattling around in the boot for months), and don't leave components out of a fault diagnosis sequence just because they are new or recently-fitted. When you do finally diagnose a difficult fault, you'll probably realise that all the evidence was there from the start.

1 Engine

Engine fails to rotate when attempting to start

☐ Battery terminal connections loose or corroded (Chapter 1).
☐ Battery discharged or faulty (Chapter 5).
☐ Broken, loose or disconnected wiring in the starting circuit (Chapter 5).
☐ Defective starter solenoid or switch (Chapter 5).
☐ Defective starter motor (Chapter 5).
☐ Starter pinion or flywheel/driveplate ring gear teeth loose or broken (Chapters 2 or 5).
☐ Engine earth strap broken or disconnected.

Starter motor turns engine slowly

☐ Partially-discharged battery (recharge, use jump leads, or push start) (Chapter 5).
☐ Battery terminals loose or corroded (Chapter 1).
☐ Battery earth to body defective (Chapter 5).
☐ Engine earth strap loose.
☐ Starter motor (or solenoid) wiring loose (Chapter 5).
☐ Starter motor internal fault (Chapter 5).

Engine rotates, but will not start

☐ Fuel pump inertia switch tripped (electric pump) (Chapter 4).
☐ Fuel tank empty.
☐ Battery discharged (engine rotates slowly) (Chapter 5).
☐ Battery terminal connections loose or corroded (Chapter 1).
☐ Ignition components damp or damaged (Chapters 1 and 5).
☐ Broken, loose or disconnected wiring in the ignition circuit (Chapters 1 and 5).
☐ Worn, faulty or incorrectly-gapped spark plugs (Chapter 1).
☐ Fuel injection system fault (Chapter 4).
☐ Major mechanical failure (eg broken timing chain) (Chapter 2).

Engine difficult to start when cold

☐ Battery discharged (Chapter 5).
☐ Battery terminal connections loose or corroded (Chapter 1).
☐ Worn, faulty or incorrectly-gapped spark plugs (Chapter 1).
☐ Fuel injection system fault (Chapter 4).
☐ Other ignition system fault (Chapters 1 and 5).
☐ Low cylinder compressions (Chapter 2).

Engine difficult to start when hot

☐ Air filter element dirty or clogged (Chapter 1).
☐ Fuel injection system fault (Chapter 4).
☐ Low cylinder compressions (Chapter 2).

Starter motor noisy or excessively-rough in engagement

☐ Starter pinion or flywheel/driveplate ring gear teeth loose or broken (Chapters 2 or 5).
☐ Starter motor mounting bolts loose or missing (Chapter 5).
☐ Starter motor internal components worn or damaged (Chapter 5).

Engine starts, but stops immediately

☐ Loose or faulty electrical connections in the ignition circuit (Chapters 1 and 5).
☐ Vacuum leak at the throttle body or inlet manifold (Chapter 4).
☐ Fuel injection system fault (Chapter 4).

Engine idles erratically

☐ Carburettor stepper motor plunger dirty (2.0 litre only) (Chapter 5)
☐ Incorrectly-adjusted idle speed (Chapter 4).
☐ Air filter element clogged (Chapter 1).
☐ Vacuum leak at the throttle body, inlet manifold or associated hoses (Chapter 4).
☐ Worn, faulty or incorrectly-gapped spark plugs (Chapter 1).
☐ Uneven or low cylinder compressions (Chapter 2).
☐ Camshaft lobes worn (Chapter 2).
☐ Fuel injection system fault (Chapter 4).

Engine misfires at idle speed

☐ Worn, faulty or incorrectly-gapped spark plugs (Chapter 1).
☐ Faulty spark plug HT leads (Chapter 5).
☐ Vacuum leak at the throttle body, inlet manifold or associated hoses (Chapter 4).
☐ Fuel injection system fault (Chapter 4).
☐ Distributor cap cracked or tracking internally, where applicable (Chapter 5).
☐ Uneven or low cylinder compressions (Chapter 2).
☐ Disconnected, leaking, or perished crankcase ventilation hoses (Chapter 4).

Engine misfires throughout the driving speed range

- [ ] Fuel filter choked (Chapter 1).
- [ ] Fuel pump faulty, or delivery pressure low (Chapter 4).
- [ ] Fuel tank vent blocked, or fuel pipes restricted (Chapter 4).
- [ ] Vacuum leak at the throttle body, inlet manifold or associated hoses (Chapter 4).
- [ ] Worn, faulty or incorrectly-gapped spark plugs (Chapter 1).
- [ ] Faulty spark plug HT leads (Chapter 5).
- [ ] Distributor cap cracked or tracking internally (Chapter 5).
- [ ] Faulty ignition coil (Chapter 5).
- [ ] Uneven or low cylinder compressions (Chapter 2).
- [ ] Fuel injection system fault (Chapter 4).

Engine hesitates on acceleration

- [ ] Worn, faulty or incorrectly-gapped spark plugs (Chapter 1).
- [ ] Vacuum leak at the throttle body, inlet manifold or associated hoses (Chapter 4).
- [ ] Fuel injection system fault (Chapter 4).

Engine stalls

- [ ] Vacuum leak at the throttle body, inlet manifold or associated hoses (Chapter 4).
- [ ] Fuel filter choked (Chapter 1).
- [ ] Fuel pump faulty, or delivery pressure low (Chapter 4).
- [ ] Fuel tank vent blocked, or fuel pipes restricted (Chapter 4).
- [ ] Fuel injection system fault (Chapter 4).

Engine lacks power

- [ ] Fuel filter choked (Chapter 1).
- [ ] Fuel pump faulty, or delivery pressure low (Chapter 4).
- [ ] Uneven or low cylinder compressions (Chapter 2).
- [ ] Worn, faulty or incorrectly-gapped spark plugs (Chapter 1).
- [ ] Vacuum leak at the throttle body, inlet manifold or associated hoses (Chapter 4).
- [ ] Fuel injection system fault (Chapter 4).
- [ ] Brakes binding (Chapters 1 and 10).
- [ ] Clutch slipping (Chapter 6).

Engine backfires

- [ ] Vacuum leak at the throttle body, inlet manifold or associated hoses (Chapter 4).
- [ ] Fuel injection system fault (Chapter 4).

Oil pressure warning light illuminated with engine running

- [ ] Low oil level, or incorrect oil grade (Chapter 1).
- [ ] Faulty oil pressure sensor (Chapter 2).
- [ ] Worn engine bearings and/or oil pump (Chapter 2).
- [ ] Excessively high engine operating temperature (Chapter 3).
- [ ] Oil pressure relief valve defective (Chapter 2).
- [ ] Oil pick-up strainer clogged (Chapter 2).

Note: *Low oil pressure in a high-mileage engine at tickover is not necessarily a cause for concern. Sudden pressure loss at speed is far more significant. In any event, check the gauge or warning light sender before condemning the engine.*

Engine runs-on after switching off

- [ ] Excessive carbon build-up in engine (Chapter 2).
- [ ] Excessively high engine operating temperature (Chapter 3).

Engine noises

Pre-ignition (pinking) or knocking during acceleration or under load

- [ ] Ignition timing incorrect/ignition system fault (Chapters 1 and 5).
- [ ] Incorrect grade of spark plug (Chapter 1).
- [ ] Incorrect grade of fuel (Chapter 1).
- [ ] Vacuum leak at throttle body, inlet manifold or associated hoses (Chapter 4).
- [ ] Excessive carbon build-up in engine (Chapter 2).
- [ ] Fuel injection system fault (Chapter 4).

Whistling or wheezing noises

- [ ] Leaking inlet manifold or throttle body gasket (Chapter 4).
- [ ] Leaking exhaust manifold gasket (Chapter 4).
- [ ] Leaking vacuum hose (Chapters 4 and 10).
- [ ] Blowing cylinder head gasket (Chapter 2).

Tapping or rattling noises

- [ ] Worn valve gear, timing chain, camshaft or hydraulic tappets (Chapter 2).
- [ ] Ancillary component fault (water pump, alternator, etc) (Chapters 3, 5, etc).

Knocking or thumping noises

- [ ] Worn big-end bearings (regular heavy knocking, perhaps less under load) (Chapter 2).
- [ ] Worn main bearings (rumbling and knocking, perhaps worsening under load) (Chapter 2).
- [ ] Piston slap (most noticeable when cold) (Chapter 2).
- [ ] Ancillary component fault (water pump, alternator, etc) (Chapters 3, 5, etc).

2 Cooling system

Overheating

- [ ] Auxiliary drivebelt broken or incorrectly adjusted (Chapter 1).
- [ ] Insufficient coolant in system (Chapter 1).
- [ ] Thermostat faulty (Chapter 3).
- [ ] Radiator core blocked, or grille restricted (Chapter 3).
- [ ] Electric cooling fan or thermostatic switch faulty (Chapter 3).
- [ ] Viscous-coupled fan faulty (Chapter 3).
- [ ] Ignition timing incorrect, or ignition system fault (Chapters 1 and 5).
- [ ] Inaccurate temperature gauge sender unit (Chapter 3).
- [ ] Airlock in cooling system (Chapter 3).

Overcooling

- [ ] Thermostat faulty (Chapter 3).
- [ ] Inaccurate temperature gauge sender unit (Chapter 3).

External coolant leakage

- [ ] Deteriorated or damaged hoses or hose clips (Chapter 1).
- [ ] Radiator core or heater matrix leaking (Chapter 3).
- [ ] Pressure cap faulty (Chapter 3).
- [ ] Water pump internal seal leaking (Chapter 3).
- [ ] Water pump-to-block seal leaking (Chapter 3).
- [ ] Boiling due to overheating (Chapter 3).
- [ ] Core plug leaking (Chapter 2).

Internal coolant leakage

- [ ] Leaking cylinder head gasket (Chapter 2).
- [ ] Cracked cylinder head or cylinder block (Chapter 2).

Corrosion

- [ ] Infrequent draining and flushing (Chapter 1).
- [ ] Incorrect coolant mixture or inappropriate coolant type (Chapter 1).

Fault Finding

3 Fuel and exhaust systems

Excessive fuel consumption

- [ ] Air filter element dirty or clogged (Chapter 1).
- [ ] Fuel injection system fault (Chapter 4).
- [ ] Ignition timing incorrect or ignition system fault (Chapters 1 and 5).
- [ ] Brakes binding (Chapter 10).
- [ ] Tyres under-inflated (Chapter 1).

Fuel leakage and/or fuel odour

- [ ] Damaged fuel tank, pipes or connections (Chapters 1 and 4).

Excessive noise or fumes from exhaust system

- [ ] Leaking exhaust system or manifold joints (Chapters 1 and 4).
- [ ] Leaking, corroded or damaged silencers or pipe (Chapters 1 and 4).
- [ ] Broken mountings causing body or suspension contact (Chapter 4).

4 Clutch

Pedal travels to floor - no pressure or very little resistance

- [ ] Badly stretched or broken cable (Chapter 6).
- [ ] Stripped pawl on pedal (Chapter 6).
- [ ] Broken clutch release bearing or arm (Chapter 6).
- [ ] Broken diaphragm spring in clutch pressure plate (Chapter 6).

Clutch fails to disengage (unable to select gears)

- [ ] Cable free play excessive (Chapter 6).
- [ ] Clutch driven plate sticking on gearbox input shaft splines (Chapter 6).
- [ ] Clutch driven plate sticking to flywheel or pressure plate (Chapter 6).
- [ ] Faulty pressure plate assembly (Chapter 6).
- [ ] Clutch release mechanism worn or incorrectly assembled (Chapter 6).

Clutch slips (engine speed increases, with no increase in vehicle speed)

- [ ] Clutch driven plate linings excessively worn (Chapter 6).
- [ ] Clutch driven plate linings contaminated with oil or grease (Chapter 6).
- [ ] Faulty pressure plate or weak diaphragm spring (Chapter 6).

Judder as clutch is engaged

- [ ] Clutch driven plate linings contaminated with oil or grease (Chapter 6).
- [ ] Clutch driven plate linings excessively worn (Chapter 6).
- [ ] Faulty or distorted pressure plate or diaphragm spring (Chapter 6).
- [ ] Worn or loose engine or gearbox mountings (Chapter 2).
- [ ] Clutch driven plate hub or gearbox input shaft splines worn (Chapter 6).

Noise when depressing or releasing clutch pedal

- [ ] Worn clutch release bearing (Chapter 6).
- [ ] Worn or dry clutch pedal pivot (Chapter 6).
- [ ] Faulty pressure plate assembly (Chapter 6).
- [ ] Pressure plate diaphragm spring broken (Chapter 6).
- [ ] Broken clutch driven plate cushioning springs (Chapter 6).

5 Manual gearbox

Noisy in neutral with engine running

- [ ] Input shaft bearings worn (noise apparent with clutch pedal released, but not when depressed) (Chapter 7A).*
- [ ] Clutch release bearing worn (noise apparent with clutch pedal depressed, possibly less when released) (Chapter 6).

Noisy in one particular gear

- [ ] Worn, damaged or chipped gear teeth (Chapter 7A).*

Difficulty engaging gears

- [ ] Clutch fault (Chapter 6).
- [ ] Worn or damaged gear linkage (Chapter 7A).
- [ ] Worn synchroniser units (Chapter 7A).*

Jumps out of gear

- [ ] Worn or damaged gear linkage (Chapter 7A).
- [ ] Worn synchroniser units (Chapter 7A).*
- [ ] Worn selector forks (Chapter 7A).*

Vibration

- [ ] Lack of oil (Chapter 1).
- [ ] Worn bearings (Chapter 7A).*

Lubricant leaks

- [ ] Leaking oil seal (Chapter 7A).
- [ ] Leaking housing joint (Chapter 7A).*

*Although the corrective action necessary to remedy the symptoms described is beyond the scope of the home mechanic, the above information should be helpful in isolating the cause of the condition, so that the owner can communicate clearly with a professional mechanic.

6 Automatic transmission

Note: *Due to the complexity of the automatic transmission, it is difficult for the home mechanic to properly diagnose and service this unit. For problems other than the following, the vehicle should be taken to a dealer service department or automatic transmission specialist.*

Fluid leakage

- [ ] Automatic transmission fluid is usually deep red in colour. Fluid leaks should not be confused with engine oil, which can easily be blown onto the transmission by air flow.

- [ ] To determine the source of a leak, first remove all built-up dirt and grime from the transmission housing and surrounding areas, using a degreasing agent or by steam-cleaning. Drive the vehicle at low speed, so that air flow will not blow the leak far from its source. Raise and support the vehicle, and determine where the leak is coming from. The following are common areas of leakage:
  - a)   *Fluid pan (transmission "sump").*
  - b)   *Dipstick tube (Chapter 1).*
  - c)   *Transmission-to-fluid cooler fluid pipes/unions (Chapter 7B).*

Transmission fluid brown, or has burned smell

☐ Transmission fluid level low, or fluid in need of renewal (Chapter 1).

General gear selection problems

☐ The most likely cause of gear selection problems is a faulty or poorly-adjusted gear selector mechanism. The following are common problems associated with a faulty selector mechanism:

a) Engine starting in gears other than Park or Neutral.
b) Indicator on gear selector lever pointing to a gear other than the one actually being used.
c) Vehicle moves when in Park or Neutral.
d) Poor gear shift quality, or erratic gear changes.

☐ Refer any problems to a Ford dealer, or an automatic transmission specialist.

Transmission will not downshift (kickdown) with accelerator pedal fully depressed

☐ Low transmission fluid level (Chapter 1).
☐ Incorrect selector adjustment (Chapter 7B).

7 Propeller shaft

Clunking or knocking noise when taking up drive

☐ Worn universal joints (Chapter 8).
☐ Loose flange bolt (Chapter 8).

8 Final drive and driveshafts

Excessive final drive noise

☐ Oil level low, or incorrect grade (Chapter 1)
☐ Worn bearings (Chapter 9)
☐ Worn or badly adjusted crownwheel and pinion (Chapter 9)
☐ Loose or deteriorated final drive mountings (Chapter 9)

Oil leakage from final drive

☐ Pinion or output flange oil seal leaking (Chapter 9)

9 Braking system

Note: *Make sure that the tyres are in good condition and correctly inflated, that the front wheel alignment is correct, and that the vehicle is not loaded with weight in an unequal manner. Apart from checking the condition of all pipe and hose connections, any faults occurring on the anti-lock braking system should be referred to a Ford dealer for diagnosis.*

Vehicle pulls to one side under braking

☐ Worn, defective, damaged or contaminated front or rear brake pads on one side (Chapters 1 and 10).
☐ Seized or partially-seized front or rear brake caliper piston (Chapter 10).
☐ A mixture of brake pad lining materials fitted between sides (Chapter 10).
☐ Brake caliper mounting bolts loose (Chapter 10).
☐ Worn or damaged steering or suspension components (Chapters 1 and 11).

Noise (grinding or high-pitched squeal) when brakes applied

☐ Brake pad friction material worn down to metal backing (Chapters 1 and 10).
☐ Excessive corrosion of brake disc - may be apparent after the vehicle has been standing for some time (Chapters 1 and 10).

Engine will not start in any gear, or starts in gears other than Park or Neutral

☐ Faulty starter inhibitor switch (Chapter 7B).
☐ Incorrect selector adjustment (Chapter 7B).

Transmission slips, shifts roughly, is noisy, or has no drive in forward or reverse gears

☐ There are many probable causes for the above problems, but the home mechanic should be concerned with only one possibility - fluid level. Before taking the vehicle to a dealer or transmission specialist, check the fluid level and condition of the fluid as described in Chapter 1. Correct the fluid level as necessary, or change the fluid and filter if needed. If the problem persists, professional help will be necessary.

Vibration when accelerating or decelerating

☐ Worn centre bearing or universal joints (Chapter 8).
☐ Bent or distorted shaft (Chapter 8).
☐ Deteriorated rubber insulator on centre bearing (Chapter 8)

☐ Rear cover leaking (Chapter 9)
☐ Cover or casing cracked (Chapter 9)

Grating, knocking or vibration from driveshafts

☐ Flange screws loose (Chapter 9)
☐ CV joints worn (Chapter 9)
☐ Driveshaft bent (Chapter 9)

Excessive brake pedal travel

☐ Faulty master cylinder (Chapter 10).
☐ Air in hydraulic system (Chapter 10).
☐ Faulty vacuum servo unit (Chapter 10).

Brake pedal feels spongy when depressed

☐ Air in hydraulic system (Chapter 10).
☐ Deteriorated flexible rubber brake hoses (Chapters 1 and 10).
☐ Master cylinder mountings loose (Chapter 10).
☐ Faulty master cylinder (Chapter 10).

Excessive brake pedal effort required to stop vehicle

☐ Faulty vacuum servo unit (Chapter 10).
☐ Disconnected, damaged or insecure brake servo vacuum hose (Chapters 1 and 10).
☐ Primary or secondary hydraulic circuit failure (Chapter 10).
☐ Seized brake caliper piston(s) (Chapter 10).
☐ Brake pads incorrectly fitted (Chapter 10).
☐ Incorrect grade of brake pads fitted (Chapter 10).
☐ Brake pads contaminated (Chapter 10).

Fault Finding

Judder felt through brake pedal or steering wheel when braking

☐ Excessive run-out or distortion of brake disc(s) (Chapter 10).
☐ Brake pad linings worn (Chapters 1 and 10).
☐ Brake caliper mounting bolts loose (Chapter 10).
☐ Wear in suspension or steering components or mountings (Chapters 1 and 11).

Pedal pulsates when braking hard

☐ Normal feature of ABS - no fault

Brakes binding

☐ Seized brake caliper piston(s) (Chapter 10).
☐ Incorrectly-adjusted handbrake mechanism (Chapter 10).
☐ Faulty master cylinder (Chapter 10).

Rear wheels locking under normal braking

☐ Seized brake caliper piston(s) (Chapter 10).
☐ Faulty brake pressure regulator (Chapter 10).

10 Steering and suspension

Note: *Before diagnosing suspension or steering faults, be sure that the trouble is not due to incorrect tyre pressures, mixtures of tyre types, or binding brakes.*

Vehicle pulls to one side

☐ Defective tyre (Chapter 1).
☐ Excessive wear in suspension or steering components (Chapters 1 and 11).
☐ Incorrect front wheel alignment (Chapter 11).
☐ Accident damage to steering or suspension components (Chapters 1 and 11).

Wheel wobble and vibration

☐ Front roadwheels out of balance (vibration felt mainly through the steering wheel) (Chapter 11).
☐ Rear roadwheels out of balance (vibration felt throughout the vehicle) (Chapter 11).
☐ Roadwheels damaged or distorted (Chapter 11).
☐ Faulty or damaged tyre (Chapter 1).
☐ Worn steering or suspension joints, bushes or components (Chapters 1 and 11).
☐ Wheel bolts loose (Chapter 11).

Excessive pitching and/or rolling around corners, or during braking

☐ Defective shock absorbers (Chapters 1 and 11).
☐ Broken or weak coil spring and/or suspension component (Chapters 1 and 11).
☐ Worn or damaged anti-roll bar or mountings (Chapter 11).

Wandering or general instability

☐ Incorrect front wheel alignment (Chapter 11).
☐ Worn steering or suspension joints, bushes or components (Chapters 1 and 11).
☐ Roadwheels out of balance (Chapter 11).
☐ Faulty or damaged tyre (Chapter 1).
☐ Wheel bolts loose (Chapter 11).
☐ Defective shock absorbers (Chapters 1 and 11).

Excessively-stiff steering

☐ Lack of steering gear lubricant (Chapter 11).
☐ Seized track rod end balljoint or suspension balljoint (Chapters 1 and 11).

☐ Broken or incorrectly adjusted auxiliary drivebelt (Chapter 1).
☐ Incorrect front wheel alignment (Chapter 11).
☐ Steering rack or column bent or damaged (Chapter 11).

Excessive play in steering

☐ Worn steering column universal joint(s) (Chapter 11).
☐ Worn steering track rod end balljoints (Chapters 1 and 11).
☐ Worn rack-and-pinion steering gear (Chapter 11).
☐ Worn steering or suspension joints, bushes or components (Chapters 1 and 11).

Lack of power assistance

☐ Broken or incorrectly-adjusted auxiliary drivebelt (Chapter 1).
☐ Incorrect power steering fluid level (Chapter 1).
☐ Restriction in power steering fluid hoses (Chapter 11).
☐ Faulty power steering pump (Chapter 11).
☐ Faulty rack-and-pinion steering gear (Chapter 11).

Tyre wear excessive

Tyres worn on inside or outside edges

☐ Tyres under-inflated (wear on both edges) (Chapter 1).
☐ Incorrect camber or castor angles (wear on one edge only) (Chapter 11).
☐ Worn steering or suspension joints, bushes or components Chapters 1 and 11).
☐ Excessively-hard cornering.
☐ Accident damage.

Tyre treads exhibit feathered edges

☐ Incorrect toe setting (Chapter 11).

Tyres worn in centre of tread

☐ Tyres over-inflated (Chapter 1).

Tyres worn on inside and outside edges

☐ Tyres under-inflated (Chapter 1).
☐ Worn shock absorbers (Chapters 1 and 11).

Tyres worn unevenly

☐ Tyres out of balance (Chapter 1).
☐ Excessive wheel or tyre run-out (Chapter 1).
☐ Worn shock absorbers (Chapters 1 and 11).
☐ Faulty tyre (Chapter 1).

11 Electrical system

Note: *For problems associated with the starting system, refer to the faults listed under "Engine" earlier in this Section.*

Lights inoperative

☐ Bulb blown (Chapter 13).

☐ Corrosion of bulb or bulbholder contacts (Chapter 13).
☐ Blown fuse (Chapter 13).
☐ Faulty relay (Chapter 13).
☐ Broken, loose, or disconnected wiring (Chapter 13).
☐ Faulty switch (Chapter 13).

Ignition/no-charge warning light remains illuminated with engine running

- [ ] Auxiliary drivebelt broken, worn, or incorrectly adjusted (Chapter 1).
- [ ] Alternator brushes worn, sticking, or dirty (Chapter 5).
- [ ] Alternator brush springs weak or broken (Chapter 5).
- [ ] Internal fault in alternator or voltage regulator (Chapter 5).
- [ ] Broken, disconnected, or loose wiring in charging circuit (Chapter 5).

Ignition/no-charge warning light fails to come on

- [ ] Warning light bulb blown (Chapter 13).
- [ ] Broken, disconnected, or loose wiring in warning light circuit (Chapter 13).
- [ ] Alternator faulty (Chapter 5).

Battery will not hold a charge for more than a few days

- [ ] Battery defective internally (Chapter 5).
- [ ] Battery electrolyte level low - where applicable (Chapter 1).
- [ ] Battery terminal connections loose or corroded (Chapter 1).
- [ ] Auxiliary drivebelt worn - or incorrectly adjusted, where applicable (Chapter 1).
- [ ] Alternator not charging at correct output (Chapter 5).
- [ ] Alternator or voltage regulator faulty (Chapter 5).
- [ ] Short-circuit causing continual battery drain (Chapters 5 and 13).

Instrument readings inaccurate or erratic

Instrument readings increase with engine speed
- [ ] Faulty voltage regulator (Chapter 13).

Fuel or temperature gauges give no reading
- [ ] Faulty gauge sender unit (Chapters 4 and 5).
- [ ] Wiring open-circuit (Chapter 13).
- [ ] Faulty gauge (Chapter 13).

Fuel or temperature gauges give continuous maximum reading
- [ ] Faulty gauge sender unit (Chapters 4 and 5).
- [ ] Wiring short-circuit (Chapter 13).
- [ ] Faulty gauge (Chapter 13).

Horn inoperative, or unsatisfactory in operation

Horn operates all the time
- [ ] Horn contacts permanently bridged or horn push stuck down (Chapter 13).

Horn fails to operate
- [ ] Blown fuse (Chapter 13).
- [ ] Cable or cable connections loose, broken or disconnected (Chapter 13).
- [ ] Faulty horn (Chapter 13).

Horn emits intermittent or unsatisfactory sound
- [ ] Cable connections loose (Chapter 13).
- [ ] Horn mountings loose (Chapter 13).
- [ ] Faulty horn (Chapter 13).

Windscreen/tailgate wipers inoperative, or unsatisfactory in operation

Wipers fail to operate, or operate very slowly
- [ ] Wiper blades stuck to screen, or linkage seized or binding (Chapters 1 and 13).
- [ ] Blown fuse (Chapter 13).
- [ ] Cable or cable connections loose, broken or disconnected (Chapter 13).
- [ ] Faulty relay (Chapter 13).
- [ ] Faulty wiper motor (Chapter 13).

Wiper blades sweep over too large or too small an area of the glass
- [ ] Wiper arms incorrectly positioned on spindles (Chapter 1).
- [ ] Excessive wear of wiper linkage (Chapter 13).
- [ ] Wiper motor or linkage mountings loose or insecure (Chapter 13).

Wiper blades fail to clean the glass effectively
- [ ] Wiper blade rubbers worn or perished (Chapter 1).
- [ ] Wiper arm tension springs broken, or arm pivots seized (Chapter 13).
- [ ] Insufficient windscreen washer additive to adequately remove road film (Chapter 1).

Windscreen/tailgate washers inoperative, or unsatisfactory in operation

One or more washer jets inoperative
- [ ] Blocked washer jet (Chapter 1).
- [ ] Disconnected, kinked or restricted fluid hose (Chapter 13).
- [ ] Insufficient fluid in washer reservoir (Chapter 1).

Washer pump fails to operate
- [ ] Broken or disconnected wiring or connections (Chapter 13).
- [ ] Blown fuse (Chapter 13).
- [ ] Faulty washer switch (Chapter 13).
- [ ] Faulty washer pump (Chapter 13).

Washer pump runs for some time before fluid is emitted from jets
- [ ] Faulty one-way valve in fluid supply hose (Chapter 13).

Electric windows inoperative, or unsatisfactory in operation

Window glass will only move in one direction
- [ ] Faulty switch (Chapter 13).

Window glass slow to move
- [ ] Regulator seized or damaged, or in need of lubrication (Chapter 12).
- [ ] Door internal components or trim fouling regulator (Chapter 12).
- [ ] Faulty motor (Chapter 12).

Window glass fails to move
- [ ] Blown fuse (Chapter 13).
- [ ] Faulty relay (Chapter 13).
- [ ] Broken or disconnected wiring or connections (Chapter 13).
- [ ] Faulty motor (Chapter 13).

Central locking system inoperative, or unsatisfactory in operation

Complete system failure
- [ ] Blown fuse (Chapter 13).
- [ ] Faulty relay (Chapter 13).
- [ ] Broken or disconnected wiring or connections (Chapter 13).

Latch locks but will not unlock, or unlocks but will not lock
- [ ] Faulty switch (Chapter 13).
- [ ] Broken or disconnected latch operating rods or levers (Chapter 12).
- [ ] Faulty relay (Chapter 13).

One solenoid/motor fails to operate
- [ ] Broken or disconnected wiring or connections (Chapter 13).
- [ ] Faulty solenoid/motor (Chapter 12).
- [ ] Broken, binding or disconnected latch operating rods or levers (Chapter 12).
- [ ] Fault in door latch (Chapter 12).

Glossary of Technical Terms

A

ABS (Anti-lock brake system) A system, usually electronically controlled, that senses incipient wheel lockup during braking and relieves hydraulic pressure at wheels that are about to skid.

Air bag An inflatable bag hidden in the steering wheel (driver's side) or the dash or glovebox (passenger side). In a head-on collision, the bags inflate, preventing the driver and front passenger from being thrown forward into the steering wheel or windscreen.

Air cleaner A metal or plastic housing, containing a filter element, which removes dust and dirt from the air being drawn into the engine.

Air filter element The actual filter in an air cleaner system, usually manufactured from pleated paper and requiring renewal at regular intervals.

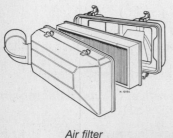

Air filter

Allen key A hexagonal wrench which fits into a recessed hexagonal hole.

Alligator clip A long-nosed spring-loaded metal clip with meshing teeth. Used to make temporary electrical connections.

Alternator A component in the electrical system which converts mechanical energy from a drivebelt into electrical energy to charge the battery and to operate the starting system, ignition system and electrical accessories.

Ampere (amp) A unit of measurement for the flow of electric current. One amp is the amount of current produced by one volt acting through a resistance of one ohm.

Anaerobic sealer A substance used to prevent bolts and screws from loosening. Anaerobic means that it does not require oxygen for activation. The Loctite brand is widely used.

Antifreeze A substance (usually ethylene glycol) mixed with water, and added to a vehicle's cooling system, to prevent freezing of the coolant in winter. Antifreeze also contains chemicals to inhibit corrosion and the formation of rust and other deposits that would tend to clog the radiator and coolant passages and reduce cooling efficiency.

Anti-seize compound A coating that reduces the risk of seizing on fasteners that are subjected to high temperatures, such as exhaust manifold bolts and nuts.

Asbestos A natural fibrous mineral with great heat resistance, commonly used in the composition of brake friction materials.

Asbestos is a health hazard and the dust created by brake systems should never be inhaled or ingested.

Axle A shaft on which a wheel revolves, or which revolves with a wheel. Also, a solid beam that connects the two wheels at one end of the vehicle. An axle which also transmits power to the wheels is known as a live axle.

Axleshaft A single rotating shaft, on either side of the differential, which delivers power from the final drive assembly to the drive wheels. Also called a driveshaft or a halfshaft.

B

Ball bearing An anti-friction bearing consisting of a hardened inner and outer race with hardened steel balls between two races.

Bearing The curved surface on a shaft or in a bore, or the part assembled into either, that permits relative motion between them with minimum wear and friction.

Bearing

Big-end bearing The bearing in the end of the connecting rod that's attached to the crankshaft.

Bleed nipple A valve on a brake wheel cylinder, caliper or other hydraulic component that is opened to purge the hydraulic system of air. Also called a bleed screw.

Brake bleeding Procedure for removing air from lines of a hydraulic brake system.

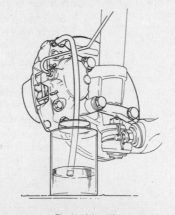

Brake bleeding

Brake disc The component of a disc brake that rotates with the wheels.

Brake drum The component of a drum brake that rotates with the wheels.

Brake linings The friction material which contacts the brake disc or drum to retard the vehicle's speed. The linings are bonded or riveted to the brake pads or shoes.

Brake pads The replaceable friction pads that pinch the brake disc when the brakes are applied. Brake pads consist of a friction material bonded or riveted to a rigid backing plate.

Brake shoe The crescent-shaped carrier to which the brake linings are mounted and which forces the lining against the rotating drum during braking.

Braking systems For more information on braking systems, consult the *Haynes Automotive Brake Manual*.

Breaker bar A long socket wrench handle providing greater leverage.

Bulkhead The insulated partition between the engine and the passenger compartment.

C

Caliper The non-rotating part of a disc-brake assembly that straddles the disc and carries the brake pads. The caliper also contains the hydraulic components that cause the pads to pinch the disc when the brakes are applied. A caliper is also a measuring tool that can be set to measure inside or outside dimensions of an object.

Camshaft A rotating shaft on which a series of cam lobes operate the valve mechanisms. The camshaft may be driven by gears, by sprockets and chain or by sprockets and a belt.

Canister A container in an evaporative emission control system; contains activated charcoal granules to trap vapours from the fuel system.

Canister

Carburettor A device which mixes fuel with air in the proper proportions to provide a desired power output from a spark ignition internal combustion engine.

Castellated Resembling the parapets along the top of a castle wall. For example, a castellated balljoint stud nut.

Castor In wheel alignment, the backward or forward tilt of the steering axis. Castor is positive when the steering axis is inclined rearward at the top.

Glossary of Technical Terms

Catalytic converter A silencer-like device in the exhaust system which converts certain pollutants in the exhaust gases into less harmful substances.

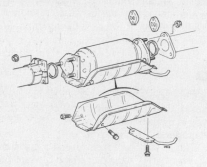

Catalytic converter

Circlip A ring-shaped clip used to prevent endwise movement of cylindrical parts and shafts. An internal circlip is installed in a groove in a housing; an external circlip fits into a groove on the outside of a cylindrical piece such as a shaft.

Clearance The amount of space between two parts. For example, between a piston and a cylinder, between a bearing and a journal, etc.

Coil spring A spiral of elastic steel found in various sizes throughout a vehicle, for example as a springing medium in the suspension and in the valve train.

Compression Reduction in volume, and increase in pressure and temperature, of a gas, caused by squeezing it into a smaller space.

Compression ratio The relationship between cylinder volume when the piston is at top dead centre and cylinder volume when the piston is at bottom dead centre.

Constant velocity (CV) joint A type of universal joint that cancels out vibrations caused by driving power being transmitted through an angle.

Core plug A disc or cup-shaped metal device inserted in a hole in a casting through which core was removed when the casting was formed. Also known as a freeze plug or expansion plug.

Crankcase The lower part of the engine block in which the crankshaft rotates.

Crankshaft The main rotating member, or shaft, running the length of the crankcase, with offset "throws" to which the connecting rods are attached.

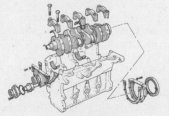

Crankshaft assembly

Crocodile clip See Alligator clip

D

Diagnostic code Code numbers obtained by accessing the diagnostic mode of an engine management computer. This code can be used to determine the area in the system where a malfunction may be located.

Disc brake A brake design incorporating a rotating disc onto which brake pads are squeezed. The resulting friction converts the energy of a moving vehicle into heat.

Double-overhead cam (DOHC) An engine that uses two overhead camshafts, usually one for the intake valves and one for the exhaust valves.

Drivebelt(s) The belt(s) used to drive accessories such as the alternator, water pump, power steering pump, air conditioning compressor, etc. off the crankshaft pulley.

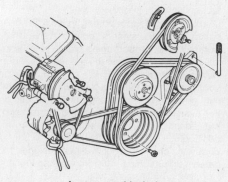

Accessory drivebelts

Driveshaft Any shaft used to transmit motion. Commonly used when referring to the axleshafts on a front wheel drive vehicle.

Drum brake A type of brake using a drum-shaped metal cylinder attached to the inner surface of the wheel. When the brake pedal is pressed, curved brake shoes with friction linings press against the inside of the drum to slow or stop the vehicle.

E

EGR valve A valve used to introduce exhaust gases into the intake air stream.

Electronic control unit (ECU) A computer which controls (for instance) ignition and fuel injection systems, or an anti-lock braking system. For more information refer to the *Haynes Automotive Electrical and Electronic Systems Manual*.

Electronic Fuel Injection (EFI) A computer controlled fuel system that distributes fuel through an injector located in each intake port of the engine.

Emergency brake A braking system, independent of the main hydraulic system, that can be used to slow or stop the vehicle if the primary brakes fail, or to hold the vehicle stationary even though the brake pedal isn't depressed. It usually consists of a hand lever that actuates either front or rear brakes mechanically through a series of cables and linkages. Also known as a handbrake or parking brake.

Endfloat The amount of lengthwise movement between two parts. As applied to a crankshaft, the distance that the crankshaft can move forward and back in the cylinder block.

Engine management system (EMS) A computer controlled system which manages the fuel injection and the ignition systems in an integrated fashion.

Exhaust manifold A part with several passages through which exhaust gases leave the engine combustion chambers and enter the exhaust pipe.

F

Fan clutch A viscous (fluid) drive coupling device which permits variable engine fan speeds in relation to engine speeds.

Feeler blade A thin strip or blade of hardened steel, ground to an exact thickness, used to check or measure clearances between parts.

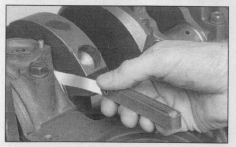

Feeler blade

Firing order The order in which the engine cylinders fire, or deliver their power strokes, beginning with the number one cylinder.

Flywheel A heavy spinning wheel in which energy is absorbed and stored by means of momentum. On cars, the flywheel is attached to the crankshaft to smooth out firing impulses.

Free play The amount of travel before any action takes place. The "looseness" in a linkage, or an assembly of parts, between the initial application of force and actual movement. For example, the distance the brake pedal moves before the pistons in the master cylinder are actuated.

Fuse An electrical device which protects a circuit against accidental overload. The typical fuse contains a soft piece of metal which is calibrated to melt at a predetermined current flow (expressed as amps) and break the circuit.

Fusible link A circuit protection device consisting of a conductor surrounded by heat-resistant insulation. The conductor is smaller than the wire it protects, so it acts as the weakest link in the circuit. Unlike a blown fuse, a failed fusible link must frequently be cut from the wire for replacement.

Glossary of Technical Terms

G

Gap The distance the spark must travel in jumping from the centre electrode to the side electrode in a spark plug. Also refers to the spacing between the points in a contact breaker assembly in a conventional points-type ignition, or to the distance between the reluctor or rotor and the pickup coil in an electronic ignition.

Adjusting spark plug gap

Gasket Any thin, soft material - usually cork, cardboard, asbestos or soft metal - installed between two metal surfaces to ensure a good seal. For instance, the cylinder head gasket seals the joint between the block and the cylinder head.

Gasket

Gauge An instrument panel display used to monitor engine conditions. A gauge with a movable pointer on a dial or a fixed scale is an analogue gauge. A gauge with a numerical readout is called a digital gauge.

H

Halfshaft A rotating shaft that transmits power from the final drive unit to a drive wheel, usually when referring to a live rear axle.

Harmonic balancer A device designed to reduce torsion or twisting vibration in the crankshaft. May be incorporated in the crankshaft pulley. Also known as a vibration damper.

Hone An abrasive tool for correcting small irregularities or differences in diameter in an engine cylinder, brake cylinder, etc.

Hydraulic tappet A tappet that utilises hydraulic pressure from the engine's lubrication system to maintain zero clearance (constant contact with both camshaft and valve stem). Automatically adjusts to variation in valve stem length. Hydraulic tappets also reduce valve noise.

I

Ignition timing The moment at which the spark plug fires, usually expressed in the number of crankshaft degrees before the piston reaches the top of its stroke.

Inlet manifold A tube or housing with passages through which flows the air-fuel mixture (carburettor vehicles and vehicles with throttle body injection) or air only (port fuel-injected vehicles) to the port openings in the cylinder head.

J

Jump start Starting the engine of a vehicle with a discharged or weak battery by attaching jump leads from the weak battery to a charged or helper battery.

L

Load Sensing Proportioning Valve (LSPV) A brake hydraulic system control valve that works like a proportioning valve, but also takes into consideration the amount of weight carried by the rear axle.

Locknut A nut used to lock an adjustment nut, or other threaded component, in place. For example, a locknut is employed to keep the adjusting nut on the rocker arm in position.

Lockwasher A form of washer designed to prevent an attaching nut from working loose.

M

MacPherson strut A type of front suspension system devised by Earle MacPherson at Ford of England. In its original form, a simple lateral link with the anti-roll bar creates the lower control arm. A long strut - an integral coil spring and shock absorber - is mounted between the body and the steering knuckle. Many modern so-called MacPherson strut systems use a conventional lower A-arm and don't rely on the anti-roll bar for location.

Multimeter An electrical test instrument with the capability to measure voltage, current and resistance.

N

NOx Oxides of Nitrogen. A common toxic pollutant emitted by petrol and diesel engines at higher temperatures.

O

Ohm The unit of electrical resistance. One volt applied to a resistance of one ohm will produce a current of one amp.

Ohmmeter An instrument for measuring electrical resistance.

O-ring A type of sealing ring made of a special rubber-like material; in use, the O-ring is compressed into a groove to provide the sealing action.

Overhead cam (ohc) engine An engine with the camshaft(s) located on top of the cylinder head(s).

Overhead valve (ohv) engine

Overhead valve (ohv) engine An engine with the valves located in the cylinder head, but with the camshaft located in the engine block.

Oxygen sensor A device installed in the engine exhaust manifold, which senses the oxygen content in the exhaust and converts this information into an electric current. Also called a Lambda sensor.

P

Phillips screw A type of screw head having a cross instead of a slot for a corresponding type of screwdriver.

Plastigage A thin strip of plastic thread, available in different sizes, used for measuring clearances. For example, a strip of Plastigage is laid across a bearing journal. The parts are assembled and dismantled; the width of the crushed strip indicates the clearance between journal and bearing.

Plastigage

Propeller shaft The long hollow tube with universal joints at both ends that carries power from the transmission to the differential on front-engined rear wheel drive vehicles.

Proportioning valve A hydraulic control valve which limits the amount of pressure to the rear brakes during panic stops to prevent wheel lock-up.

R

Rack-and-pinion steering A steering system with a pinion gear on the end of the steering shaft that mates with a rack (think of a geared wheel opened up and laid flat). When the steering wheel is turned, the pinion turns, moving the rack to the left or right. This movement is transmitted through the track rods to the steering arms at the wheels.

Radiator A liquid-to-air heat transfer device designed to reduce the temperature of the coolant in an internal combustion engine cooling system.

Refrigerant Any substance used as a heat transfer agent in an air-conditioning system. R-12 has been the principle refrigerant for many years; recently, however, manufacturers have begun using R-134a, a non-CFC substance that is considered less harmful to the ozone in the upper atmosphere.

Rocker arm A lever arm that rocks on a shaft or pivots on a stud. In an overhead valve engine, the rocker arm converts the upward movement of the pushrod into a downward movement to open a valve.

Rotor In a distributor, the rotating device inside the cap that connects the centre electrode and the outer terminals as it turns, distributing the high voltage from the coil secondary winding to the proper spark plug. Also, that part of an alternator which rotates inside the stator. Also, the rotating assembly of a turbocharger, including the compressor wheel, shaft and turbine wheel.

Runout The amount of wobble (in-and-out movement) of a gear or wheel as it's rotated. The amount a shaft rotates "out-of-true." The out-of-round condition of a rotating part.

S

Sealant A liquid or paste used to prevent leakage at a joint. Sometimes used in conjunction with a gasket.

Sealed beam lamp An older headlight design which integrates the reflector, lens and filaments into a hermetically-sealed one-piece unit. When a filament burns out or the lens cracks, the entire unit is simply replaced.

Serpentine drivebelt A single, long, wide accessory drivebelt that's used on some newer vehicles to drive all the accessories, instead of a series of smaller, shorter belts. Serpentine drivebelts are usually tensioned by an automatic tensioner.

Serpentine drivebelt

Shim Thin spacer, commonly used to adjust the clearance or relative positions between two parts. For example, shims inserted into or under bucket tappets control valve clearances. Clearance is adjusted by changing the thickness of the shim.

Slide hammer A special puller that screws into or hooks onto a component such as a shaft or bearing; a heavy sliding handle on the shaft bottoms against the end of the shaft to knock the component free.

Sprocket A tooth or projection on the periphery of a wheel, shaped to engage with a chain or drivebelt. Commonly used to refer to the sprocket wheel itself.

Starter inhibitor switch On vehicles with an automatic transmission, a switch that prevents starting if the vehicle is not in Neutral or Park.

Strut See MacPherson strut.

T

Tappet A cylindrical component which transmits motion from the cam to the valve stem, either directly or via a pushrod and rocker arm. Also called a cam follower.

Thermostat A heat-controlled valve that regulates the flow of coolant between the cylinder block and the radiator, so maintaining optimum engine operating temperature. A thermostat is also used in some air cleaners in which the temperature is regulated.

Thrust bearing The bearing in the clutch assembly that is moved in to the release levers by clutch pedal action to disengage the clutch. Also referred to as a release bearing.

Timing belt A toothed belt which drives the camshaft. Serious engine damage may result if it breaks in service.

Timing chain A chain which drives the camshaft.

Toe-in The amount the front wheels are closer together at the front than at the rear. On rear wheel drive vehicles, a slight amount of toe-in is usually specified to keep the front wheels running parallel on the road by offsetting other forces that tend to spread the wheels apart.

Toe-out The amount the front wheels are closer together at the rear than at the front. On front wheel drive vehicles, a slight amount of toe-out is usually specified.

Tools For full information on choosing and using tools, refer to the *Haynes Automotive Tools Manual*.

Tracer A stripe of a second colour applied to a wire insulator to distinguish that wire from another one with the same colour insulator.

Tune-up A process of accurate and careful adjustments and parts replacement to obtain the best possible engine performance.

Turbocharger A centrifugal device, driven by exhaust gases, that pressurises the intake air. Normally used to increase the power output from a given engine displacement, but can also be used primarily to reduce exhaust emissions (as on VW's "Umwelt" Diesel engine).

U

Universal joint or U-joint A double-pivoted connection for transmitting power from a driving to a driven shaft through an angle. A U-joint consists of two Y-shaped yokes and a cross-shaped member called the spider.

V

Valve A device through which the flow of liquid, gas, vacuum, or loose material in bulk may be started, stopped, or regulated by a movable part that opens, shuts, or partially obstructs one or more ports or passageways. A valve is also the movable part of such a device.

Valve clearance The clearance between the valve tip (the end of the valve stem) and the rocker arm or tappet. The valve clearance is measured when the valve is closed.

Vernier caliper A precision measuring instrument that measures inside and outside dimensions. Not quite as accurate as a micrometer, but more convenient.

Viscosity The thickness of a liquid or its resistance to flow.

Volt A unit for expressing electrical "pressure" in a circuit. One volt that will produce a current of one ampere through a resistance of one ohm.

W

Welding Various processes used to join metal items by heating the areas to be joined to a molten state and fusing them together. For more information refer to the *Haynes Automotive Welding Manual*.

Wiring diagram A drawing portraying the components and wires in a vehicle's electrical system, using standardised symbols. For more information refer to the *Haynes Automotive Electrical and Electronic Systems Manual*.

Conversion Factors

Length (distance)

Inches (in)	X 25.4	= Millimetres (mm)	X 0.0394	= Inches (in)
Feet (ft)	X 0.305	= Metres (m)	X 3.281	= Feet (ft)
Miles	X 1.609	= Kilometres (km)	X 0.621	= Miles

Volume (capacity)

Cubic inches (cu in; in3)	X 16.387	= Cubic centimetres (cc; cm3)	X 0.061	= Cubic inches (cu in; in3)
Imperial pints (Imp pt)	X 0.568	= Litres (l)	X 1.76	= Imperial pints (Imp pt)
Imperial quarts (Imp qt)	X 1.137	= Litres (l)	X 0.88	= Imperial quarts (Imp qt)
Imperial quarts (Imp qt)	X 1.201	= US quarts (US qt)	X 0.833	= Imperial quarts (Imp qt)
US quarts (US qt)	X 0.946	= Litres (l)	X 1.057	= US quarts (US qt)
Imperial gallons (Imp gal)	X 4.546	= Litres (l)	X 0.22	= Imperial gallons (Imp gal)
Imperial gallons (Imp gal)	X 1.201	= US gallons (US gal)	X 0.833	= Imperial gallons (Imp gal)
US gallons (US gal)	X 3.785	= Litres (l)	X 0.264	= US gallons (US gal)

Mass (weight)

Ounces (oz)	X 28.35	= Grams (g)	X 0.035	= Ounces (oz)
Pounds (lb)	X 0.454	= Kilograms (kg)	X 2.205	= Pounds (lb)

Force

Ounces-force (ozf; oz)	X 0.278	= Newtons (N)	X 3.6	= Ounces-force (ozf; oz)
Pounds-force (lbf; lb)	X 4.448	= Newtons (N)	X 0.225	= Pounds-force (lbf; lb)
Newtons (N)	X 0.1	= Kilograms-force (kgf; kg)	X 9.81	= Newtons (N)

Pressure

Pounds-force per square inch (psi; lbf/in²; lb/in²)	X 0.070	= Kilograms-force per square centimetre (kgf/cm²; kg/cm²)	X 14.223	= Pounds-force per square inch (psi; lbf/in²; lb/in²)
Pounds-force per square inch (psi; lbf/in²; lb/in²)	X 0.068	= Atmospheres (atm)	X 14.696	= Pounds-force per square inch (psi; lbf/in²; lb/in²)
Pounds-force per square inch (psi; lbf/in²; lb/in²)	X 0.069	= Bars	X 14.5	= Pounds-force per square inch (psi; lbf/in²; lb/in²)
Pounds-force per square inch (psi; lbf/in²; lb/in²)	X 6.895	= Kilopascals (kPa)	X 0.145	= Pounds-force per square inch (psi; lbf/in²; lb/in²)
Kilopascals (kPa)	X 0.01	= Kilograms-force per square centimetre (kgf/cm²; kg/cm²)	X 98.1	= Kilopascals (kPa)
Millibar (mbar)	X 100	= Pascals (Pa)	X 0.01	= Millibar (mbar)
Millibar (mbar)	X 0.0145	= Pounds-force per square inch (psi; lbf/in²; lb/in²)	X 68.947	= Millibar (mbar)
Millibar (mbar)	X 0.75	= Millimetres of mercury (mmHg)	X 1.333	= Millibar (mbar)
Millibar (mbar)	X 0.401	= Inches of water (inH₂O)	X 2.491	= Millibar (mbar)
Millimetres of mercury (mmHg)	X 0.535	= Inches of water (inH₂O)	X 1.868	= Millimetres of mercury (mmHg)
Inches of water (inH₂O)	X 0.036	= Pounds-force per square inch (psi; lbf/in²; lb/in²)	X 27.68	= Inches of water (inH₂O)

Torque (moment of force)

Pounds-force inches (lbf in; lb in)	X 1.152	= Kilograms-force centimetre (kgf cm; kg cm)	X 0.868	= Pounds-force inches (lbf in; lb in)
Pounds-force inches (lbf in; lb in)	X 0.113	= Newton metres (Nm)	X 8.85	= Pounds-force inches (lbf in; lb in)
Pounds-force inches (lbf in; lb in)	X 0.083	= Pounds-force feet (lbf ft; lb ft)	X 12	= Pounds-force inches (lbf in; lb in)
Pounds-force feet (lbf ft; lb ft)	X 0.138	= Kilograms-force metres (kgf m; kg m)	X 7.233	= Pounds-force feet (lbf ft; lb ft)
Pounds-force feet (lbf ft; lb ft)	X 1.356	= Newton metres (Nm)	X 0.738	= Pounds-force feet (lbf ft; lb ft)
Newton metres (Nm)	X 0.102	= Kilograms-force metres (kgf m; kg m)	X 9.804	= Newton metres (Nm)

Power

Horsepower (hp)	X 745.7	= Watts (W)	X 0.0013	= Horsepower (hp)

Velocity (speed)

Miles per hour (miles/hr; mph)	X 1.609	= Kilometres per hour (km/hr; kph)	X 0.621	= Miles per hour (miles/hr; mph)

Fuel consumption*

Miles per gallon, Imperial (mpg)	X 0.354	= Kilometres per litre (km/l)	X 2.825	= Miles per gallon, Imperial (mpg)
Miles per gallon, US (mpg)	X 0.425	= Kilometres per litre (km/l)	X 2.352	= Miles per gallon, US (mpg)

Temperature

Degrees Fahrenheit = (°C x 1.8) + 32

Degrees Celsius (Degrees Centigrade; °C) = (°F - 32) x 0.56

It is common practice to convert from miles per gallon (mpg) to litres/100 kilometres (l/100km), where mpg (Imperial) x l/100 km = 282 and mpg (US) x l/100 km = 235

Note: *References throughout this index are in the form - "Chapter number" • "page number"*

Preserving Our Motoring Heritage

< The Model J Duesenberg Derham Tourster. Only eight of these magnificent cars were ever built – this is the only example to be found outside the United States of America

Almost every car you've ever loved, loathed or desired is gathered under one roof at the Haynes Motor Museum. Over 300 immaculately presented cars and motorbikes represent every aspect of our motoring heritage, from elegant reminders of bygone days, such as the superb Model J Duesenberg to curiosities like the bug-eyed BMW Isetta. There are also many old friends and flames. Perhaps you remember the 1959 Ford Popular that you did your courting in? The magnificent 'Red Collection' is a spectacle of classic sports cars including AC, Alfa Romeo, Austin Healey, Ferrari, Lamborghini, Maserati, MG, Riley, Porsche and Triumph.

A Perfect Day Out

Each and every vehicle at the Haynes Motor Museum has played its part in the history and culture of Motoring. Today, they make a wonderful spectacle and a great day out for all the family. Bring the kids, bring Mum and Dad, but above all bring your camera to capture those golden memories for ever. You will also find an impressive array of motoring memorabilia, a comfortable 70 seat video cinema and one of the most extensive transport book shops in Britain. The Pit Stop Cafe serves everything from a cup of tea to wholesome, home-made meals or, if you prefer, you can enjoy the large picnic area nestled in the beautiful rural surroundings of Somerset.

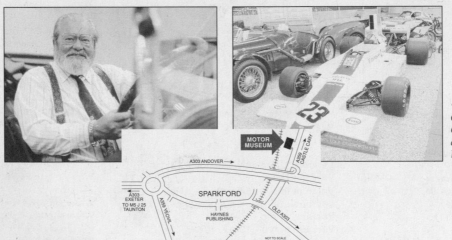

John Haynes O.B.E., Founder and Chairman of the museum at the wheel of a Haynes Light 12. >

< Graham Hill's Lola Cosworth Formula 1 car next to a 1934 Riley Sports.

The Museum is situated on the A359 Yeovil to Frome road at Sparkford, just off the A303 in Somerset. It is about 40 miles south of Bristol, and 25 minutes drive from the M5 intersection at Taunton.
Open 9.30am - 5.30pm (10.00am - 4.00pm Winter) 7 days a week, *except Christmas Day, Boxing Day and New Years Day*
Special rates available for schools, coach parties and outings Charitable Trust No. 292048